CANTERBURY
UNDER THE
ANGEVIN KINGS

by

WILLIAM URRY

UNIVERSITY OF LONDON
THE ATHLONE PRESS
1967

Published by
THE ATHLONE PRESS
UNIVERSITY OF LONDON
at 2 Gower Street London WC1
Distributed by Constable & Co Ltd
12 *Orange Street London* WC2

Canada
Oxford University Press
Toronto

U.S.A.
Oxford University Press Inc
New York

Printed in Great Britain by
WESTERN PRINTING SERVICES LTD
BRISTOL

CANTERBURY UNDER THE
ANGEVIN KINGS

By permission of the Dean and Chapter of Canterbury

THE CENTRAL AREA OF CANTERBURY ABOUT A.D. 1200

Buttermarket (*forum*), Mercery Lane (*Merceria*), Parade (*magna strata*)

From the survey evidently made following the fire of 1198 (Rental D, §§104–11)

TO MY WIFE

PREFACE

IT is three and a quarter centuries since William Somner published his *Antiquities of Canterbury*, the most scholarly among early printed accounts of an English provincial borough. With this admirable lead it might well have been expected that a full-length definitive History of the city would long since have seen the light. This has not been the case though great numbers of books and articles have appeared on individual subjects. A major difficulty is the versatility required of any writer, owing to the intrusion of Canterbury into so many different fields of study. A specialist knowledge of ecclesiastical history, urban history, monasticism (in itself embracing a wide range of different studies), of art and of architecture, is demanded of the local historian. Again, there is the daunting bulk of material surviving from the Middle Ages, and from later centuries. Two vast Benedictine abbeys, a priory, a nunnery, three friaries, five very ancient almshouses, and a score of parish churches, not to mention one of the greater medieval boroughs, can produce between them an embarrassing amount of records, and, independently of any materials at or emanating from Canterbury, a large History could be constructed from information relating to the city's past to be found in the central archives at the Public Record Office. Perhaps one day someone will attempt a synthesis of the various individual studies which have been made; but it is to the latter category that the present book belongs—a contribution towards a future History of Canterbury.

An earlier version of this work was approved by the University of London for award of the degree of Ph.D. in 1956. Publication has been made possible by grants from a number of bodies to whom particular thanks are owing. These are: the Dean and Chapter of Canterbury; the Mayor and Corporation of Canterbury; Birkbeck College, University of London; the trustees of the Isobel Thornley Bequest Fund and the British Academy.

There remains the pleasant task of offering thanks to the very many friends, scholars and teachers who have given help and encouragement. The book has been a long time in making, and pleasure is now mixed since there are several to whom gratitude can no longer be expressed in person, but only placed on record. Such thanks are due first of all to my Mother, who taught me *ab incunabulis* of history in Canterbury; then to

James Adams and Donald MacGillivray, teachers; to Claude Jenkins, late Regius Professor of Ecclesiastical History in the University of Oxford, sometime Canon of Canterbury; to Henry Thomas Mead, once Librarian of the City of Canterbury; and to Dorothy Gardiner, antiquary. Like so many other students of the medieval city, I owe an immense debt to William Blore, Cathedral Librarian from 1936 to 1948, not least for the privilege of serving as his assistant for two years.

The Dean and Chapter of Canterbury, and the Mayor and Corporation of the City, whose financial help has already been gratefully acknowledged, must be thanked again, for permission to make use of their respective archives and to publish documents. Here I may take occasion for thanking Mr John Boyle, LL.B., F.S.A., Town Clerk of Canterbury and official custodian of the borough archives. I likewise offer thanks for the use of documents to the Reverend Derek Ingram Hill, M.A., Master of Eastbridge Hospital, and a distant successor in office to *Radulfus, nepos sancti Thome martiris*. I am grateful for help over many years to Mr Frank Higenbottam, B.A., F.L.A., City Librarian of Canterbury; likewise to Mr Frank Jenkins, F.S.A., who has ever allowed me to draw on his great learning in matters relating to the world of Rome, and to Roman Canterbury in particular. Professor Norma Adams of Mount Holyoke has given me much help, especially in connection with tenures, and has extended me much kindness, on both sides of the Atlantic. Like all his students, I am indebted to Professor V. H. Galbraith for a vivid insight into the early medieval world. Dr Avrom Saltman and Dr Cecil Roth have helped me on questions relating to the Jews of Canterbury. Professor C. R. Cheney and Professor Bruce Dickens have given counsel in connection with texts, and hospitality at Cambridge which enabled me to work there at leisure on Canterbury MSS. Dr Reginald Dodwell of Trinity College has offered much advice on Canterbury handwriting and illumination. Mr Nicholas MacMichael, F.S.A., of the Westminster Abbey Muniment Room, has aided me in questions relating to Kentish manorial history. Dr Felix Hull, Kent County Archivist, has always been ready to answer questions and produce documents. To the staff of the British Museum Manuscripts Department, the Bodleian Library, the Cambridge University Library and the Public Record Office I am under much obligation. In particular I would wish to thank Dr Patricia Barnes of the P.R.O., and Dr G. C. R. Davis at the British Museum. Mr Geoffrey Bill, M.A., and his staff at Lambeth Palace Library have been tireless in dealing with problems presented to them. Dr William Pantin has engaged in many discussions on the ground-plan of medieval Oxford, while Dr Pierre Chaplais, University Reader in Diplomatic, has helped me with points relating to charter-forms. With Professor Raymonde Foreville of the University of Caen I have had many exchanges, most valuable to me, on the age of Thomas Becket, and owe to her the opportunity of making a close acquaintance with the Norman countryside. Mr Peter Sawyer, M.A., of Leeds University, has given much advice in connection with Domesday Book. To Professor R. R. Darlington, F.B.A., my debt is considerable. As the supervisor of my thesis he might well have thought that his obligations would end with its completion; but throughout the years of revision his great patience and kindness have been unvarying.

Mr A. Bell, Borough Treasurer of Canterbury, performed a singular service in passing twelfth-century rents through his modern computers, thereby saving me infinite labour. It is not easy to express my gratitude to Mr Jack Maple, repairer of MSS in the Cathedral Library, Canterbury, for long-sustained tolerance of both author and book, and for actual practical help and advice on questions of arrangement, presentation and indexing. Dr John Shirley, 'one of the Prebendaries of this Church', has given encouragement and stimulus over many years. Mr Philip Wardle Richards, B.A., indicated and inspired lines of study at a very early stage of my researches. Finally I return illimitable gratitude to my Wife and family, who have been compelled for so long to live in company with Terric the Goldsmith and Solomon the Mercer.

I can perhaps conclude this preface no more fittingly than with the words in which William Somner ends his own charming and ingenuous *Preface to the Reader* in 1640.

This worke is chiefly collected from old *Manuscripts, Leiger-bookes* and other *Records* of credit, exhibited to me for the most part by the Treasury of our *Cathedrall*; which, as it exceeds most of the Realme, if not all, in beauty, statelinesse, and magnificence of building; so in this particular kinde of unvaluable treasure, is, as I conceive, inferior unto none. . . . If the Worke may not deserve thine acceptance (courteous Reader) for itselfe, let then the *Authors* love to *Antiquities*, his *thankfull intentions* towards the *place* of his *birth*, *education* and *present abode*, and the *encouragement* of *worthy friends*, serve for his *Apology*. If otherwise it give thee some content, and mine endeavours prove acceptable unto thee, I shall desire thou wouldest be thankfull to them, without whose *helpe*, as I had not been *able*, so without whose *encouragement* I had neither beene *willing*, thus to have adventured forth in publike.

Chapter Library,   WILLIAM URRY
Canterbury Cathedral,
ad mediam quadragesimam,
1966

CONTENTS

MAP FOLDER

ABBREVIATIONS

A–G	Rentals thus designated, printed *in extenso* below. Numbers refer to paragraphs in the transcript.
X 1, X 2, Y, Z	Rentals, thus designated.
I, II, III, etc.—LXX	Charters printed *in extenso* below.
BBC	British Borough Charters. Vol. i., edited by A. Ballard. (Vol. ii, edited by A. Ballard and J. Tait)
BBSA	Black Book of St Augustine's Abbey, Canterbury, ed. G. J. Turner and H. E. Salter (British Academy)
Birch, *CS*	Birch: *Cartularium Saxonicum*
CAC	Chapter Archives, Canterbury
Ch. Ant.	Chartæ Antiquæ (among Chapter archives)
CCR	Calendar of Close Rolls (HMSO)
CRR	Curia Regis Rolls (HMSO)
CS	Camden Society
DB	Domesday Book (Record Commrs.)
DMon	Domesday Monachorum of Christ Church, Canterbury, edited by D. C. Douglas, 1944
EBH	Eastbridge Hospital, Canterbury
Eng. Hist. Docs.	*English Historical Documents*, edited by D. C. Douglas
Epp. Cant.	Epistolæ Cantuarienses. Edited by W. Stubbs (*RS*)
EHR	*English Historical Review*
Greg.	Cartulary of the Priory of St Gregory, Canterbury. Edited by A. M. Woodcock. Camden Third Series, vol. lxxxviii, 1956
Guernes	Guernes de Pont Ste Maxence, *Vie de Saint Thomas*, ed. Walberg
Hist. Eng. Law	Pollock, F., and Maitland, F. W., *History of English Law before the time of Edward I*, 1923

HMC	Historical Manuscripts Commission
Kemble *CD*	Codex Diplomaticus Ævi Saxonici opera J. M. Kemble
Materials	Materials for the History of Thomas Becket (*RS*)
MEB	Tait, J., *Medieval English Borough*
PR	Pipe Rolls, cited in printed edition of Pipe Roll Society
RBE	Red Book of the Exchequer. Edited by H. Hall (*RS*)
Regesta	Regesta Regum Anglo-Normannorum. Vol. i, edited by H. W. C. Davis and R. J. Whitwell. (Vol. ii, ed. by C. Johnson and H. A. Cronne)
Reliefs	Reliefs paid on holdings of monks of Christ Church, Canterbury, 1215 ff. From MS. Lit. D 4, Cathedral Library, Canterbury (cited by year)
RS	Rolls Series
TA	Treasurers' Accounts, in Chapter Archives, Canterbury
Thorne	Thorne, *Chronicle*, in Twysden, *Scriptores Decem* (page numbers refer to translation of A. H. Davis)
VCH	Victoria County History

CHAPTER I

Introduction

IT is possible in the case of Canterbury to escape from that 'arid atmosphere of legal archaeology', which, as Sir Frank Stenton says, is usually encountered when one attempts to investigate the history of the early English borough.[1] The monks of Christ Church have bequeathed to us a long series of rentals, some in great detail, listing the extensive property in the city from which they drew income. Canterbury is, of course, not the only borough where material other than perhaps an early charter or a not over-informative entry in Domesday can be discovered. London boasts of the *Description* prefixed by William FitzStephen to his account of Thomas Becket, her most famous son.[2] The monk Lucian did on a smaller scale for Chester[3] what FitzStephen did for London, but the information provided is embedded in a mass of allegory and homiletic matter. Winchester is missing from Domesday Book, but the want is more than made good by two special descriptions, one of c. 1110, and the other of 1148.[4] Short descriptions are available for Gloucester and Winchcombe in the age of Domesday,[5] while the inhabitants of the little township at the gates of Battle abbey are listed in the abbey Chronicle.[6] A charter of 1111 relating to the 'little borough' of Fordwich,[7] on the river below Canterbury, gives the names of twenty-five of its townsfolk, a substantial

[1] Stenton, *Norman London*, p. 22.

[2] See Stenton, *Norman London*, p. 25, for notes on the editions of FitzStephen, in conjunction with a translation by N. B. Butler. The translation is reprinted in *Eng. Hist. Docs.*, ii, No. 281. *Norman London* has been republished in *Social Life in Early England*, ed. G. Barraclough (1960).

[3] *Liber Luciani de Laude Cestrie*, ed. M. V. Taylor (*Lancashire and Cheshire Record Society Publications*, lxix, 1912).

[4] The surveys in the Winchester Domesday are printed in *DB*, (Rec. Com.), iv, 531–62. They are discussed by J. H. Round in *VCH, Hants*, i, 527 ff.

[5] See Ellis, *A General Introduction to Domesday Book*, ii, 446–7.

[6] *Chronicon Monasterii de Bello (Anglia Christiana)*, pp. 12–16.

[7] BM. MS. Cotton, Claudius D X, 175r. Grant by Hamo 'dapifer', sheriff of Kent, of the *villa* of Fordwich to St Augustine's abbey. Most of the names are English. There is a moneyer (Hagemund). Domesday calls Fordwich 'parvum burgum', and says that it contains 73 (formerly 96) burgages (*DB*, i, fol. 12r).

proportion of them. In recent years a late twelfth-century rentroll has come to light evidently relating to Newark, and embodying some five hundred entries.[1]

London has produced surprisingly little in the way of early rentals and surveys, in view of the number of dwellings in the hands of clerical lords. There are a few short specimens, such as the list of lands and churches, compiled c. 1100, rendering income to Canterbury cathedral, supplying the name of the earliest London alderman.[2] Thirty years later we have the list of tenants of St Paul's, offering valuable evidence as to the existence of wards.[3] To the monks of Canterbury are owing two other, and neglected, London rentals, of c. 1180[4] and of c. 1230,[5] the latter in considerable detail. Mary Bateson published a short rental of London at the end of the twelfth century.[6]

Brief lists exist of townsfolk at Sandwich and Dover paying rents to Canterbury cathedral about 1206 and 1218.[7] Hull, 'a new Liborne in a colder and flatter land', has been mapped from the Edwardian surveys.[8] The groundplans of Winchelsea and New Sarum offer themselves as important documents in the history of town-planning.[9] In the fifteenth century there are two descriptions of west-country boroughs in the detailed rental of Gloucester (1455)[10] and in the account of Bristol in the *Itinerary* of William of Worcester.[11] William was preoccupied with figures and

[1] St John's College, Oxford, MS. No. 39. Published in *Thoroton Society Record Series*, xvi (Documents relating to the Manor and Soke of Newark on Trent, ed. M. W. Barley, the late W. H. Stevenson and K. Cameron), 1955.

[2] B. W. Kissan, 'An Early List of London Properties' (in *Trans. of London and Middlesex Archæological Society*, NS, viii, 57–69); *Eng. Hist. Docs.*, ii, 954–6.

[3] H. W. C. Davis, 'London Lands and Liberties of St Paul's 1066–1135' (*Essays in Mediaeval History presented to T. F. Tout*). For London material see *Bibliographical Note*, prefixed to Stenton, *Norman London*, and see *Eng. Hist. Docs.*, ii, § iv, D.

[4] Canterbury Cathedral Library, Lit. MS. B.15, ff. 14–17. This rental is embodied in X 1. See pp. 15 ff. below. It has been used by B. W. Kissan in 'The Earliest Mention of Bow Church' (*Trans. of London and Middlesex Archæological Society*, NS, vii, 439). There is a version, very close in date, in Canterbury Lit. MS. B.16.

[5] CAC, Reg. K, ff. 66v–69r.

[6] 'A London Municipal Collection of the Reign of John' (*EHR*, xvii (1902), pp. 483–4).

[7] CAC, Reg. K, ff. 47r–v.; Reg. H, fol. 15v.

[8] J. Bilson, 'Wyke upon Hull in 1293' (*Trans. of the East Riding Antiquarian Society*, xxvi, 37–105).

[9] Tout reproduces the O.S. plan of Winchelsea in his *Mediæval Town Planning* (opp. p. 24).

[10] *Rental of all the Houses in Gloucester, A.D. 1455*. Compiled by Robert Cole. Ed. by W. H. Stevenson (1890).

[11] *Itineraria Symonis Simeonis et Willelmi de Worcestre ... edidit ... J. Nasmith* (1778). A new edition of W. of Worcester is in preparation by Mr John Harvey.

supplies the measurements of streets, dimensions of buildings, heights of church towers and even the number of steps therein.

By unexplained coincidence it is at the two older University towns that the greatest riches of urban topography may be encountered. Here the Hundred Rolls provide, instead of the querulous complaints which serve for an entry at places like Canterbury, the most detailed, large-scale, and systematic surveys made in boroughs before the end of the Middle Ages.[1] Perhaps the accounts of both University towns are in such detail because large numbers of clerks were available to assemble the evidence. Not only have the two boroughs such admirable entries in the Hundred Rolls but colleges have preserved vast numbers of deeds relating to their urban property, estimated at the number of 50,000 in the case of Oxford. Dr Salter prepared his map of medieval Oxford from such material,[2] and at Cambridge Professor Willis and Mr Clark produced their excellent plans showing how ever-expanding colleges had obliterated the layout of ancient burgess-tenements.[3]

The monks of Canterbury cathedral accumulated extensive archives in administering their local property. More than five hundred charters,[4] mostly of a date before 1300, relate to their holdings in the city, while from the twelfth century they were compiling rentrolls and surveys of these holdings. They must be credited with an important contribution to early cartography. Bound into the Psalter of Eadwine is the mid-twelfth century plan of the cathedral waterworks system, 'one of the most famous documents of its kind'.[5] It is closely related to the surveys reproduced below and indeed, a great deal of the

[1] See Maitland, *Township and Borough*, p. 69. The material for Canterbury in the Hundred Rolls is disappointing in the extreme. There is little but reports of petty encroachments, misconduct of royal officials, and so forth (*Rotuli Hundredorum*, i, pp. 203-4). The Canterbury rentals (below) offer great detail, but they are not so extensive, because they refer only to cathedral property and again, the borough was not so large.

[2] H. E. Salter, *Map of Medieval Oxford*, 1934. This has now been republished with copious notes (H. E. Salter, *Survey of Oxford* . . . Ed. by W. A. Pantin. Vol. i. Oxford Historical Society, NS, xiv, 1960).

[3] R. Willis and J. W. Clark, *Architectural History of the University of Cambridge*, etc., 1886.

[4] CAC, Ch. Ant., series C, nos. 693 ff. The cathedral was not the only local house which had urban property and consequently produced charters and rentals. Eastbridge Hospital has kept together its archives, which embody some late rentals, with an extensive collection of early charters, of which about 80 relate to Canterbury (some within the twelfth century). The archives of St John's Hospital, and of Harbledown Hospital were largely destroyed in the air-raid of 1 June 1942. The archives of St Augustine's abbey were scattered at the dissolution. Charters and registers of the abbey survive, such as the great cartulary BM. MS. Cotton Claudius D X. See Chapter III.

[5] *The Canterbury Psalter*. Edited by M. R. James, 1935. Introduction p. 53.

information in them would not be intelligible without reference to this plan.[1]

The documents which have been edited in this work have been selected on two grounds: age and fullness of information. Consequently informative rentals such as D (c. 1200) and F (c. 1206), have been preferred to rentals of c. 1180 (X 1 and X 2)[2] which are hardly more than bald lists of names and rents. The oldest rental is A, representing a list of acquisitions, mainly dwellings in Canterbury, made by prior Wibert (1153–67). The next in date, B, may be assigned to about 1166, and ranks high among material relating to the early English borough. It was compiled about twenty years after the second Winchester survey, but is much more informative. B is not complete as it stands, since it describes only three of the six city wards in Canterbury, but includes much of the populous central area. Rental D is the most outstanding of the Canterbury documents, and it is hard to find anything comparable at this point of time (c. 1200). It provides a detailed description of some four hundred holdings in the borough with definition of adjacent premises, complete with the measurements of nearly every holding surveyed. Rental D is close in date to F, which is a schedule at great length, prepared by the monks about 1206, of rents received at various times during the year, from dwellings in Canterbury. It is not a systematic survey, but descriptive paragraphs are supplied, indicating the site where the rent arises, and the whole forms a valuable adjunct to D, in many cases amplifying its descriptions, and explaining its less-clear passages. The monks were mesne tenants in respect of many holdings, and drew up lists of rents due from them to various lords, lay and ecclesiastical. Rentals C (c. 1180), and G (c. 1200) reproduced below, are such schedules.

A collection of charters illustrating and amplifying evidence from the rentals has been added. The earliest charter is the record in Old English of the well-known exchange in the days of St Anselm between the merchant gild of Canterbury and the cathedral monks. Many of the charters will show how holdings in Canterbury were acquired. Others have been selected since they illustrate tenurial points. A few add to the evidence available for compiling the maps appended to this study.

---

[1] This plan has been reproduced many times, as in *Vetusta Monumenta* of the Society of Antiquaries (ii, xv, 1755); Willis, *Conventual Buildings of the Monastery of Christchurch, Canterbury; The Canterbury Psalter* (facsimile edition), ed. M. R. James (1935), p. 53.

[2] For Rentals X 1, X 2, see pp. 15 ff. below.

RENTAL A

Rental A (Rental 87 in the Chapter archives) is a roll consisting of two membranes glued together giving a total length of 3 feet 7⅝ inches with an average width of 7¾ inches. The writing (apart from that in two sections) is a fine example of the Christ Church hand of the mid-twelfth century. The bulk of the text may be the work of a single scribe but variations in size and in colour of ink show that the roll was not compiled at one point of time. The front of the roll is fairly uniform and may have been put together within a short space, but the entries on the back give the impression that they were made as the transactions which they record were effected. Two sections on the back (A 32, 33) are in a hand which has strong affinities with the chancery script. At the end of the visible text, a passage, evidently of six paragraphs, has been erased, though small sections can be recovered beneath an ultra-violet ray lamp. The total number of sections, including those erased, amounts to forty-four.

The roll records acquisitions made by Wibert, prior of Canterbury 1153–67. We know that some of these acquisitions were made while he was as yet sub-prior, but he is referred to as prior at the beginning of the document, so the earlier limit for the roll is 1153.[1] If the entries on the back were made closely following the respective transactions, then they were probably added through the later years of the priorate. It may be pointed out that one acquisition, ground close to the road junction 'Tierne' in central Canterbury, said in Rental D (D 261), to have been bought by prior Wibert, finds no place in the roll.

RENTAL B

Rental B is Rental 31 in the Chapter archives. It is in a very fine state of preservation and consists of a roll of an average width of 11½ inches, formed of five skins attached by contemporary stitching, giving a total length of 6 feet 11 inches. The hand is a small, well-formed, and on the whole regular bookhand in a black ink. This hand has close affinities with that of the running commentaries in the great Psalter of Eadwine. In fact it is very tempting to speculate whether we have here another example of the work of the famous 'scriptorum princeps' as he styles himself. There is indeed suggestion that an English scribe wrote out the roll because of the occasional use of Old English characters. A certain amount of irregularity creeps in towards the bottom of the roll in either column, suggesting that

[1] For the date of Wibert's accession to the priorate see p. 6 n. 1 below.

the first column was not completed before the second was started. The information in the compiler's hands was not quite complete and occasionally facts and figures are left out. The blank spaces left as a result of such omissions are marked in each case with a symbol resembling 'c' reversed. At the beginning of each section there is a paragraph mark. The material is arranged under wards in the city of Canterbury where the property lay, while the property is further divided under the monastic departments taking the rents. Space was left for headings, while a note in a very small hand was inserted to indicate what was wanted. The headings proper have been supplied in a bright red, in a hand which again can probably be found in the Canterbury Psalter, and which can again be attributed, without much doubt, to Eadwine the scribe. On the grounds of handwriting and general appearance the document can be referred to a date not far from the middle of the twelfth century.

The roll is singularly free from additional entries such as disfigure most Christ Church rentals, made in efforts to bring the record up to date. There are two notes of the fifteenth century, while some odd letters in the margin added to indicate sections separated in the manuscript, but relating to each other, seem to have been written by William Somner (1606–69), the Canterbury antiquary and Keeper of the cathedral archives, who has also added a note at the end. An endorsement has been made by C. R. Bunce who sorted and arranged the cathedral and city archives c. 1800.

Internal evidence corroborates the date suggested on grounds of handwriting and appearance. Wibert is named as prior in the present tense.[1] Two holdings are said to have been given 'with Gervase our fellow-monk' (B 54, 55). The only Gervase traced in the twelfth century is the historian, who tells us he was professed at the hands of Becket himself, 16 February 1163.[2] If there were more than one Gervase at a time in the cloister, some distinguishing mark or title would be expected, essential in a small community. It is significant that c. 1200, when the same holdings are surveyed, Gervase is mentioned again, still without a distinguishing title.[3] An early cure effected (before Easter 1171) by the virtues of St Thomas Becket, according to Benedict of Peterborough, was the restoration to health of the children of Godefrid the baker.[4] A man of this name occurs in the roll

---

[1] B 32. W. G. Searle gives 1150 for the accession of Wilbert as prior (*Christ Church, Canterbury* ... ii. *Lists of Deans, Priors, and Monks*, etc. Cambridge Antiquarian Society, 8vo. series, 1902, p. 158.) Wharton, *Anglia Sacra*, i, 137, and Dart, *Canterbury Cathedral*, p. 180, give 1153. Searle was evidently misled by the fact that Gervase gives the story of the deposition of prior Walter under 1150–1, though he ends with an explanatory note showing that it occurred in 1153. *Opera, RS*, i, 146).

[2] Gervase, *RS*, i, 173. [3] D 26–28. [4] For Godefrid, see pp. 162, 183 below.

as holder of a tenement in central Canterbury (B 118). Near St George's Gate there are tenements in the possession of Hamo, provost of Canterbury (B 100, 213) who was in the hands of William Cade the moneylender 1160–1 and is mentioned several times in the twenty years running from 1155.[1] Another tenant named in the rental, John Calderun (B 73), is a witness when Hamo pledges his property to Cade, and (by Charter XLVII) assigns his holdings to the Cathedral in 1177. Lambin Frese the moneyer, who was persuaded to move from his holding beside the cathedral gate (B 79) by 1177, is still in occupation of this holding in the rental. Other burgesses who were induced to move from ground not far off, close to the cathedral, following the fire of 1174, are as yet in possession of their dwellings (B 72–4). There is nothing to suggest that the rental cannot belong to the priorate of Wibert, and we may assign it to the period from February 1163 (the date of the profession of Gervase), to September 1167 (death of prior Wibert). If the suggestion made below is valid that the Canterbury wards had an origin in the police measures incorporated in the assize of Clarendon, then a further limit, from early in 1166, may be offered for the rental.[2]

An ambitious piece of work like Rental B was probably not made without some great occasion. There was a conflagration which almost completely devastated Canterbury in 1161,[3] and the rental may have been put together to clarify the rights of the cathedral monks and of their tenants in ground where rebuilding was taking place.[4]

RENTAL C

Literary MS. D 4 in the Cathedral Library, is a volume bound in calf, containing a number of unrelated items, such as the earliest monastic accounts surviving in this country, an early twelfth-century version of

[1] For Hamo see pp. 84, 156 below. [2] In account of wards, Chapter IV.

[3] *Annales Monastici* (Winton), RS, ii, 56. 'Londonia combusta est . . . et Cantuaria.' Ibid., p. 238 (Waverley): 'Cantuaria paene tota arsit'.

[4] It is difficult to assess the relative dates of A and B. Rental A, at least in its later stages seems to represent a record of acquisitions made from time to time as they occurred. If B were compiled late in Wibert's priorate then an absence of entries from B ought to indicate at what point, in relation to A, the former (B) was compiled. Everything in A which might be looked for in B is in fact there, except the ground of Cophin next to Northgate (A 9) and the rent of 20s. (A 34) due to the cellarer outside Newingate. The former item is high on the list in A, and evidently acquired early in the priorate or even before, and therefore before the compilation of B, while the 20s. is an old rent due to the cellarer even before Wibert secured the holding. It is impossible to make any deductions connected with holdings in the three southern and western wards of the city, mentioned in A, since B does not survey them.

Domesday Book as far as it covers the manors of Christ Church, Canterbury; an extent of the manor of Chartham, Kent, (c. 1200); reliefs taken by the treasurers of the cathedral (from 1216), together with transcripts of miscellaneous law-proceedings. The volume contains rentals of church property in Canterbury as follows:

Outpayments by the monks in respect of their holdings, principally in Canterbury (ff. 17–24).

Rents bought by Nigel the almoner from the heirs of Stephen the clerk (fol. 61 r.–v.), late twelfth century.

Rental of Colton manor, north Canterbury, of the earlier thirteenth-century (ff. 71–76).

Rents 'formerly received by the cathedral treasurers', of late thirteenth-century date (ff. 77v.–78r.).

Rental of cathedral property in Canterbury, of the late thirteenth-century (ff. 79–95).

Rental close in date and form to the last-mentioned (ff. 96–118).

We are here concerned only with the first item. This rental occupies eight folia each of an average size $9\frac{4}{5}$ inches by $6\frac{2}{5}$ inches. The handwriting is of the late twelfth century. The first page was carried out by the scribe in a very large script, the taller letters reaching a height of $\frac{3}{10}$ inch. At the head of the second page, he started the text again in a handwriting of more normal proportions. The rental consists of a schedule of outpayments made by the monks to their lords in respect of property (nearly all in Canterbury) held by the former and let out to tenants. An almost identical text is found incorporated in Rental X 2, which can be assigned to a date c. 1180. There is nothing in Rental C to conflict with such a date and it may accordingly be likewise assigned thereto. The names of tenants indicate that C is older than D (of c. 1200). Wibert, chamberlain to the abbot of Battle is still in possession of ground in St Alphage parish (C 16), which he bestowed (in Charter LIII) towards the end of the century upon the nuns of Minster in Sheppey, who are in possession in Rental D (D 76). Paulina, widow of Alderman John, occupies (in C) her holding (C 26) in Burgate Street, granted to her between 1175 and 1177, by the terms of Charter XXIII. Hukelot se frode (C 68) holds his ground in Ruttington Lane in C while D (D 30) shows his widow as in occupation.

RENTAL D

Register H[1] in the Chapter Archives contains a great deal of miscellaneous matter, from c. 1200 until c. 1420. The text of Rental D occupies ff. 218–29

[1] Reg. H is described in HMC, viii, app. 340–4.

of the register and forms the last element therein. A blank leaf, of the same texture and shade of colour as the folia of the rental, follows the last leaf and is clearly part of the item. The tight condition of the sewing does not allow an examination of the way in which the leaves are assembled but the occurrence of the hair- and flesh-sides of the parchment indicates an arrangement as follows. Folia 218–25 are four bifolia, one within the other. Folia 226–30 were originally four bifolia, again one within the other. The bifolium formed by ff. 226 and 230 is complete, folio 230 being the last, blank, leaf mentioned above. Within this bifolium lie ff. 227, 228, 229, originally bifolia, but owing to the removal of most of the second sheet in each case, each consists only of a single folio with a stub. The three stubs may be seen projecting after folio 229. Each folio is ruled with a lead point. There are forty-three horizontal lines on a full page, allowing for forty-two lines of text, while four vertical lines regulate the columns. The handwriting is a very well-formed and regular bookhand of the period c. 1200. It is executed in a black ink, while headings (showing in which Canterbury parish the holdings lay, or whether they were within or without the walls) are supplied in bright red, in a hand which appears to be different from that of the main text. The rental is the work of a highly-skilled and practised scribe, and it is curious that the handwriting has not been noticed in any other book or document surviving from the Canterbury scriptorium.

The text constitutes a detailed survey of a large proportion of the city of Canterbury, principally of holdings whence rent arises to the cathedral monks, and is arranged (as indicated) in four columns. 1. Name of tenant. 2. Annual rent paid, usually divided into instalments. 3. Term of year (always a religious feast) when rent falls due. 4. Description of the holding in question, often in very considerable detail, supplying measurements. There are 388 sections in the document, each normally covering one holding, though in certain cases one section will cover several. The question of dating this rental is bound up with the dating of Rental F and the reasons for assigning it to c. 1200 are given below.

RENTAL E

Rental 33 in the chapter archives comprises three rolls (33, i, ii, iii) stitched together at the foot. Each is a rental of cathedral holdings in Canterbury. Rental E is the oldest of the three (33, ii) and may be dated about 1200. The next in date (i) was written up c. 1230–35, and is the surviving portion of a much longer roll called 'Gregory's roll'. This (Rental Z) is discussed in more detail below. Roll iii is a fragmentary rental covering a few parishes in Canterbury and was put together (judging from the handwriting and names occurring) in the later thirteenth century.

Rental E consists of one membrane with a total length of 17 inches with an average width of 7 inches. The bulk of the text is in a very small current hand of about 1200, while there are some additions made at the end of the thirteenth century. There are no rulings of any kind. The whole is divided into forty-seven sections of which forty-four are in the earlier hand while the last three are in the later. Each section is provided with a paragraph mark. Caught into the stitching at the bottom is a slip of vellum in the same hand as that of the main text, bearing the couplet:

> Raptus ad incestus, explensque libidinis estus
> Fit pater ex matre natus, cui filia proles.

This rental is a survey of the parish of St Margaret, Canterbury, and is very closely related to the corresponding section in Rental D, so closely, that it must be based on the same material, though the information is set out in a different way, and the paragraphs do not always follow the same geographical order. The contents and handwriting point to a date close to that of Rental D (c. 1200).

RENTAL F

The first twenty-four leaves of Register H are occupied with a great schedule of miscellaneous payments, principally rents due to the monks of Christ Church. The whole schedule is drawn up in an untidy fashion, contrasting with the almost mechanical neatness of Rental D. The various groups in the schedule are as follows:

Rents in Canterbury (ff. 1–15r.).
Rents in Dover and Sandwich (fol. 15v.).
Rents *de diversis locis* (rents from various places in Kent and throughout the realm, including odd rents in Winchester and Exeter) (ff. 16–17).
Income *de sinodis* with pensions from churches (fol. 184).
Redditus from manors (fol. 18v.).
Gabulum from manors (fol. 19r.).
Denarii ad coquinam, apparently a render from manors originally in kind and now commuted (ff. 20v.–21r.).
A page left blank in the original draft of the schedule, whereon have been entered pensions due to individuals, anniversaries celebrated in the cathedral, paid by the treasurers; others, not paid by the treasurers, etc. (fol. 21v.).

Outpayments made by the monks *pro defensione terrarum*, almost exclusively relating to Canterbury. This is in effect a later version of Rental C. It is Rental G and it is discussed below (ff. 22r.–24r.).

Rents from tenants of sheepruns at Cliffe, Kent (fol. 24r.[1]).

Rental F is the first item mentioned above. This Rental is not, like B and D, a survey or inventory of burgess-holdings, but is an instrument to be used in the collection of rents. It is not drawn up on a geographical basis, like B or D, working from ward to ward or from parish to parish, but embodies entries arranged under the dates during the year at which rents fall due, usually religious feasts.

The leaves on which the schedule is written are of an average size of 12 inches in height with a breadth of 9 inches, apart from two gatherings (ff. 11–17, 13–14) appreciably narrower ($8\frac{1}{8}$ inches) than the rest, set out on guards. The binding of Register H is tight (as noted above) and does not allow an examination of the arrangement of the leaves. It is not possible in this case to make certain deductions from the occurrence of hair- and flesh-sides of leaves. Many of the earlier leaves have been extensively damaged in a fire, probably that in the cathedral audit house in June 1670, making examination more difficult still.

The vellum is pricked at the edges for ruling, which has been done in a careless fashion with a lead point. There are forty horizontal rulings and seven vertical. There are three columns of text: 1. Name of tenant. 2. Rent due. 3. Description of the holding, in varying degrees of detail. One page (2v.) has the column, normally placed third, on the left hand while names of tenants are on the right. The impression gained from a study of the rental is that columns 1 and 2 were first written up and the descriptive accounts of holdings added at a later date.

Two principal hands may be distinguished. The first is found as far as folio 11v. (inclusive), while the second takes over at folio 12r. and carries on to the end. The great numbers of notes and additions made to keep the rental up to date are in many different hands.

Rentals D and F present in their different way substantially the same picture of Canterbury. The great mass of names is the same and the dates of the documents cannot be very far apart. However, differences can be traced from which it must be deduced that Rental F is a little later in date than Rental D. Differences are as follows:

---

[1] A scrap of vellum is caught into the binding between ff. 11 and 12, bearing the note, 'Promissio facta conuentui ecclesie Christi Cant' per maneria', followed by a list of payments, all in a hand of the early thirteenth century.

	D		**F**
Para.		*Para.*	
33	Nigel s. of Albri	103	Widow of Nigel s. of Albri
61	'De fabrica extra Northgate super fossam'	76	'De terra quadam super fossam ubi fabrica quondam fuit'
109	Solomon mercator	294	William Silvester occupying ground 'que fuit Salomonis merceir'
110	Solomon mercator	662	Godelief widow of Solomon mercator
112	William s. of Pagan	29	Heirs of William s. of Pagan
126	Robert Polre	176	Heirs of Robert Polre
178	William s. of Odo	241	Heirs of William s. of Odo
186	Osbert Pret	27	Widow of Osbert Pret
211	Mainer the rich	30	Heirs of Mainer the rich
315	Solomon the clerk	146	Heirs of Solomon the clerk
346	Hubert Calvel	410	Heirs of Hubert Calvel

The monks of Christ Church were expelled by John for their part in the archiepiscopal election controversy in July 1207 and did not return to Canterbury until June 1213.[1] A note in red ink written in over an erasure at the head of the last item in the great schedule in Register H described above, indicates the state of affairs in the sheepruns at Cliffe as obtaining 'ante exilium'. If the last item dates from before the great exile, then the rest of the schedule must likewise be pre-exilic, in which case the date for the document as a whole must fall before the middle of 1207. It was certainly not the work of royal agents during the exile, for the whole atmosphere of the compilation is plainly monastic, and if it were the work of such agents then amid a thousand entries there would surely be some sign of secular and curial origin.[2] The constant use of 'nos, nobis', in such expressions as 'hanc terram dedit nobis' (F 138) as in connection with ground given to the monks by William of Eynesford, or a reference to Barton mill as 'molendinum nostrum' (F 287) shows that the compilers were monks of Canterbury cathedral.

The leading citizen Terric the goldsmith is named as tenant of ground in Rental F (F 30, etc.). Terric was definitely dead within the monastic financial year Michaelmas 1213–Michaelmas 1214, when payments were made to his widow, who in January 1214 with her son made fine with the king for seisin of Terric's chattels and debts. Terric was probably dead by 1208.[3] Another citizen, Ingenulph the plumber (F 199, 200, etc.), was dead in or before the end of the financial year 1214–1215, for a relief was

---

[1] See *Interdict Documents*, ed. P. M. Barnes and W. R. Powell (PRS, NS, 34, 1960), pp. 37 ff.

[2] For the story of the exile and confiscations, see *Interdict Documents, ut supra*.

[3] For Terric the goldsmith and family, see pp. 85, 118, 174–6.

paid in this year for his holding.[1] He seems in fact to have died before the return of the monks from exile, for his salary as monastic plumber was paid down until their departure, but does not reappear in the accounts on their return.[2] Most significant is the occurrence of the name Adam of Charing, a well-known figure in Kent, the repentant enemy of Becket and founder of the hospital at New Romney. Adam was dead by 1207 and possibly by 1206, and it is hardly conceivable that a monk of Christ Church would not know of the death of a man of his status.[3] It seems possible, therefore, to refer Rental F to c. 1205–6, or a short time before.

Since Rental D is patently earlier in date than F, the later limiting date for D will fall a few years before, and in fact what evidence there is does point to a date about 1200. It has been suggested above that Rental B was prepared in order to record rights both of monks and their tenants in Canterbury after the fire of 1161, and D may well be a parallel record compiled after the disastrous conflagration of 1198.[4] The Pipe Roll of that year gives a list of citizens of Canterbury, a sum of money being entered against each name, apparently representing amounts still to be paid towards a tallage. Of the seventy-six names given, perhaps twenty-four may be found in Rental D.[5] Some of the tenants in the Rental may be discovered elsewhere in the Pipe Rolls at the end of the twelfth century and early in the thirteenth. Jacob the Jew occurs in 32 Henry II[6]; Wiulph son of Meiner the rich in 3 John;[7] Terric the goldsmith in 8 Richard I and many other years;[8] Reginald son of Roger Blund in 33 Henry II;[9] Richard Deudune in 31 Henry II;[10] Henry Barate in 5 Richard I,[11] while Adam of Charing, in possession in D[12] of the holdings of Lambin Frese (himself mentioned in several years from 26 Henry II)[13] may be found in the Roll for 28 Henry II.[14]

Again, the *Epistolæ Cantuarienses*, recounting the epic struggle between

[1] Reliefs, *sub anno*.

[2] Accounts, in Cathedral Library, Lit. MS. D 4 and in CAC, *TA*, *sub annis*.

[3] For Adam of Charing, see pp. 180–1.

[4] *Annales Monastici* (Winton), *RS*, ii, 67. 'Cantuaria fere tota combusta est.'

[5] PR, 10 Richard I, pp. 207–9. Robert s. of Richard, Terric the goldsmith, Wilard of Flanders (probably the Wilard 'mercator' of D 204), Mainer le Riche, Reginald Blund, John le Volt, Arnold Ferre, Roger Blund, Robert Pollard, Ingenulph the plumber, Suan the merchant, William the cook (his widow is named in D), Gilbert 'de aula' (probably representing the heirs of H. 'de aula' in D 40), Simon Chiche, Robert s. of Emma, Robert s. of Hamo, Nicholas the glasswright, Walter Buef, William the marshall, Henry Cokere, (Henry 'cocus' of D 92?), Wiulf s. of Mein[er], Henry Barate, Henry Cod, Blakeman (the Blakeman 'burarius' of D 195?).

[6] p. 191; D 304. [7] p. 290; D 283. [8] p. 20; D 99.
[9] p. 228; D 101. [10] p. 227; D 151. [11] p. 165; D 200.
[12] D 225. [13] p. 148. [14] pp. 88, 106, and many other years.

archbishop and monks in the days of Baldwin and Hubert, mention names found in D such as those of Arnold Ferre (1189),[1] Ralph, nephew of St Thomas (1188),[2] Master Feramin (*passim*),[3] William the skinner (1189),[4] and again, Adam of Charing at the same time.[5] Corroborative evidence may be extracted from references in D to the 'new gate', the structure put up at the western end of the Buttermarket to replace the old and inconvenient entrance to the cathedral at the eastern end of the market.[6] Now the cathedral treasurers' accounts record payments 'pro nova porta' of 111d. in the financial year 1198–9, of 14s. (1199–1200), of £50 (1200–1), and of £140 6s. 8d. (1201–2), when the gate disappears from the accounts.[7] The gate seems to have been a considerable time in building, and the total spent is large, all of which points to some big structure, such perhaps as the main entrance.

RENTAL G

The rental is headed *pro defensione terrarum* and is one of the later components (ff. 22r. 24r.) of the great schedule (which also embodies Rental F) at the beginning of Register H. It may be referred to the same date (not later, it appears, than 1207). Rental G is a later version of Rental C, providing a list of lords of ground held by the monks and in turn let out to sub-tenants, showing the manifold changes in tenancy after twenty-five years. Further changes have been recorded in G in the years following its compilation, with the result that it offers a most untidy appearance as the result of extensive corrections, erasures, and so forth. Almost the whole of the original text on the first page has been scratched out and written in again.

SOME OTHER CANTERBURY RENTALS

Considerable use has been made of early rentals not transcribed in this work, but requiring some description. Mention may be made at this point of an apparently lost Rental, called *Rotulus Symonis*, evidently some roll compiled by one Symon, presumably one of the monks.[8] It finds mention in a marginal note on fol. 13v. in Rental X 2, discussed below. The roll

---

[1] Ep. cccxxvi; D 311.   [2] Ep. ccxxvii; D 209.   [3] D 237, 253, 290.
[4] Ep. cccxxii, D 331.   [5] Ep. cccxxiv.   [6] D 110.
[7] Treasurers' Accts., in Lit. MS. D 4, *sub annis*. The gate cannot be the back gate as that, still standing today, is of mid-twelfth-century date.
[8] It does not appear to be possible to identify Symon for certain. There were many monks of the name.

must be older than c. 1180, the date of X 2, but the note in the last-mentioned is not intelligible as a reference to Rental B, c. 1166. The 'Roll of Symon' is probably some compilation falling in date between B and X 2.

RENTALS X 1, X 2

These rentals are not comparable with B, D or F, being hardly more than bald lists of names and rents. They are to be found in Lit. MSS. B 15 and B 14 respectively, in the Cathedral Library.[1] X 1 is composed of three gatherings of four bifolia each. At the beginning and end are single sheets, the guards of which appear at ff. 9-10 and ff. 17-18 respectively. The total number of folia therefore amounts to twenty-six. The average size of the leaves is $11\frac{1}{2}$ inches (vertical) by $7\frac{1}{2}$ inches. The true breadth must originally have been greater since the fore-edges are largely destroyed by damp. Rental X 2 is composed of a single gathering of eleven bifolia. Half a sheet is inserted between ff. 3 and 4, the guard projecting between ff. 19 and 20. The average size of the leaves is approximately $11\frac{3}{8}$ inches (vertical) by $6\frac{3}{8}$ inches. Both MSS. are bound in handsome modern covers of dark calf.

Each rental is substantially the same schedule of names of tenants holding ground in Canterbury, supplemented by information about income from other sources, as from manors, or from property in London. Each is the work of a different scribe, the handwriting in both cases indicating a date late in the twelfth century. It seems that both lists were in use at the same time, for corrections made to bring the information up to date following changes in tenancy are found in corresponding entries in each version. However, one list (X 1), is evidently slightly earlier in date than the other, as is suggested by the entries given below.

X 1	X 2
John s. of Vivian (fol. 1v.)	Heirs of John s. of Vivian (fol. 2v.)
William of Pluckley (fol. 4r.)	Heirs of William of Pluckley (fol. 4r.)

Differences of this kind are few in number, emphasizing that the rentals are not far apart in date. The case of John son of Vivian is by itself alone sufficient to establish relative dates between the two. He was a leading citizen, borough reeve, an actor in a miracle story of St Thomas Becket, and a member of the cathedral gild of St Anselm, no doubt frequenting the shrine of that saint in the cathedral. His death must have been well-known to the monks.

[1] They were formerly components of Lit. MS. B 7. See Woodruff, *Catalogue of the MS. Books in the Library of Christ Church, Canterbury* (1911), pp. 31-32.

The earlier limiting date for both documents is 1170 since Thomas Becket is mentioned more than once and styled 'Saint'. The ground in Wincheap granted to St Thomas and the monks by Osbert of Thanington (by the terms of Charters XLI, XLII) is in their hands (X 1, fol. 7v., X 2, fol. 8r.–v.), while Rohesia 'sister of St Thomas' and Ralph his nephew are named as tenants (X 1, ff. 5r. 6v.). There is a passage in Rental X 1 (ff. 19–20), devoted to what are called the 'Rents of St Thomas'. A new generation of Canterbury tenants has come into possession since the date of Rental B (c. 1166). For example, while B (B 75) shows William son of Pagan as holding his ground in the Buttermarket, Rental X 2 (fol. 7r.) indicates that his heirs are in possession. Pagan, servant in the monastic bathhouse, is alive in Rental B (B 114), while his heirs pay his rent in X 1 (fol. 2r.).

While X 1 and X 2 are patently later in date than B, they are in turn demonstrably earlier than Rental D, as the following examples will show.

Tenant in X 1 or X 2	Tenant in D
Hulot se frode X 2, fol. 4v.	Widow of Hugo le frode, D 30
Robert Godivere X 2, fol. 7v.	Heir of Robert Goddivere, D 3
Hugo Fagard X 2, fol. 9v.	Daughter of Hugh 'Flagard', D 72
Alan the alderman X 2, fol. 6v.	Heirs of Alan the alderman, D 130
Ailric Sokere X 2, fol. 3v.	Heirs of Ailric Seocher, D 131
Norman the plumber X 1, fol. 3r.	Ingenulph the plumber son of Norman the plumber, D 95

We have seen that Rentals X 1 and X 2 are later in date than the murder of Becket, and earlier in date than Rental D, giving a range of thirty years. They can evidently be further limited. The moneyer Lambin Frese had occupied a holding just before the cathedral gate, from which he had removed by 1177 to his dwelling in Stour Street as recorded in Charter XXXVI. His name may be found in X 1 and X 2 as occupant of this last-mentioned dwelling. It is probable that his move from the Buttermarket was connected with the great conflagration at the cathedral in September 1174, which will in such case offer an earlier limit for X 1 and X 2. We know that Lambin Frese had fled from Canterbury by the autumn of 1180, and the fact that his name stands in X 1 and in X 2 means that they must have been compiled at the latest by that point of time, since Lambin's flight, that of a well-known man in business circles in a small community can hardly have gone by unknown to his lords the monks.[1] His great stone house in Stour Street was taken over by the crown and eventually bestowed on Adam of Charing, Becket's enemy.[2] The name of Lambin Frese occurs both in X 1 (fol. 2v.) and X 2 (fol. 3v.) under the entry for Midlent, but where we should expect his name at Michaelmas in either version, there we find an erasure (X 1, fol. 12r., X 2, fol. 12r.) above which the name of Adam of Charing has been written. It is probable that the keeper of the rentbooks made the necessary alteration of tenancy at Michaelmas in each case but overlooked the Midlent entries. On the face of it, the earlier limit for the rentals is 1177, the date of Henry II's charter confirming Lambin in his house in Stour Street, though it is possible that the charter may be retrospective in which case the limit can be pushed back a little, though not beyond 1174, while the later limit for the unaltered draft of the two rentals must be September 1180.

The subject matter of X 1 and X 2, as indicated, is mainly confined to Canterbury, though there are payments from housing in Sandwich and Dover, and miscellaneous items of income from various places in the realm. The material is in fact very much like that in the schedule of c. 1206 in Register H, embodying Rentals F and G.

Some important differences may be found between X 1 and X 2, such as the passage headed 'Redditus sancti Thome' in the former, not to be found in the latter. In both there is the valuable if short rental of Canterbury cathedral housing in London.[3] Rental X 2 alone embodies (ff. 23–26) a passage headed: 'Hoc est gablum quod debemus diuersis hominibus de diuersis terris quas tenemus de eis.' This is in effect another draft of Rental C, the outpayments made by the monks.[4]

RENTAL Y

There is in Register K in the Chapter Archives a long schedule of various sources of income received by the monks, close in nature and content to the schedule at the beginning of Register H, being more or less a later version thereof. A very considerable proportion of the schedule in Register K is therefore devoted to rents in Canterbury. The size of the sheets on which the schedule under discussion is written is 13 inches (vertical) by $9\frac{1}{4}$ inches. Every leaf has been slightly damaged by fire, evidently that which happened in the Chapter Audit House in 1670. The hand is a handsome bookhand of the earlier thirteenth century. The uprights slope back

---

[1] For Lambin Frese, see p. 115.   [2] See pp. 180–1.   [3] See p. 35.
[4] Rental C and this passage have been collated below, and significant differences noted.

slightly. Initials are supplied throughout in red and blue, sometimes adorned with hairlines. At the beginning is a beautifully illuminated letter 'R' serving as the first letter of a tenant's name (Robertus aurifaber), incorporating animal and plant motifs and the little white lions characteristic of Canterbury work. It is strange that an accomplished artist should have expended his talents on a purely business document, bound soon to go out of date. The rental must have presented when new a fine example of products of the Christ Church scriptorium, but alterations made in attempts to keep it up to date as tenancies changed have disfigured it very badly, as has happened in the case of Rental F.

The style of handwriting and of the initial at the beginning point to a date early in the thirteenth century. A substantial change of names indicates that some years have elapsed since the compilation of Rental F (c. 1206). Often where in F a name has been altered and that of a later tenant has been put in, this latter name will be found in the original draft of Y. For example, the name of Goldwin the mercer has been substituted for that of an earlier tenant in F (F 258), while Goldwin is tenant at the date of compilation of Y (fol. 29r.). In the same way, Milo 'de balneario' is the name given following an alteration in F (F 257), while this is the original name in Y (fol. 27v.). Examples can be multiplied. Furthermore, certain citizens who are alive in F, like Terric the goldsmith (F 193), are dead in Y (fol. 40r.). Ingenulph the plumber's daughters have succeeded to their father in Y (fol. 28r.) while he is alive and enjoying his holdings in F (F 199).

That Y was compiled by monks, and not by royal agents in occupation during the great exile is clear from the use (as in F) of the words 'nos, nobis'. It must therefore lie in date after June 1213, when the brethren came back from exile. There was a tenant of the monks evidently alive when mentioned in Y, named Alphage Frode (fol. 39r.). A man of this name was dead late in 1216, when there is record of a relief exacted for his holding.[1] It is not safe to rely on a single entry for dating these documents, unless the man in question is of some importance, and it is quite possible that there were a father and son of the same name. However, Dionisia, daughter of Rucheved, and Simon de la Tune, named as alive in Rental Y (ff. 41v., 29r.), are dead according to the reliefs, by late in 1218, while Peter the cordwainer, another tenant alive in Y (fol. 40r.), is dead by late in 1219. It seems probable that the rental must have been put together very soon indeed after the return of the monks in 1213, possibly by 1216, if we can rely on the evidence of the name of Alphage Frode (who was in fact a

[1] Reliefs, *sub anno.*

citizen of some wealth and importance and undoubtedly well known), and certainly within a year or two later. We may suppose that Y is the great new standard rentroll drawn up by the monks as part of their general reorganization on return from exile.

RENTAL Z

The next great survey, that is a description of housing, made moving from parish to parish, or from ward to ward (as opposed to a rent-collector's book, where rents are arranged under times within the year when they fall due, like Rentals X 1 and 2, F and Y), is to be found in the 'Roll of Gregory', already mentioned. This is the largest element in Rental 33 in the Chapter archives, and consists of a roll of five membranes stitched together with a blue thread, apparently original, approximately $8\frac{3}{10}$ inches wide, apart from in the case of the first membrane, which has an average width of only $7\frac{9}{10}$ inches. The total length of the roll is 7 feet $1\frac{1}{2}$ inches.

The first two membranes are not in their correct order, for though the parish of Holy Cross in Canterbury is dealt with in the first, the second membrane bears a title: 'Redditus prioris et conuentus ecclesie Christi Cantuar'. vltra Eastbrege in Cantuar'. in parochia sancti Petri et sancte Crucis de Westgate.' Despite the limitations of this title the rental is not by any means confined to these two transpontine parishes, but covers as well the parishes of All Saints, SS Mary Breadman, Andrew and Mary Magdalen. The information is distributed into columns: 1. Name of tenant; 2. Term of payment and rent; 3. Description of the holding, with (occasionally) the dimensions. The principal hand found in the document is a small and slightly irregular bookhand of the earlier thirteenth century. There are very considerable alterations in many different hands.

In Register K[1] there is to be seen a long list of monastic property in Canterbury headed: 'Transcriptum rotuli Gregorii in thesauraria'. It is written in a large and clumsy hand of c. 1300, the same hand in which a rental of Whitstable is set out in the same Register, bearing the date 24 Edward I. The 'Transcriptum' contains material over and above that to be found in Rental Z, though where they cover the same ground the texts are almost identical. A conspicuously corrupt passage in the 'Transcriptum'[2]

---

[1] Reg. K, ff. 191–208.

[2] Reg. K, fol. 201r. A note written in the roll in two columns is written as one in the register, but the scribe has made nonsense of the passage by copying straight across the top line, then the second line, and so on, of each column. As his own lines embodied a number of words different from the combined total in each line in the two columns, the final result is unintelligible.

can be explained with reference to Rental Z. We may therefore conclude that Rental 33 bore the name 'Gregory's Roll', a name which must have been current in the cathedral archives for some sixty or seventy years. The name was most probably acquired from the monk Gregory who served as cathedral treasurer for the year 1232–33,[1] just at the moment when this roll must have been drawn up, and it may be assumed that Gregory compiled it.

There is a long erasure in the original draft of the rental, that is, in the roll. A passage has been written in, in the same hand as that of the original draft, recording that a holding in St Mary Magdalen parish was 'gavelet' from Michaelmas 1230 by decree of the borough court, and was sold to one John Prude safeguarding the rights of the original tenants should they turn up ready to pay arrears. Part of the payment made by John Brand the new tenant is entered in the cathedral treasurers' accounts for the year 1232–3.[2] This is suggestive that the original draft of the rentroll was made before the end of the financial year running to Michaelmas 1233. There is a note in the accounts for the same year mentioning a payment of 8s. and running 'in restitucione pro domo Rogeri de Yrelande quam vendidimus Radulfo aurifabro', while the roll embodies a note indicating that the treasurers have granted ground described as of Roger of Ireland to Ralph the goldsmith at 6s. *per annum*. It is not quite clear how this transaction should be interpreted in light of the two entries, but it is at any rate quite clear that the 'Roll of Gregory' cannot lie in date far from the years 1230–33.

THE COLTON RENTAL

Among the miscellaneous items bounded up in Lit. MS. D 4 in the Cathedral Library is a rental[3] of six leaves listing rents, names of tenants, with a short note on holdings, belonging to the Christ Church manor of Colton in the suburbs beyond the northern walls of Canterbury. Many of the holdings clearly lie in Baggeberi (now New Ruttington Lane), and in the Northgate Street area. Frequently the same entries can be identified (some sixty years or more earlier) in Rental B, though this area is neglected by the compilers of Rental D (c. 1200).

The leaves of the rental measure $9\frac{9}{10}$ inches (tall) by $6\frac{4}{10}$ inches. It is difficult to see how they are arranged owing to the tightness of the binding, but the occurrence of the hair- and flesh-sides suggests there are three

---

[1] CAC, Misc. Accts, 1, *sub anno*. [2] *TA, sub anno.*
[3] Lit. MS. D 4, ff. 71–76.

bifolia, each within the other. The writing is a handsome bookhand, evidently of the early thirteenth century. There were originally one hundred sections in the rental but erasures have been made and additions effected. Entries are distributed under church feasts, noted in red, within the year, at which payments fall due. The latest possible date for the document appears to be 1227 since there is reference to the 'via qua itur in curiam domini archidiaconi.'[1] The archdeacon had a dwelling close to the housing described in the rental, just south of Baggeberi, but had left this dwelling and had moved across the river to Hackington by 1227.[2] A note added in another hand at the end of the rental states: 'anno quarto post translationem beati Thome. eo anno combusta est magna pars ciuitatis et omnes qui tenebant de Coltona destruxit ignis. die sancti Johannis ante portam Latinam'. Perhaps this rental was compiled to record rights of the monks and tenants within the devastated area, so falling in date after 6 May 1224. On the other hand it may date from before the disaster, and the note have been added afterwards.

A FRAGMENTARY RENTAL AT CAMBRIDGE

This item forms part of the binding of a volume containing a number of tracts of the twelfth century, once at Canterbury and now at Trinity College, Cambridge. It was originally a single sheet and is divided in two, each portion serving as a fly-leaf. The entries in the fragment have been printed by Dr James, not altogether accurately, in his description of the volume.[3] It has formed part of the volume since at least c. 1300, for the pressmark of the Cathedral Library at Canterbury (D[istinccio]. iiij[a] G[radus]. vij.) is written in on the portion of the rental at the front of the volume, in a hand of that date. The date of the rental, of which the fragment at Cambridge forms a part, must be towards 1180 since Lambin Frese the moneyer is named as a tenant paying 42d. half yearly (the rent of his great stone house in Stour Street, Canterbury).

THE SHADWELL FRAGMENT

This fragment[4] consists of a single sheet of parchment, 6 inches by 4 inches, evidently the sole surviving leaf of a Christ Church rental. It

---

[1] Ibid., fol. 72r.

[2] *Acta Stephani Langton Cantuariensis Archiepiscopi* ... Edited by K. Major (Canterbury and York Society Publications), p. 121.

[3] Trinity College, Cambridge. MS. B. 1. 25. *Catalogue of Western MSS., Trin. Coll. Camb.*, i, 28–9.   [4] CAC, Shadwell MSS., no. 13.

covers five holdings in Canterbury with some near Sandwich and at Dover.[1] The handwriting is a well-formed bookhand with headings in red ink. It is clearly not far removed in date from Rentals X 1 and X 2, of c. 1180. The entries in the fragment are slightly more informative than those in X 1 and X 2. For example where X 1 merely gives Vitalis Pacoc as paying 4d. 'in parochia sancti Petri', the fragment observes that this payment arises 'de duabus terris que sunt prope Crinemelle in parrochia sancti Petri una illarum fuit Eadilde. Hornodes. 7 altera Radulfi Elfwines sune.' The loss of the remainder of this rental is much to be regretted as we would clearly have, if it were complete, a view of the city of Canterbury in some detail falling between B and D and, since B does not cover three (Ridingate, Worthgate, Westgate) of the six wards, we should have the earliest body of information in such detail relating to such areas.

It is curious that the Canterbury surveys and rent lists have not attracted much attention. Rentals A and B have indeed never appeared in published catalogues or guides to the cathedral archives, but attention was drawn to Rentals D and F in the account of Register H in the archives, by Dr Brigstock Sheppard, prepared for the Historical MSS. Commission in 1881.[2] William Somner (1606–69), the Canterbury antiquary, knew Rentals A and B. He added some notes to the latter in which he referred to the former, but there is nothing in his *Antiquities of Canterbury* which suggests that he had found them by the date he published his volume (1640). Somner certainly knew Rental D for he added remarks to it, and wrote a whole mass of comments and notes about it, with identifications of dwellings with those of his own day, added (curiously enough) on the back of the draft copy of the annual cathedral treasurers' accounts for the year 1663–4. Again, there is little to indicate that Somner made use of this rental in his *Antiquities*.

---

[1] Of the five Canterbury entries four relate to ground near the river in what became the Greyfriars' precinct. One piece of ground lies in St Alphage parish.

[2] HMC, viii, app. I, pp. 340, 344.

CHAPTER II

The Place of the Urban Property in the Economy of Christ Church, Canterbury

BY the end of the twelfth century the monks of Canterbury Cathedral were lords of between one third and one half of the domestic property of the city. It may be inferred from the words of Bede that the early missionaries received territory in Canterbury and in time such territory may have become covered with housing. The surviving Old English charters do not tell very much about acquisition of ground and dwellings in Canterbury by the community of Christ Church. No doubt the conflagration of 1067 destroyed much of the accumulated muniments of the pre-Conquest cathedral, such as had been spared by the Danes.[1]

An early twelfth-century obituary states that archbishop Æthelheard had (about 800) helped Christ Church recover certain property including six *mensurae* in Canterbury near 'Eadburgwelle'.[2] A record, preserved in a contemporary text, survives of a transaction whereby his successor archbishop Wulfred purchased in 811 from Cœnwulph king of Mercia, certain estates in Kent including properties in Canterbury described as

in civitate Dorovernia in australe parte ecclesiae salvatoris duas possessiunculas et tertiam dimediam id est in nostra loquella ðridda half haga et prata duo ad eas prius et modo pertinentia in orientale parte Sture fluminis sita.[3]

It is stated in a late memorandum concerning grants made by archbishop Wulfred to his cathedral that he gave

villam quæ nominatur Eastur. Waldingtun in occidentali plaga ecclesie Christi infra menia urbis Dorobernie intra ripam fluminis Sture.

---

[1] There was loss of muniments at St Augustine's abbey in 1168, when 'many ancient documents perished'. *Thorne*, col. 1815, p. 94.

[2] BM. MS. Cotton, Galba E III, printed Dart, *Canterbury Cathedral*, app. viii.

[3] Birch, *CS*, 335. A later memorandum of the transaction in a cartulary (Lambeth 1212) states that the estates including the properties in Canterbury ('duas mansiones et dimidiam quod Angli dicunt thridda hialf haga. et duo prata in orientali parte fluminis Sture sita'), were bought 'ad opus ecclesiæ Christi' (Birch, *CS*, 336), but this has no independent authority.

23

This follows a brief summary of a surviving document dated 824, but the date of the grant of the *villa* is unknown.[1]

The monks preserved a document purporting to be a testamentary disposition by archbishop Wulfred's kinsman the priest Werhard in 832 of a *mansio* in north Canterbury, with a *clausula* which the English call 'teage'.[2] There survives an original charter by which king Æthelred granted in 1002 to his faithful man Æthelred and his wife, with reversion to Christ Church, a little property fifteen rods by eight, called a haw (haga) in the endorsement, within the ambit of the city of Canterbury, together with six acres for ploughing outside the wall.[3]

The early twelfth-century martyrology cited above states that seventy-two *mansiones* in Canterbury, in conjunction with estates in Essex and Kent, were acquired from a certain Osbern Bigge, evidently the Kentish magnate who is mentioned in the Canterbury entries in Domesday Book.[4]

Domesday refers to burgesses of the archbishop and of the abbot of St Augustine's but says little about burgesses of Christ Church or of their dwellings. There is mention of the land of 'Holy Trinity' (i.e. Christ Church), stated to be exempt from the king's sake and soke. There were, says the Exchequer text, two *domus*, of two burgesses, one within and one without the city, on the highway, which a certain monk of the church of Canterbury removed (abstulit).[5] The version in the White Book of St Augustine's relates that the monks of the cathedral were concerned here and that they destroyed one house and prevented another from being rebuilt (facta).[6] Under the heading in Domesday 'land of the archbishop's monks', it is affirmed that 'Nordevde' is held by the archbishop and that to this manor there pertain ninety-seven burgesses rendering £8 4s. *de gablo*.[7] Domesday Monachorum says that 'Nordwda' is a manor of the monks, and that thereto belong a hundred burgesses less three, rendering £8 6d.[8] The St. Augustine's version states that the archbishop has the

---

[1] Birch, *CS*, 382. The statement that the grant was made 'monachis' does not necessarily throw doubt on the genuineness of the tradition, for 'monachi' have been substituted for the 'familia' in the summary of the exchange dated 824 (Birch, *CS*, 381).

[2] Birch, *CS*, 402.

[3] Birch, *CS*, 1002; *Eng. Hist. Docs.* i, part ii, no. 124.

[4] BM. MS. Galba E III, printed Dart, *Canterbury Cathedral*, app. viii.

[5] *DB*, i, fol. 2r.

[6] PRO, Misc. Books of Exchequer (E 164/27), fol. 22v. Ed. Ballard (as *Eleventh Century Inquisition of St Augustine's*, British Academy), p. 10.

[7] *DB*, i, fol. 5r.

[8] *DMon*, p. 88.

manor of Norgate and that thereto now belong ninety-seven burgesses rendering £9 6d. *de gablo*.[1]

As may be seen, it is not clear whether it is the monks, or the archbishop, who is lord of the manor and its dependent burgesses.

The identification of Nordevde, Nordwde or Norgate offers some difficulty. Whitstable, six miles from Canterbury, anciently bore the name 'Northwood', but this lay in the hundred of Reculver[2] whereas 'Nordevde' lay in Canterbury hundred. Somner readily identifies 'Nordevde' with the Barton, which lay half a mile from the Northgate of Canterbury.[3] It is probable that the true form of the name 'Nordevde' was Norgate or Northgate, and that it took its name from the city gate outside which it was to be found, in the same way that the manor of Westgate took its name from another gate. Barton was not in actual fact a manor, but was confused with, or assimilated to, the adjacent manor of Colton, the nucleus of which seems to have been on the Sturry Road, opposite the Barton.[4]

The question arises, if there were almost a hundred burgesses in Canterbury dependent on the manor of 'Nordevde', where were their holdings sited? Other external manors had ground in Canterbury and, as will be shown below, several such manors and their dependencies enjoy a mention in the rentals within the twelfth century, yet no trace at all of this considerable mass of housing, said to be attached to 'Nordevde' is to be found.

Rental B shows that between the northern city walls and Barton-Colton there are very considerable suburbs, comprising *mansure*, in Northgate Street, Broad Street and the area around 'Drutintune', or Old Ruttington Lane. Is it possible that these suburbs have grown up on fields belonging to 'Nordevde' i.e. Barton-Colton, and that the holdings which lie in Canterbury according to Domesday, and produce £8 or £9 or more in rent to the manor, are in actual fact these extramural suburban *mansure*? If the whole block were transferred bodily to a general urban Christ Church Rental for Canterbury, this would account for the absence of any

---

[1] White Book, fol. 22v.; ed. Ballard, p. 12; *DMon*, p. 88. Both the printed versions (*Eleventh Century Inquisition* and in *DMon*) give the number of the burgesses as 100 minus, not 3, but 19. The word 'tres' has been altered slightly in the MS. and resembles xix. The text runs in the MS. of White Book 'cui nunc subiacent c. burgenses tres minus qui reddunt ix. lib. et vi d.'

[2] The schedule in Reg. K glosses Northwood as Whitstable. See p. 26 below.

[3] *Antiquities*, ed. of 1703, p. 47. There is some confusion in the account of Barton in R.A.L. Smith. 'The Barton and Bartoner of Christ Church, Canterbury' (*Archæologia Cantiana*, lv).

[4] The MS. materials in the Chapter Archives point to the assimilation. At the beginning of the thirteenth century there was a monk who acted as 'custos' of the Colton and a 'hallimotum' was held, in which conveyances of ground were published (Reg. E, ff. 85–92).

mention of a connection with the manor of 'Nordevde' (or Colton-Barton, if identical with 'Nordevde').[1]

In Register K, among the Chapter Archives at Canterbury, is to be found a text (in a hand of c. 1200) of Domesday Monachorum, apparently independent of that published by Professor Douglas.[2] Prefixed to this version in Register K is a schedule headed:

Iste sunt firme monachorum sancte Trinitatis Cantuarie quas bone memorie Lamfrancus archiepiscopus sic constituit et ordinauit tam de maneriis que reddunt bladum et denarios quam de illis que reddunt denarios tantum.[3]

There are three lists within the schedule: one without special heading, giving food farms and other renders in kind from various manors, together with sums of money; a second list headed 'Gablum maneriorum', showing money renders from manors, and a third list: 'Firma in denariis tantum'. The schedule, of great value for the elucidation of Domesday problems, has been discussed by Mr Lennard.[4] There are three items which relate to Canterbury under the heading 'Gablum maneriorum'.

> De hac ciuitate viij lib. et ij den.
>
> De vij acris que ciuitati adiacent x sol.
>
> De hac ciuitate xvj sol. viij den.

Lanfranc is mentioned and the entries can probably be referred back to the age of Domesday though the natural tendency must be borne in mind to associate any enactment of importance with a great name in the past.

It will be noted that the first entry embodies a figure of £8 2d., remarkably close to the render of £8 4s. or £8 6d. given for income derived from urban property from 'Nordevde' or 'Norwde' in the Exchequer and Christ Church versions of Domesday respectively. It is conceivable that the same render is involved. The 'seven acres' whence the sum of 10s. arises in the second entry can hardly be other than the field called 'Seven Acres' in Wincheap, outside the southern walls, which may be found

---

[1] There is a list, headed 'Istos redditus de Coltona solebant thesaurarii quondam recipere' in Lit. MS. D 4 (ff. 77v–78r). It is in a hand of the middle or later thirteenth century but mentions tenants alive early in the same century. Have the rents arising in the northern suburbs been transferred at some date after Domesday to the main treasury account, and transferred back at a later period?

[2] CAC, Reg. K, ff. 70–72. This version follows the principal text, published by Professor Douglas, very closely, but there are occasional differences, e.g. in the case of Wingham manor, where the words 'suus filius' are added to the name Arnoldus.

[3] Ibid. fol. 69v.

[4] R. Lennard, *Rural England*, chapter V, 'The farming out of manors'. See pp. 120, 135 ff.

divided among tenants by c. 1180 (in Rental X 1)[1] and likewise divided at the end of the century (as in Rental F).[2] Within this period 'Seven Acres' may be found producing 9s. 9d.[3] falling closely into line with the figure from the seven acres given in the schedule in Register K. It is curious that there should be two sums derived 'from this city'. The second may perhaps be explained by reference to a late twelfth-century version of the schedule. We shall find (c. 1180) that four sums are due 'five days before Michaelmas'. They are (as given in Lit. MS. B 14),[4] £7 9s. 5¾d. from Monkton; £8 os. 4d. from Little Chart; 16s. 11½d. from 'Wadland'; and 16s. 8d. from Whitstable or Northwood, not to be confused with 'Nordevde' or 'Nordwde'. The figures are very close to, or even identical with, figures in the schedule in K (where we find the four entries all grouped together), and we may draw a conclusion that the second entry in Register K 'de hac ciuitate' relates to Wadland or Wodland, another of the big fields flanking Wincheap on the east, outside Worthgate at Canterbury, close by 'Seven Acres'.[5]

A fourth item relating to Canterbury may be discovered in the schedule in Register K. Within the first group which includes farms in kind from manors is the entry 'Baggeberi reddit xxj sol'. 'Baggeberi' is the name of New Ruttington Lane, in the northern suburbs, connecting 'Drutintun' with Northgate Street. It is almost completely surveyed on both sides in Rental B at which date (c. 1166) it is largely flanked with dwellings and produces 22s. 7d. *gabulum*, close to the figure given in K. The form of the name points originally to some sort of rural settlement rather than an urban street. Mr Lennard indicates that since the entry finds a place in a list predominantly composed of renders in kind, commutation into cash has doubtless been the result of urbanization.[6]

Early in the twelfth century the cathedral obituary[7] affords mention of eleven *mansure* given by Hugh Maminot together with St Mary Queningate church. The martyrology has value as evidence since it can hardly be far removed in date from the event it purports to record. These *mansure* are probably identical with ground granted to enlarge the monastic

---

[1] X 1, fol. 13v.　　　　[2] F 601–7.　　　　[3] X 1, fol. 13v; F 601–7.
[4] fol. 20v. B 14 embodies, *inter alia*, Rental X 2.　　　　[5] F 585, etc.
[6] If the list as it stands does in fact date from the days of Lanfranc, and if the commutation is due to urbanization, then it may be remarked that an extra-mural suburb, some considerable distance from the city walls, had grown up by an early date. There was substantial 'development' of the district outside Northgate at such a date as we know for a fact, since Lanfranc established here the hospital of St John Baptist, the house of canons of St Gregory, and the dwelling of the archdeacon, in all occupying a wide area.
[7] In BM. MS. Galba E III, printed Dart, *Canterbury Cathedral*, app. viii, cited above.

cemetery, a grant confirmed by Henry I.[1] If such is the case, the dwellings cannot be regarded as a source of income to the monks. About 1100 the brethren are disclosed as in possession of two 'haws' at Ridingate, and seven at Newingate, which they surrender to the merchants' gild in exchange for eight 'haws' within Burgate.[2] Rental B[3] makes casual mention of ground in Broad Street, bought by Prior Walter (either Walter I, 'durus dens', 1143–49, or Walter II, 1149–53).

With Prior Wibert (1153–67) much clearer light dawns. We find the monks in control of wide possessions in the shape of urban housing and we have, moreover, in Rental A, the record of Wibert's acquisitions in this field. He had apparently two main objectives, first to establish a scientific frontier for the cathedral precincts, which he did effectively on the northern flank by evicting alien, secular, elements within the line of the city wall, and secondly to build up the endowments. He was already at work when sub-prior. Before the end of his priorate it is disclosed (in Rental B) that the monks control about half the burgess-dwellings in the northern and eastern section of the city of Canterbury. They certainly had some ground in the other, unsurveyed, part of the city at the same date, and are shown in Rentals D and F, thirty or forty years later, to have many possessions there.[4] Little evidence may be found to indicate how this great rentroll was accumulated. Wibert followed a systematic policy of acquiring holdings, yet his total achievements in this direction, as recorded in Rental A, amount to less than forty tenements secured in a period of more than twenty years. Probably much of the rentroll was built up through the fact that construction of houses took place on agricultural ground belonging to the monks. Outside the city walls the layout strongly suggests that this is in fact the case. Between Northgate and Old Ruttington Lane the *mansure* seem to be cut out of a couple of fields, while outside Worthgate, along Wincheap, the names survive of ancient fields (divided into plots, many bearing *mesagia* by the early thirteenth century), such as 'Holtege', 'Seven Acres', and 'Wadland'.[5]

It does not seem that charitable gifts can account for much of the property. By the twelfth century, when documents are plentiful, it is patent that the monks obtain their urban housing through straightforward purchase. Enthusiasm for the cult of Becket resulted in a few donations, such as that of Osbert of Thanington,[6] of Hamo son of William

---

[1] IV, V, VI.   [2] I.   [3] B 18.
[4] See A 10–18 (ground without Ridingate), A 19, 20 (without Worthgate), A 27 (within Worthgate).
[5] See pp. 188–9 below.   [6] XLI, XLII.

le Bof,[1] or of Philip of Hardres, whose enthusiasm for the Saint was stimulated by the prospect of perils about to be encountered on the Crusade.[2] On occasion that which appears to be a gift to the monks is in effect a sale. Ralph de Ældeham grants ground in perpetual alms on the north side of the Precincts, at the middle of the twelfth century, for the health of his soul, and of the souls of his kin, as he affirms,[3] yet Wibert's roll[4] records that he was given 10s., and a 'cuppa mazarina' despite the pious protestations of his charter. Robert, son of Richard who heads the Canterbury tallage roll of 1198,[5] made a grant of four shops in Burgate Street to the monks.[6] An entry in Register K in the cathedral archives says that 112s. being rent from the shops is to be expended on 8 October, Robert's anniversary,[7] while the entry in the obit roll tells how he died on 8 October, and bestowed on the cathedral not only the four shops but a 'ciphum' of silver weighing six and a half marks, together with five marks of silver in cash.[8] The income from the shops was expected to be laid out in extra delicacies for the monks in the refectory. There are similar benefactions from ecclesiastics. It is remarkable how many bishops and abbots in the later twelfth and earlier thirteenth centuries came from Christ Church, Canterbury.[9] Two of them had grateful memories of their old home. Herlewin, former monk of Christ Church and bishop of Leighlin in Ireland from 1202 (or before) until 1217, gave an income of 30s. produced from five shops in Canterbury, to be expended in the proportion of 20s. for a treat for the monks, and 10s. on alms.[10] A parallel benefaction was that of 'Abbot Robert's shops'. Robert of Hastings, monk of Christ Church, was appointed abbot of Chester, with support of Henry II and of Archbishop Baldwin. He vacated the office under pressure from earl Ranulph but was, however, assigned a pension of twenty marks.[11] With his own funds he built four shops in Burgate Street, Canterbury (opposite the shops of Robert son of Richard), and bought the house of Liefwin the carpenter in the same street, bestowing the property on the monks. The combined rents amounted to 60s. and were expended in a similar way to the rents from Herlewin's shops. Forty shillings were allocated to feed the monks

[1] XLV.   [2] LV.   [3] XII.   [4] A 3.
[5] PR, 10 Richard I, pp. 207–9.   [6] LIX.
[7] CAC, Reg. K, fol. 60v; Reg. H, fol. 21v.
[8] Obituary of Christ Church, Canterbury, BM. MS. Galba E III, printed in Dart, *Canterbury Cathedral*, app. viii.
[9] Knowles, *Monastic Order in England*, p. 177 n.
[10] CAC, Reg. K, fol. 60v. 'In anniuersario Herlewini episcopi octauo kal. Aprilis ad refectionem conuentus xx sol. Ad elemosinam x sol. sc. de redditu v scopparum quas ipse suis expensis fieri fecit super terram huius ecclesie.'
[11] *Epp. Cant. RS*, p. xl. *Monasticon*, ii, p. 372.

on the donor's anniversary, while the sum of 20s. was assigned to sustain the truly poor.[1] The brethren certainly made the most of their specious pretext of poverty.

It is possible that the monks owed one small corpus of holdings to Becket himself. Rental X 2 (c. 1180) embodies a short list of tenants with their rents, headed 'Redditus sancti Thome'.[2] Since other blocks of rents are named after their donors it would seem reasonable to suppose that the case is the same here. There is support for this view in the actual site of the holdings, for some of them are at the upper end of Ruttington Lane, very close indeed to the official residence of the archdeacon of Canterbury. The ground might well have been part of the curtilage of the archdeacon, granted away by Becket during his tenure of that office. Some tenements in Canterbury were acquired by the monks as patrimony when a recruit joined the house. Seven holdings described in the rentals fall into this class.[3]

While the monks were at work trying to enlarge their holdings, they suffered some self-imposed losses chiefly in their attempt to extend their precincts and consolidate their boundaries. Hugh Maminot's *mansure*, as suggested above, were evidently wasted in the enlarged cemetery. Prior Wibert levelled a row of dwellings to the north of the Precincts and carried the boundary wall up to the road running along the inside of the city wall.[4] An important landmark in the history of monastic housing in Canterbury is represented by the great exchange of 1177 when a block of dwellings near the cathedral affording 20s. 11d. in rent, was acquired from St Augustine's abbey with support from Henry II, in return for ground of comparable value belonging to Christ Church elsewhere in Canterbury.[5] The ground taken over from the abbey was cleared of housing, and thrown into the monastic cemetery, to avoid (as the charters explain) the frequent fires which had taken place among the housing. Not only was the ground in Canterbury sacrificed for the purpose of enlarging

---

[1] CAC, Reg. K, fol. 60v. 'In anniuersario Roberti quondam abbatis Cestrensis vij⁰ kal. Octobris ad refeccionem conuentus xl sol. ad elemosinam xx sol. de redditu iiii scopparum quas suis expensis fieri fecit super terram huius ecclesie et de domo quam ipse emit de Lefwino carpentario.' See D 98.

[2] Rental X 1, ff. 19v–20r. The archdeacon's house lay south of Baggeberi, outside the northern city walls. It was acquired by the monks in 1227. See p. 201.

[3] An eighth (within the twelfth century) may be added from the 'Shadwell' fragment (CAC, Shadwell MS). See p. 21. At the end of the thirteenth century the monks obtained at least thirteen houses or pieces of ground of the dispossessed Jews (CAC, Ch. Ant., C 770b, printed with some inaccuracies by Adler in his 'Jews of Canterbury' in *Jews of Medieval England*, p. 119. CAC, Ch. Ant. C 80 is record of an inquisition 35 Edward I, which discloses that the monks had obtained twenty holdings of Jews of Canterbury, some of which were meadowland on the edge of the city.

[4] A 1–8; see account of Precincts, Chapter IX.   [5] XXVI–XXVIII.

the Precincts, but the monks gave up their property in Friday Street in London to the Cornhill family, in exchange for ground and buildings in the hands of that family flanking the Precincts on the north side of Burgate in Canterbury. Fear of fire is again stressed in the relevant charters.[1]

Before the death of Becket the great body of property in Canterbury controlled by the monks had been divided up among the various monastic departments, as is shown by Rental B. There is evidence to suggest that about the year 1100, rents in Canterbury had already been allocated to departments, since the rent due from a tenement granted to William Cauvel by the prior and monks, and confirmed by Anselm, was assigned to the cellarer.[2] Half a century later Wibert the sub-prior acquired two small *mansure* in central Canterbury.[3] The vendor undertook to pay 18½d. *per annum* to the cellarer for these properties and his own dwelling, with 2d. evework, and it seems likely that the holdings were already burdened with the cellarer's rent before Wibert's purchase. Ground at St Sepulchre's, without Ridingate, bought by Wibert in 1152 was charged, even before the purchase, with *gablum* due to the cellarer.[4] The cellarer likewise drew *gablum* from ground without Newingate, bought by Wibert in or after 1153.[5] Territory in Wincheap (cut up into plots),[6] secured by Wibert, furnished 32d. to the *camera* of Christ Church. It is clear therefore that at least two obedientiaries of Christ Church controlled property at Canterbury by the middle of the twelfth century. In 1158 Adrian IV confirmed to Wibert, prior of Holy Trinity (i.e. Christ Church), Canterbury, and his brethren possessions conceded to them by archbishop Theobald, viz., the offices of sacrist and cellarer, 'cum omnibus ad easdem obedientias pertinentibus'.[7] In 1163 Alexander III issued another bull[8] in parallel terms. Within a year or two we have an excellent picture of the division of the great mass of dwellings in Canterbury, held by the cathedral, among the different departments.

Rental B, compiled not later than September 1167, shows that more than two hundred and twenty buildings lying in the northern half of Canterbury had been distributed among six departments: that of the cellarer, and of the sacrist; the 'garden', the guest house, the almonry, and the priory. The chamberlain, despite the fact that, as noted above, his office is found receiving rents earlier in the century, has no holdings allocated to him in Rental B. The explanation may be that the rental does not

---

[1] XXIX–XXXII. The ground at Canterbury became part of the Precincts.

[2] II, III.   [3] XI.   [4] IX, X.   [5] A 34.   [6] A 35.

[7] Holtzmann, *Papsturkunden in England*, ii, 228–9; R. A. L. Smith, *Canterbury Cathedral Priory*, p. 14, and note.

[8] Holtzmann, op. cit., ii, 298–9.

cover Wincheap where lay the land from which the *camera* drew rents, and that perhaps no rents were received by that department from those parts of Canterbury covered by Rental B.

A central monastic treasury was established by 1179, in which year Alexander III issued three separate bulls, confirming firstly to the cellarer's department, secondly to the chamber, and thirdly to the sacristry, their respective possessions.[1] Properties of the departments are set out, and embody in the first case Barton 'in the north part of Canterbury', with its mills and meadows, St Mildred's mill, Shalmsford mill, Guthwold's mill, 'Munkemelle', 'Hottemelle', 'Crienemelle', and Shelford mill (all in and around Canterbury), 'cum ceteris redditibus et mansionibus infra civitatem Cantuariensem et extra'. To the chamber pertain 'predia et prata et possessiones et redditus' within the city of Canterbury or without, while the sacristry is to enjoy 'certain rents' in Canterbury, and churches, namely St Sepulchre's, St Peter's, St Mary 'de Andresgate' (i.e. St Mary Breadman), St George's and St Mary Queningate, 'with its chapel of Burgate' (? St Michael). In the case of all three departments it is now laid down that income is to pass into the hands of treasurers appointed by the prior and convent, and that they shall ordain or lay out nothing but by the command of the prior and convent or of the 'maior et sanior pars' thereof.[2] The almonry escaped control by the central treasury, and managed to maintain itself and its revenues more or less intact for the rest of the middle ages. It formed in effect a separate house, a fact recognized by Henry VIII, who, though he left the newly-established secular cathedral in possession of the bulk of the priory's endowments, confiscated the almonry and its holdings.

Of the small endowments in the monastery supporting anniversaries, some fell into the hands of the treasurers, while certain others were under the control of an individual monk appointed for the purpose. A schedule[3] in Register K headed 'Anniuersaria que fiunt de thesauraria' comprises the anniversaries of bishop Herlewin, maintained by rent from shops in Canterbury, of prior Wibert and Robert son of Richard, likewise maintained by rent from the shops, and of Eldrith, wife of Ingenulph the plumber. The anniversary of Hugh de Dovera (the donor of St Mildred's

---

[1] Holtzmann, *Papsturkunden*, ii, 370–8. R. A. L. Smith, *Canterbury Cathedral Priory*, pp. 14–15, and notes. It is stated that Rental 31 (Rental B) 'enumerates certain small rents apportioned to a *dispensator* or *thesaurarius*'. A treasurer is not named in Rental B, while the William 'dispensator' who finds a mention (B 10, 160) does not receive rents, but on the contrary pays them. He seems to be an ordinary lay tenant of Cathedral property.

[2] See R. A. L. Smith, *Canterbury Cathedral Priory*, p. 15.

[3] CAC, Reg. K, fol. 60v.

mill) is, however, administered 'per manum monachi qui custodit molendinum de sancta Mildritha'. Another schedule, close in date (in Register H), shows that rearrangement might take place, for control of the anniversary of Robert son of Richard is now vested in a monk specially commissioned for the purpose.[1] Other small endowments which evaded control by the treasurers, or greater obedientiaries, were properties attached to the various altars, like those of SS. Dunstan and Alphage, which possessed a corpus of property out in the county and in Canterbury, the most conspicuous being the Great Hall of St Dunstan in St George's parish, a few yards below the church, acquired from the Cornhill family.[2] St Michael's altar drew small rents from housing[3] while the altar of St Mary the Virgin in the cathedral nave was endowed with rents, arising in the various city parishes, worth 22s. 7d. plus five chickens, granted by Susanna de Planaz, daughter of John son of Vivian, the borough reeve c. 1175.[4] Other altars, such as those of St John and of St Mary 'in cryptis' each controlled an odd dwelling.[5] St Andrew's altar took an appropriate rent in kind, two pounds of wax, from a holding in Northgate Street.[6]

The almoner's rents enumerated in Rental B amount to but 8s. 6d. drawn from eight holdings.[7] The rents were expanded as time went on. By c. 1200 the almonry possesses twenty-four holdings in Canterbury producing 30s. 7d.[8] Nigel the almoner bought a block of holdings about 1230, worth (after deductions for quitrents) 24s. 3d., plus four chickens.[9] His successor Robert of Wheathampstead purchased a further group of holdings, producing (after deductions) 7s. and one chicken.[10] A fine rental of almonry holdings compiled in 1305 by John de Gore the sub-almoner shows that the department at this date enjoys an income of £4 2s. 3½d. from local house property.[11]

It is not easy to gain any certain information about total income accruing to the monks from urban property before the middle of the twelfth century. As we have seen, sums of £8 0s. 2d. and of 16s. 8d. arise 'de hac ciuitate' according to the schedule (claimed for the days of Lanfranc) in Register K, which also tells us of 10s. from 'Seven Acres', and of 21s. from 'Baggeberi'. The first figure may represent rents from the manorial

---

[1] CAC, Reg. H, fol. 21v.

[2] LXVII, LXIX. CAC, Rental 39 (of the early thirteenth century) lists rents due to these altars. Endowments are recorded in CAC, Reg. E, ff. 145-51.

[3] CAC, Reg. E, fol. 160.   [4] Ibid., fol. 173r.

[5] Ibid., ff. 157, 167.   [6] Z, fol. 191v.

[7] B 43-49. There is another entry (50) but only the first name of the tenant is given.

[8] Cathedral Library, Lit. MS. D 4, fol. 58v.

[9] Ibid., fol. 61.   [10] Ibid., fol. 62.   [11] CAC, Reg. B, fol. 438.

tenements of 'Nordevde', which are probably outside the walls. Baggeberi, beyond the northern walls, may possibly be 'built up' at this date, though it seems unlikely that 'Seven Acres', or 'Wadland', whence arises almost certainly the smaller of the rents 'de hac ciuitate', can in the eleventh century represent urban property. It is with Rental B in the mid-twelfth century that some light appears. This rental, unhappily covering only half of Canterbury, shows that this half produces rents for the monks amounting to £17 3s. 7¾d. plus half a seam of salt.[1] We know well that the monks had property in the other half of Canterbury, and consequently we may believe that the rents approached double the figure above. There is a valuable conspectus of income secured by the monks incorporated in Rental X 2 (c. 1180)[2] and available with a few modest variations in another MS.[3] This conspectus is more or less a later version of the schedule, alleged to be associated with Lanfranc, in Register K. The renders in kind have now been commuted into cash, and other sources of profit have been incorporated such as rents in London, and from other places. The total receipts in cash are set down as £714 5s. 6½d. The largest single item is *redditus maneriorum*, at £357 13s. 4d., evidently the income set out as farms in terms of months, weeks or days in Register K, and now commuted. Other commutations are £86 5s. for *denarii ad coquinam*, and £44 1s. 6d. for *denarii ad porcos*.[4] Rents from London properties amount to £44 3s. 9d., while there are small sums derived from Romescot and from possessions at widely different points in the realm, a mill here, a meadow there, rents from Dover and Sandwich, and even from as far away as Norwich. Rents from Canterbury come to £37 3s. 9d.

The figures for Canterbury rents from the rentals themselves are as follows: Rental B, as indicated, embodies entries amounting to over £17, suggesting about £34 from the whole city. Rental X 2, of c. 1180, is concluded by a total of £35 3s. 9¾d. (close to the figure in the conspectus) to which must be added 66s. 3d. from prior Wibert's rents, and 16s. 11½d. from the ground called Wadland outside Worthgate, with 9s. 9d. from 'Seven Acres', not far off. Rental D is manifestly incomplete, and the total from its various figures comes but to £27 18s. 4d. The sums listed in Rental F amount to £42 1s. 3¾d.[5] At the end of Rental Y (compiled towards 1220) there is given a total £41 (incomplete, since shillings and pence are not given), plus 59s. 6½d. from Wibert's rents. The rents paid to Colton manor, given in the rental compiled about 1224, show that

---

[1] See p. 142.   [2] X 2, ff. 20–23.
[3] Lit. MS. B 16, ff. 9v–10v.   [4] See Lennard, *Rural England*, pp. 135 ff.
[5] For totals of rents in the Rentals, where a total is not supplied by the compiler, see Preface.

about £4 is drawn from holdings in the outer northern suburbs.[1] These holdings are included in B, but only partly included in D, F, and Y.

It is curious that the schedule in X 2 (c. 1180), which seems to be intended as a conspectus of income in cash, makes no mention of what was a profitable source of revenue in later years, that is the rents derived *de domibus et scoppis* in Canterbury. These are discussed below, but it must be pointed out here that less than twenty years from the date of the schedule in X 2, income is already £24 11s. 9¾d.[2] However, takings from this source are rising greatly in the thirteenth century and it is possible that c. 1180 they were inconsiderable.

It will be seen that the Canterbury rents form but a modest proportion of the total income collected by the treasurers and an even more modest proportion of the total income of the monastery, if the substantial renders in kind brought in from the manors are considered.[3] In terms of actual cash the Canterbury rents form about five per cent of the whole, and this proportion is maintained through most of the Middle Ages. The figures given c. 1180 for rents in Canterbury fall fairly into line, it will be noticed, with figures for half Canterbury disclosed fourteen or fifteen years before in Rental B. It is interesting to observe that the monks' income from rents in London is actually greater than that derived from Canterbury for, though the holdings in London are much smaller in number, individual rents are far higher. The rental of London embodied in X 1 shows that the monks possessed twenty-five dwellings there[4] as opposed to four hundred holdings at Canterbury, while rents from the London dwellings amount (c. 1180), to £44 3s. 9d.[5] One London house alone, in the busy commercial quarter of 'Westcheape' (Cheapside), furnishes an enormous (by Canterbury standards) rent of £9 12s. There are (as indicated above) rents derived by the monks from other boroughs. Dover produces 16s.

---

[1] In Cathedral Library Lit. MS. D 4. It is difficult to arrive at an exact figure. The total given in the MS. is 104s. 2d. but from this must be deducted a payment made from the manor of Harty (across the Swale, ten miles away), probably a commuted labour service, amounting to 20s. 8d. *per annum*. An early-thirteenth-century note in CAC, Reg. K, indicates that 16d. is received by Christ Church 'De Sullinga de Witstapele' (five miles away) because the men of Whitstable 'solebant antiquitus metere ad Bertonam' [the Christ Church home farm, Barton, north of Canterbury, next to Colton] (K, fol. 48v). Rents for access to a 'fossa' apparently irrigating certain holdings must also be deducted.

[2] In the Treasurers' accounts (CAC, *TA*) under 1198–99.

[3] It might be possible to calculate very roughly the value of the food renders, from the *Assise Scaccarii*, which survive intermittently from 1225. However, there are supplies other than food such as the great masses of wood for fuel, evidently cut in woods belonging to the monks. The treasurers account for its transport annually (CAC, Accts. of Priory, Treasurers, *passim*).

[4] X 1, ff. 14v–17r; also X 2, ff. 15v–18r.   [5] X 2, fol. 22v.

6d. from ten holdings, Sandwich 4s. 7d. from five houses, while a holding in Norwich styled 'managium' renders 10s.

When at the end of the twelfth century figures for annual receipts from rents first become available we find that income from housing in Canterbury falls into two groups: *gablum*, from property held at gavelkind, and rents *de domibus et scoppis*. The former represents income from retained rents where property (ground, rather than ground with buildings) is sold in return for a substantial *gersuma*, together with an annual rent, while the latter group represents income from another class of property (houses and shops, as its name suggests) let (locata). Already in the financial year 1198–9 receipts from 'houses and shops' amount to £24 11s. 9¾d. as compared with £31 10s. 7½d. from gavelkind rents. While the gavelkind rents remain almost static or even fall during the thirteenth century there is a remarkable increase in income *de domibus et scoppis*. By 1223–4 takings have reached over £60 from this source and in the thirties figures of over £70 are common. In the year 1281–2 more than £101 is collected, while by 1300 more than £110 is received (in which year £26 11s. 1¼d. is received from gavelkind rents).[1] By this date the total income taken by the treasurers in cash is over £2,000 *per annum*. If the urban rents are but a small proportion of the total income it must be pointed out that they will bear comparison with receipts from what is popularly regarded as a chief source of revenue to the monks of Christ Church. Much has been said of the 'vast profits' derived from offerings at the shrine of St Thomas, yet in many years within the thirteenth century this income was no greater than that secured from the local rents, and in many years Canterbury tenants actually paid more than the pilgrims offered. In 1220 offerings to St Thomas amount to £383 5s. or nearly five times receipts from rents,[2] but this was the year of the splendid translation when the saint's bones were removed to the new shrine, in the presence of great men from all over Europe, from whom large gifts might be expected. However in 1270, the second Jubilee year, offerings by pilgrims amount only to £204 2s. 10d., not even twice the sum taken from Canterbury rents at the same time. Figures for takings at the shrine such as £109 (1250), £72 14s. 10d. (1258), £95 11s. 3d. (1264) are often exceeded in the rentrolls, as by £116 6s. 1d. (1235–6), £112 1s. 11½d. (1237–8), and £123 8s. ¾d. (1255–6).

Moreover, figures for rents are merely those entered under such heading in a given year, and take no account of the often considerable sums in arrear from a previous year. Unfortunately since the figures for arrears in the treasurers' accounts are seldom broken down, it is not possible as a

[1] *TA, sub annis.*   [2] *TA, sub annis.*

rule to ascertain the true proportion for rents. In one year (1229–30) the arrears are exceptionally high, and the treasurers break them down in the accounts. We find that arrears *de domibus et scoppis* come to £23 14s. 11½d. as against £46 11s. 9½d. received when due. Even so, figures for arrears are merely what the treasurers managed to collect, and there may be further sums due from tenants.[1]

The takings on urban rents did not represent pure profit. Large numbers of monastic holdings were charged with rents to other lords. Wibert acquired ground thus encumbered, and in Rental A he may be seen attempting to buy out claimants, not always successfully. From one holding as many as three lords drew rents. Two of them, both laymen, allowed themselves to be bought out, but the third, archbishop Theobald, in his capacity as lord of the manor of Westgate, evidently would not consent, and held on to his rent of 6d. *per annum*.[2] Some thirty lords exacted rents from the monks, amounting to a total of 116s. 11½d. c. 1180 and about the same figure c. 1205, as is shown by Rentals C and G respectively.

The recipients comprise a number of private individuals, some of them manorial lords out in the countryside; and a group of religious houses, such as Faversham abbey, St Sepulchre's nunnery, Canterbury, Minster abbey in Sheppey, and Barking abbey. Certain rents were due to the courts of various manors, like Westgate and St. Martin's. Certain other rents were due to other departments within the monastery itself.[3] The king, through the borough reeves, drew rents in respect of two holdings.[4]

When the monks let out buildings, as opposed to ground, they became involved in other expenses. It is clear that they accepted liability for repairs to housing, and accordingly the treasurers' accounts incorporate under expenditure an annual entry headed 'opera in villa', sometimes showing a heavy total. Already in the year 1198–9, when income *de domibus et scoppis* is £24 11s. 9¾d., costs of repairs are £5 3s. 1d.[5] In 1207 came the great crisis in the history of Christ Church, when the monks were forced into exile because of their support for Langton in the struggle over the primacy. Fulk de Cantilu and Reginald of Cornhill were ordered to take over the possessions of the monks, apparently including the urban

---

[1] It is probable that (as suggested above) rents in the northern suburbs are assigned to Colton manor beyond Northgate. [2] A 3.

[3] There were some absurdities involved in the payment of rents *pro defensione terrarum* by the monks. One obedientiary might stand in relation of lord to another. The sacrist, a great official, was tenant to a very minor official, the 'ortolanus'. The former held ground from the latter, and let it to a citizen (B 131, 165). Sometimes there seems to have been but little interdepartmental co-operation. See B 208.

[4] C 2, 39; G 2, 37. [5] *TA, sub annis.*

property.[1] When the brethren came back (June, 1213) they found that their estates had suffered serious depreciation owing to mismanagement and exploitation, and drew up a long list of 'deteriorations' on each manor. An estimate was added of damage to their housing in Canterbury, at a figure of £20.[2] This, as it turned out, was a serious under-estimate, for the brethren were compelled to expend within a few months no less than £58 14s. under the heading 'opera in villa'. All through the thirteenth century the monks had to spend an average of £25 *per annum* on repairs to housing in Canterbury, or about a third of their income from houses and shops.[3]

The normal place for collection of rents was the cathedral treasury, and a clause often embodied in charters lays down that the grantee must pay his rent here at the appropriate time. Not only was rent due to the monks to be paid in the treasury, but the brethren insisted that rent due from them was to be collected there. The nuns of Minster far away in the Isle of Sheppey were obliged to send into Canterbury for their rent of 4s. by terms of an agreement made towards 1167.[4] However, when the monks came into contact with some strong-minded individual like one of the Crèvecœurs up at Blean, he insisted that they were to come up and collect their rent at his house.[5]

Income from housing and ground in Canterbury was coming in all the year round. Rental B shows that soon after the middle of the twelfth century *gablum* fell due on seventeen different days within a twelvemonth, all of them festivals of saints, or other ecclesiastical occasions. On most of such days there can have been but few callers at the treasury, but there were two great accounting days, Midlent and Michaelmas, when the crowd would have been great had all the tenants come together, and accordingly from the later twelfth century three separate sessions were held called *capitula*. Rents on the two great settlement days are so divided in Rentals X 1, X 2 of c. 1180. Rental F, c. 1206, records no less than two hundred and twenty-nine payments as due at Midlent, broken up into *capitula* of seventy-nine, eighty-four and sixty-six. At Michaelmas there are due one hundred and fifty-six rents, distributed into *capitula* of fifty-one, fifty-two and fifty-three.

It would be expecting too much of human nature to suppose that every-one would turn up on the appointed day bearing his rent, and the treasurers

---

[1] Cornhill evidently took part in his capacity as sheriff of Kent. Fulk's period of office was ended by writ dated 23 January 1208. For the story of the confiscation, see *Interdict Documents*, ed. P. M. Barnes and W. R. Powell (PRS, NS, 34, 1960).

[2] CAC, Rental 38, part 2. *Interdict Documents*, p. 55.

[3] *TA, sub annis*.   [4] XVI.   [5] G 49.

were compelled to maintain 'duo servientes pro redditibus colligendis', at salaries which suggest that they were available for continuous duty.[1] Sometimes still more drastic sanctions were invoked. In 1249 the monks hired the archdeacon's apparitor (preco) to go through the city and denounce as excommunicate those who would not pay their rent.[2]

The surviving rolls of arrears[3] in the cathedral archives running from 1230 show rents in process of collection. The rolls were actually used in gathering rents, as is clear from their appearance. Figures are altered, reduced, and scratched out. Every year there are scores of individuals whose rents are overdue at sums often under a shilling. They may be seen in these lists of arrears paying off debts at a penny or a halfpenny a time.

The cathedral archives contain great numbers of rentbooks and rolls running to the end of the Middle Ages.[4] A curious feature emerging from a study of them is that names of tenants with whom we are familiar in the age of king John or of Henry III are still in the lists in the days of Henry VIII. In the reign of this last-named king, among tenants of the cathedral, we may find the 'heirs of Terric the goldsmith'.[5] It is unlikely that the tenants of the ground in question were descendants of Terric, or Theoric, craftsman and financier of the later twelfth century, or, even if they were, that they were conscious of their ancestry. It is clear that the name of a remote occupant has remained attached to the ground, in the same way that out in the county of Kent names of ancient cultivators remain attached to their holdings.[6] In 1530 one Henry 'de Eastria' appears to be paying rent for a tenement in Canterbury.[7] The archaic form of the name makes the entry suspect, and we may trace it back into the thirteenth century, to the days when the property was held by Henry of Eastry, namesake of the great prior of Canterbury cathedral.[8] Indeed, one example of such survival of a name remains today in 'Meister Omers', the great house near the east end of the cathedral, which perpetuates the memory of an occupant in the mid-thirteenth century, Magister Homerus the lawyer.[9]

---

[1] CAC, Reg. K, fol. 217. Each has 26s. 8d. *p.a.* The schedule in which they are mentioned is dated 1322, but they appear in the lists of arrears (CAC, Arrears) of 1233, 1234, etc.

[2] CAC, Domestic Economy, no. 1, ii.   [3] CAC, Arrears.

[4] In the series CAC, Miscellaneous Accounts, and CAC, Rentals.

[5] CAC, Misc. Accts., 29, under 2 Henry VIII. See pp. 174–6.

[6] Jolliffe, *Prefeudal England*, pp. 26–7.   [7] CAC, Rental 81, fol. 6.

[8] Lit. MS. D 4, fol. 87r. Henry of Eastry, the tenant, pleaded in the local borough court c. 1280 (CAC, Ch. Ant. C 79).

[9] See *Archæologia Cantiana*, xiii, pp. 116–21.

CHAPTER III

The Holders of Land in Canterbury

THE lords of ground within Canterbury fall into many different categories, ranging from the king to some widow dwelling on her small plot of earth held from a citizen who in turn holds perhaps from the church, or from another citizen. The lords may be divided roughly into classes as follows. At the head stands the king, lord of the whole borough, yet possessed of the most modest income (embodied in his farm) from land within the city. There is a group of lords dwelling on, and taking their names from manors out in the countryside, each of whom controls a few tenements in Canterbury. Several religious houses, within and without the city, have holdings running from the vast accumulations of Christ Church (up to half the borough) to the solitary tenement of a distant nunnery. Some of the citizens enjoy a substantial rentroll from dwellings let out to their fellows, while there is the little man or woman holding only the few square yards where he or she dwells.

Some light may be thrown on to the sources of the royal farm in Canterbury by the Rentals and Charters, since certain tenements in the hands of the monks stand charged with rents contributory thereto.

The income derived from the borough by its lord, the king, is unimpressive. At the date of Domesday Book he has but nineteen burgesses[1] rendering £1 17s. 3d. *gablum*, survivors of fifty-one T.R.E., who rendered £3 17s. 5d.[2] The cause of the reduction in numbers was due to destruction of eleven dwellings 'in fossato ciuitatis',[3] according to the Exchequer text, or 'infra fossatum castelli', according to the St Augustine's abbey version.[4] Seven dwellings of the original fifty-one have been transferred to the archbishop, and fourteen to the abbey 'pro excambio castelli'.[5]

---

[1] *DB*, i, fol. 2r.

[2] These amounts are supplied from the text in the White Book of the abbey (PRO, E 164/27, fol. 22r; ed. Ballard, *Eleventh Century Inquisition*, p. 9). The MS. says that the fifty-one burgesses paid £3 17s. 5d. and that the missing thirty-two paid £2 0s. 2d. to the king; giving the figure of £1 17s. 3d. for the remaining nineteen. Ballard's figures, and whole printed text, are most inaccurate.

[3] *DB*, i, fol. 2r. [4] White Book, fol. 22r; ed. Ballard, p. 9. [5] *DB*, i, fol. 2r.

The holdings of the churchmen have been wasted to build the castle and they have been compensated with other dwellings elsewhere in Canterbury whence rent is due to the king, henceforth paid to them. Domesday discloses at Canterbury no low regular burgage rent[1] due to the king as lord of the borough. Maitland asks in his discussion of the borough of Cambridge, why it is that in borough after borough certain houses pay landgafol, while others do not. Was the burden once general and have we a mere survival? Is the payment of the gafol a relic of commendation?[2]

At Winchester the surveyor can work up and down the principal streets enumerating dwelling after dwelling where rent is due to the king.[3] A considerable proportion of houses in Cambridge produces landgafol, at £7 2 ores, plus 2d. in Domesday, and at a figure under £8 in the Hundred Rolls, but even here the incidence of payment is on less than half the holdings.[4] At York only a modest proportion of the holdings within the city is charged with a rent to the crown, and here a special term, 'haimald' is employed to denote both the rent and the tenement from which it is due.[5] In the case of Bristol figures for rents are available at no less than three different dates (1295, in the fourteenth century, and c. 1488).[6] At London the king's landgable was exacted from an undefined number of tenements, and in case of non-payment a special version of the gavelet process of distress could be invoked.[7]

There are other royal sources of income in Canterbury at the date of Domesday, beside burgess-dwellings.[8] Eight acres of meadow, once used as pasture by royal messengers, produce 15s. de censu. One thousand acres of 'silva infructuosa' otherwise called 'minuta silva'[9] afford 24s. Three mills produce 108s. while toll renders 68s. Domesday says that altogether (inter totum) the city was worth £51 T.R.E., as much when Haimo the sheriff took it over, and now, at the date of the survey, £50. However the farmer (qui tenet nunc) pays £30 blanch and £24 tale, above which the sheriff gets 110s.[10]

Following Domesday Book the next material information which can be recovered about royal profits from Canterbury is in the Pipe Roll of 31 Henry I, when the sheriff of Kent renders account of £27 8s. 10d.

---

[1] See Hemmeon, *Burgage Tenure*, pp. 61 ff.   [2] *Township and Borough*, pp. 70–1.
[3] *DB*, iv (in the Winton Survey).   [4] *Township and Borough*, pp. 70–71, 180–2.
[5] Farrer, *Early Yorkshire Charters*, i, p. xi.
[6] See Veale, *Great Red Book of Bristol* (Bristol Record Society), appendix C.
[7] Bateson, 'A London Municipal Collection of the Reign of John, Part i' (*EHR*, xvii, 495).
[8] *DB*, i, fol. 2r.   [9] White Book of St Augustine's, fol. 21v; ed. Ballard, p. 7.
[10] *DB*, i, fol. 2v.

ad pens' of the farm of the city and is quit.[1] The roll of 2 Henry II mentions £29 blanch 'in Cantuar',' 'which William of Ypres has' and £20 tale which William of Ypres likewise has.[2] In the next year there is an entry of £14 10s. blanch (just half the figure for the previous year) 'for the half year when William of Ypres had it', plus £10 tale 'quas Willelmus de Ipra habuit' (i.e. for the half year when William had it?).[3] The figure for the farm appears therefore to be, by the reign of Henry II, £29 blanch and £20 tale, not far from the Domesday figure, the diminution being accounted for, no doubt, by conditions in the anarchy. The figures for the farm are not disclosed in later Pipe Rolls, though as will be seen below the 'prepositi' of Canterbury are found collecting some components of the royal revenue in the later twelfth century.

A chance survival of a document discloses the process of reduction or the king's rentroll in the city. Charter xxv shows that there was a woman called Athelisa who occupied ground outside Worthgate opposite the castle, on the moat. She was a tenant of Christ Church to which she paid 4s. *per annum*, and had, according to the charter, 3s. to her own use, from which it seems evident that she had tenants who paid her 7s. This ground was requisitioned to extend the outer fortifications, and the question of compensation was undertaken by the royal justices.[4] They decreed that royal rents to the same value should be assigned to Christ Church and to Athelisa, and a jury of local *probi homines* was empanelled to select the same. They designated certain holdings lying on the north side of Burgate Street, producing to the crown gable of 16d., 20d., 17d., 12d. and 20d., making a total of 7s. 1d. Of this Athelisa was to receive 3s. while the brethren took their share of 4s. Athelisa owned other rents near Worthgate worth 5s. or some sum close thereto. Her ground here was likewise requisitioned for strengthening the fortifications, though in this instance she was not assigned other ground, but was granted 5s. *per annum*, which figure will be found in the Pipe Rolls every year for a very long time.[5] The allowance is first to be seen in 15 Henry II when she receives 15s. for three years, so it may be assumed that the appropriation had taken place in or before 1166.[6]

In 1234 Canterbury was granted to its citizens in fee farm for £60 *per*

---

[1] PR, 31 Henry I, p. 63.

[2] PR, 2, 3, 4 Henry II, p. 65; William of Ypres is the grantor of Charter XIV.

[3] Ibid., pp. 101, 102.

[4] There is some difficulty over the names of the justices, as recorded in Charter xxv. See notes to this charter.

[5] See PR, 14 Henry III, p. 111.

[6] PR, 15 Henry II, p. 161. She is called Adelizia f. Simonis.

annum payable in two instalments (Easter and Michaelmas).[1] We have an admirable analysis of royal revenue arising in Canterbury, drawn up at a date so close that it can hardly be considered as anything but the inquisition commissioned by the crown preparatory to the grant in fee farm. This document (which is available in a transcript of the fifteenth century) purports to be the findings of a group of local knights and citizens who all flourished, as far as may be traced, in the earlier thirteenth century. The schedule of sources of profit drawn up at their behest, is described as 'Particulars whence the farm of the city of Canterbury ought to arise *per annum*', and may be conveniently referred to as the 'Particulars of the Farm'. The whole is reproduced as Appendix A below.

The sources of revenue fall into four groups, and amount to a total of £54 0s. 5½d. The groups are: pleas and similar cases, producing £20 13s. 2d.; stallage, producing twenty marks; a mill, with meadowland, valued at £18;[2] dwellings, plots of ground and the like, in Canterbury, producing the balance (£2 0s. 7½d.).

The pleas specified in c. 1234 may be roughly equated with sake and soke enjoyed by the king in Domesday. A round figure would be expected in the 'Particulars' since income from such a source is unpredictable, in which case the figure for pence in the sum £20 13s. 2d. should probably read '4d.' Stallage, the next source of income, is not mentioned in Domesday, though on the other hand toll named in Domesday, strangely enough, finds no place in the 'Particulars'.[3] Probably 'stallage' comprehends toll. It will be noticed that a sum of twenty marks from stallage is annually paid to the leper hospital at Harbledown c. 1234.[4] This benefaction was made to the hospital as part-penance for the murder of Thomas Becket by Henry II, the very day (12 July 1174) he performed his pilgrimage.

> Pur amur saint Thomas ad otrïe en dun
> Vint marchies de rente a la povre mesun.[5]

The payment (£13 6s. 8d.) was taken over by the citizens when Canterbury was granted to them in fee farm in 1234 and is still being paid

---

[1] The charter is preserved among the city archives. See p. 87.

[2] This figure seems to be annual render. As a mill is included it appears much too low for capital value.

[3] Toll is an important source of income in the medieval borough accounts. It amounts to an average of 3s. per day in the earliest surviving Canterbury borough account (c. 1270, City Archives, F/2/2).

[4] 'Particulars' (App. A) § 2.

[5] *Guernes*, vv. 1185, 1186.

regularly to Harbledown Hospital every year, past the middle of the twentieth century.[1]

Domesday specifies three mills of the king, though only one mill is mentioned in the 'Particulars'. It is said to render (as indicated) in conjunction with ten acres of meadow (probably substantially the eight acres in Domesday), £18 *per annum*.[2] The mill can be recognized by its name as King's Mill, standing at King's Bridge, in the centre of the city. The meadow can likewise be recognized from its name, as Kingsmead, on the river below Canterbury, still today in the hands of the citizens.

The various plots of ground in the hands of the king all round the city are specified individually. Some are classed as 'terra', some 'tenementum', others as 'domus' or 'curtillagium'.

In the case of these various tenements of c. 1234 there is a singular lack of correspondence with the information in Domesday, and modifications disclosed by such documents as Charter XXV. Between 1066 and 1086 the royal rentroll was reduced from £3 17s. 5d. to £1 17s. 3d., through (as shown above) demolitions of dwellings to extend the fortifications, and compensations to churchmen. Henry II abandoned claim to seven other dwellings to compensate the monks, and Athelisa, for their holdings requisitioned at Worthgate, again to develop the fortifications. It is highly improbable that there were no other losses to the royal rentroll in the twelfth century, and it would appear that hardly anything can be left to the king. However, the 'Particulars' disclose an income of £2 0s. 7½d. from as many as thirty miscellaneous patches of ground around the city. Doubtless much of this had been acquired at no remote date from such sources as escheat or forfeiture, or again, from squatters on waste ground, or in the city ditch. Several of the holdings mentioned in the 'Particulars' can be identified. One may be easily located for it is the church of St Mary Magdalen, Burgate, which must have been founded on royal territory since a rent of 20d. arises therefrom.[3] It may be pointed out that close to this church lie other pieces of ground owing rent to the crown, like the 'ground of Kenting' also furnishing 20d. and the block of dwellings worth 7s. 1d. with which Christ Church and Athelisa daughter of Simon were compensated for their ground expropriated at the castle.[4] There are two pieces of meadow, one, of ten acres, mentioned already,[5] and another, held by Christ Church, at 18d. *per annum*.[6] It is worth noting that one

---

[1] For a fuller account of this payment see W. Urry, 'Two Notes on Guernes de Pont Ste-Maxence, *Vie de Saint Thomas*' (*Archæologia Cantiana*, lxvi, 1953, pp. 92–97).

[2] 'Particulars', § 1.   [3] § 4.   [4] C 2; G 2; IV, V, XXV, XXVI, XXVII.

[5] 'Particulars', § 1.   [6] § 6.

piece of ground is not in Canterbury at all, but lies well beyond the city liberty at St Dunstan's, and must have been included in the city farm for administrative convenience.[1]

One render of 5s. does not seem capable of a straightforward explanation. The entry says that the 5s. is derived from the Barbican 'qui debentur in compoto super scaccarium'.[2] It was at the Barbican, outside the castle, that Athelisa's property lay, and indeed she is called Athelisa of Barbican. For ground belonging to her and requisitioned here (as shown above) she was allowed 5s. every year, an allowance which finds a place in the Pipe Rolls.[3] We should rather expect to find a reduction made on the total for royal receipts in Canterbury, than an entry on the credit side. Perhaps the 5s. in the 'Particulars' forms part of some bookkeeping arrangement in connection with the annual sum due to Athelisa, or (by this time, c. 1234) to her heirs.[4]

The royal interest in certain groundplots in Canterbury can readily be explained, for these constitute encroachments upon the fortifications of the city. The house of the heirs of Bartholomew the smith, with adjacent holdings, stands on the moat at Northgate.[5] The house of the abbot of St Radegund's stood[6] very close at hand to these, upon the ditch, under the wall, in Duck Lane. Some dwellings abut on to the city wall outside and inside, as that of Alfred Hocholte outside at Westgate,[7] and that of Alfred Markare inside at Newingate,[8] a dwelling which can be accurately sited from the Rentals.[9] William Somner lamented the want of a *pomœrium* inside and outside the walls in 1640,[10] but it is obvious that the essential clear space either side of the fortifications was disappearing in the twelfth and thirteenth centuries, and that the crown connived at the practice, endangering the safety of the city, in accepting rents from the squatters.

Sums contributory to the royal farm can sometimes be traced in the archives of those who paid. St Augustine's abbey owed 20d. *per annum* to the farm for ground of William son of Richild (Richard) until 1177, when the ground in question was ceded to the cathedral monks.[11] Christ Church owed 20d., undoubtedly the same due, for ground absorbed into

---

[1] 'Particulars', § 7. [2] 'Particulars', § 3.

[3] See above. It is curious that the word Barbican emerges in the Pipe Roll of 14 Henry III (p. 111), whereas it is not used in the Rolls temp. Henry II.

[4] It is possible that the 5s. was delivered to her locally and that a quittance was exhibited at the royal exchequer.

[5] 'Particulars', §§ 10–13. [6] § 14. [7] § 24. [8] § 30.

[9] B 69; D 88. [10] Somner, *Antiquities of Canterbury* (1640), p. 32.

[11] XXVI, XXVII.

the enlarged monastic cemetery south of the cathedral belltower, enclosed within the new boundary wall,[1] and also owed 2s. 6d. for the ground of Alfred the parmenter 'in front of the old cemetery gate'.[2] It would be reasonable to expect these entries to find a place in the schedule of components of the farm of c. 1234. There is indeed an entry which embodies some of the same names and figures. Section 5 of the 'Particulars' states that 20d. is received towards the farm 'from the house of David of Burgate, from the convent of Holy Trinity [i.e. Christ Church] from the stone house opposite the old gate.' Now while 20d. is paid as shown according to the cathedral evidence,[3] this sum is due, not from the house at the old gate, but for the ground some way off enclosed within the new conventual wall, opposite the house of David of Burgate.[4] For the house at the old gate a figure of 2s. 6d. in fact was due.[5] It almost looks as if this entry c. 1234 in the 'Particulars' is a conflation of the two of an earlier date. Probably the figure of 2s. 6d. has been liquidated at some point of time in the interval; the facts have grown dim and confused in the communal memories of monks and citizens, and a payment of 20d. due from an obliterated holding now lying unidentified somewhere in the cathedral graveyard has been connected with a more tangible stone house. There is some confusion, it should be remarked, even at an earlier date about the 20d. It seems clear that it must have been originally the figure due to the crown from the holding of St Augustine's abbey held by William son of Richild (Richard) which was assigned to the cathedral in 1177 when the effort was made to clear all the territory south of the great church for fear of fire (following the disaster of 1174).[6] It was specifically enacted that 20d. due 'to the king's farm' for this holding, paid in the past by the abbey monks, should be paid in future by their brethren at the cathedral.[7] Now Rental C says[8] that the money is due 'from the ground of Kenting' while a quarter of a century later Rental G[9] says that it is due for the ground of Kenting, 'enclosed within the new wall'. There was indeed territory in the hands of 'Kenting' here for William of Ypres conveyed to Christ Church, in or before 1155, rent of 20d. from the ground of Leuwin Chentingessune.[10] One of the rents from holdings close to the cathedral belltower with which Athelisa and the monks were compensated for loss of their ground at the castle, was of 20d. 'from the land of Lifwin Kenthing'.[11] Neither the

---

[1] C 2; G 2.   [2] C 39; G 37.   [3] C 2; G 2.

[4] This house serves as a landmark in rentals and charters of the earlier thirteenth century and stood west of St Mary Magdalen church, on the north-eastern corner of Iron Bar Lane (Rental Y, fol. 24r).

[5] C 39; G 37.   [6] XXVI, XXVII.   [7] Ibid.   [8] C 2.
[9] § 2.   [10] XIV.   [11] XXV.

20d. from ground of Chentingessune granted by William of Ypres, nor yet 20d. from that of Lifwin granted by Athelisa to the monks is a contributory to the farm late in the twelfth century for (at least as far as the documents show) the former is not rendered to the king, while the latter was definitely assigned away by the royal justices by 1168.[1] The ground of 'Kenting' held from William of Ypres, and that held from the crown might be the same, as there is a parallel example at the same date not far off[2] of ground held from more than one lord, but it is hard to identify either with the ground of Richild, held first from St Augustine's abbey and then from Christ Church, for which 20d. was due to the crown. Obviously there is confusion, arising from fading memories as to which piece of ground actually bore this charge.

The other piece of ground burdened with a charge to the royal farm can be discovered in the Rentals. The ground was, as indicated above, that of Alfred the parmenter, and it lay at the old gate of the cathedral cemetery.[3] Rental A shows[4] Alfred the parmenter in occupation of a holding at this gate, bought by prior Wibert, while the same entry can be found in Rental B.[5] One difficulty is however, that the rent due to the crown (2s. 6d.) is equalled by the rent paid by the tenant, and therefore the cathedral would make no profit, though of course relief would occur from time to time.[6]

The 'Particulars' embody a payment, as mentioned above, of 18d. from Christ Church 'from a certain meadow'.[7] This amount has not been traced in the cathedral archives, and it is not clear where the meadow lay. Possibly it was held by a monastic department, for which, at this early date (c. 1234) no archives are available.

The schedule of outpayments in Rental X 2 (c. 1180) embodies an entry mentioning a payment of 20d. made to the 'prepositi' of Canterbury 'for the ground of the priest of Brook'.[8] This may be probably equated with the ground given by John Calderun[9] to Christ Church, whence rent was due to Agemund of Wye (near neighbour to Brook, ten miles from Canterbury), lying almost next to the city prison. The subsequent history of this rent to the 'prepositi' cannot be traced. It

---

[1] Ibid.   [2] A 3.   [3] C 39; G 37.
[4] A 28.
[5] B 89.
[6] The 'ground of Dunstan' outside Northgate was a similar case (B 56).
[7] 'Particulars', § 6.
[8] C, variant readings to § 75.
[9] XLVII, XLVIII. A rent of 13d. reserved to A. of Wye in these charters appears to be the rent of 13d. paid to the priest of Brook (C 40; G 38).

does not seem to be possible to identify it among the rents in the schedule of 1234.[1]

The manorial lords mentioned at the beginning of the chapter will well repay study. Many of the families concerned are of exceptional interest since in more than one case they can be traced back from the lord who is, in the later twelfth century, collecting rents in Canterbury, to a landowner mentioned in the Kentish section of Domesday Book. Some of the families are involved in the story of archbishop Thomas Becket, and again, some of them supply a knight to the honour of the archbishop.

St Mildred's mill, close to Canterbury Castle, was granted, together with some ground in the city, to Christ Church by Hugh de Dovera, a grant confirmed by his nephew John soon after the middle of the twelfth century.[2] John de Dovera, possibly the same man, holds ground in St Peter's parish about 1200,[3] while Fulbert, son of John de Dovera is involved in a dispute over ground in Canterbury at much the same date.[4] Hugh and his nephew John are distinguished men. John with his colleagues charged an 'assize' on the royal demesne in 1172–3.[5] Hugh served as sheriff of Kent from Christmas 1160 until 1168, his term of office coming to an end by Easter in that year.[6] In 1163 he attested a charter settling services due from knights of the count of Flanders to the king of England.[7] By his *carta* in 1166 he made return of fifteen knights in Kent,[8] one of them being Elias of Shillingheld, a name which may be found among witnesses to the charter of John de Dovera confirming St Mildred's mill to Christ Church.[9] Hugh de Dovera made a return of knights (five and a half fees all told) in Cambridgeshire, as of the inheritance of his wife at the same date, and had five knights of the honour of Bourne.[10] In 1167–8 he paid £9 6s. 8d. scutage from old enfeoffments, and one mark from new.[11] In 1171–2

---

[1] The entry was cancelled in Rental C, in the variant reading, § 75 (c. 1180), at an early date. The history of the royal farm in Canterbury can be traced right down to the present day. The receipts were until the nineteenth century kept in a separate section of the annual borough accounts headed 'Pipe Rents', though they were confused in some measure with the block of rents acquired from the crown after the dissolution of St Augustine's abbey. Some of the farm rents were being paid as late as 1943, when they were liquidated for a capital sum. As shown above, the charge upon the farm of twenty marks to Harbledown Hospital, enacted by Henry II in 1174, is still a reality.

[2] XLVI; Hasted, *Kent*, 8vo edition, xi, 143. [3] D 317.

[4] CRR, Hilary, 1 John, p. 124. [5] Eyton, *Itinerary*, p. 176.

[6] Ibid., p. 338. [7] Ibid., p. 61.

[8] RBE, pp. 191–2. This Elias is probably the Elias 'dapifer Hugonis de Doura' who renders account *de misericordia* in 16 Henry II. See PR, *sub anno*, p. 160.

[9] XLVI.

[10] RBE, pp. 368, 372. The wife's name is Matilda, according to the cartulary of St Bertin. See below. [11] RBE, p. 35.

John his nephew produced £14 and 20s. under the same headings.[1] John had evidently succeeded to headship of the family in the interval. Hugh's shrievalty, as noted above, had finished by Easter (31 March) 1168 and, since the cathedral obituaries indicate that his commemoration took place on 2 March, we shall probably not be wrong in supposing that he died 2 March 1168.[2]

Hugh apparently had no son. John his nephew had (as shown above) a son Fulbert (II). He (John) had two brothers, William (II) and Ralph, and all three were sons to William (I) de Dovera.[3] This William, a soldier of the Empress, 'vir studii militaris, calidus et acer', suddenly became full of remorse for all the evil and afflictions he had brought on the populace in the Civil War, joined the Crusade, and was slain in the East.[4] He and his brother Hugh (the grantor to Christ Church of St Mildred's mill), were sons of Fulbert de Dovera.[5]

The alternative name of the family was 'of Chilham'. There are of course many cases where a family bears more than one surname derived from scattered possessions, as in the case (in Kent) of the line of Vitalis, known as 'de Soford', and as 'de Sturmuth' or in the case of the line of Godefrid styled 'of Malling' (Sussex), or 'of Thanington' (Kent). However, certain families bear two names, one derived from a possession in England, and the other from a place of origin in Normandy, as in the case of the Vaubadons or Dentons, and the Crèvecœurs or Bleans.[6] In the case of the 'de Dovera' or Chilham family we have territorial names, one (so it may be assumed) derived from Dover, and the other from Chilham, six miles from Canterbury. The connection with Chilham can easily be demonstrated,

[1] Ibid., p. 48.

[2] Obituary of Christ Church, Canterbury, BM. MS. Cotton, Galba E III, fol. 32r (printed Dart, *Canterbury Cathedral*, 1726, app. viii). In addition to St Mildred's mill Hugh de Dovera gave to the monks 10s. *p.a.* from the mill at Shalmsford in Chartham, near Canterbury (ibid.). Hugh's name is mentioned in the Pipe Rolls in many years after 1168, but the mention of a man's name therein is no proof that he was still alive. It seems likely that there may have been two Hughs, sons of Fulbert. The Domesday entry for Eastling (i, fol. 10v) says that Odo gave the manor to Hugh son of Fulbert, though the tenant is named (1086) as Fulbert. It is most likely that the transfer by Odo of the manor to Hugh took place before the bishop's fall in 1082. Thorne, the chronicler of St Augustine's, says that abbot Scolland (d. 3 September 1087) assigned two ploughlands at Shepherdswell (near Dover) to Hugh son of Fulbert (col. 1789, p. 53). Is this Hugh an earlier son of Fulbert who has died before his father, as may be suggested by the Eastling entry in Domesday? Perhaps Hugh (d. 1168) is son of a second and late marriage.

[3] *Archæologia Cantiana*, iv. Notes from the [eighteenth-century] cartulary of St Bertin [printed by an anonymous editor]. Charters I and xv.

[4] *Chronicles of the Reigns of Stephen, Henry II and Richard I* (RS), in *Gesta Stephani*, iii, pp. 109, 114.

[5] *Archæologia Cantiana, ut supra*.   [6] For these families, see below.

but the surname 'de Dovera' is less easily explained. It is true that the family owed castle-guard at Dover, but this is not distinctive enough, it may be argued, since several families owe the same service.

Fulbert, named as lord of Chilham in Domesday Book, is one of the men of Odo of Bayeux. Round suggested that 'Dovera' whence he takes one of his names is not the Kentish Dover, but the Norman Douvres (la Délivrande) north of Caen, and some thirty miles from Bayeux. As he points out, the rare Christian name Fulbert is found attached to ground at Douvres in the days of Henry II.[1] The place-name is rendered Dovera in early charters. The barony of Douvres belonged in the twelfth century to the bishop of Bayeux, and was made up of a group of holdings stretching into the parishes of Douvres and Bernières. As early as 1035 the bishop had ground at Douvres. Odo himself bought the fief of Bernières from William de Courseulles.[2] It seems likely that Douvres may be added to the list of places whence came one of the first generation of Norman invaders.

Hugh the sheriff, son of Fulbert 'of Chilham', granted Hougham Church (Kent, near Dover) to the monks of Dover at some date between 1155 and 1162,[3] and bestowed Chilham church on St Bertin, perhaps in the period 1151–4, by a charter in which he mentions his wife Matilda and his mother Adelit.[4]

Domesday Book shows that Fulbert held (under bishop Odo) Chilham together with Hougham and Barham, Luddenham and Eastling, with a mill in the manor of Eastry.[5] Folbert of Chilham is witness to the charter (c. 1100) of prior Ernulf and the convent of Christ Church granting ground at Canterbury to William Cauvel.[6] On 27 March 1111, Fulbert de Cilleham, in company with his 'miles' Hugo, attests on the side of the sheriff of Kent, a transaction relating to St Augustine's abbey.[7] This may well be the Fulbert of Domesday Book, though it is unlikely, yet far from impossible, that the last-mentioned should be the Fulbert who is father to Hugh of Chilham who dies more than eighty years after the date of Domesday.

The holdings of Fulbert in Domesday are long afterwards grouped

---

[1] Round, *Family Origins*, p. 213, citing Bourienne, *Antiquus Cartularius Ecclesiae Baiocensis*, i, 144 ('. . . terra apud Doveram quae dictur . . . terra Fouberti').

[2] I am very grateful to Professor M. de Bouard for this information. Douvres is called Dovera in several twelfth-century documents, as in the archives of St Stephen, Caen. It is called Dovera in a charter of Richard de Hommet to the Chapter of Bayeux (*Antiquus Cartularius Ecclesiae Baiocensis*, i, 54). See last note.

[3] Saltman, *Theobald*, no. 96.   [4] *Archæologia Cantiana*, iv, *ut supra*, Charter i.

[5] *DB*, i, ff. 9v–10v, 13r.   [6] III.

[7] BM. MS. Cotton, Claudius D X, fol. 175r. The charter relates to Fordwich, the 'parvum burgum' of Domesday Book, lying on the river, a mile below Canterbury.

together for service at Dover Castle.[1] Even in the twentieth century the name of Fulbert's Tower there still commemorates him.

According to Rental D there is a certain Hamo de Soford who holds ground at Canterbury in Dover Street, between Newingate and Ridingate,[2] and other ground just without Ridingate.[3] At much the same date one William de Soford has ground close to the same gate, in the hands of a tenant.[4] The family evidently takes its name from Shoford, the old name for the 'Mote' at Maidstone. There is sound reason for drawing their descent from one of the invaders of 1066.

When William landed in 1066 a knight, Vitalis, went forth on reconnaissance to locate the English army. The Bayeux tapestry depicts his return to William, while the duke asks him if he had seen Harold's army. Vitalis may be identified with bishop Odo's man Vitalis, who is an extensive landholder in Kent.[5] Vitalis, who is supplied with the title 'de Canterbires' in the St Augustine's abbey Domesday, shared with Ranulph de Curbespine in plundering the Canterbury gild of burgesses.[6] He had a son Hamo who is characterized by pious benefactions. Hamo ceded Stourmouth church with pasture on that manor to Rochester cathedral for the souls of his father and mother, and because his brother had become a monk.[7] Vitalis evidently had a son in addition to Hamo. Hamo was required in the period 1116–18 to investigate, in company with the 'probi vicini' of Sandwich, certain business connected with a ship of the abbot of St Augustine's.[8] He witnesses a grant to Leeds priory (Kent) during the archiepiscopate of William of Corbeil (1123–36).[9] Hamo had a son William who imitated his father's religious benefactions by granting

---

[1] F. W. Hardman, 'Castle-guard Service of Dover Castle' (*Archæologia Cantiana*, xlix' 96–107). The story of the Chilham-Douvres family is continued in the valuable article by G. A. Moriarty, 'The First House of Chilham', in *New England Historical and Genealogical Register*, cv. King John's illegitimate son Richard of Chilham took his name from the heritage of his wife Roesia (whom he married c. 1214). She was daughter of Fulbert (II) of Chilham, de Douvres.

[2] D 138.   [3] D 153.

[4] Eastbridge Hospital, Canterbury, Charter A 28.

[5] He holds Nortune (Northwood, Whitstable) in Reculver hundred (*DB*, i, fol. 3v.); in Wingham (*DMon*, p. 83); in Sifflington (*DB*, fol. 7r); in Preston (ibid., fol. 12v); in Swalecliff (ibid., fol. 10r); in 'Stursæte' (Westgate, Canterbury? *DMon*, p. 81), etc. See *DMon*, p. 57; W. Urry, 'The Normans in Canterbury' (*Canterbury Archæological Society Occasional Papers*, no. 2, pp. 12–14).

[6] PRO, E 164/27 (the White Book), fol. 22v; ed. Ballard, p. 10; *DB*, i, fol. 2r.

[7] Evidently at Rochester (*Textus Roffensis*, fol. 108). It may be deduced that Hamo met St Anselm at least once, for the transaction recorded in the charter is effected in his presence.

[8] Davis, *Regesta*, i, no. 108, where the document is dated 1078–83. For the revised dating see *EHR*, xxix, 251; *DMon*, p. 55.

[9] Kent County Record Office, Cartulary of Leeds priory, fol. 3v.

Chilston (near Maidstone) to Leeds priory, by a charter in which he refers to his son 'H', indicating that he has other sons.[1] He grants Bletchenden in Kent to Leeds by another charter in which he names his brother John and Gilbert.[2] He himself is named as a knight of William, Earl of Gloucester in 1166,[3] and is apparently dead by 1173, when Sybilla, wife of William son of Hamo, renders account of forty marks to have her dowry at Stourmouth, where both Vitalis and Hamo once held.[4] The names of the heir of William, 'H', may be expanded to Hamo, for Hamo son of William 'of Stourmouth' abandoned claim in or before 1184 to St Augustine's abbey to any right in the church of St Edmund Ridingate Canterbury.[5] There is a curious note in the cartulary of St Laurence priory, Canterbury, lying on the Dover Road, half a mile from the Ridingate of Canterbury, running:

Hamo filius Viel de Soford qui fecit ecclesiam sancti Edmundi cui assignauit iiij^or acras terre ad panem benedictum. Qui venit conquestu Anglie et assignauit ecclesie sancti Laurentii vnam acram ad idem officium cuius filius dicebatur Willelmus qui fecit ecclesiam sancte Marie de Bredene et eius filius dicitur iste Willelmus de Soford miles comitis Gloecestrie.

The entry is preceded by a note stating:
'Hoc subsequens scribitur in dorso carte predicte. vide in carta.'[6]
    The charter in question is a quitclaim to St Laurence priory by Godard, priest both of St Mary Bredin church and of St Edmund Ridingate church, Canterbury, of certain tithes received in the parishes in question. The charter, judged from the names within it, must date to about 1200. On the face of it it would seem that the invader at the Conquest was Hamo, son of Viel, Vitalis, but since he is specifically named as benefactor to St Laurence priory, which was not founded until 1137,[7] it is unlikely that he can be the invader. It is not improbable that confusion has arisen in a tradition some hundred and thirty years old.
    We see that the name 'Soford' is applied to Hamo (II). There can indeed be little doubt that the Shofords and the line of Vitalis, lord of Stourmouth,

---

[1] Ibid., fol. 2v.   [2] *Cal. of Charter Rolls*, v, 207.   [3] *RBE*, p. 189.
[4] PR, 19 Henry II, p. 87. She is quit in the roll for 23 Henry II (p. 204).
[5] BBSA, p. 542.
[6] Cambridge University Library, Add. 6845, no. 32 (G. R. C. Davis, *Medieval Cartularies*, no. 211).
[7] A version of the charter is found in the fifteenth-century cartulary of the priory (Cathedral Library, Lit. MS. C 20; Davis, *Medieval Cartularies*, no. 212). Mr S. E. Rigold observes that since it must have been almost impossible to found a new parish as late as 1137 then the churches (of St Edmund and St Mary Bredin) were founded earlier than that date, and the foundations and endowments named in the endorsement may be assigned to Vitalis himself and his son (*Journal of Medieval Archæology*, iv, p. 175).

are one and the same family. Hamo, son of William of Stourmouth, surrenders claim, towards 1184, upon St Edmund Ridingate church, founded according to the St Laurence cartulary by an earlier Hamo, son of Viel de Soford. It is remarkable to record that the name of the founder of the line is (so it appears) in current use even today. In the fourteenth century 'Vieleston', that is Filston in Shoreham, Kent, was held of the Shoford family. The name of Viel, Vitalis, patently stands embedded in this place-name.[1]

As indicated above, Hamo de Soford holds ground c. 1200 in Dover Street, Canterbury, while William de Soford has other ground hard by, without Ridingate. This last-mentioned piece of ground is only a stone's throw from St Edmund's church, and the other ground is less than four hundred yards from St Mary Bredin church.

Holding at the corner of St Margaret's Street about 1166 (according to Rental B), may be found the 'daughter of Godefrid of Malling'. She can claim descent from a Domesday knight. Her father must be the Godefrid who came to terms with the monks of Christ Church on Easter Monday 1155 in the *camera* of archbishop Theobald, and in his presence, in connection with the manors of Patching and Wootton (Sussex).[2] Domesday Monachorum affirms that Godefrid dapifer holds a 'sulung' from the archbishop at Thanington (on the river, just above Canterbury).[3] He can hardly be other than the Godefrid of Thanington who attests Charter II, almost contemporary with Domesday. Godefrid dapifer holds elsewhere in Kent, as at Swarling near Canterbury.[4] The Exchequer version of Domesday says that Godefrid holds at 'Lerham' (Lenham) while Domesday Monachorum says that the tenant is Godefrid of Malling.[5] Now at South Malling (Sussex) there is a Godefrid holding of Lanfranc, who, in his charter to St Gregory's priory, Canterbury, concedes tithes of demesne of manors of his knights, specifying those of Thanington 'quam villulam Godefrido contulimus', as he says, and of Lenham 'quam Godefrido donauimus.'[6] He makes no differentiation between the Godefrid in either instance and we are left with the strong impression that Godefrid in all the cases above is the same man. There is, however, a difficulty, since the list of knights of the see of Canterbury in Domesday Monachorum embodies the names of both Godefrid of Thanington and Godefrid of Malling, but it is to be noticed that the assessment (three fees) is the same in each entry,

[1] Mr N. H. MacMichael has now extended the family history by study of the archives of Rochester Cathedral. See his 'Filston in Shoreham'. (*Archæologia Cantiana*, lxxvii, 1963, pp. 133 ff.)

[2] CAC, Ch. Ant. W 50, i and ii. Saltman, *Theobald*, app. A.   [3] *DMon*, p. 81.

[4] Ibid., p. 83.   [5] *DB*, fol. 4v, *DMon*, p. 93.   [6] Greg., no. 1.

making it possible to ask if the same man has been mentioned twice.[1] Some substantial connections between the Sussex Malling and Thanington can be adduced in support of this view.

Godefrid of Malling (most likely the Godefrid of Domesday) had a son William. Writing from Bec, probably in 1103, archbishop Anselm asked Gundulph, bishop of Rochester, to settle some debts and payments on his behalf, among them 20s. which Gundulph was to ask Godefrid of Malling to pay to his own son William.[2] Archbishop William (1126–36) issued notification that William of Malling had granted him all his rights in the church of Thanington and that he had in turn bestowed them on St Gregory's priory, Canterbury.[3] Prior Walter and the monks of Christ Church entered into agreement in 1144 with William of Malling over the farm of Patching,[4] while in the period 1139–48 William of Malling with his son Godefrid consented to the grant made by Philip, canon of Malling, brother of William, and uncle of Godefrid, of rights in the church of Glinde (in Malling, Sussex) to the abbey of Bec.[5] This younger Godefrid can without any doubt be equated with the man whose daughter holds at St Margaret's Street, Canterbury, c. 1166,[6] and again with the individual who came to terms over Patching and Wootton in 1155. The relevant charter indicates that he is son to William of Malling (who was, as will have been seen) negotiating with Christ Church over Patching eleven years before. This charter, in the form of a splendid cirograph, both portions of which are preserved together at Canterbury, is actually signed by Godefrid of Malling with a rude cross.[7]

The ancestry of William of Eynesford, holding ground in Rental B and of his namesake holding in Rental D,[8] may readily be carried back to the date of Domesday Book. Professor Douglas has shown that though this family exhibits all the signs of membership of the ruling, land-owning Norman caste, yet it derived from an ancestor with a Scandinavian name.[9] Domesday states that Ralph, son of Hospac, holds at Eynesford, Kent,[10] while he is listed among the knights of the see of Canterbury.[11] The son of Ralph, William (William I, of Eynesford) had a wife named Hadewisa,[12]

---

[1] *DMon*, p. 105.   [2] Anselm, *Opera*, ed. Schmitt, iv (*Epistolæ*), p. 207.
[3] Greg., no. 3.
[4] CAC, Ch. Ant., P 10. Does a connection with Glinde account for the presence in Canterbury of Robert, clerk of Glinde, c. 1160 (XIX)?
[5] Saltman, *Theobald*, no. 177; see also nos. 59, 86.   [6] B 112. See above.
[7] Saltman, *Theobald*, app. A. See above.   [8] B 223, D 307.
[9] *DMon*, p. 47.   [10] *DB*, i, fol. 4.   [11] *DMon*, p. 105.
[12] CAC, Ch. Ant. R 1. This charter (late twelfth century) relating to Ruckinge, Kent, carefully distinguishes between the various Williams, calling them 'senex', 'filius', 'tercius', etc. It enables the initial 'H.' (wife of William I) to be extended to Hadewisa (cf. *DMon*, p. 47).

and after an active career in the world, including service (probably) as sheriff both of Essex and of London, became a monk at Canterbury.[1] He evidently died in some unspecified year on 8 March, on which day he was annually commemorated by the brethren.[2] He in turn had a son William called 'Gurham', who had a son, William III, who enters history as surety for Becket to the extent of one hundred marks. On Becket's flight he lost his money and only recovered it (with papal support) more than ten, and perhaps nearly twenty, years later from offerings at the tomb of the Saint.[3] Other members of the Eynesford family were involved in the crisis. William's brothers, John and Robert, suffered excommunication at Becket's hands in 1169.[4] It must be William of Eynesford III who holds ground in St Margaret's Street, Canterbury, according to Rental B, about four years before the murder.[5] The ground in Stour Street, close to the back of Eastbridge Hospital, named in Rental D[6] as that of William of Eynesford, may be connected with William of Eynesford IV (d. 1197), or perhaps with William V, who came of age between Hilary 1199 and Michaelmas 1200.[7]

There were two other pieces of ground very close at hand to the last-mentioned, associated with the family. A William of Eynesford bestowed upon Leeds priory (Kent) the site of St Helen's church, held of him *in burgagio*, together with 2s. rent arising from ground next to Eastbridge in Canterbury, whereon Edward son of Odbold had established the Hospital of St Thomas. The mention by the grantor of his brother Bartholomew shows that this William is William of Eynesford IV.[8]

The Eynesfords are, like other county holders of land in Canterbury, knights of the see. The progenitor of the line, Hospac, is (as indicated above) named in the list in Domesday Monachorum, while there is a William of Eynesford (William V) mentioned among the 'milites archiepiscopi' in 1210–12.[9]

The Ratlings are another Kentish manorial family holding ground in Canterbury, and having a place in a list of knights of the see. They take their name from Ratling in Nonington, six miles from Canterbury. Thomas of Ratling is assessed at one fee in the schedule of knights of 1210–12.[10] He is probably identical with the Thomas of Ratling who holds ground beside St George's church in Canterbury c. 1200.[11] The name

---

[1] *DMon*, p. 46.

[2] BM. MS. Cotton, Nero C IX, printed Dart, *Canterbury Cathedral*, app. xii.

[3] PR, 11 Henry II, p. 105. He gave a quittance to prior Alan (1179–86) and the monks (*DMon*, p. 110). See remarks on date of the quittance (ibid., p. 45).

[4] *DMon*, p. 45. [5] B 223. [6] D 307. [7] *DMon*, p. 47.
[8] See family tree in *DMon*, p. 47. [9] *RBE*, p. 726. [10] Ibid., pp. 469, 724. [11] D 123.

associated with this ground forty years or more earlier is that of Alan of Ratling, who moreover controls ground north of the Precincts,[1] just within the city wall, and is evidently the Alan who is lord of ground occupied by Isaac son of Benedict, near King's Bridge, some years later.[2] In his spate of excommunications issued in 1169, Becket names Alan of Ratling as invading rights of the see during his exile.[3] In 1176–7 Alan is amerced two marks 'pro falso clamore' according to the Pipe Roll.[4] He may be the Alan of Ratling who attested the judgment reached in the county court of Kent in 1176 when the abbey of St Augustine secured a victory over its tenants in Thanet, in connection with the question of their attendance at the abbey court in Canterbury.[5] The father of Alan, named Asketill, occurs in the same list of witnesses. He is probably identical with the man of the same name mentioned in Canterbury charters of 1144 and 1148,[6] though it seems unlikely that the Asketill of 1176 can be identical with Asketill of Ratling who was present at Sandwich in 1127 when rights of Christ Church, Canterbury, in the port were vindicated.[7] However he may have attended as a young manorial lord.

Alan of Ratling offended Becket, yet it seems that it must be he whose wife was cured by the Saint of illness. Æliz, wife of Alan 'de Redingis', convulsed with suffering, was about to die when the water of St Thomas was brought to her, restoring her to health.[8] 'Reding', and its variants, is a not uncommon misrendering of Retling, Ratling, through conjunction of *t* with *l* in the name, and the rapid production of the water impregnated with the holy blood, points much more to a village near Canterbury than to Reading in distant Berkshire.

The descent of the family would appear to run as follows (though we cannot be completely certain that the list carries on from father to son in every case): Asketill (of age 1127, and possibly identical with Asketill of 1144, 1176); Alan (occurs 1148, 1160, 1169, 1176–7, and about 1180); Thomas (alive c. 1200, c. 1216, dead by 1232); Alan (occurs 1232).

Conspicuous among the knightly clans holding ground in Canterbury are the Cornhills, who were great men not only in London, but in Kent, where no less than five of them served as sheriff.[9] In the later twelfth

[1] A 7; XIX. [2] LI.
[3] *Materials*, vi, p. 602. [4] 23 Henry II, p. 206.
[5] *Facsimiles of Royal and other Charters in BM*, i, no. 57.
[6] CAC, Ch. Ant., p. 10; M 190. [7] Boys, *Sandwich*, p. 553.
[8] *Materials*, ii, pp. 152–3.
[9] The Cornhills have been made the subject of a study by Mr W. R. Powell in 'English Administrative Families in the 12th and 13th Centuries with Special Reference to the Cornhill Family' (B.Litt. thesis, Oxford, 1952).

century members of the family have ground on the north side of Burgate Street in Canterbury, partly bought by Gervase of Cornhill (the justiciar of London, itinerant justice and the sheriff of Kent who confronted Becket at Sandwich on his return from exile in 1170), and partly of the inheritance of Matilda, daughter of Hamo 'dapifer' wife to Gervase' son, Reginald of Cornhill (I).[1] This lady is apparently daughter of Hamo, son of Roger the cook, for Reginald came to terms with abbot Roger of St Augustine's over 'haws and all lands at burgage' held on the day of his death by 'Haymo, son of Roger the cook'.[2] North Holmes, in the suburbs of Canterbury, adjacent to the abbey is mentioned in the agreement, and it was near here that Roger 'cocus' held a 'barton', at the date of Rental B.[3]

In 1197 another agreement was entered into over the office of seneschal of St Augustine's, between Reginald of Cornhill, with his wife Matilda on the one part and the abbot and convent on the other.[4] Reginald and Matilda quitclaimed the office of seneschal to the monks, receiving in exchange 80 marks and 50 acres of ground 'between the park of Littlebourne and Wootton' (east of Canterbury), which Cleranbaud (evidently the evil abbot who gave hospitality to the four knights on the day of Becket's murder) had bestowed on Hamo son of Roger. It may reasonably be deduced that Matilda is daughter of Hamo (the steward, seneschal, of the abbey), who was son to Roger the cook, holding the 'barton' near the abbey. John son of Roger the cook, and Hamo son of Roger who hold, c. 1166, adjacent pieces of ground at the bottom of Ivy Lane outside Newingate, close to St Augustine's, seem to be uncle and father of Matilda.[5] Roger is patently no mere lowly menial, and indeed these household officials are often great men, like James the archiepiscopal porter, alderman of Northgate ward, and mayor of Canterbury.[6] Moreover, the Cornhills themselves were of burgess and mercantile origin, and William of Canterbury sneers at Gervase for being more at home with his percentages, than in promoting equity and justice.[7]

The monks of Christ Church, Canterbury, were anxious to get possession of the Cornhills' ground in Burgate Street as it lay uncomfortably near the cathedral, and the buildings thereon were a source of danger from fire. In (probably) 1177 an exchange was made for other territory in Friday Street, London, with the approval of Henry II.[8]

Reginald of Cornhill (evidently Reginald I) acquired ground in the

---

[1] XXIX–XXXII.   [2] XL.   [3] B 194.
[4] BM. Cotton, Claudius D X, fol. 73v; BBSA, pp. 530–1.   [5] B 91.
[6] See pp. 87–8.   [7] *Materials*, i, p. 100.   [8] XXXI, XXXII, and see XXIX.

High Street in Canterbury, next to that of Hugh de Neville, occupied by the minters, from alderman Thomas, and sold it to Christ Church for sixty marks, where it served as part of the endowment of the altars of SS. Dunstan and Alphage.[1] Reginald of Cornhill is entered in Rental F as occupant of ground in White Horse Lane, Canterbury, but since the corresponding entry in Rental D states that the tenant is the 'vicecomes', it is probable that Reginald has entered into the holding in his capacity as sheriff.[2] Rental F indicates that Reginald of Cornhill is joint-tenant with Peter 'de castello' of some acres of ground in the Wincheap area, outside the city walls not far from the castle.[3] The possessions of the family in Canterbury must have been very extensive as Reginald III sold ground producing an annual income of £9 3s. 7½d. to St Augustine's abbey to raise money to liquidate the colossal sums owing for his father's defection from John's cause at the close of the reign.[4] The six marks' worth of income sold to the abbey for the same reason seems to have been disposed of by Reginald III. Matilda of Lukedale, wife of Reginald III, gave legacies of rents (worth 13s. 6d. *per annum*) in the city, increased out of affection to her by her husband to 20s. *per annum*.[5]

It is of interest to observe the name Neville in close conjunction with that of Cornhill. It is tempting to see in the Hugh de Neville with a holding next to the Cornhill ground in the High Street, the Forester of England, ancestor of the Earls of Essex, and husband of Reginald of Cornhill's niece Joan.[6]

Another knight of the see of Canterbury may be found in Canterbury, holding in White Horse Lane, close to the ground which was at one stage in the hands of Reginald of Cornhill, sheriff of Kent. Late in the twelfth century a woman named Hachenild, followed by her son Frumbold (Frumelin), holds from the monks of Christ Church, who in turn hold from Richard of Graveney (the manor near Faversham).[7] By about 1216 another Richard receives rent for the ground[8] and may be identified with the man of the name who is assessed at two fees in the schedule of 1210–12.[9] He is probably the Richard of Graveney who in 1202 receives a quitclaim from Guncelin of Ospringe (the manor very close to Graveney) for a seam of salt,[10] and may again be the knight who defaulted from the grand assize in 1203.[11] The family seems to imitate the usage among man-

[1] LXVIII.   [2] D 282, F 16.   [3] F 24.
[4] BBSA, pp. 164–70. See *Thorne*, col. 1878, p. 191.   [5] BBSA, p. 602.
[6] LXVIII; Page, *London, its Origin and Early Development*, pp. 151, 243.
[7] C 1, G 1, D 281, 282.   [8] Y, fol. 58v; Z, fol. 199v.
[9] RBE, p. 471.   [10] *Pedes Finium*, Kent, printed *Archæologia Cantiana*, iii, p. 226.
[11] CRR, 5–7 John, p. 5.

orial clans, and repeats the same Christian name in successive generations. It would be instructive to know how far back a succession of Richards could be traced.

At the date of Domesday Richard, 'homo archiepiscopi' otherwise called Richard the constable, holds Graveney from the archbishop with Leaveland, both close to Faversham.[1] Domesday Monachorum names Wimund of Leaveland as a knight of the see.[2] It is clear, however, that the history of these two manors diverges at an early date.[3]

There is a group of Canterbury lords taking their names from manors lying close together in the hills south-west of Canterbury. Gregory and Simon of Kenfield (near Petham) have ground without Worthgate worth 4s. *per annum*, and jointly possess the holding on the corner of Mercery Lane conveyed to Christ Church and held by Solomon the mercer at 13d.[4] Simon and Nigel of Sappington, a quarter of a mile from Kenfield, are lords of the ground at the corner of Castle Street,[5] where Reginald of Tonford (the manor on the way from Kenfield to Canterbury) also has an interest.[6] Emma, of Whiteacre (Wettekera), close to Petham and Waltham (together with her husband Geoffrey de Lisores), has ground at the fringe of the Christ Church precincts.[7] Emma probably derives descent from Nigel 'de Huatacra', enfeoffed by Lanfranc in Whiteacre, listed among knights of the see in Domesday Monachorum, and probably identical with the Nigel named as the archbishop's tenant in Petham.[8] The plea held at Sandwich in 1127 concerning the tolls of Sandwich and Stonar was attended by a concourse of knights among whom we find Niel de Hwetacre, possibly son to the above.[9]

Emma of Whiteacre's husband has patent continental connections. He probably derives his name from Lisors (dépt. Eure, arrond. les Andelys, canton Lyons la Forêt). It is very likely that Nigel, for long called 'Wireker' (Witeker?), monk of Canterbury and satirical poet, is a member of this family.[10] Emma and her husband evidently had a son Tomas de Lisures, who in the Pipe Roll for Michaelmas 1205 owes ten marks and one palfrey to have his relief and seisin of the fee of half a knight in Whiteacre in which his mother Emma was seized on the day of her death.[11]

---

[1] *DB*, fol. 4r; *DMon*, p. 85. [2] *DMon*, p. 105.

[3] The family deriving its name from Leaveland became hereditary keepers of the Palace of Westminster and of the Fleet Prison (C. T. Clay, 'The Keepership of the Old Palace of Westminster', in *EHR*, lix, 1–21; Hasted, *Kent*, iii, 17).

[4] A 19, 20. [5] A 27. [6] Ibid. [7] A 6.

[8] *Monasticon*, vi, 615; *DMon*, p. 51; *DB*, i, fol. 3v.

[9] Boys, *Sandwich*, p. 553; *Regesta*, ii, no. 1511.

[10] See pp. 153–4. [11] PR, 7 John, p. 117.

The William Capel who holds contiguous tenements on the north side of the precincts of Christ Church is apparently the tenant of Preston next Wingham, holding from St Augustine's abbey. His name may be derived from Capel in Petham, close to Sappington, Kenfield and Whiteacre. He was present in the Infirmary Cloister at Canterbury in 1148 when arrangements were made about the Christ Church manor of Monkton. He may be the William Capel who sold Berewick (Kent) to William de Alberville. William Capel had a kinsman, Ivo of Wyke (the manor adjacent to Canterbury).[1]

Most of the secular lords holding in Canterbury come from manors not far away. Eustace of Mereworth, however, comes from the other side of the River Medway. In Rental D he is found holding ground west of Eastbridge Hospital, evidently the three dwellings whence rent was given to the hospital by Gunnora, daughter of Eustace of Mereworth, early in the thirteenth century.[2] One Eustace of Mereworth is listed among knights of William Earl of Gloucester in 1166.[3] In 1168-9 Paulina, daughter of Eustace of Mereworth, pays 30s. for custody of her son and his land, a payment continued annually until 1172-3, when the boy probably came of age.[4] He may be the Eustace of Mereworth who gave the advowson of Mereworth church to Leeds priory (Kent) by a charter which, confirmed by Gilbert Glanville as bishop of Rochester, was in dispute in the *curia regis* in 1214, when the litigants were the prior of Leeds and Roger, son of Eustace.[5] A Eustace of Mereworth was a benefactor to Combwell priory, Kent.[6]

The great family of Hardres, which for some seven hundred years held the manor of that name five miles from Canterbury, may be found in control of ground in the city. Philip of Hardres held a groundplot in St Peter's parish and another in St Alphage.[7] In the last-mentioned, he had a tenant whom he ceremoniously handed over, together with the ground, on the tomb of St Thomas just as he was setting off for the Third Crusade.[8]

---

[1] BBSA, pp. 549, 550; A 37; CAC, Ch. Ant. M 190. If his name is in fact territorial, it is odd that it is not supplied with a 'de', customary at the date.

[2] D 369; Duncombe and Battely, *Three Archiepiscopal Hospitals*, p. 378: two dwellings here were occupied by Hamo and Ralph, sons of Arnold of Eastbridge the dyer (Eastbridge Hospital MSS. A 59, J 34).

[3] *RBE*, i, p. 190. [4] PR, 15 Henry II, p. 162, and following years.

[5] CRR, 15-16 John, p. 69. *Pedes Finium*, printed in *Archæologia Cantiana*, vi, p. 230.

[6] *Archæologia Cantiana*, vi, p. 222. It is claimed that William of Mereworth, a knight of Kent, was present at the siege of Acre (Philipot, *Villare Cantianum*, p. 236). This remark seems to depend only upon the so-called Dering Roll. (See Wagner, 'Catalogue of English Medieval Rolls of Arms'; *Aspilogia*, i.)

[7] D 73, 354. [8] LV.

In the case of the other holding, which lies at the far end of Criene Mill Lane, close to the inner side of the city walls, it almost seems that he holds it in demesne.[1] At any rate his own name is associated with the ground, and property opposite is said to be sited 'opposite Philip of Hardres' gate'. The ground is not likely to have incorporated a dwelling (in this low-lying marshy area) and perhaps Philip kept it for grazing. A connection between Philip and Upper Hardres is underlined by the occurrence of his Christian name in the ancient glass in the church there.[2] Possibly he sur-vived the Crusade (unless the same Christian name is repeated, as so often, in a manorial family), for Philip of Hardres was involved in litigation with the Hospitallers over Hardres church in 1199–1200 in the *curia regis*.[3] In 1202 he served on a grand assize.[4] He may have been dead by June 1218 when orders were given for seizure of all the land which was (fuit) of Philip of Hardres,[5] while next year a writ was sent to the 'prepositi' of Canterbury commanding them to enquire according to the custom of the city by the oath of twenty-four legal men what lands and rents Philip of Hardres had in the city and who held such lands and rents from him. Orders were given for delivery of seisin to Constance his sister and heir.[6]

Prior Alan of Christ Church, who succeeded as abbot of Tewkesbury in 1186,[7] wrote while still at Canterbury to Robert of Hardres in connec-tion with a quarrel over some property of Christ Church. Robert, merely on the basis of an entry in Domesday Book, considered that he had a claim to the property in question. Alan reproached him, reminding him that they had suffered want together when young and, now that they had both got on in the world, Robert might show a proper gratitude to the church which had nourished them.[8]

The early history of this distinguished family is obscure, and matters are not made easy by the existence of another family named Hardres at Lower Hardres nearby. This family (in the persons of Luke and Paulinus) draws rents in Canterbury from ground in Stour Street.[9]

There is a group of families in Canterbury which seem to have more

[1] D 354, n.
[2] The name PHILIPP[   ] is to be seen in the border of the roundel depicting the Virgin and Child. Philip de Heac Hardre witnesses CAC, Ch. Ant., G 183.
[3] *Rotuli Curiæ Regis* (Rec. Commrs.) ii, pp. 127, 259.
[4] CRR, 3–5 John, p. 126.   [5] *Excerpta e Rotulis Finium*, i, 13.
[6] *Rotuli Literarum Clausarum*, i, 388.
[7] *Annales Monastici*, RS (Tewksbury), i, pp. 53, 54.
[8] *Alani prioris Cantuariensis . . . scripta*, ed. I. A. Giles, 1846, Ep. vi. Alan was 'natione Anglus' (Gervase, RS, i, p. 335) which is of considerable interest if any suggestion of re-lationship with R. de Hardres can be read into the letter.
[9] LXV. See BBSA, pp. 488–96.

affinities with the country knights, than with their fellow-citizens. Chief among such families are the Cauvels. The founder of the line was named William Cauvel, Calvellus. He is undoubtedly identical with Calveal the portreeve, who with the 'eldest men' of the merchant gild of Canterbury on the one hand, as opposed to Anselm and brethren of Christ Church on the other, attests the well-known exchange of property at Burgate, Newingate and Ridingate, Canterbury about 1100.[1] It is hardly likely that the name 'Calveal' is baptismal. In a letter written 1104–5 Anselm refers to Calvellus, mentioning him again a few lines away as William Calvellus.[2] Again Anselm names an individual, evidently this same man, both as William Calvellus and Calvellus in a charter of much the same date.[3] We are safe in assuming that Calveal in the exchange document is William Calvel, Cauvel. It is worth comment that a man whose name stamps him as a foreigner has stepped into the shoes of the Old English reeve in the same way that Norman barons took over the office of sheriff out in the shires. Another appearance as portreeve may perhaps be connected with Calvel. Anselm addresses a severe admonition to William Calvel reproaching him for moving the site of a market to the detriment of the monks, and threatening excommunication if the matter is not put right. It is noteworthy that the archbishop calls Calvel 'friend'.[4]

Another claim to fame may be the foundation of a nunnery. Until the end of the middle ages the sisters of St Sepulchre's, Canterbury, were wont to give away 6s. 8d. in lieu of a quarter of wheat every Maundy Thursday, for the sake of the soul of their founder, William Calwell, 'citizen of Canterbury', and 'first founder of this nunnery'.[5] The establishment of the house has usually been attributed to Anselm himself, but there is an entry in Domesday Book disclosing the existence of a group of four nuns, who hold ground close to Canterbury from St Augustine's abbey.[6] This description does not conflict with a description of the ground whereon the nunnery stood.[7] If the entry in Domesday does in fact refer to St Sepulchre's then the date of its foundation must be moved back before 1087, and therefore before the arrival of Anselm at Canterbury as archbishop. If the tradition among the sisters were true, then William Calvel

[1] I.   [2] See below.   [3] II.

[4] Anselm, *Opera*, ed. Schmitt, v, Ep. 358. Cf. nos. 356, 359. W. Urry, 'The Normans in Canterbury' (*Canterbury Archæological Society Occasional Papers*, no. 2), p. 15.

[5] *Valor Ecclesiasticus*, i, p. 30; Leland, *De Rebus Britannicis Collectanea* (ed. 2, 1774), p. 89. Urry, p. 17. Cf. *Monasticon* (ed. 1, 1655), i, p. 545.

[6] *DB*, i, fol. 12r.

[7] The chronicler of St Augustine's abbey says that the nunnery was sited 'infra limites feodi beati Augustini . . . tamen in solo archiepiscopatus' (*Thorne*, col. 1893, p. 215).

the founder must be among the first generation of invaders, probably born overseas. Anselm would take a place as joint-founder at a slightly later date. On Monday before Easter, 1111, Hamo sheriff of Kent granted the little borough of Fordwich near Canterbury to St Augustine's abbey. Among the *familia* of the abbot attesting are to be found William Calvel with Robert and Baldwin his sons.[1] In the period 1115-22 archbishop Ralph issues notification addressed to Ernulph, bishop of Rochester, and to the hundred of Westgate, that he has granted to his sister Azeliz two mills acquired from Calvellus, who is mentioned in the past tense.[2]

In a case in the *curia regis* in 1206 a jury was required to determine whether Hamo son of Vitalis gave to William Cauvel one carucate of land with appurtenances 'in Cant'' in marriage with Matilda sister of the said Hamo. At that date a William Cauvel was suing his brother Richard for half the ground, which lay at Iffin, south of Canterbury. The jury decided that Hamo gave all the land with Matilda to be held as one eighth of a knight's fee, adding moreover that William Cauvel the husband had several (plures) sons, of whom the eldest was Ralph, who held the ground all his life without any claim from his brethren.[3] The marriage had evidently taken place a long time before 1206. Some light on the case may be thrown by a charter of St Gregory's priory, which records the grant by William son of Hamo, on 29 January 1169, of the wardship of his kinsman Ralph 'Cavel' to the priory.[4] The sequence of names: William son of Hamo, son of Vitalis, indicates that we have here the distinguished Kentish family which draws descent from a knight in the host of William the Conqueror. We have been told that Hamo son of Vitalis has a sister Matilda, who is presumably daughter to Vitalis himself. Her marriage with a William Cauvel will account for the mention of kinship between the two families in 1169. Since Matilda is apparently daughter of one of the invaders, the marriage could have taken place at an early date. It is tempting to identify the husband with the William Cauvel who was evidently portreeve of Canterbury about 1100, a friend of St Anselm, and founder of the nunnery. However, the fact of repetition of Christian names in Anglo-Norman families will impose extreme caution, though it may be pointed out that a William has not been noticed in the family between the supposed portreeve and the William son of Baldwin Cauvel alive about 1150.

In 1127 by order of the king[5] the great enquiry was held to determine

[1] BM. MS. Cotton, Claudius D X, fol. 175r. [2] Cal. Charter Rolls, v, p. 62.
[3] CRR, 7-8 John, p. 243, and see ibid., p. 202. [4] Greg., no. 143.
[5] *Regesta*, ii, no. 1127.

rights of Christ Church, Canterbury, in the haven of Sandwich. The plea was held by William, sheriff of Kent, in the presence of archbishop William, John, bishop of Rochester, and a company of knights and others, clerical and lay, 'whereof the multitude was without number'. The knights include great men of the county, like William of Eynesford, Hugh of Chilham, Hamo son of Vitalis, and so forth. Among these men with knightly, manorial names occurs Rauf Cauvel. Possibly this man is the Ralph, brother of William Cauvel, attesting the charter of Anselm of c. 1100.[1]

William Cauvel, named in the Fordwich charter of 1111, had, as shown above, two sons, Robert and Baldwin. The latter may be the Baldwin, son of William Cauvel, who was granting away stretches of ground at St Sepulchre's bar, Canterbury, opposite the nunnery in 1149 and 1152.[2] This Baldwin had at least two sons, William and Stephen.[3] William son of Baldwin may be the William Cauvel whose daughter Margaret married William Cokin, son of Augustine of London, and carried to him the family ground beside St Margaret's church in central Canterbury.[4] This Margaret appears to be the Margaret (Margery) who with her sister Christina entered into final concord with John le Taillur son of Jordan[5] over a messuage in Canterbury in 1201, and in the same year with Alphage Lamb[6] the burgess, over twenty-one acres of ground at Yoclete near St Laurence, Canterbury, half a mile beyond the nunnery, of which their father William Cauvel had been seized in the days of Henry II.

Another family having affinities with the country knights is that of John son of Vivian. The first-recorded member of the line is Vivian of Wiht, taking his name from the island in the lower area of the city. He is probably the Vivian who with Gregory the moneyer attests a charter in the days of abbot Hugh II of St Augustine's (1126–51).[7] Vivian 'set out for Jerusalem' from Canterbury, and it is tempting to guess that he went with

---

[1] II.

[2] VIII, IX, X. Stephen may be identical with the Stephen appearing some time after the death of Becket (XLV).   [3] Ibid.

[4] D 266, 267. The family may have been established at St Margaret's by 1150 or earlier, for one Robert Cauvel attests the charter of archbishop Theobald relating to ground of Wibert priest of St Margaret's (VII). Among hostages given to Saladin in July 1192 at the siege of Joppa was an Augustine of London (Landon, *Itinerary of Richard I*, PRS, NS, 13, p. 67).

[5] Feet of Fines, Kent, printed *Archæologia Cantiana*, ii, p. 260. See CRR, 3–5 John, p. 8.

[6] Feet of Fines, Kent, *ut supra*, p. 261. See also CRR, 3–5 John, p. 50, and Introduction to *Curia Regis Rolls* (Selden Society), p. 189. Alphage Lamb holds close to the Cauvel family in Canterbury in St Margaret's parish (D 261).

[7] BM. MS. Cotton Claudius D X, fol. 98.

the Kentish contingent on the Second Crusade.[1] John, his son, served as borough reeve of Canterbury in the years following the murder of Becket, and may have been reeve as early as 1169.[2] He had a brother named William[3] and a son called Theobald.[4] This son probably predeceased his father. Three sisters, daughters of John, are frequently named in local charters and in the rentals. One, Eugenia, evidently did not marry. Another, Mary, married Adam, lord of the Surrey Tolworth, who is with little doubt the crusader who was excused scutage in 1191 because at the siege of Acre with Richard, in company, it may be remarked, with Simon de Vaubadun, a Kentish knight who had interests in ground at Butchery Lane, Canterbury.[5] John left a widow named Leticia with a house, embodying a *camera*, together with an orchard close to the central crossroads in Canterbury, just below St Margaret's Street.[6]

Susanna, daughter of John son of Vivian, married Ralph de Planaz, another man of knightly status. After John's death the three daughters may be found in occupation of their father's possessions in Canterbury,[7] and the record of the litigation in which they were involved suggests that, beyond the walls out on the downs towards Dover, their father must have been in control of some hundreds of acres.[8] The burgess seems to have been as wealthy in terms of land as many a knight. Indeed it is probable that he enjoyed such a status, since he is once referred to as a 'dominus'.[9] John was a member of the Canterbury gild of St Anselm, banded together to prosecute the cult of the saint.[10]

The property of the manorial lords and even of the king is negligible compared with the vast possessions of the church in Canterbury. The archbishop, however, the most important among the clerical holders of land, has surprisingly little ground in the city. Domesday discloses that as lord of the manor of Estursete (Westgate?) he has fifty-two dwellings

[1] Eastbridge Hospital MSS, Charter no. A 26. A grant had been made by Vivian 'antequam Jerusol' adiret'. For the Kentish contingent see Osbern, *De expugnatione Lyxbonensi* in *Chronicles and Memorials, Richard I, RS,* i, p. cxliv.

[2] When he attests a charter of St Gregory's priory at the head of a list of burgesses (Greg., no. 143).

[3] Eastbridge Hospital MSS. Charter no. A 26.

[4] Greg., no. 143; Cartulary of Dover Priory (Lambeth MS. no. 241), fol. 171v. See below.

[5] Landon, *Itinerary of Richard I* (PRS, NS, 13), p. 59. Cf. CRR, 3–5 John, p. 303.

[6] F 263, 349; D 286. Cf. D 350.   [7] Z, fol. 200r.

[8] CRR, Richard I–1 John, p. 363.

[9] Cartulary of Dover Priory (Lambeth MS., no. 241), fol. 171v. Godeleva d. of Wolnod of Canterbury grants to Dover prior ground near Hottemelne in central Canterbury held 'de domino Johanne filio Viviani'. The charter is witnessed by Theobald s. of John s. of Vivian, and Ralph Planaz, evidently John's son-in-law.

[10] W. Urry, 'St Anselm and his Cult at Canterbury' (*Spicilegium Beccense*, i, pp. 579–81).

T.R.E., reduced to twenty-five in the days of Lanfranc through the building of the palace.[1] Domesday also shows that the archbishop has burgesses, in two groups of twelve and thirty-two, both apparently passed over to the newly-established priory of St Gregory.[2] He has, furthermore, a few burgesses at the castle[3] and seven more in his capacity as lord of St Martin's.[4] By the twelfth century, however, the archbishop has little or nothing in Canterbury, unless the rent is counted which was acquired by Theobald from St Augustine's to liquidate the claim for the holy oils, though this has been assigned for purposes of collection to Westgate manor, to which also a few other small rents are still due.[5] The archbishop at one time controlled a great stretch of the open country north of Canterbury, running out from the city walls, beyond the fringe of housing. Lanfranc's three foundations here, St John's Hospital, the priory of St Gregory, and the house of the archdeacon, cover between them a large area, running all the way (apart from intersection by roads) from the river to Ruttington Lane.

Among the religious the nearest rival to Christ Church in possession of urban property is St Augustine's abbey. It is curious that its riches in this respect are not greater, as by 1200 the abbey has been established for six hundred years, and one might have expected that investments and gifts of the pious would have resulted in a large rentroll in the city. A charter of 762 relates to ground given to the abbey at Queningate, opposite the abbey, by the city wall.[6] Domesday discloses that the abbey has held, in virtue of its lordship of Longport, alias Barton (the suburban manor), seventy burgesses in Canterbury,[7] and records that the abbot has (1087) fourteen burgesses until of late rendering gable to the King 'pro excambio castelli'.[8] The royal holdings have been given to the abbot in compensation for property requisitioned and wasted to make room for the castle. In two MSS. of the abbey, one of the twelfth and another of the thirteenth century, may be found a note relating to eleven burgesses 'at the castle', and their rents, surrendered in exchange not for other dwellings elsewhere, but for the churches of SS. Mary de Castro and Andrew, Canterbury.[9] It appears that another transaction, different from that recorded in Domesday Book, is involved here. The writ of Henry I confirming the exchange of ground between abbey and cathedral indicates that the former had property very close to Christ Church.[10] In the middle of the twelfth cen-

[1] *DB*, fol. 3v. [2] Ibid., fol. 3r. [3] Ibid., fol. 2r. [4] Ibid., fol. 4r.
[5] See pp. 76–9. [6] Birch, *CS*, 192. [7] *DB*, i, fol. 12r.
[8] Ibid. fol. 2r.
[9] BM, MS. Roy. I B xi, fol. 146v.; PRO E 164/27 (the White Book), fol. 22r. See Appendix B. [10] v, vi.

tury Rental B makes casual mention of a few holdings of the abbey, one within and three without the walls,[1] while Rental D shows that by 1200 the abbey has patches of ground here and there, such as the strip of waste within Burgate,[2] a long stretch of valuable business property in Mercery Lane,[3] a piece of ground whereon stands a house in St Helen's,[4] and a few tenements in streets near the Westgate.[5]

The documents relating to the exchange of 1177 between Christ Church and the abbey show that the latter abandoned to the former seven holdings in Burgate, while the former gave the latter in compensation ground of comparable value elsewhere, some lying close to the abbey precinct.[6] A schedule of properties (of the early thirteenth century) entered in the Black Book producing rents to the abbey sacristry enumerates holdings in Canterbury producing some £15 *per annum*.[7] Another rentlist (of a similar date) in the volume comprises about seventy holdings, but does not supply figures for rents.[8] The impression gained is that the abbey has urban property equal to about one quarter of that of Christ Church. Numbers of charters entered in the cartularies of St Augustine's show how the rentroll was increased in the later twelfth century and in the early thirteenth.[9] Some citizens make grants for the sake of their souls, but many acquisitions are straightforward purchases by the monks.[10] The urban holdings of the abbey have had a long history. They fell to the crown at the dissolution, and before long were purchased, together with the abbey mill in St Radegund's, close by the watergate, by the Corporation of the city of Canterbury to supplement the common stock of the city. Henceforth the Corporation rent-collector received the rents which by the passage of time and fall in the value of money became trivial, and not worth collection. Since 1942 many have been liquidated for a capital sum. However, some still survive today, such as the rent of 6s. *per annum* paid out of the shop at the north-east corner of Mercery Lane, as a holding of the 'late dissolved abbey of St Augustine'. The Corporation moreover still collects 6s. 8d. from no. 13 Mercery Lane, part of the 'terra' of the abbey mentioned at this point in Rental D.[11]

St Gregory's priory has a modest rentroll within Canterbury. The cartulary of the house records acquisitions of domestic properties, about sixteen in number. The priory rentlists show that the brethren have some holdings

[1] B 56, 91, 99.   [2] D 89.   [3] D 110, n.
[4] D 292.   [5] D 370, 377, etc.   [6] XXVI–XXVIII.
[7] BBSA, pp. 335–45. Another version of substantially the same rental is to be found in the abbey register Cott. Julius D I, ff. 139–42.
[8] BBSA, pp. 176–80.   [9] BBSA, pp. 577, 580, 595, 597, 599, and *passim*.
[10] Ibid., pp. 576, 579, 581, etc.   [11] See D 110 n.

strung out along the track leading across the marshy district in the south-western quadrant of the walled area.[1] Some are dwellings. St Gregory's priory, furthermore, has interest in a number of houses in the suburb beyond Westgate running towards St Dunstan's.[2] To the property above-mentioned (perhaps thirty dwellings all told) may be added the mill called Crienemeldne, on the river Stour, where the Greyfriars built their house in the thirteenth century.

Dover priory has a stone house just within Northgate,[3] while its cartulary discloses that it possesses other holdings, an 'aula' and shops near Northgate, a house on the Stour and another held from the Planaz family in the central area, near St Andrew's church.[4] About 1200 Leeds priory (Kent) has ground just within Westgate and acquires more ground not far from King's Bridge in 1278.[5] William of Eynesford IV (d. 1197) bestowed upon the priory the church of St Helen (which ceased to be a church in the earlier thirteenth century).[6] The priory was possessed of half the tithes of the castle of Canterbury from a very early date.[7]

The monks of Faversham are lords of two holdings in St Peter's Street,[8] while the canons of St Radegund's abbey near Dover, have a tenement in Burgate Street.[9] Even today the name of St Radegund's Street perpetuates the memory of their dwelling under the city wall near Northgate.[10]

The military orders are represented by the Hospital of St John of Jerusalem, which holds, about 1200, a couple of tenements in St Peter's and one in Castle Street,[11] both in the hands of Robertson of Richard, a leading citizen.

There is a religious house a long way from Canterbury which is shown to have property there. A writ of Henry I (issued in the period 1129–33)

---

[1] See Greg., app. iv. See also D 214. Half a citizen's house stands on a plot held of St Gregory's.

[2] Ibid., nos. 57, 60, 61, etc.   [3] D 4 n.   [4] Lambeth MS. 241, ff. 168–74.

[5] D 326, 388; CAC, Ch. Ant. C 765. See *Archæologia Cantiana*, liv, p. 7.

[6] Cal. Charter Rolls, v, pp. 200–1.

[7] Cartulary of Leeds priory, Kent County Record Office, fol. 2v; Saltman, *Theobald*, no. 148.

[8] D 366, 367. See p. 75.   [9] D 98.   [10] See Appendix A, § 14.

[11] D 218, 312. The Hospitallers paid 20 marks in 10 John for licence for the marriage of their 'hospes' Robert son of Richard (PR, 10 John, p. 101). The Memoranda Roll for 1 John (Michaelmas, 1190) observes that Robert s. of Richard owes 60 marks 'de taillagio facto per Stephanum de Turneham' (i.e. that of 10 Richard I, pp. 207–9 in the Pipe Roll of that year, where R. s. of Richard owes 60 marks) and goes on to say: 'Vic' dicit quod debet esse quietus per libertatem Hospitalariorum quia dicit quod est homo eorum et ostendit breve Justic' per quod precipiatur ut faciat eis habere in singulis burgis unum hominem qui debet esse quietus de huiusmodi tallagiis et exaccionibus.' (Memoranda Roll, 1 John, PRS, p. 22). The Templars make a parallel claim (ibid.).

addressed to Rualon, sheriff of Kent and the 'prepositus' of Canterbury, reveals that the canons of SS. Julian and Botulph, Colchester, had land and houses at Canterbury acquired when Edmund, son of Bristerd and Lunna, became a canon there.[1] No evidence has been traced which would show that the canons possessed the property at a later date.

A modest amount of ground has come into the hands of a group of nunneries by the beginning of the thirteenth century. The local house, St Sepulchre's, is naturally richest in this respect. The nuns here have a plot of ground in St Alphage parish by the middle of the twelfth century, and later on may be found holding this, together with a tenement in Broad Street, and another in Castle Street.[2] Outside Ridingate they hold ground, apparently from a citizen, alderman John son of Roger,[3] while in Wincheap, half a mile beyond the walls, they control the long stretch of ground (from which they draw 3s. rent), given by their tenant Osbert priest of Thanington to Christ Church in honour of St Thomas.[4] The schedule of gifts to the nunnery entered in the Charter Rolls under 1247 embodies half a dozen entries relating to Canterbury. Other holdings may be referred to under the heading 'land in Canterbury'.[5]

The nuns of SS. Mary and Sexburga in Sheppey owned a holding in Mercery Lane let out to Arnold Chiche at 8s. *per annum* and another in the Burgate area, let out to Ingenulph the plumber at 3s. These they exchanged in 1187 with Christ Church for a marsh called Leffleddehope probably lying in the Sheppey levels near their nunnery, increasing ease of administration on either hand.[6] Some years before this the nuns had acquired three holdings in the city when a novice took the veil among them. The donors were her parents, who received from the holdings an annual total of 44½d. presumably received henceforth by the nuns.[7] Wibert nephew of, and clerk to, Odo abbot of Battle, formerly a monk of Christ Church, and *de facto* prior from 1167 until 1175, gave the nuns ground in St Alphage in the last years of the century.[8] Less easy to explain is the possession in the later twelfth century by Barking abbey (Essex) of a plot of ground in Butchery Lane held from the sisters by Christ Church at the substantial rent of 5s. 2d., and let out with adjacent ground to a tenant.[9] This rent was still being paid to the nunnery at the end of the Middle Ages.[10] The possession of ground by Barking abbey at Canterbury

---

[1] *Regesta*, ii, no. 1734. [2] B 5; D 63, 265. [3] D 152.
[4] D 167ff.; F 167–76; C 55; G 56; XLI, XLII. Juliana, named as prioress in XLI, cannot be Juliana, prioress, d. 1258 (*VCH, Kent*, ii, p. 143), and her name can accordingly be added to the list of prioresses.
[5] Cal. Charter Rolls, i, pp. 318–20. [6] LII. [7] XVI. [8] LIII, LIV.
[9] C 53; G 55. [10] CAC, Misc. Accts., 30, fol. 105 (1516).

may possibly be connected with the fact that Becket's sister was abbess of that house. Not far off, in Burgate Street, the nuns of Malling abbey, Kent, have a dwelling held from them by Christ Church and let out to a leading citizen.[1] This 'managium', as it is called, was bestowed upon Christ Church by Lambert Garegate its tenant when he became a monk, in or before 1167. The charter made it clear that the rent of 4s. owing to the nuns was still to be paid to them.

The Canterbury almshouses have some tenements, the richest in this group being Eastbridge Hospital, which probably received some as original endowment from its founder, Edward son of Odbold. However, the large collection of charters in the Hospital chest shows that there was systematic investment in house property in the earlier years of the thirteenth century.[2] The loss of the muniments of three hospitals, St. John's, St Nicholas of Harbledown, and Maynard's, renders difficult any estimate of their holdings.[3] St Laurence priory had a *mansio* in Wincheap, given by Lambert Garegate (the benefactor of Christ Church and Malling abbey, who died in 1167 or before).[4] The priory has interest in some other property around the city, as in Mercery Lane,[5] and beyond the walls, near the priory itself.[6]

Certain of the Canterbury churches (such as SS. George, Edmund, Mary Bredin, Michael, and Mildred) enjoy glebe in the form of dwellings and agricultural ground.[7]

There are considerable holders of ground in Canterbury among the citizens themselves. For example the leading citizen Robert son of Richard is rich in ground. He has, as disclosed by the rentals, at least eight pieces of property within and without the city walls.[8] These are only casually mentioned, and there may have been many others, as is shown by his charters recording benefactions to religious houses, like the four shops in Burgate given to Christ Church to establish his anniversary,[9] or the ground worth 10s. *per annum* bestowed upon St Augustine's abbey, again to found an anniversary (for himself and his wife).[10]

---

[1] xx.

[2] Archives of Eastbridge Hospital, deposited in Cathedral Library, Charters, series A.

[3] The archives of SS. John and Nicholas were destroyed in a lawyer's office during the great air attack of 1 June 1942. Those of Maynard's Hospital were removed to London for a lawsuit in 1666 and perished in the Great Fire.

[4] Cartulary of St Laurence priory, Lit. MS. C 20 in Cathedral Library, p. 76.

[5] Ibid., p. 75.

[6] Ibid., *passim*. St Laurence priory had ground incorporated in the vineyard of St Augustine's abbey, close to the top of Old Ruttington Lane (BBSA, p. 154), with a messuage at another point (ibid., p. 166).   [7] See pp. 211–12.

[8] D 86, 114, 218, 296, 312, 365; Y, fol. 27r; Z, fol. 220v.   [9] LIX.   [10] BBSA, p. 590.

The family descended from Roger, alderman of Canterbury, is well-endowed with land in Canterbury. Alderman John son of Roger has c. 1200 five plots of ground,[1] while his son alderman William has as many as eighteen holdings, lying at different points, from which he draws 24s. 8½d. rent, minus 9s. 2d. paid to St Augustine's abbey.[2] He or his father must have had some interest in other ground, affording 14s. rent., as is evident from a quitclaim exacted by the monks.[3] Alderman John had interest in the advowson of St John's church, probably indicating that the family had some part in endowing this church.[4] The evidence above, which is again merely casual, arising by chance, shows that the family had claims of some kind on at least thirty properties in Canterbury.

There remains the difficult question of the sitting tenant. The rentals are not primarily concerned with this class but merely with the man, woman or institution paying rent to Christ Church. It is quite clear that the rent is not paid by the actual occupants in many cases, for those religious houses which hold dwellings must let them out to citizens, whose names are not necessarily given in the rentals. Again, the country knights who have ground in the city are not likely to dwell upon it, though of course (as in the case of Philip of Hardres) they may keep a plot of ground in their own hands, perhaps for accommodating horses.[5]

We sometimes have the names of tenants of these country knights. Gilbert of Barham's house in the Buttermarket is occupied by Simon fenier,[6] while his other ground has as tenant William son of Elfric.[7] Winedei Butercluncc occupies Alan of Ratling's holding near St George's church, and his other holding lower down the High Street is in the hands of Isaac the Jew.[8] The Graveney family have a citizen tenant in White Horse Lane,[9] and the Kenfields have as tenant Solomon the mercer, at the corner of Mercery Lane.[10] The occupants of the ground of Paulina of Mereworth, next to King's Bridge, are shown by charters of Eastbridge Hospital to have been Ralph and Hamo, sons of Arnold of Eastbridge the dyer.[11]

Occasionally a citizen may occupy two or more holdings as sitting tenant if they are adjacent, as in the case of Jacob the Jew whose big stone house covers as many as three holdings, running up the High Street from the corner of Stour Street.[12] It is possible that even where a citizen's plots of ground are not adjacent he may be sitting tenant in respect of more than

[1] D 91, 152, 153, 154, 156. [2] BBSA, pp. 161–4. [3] Ibid., p. 599.
[4] Ibid., p. 542. [5] See account of Hardres family above.
[6] D 112. [7] LVIII. [8] XIX, LI. [9] C I; G I.
[10] B 222. [11] Eastbridge Hospital Charters, A 25; D 369. [12] XLIX–LI.

one. Solomon the mercer has his ground in Mercery Lane, and his quasi-surname suggests strongly that he dwells here.[1] However, he has other ground far away in Criene Mill Lane.[2] It is unlikely that anyone can dwell in this marshy area, and it is not improbable that this last-mentioned holding is agricultural in nature like a modern allotment garden. Solomon's close neighbour, Goldwin the mercer, also has ground near the river and may cultivate it in his spare time.[3] Again, it is likely that many of the merchant class have stores or yards not necessarily adjacent to their actual dwellings.

We can be fairly certain where some of the citizens lived; in fact we are specifically told in some cases. Edward son of Odbold lived on his groundplot north of St Peter's church.[4] John son of Terric the goldsmith lived by the river Stour,[5] while Robert son of Richard occupied his own groundplot in All Saints' Lane.[6] Robert Polre dwelt just inside Newingate.[7] The names of citizens often betray the place where they dwell. We may be sure that Robert of Hottewell, with a groundplot next to Hottewell actually lives here.[8] Adam 'de cruce' with ground next to Newingate Cross can hardly have derived this distinctive title if he merely owned the ground and let it out to someone else.[9] Luke del Bar, with ground at Barton Bar, must take his name from this obstruction,[10] Arnold of Eastbridge,[11] Fulco of Wincheap,[12] Liefwin of Westgate,[13] unquestionably dwell beside the landmarks which provide them with a name. Conversely the trades practised by the citizens supply a name to thoroughfares and other topographical features. Solomon the mercer and his neighbours, Baldwin, Luke and Charles,[14] mercers, all holding in Mercery Lane, must carry on trade there. Martin 'sæltere' patently dwells close to Salt Hill.[15]

[1] D 111. This is in fact composed of two adjacent plots.
[2] D 348.
[3] D 349. Edward the fuller can hardly live out on the moors at Horsfold (F 634).
[4] '. . . terra ubi mansit Edwardus filius Odboldi . . . in vico iuxta ecclesiam sancti Petri' (Z, fol. 199r).
[5] '. . . terra que fuit Radulphi nepotis sancti Thome martiris [i.e. Rental D, 66] super Sturam vbi Johannes filius Terrici manet' (Z, fol. 197v).
[6] F 133.
[7] F 50.
[8] D 228.
[9] F 657.
[10] Z, fol. 191v.
[11] Duncombe and Battely, *Three Archiepiscopal Hospitals*, p. 317.
[12] F 45.
[13] D 382.
[14] D 110 n.
[15] BBSA, p. 161.

A NOTE ON CERTAIN RENTS PAID BY THE MONKS OF CHRIST CHURCH TO OTHER LORDS

A

(*i*) Domesday Book records that there were pertaining to the manor of 'Estursete', which can hardly be other than the manor of Westgate just outside the city walls of Canterbury, on the river Stour, fifty-two *masuræ* of which twenty-seven had been destroyed by 1087 in the construction of the archiepiscopal palace.[1] The destroyed twenty-seven must have lain in the wide area of the old Palace, east of Palace Street. Around the site of these destroyed *masuræ* there lie in the twelfth century certain dwellings owing rent to the manor of Westgate.[2]

Charter XVII (1157–61) shows that the patrimony (a house and ground by the almonry wall) brought by John son of Walter as a new monk was held 'of the fee of Westgate'. Archbishop Theobald, confirming the donation, retained an annual 'census' of an unspecified amount. The same ground is a subject of Charter XVI, from which we learn that the monks owed another rent to Liviva the widow (C 17, G 19), and that when she had (with her husband) assigned it to Minster abbey in Sheppey, at the time her daughter took the veil there, the nuns were charged with the responsibility of acquitting the monks 'versus curiam de Westgate', both for this ground and the ground next door.

(*ii*) South of (*i*), above, lay another holding. This is C 22, G 23, divided, by the date of Rental D, into two (D 1, 2). In fact it is held by two tenants in C and G, where it is shown that it produces a rent of 4d. to Westgate.

---

[1] *DB*, i, fol. 3v.; *DMon*, p. 81.

[2] 'Estursete' in *DB* and 'Stursæte' in *DMon* are usually identified with the manor and hundred of Westgate, outside the Canterbury gate of that name (N. Neilson in *VCH, Kent*, iii, p. 258; Douglas in *DMon*, p. 18, etc.) See Hasted, *Kent*, iii, p. 571. Somner (*Antiquities of Canterbury*, 1640, p. 89) makes the identification and has been followed ever since. As Hasted says, it is difficult to see what 'Estursete' might have been, other than Westgate. St Martin's, east of Canterbury, is said to be of the hundred of Westgate (*DB*, i, fol. 4r.) though it must have been of the hundred only from an administrative point of view, since it was physically detached. In the later middle ages one of the 'borgs', or units in the Kentish frankpledge system, of the hundred of Westgate was called 'Stoursete' (Lambeth MSS. roll 1788). Presentments are made *temp.* Henry IV, V, that the road 'apud Stoursete', and the way between 'Stoursete' and the prior's meadow (Kingsmead?), and the way between Hackington vicarage and 'Stoursete', are in bad condition. This seems to suggest that the name 'Stoursete' applies in the later middle ages to the district around the group of early dwellings in St Stephen's Road, south of the road-junction with Broad Oak Road. Evidently, as happens elsewhere, one of the borgs within the hundred bore the same name as the hundred.

It is clearly not to be identified with the adjacent tenement mentioned in Charter XVI.

(*iii*) Charter XVI says that there is an adjacent tenement for which the nuns are to acquit 'versus curiam de Westgate'. There is no statement of rent forthcoming, though it sounds as if something is due, and we can see that this urban holding (covered by a stone house c. 1230—see D 4, n.) is positively connected with Westgate.

(*iv*) Next to the north lay the holding of Vavasur, later of William of Maidstone (B 52, D 4; F 114). This ground was charged with 12d. *per annum* to Westgate court (C 20, G 21).

(*v*) A little to the east, within the city walls was dwelling c. 1160 Goditha daughter of Elfwin and her husband Vavasur (A 3, XII, XIII). At that date 6d. *per annum* was due to the archbishop, clearly the 6d. paid c. 1180 and c. 1206 to Westgate court (C 21, F 22).

(*vi*) Early in the thirteenth century a house apparently in King's Street, and close to the palace, bought by St Gregory's priory, was charged with 12d. annually to Westgate court (Greg., no. 74).

We have therefore within a narrow radius, clustered round the palace and the site of the twenty-seven lost *masuræ* named in Domesday Book as dependent on 'Estursete', six holdings connected with Westgate Manor. It does not seem inconceivable that we have here some of the remaining twenty-five *masuræ* dependent on 'Estursete' in Domesday.

It will be convenient at this point to consider other cases where there is a connection between a dwelling in Canterbury in the twelfth century, and a country manor, with a parallel in Domesday Book. Rental B describes as 'terra de Wicham' certain ground at or very near the southern end of Butchery Lane.[1] 'Wicham' must be Wickhambreux, a few miles from Canterbury. At the date of Domesday, Wickhambreux was held in demesne by Odo of Bayeux who must therefore be lord of the three *masuræ*, belonging to this manor in Canterbury. There is curious evidence relating ground at Butchery Lane with Bayeux, and hence with Odo. Next to, or very near the 'terra de Wicham' is ground of Simon de Valbadun (*alias* de Denton?),[2] probably a descendant of one of two brothers with the name Valbadon holding successively at Hamstede in East Kent, given to one of them by Odo.[3] The name Valbadun may be found con-

---

[1] B 221.
[2] For the Valbadun-Denton family, see W. Urry, 'The Normans in Canterbury' (*Canterbury Archæological Society Occasional Papers*, no. 2, pp. 8–9).   [3] *DB*, i, fol. II v.

nected with ground in Butchery Lane, Canterbury, next to, or close to, ground bearing the name of Odo's manor of Wickham, while far away in Normandy there is to be found, a few miles from Bayeux, a hamlet called Vaubadon.

King Stephen gave the manor of Faversham to his abbey there. Domesday says that the manor of Faversham has in Canterbury three haws worth 20d.[1] Late in the twelfth century two tenements in St Peter's Street, Canterbury, are held of the monks of Faversham, one of the tenements producing a rent of 5d.[2] These may well be two of the haws named in Domesday.

According to Domesday the manor of Newington,[3] near Faversham, has in Canterbury four haws with two in Rochester, rendering 64d. The version in the White Book of St. Augustine's Abbey says nothing of the Canterbury haws but observes that the Rochester haws are worth 24d., from which it may be assumed that those at Canterbury produce 40d.[4] The schedule in the abbey White Book headed 'Noticia terrarum sancti Augustini in comitatu de Kent', a neglected Domesday satellite, indicates that a rent of 30d. arose 'de quatuor aghis in Canterburia . . . et una ecclesia'.[5] Register P among the Chapter Archives at Canterbury contains an account of Newington in a hand of the later twelfth century, close in content to the entry for this manor in Domesday Book. The passage relating to the urban property runs:

Due . . . in Rofecestra mansiones que reddunt ij sol. Tres quoque mansiones in ciuitate Cantuar' in occidentali parte Eastbregge 7 ecclesia que ibi est reddunt xxx denarios.[6]

The passage in Register P relating to Newington may also be found in Lambeth MS. 1212, in a hand of the thirteenth century. There is no material variant in the section relating to the urban dwellings, except for the fact that the Lambeth copy bears a gloss: 'id est hagan'.[7]

The value of the entries in Register P and in Lambeth MS. 1212 lies in the fact that we are given some idea of the site of the Canterbury 'haws', west of Eastbridge, or King's Bridge, and that we may reasonably assume

---

[1] DB, i, fol. 2v.　　　　　　　　　　[2] Rental D 366, 367; Rental C 45; G 45.
[3] DB, i, fol. 14v.　　　　　　　　　　[4] PRO, E 164/27, fol. 20v.
[5] Ibid., fol. 16v. The entry relating to the Canterbury *mansiones* is followed by a list of eleven names, with rents headed: 'Hoc est gablum de burgensibus de Newentune.' It seems highly improbable that the inhabitants of Newington can have been called burgesses at any time, and it would be tempting to speculate whether we may have here names of individuals dwelling on the haws at Canterbury and Rochester, were it not for the fact that the combined rents amount to over 16s. The term 'dimidia agha' is used of one holding.
[6] CAC, Reg. P, fol. 28.　　　　　　　[7] Lambeth MS. 1212, ff. 335–6.

that at one of the four in Domesday Book has been constructed a church. Unless some lost building is concerned, the church would seem to be St Peter's, which embodies some very early Norman work.

B

An entry in Rental B[1] relating to a tenement in Northgate Street records that it had been ceded to the archbishop with ground adjacent by the monks of St Augustine's 'for sheep and bread and mead'. This entry harks back to the ancient organization of the pre-conquest English church.

On Maundy Thursday the diocesan bishop consecrates *oleum catechumen-orum* (chrism) and *oleum infirmorum*. The abbey of St Augustine having largely established an independence of the archbishop, was yet obliged to admit intervention on certain indispensable occasions, one of which was for the receipt of the holy oils. Domesday Monachorum incorporates lists showing the way in which these oils were distributed in the diocese of Canterbury.[2] The scheme is that obtaining in the post-conquest period and no doubt far back into the past. The distribution is based on a series of 'minster churches', each standing at the head of a species of rural deanery.

In the lists in Domesday Monachorum, the churches dependent upon St Augustine's abbey are as a general rule omitted, and it may be guessed that distribution of the sacred oils to such churches was undertaken by the abbey itself, which would consequently make a gross payment to the archbishop. We may indeed find such a gross payment, of considerable size, comprising both a money element and renders in kind. We learn that 7d. is placed on the High Altar of Canterbury cathedral, or passed between the sacrists of either house, while a further render is effected from the abbey as follows:[3]

> 30 loaves worth 4 a penny
> 2 best sheep
> 2 amphorae of mead
> 1 amphora of ale
> 600 pence.

The narrative of the dispute depends very largely on the chronicle of William Thorne, monk of St Augustine's abbey, writing as late as the

[1] B 56
[2] See *DMon, Introduction*, § ii, for a discussion of the problem. Professor Douglas bases his discussion on the work of Dr G. Ward in *Archæologia Cantiana*, xlv, pp. 60–89. See Saltman, *Theobald*, pp. 66–69.   [3] *DMon*, p. 78.

fourteenth century. However, he had access to contemporary materials such as papal bulls, and letters of such figures as Henry, bishop of Winchester. Thorne says that a money render of 50s. 7d. (i.e. 600d. plus 7d.) was made both for chrism and oil,[1] losing sight of the fact that the render in kind was in part-payment. He does in fact mention the render, but indicates that it was commuted at some point of time for an annual payment of 3s.[2] The fees paid by the cardinal or minster churches in Kent for chrism and oil in the lists in Domesday Monachorum are very similar in nature to those produced by the abbey, since they involve renders in kind of the same nature, and large and small money payments. The payment made by the monks of St Augustine's to the archbishop must have been very irksome indeed, and they evidently took steps to free themselves.

In 1120 Pope Calixtus liberated the abbey from what he called a 'base extortion of rams, bread and drink, which the monks of Holy Trinity . . . strive to claim for themselves',[3] including, no doubt, the archbishop, and furthermore sent word to the archbishop and his monks to stop the exaction.[4] At some juncture between 1123 and 1136 the abbey and archbishop William came to an agreement over the payment in kind. It is possible, since the agreement seems to embody the first mention of a figure of 3s. in commutation, that this was the occasion upon which it was fixed.[5] In 1139 Innocent II reaffirmed the exemption of St Augustine's from the payment in kind, as laid down earlier by Calixtus, in a bull addressed to abbot Hugh, and informed him that he had notified archbishop Theobald that he was no more to demand 50s. 7d. paid for chrism and oil.[6] There was some confusion, it is clear, even in the eyes of contemporaries, as to the precise nature of the payments. Meanwhile in 1138 the Council of Westminster had laid down as its first canon, that nothing was to be paid for the holy oils, nor for other sacraments.[7]

Theobald treated the commands of Innocent II with complete contempt, and received a summons to Rome.[8] He evaded going thither by producing the excuse that he was unable to comply owing to the civil war in England, and was given until the octave of St Martin, 1142, to appear either

---

[1] *Thorne*, col. 1800, p. 77.   [2] Ibid., col. 1804, p. 77.
[3] Ibid., col. 1797, p. 65.   [4] Ibid., col. 1797, p. 66.
[5] Elmham, *Chronicle*, RS, p. 404. The concluding remarks of the bull of Eugenius printed here indicate that this agreement had been effected (by charter), between abbot Hugh (I or II?) and Theobald's 'predecessor'. The limiting dates given are those of archbishop William.
[6] *Thorne*, col. 1800, pp. 69–70.
[7] Gervase, *Opera*, RS, i, p. 107; Wilkins, *Concilia*, i, p. 415.
[8] *Thorne*, col. 1802, pp. 73, 74.

in person or by proctors.[1] Finally his agents, with those of the abbey appeared before the pope, and engaged in long argument.[2] The latter made formal complaint, but the former refused to answer until all arrears had been paid up to date.[3] The others rejoined that they were unable to pay, because of the canon enacted at Westminster, and of the bulls issued by the pope's predecessors. The archiepiscopal party affirmed that the dues were in the nature of a rent (census).[4] After more charges and counter-charges Innocent announced that it was quite impossible to learn the truth of the matter on the spot, and committed the case to the legate Henry of Winchester and to Robert bishop of Hereford, for determination in England.[5]

Accordingly a council was held at Winchester in 1143 under the presidency of bishop Henry, and in the presence of many other bishops, including Robert of Hereford and Theobald.[6] The discussion was confined to the render of 50s. 7d., and it was decided that the claim should be waived by Theobald in return for some property worth 60s. *per annum*. Two mills at Dover belonging to the abbey of St Augustine were suggested, producing this figure. Theobald resisted, and secured a further concession in the shape of 20s. *per annum* from a prebend in St Martin's at Dover belonging to the abbey, whereby, as William Thorne bitterly notes, he obtained a very excessive compensation.[7]

The question of the 3s. still remained, however, unsettled. In the next year (1144), a deputation of monks from St Augustine's arrived at the curia, where they found Theobald sitting with the pope.[8] Among other business they requested papal confirmation of the arrangements made at Winchester, to which Theobald objected, complaining that he was still being robbed of 3s. *per annum* 'for bread, drink and rams'. Under the direction of Lucius, made *viva voce* in the first instance, agreement was reached involving the transfer from the abbey to the archbishop of three shillings-worth of land,[9] 'three plots (*mansure*) of land,' as Thorne describes it, 'outside the Northgate of the city of Canterbury, opposite the southern angle of the cemetery of St Gregory, close to the highroad on the right as you go into the city'.[10]

By a bull of 17 April 1144, Lucius confirmed *inter alia* both the new

---

[1] Ibid., col. 1802, p. 74. [2] Elmham, *Chronicle*, RS, p. 375; *Thorne*, col. 1802, p. 73.
[3] *Thorne*, col. 1802–3, p. 74. [4] Ibid., Elmham, *Chronicle*, RS, p. 376.
[5] Elmham, *Chronicle*, RS, p. 377; *Thorne*, col. 1802–3, pp. 73–74.
[6] Wilkins, *Concilia*, i, pp. 422–3; *Thorne*, col. 1803–4, pp. 75 ff.
[7] *Thorne*, col. 1805, p. 78.
[8] Ibid., col. 1804, p. 77. Thorne is using a letter of Henry, bishop of Winchester.
[9] *Thorne*, col. 1804–5, p. 77. [10] Ibid., col. 1806, p. 79.

arrangement and the agreement already reached about the payment of 50s. 7d.[1] Subsequently pope Eugenius III reminded Theobald of the instruction given *viva voce* by Lucius, commanding him to implement it, and to hand back to the abbey a charter of agreement made to archbishop William by abbot Hugh concerning the 3s.[2]

---

[1] Holtzmann, *Papsturkunden*, ii, pp. 179–81.

[2] Elmham, *Chronicle*, RS, p. 404. The actual ground surrendered by the abbey to the archbishop to liquidate the claim for 3s., the commuted render, can be identified with some certainty. The southern angle of the cemetery of St Gregory mentioned by Thorne (note 1, above) is a fixed point. D 7 says that it is 132 feet from the corner of Broad Street. The ground opposite to this, on the western side of Northgate Street 'on the right, as you go into the city', is Rental D 9–10. Section 9 is classed as 'terra', 36 feet by 222 feet, yielding 26d. *per annum*, and is in fact Rental B 56, yielding 26d. *per annum*, to the monks of Christ Church, who pass this sum on to the archbishop's court of Westgate. This is the precise holding, as will have been seen, passed over from the abbey, with ground adjacent, 'pro multonibus 7 panibus 7 medone' (see A 5, C 19, F 59, and G 20). The monks of Christ Church had acquired the ground from the tenant, the widow of Warin the mason, and thereby incurred responsibility for the rent due to his lord, the archbishop, formerly the abbey. It is not clear which side the 'ground adjacent', affording the odd 10d. to the archbishop, lay. The ground to the north is D 10, which produces 10d. to Christ Church, though there is no mention of a payment of this sum to the archbishop. The ground has the same depth as § 9 (222 feet). D 9 is represented today (1966) by nos. 61a and 62 Northgate Street. The payment of 26d. was still being made by Christ Church to the archiepiscopal court of Westgate (evidently to this court, for administrative convenience) in 1318 (Lambeth MSS., Roll. 1105. *Thessurariis sancte Trinitatis* [i.e. Canterbury cathedral] *ijs. ijd.*).

CHAPTER IV

Borough Government

S O M E limited but valuable information on the subject of local government can be extracted from the rentals and charters. In Domesday Book Canterbury appears as a hundred, probably surrounded by the limits (embracing the walls and a wide tract of countryside) which enclosed it until 1835, and indeed which to a great extent enclose it today. The first surviving charter (long when compared with most borough charters of the age) is that of Henry II, issued at Westminster possibly in 1155.[1] The provisions of the charter are as follows:

No citizen is to be impleaded without the walls on any plea except pleas relating to external tenures, apart from the king's moneyers and ministers.

The citizens shall have quittance of the murderfine within the city and in the portsoke.

None of the citizens shall fight a 'duel'.[2]

The citizens may deraign pleas of the crown according to the ancient custom of the city.

Within the city walls none shall take his hospitality by force but [?sed for vel in error in MS.] by assignment of the marshal. [N.B. Cal. Charter Rolls, ii, p. 472 (see note 1 below) gives sec (sic)]

---

[1] The charter is printed, with substantial inaccuracies, by J. B. Sheppard in HMC, ix, app. i, p. 166. It is printed with some small variations from the text as it appears in the original charter, in Cal. Charter Rolls, ii, p. 472. Facsimile in Friends of Canterbury Cathedral, Annual Report, xxi, 1948, opp. p. 32. It was issued at Westminster, and is attested by Becket as chancellor. It appears that he was in office as early as January 1155, and probably from the previous month. (R. Foreville, 'Tradition et Comput dans la Chronologie de Thomas Becket', in Bulletin Philologique et Historique du Comité des Travaux Historiques et Scientifiques, 1955 et 1956, p. 9). The names of other witnesses do not positively establish for the Canterbury charter a much later limit than December 1154. Warin f. Gerald is named as 'camerarius' in a charter, issued at Westminster, assigned (Eyton, p. 2) presumably to a point of time after the coronation (19 December 1154). Eyton's Index gives him an earlier limit of 1155. Henry was at Westminster again in March 1155 and December 1155, but not again until (possibly) April–August 1158. Warin f. Gerald had been succeeded as 'camerarius' by his brother Henry by August 1158. Charters to other boroughs (Exeter and Gloucester) were issued in 1155 (Eyton, pp. 6, 7). The Winchester charter is assigned to 1155–8 (BBC, i, p. xxxii).

[2] It is worth pointing out in connection with this mention of trial-by-battle, that there is some evidence for the existence of an ordeal-pit at Canterbury. See p. 198.

The citizens are quit of toll and lastage throughout England and the ports of the sea.

Of scavage [escewinga, i.e. tolls for exposing goods] it is to be the same as in the days of Henry I.

None is to be judged in a money amercement except as judgment was given in the time of Henry I.

There shall be no miskenning in any plea within the city.

The 'Burghimot' is to be held once only in fifteen days.

The citizens shall have their lands and tenures and all pledges and debts justly, whosoever shall owe them to them.

Concerning their lands and tenures within the city right shall be done to them according to the custom of the city.

Of all their debts contracted at Canterbury, and mortgages (vadimonia) made there, the pleas shall be held at Canterbury.

If anyone in England shall take toll or custom from the men of Canterbury, after failure to make amends, the sheriff of Kent ['Canthuar.', the word used above for Canterbury, but clearly meaning Kent in this instance], shall take a distress at Canterbury.

The citizens are to have their hunting wheresoever they held it in the time of king Henry I.

For the better state of the city (ad emendationem ciuitatis) the citizens are made quit of brudtol, childwita, eresgieua, and scotale, so that neither the sheriff of Kent, nor any other of the king's 'bailiffs', shall hold scotale.

All the above are conceded on the most advantageous terms at which they were enjoyed in the time of Henry I, together with all other liberties and free customs as held in the same reign.

The chief comment on the above seems to be that there is every suggestion that extensive rights of self-government have been enjoyed for a long time. It will be remarked that in five clauses out of the sixteen and in the concluding remark, there is mention of custom of the city, or there is harking-back to the days of Henry I. The clause relating to the burghmoot clearly indicates that the institution had been in existence before the date of the charter. The most important clause, empowering the citizens to deraign pleas of the crown, actually refers to the ancient custom of the city in this respect. A substantial proportion of the charter is patently confirmatory.

The witnesses to the charter include some men of considerable interest in a study of Canterbury. They comprise archbishop Theobald, Hugh 'de Dovera', a benefactor to Christ Church,[1] who probably died in office as sheriff of Kent in 1168, Walchelin Maminot the local magnate, Ralph

[1] XLVI.

Picot, who served as sheriff of Kent, and Thomas Becket himself, in his capacity as chancellor. A striking illustration of the fact that charters of the age are by no means exhaustive is the absence of any mention of the Canterbury gild of merchants, which we find in existence and in possession of property only ten years later, and which, if identical, as is probable, with the urban gild named in Domesday Book, was in existence long before the date of the charter.[1] The merchant gild is often a conspicuous feature in other borough charters, and at Canterbury one might well expect a clause either empowering its establishment, or confirming it. The next surviving charter is that of 1234, when the city was granted in fee farm at £60 per annum.[2]

The names of some pre-conquest reeves are known in the case of Canterbury. William Somner says that '. . . in the yeare 780. in certaine Charters of Christ-Church bearing date at *Canterbury*, mention is made of one *Aldhune hujus Civitatis Præfectus*, as in one, *Regis Præfectus in Doroberniâ*, as in another of them, who having purchased *Burne*, consisting of foure plough-lands, of his Master the Kentish King *Egbert*, for two thousand shillings, gave it all to the Monkes of that Church, *ad mensam* . . .'[3] It is evident from existing charters that the grant was made by Aldhune (Ealdhun), confirmed by Egbert of Kent, and cancelled by Offa, but the date 780 does not occur in them.[4] We may suppose therefore that Somner had access to documents existing in 1640, but now lost. A charter of 860–6 includes among the witnesses 'Æthelstan 7 ingan [for 'innan'] burgware'. Professor Tait suggests he was reeve of the borough.[5] Hlothwig 'portgerefa' is named in a charter of 968.[6] Æthelred 'portgerefa on byrig' is found c. 995.[7] When the Danes attacked Canterbury in 1011, Ælfword

[1] For the early Canterbury gilds see below, Chapter V.

[2] HMC, ix, app. i, p. 166; *BBC*, ii, p. xxvi.

[3] Somner, *Antiquities of Canterbury*, 1640, p. 363.

[4] Birch, CS 319, 312. Birch, *CS*, no. 319 refers to Ealdhun as a 'good man', who in this royal *villa* was 'præfectus'. It is clear that the *villa* is in fact Canterbury. Birch, *CS* no. 332 calls Ealdhun 'comes', and further indicates that he was kinsman (propinquus) to Archbishop Iaenberht (765–92). Birch, *CS* no. 293 indicates that Ealdhun made his grant as he was about to go overseas. For the nature of Ealdhun's office see Jolliffe, *Prefeudal England*, p. 47.

[5] Birch, CS, 515. See MEB, p. 9.

[6] The charter of 968 is Birch *CS* 1212. Somner quotes from a charter of 956 (*Antiquities of Canterbury*, 1640, p. 364) in which Hlothwig, portreeve, is witness. The document is clearly not Birch, *CS* 1212, and we may assume that this is a case where Somner had before him a now lost charter. Possibly charters known to Somner and now untraced were destroyed in the fire in the Cathedral Audit House, 1670, just after his death.

[7] Robertson, *Anglo-Saxon Charters*, LXIX.

the king's reeve was among the captives.[1] The charter (between 1044 and 1048) relating how Godric of Bourne acquired the estate at Offham tells that the purchase was completed at Wye before the whole shire of Kent.[2] Among the witnesses was Godric 'portgerefa', with Wulfsige the king's reeve. The former is probably connected with Canterbury. The latter may belong to Wye which appears elsewhere as an administrative centre.[3] At the date of the Norman Conquest the borough reeve at Canterbury was Bruman, who earns an adverse mention in Domesday Book for unjust exaction of tolls.[4] The St Augustine's version contributes a further adverse mention, disclosing that if bread and ale were sold otherwise than in ancient times then forfeits were to be exacted from offenders. A certain 'prepositus', Brimannus, however, 'took the forfeit as toll', that is apparently he connived at the breaking of the regulations, accepting the forfeit money.[5]

After Bruman, the next portreeve known is Calveal (evidently identical with William Calvellus of contemporary charters), who attests the well-known exchange between Christ Church and the chapmangild of Canterbury.[6] From the occurrence of his name in conjunction with the seniors of the gild it seems as if he may preside over the organization. Calvel is much more than a mere name. We know he was acquainted with St Anselm, and was part-founder of the local nunnery. He suffered severe reproof from the saint for moving the market to the inconvenience of the monks.[7]

So far we have had only names of single reeves, but half a century later we find two joint reeves called 'prepositi'. About the beginning of 1156,

---

[1] *ASC, sub anno.* Plummer, *Two of the Anglo-Saxon Chronicles Parallel,* i, p. 141. Verses embodied in the *Heimskringla,* apparently referring to events of 1009, recount:

> The portreeves (portgriefar) could not
> Hold the proud Olave
> From the town, the fort of the Kentish men.
>
> *Heimskringla,* ed. E. Monsen (English Translation, 1932)

It is curious that the plural is used in reference to the portreeve.

[2] Robertson, *Anglo-Saxon Charters,* no. CIII.

[3] See Robertson, *Anglo-Saxon Charters,* p. 439.

[4] *DB,* i, fol. 2r.

[5] White Book (PRO E 164/27), fol. 21v. Ed. Ballard, p. 8. *Thorne* (col. 1780, pp. 38–39) mentions a 'prefect' called Bruman, a benefactor of St Augustine's abbey, but dates him to the time of abbot Wulfric I (985–1006). He gave to St Augustine's two 'hagas' and a meadow. If, however, abbot Wulfric II (1047–59) is involved, we may have the Bruman who was reeve at the Conquest. But Thomas of Elmham (*Historia, RS,* p. 23) assigns the donation of Bruman (who is not styled 'prefect') to 991. Is it possible that we have yet another 'prefect' (of Canterbury?) called Bruman at this date?

[6] I, II, III.

[7] See pp. 62–3.

Henry II when at Canterbury issued a writ addressed to Hamo and John 'prepositi' ordering them to put right encroachments during the Anarchy made on a pathway belonging to the monks near Burgate Street.[1] Hamo the reeve is frequently named. In the period 1153–61 he attests a charter[2] relating to the Christ Church manor of Illeigh (Essex), while late in 1160 or early in 1161 he contracts debt to the extent of 41½ marks with William Cade the financier, pledging in case of non-payment his mill and all his tenements, within and without Canterbury. His son Robert joins with him in the guarantee.[3] Rental B shows that he is paying rent for ground just within Newingate, Canterbury, where he probably dwells.[4] It is of interest to note that his father Henry had given the ground to Christ Church on taking the cowl there. Hamo was alive and in office as late as 1167, and if the suggested date of Charter xxv is correct then he was still performing his duties about 1177. John 'prepositus', presumably the colleague named above, appears in the Pipe Roll[5] for 1166–7 as member of a board of four comprising himself, Adam of Charing, John son of Vivian (soon to serve as reeve) and the prior of St Augustine's, concerned with repairs to the city walls, expending £20 for the purpose from funds of the see of Canterbury appropriated during Becket's exile. Benedict of Peterborough recounts an anecdote among his great collection of miracles of St Thomas showing John son of Vivian performing the office of reeve (preposituræ . . . officium). John intercepted a man leaving Canterbury with a cart empty but for two sick pilgrims, demanding whether toll had been paid on goods brought to the city. The driver replied that all the goods brought were sick folk, who had been cured at the tomb of St Thomas, apart from the two in the cart.[6] The incident is of great value in showing a borough reeve concerned with collection of toll. The Pipe Rolls show John son of Vivian performing duties which (if he is not actually called 'prepositus' in such connection), strongly suggest he is carrying out the duties of this office. He collects in 1179–80 the last instalment paid of the colossal amercement suffered by the Canterbury moneyer John son of Robert,[7] and is himself amerced in year 1181–2 in the great sum of two

[1] xv. Hamo witnesses the almost contemporary charter of William of Ypres, no. xiv.

[2] CAC, Ch. Ant. H 123, temp. prior Wibert, and archbishop Theobald, executed in the Chapter House at Canterbury.

[3] H. Jenkinson, 'A Money-Lender's Bonds of the Twelfth Century' (in Essays presented to R. L. Poole), pp. 206–7.   [4] B 100, 213; XXI, XXII, XLIII.

[5] PR, 13 Henry II, pp. 201–2. For Adam of Charing, the repentant enemy of Becket, see pp. 180–1.

[6] Materials, RS, ii, p. 138. J. F. Vivian may have been reeve by 1169. See p. 65 above.

[7] PR, 26 Henry II, p. 145. For J. son of Robert and other Canterbury moneyers, see Chapter V.

hundred marks for allowing a forger to escape and for handing over a dowry without authorization.[1] The roll for 1182–3 shows him taking charge of the goods of a delinquent, a debt which drags on for years,[2] finally collected at the beginning of the next reign from his daughter, Susanna de Planaz, from which we may deduce that John was dead by 1189.[3] He is named at the head of a list of burgesses as witness to a grant of wardship to St Gregory's priory in 1169,[4] and may well then have been serving as 'prepositus', in which case he must have been one of the reeves who were charged by the four knights to bring out the citizens in service for the king on the day of Becket's murder.[5]

Towards 1200 several names of reeves may be recovered. Eun, 'prepositus civitatis', witnesses charters to the priory of St Laurence[6] and to the cathedral,[7] while other witness-lists provide the names of Eudo son of Sigar,[8] Arnold Ferre,[9] Theoric the vintner,[10] and Terric the goldsmith.[11] Somner supplies the names (without citing a source) of Mainer the rich[12] and of his son Wiulph the rich.[13] The name of Eudo the sheriff's clerk, occurring in more than one charter, is of extreme interest in its suggestion of county influences at work within the borough.[14] It is clear that by 1200 a change is taking place, for no longer do reeves serve for years together, but a rapid alteration in names points to annual election. Now and then the term of office can be dated, as in the case of Samuel the dyer and John the mercer who attest a charter of 1204.[15] Increasingly the 'prepositi' are called bailiffs (ballivi) following the fashion in other boroughs.

Some inferences may be drawn about the function of the reeve. In the age of the conquest he is concerned with collection of tolls, and must pursue and exact amends 'whithersoever he shall go' from any delinquent

[1] PR, 28 Henry II, p. 154.
[2] PR, 29 Henry II, p. 158. The delinquent, William son of Hubert, is called 'assayer, of Canterbury'. See PR, 28 Henry II, p. 146.
[3] PR, 1 John, p. 61. [4] Greg., charter 22. [5] See below.
[6] Cathedral Library, Lit. MS. C 20, p. 82. [7] LIX. [8] Greg., charter 42.
[9] Ibid. A. Ferre serves with E. son of Sigar. He also serves with Terric the goldsmith (CAC, Ch. Ant. C 735).
[10] The MS. evidence cannot be traced. Somner gives the name, citing a cartulary of St Radegund's priory, Dover (Somner, Antiquities of Canterbury, 1640, p. 21). The name has not been found in Bodleian MS. Rawlinson B 336 (cartulary of St Radegund).
[11] CAC, Ch. Ant. C 735.
[12] Somner, Antiquities of Canterbury, 1640, p. 142. [13] Ibid.
[14] LXV; BM. MS. Cotton Claudius D X (cartulary of St Augustine's), fol. 75. Grant of ground in St George's parish, Canterbury, published in Newingate hundred (i.e. ward) court, and in Burghmoot. These being witnesses: 'Eudone clerico vicecomitis preposito ciuitatis', and others.
[15] CAC, Ch. Ant. C 713.

who shall have dug, or fixed a stake, in the road.[1] Calveal the reeve of 1100 appears to be leader of the merchant gild of Canterbury, and controls the market, or at least has powers to move it, as we learn from the correspondence of St Anselm.[2] John son of Vivian late in the twelfth century collects tolls and has custody of the goods of delinquents. Henry II charges the reeves with the duty of putting Christ Church back in control of some of its property lost during the Anarchy, adding that if the reeves did not do it then 'my justiciar or sheriff of Kent will do it'.[3] The reeves have fiscal duties. We have seen John son of Vivian ensuring collection of toll, and we find that rents, apparently royal rents, are paid into the hands of the 'prepositi' in the twelfth century.[4] The 'prepositi' have evident military duties, since the four knights commanded 'li provoz' to bring out the citizens in service for the king on 29 December 1170.[5] It may at this juncture be remarked that their military functions were probably superseded for the time being when the local constables were established at the council held at London in 1205.[6] Ralph of St Clement's 'constabularius', apparently the local Canterbury constable, appears in Charter LXV, and may be identical with the 'Rand' tunc constabularius Cant' ' named as witness, in company with Reginald of Cornhill (I or II?), and James 'de porta', apparently the mayor of Canterbury of that name (dead by late in 1216), in the cartulary of Leeds priory (Kent).[7] Another constable is Colin, who appears to be not only 'constabularius', but also alderman of Ridingate ward in Canterbury.[8]

Probably the reeves in earlier days were nominees of the king. Eudo the reeve, 'clericus vicecomitis', might possibly be the nominee of the sheriff. However, it is worth pointing out that certain of the reeves seem to be local men, if the possession of property locally by their fathers may be relied upon. Hamo the reeve in office from 1156 until perhaps 1177 has a father with ground just inside Newingate,[9] while John son of Vivian has a father who takes a name from 'Wiht', the island in the Stour within the city walls and has ground in Stour Street nearby.[10] Men in office for years together may have been appointed by the crown, but it is less likely that their successors, who from about 1200 seem to change every year, can owe their office to appointment in this way, especially when these reeves are so often quite clearly local men. However, the sheriff of Kent

[1] DB, i, fol. 2r.   [2] See above, p. 62.   [3] XV.
[4] C 2; G 2.   [5] Guernes 11. 5171 ff. The term 'li provoz' is in the singular.
[6] Gervase: Opera (RS), ii, 96–97.
[7] Kent County Record Office MS. fol. 2.
[8] BM. MS. Cotton, Claudius D X, fol. 76r.
[9] See above.   [10] See p. 64.

was usually at hand and may have taken a part in elections. From 1234, by virtue of the royal charter, the bailiffs were in fact elected freely, and this concession probably confirms an arrangement already long in practice.

The evidence discussed above as to the function of the reeves at Canterbury offers useful comment on the question whether a grant in fee farm did in fact bestow powers of local government. The Canterbury charter of 1234 makes a bald grant of the city in fee farm, lays down the farm at a figure of £60, and says that the citizens are to produce this sum at the exchequer in instalments at Easter and at Michaelmas.[1] The charter says that the citizens may elect the bailiffs but says nothing else on the subject of administration, though we know that the citizens had enjoyed some rights of local government for about a century and possibly longer.

AN EARLY MAYOR OF CANTERBURY

Many English boroughs, following the example of London, were setting up a mayoralty in the early thirteenth century. The office of mayor of Canterbury dates continuously only from 1448, though this is not the only important borough in which a mayor was late, or apparently late, in appearing. However, there are two charters[2] which have come to light where there is named among the witnesses 'Jacobus de porta maior Cant' ', or 'maior ciuitatis Cant''. It seems unlikely that this is a slip of a scribe's pen for 'balliuus' or 'prepositus' especially as James 'de porta' is named alone with no colleague in office. The citizens have evidently followed the fashion in other boroughs and have adopted a single mayor in place of the two joint-reeves. One of the charters[3] recounts the grant by Robert 'camerarius' to Robert of Abingdon 'clericus', of ground held of Christ Church on the north side of the 'Parade' (near Mercery Lane) at 3s. *per annum*. In the financial year ending Michaelmas 1217 the monks exact 3s. relief from the daughters of Robert 'camerarius', and register another relief of 3s. 'de Roberto clerico de Abind'' for ground of R. 'camerarius'.[4] It is difficult to interpret these two entries, and on the face of it it would appear that Robert of Abingdon got the ground from the daughters who had become possessed of it at their father's death. However, it is clear in

[1] *BBC*, ii, p. 311; Cal. Charter Rolls, ii, p. 472.

[2] Of the two charters one (CAC, Reg. A., fol. 421r.) is a copy in a hand of the early fifteenth century. The other (Archives of Eastbridge Hospital, Canterbury, Charter A 13) is an original. The former is grant by R. 'camerarius' to R. of Abingdon. See below. The latter records grant by Hugo Godeshall to Eastbridge Hospital. The grant was published 'in hundredo de Westgate', probably the urban ward court, rather than that of the extra-mural hundred of Westgate.

[3] CAC, Reg. A, fol. 421r.   [4] CAC, Reliefs, *sub anno*.

the charter that their father made the grant to Robert of Abingdon. Perhaps he died very soon and the daughters paid relief and later made an effective conveyance. It seems probable that we have the same piece of ground both in the list of reliefs and in the charter. Reliefs are not uncommonly paid later than the date of the transaction with which they are connected (death or alienation), and we may suppose that the ground has been conveyed to Robert of Abingdon within a few years before 1217. James 'de porta' himself, the mayor, was dead by the autumn of 1216, when his son paid relief on his holdings.[1] At the latest he must have served the office of mayor in 1216, and if for a complete year, then probably from the autumn of 1215. The office cannot be traced in the succeeding period, and James 'de porta' may have been its only holder before it was revived in the fifteenth century.

James 'de porta' was a man of some consequence. He held from the monks the valuable flesh-shambles in the Buttermarket,[2] was in occupation of ground incorporating stone buildings in Palace Street, opposite the gate of the archbishop's Palace.[3] He was 'portarius'[4] of the palace, and may have lived on his property adjacent to the gate. He was alderman of Northgate ward,[5] and probably held office in the 'borough gild'. Certainly it appears that for many years he collected rents due to the gild.[6] It is of interest to note that his father, William 'de porta', is named among the votaries of St Anselm c. 1166, his name standing high in the list, among leading citizens.[7]

COURT AND COUNCIL

In the twelfth century a great many boroughs possessed a borough court,[8] while by the end of the next century they have a court of law and an administrative council. Round was inclined to see at London and many south-eastern boroughs an imitation of the institutions of foreign communes,[9] while Maitland on the other hand advanced a theory of purely native development.[10] He affirmed that in the boroughs court and council were slowly differentiated, the borough court becoming a mere tribunal, while by its side a distinctly conciliar organ is developed. At Ipswich in

---

[1] CAC, Reliefs, sub anno.   [2] D 112.   [3] LIII, LIV.   [4] He is so-called in Charter LIV.
[5] Greg., nos. 42, 43, etc.   [6] For the Canterbury gilds, see Chapter V.
[7] W. Urry, 'St Anselm and his cult at Canterbury' (in Spicilegium Beccense, i, p. 578).
[8] Husting, husteng at London, Northampton, Norwich, Grimsby, Lynn and Yarmouth; burghimot, burwaremoot at Canterbury, Lincoln and Winchester; hundred at Bristol, Dublin, Kilkenny, Sandwich. See BBC, pp. 142–3.
[9] Commune of London, pp. 219 ff; Feudal England, pp. 552 ff.
[10] Hist. Eng. Law, i, p. 659.

1200 a council is set up by the burgesses (following a grant in fee farm), with authority to elect the two bailiffs, hitherto crown nominees, and also the newly-created coroners, instituted to watch over royal rights in the borough. The men of Ipswich did not stop there for they chose twelve men styled 'capitales portmanni jurati' or perhaps merely 'jurati', 'such as there are in other free boroughs in England'.[1] In February 1215 John told the *probi homines* of Northampton that he had accepted William Thilly as their mayor, ordered them to be intendant to him as such, and to elect twelve of the more discreet and better men of the town to despatch their affairs with him.[2] It seems improbable that these populous boroughs can have acquired a governing body only in the age of John and the readiness with which the men of Ipswich establish their 'jurati' without any special royal permission, and the fact that, as they remark, other free boroughs of the realm have such bodies, makes it not improbable that they were only carrying on some arrangement already long in force. Perhaps the number of 'jurati' was altered at this juncture. Again at Northampton it is unlikely that a borough with a long history and a mixed population can have been controlled by a virtual dictatorship of royal reeves.

Since Canterbury was a hundred-borough in the eleventh century, it presumably had at that time an urbanized hundred court. The first positive mention of a court or of a governing body is in the charter of c. 1155. There, as has been pointed out, it is clear that the body has already been in existence for some time, since its sessions are now limited to once a fortnight. This frequency of sessions and the indication that (as may be inferred) they have evidently been held at even shorter intervals is of value, since a body which met in that age with such frequency sounds more like a court of law than a deliberative assembly. We have many mentions of the boroughmoot evidently functioning as a court, from the later twelfth century, for it was customary to publish conveyances of property within the city, both in the appropriate ward court, and in the boroughmoot.[3] There is an instance of c. 1200 where the last-mentioned may be

---

[1] Gross, *Gild Merchant*, ii, pp. 116 ff. from the 'Little Domesday of Ipswich'. See MEB, pp. 270 ff.

[2] *Rotuli Litterarum Clausarum* (Rec. Commrs.), i, p. 188a. See MEB, pp. 272 ff.

[3] E.g. 'Pro hac . . . donacione mea facta et recordata in burgemoth' ciuitatis Cantuarie et postea in hundredo de berthe de Burgate' (BBSA, p. 598); 'pro . . . donacione . . . facta et recordata in burgimoto ciuitatis Cantuarie et in hundredo berthe de Redingate' [32 Henry III] (ibid., p. 397); cf. BBSA, p. 391. There are many other instances among the archives of Canterbury Cathedral and of Eastbridge Hospital, etc. A charter of the early thirteenth century in the Dover Priory cartulary (Lambeth MS. no. 241, fol. 169r.) records a grant relating to ground south of St Andrew's church, Canterbury, made 'teste toto burhimoto nullo obsistente uel contradicente'.

seen acting as a deliberative assembly. Terric the goldsmith granted ground near Burgate to Amfrid of Burgate, moved thereto, as is affirmed, by the inspiration of God and petition of the whole boroughmoot.[1] It is possible, however, that this marks the end of litigation.[2]

Unhappily we are left entirely in the dark as to the composition of the boroughmoot. The great Christ Church rental of c. 1230 shows a clear instance where the boroughmoot is acting as a court of law, for after a tenant has not paid his rent for fifteen years the Kentish process of gavelet is invoked and the land assigned to its lords, the monks, 'per consideracionem borchemott'.[3] In 1257 the abbot of St Augustine's made an arrest in the fields of Longport manor. The city bailiffs (flourishing their white wands of office) claimed the prisoner and summoned the abbot as their peer to the boroughmoot for the next day. The abbot refused to come, making claim that the day was not Tuesday, the accustomed day for the boroughmoot. We can see that this is the boroughmoot in its judicial capacity, and also that Tuesday is already the day for business, as it will be until 1835. We discover, moreover, that the Boroughmoot Horn, undoubtedly the same venerable instrument which even today resounds on civic occasions, was used to rouse the city in 1257.[4] In 1275 the boroughmoot may again be found delivering judgment in a case relating to tenures, as c. 1230.[5] At the end of the century, when rolls of pleas become available, they are all headed 'curia ciuitatis Cant'.[6] The old undifferentiated court has apparently bifurcated into court and council. From the mid-fourteenth century the expression boroughmoot is definitely confined to the administrative body, and will remain attached to it until 1835.

Notice must be taken to two non-judicial acts in the mid-thirteenth century. In 1259 it was alleged *coram rege* that whereas John Dodekere had been elected 'per communitatem ciuitatis' as bailiff of the city, he had been ejected from office by sixteen men, whose names are those of leading citizens of the age. The jury found that the 'maior pars et sanior' among the citizens had elected as bailiffs Thomas Chiche and Daniel le draper (who occur among the sixteen above), while the 'minor pars et infirmior' had elected John Dodekere.[7] Two years later (1261), a byelaw is enacted

[1] LXIII.

[2] Christina of Canterbury offered half a mark in the *curia regis* for an inquisition over ground at Nackington (just outside Canterbury) in 1 John, by testimony of the neighbourhood and of the portmoot. *Rotuli Curiæ Regis* (Rec. Commrs.) 1 John, p. 72.

[3] Rental Z, fol. 199v.

[4] Canterbury City Archives, Charter no. 29 (exemplification of record of case of 1257).

[5] CAC, Ch. Ant. C 79.   [6] Canterbury City Archives, J/B/100 ff.

[7] *Select Cases of Procedure without Writ under Henry III*, ed. H. G. Richardson and G. O. Sayles (Selden Society), pp. 38–39.

by Hamo Doge, alderman of Westgate, with four other aldermen, and thirteen leading citizens, together with the whole 'communitas' of Canterbury. The byelaw revokes a rate imposed on bakers' stalls and windows, grievous to the poor, said to have been imposed by certain 'concives'.[1] The body enacting the new byelaw embodies only two names occurring among those in the list of 1259, and there is strong suggestion that rival factions are at work. It is highly significant that the oath of bailiff was administered to John Dodekere the unsuccessful claimant in the former case by Hamo Doge, the leading local lawyer, whom we see heading the list of enactors in the later case. Unfortunately neither body is given any title, though we may note that eighteen[2] men are involved on the former occasion and the same number on the latter. In this latter case one of the six aldermen is missing.

It is tempting to believe that we have here (in 1261) substantially the six aldermen, with the twelve jurates of Canterbury, who were as we know in existence before 1300.[3] It may be remarked that since the number involved in the events of 1259 is apparently the same it is not inconceivable that we have at that date approximately the six aldermen and the jurates. If this is so, then it means that both benches could largely be thrown out of office, an argument against the inheritability of the office of alderman.[4]

We have no certain information about the composition of the borough-moot before the fourteenth century. In its judicial capacity, before its divergence, it was probably very small and there is unsubstantial evidence to suggest that in its deliberative capacity it was not large. About 1230 a lane in St George parish, evidently Iron Bar Lane, is called 'parvus vicus iuxta spechhus',[5] while the name 'Speechhouses' is attached to buildings at the western corner of the lane on the High Street even in the sixteenth century.[6] The Red Book of St Augustine's embodies a charter of 49 Henry III relating to rent arising 'de pretorio',[7] without any indica-

[1] Canterbury City Archives, Charter no. 6.

[2] If H. Doge and John Dodekere are added to the sixteen. Doge was presumably a member of the governing body. He is named as alderman only two years later.

[3] Pleas of Crown before J. de Berewyk and colleagues, Justices itinerant at Canterbury, 21 Edward I. (Printed Somner, *Antiquities of Canterbury*, 1640, pp. 502 ff.; Discussed W. Urry, Ph.D. thesis, London, 1956, i, 245 ff.)

[4] Discussed below. If almost a whole governing body has in fact been thrown out, is this a reflection of the convulsions at London at the same date?

[5] Rental Z, fol. 196v.; Somner, *Antiquities of Canterbury*, 1640, p. 28. Cf. Cal. Fine Rolls, 1413, p. 91; Jacob, 'Chichele and Canterbury' in *Studies in Medieval History, Presented to F. M. Powicke*, p. 402.   [6] CAC, Bunce, *Schedule*, ii, p. 289.

[7] BM. MS. Cotton Claudius D X, fol. 97r. The grantee of a messuage granted by the citizens in Queningate parish in or before 1269 was required to pay his rent half yearly at their 'pretorium' (Cal. Charter Rolls, ii, p. 123).

tion as to where this structure was to be found, while another charter (undated, but of the thirteenth century) makes mention of a tenement between St Margaret's church and the 'locutorium' of Canterbury.[1] This 'locutorium' is clearly the site which became the fishmarket, and is even today city property. The Black Book of St Augustine's incorporates a Canterbury rental, perhaps of the mid-thirteenth century, mentioning a 'loquitorium',[2] but this cannot be the same building as that in St Margaret's as it is on a frontage running east-west, while that in St Margaret's runs north-south. One point which may be evoked is that the body which met together in the speech-house can hardly have been of great size. It was patently not a full assembly of the citizens.

WARDS

Domesday Book discloses that a ward system had been evolved in many boroughs. York was divided into 'shires'.[3] Cambridge[4] and Stamford[5] were cut up into ten and six 'custodiæ' respectively, while at Huntingdon there are four 'ferlings'.[6] There is no hint that the 'hundred' of Canterbury is cut up into smaller units. Ballard, in his edition of the St Augustine's version of Domesday, suggests that aldermen, and by implication wards, were established here in the eleventh century.[7] The 'seniores' who control river banks near mills,[8] and whose interests must evidently be regarded when adjustments are made in connection with sluices, may he says, be 'seigneurs' (which is the more likely interpretation) or may alternatively be aldermen. There is certainly nothing to support his latter view, and we have no substantial evidence for the existence of these officials for another eighty years. Rental B, drawn up about 1166, surveys the eastern and northern sections of Canterbury, and shows that this area has been cut up into three wards, those of Northgate, Burgate and Newingate. We may assume that the remaining area of the city has been divided into the wards of Ridingate, Worthgate and Westgate, which were in existence at the end of the twelfth century. There are three aldermen named in the survey, though they are not specifically connected in Rental B with wards; yet we may readily believe that they were heads thereof, since by about 1170 one alderman (John) is specifically named in connection with a given ward

---

[1] Ibid., fol. 95v.   [2] BBSA, p. 180.   [3] DB, i, fol. 298r.
[4] Ibid., fol. 189a.   [5] Ibid. fol. 336v.   [6] Ibid. fol. 203r.
[7] Ballard, Eleventh Century Inquisition of St Augustine's (from PRO, E 164/27, the White Book of St Augustine's), p. 8.
[8] Ibid.

(Burgate)[1] and since at least by 1200 the term 'aldermaneria' (alderman-ria) is regularly used to describe wards.[2]

The London wards were more or less urban versions of the rural hundreds.[3] The Canterbury wards give the impression that they were copied bodily from their London counterparts, and indeed what we know of the functions of the Canterbury wards does strongly suggest that these were civic hundreds, the most striking and obvious evidence being the use of the term *hundredum* used continually to describe the wards.[4] The equation between the rural hundred and the urban ward is emphasized at the Westgate of Canterbury. Within the walls lies the city ward or hundred of Westgate and without lies the archiepiscopal hundred of the same name, 'hundredum infra Westgate' and 'hundredum extra Westgate' as they are termed in charters. There is a difference in the name of the chief officer, it is true, for an alderman presides within the gate, and a 'ballivus' without, but the second officer in either case is the 'bedellus,' and it would be quite impossible to tell from the language of charters (unless the chief officer is mentioned, and the geography of a holding is made clear) whether a conveyance of ground is being conducted within or without the walls. However, the hundred court is clearly of greater status than the ward court.

The focus of ward activity was its court, undoubtedly as old as the ward itself. We have numerous mentions of the court from the later twelfth century, for conveyances were published therein, and innumerable charters recount that a sale has been recorded in the appropriate ward court, usually followed by publication in the boroughmoot. In the post-medieval period a small fine for alienation was exacted in sales, and prob-ably this practice is of great antiquity. Apart from publication of charters, activity of the ward court is obscure before the fifteenth century, when we find that ward courts are collecting information about offences and nuis-ances within their jurisdictions and passing them up to the 'Inquisition' which becomes known, by the reign of Edward IV, as the Sessions. The wards are in fact performing the function of the view of frankpledge. There is a valuable piece of evidence for police activity of the ward and of its alderman in 1241. Among pleas of the crown conducted in that year at Canterbury it is related that a group of men broke into a house and

[1] XLV. See under 'Ward Officer', below.

[2] See discussion of nomenclature of wards, below.

[3] 'London Lands of St Paul's,' by H. W. C. Davis, in *Essays . . . presented to T. F. Tout*, pp. 48–49; Stenton, *Norman London*, p. 10. *Calendar of Plea and Memoranda Rolls, London, 1413–37*, Intro., pp. xxiv–xxx.

[4] E.g. in 1197 (Burgate 'hundred'). BBSA, p. 602.

maltreated the occupant. The victim brought an action against them. One man answered the summons but pleaded his clergy, and was handed over to the archdeacon. One was arrested and amerced. Two others, John Fareman and Adam le Waller, fled to sanctuary at the cathedral. 'et Johannes fuit in aldermanria Nicholai de Hathlou de Radegate et Adam fuit in aldermanria Willelmi Cokin in Wurgate. Ideo in misericordia.'[1] Hathlou and Cokin were aldermen of Ridingate and Worthgate and are respectively, so we see, responsible for delinquents in their wards, as much as a head of a borg, or a tithingman, in the countryside.[2]

The police activity of the ward will remain prominent in all its history until 1835. Indeed, since the ward first emerges without ambiguity in local history at some point of time shortly before September 1167 (in Rental B) it is tempting to ask whether it might not have had an origin in the Assize of Clarendon, 1166 (in February of that year?) in which case the date for Rental B may accordingly be narrowed.

THE NOMENCLATURE OF THE WARD

The term 'ward' is not found employed in Canterbury before the fifteenth century, and it is then clearly an importation from London. The first term noticed (in Rental B) is *bertha*, which seems to be peculiar to Canterbury. It may be cognate with the term borg, borh, and variants, used out in the Kentish countryside to denote a subdivision of the hundred, both personal and territorial, corresponding largely with the tithing in other parts of the realm.[3] *Bertha* is usually declined as a feminine noun, though indeclinable forms (as *berthe*) occur.[4] An isolated gallicized rendering has been found in *la birthe*.[5] A rental of St Augustine's abbey of c. 1216 affords the spelling *burtha*, while a late rendering *birtha* has been noticed.[6] The main life of the term lies within the century running from c. 1166, though it is found intermittently for another hundred years. Legal conservatism pre-

---

[1] *Select Cases of Procedure without Writ under Henry III*, ed. Richardson and Sales (*Selden Society*, vol. lx), p. 67.

[2] 'Dominus N. de Allou' was alderman of Ridingate in 1250 (BM. MS. Cotton, Claudius D X, fol. 76r.). William Cokin was alderman of Worthgate (CAC, Reg. E, fol. 94r.).

[3] If there had been an Old English abstract in -iþu, related to borg, byrgea, it would have been *byrhþ(u), which would have given the middle Kentish berth(e). Since the functions of the rural 'borg' and the urban *bertha* are in some measure parallel, it seems that *bertha* has this origin, in an abstract connected with borg. I am very grateful to Professor D. Whitelock for this note.

[4] '. . . in hundredo de berthe de Burgate' (BBSA, p. 598).

[5] CAC, C 1194.

[6] See below.

serves it in use in the borough court (in the form *birtha*) as late as c. 1400.[1]

The word *borgum* and variants is found applied through the middle ages to Canterbury wards, though this usage is very rare. One instance has been found in the thirteenth century. The hamlet of St Martin's, which is not a ward but an enclave of ambiguous status within the geographical area of Burgate ward, is called *borga* on one occasion.[2] It is difficult to follow Professor Tait's remark that after the Conquest the division in Canterbury corresponding to wards was the borgh, 'the usual local name for the tithing', and that before the thirteenth century these borghs were reorganized as aldermanries with hundred courts 'in pretty obvious imitation of the London wards and wardmoots.'[3] The conclusion cannot be avoided that the Canterbury wards are in fact an imitation of those of London, but it is not easy to follow the remainder of the passage. The references supplied lead to the form *bertha*, not borgh,[4] and the suggestion of any reorganization seems to be without basis. *Hundredum* and *aldermanria* are both found within the twelfth century.[5] Both terms were in common use in the thirteenth and fourteenth centuries but disappear in the fifteenth. Three of the terms, *borgum*, *bertha* and *hundredum*,[6] are found used to describe the geographical area of the ward. The ward court is commonly designated *hundredum* though *bertha* may also be used in this sense while the terms are found in apposition. *Hundredum* may mean the suitors at the ward court.[7] *Aldermanria* occurs in the sense of tithing,[8] while all the terms for a ward, in varying senses may be found in conjunction and apposition.

The naming of the wards in Canterbury is quite simple. There were six principal gates and the six wards are called after these gates: Westgate,

---

[1] Corporation Archives, Canterbury, 1380–1; J/B/181. 'J. Strete queritur de M. Bracy de placito transgressionis . . . in birtha de Redyngate.'

[2] In the enquiry of 1293 (*Quo warranto* proceedings, printed in Somner, *Antiquities of Canterbury*, 1640, pp. 502 ff., from exemplification, being Charter no. 13, among City Archives).

[3] MEB, p. 60, n., and cf. p. 292, n.

[4] BBSA, pp. 394, 397. The term 'borgh' in the sense of urban ward is not found under the reference HMC, ix, pt. 1, *passim*. 'Borgh' does not occur under another reference (to BBC, i, p. 130).

[5] BBSA, p. 602. Charter dated 2 February 1197. The transaction is said to be 'recordata . . . in hundredo de Burgat'. Richard I makes grant (1197) of the aldermanry of Westgate (*BBC*, i, p. 130).

[6] BM. MS. Cotton, Julius D, fol. 139v. (*borgum*); Rental B, *passim* (*bertha*); Eastbridge Hospital Charter A 10 (*hundredum*).

[7] XLIX: 'Hiis testibus . . . [9 names] . . . et totum hundredum' [sic].

[8] In the case of 1241, cited above.

Northgate, Burgate, Newingate, Ridingate and Worthgate. For the modern student this has immense advantages over the London system in earlier times, whereby wards are named after their aldermen, and cannot therefore always be identified.

WARD OFFICERS

The chief officer of the Canterbury ward is regularly the alderman. Aldermen are first mentioned in Rentals A and B, both of the days of prior Wibert (d. 1167). Alan the alderman is found in A,[1] and in B which also supplies the names Gregory and Wulnoth.[2] If an emendation by William Somner to B is correct then we have another name, Roger, at this early date.[3] There is nothing positive to connect these aldermen with wards, but we may assume that they are so connected. Soon after 1170, and within ten years of the date of Rentals A and B, a witness to a charter[4] is named as John 'ælderman de Burgate'. He is without doubt the alderman John named in another charter relating to ground in this ward, at much the same date.[5] The phrases 'aldermanry of Westgate', or 'of Burgate',[6] used in the later twelfth century, adequately identify ward and alderman.

At the end of the same century a vice-alderman makes an appearance, but only in the ward of Westgate, which ward exhibits abnormal features. Hugo, 'qui est in loco aldermanni', attests a grant of property in this ward towards 1200.[7] Humphrey 'vicealdermannus' is named in Rental F (c. 1206).[8] He is not identified with Westgate ward in this context, but is undoubtedly the Humphrey, alderman of this ward attesting a charter of 1207.[9] It is possible that he may have achieved promotion, yet it is possible that he is acting as deputy for an absentee alderman proper, and is loosely known in Canterbury as alderman. It is significant that the tallage roll of 1198, earlier in date than Rental F, names Humphrey the alderman.[10] The actual alderman at this date was, we know, an official of the royal household, Baldwin de Werreval, 'pincerna', whose daughter married another official, the royal robemaker, who succeeded to the aldermanry.[11] Neither the butler nor the robemaker was likely to stay in Canterbury and the vice-alderman was evidently appointed to carry out on the spot the duties of the post.

---

[1] A 34.   [2] B 86, 99, 213.   [3] B 201.   [4] XLV.   [5] XXI.
[6] As in the grant by Richard I, cited below (Westgate); in Charter XLV (Burgate).
[7] LI.   [8] F 147, 475.   [9] CAC, Ch. Ant. C 1100.
[10] PR, 1 Richard I, p. 207.   [11] See below.

Among witnesses to charters relating to ground in Canterbury there frequently appear officials styled 'bedelli, budelli', especially in cases where conveyances are said to have been published in a ward court. The name of a given 'bedellus' will appear and reappear in conjunction with the same ward. Martin the bedel witnesses sales in Newingate ward,[1] while Arnold the bedel occurs as witness to transactions in Westgate ward.[2] He makes a grant on his own account calling himself 'bedellus de Westgate'.[3] Robert the bedel attests two transactions in Northgate ward,[4] where also William the bedel is found.[5] Solomon the bedel can be identified with Ridingate ward, where he appears in two charters.[6] Engeland 'bedellus de Burgate' appears in a charter of the time of Abbot Roger (evidently Roger I, 1176–1212).[7] A Richard the bedel in Burgate ward must be serving that office before the end of 1225.[8]

It is quite clear that these bedels were officials of the wards, and were imitated, like the wards themselves and the aldermen, from London, where the bedel was more or less the constable of later centuries. London bedels were heavily burdened with duties, for it is obvious from the passage devoted to them in the *Liber Albus* that their office was no sinecure.[9]

THE ENDOWMENT OF THE ALDERMANRY

An endowment is found associated with one of the six ancient wards of Canterbury, namely Westgate. Ground enjoyed by aldermen of all wards in a personal capacity is naturally encountered, since they tend to be men of wealth, but Westgate is the only case where a corpus of property bound up with the office of alderman can be discovered. Westgate is an abnormal aldermanry, and must be considered apart from the rest. 'I conceive it to have beene,' says William Somner, 'if not absolutely the chiefe, yet one of more respect and consequence than the rest.'[10]

[1] Greg., nos. 17, 53.
[2] Archives of Eastbridge Hospital, Canterbury, Charters A 22, 25.
[3] Ibid. no. A 43. [4] Greg., nos. 42, 43.
[5] Archives of Eastbridge Hospital, Charter J 33.
[6] Cartulary of Poor Priests Hospital Canterbury, BM. Additional MS. 29,437, fol. 183r.; Cotton Claudius D X, fol. 78.
[7] BM. M.S. Cotton Claudius D X, fol. 91v. 'John medicus filius Petri medici' is mentioned. P. 'medicus' is evidently the man of the name occurring in Rental B, while J. 'medicus' seems to be the individual named in BBSA, pp. 601–2, under 1197. The charter is clearly too early for Abbot Roger II to be concerned.
[8] BM. MS. Cotton Claudius D X, fol. 94v Martin the tanner is mentioned, who seems to be the man who died by 1225 (Reliefs, *sub anno*).
[9] *Liber Albus*, ed. Riley, pp. 272–3. [10] *Antiquities of Canterbury*, 1640, p. 98.

The rentals disclose that the alderman of Westgate receives miscell-aneous sums of money from holdings in Canterbury, apparently *ex officio*. Endowment for public office is found in medieval towns, but it is odd that an endowment is found at Canterbury only for one of six parallel institutions. If an endowment were required to sustain one alderman, then such endowment might well be expected for the rest. The question natur-ally arises: what was the origin of the estate identified with the aldermanry of Westgate?

Rental Z, drawn up about 1230, and documents of later dates show that the alderman of Westgate controls much property in Canterbury. This property exhibits an appearance of having been brought together over a period of time, since it is miscellaneous in character and scattered at many points, not always within the aldermanry of Westgate.[1] There is no evidence for what might have been expected, something in the nature of a regular charge levied upon each holding within the ward. We may expect to find trace of holdings shown to belong to, or to render rent to, the aldermanry in documents earlier than Rental Z. We may indeed find the holdings in earlier documents, like Rental D. These holdings are not now described as holdings of the alderman but are all said to be land either of Odbold, or of Edward son of Odbold. Odbold was living in the middle years of the twelfth century while his son Edward was flourishing in the years following the murder of Becket.[2] Edward dwelt on some ground just north of St Peter's church,[3] and in Westgate ward, and founded (before 1180) the hospital of St Thomas upon Eastbridge in the centre of Can-terbury.

Between 1196 and 1199 a charter was issued by Richard I to Baldwin de Werreval the royal butler, bestowing upon him whatsoever belonged to the king of the *aldermanneria* of Westgate in Canterbury within and without the walls. The king also confirmed to Baldwin whatever had been granted to him by archbishop Hubert within and without the walls, Baldwin being bound to render service (unspecified) due to king and archbishop, in such manner as it was held at any time in his life by Edward son of 'Albald'.[4] In 1200 king John granted a further charter in much the

---

[1] Most of the tenements, said to be in the hands of the alderman of Westgate, lie in Holy Cross parish (around the Westgate), or in St Peter's parish (close thereto). There is a group of nine holdings at the other end of the city, outside Newingate, in St George's parish (Rental Z, CAC, Rental 33, under parishes in question). See Appendix A, § 23; Eastbridge Hospital MSS., Charter A 43; CAC, Ch. Ant. C 1105.

[2] D 138, 311, 312, 316, 320, 375, 386; F 55, 526.

[3] Rental Z, under St Peter's parish.

[4] *Chartæ Antiquæ*, ed. L. Landon, PRS, NS, 17, no. 166; BBC, i, p. 130.

same terms, again confirming to Baldwin whatever had been granted by Hubert of the aldermanry, of the fee of the archbishop, as held by Edward son of 'Albod' on the day of his death, together with whatever was held in fee of the crown.[1] It is not clear whether the last-mentioned element were or were not part of the aldermanry but is probably intended to convey the royal interest in the aldermanry. In Edward son of Albald or Albod we may unquestionably recognize Edward son of Odbold, and we may safely deduce that Edward was alderman of Westgate ward (where we know he dwelt), and that he had died by c. 1196. No heir of Edward has been traced in local documents and perhaps his property had escheated to the crown, and somehow or other his office had likewise escheated, to become identified with his property down to the end of the Middle Ages. It is not easy to see how the archbishop acquired any interest in the property or the office, but we may perhaps suppose that Edward had some holdings outside the western limits of his aldermanry, which marched for a long distance with the boundary of the archiepiscopal hundred of Westgate, just across the narrow river. Indeed, in the fifteenth century, when a rental was drawn up of the aldermanry,[2] we may see therein houses in North Lane (within the archiepiscopal hundred), while 5s. 2d. is due to the archbishop, and 16d. or a ploughshare is due to Westgate, either the manorial or hundred court. Possibly these houses in North Lane and the rent due to Westgate date from the twelfth century, accounting for the connection of archbishop Hubert with the original grant.

The transfer of the aldermanry to Baldwin de Werreval by Richard I was not a gift but a sale. Notice of the transaction appears in the Pipe Roll for 1197–8, when the price is given as twenty marks.[3] We have seen that John granted the aldermanry to William the robemaker, whose connection with Baldwin de Werreval was, so we find, close. They were father- and son-in-law. John bestowed Alice daughter of Baldwin, in conjunction with a 'serjeantry', evidently the aldermanry, upon William the robemaker.[4] The pair seem to have had a son called William 'filius Willelmi scissoris de Godestede'.[5]

[1] *Rotuli Chartarum*, ed. T. D. Hardy, 1837, I, pt. i, 1199–1216, p. 68; *BBC*, i, p. 131; Philipot *Villare Cantianum*, 1659, p. 93; *Cartæ Antiquæ*, PRS, no. 165.

[2] Available in an eighteenth-century transcript in a register of miscellaneous documents relating to Canterbury among the City Archives (p. 53).

[3] PR, 10 Richard I, p. 210; 1 John, p. 66; 2 John, p. 213; 3 John, p. 287.

[4] *Book of Fees*, pt. i, p. 271. 'Filia Baldewini de Verevall' est de donatione domini regis et Willelmus Taillur habet eam de dono domini Johannis Regis. et seriantia illa infra Cantiam valet per annum xv m.' It may be inferred that the serjeantry was the aldermanry.

[5] CAC, Ch. Ant., C 629.

In the reign of Henry VII the aldermanry enjoyed a rental of £7 16s. 11d. (less 5s. 2d. due to the archbishop).[1] It is then stated that the whole aldermanry 'with leets and rents as well within the city of Canterbury as without, with the casualties' is worth £13 6s. 8d.

This is patently a round sum (twenty marks) and is obviously an estimate. The sergeantry (clearly the aldermanry) associated with Alice, daughter of Baldwin de Werreval, was valued at fifteen marks, according to the Book of Fees.[2] By some means the aldermanry came into the hands of the abbot and monks of St Augustine's, and was granted and leased by them to Hamo Doge, the Canterbury lawyer, for £10 *per annum*.[3] William Thorne, the abbey chronicler says that the grant was made in 1278, but we find Hamo Doge, styled 'alderman of Westgate' in the enactment (discussed above) relating to the bakers in 1261.[4] When *quo warranto* proceedings were brought in 1293, one Master William de Godestede answered for the aldermanry, and the office is clearly back in the line of William the robemaker.[5]

THE INQUISITION OF 1293

Justice J. de Berwick and his colleagues sat at Canterbury in 21 Edward I, 'a die Pasche in quindecim dies', and amongst other business asked a local jury to report on 'serjeantries'. The answers were wholly occupied with a discussion of the city aldermen, their wards, and their functions.[6]

The aldermanries of Canterbury, then, were regarded as serjeantries. The jurors affirmed that the Westgate aldermanry was held in chief by William of Lynstede, rector of Sturry (two miles from Canterbury) by serjeantry of one 'sore' hawk, worth *per annum* ten marks. Likewise they affirmed that John son of John de Handlo (Hadlow?) held the aldermanry of Ridingate of the king in chief, doing no service to him, and that it was worth 2s. *per annum*. Edmund de Tyerne held the aldermanry of Worthgate in chief from the king, doing no service, and it was likewise worth 2s. *per annum*. Thomas Chicche held the aldermanry of Burgate worth 40d. *per annum*. John de Holt held the aldermanry of Newingate worth 2s. rendering no service to the king. The sheriff of Kent was ordered to summon them, and they all appeared except Master William of Lynstede,

[1] See p. 99, n. 2.　　　　　　　　　　　　[2] *Book of Fees, ut supra.*
[3] *Thorne*, col. 1927, p. 267.
[4] Canterbury City Archives, Charter 6. See above.
[5] Ibid., Charter 13, an exemplification of 19 Richard II; printed Somner, *Antiquities of Canterbury*, 1640, app., no. xxxvi.
[6] See last note.

and made statement that the aldermanries were pertaining to, and were annexed to, the farm of the city of Canterbury, viz. £60 *per annum*. With this the jurors agreed and the aldermen were dismissed *sine die*. Lynstede then appeared and affirmed that he held the aldermanry of Westgate from Master William de Godstede, paying him 100s. *per annum* and that without him he could not answer. William was summoned, and appeared by attorney, who said on behalf of his client that he held the said serjeantry from the community (de communitate) of the city of Canterbury, paying 40d. towards the farm of the city, and this from time out of mind. The jury agreed once more, and he too was dismissed *sine die*.

The difficulties disclosed are considerable. In the case of Westgate, the jurors declare that the service rendered by Lynstede is the 'sore' hawk, worth ten marks, though this is not mentioned at the later stages, and the bench does not press the point. The purchase price of the aldermanry when it was acquired by Baldwin de Werreval nearly a hundred years before was but ten marks (reduced from twenty), but in 1293 we find William de Godstede farming it out for £5. Moreover, in 1278, as shown above, Hamo Doge was farming the aldermanry from St Augustine's abbey for £10 *per annum*. Probably the capital value was very much greater when Baldwin de Werreval acquired it than is indicated by the sum he paid for it to the crown.[1] It is difficult to make much of the affirmation that the aldermanry of Westgate was held from the community of the city, as it seems clear that it was held from the crown. There is certainly no suggestion in the schedule[2] associated, so it is supposed, with the grant of the city in fee-farm in 1234, that the aldermanry of Westgate was held from the community. It was granted by Richard I to Baldwin, granted again by John, and with little question granted to William the robemaker by the same king with Baldwin's daughter. It may have been partly held from the archbishop. If the render of 40d. is in fact contributory to the city farm, we might expect to find it in the schedule assigned to 1234, but it does not appear therein. The alderman of Westgate does in fact pay 4s. 6d.,[3] but this is merely for a single tenement, and is not some form of rent or farm for the aldermanry as a whole.

The presentments made in connection with the other aldermanries are far from lucid. Three of them are said to be held in chief from the crown. The small sums named as values of the aldermanries may be profits of ward courts, which in later centuries arise chiefly from alienations of

---

[1] The *Book of Fees* (see p. 99, n. 4) says that the serjeantry was worth 15 marks *p.a.*
[2] Appendix A.   [3] Appendix A.

holdings within the ward.[1] It is not easy to comprehend the way in which aldermanries are said to be annexed to the farm of the city. By the charter of 1234 the citizens are stated to be responsible for payment of the farm (at £60 *per annum*)[2] and when relevant documents become available (in the fourteenth century) we find it is the two bailiffs who make payment at the exchequer.[3] However, the answers given seem to have satisfied the court in 1293.

THE INHERITABILITY OF THE OFFICE OF ALDERMAN

It is not easy to substantiate the remarks of William Somner about the inheritability of the office of alderman in Canterbury, apart from the abnormal case of Westgate. Somner claims that aldermanries descended in given families and offers examples, associating the wards of Burgate, Northgate, Newingate, and Worthgate with the families of Chiche, Polre, Digges, Cokyn, (later Tierne), respectively.[4] It is true that occasionally a man's son, or even grandson, may be found in occupation of the same aldermanry but there seems to be nothing to prove that it was an actual possession of the family in question. The ward of Ridingate will provide a case where the office may be traced in the same family for three generations. Late in the twelfth century the alderman was one Roger. He was followed by John, son of Roger, in office c. 1200, while he in turn is followed by William son of John, named as William le alderman in a charter of 1226–7 or later.[5] It is possible that Richard de Lynstede, alderman of Ridingate at a later date, may have had some family connections with Roger since he confirms gifts made by 'W. aldermannus, filius I. alderman de Radyngate' to Eastbridge Hospital, though he may have made the confirmation *ex officio* since the ground in question lay within his ward.[6] By 1241 the aldermanry has passed out of the family, since Nicholas of Hadlow is alderman, or is at least performing aldermanic duties.[7] It must be observed that another member of the Hadlow family is alderman in 1293.[8]

It is hardly a matter for surprise when the same office appears and reappears in a given medieval burgess family. The number of offices was large while the number of men available to fill them was small, and it could not be difficult for anyone to get himself nominated to his father's

---

[1] As is shown in proceedings in ward courts, available from the seventeenth century.
[2] See p. 87 above.   [3] Files of *quietus* for the farm, City Archives
[4] *Antiquities of Canterbury*, 1640, p. 97.   [5] D 152, F 190, 191, 512; BBSA, p. 163.
[6] BBSA, pp. 163, 164.   [7] As may be deduced. See p. 94 above.
[8] City Archives, Charter 13 (the *quo warranto* proceedings of 1293).

position, all the more so, since it might involve arduous and unwanted duties.

THE GEOGRAPHY OF THE WARD

No maps of the pre-1835 wards of Canterbury have been traced apart from an admirably-executed survey of Westgate ward of about 1830, and another of the same date of Worthgate ward.[1] These maps were evidently prepared in connection with projected changes at the date of the Municipal Corporations Reform Bill. They show that in the case of Westgate and Worthgate there has been no change (as far as evidence is available) from the earlier Middle Ages. The two maps of c. 1830 provide parts of the boundaries of Northgate, Newingate, Burgate and Ridingate wards, where they flank those of Worthgate and Westgate.

The Canterbury wards exhibit none of the strange shapes assumed by the London wards upon the maps, and are admirably laid out in relation to the ground. The main scheme adopted by the original planners (probably about the date of Rental B), was to take as an axis for each ward the main road running out through a principal gate after which the ward was named. The boundary between each ward was designed to run up between each road, carrying on over the city wall, and so out into the open country as far as it formed part of the city area. However, the arrangement was complicated by the fact that the religious had large precincts exempt from the system of local secular government. Most of the quadrant within the north-eastern walls was taken up by the liberty of Christ Church, while outside the walls the great area within the *fossa* of St Augustine's occupied much of the extra-mural Burgate ward, while the abbey home-farm of Longport with the archiepiscopal hamlet of St Martin's, and the Christ Church manor of Calcot, occupied much of the rest. It was natural to take the island within the walls in the western quarter of the city as the ward of Westgate, but here there was no extra-mural suburb since the archbishop's manor and hundred of Westgate came right up to the walls and moreover, the built-up area on the island was not as great as that within other wards. A long strip of ground, therefore, embracing each side of the High Street, was cut out all the way up to the central cross-roads at Mercery Lane, and thrown into Westgate ward.[2]

Some further hints may be gathered as to the methods adopted by the

[1] City Archives.

[2] The fact that the survey of c. 1166 (Rental B) stops short of the High Street in Best Lane, strongly suggests that Westgate ward enjoyed its peculiar layout already at this date.

surveyors of c. 1166. Old Ruttington Lane, outside the walls about half-way between Northgate and Burgate, roughly at right angles to the fortifications, was taken as the boundary between the two wards of those names.[1] Rental D shows that the back-garden wall of houses on the west side of Mercery Lane lay on a line 105 feet back from the lane.[2] Now the map of c. 1830 in the City Archives discloses that the ancient ward-boundary lay along this same line, and it is clear that the surveyors of the twelfth century, when (evidently) the wards were delimited, selected this wall as a convenient frontier. Their decision would have had a length of life which might have surprised them, for the revision of ward-boundaries in 1835 perpetuated the arrangement, and even today the boundary, now separating Dane John and Northgate Wards, follows the ancient line, though it now runs through the display cases of a large store.

SOKES

There is little at Canterbury which resembles the secular private soke so evident at London, breaking up the symmetry of the ward-system. The archbishop has his hamlet at St Martin's, on one occasion at least referred to as 'soca sancti Martini'.[3] Its status was in dispute more than once during the Middle Ages. The only enclave which has any resemblance to the London soke is the district of Staplegate (Stablegate), just within North-gate, which appears to be the old archiepiscopal stables,[4] built-over and inhabited as time went on. It lay outside the jurisdiction of the borough until 1835, being regarded as a detached member of the manor and hundred of Westgate.

[1] B 31, 57.   [2] D 115.   [3] F 352.   [4] F 462.

CHAPTER V

Trades and Occupations

THE general thesis of Carl Stephenson's *Borough and Town* that the borough proper, where inhabitants live by trade rather than by agriculture, can only be traced from the Norman Conquest, is not supported by the evidence from Canterbury. Dr Stephenson's theories have been challenged by Professor Tait, Sir Frank Stenton and other scholars.[1] Stephenson's interpretation has been found unsatisfactory when the evidence for individual towns has been subjected to criticism, as in the case of Lincoln by Sir Francis Hill,[2] and at Cambridge by Professor Cam.[3]

Canterbury has been a place of trade from a remote date. There was a market at Queningate, between the cathedral and St Augustine's abbey, in 762.[4] The city is called 'port' in the ninth century,[5] while in the same age there is a 'merkator', called in English 'mangere'.[6] There are moreover gilds of burgesses, which, if not trade-organizations, at least indicate a certain amount of population to provide membership.[7] In the earlier tenth century there is a cattle market under the eastern walls.[8]

In the age of the Conquest there are several hundred dwellings and by 1100 a 'cepmannegild' owning houses.[9] This institution is probably identical with the gild named in Domesday Book, which had extensive possessions, of which it was robbed by Odo of Bayeux and his men.[10] The old English name of the gild of c. 1100 does not point to an institution created by Norman settlers.[11]

One economic feature found in boroughs such as Cambridge is wanting in Canterbury, namely the common fields. The oldest Canterbury charters show that tenements within the walls had appendant land outside, but there is nothing to suggest that these are allocations in the common field, and indeed they look like private estates.[12] No definite mention of

---

[1] *EHR* (1933) pp. 642–8; MEB, especially chapters III, IV, *History*, xviii, pp. 256–7.
[2] *Medieval Lincoln*, pp. 256 ff.
[3] *Liberties and Communities in Medieval England*, chapter I.
[4] Birch, *CS*, 192.   [5] Ibid., 426.   [6] See p. 148.
[7] See pp. 124–5.   [8] Birch, *CS*, 497.   [9] See p. 126.
[10] I.   [11] Cf. MEB, p. 120.   [12] Birch, *CS*, 373.

common fields and meadows can be read into 'burwara meda' lying north of Canterbury in 895.[1] There is certainly nothing in the Domesday evidence for Canterbury suggestive of the existence of common fields.

There is little to support a contention that the borough of Canterbury in the twelfth century was still, or at a recent date had been, inhabited by a population with a primarily agricultural preoccupation. The wide boundary of Canterbury, far beyond the walls, embraced several manors, but the urban nucleus within and just without the walls numbers no one (as far as the rentals show) depending mainly on agriculture for a living, though quite probably citizens grow food as a sideline. Some of the big plots in the marshy area along Criene Mill Lane look very much like agricultural ground,[2] and we may observe that they are, as has been observed above, in the hands of citizens dwelling in the central business area, like Solomon the mercer,[3] or Goldwin the mercer.[4] That some of the inhabitants took part in part-time and seasonal agricultural work is certain. Many of them owed a service called 'evework', due at Lammas, and may have performed this service in person.[5] In the sixteenth century the poorer womenfolk of Canterbury still went gleaning in Barton Fields and on Milton manor fields.[6]

Some indication of the relative economic position of Canterbury can be drawn from figures for aids and tallages in the twelfth century. In the year for which returns are fullest (23 Henry II) we find that Canterbury pays 100 marks, in common with Bedford, Exeter, Oxford, Norwich and Gloucester. This group is exceeded by London (1,000 marks), Northampton (300), York (200), Dunwich, Winchester and Lincoln (150 marks each). In the table prepared by Dr Stephenson presenting averages for aids, Canterbury with an average of 61 marks stands eleventh out of thirty-five boroughs listed, being placed below London, York, Norwich, Lincoln, Northampton, Dunwich, Exeter, Winchester, Gloucester and Oxford (in that order) with averages ranging from 997 marks to 76 marks.[7]

[1] Birch, CS, 497; MEB, p. 9, n. Cf. Birch, CS, 449.
[2] D 343, 357.
[3] D 109, 110, 348.
[4] D 349.
[5] For evework, see pp. 137–42.
[6] As is shown in cases in the archidiaconal court records. There is still much seasonal agricultural work done in the twentieth century.
[7] Borough and Town, apps. iv, v. Some indication of the status of Canterbury at an early date is given by its inclusion in the small group of cities which sent citizens to do service at the coronation. At Richard I's coronation the citizens of London occupied the butlery, those of Winchester the kitchen, and those of Canterbury the pantry. The citizens of Canterbury are not named at later coronations. (Taylor, Glory of Regality, 1820, p. 142, citing notes in BM. MS. Cotton, Vespasian C XIV).

SHOPS

There is valuable evidence for retail trade in Canterbury in the mention of numerous shops. The greater part of the northern side of Burgate Street is occupied in the early thirteenth century by an intermittent row of shops, at least thirty-seven in number.[1] Charter XXXIX shows that two shops here were taken over by a 'piscator' late in the twelfth century. The Burgate shops, together with others, probably all along the northern (cathedral) side of the street, to a total of no less than eighty, formed the subject of a lawsuit between the citizens and the cathedral in 1307.[2] In Mercery Lane the holding of Goldwin the mercer c. 1200 is cut up into eight shops soon after that date.[3] It seems unlikely that at a most generous estimate these shops can be more than 7 feet wide. The shops given to Christ Church by Robert son of Richard in Burgate Street are of much the same width.[4] Rental B, soon after the middle of the twelfth century, shows that there is a row of shops, at least three in number, apparently lying in the middle row in the main street, along the 'Parade'.[5] The great stone house between the Buttermarket and Butchery Lane is divided into eleven shops (at least) by 1234, and another stone house at the south-eastern corner of Butchery Lane is divided into shops by the same date. These shops must have been in the form of openings in the wall. One stone house on the western side of Mercery Lane is cut up into six shops and a wooden building there embodies three.[6] There are three suburban shops in 'Baggeberi', beyond the northern walls[7] and some wooden shops in Criene Mill Lane, leading away into the riverside marshes—not a place where one would expect much business.[8] We only know of these shops because they owed a rent to Christ Church. The long list of arrears of rent, drawn up in 1234, discloses the existence of well over one hundred shops, and these are merely those where the tenant is behind with his rent, and the list is confined again to shops belonging to the monks. There are long stretches of frontage unaccounted for in the surveys in the central business area, where there must have been many more shops. For example, it seems from a note in Rental Z that there are (c. 1230) shops at the north-east corner of St Margaret's Street, and it may be seen from the lists of arrears of 1234 that there are shops, at least nine in number, called the

---

[1] The evidence below, relating to shops, is taken, unless otherwise stated, from CAC, Arrears, *de domibus et scoppis*, 1234.

[2] Madox, *Firma Burgi*, pp. 254–5.　　　　　　　　　　　　　　[3] D 110, n.

[4] LIX.　　　　　　[5] B 219–21.　　　　　　[6] CAC, Arrears, *de domibus et scoppis*, 1234.

[7] Z, fol. 192v.　　　　　　　　　　　　　　　　[8] Ibid., fol. 199v.

'shops of Susanna de Planaz', running up to the corner of Rose Lane, some distance to the east.[1] It would hardly be rash to assert that there must have been something like two hundred shops in Canterbury about 1234, this alone pointing to a vigorous retail trade. Unhappily the lists of arrears rarely give the trade of the holder of a shop, though we may gather from the arrears of 1234 that there were two mercers (Adam and Alexander) on the north side of the Buttermarket opposite Mercery Lane, two saddlers (James and Nicholas) in the High Street, east of Butchery Lane, with a lorimer called John, opposite, at the corner of Rose Lane. Thomas the glasswright occupies one of Susanna de Planaz' shops close at hand.[2]

MARKETS

Several markets can be identified around the city. There is the 'forum' at Queningate in 762,[3] while there is mention in 923 of a cattle market (ryther ceap) evidently close to the eastern walls, and no doubt identical with the Ritherchieape—chiape (Dover Street), in the rentals of the twelfth and thirteenth century.[4] The Buttermarket is in existence in the twelfth century, when it is called 'forum'.[5] It is not associated with any particular commodity, though the documents disclose that there is a flesh-shambles in the south-western corner.[6] The fish-market lies west from St Andrew's church in the thirteenth century, though it does not find a mention in the rentals. The name of Wincheap, possibly an ancient wine-market, can be taken back to the beginning of the thirteenth century.[7] Rental F refers to a timber-market (timbercheppe),[8] otherwise quite unknown, half-way along Wincheap. Oaten Hill (the tumulus at the top of Dover Street) seems to perpetuate the name of an early oat market,[9] while at another tumulus, Salt Hill, just without Newingate, there may have been a salt market, unless the solitary salt-merchant Martin 'sæltere', supplied it with a title.[10]

Unfortunately the rentals and charters conceal more than they reveal

[1] Z, under St Andrew's parish.   [2] CAC, Arrears, *de domibus et scoppis*, 1234.
[3] Birch, *CS*, 192.   [4] See account of street names, Chapter IX.
[5] D 110. The name Buttermarket is of the period c. 1700.
[6] B 83, D 109.
[7] The earliest instance given by Wallenberg is of 1226 (*Kentish Place Names*, p. 5). He suggests an origin 'wain-market' (wægn+cēap).
[8] F 638.   [9] Somner, *Antiquities of Canterbury*, 1703, p. 80.
[10] For Salt Hill, see below, pp. 199–200. For M. the salter, see BBSA, pp. 166, 177, 180. Somner found evidence for a cloth-market in St George's Street (*Antiquities of Canterbury*, 1703, p. 80). In the later thirteenth century the area just outside Burgate was called 'Whete-market'. (Rental transcribed into CAC, Reg. A, fol. 364r).

in connection with trades practised by citizens, since they usually distinguish a man by giving his father's name, rather than his trade. However, in the case of some professions they break silence, as when they mention priests and clerks. Members of knightly families can be detected by the use of territorial quasi-surnames. The list of occupations which can be recovered is apparently fairly comprehensive. The evidence available does not suggest that there was any one outstanding characteristic trade or industry associated with Canterbury, unless it were that of the moneyers.

PRIESTS AND CLERKS

There were as many as eighty priests, chaplains and clerks in Canterbury in the later twelfth and earlier thirteenth centuries.[1] The names we have are merely revealed by the chance evidence of the rentals and charters, and there may have been very many more. This preponderance is only to be expected in the ecclesiastical capital of England. Some of the priests can be connected with parish churches, such as Thomas priest of St Martin's, who can hardly be other than Becket's flagellant.[2] He had a successor at St Martin's named Augustine.[3] Wibert was priest of St Margaret's, in or before 1161,[4] while Henry was priest of St George's at about the same time.[5] Osbern was priest of St Michael, Thanington,[6] William, of St Michael, Burgate,[7] and Alfred, of St Edmund, Ridingate.[8] About 1200 Godard the priest served this last-named church together with St Mary Bredin.[9]

In the twelfth century clerical marriage was still common, and it cannot be assumed that the children of priests were born before their father's ordination. We learn that Osbert the priest had a son Solomon the priest.[10] Henry the priest had a son John,[11] and Jakin the priest (c. 1180) had a daughter Matilda.[12] One priest, Walter, was son of Alwold the Smith.[13] Some names of higher clergy can be recovered. Rental D[14] indicates that the tenant of ground outside Ridingate is Master Ralph, vice-archdeacon,

[1] See index to documents, PRESBYTER, CAPELLANUS, CLERICUS. Others may be added such as: Turbin the priest (X 2, fol. 8v.); Gerard the priest (X 2, fol. 11v.). It would be of interest to know how Robert 'predicator' named in X 2 (fol. 13v) c. 1180, obtained his distinctive title. He has ground in Holtege, one of the fields flanking Wincheap. He might be R. 'spellere' who holds in Wincheap c. 1205 (F 243, etc.).

[2] B 209. See p. 181. [3] D 359. [4] VII. [5] XI.
[6] XLII. [7] A 22. [8] XLV.
[9] Cathedral Library, Lit. MS. C 20, fol. 20v. [10] B 14, D 60.
[11] Ibid. [12] X 2, fol. 4. [13] B 14.
[14] D 150; F 320.

whose name occurs some years earlier.[1] Since the twelfth-century archdeacon of Canterbury was usually an absentee, a vice-archdeacon was necessary to carry out his duties on the spot.[2] There are some 'decani' named in the documents, such as Ralph (c. 1145),[3] Roger (c. 1200),[4] Lifwin (c. 1206),[5] and William (c. 1227).[6] These are evidently deans of the Christianity, since there seems to be no local collegiate institution to which they can be assigned.

DOCTORS

We have the names of some physicians. Peter 'medicus' (c. 1166) has ground in Bridge Street.[7] Master Feramin, an active figure in local ecclesiastical politics, sees to the sick monks (fratrum infirmorum res administrat).[8] Master W. 'physicus' receives a salary of two marks from the cathedral treasurers at the beginning of the thirteenth century, and may well be a local doctor giving attendance to the brethren.[9] As might be expected, a son carries on his father's profession and we find Master John 'medicus' son to Peter 'medicus'.[10]

VICTUALLING TRADES

It is difficult to determine whether tradesmen under this heading are independent workers on their own account out in the streets of Canterbury, or are on the staff of one or other of the great religious houses. For example it is certain that many of the fifteen cooks named in the documents work for the monks.[11] The same is true of the bakers. Godefrid the baker named in Rental B with ground in Palace Street was ringleader among the revolted monastic servants in 1188,[12] while the names of bakers and cooks appended as witnesses to charters where the monks are parties, following the expression 'ex parte nostra', point to a post in the household.[13] The

---

[1] In a charter of 1184 (where he is named as a witness) relating to St Edmund's church (BM. MS. Cotton, Claudius D X, fol. 71v.).

[2] Cheney, *English Bishops' Chanceries*, App. i. Ralph may be added to the list. Robert 'vicarius' of Geoffrey Ridel archdeacon of Canterbury, named in Becket's excommunication-list in 1169, is evidently a vice-archdeacon (*Materials*, vi, pp. 601–2; *Eng. Hist. Docs.* ii, no. 143).

[3] vii.   [4] D 133.   [5] F 56, 325, 358, 562.
[6] xxxvii.   [7] B 93.   [8] *Materials*, i, p. 143.
[9] As in 1216–17, and in other years (CAC, *TA, sub annis*).
[10] BBSA, p. 602.   [11] See Index to documents, COCUS.
[12] See pp. 162, 183.   [13] E.g. in Charters XIX, XXV.

existence, however, of a body of ordinary non-monastic bakers engaged in selling bread to the public is demonstrated by a byelaw of 1262 removing a rate imposed on windows or 'corbels' where bread is displayed for sale.[1] Christ Church has its own brewhouse staff but there are alewives out in the town who supplement the family income by brewing for the monks, like the wife of Hugh the goldsmith.[2] It is difficult to draw a line between domestic staff and tradesmen catering on a larger or smaller scale for the religious houses.

Simon 'fenarius' might be a fodder-merchant on his own account or again might work in the monastic stableyard.[3] Godwin the cornmonger is clearly an independent merchant.[4] A group of 'piscatores' belongs more probably to the staff of Christ Church.[5] An absentee from the documents, curiously enough, is the vintner. If the average citizen were satisfied with ale, his monastic landlord was not. It is improbable that the monks ever got much wine from their vineyard on the slopes outside the northern city walls, and it seems to have been out of action by about 1200.[6] The names of a few vintners may be recovered from the Kentish sections of the Pipe Rolls, such as Paul and Terric the vintners.[7] The former is probably father to the family granting ground in St George's parish to St Augustine's abbey early in the thirteenth century,[8] and the latter may be the Theoricus the vintner who served c. 1200 as 'prepositus' of the borough.[9] The absence of much mention of this trade is perhaps due to limitation on the number of wine-vaults permitted in Canterbury. The Act of 7 Edward VI allowed only four[10] and there is strong suggestion that there were no more three hundred years earlier, when (at the great Translation of Becket's remains) archbishop Stephen Langton ordered (according to the French chronicle of Canterbury) free wine to be distributed at his own expense from 'les iiij. celers de vin.'[11] The names of butchers are found rarely in the rentals and charters, though the mention of two distinct flesh-shambles

---

[1] Canterbury City Archives, Charter no. 6. See p. 91.   [2] See p. 163.
[3] F 358.   [4] A 36.   [5] See p. 158.
[6] At least, the winepress was no longer on its site. Ground is said to lie 'beyond where the winepress of our vineyard used to be'. (F 20.) The vineyard seems never to appear in accounts of the thirteenth century.
[7] PR, 8 Richard I. There is another, Joseph, but there is nothing to connect him with Canterbury. There is a Gilbert vinetarius in Canterbury Lane in the thirteenth century (CAC, Reg. E, fol. 159).
[8] BBSA, pp. 391–2.
[9] For Theoric prepositus, see p. 85.
[10] 7 Edward VI, cap. 5, where specific numbers of wine-sellers are allotted to each borough.
[11] BM. MS. Harley 636, fol. 202v. as printed in Stanley, *Memorials of Canterbury Cathedral*, ed. of 1880, p. 307.

(scorcheria, macellaria), one in the Buttermarket[1] and another at the upper end of Burgate Street,[2] proves the existence of slaughtermen.

GOLDSMITHS

A dozen members of this most distinguished among the crafts can be found in the documents. The earliest (1149) is Arnold, occurring as witness to a charter.[3] It is not impossible that he is the individual who became a monk in Christ Church and, still called Arnold the goldsmith, came back early to the scene after the murder of Becket.[4] This man seems to have been a member of a family of goldsmiths.[5] The great man among the Canterbury goldsmiths at the close of the twelfth century is Terric, Theoric, 'aurifaber'. He was not only a craftsman but was a financier as well. He farmed the *cambium regis* of Canterbury, and was employed by king John, as in the ninth year of the reign, when he handled forty marks spent on buying horses for the royal use.[6] His dealings with the crown stretched to the other end of the kingdom.[7] The monks contracted large debts with him, paid off to his widow.[8] He maintained staff, such as Robert the goldsmith, 'serviens Terrici,' and Humphrey the goldsmith, 'homo Tieri', with Alexander, named in 1219 or 1220 as 'quondam serviens Terrici aurifabri'.[9] Another local goldsmith was evidently working for the crown as Arnold aurifaber (possibly Arnold Chich of Best Lane) received two marks in 7 John 'pro operatione cuppe R. auree'.[10] Beside chance commissions for the king or for great men, the goldsmiths enjoyed a permanent market for their wares in the local monasteries, with a good scope for profit when a chalice might be worth £16 6s. 8d.[11] Of course the goldsmiths worked as well in silver as in gold, and must have provided tableware for better-off citizens. Individual monks at Christ Church used silver cups, many of which bore a special name. Terric the goldsmith's son, Master William, became a monk, and long

---

[1] B 209, D 112.

[2] D 86, 88. Robert le macecrier has ground just within Burgate (B 68), while other ground very near at hand is described as 'inter carnifices' (A 23). Sunewin carnifex occurs in F 101.

[3] VIII.   [4] See p. 155.

[5] He seems to have a brother William the goldsmith.   [6] PR, 9 John, p. 30.

[7] See p. 118, below. Terric handled income of the see of Canterbury during the election crisis (in 1208) (*Rotuli Literarum Clausarum*, i, p. 108).

[8] See p. 163.

[9] D 167; XLIX; CAC, Ch. Ant. I 130 (dated 4 Henry III).

[10] PR, 7 John, p. 112. The king, judging from the modest price, clearly supplied the metal. For A. Chich, see D 295. He is called 'aurifaber' in X 2, fol. 13r.

[11] CAC, *TA. sub anno*. This is the price of a chalice acquired for the shrine of Becket.

years after his death there was still a silver-gilt cup in use in the cathedral refectory, called 'cuppa W. Terri.'[1] Perhaps it was one of his father's productions. In the earlier thirteenth century more goldsmiths may be found. One of them is described in a witness-list as 'Nigellus qui fecit sigillum.'[2] This seal is undoubtedly the great new seal of Christ Church, introduced c. 1220.

Goscelin[3] provides an instructive story in his Miracles of St Augustine, about a sideline to the metal industry, possibly within the eleventh century. Three Canterbury men, Wilfronius and Ælred, two brothers, with Sired son to the second, made a fair amount of money (dives sufficiencia), by going round England offering good prices to money-changers, goldsmiths, moneyers, minters, and other metal workers, for their castings, ashes, dross, litharge, slag, broken crucibles and so forth, commonly called 'skewings' (scopaturas). These they used to treat by burning, beating and scraping to extract the vestiges of precious metal. One day they came to Bath, where they bought some 'skewings', and carried them down to the river bank to treat. On the way they dug a big stone out of the highway for their work, were consequently arrested, and subjected to very bad treatment. The two older men bought their way out for 20s., while the young man was only loosened from prison bonds by intervention of St Augustine.

THE MONEYERS

The Canterbury mint occupies an exceptional place in the history of English coinage. By common consent the familiar penny was first struck at Canterbury in the age of Offa.[4] The number of moneyers assigned to Canterbury by Athelstan (seven: four to the king, two to the archbishop, and one to the abbot of St Augustine's) is exceeded only by the number assigned to London (eight). The Canterbury mint enjoyed a continuity across the period of the Norman conquest, as is shown by the occurrence of moneyers' names. In 1218 Canterbury and London were maintained almost alone as minting places when a policy of centralization was adopted by the government. The figures for surviving coinage speak volumes, and show that the manufacture of money must have been a characteristic outstanding industry of the city in the twelfth and earlier thirteenth centuries. A large proportion of the enormous Tealby hoard (5700 silver

---

[1] Dart, *Canterbury Cathedral*, app. vii.   [2] CAC, Reg. E, fol. 140.
[3] *Acta Sanctorum*, May, vi, p. 405.
[4] Mr Dolley of the British Museum is at work on the early Canterbury coinage.

pennies, found in 1807) was struck in Canterbury.[1] Of the Eccles find (mainly of the short-cross type, running down till c. 1228), comprising 5715 pence, 2643 came from London, and 2278 from Canterbury.[2] The still more bulky Colchester hoard (buried about 1230) contained (among 11,000 coins) some 5000 London specimens against 4122 from Canterbury.[3] No other minting boroughs even approach such figures. Oman says that these hoards would seem to show that an immense preponderance of the coinage was being made at London and Canterbury with York as a bad third.[4] The latest study of Henry II's coinage describes Canterbury as the most prolific mint of the reign.[5]

Moneyers responsible for producing this mass of coinage can be found in the documents. Gregory the moneyer is named in a charter of the time of abbot Hugh II of St Augustine's (1128–51).[6] Robert the moneyer[7] occurs about the middle of the twelfth century, and about the same date we find Freawin the moneyer with ground near Newingate.[8] Solomon and Luke, moneyers, have ground near St Helen's church at the end of the century.[9] The individuals actually described in the rentals and charters as 'monetarii' are not many, but we may learn from other sources that citizens not so specified are carrying on the industry. Lambin Frese, builder and occupant of the great stone house in Stour Street, is shown by the Pipe Roll to have been a moneyer.[10] The coins themselves offer identifications. Ulard, signing coins in the reigns of Richard and John, may be the Wilard mercator in Hawks' Lane.[11] Meinir, whose name is found on coins of the same age can hardly be other than Mainer 'the rich' with a dwelling a little way off in Stour Street, where the almshouse (Maynard's Hospital) which he founded is still to be seen.[12] His son Wiulph 'the rich' (not named as a moneyer in the documents) has a great stone house on the corner of the street called 'The Mint' (now White Horse Lane),[13] and can with little doubt be identified with Wiulph signing coins of the Henrician 'Tealby' type.[14]

The occurrence of names in the documents is of value in showing that the coinage by itself, despite the enormous amount found, does not give a

---

[1] Brooke, *English Coins*, p. 105.　　　　[2] Oman, *Coinage of England*, p. 141.
[3] Ibid.　　　　[4] Ibid., p. 135.
[5] D. E. Allen, *Catalogue of English Coins in the British Museum. The Cross and Crosslets (Tealby) type of Henry II* (1951), p. cxviii.
[6] BM. MS. Cotton, Claudius D X, fol. 98v. The charter of 1111 relating to the borough of Fordwich (ibid., fol. 175r.) gives the name of a moneyer there (Hagemund) in a list of burgesses.
[7] A 32.　　　　[8] B 218.　　　　[9] D 291; F 579.　　　　[10] PR, 27 Henry II, p. 151.
[11] D 254; Brooke, *English Coins*, p. 133.　　　　[12] D 211; Brooke, p. 113.
[13] D 283; F 308; Y, fol. 33v.; Z, fol. 200r.　　　　[14] Brooke, p. 112.

complete list of moneyers. On the face of it the Solomon the moneyer with ground, c. 1200, near St Helen's church,[1] would seem to be the man with the same name[2] signing coins, but the dates will not agree and there must be therefore two Solomons minting at Canterbury. Freawin, mentioned above, has a name not found on coins. Luke, in Rental F[3] (c. 1206), apparently has no surviving coinage to his credit, nor have Luke monetarius (who might be the same man) and Ordlief monetarius, who have respectively (c. 1230) a stone house in Crienemeldnelane[4] (St Peter's Grove), and a dwelling in 'The Mint'.[5] Seman the moneyer, whose heirs have ground at the same date in St Peter's parish, does not occur in printed lists of Canterbury moneyers.

It is not improbable that Lambin Frese the moneyer may have played a part, all unintentionally, in an episode famous in architectural history. Originally he had a workshop (fabrica) in the alleyway in front of Christ Church Gate.[6] About 1177 he moved to a new site in Stour Street, far away from the cathedral. The monks seemed singularly anxious to get rid of him, for they bestowed on him ample ground, far more commodious than the cramped patch he occupied before the gate, gave him a present of ten marks, and went to the length of securing a charter from Henry II himself, confirming the arrangements.[8] The chronicler Gervase in his 'Burning and Repair of Christ Church, Canterbury', says that the house-fire of September 1174 started among 'domunculæ' before the cathedral gate, and that three of these structures were destroyed before the fire was put out. All unseen, sparks or embers, blown up into the roof of the cathedral choir by a south-west wind, had started a conflagration which very soon blazed up, resulting in the destruction of the splendid choir consecrated forty-four years before. The story of its rebuilding is an outstanding document in the history of medieval architecture,[9] while the building itself is one of the most important transitional works in Europe. Since the monks took such elaborate measures to rid themselves of Lambin Frese and his workshop, and since the fire started at the most a few yards therefrom, it is indeed tempting to ask whether or not sparks from his furnace set fire to the workshop and hence to the cathedral.

In 19 Henry II Richard the treasurer and his colleagues charged an

---

[1] D 291. [2] Brooke, p. 113. This Salemun, signing coins, is far too late.
[3] F 579.
[4] Luke, in Z, under St Peter's parish; Ordlief, ibid., under St Mary Breadman parish. Ordlief bought the house of Frumelin (Frumbold f. Hagenild) in 'The Mint' (D 280).
[5] Z, under St Peter's parish. 'The Mint' is White Horse Lane.
[6] B 79. [7] xxxv. [8] xxxvi.
[9] Gervase, *De Combustione et Reparatione*, in *Opera* (RS) p. 3.

'assize' on the royal demesne.[1] Some of the Canterbury moneyers are named individually in this connection in the Pipe Roll. Richard the moneyer renders account for four marks, Ralph of Rye for three, Richard Deudune for two, and Roger, the archbishop's moneyer, accounts for chattels of the Flemings and foreign merchants.[2] Something terrible happens in the year 1176–7, for colossal impositions are recorded as follows:[3]

Ralph of Rye, moneyer of Canterbury, with his wife renders account of	1,000 marks
John son of Robert owes from his amercement	400 marks
Richard Corbeill owes	500 marks
Solomon and Richard Deodatus (i.e. R. Deudune, below)	600 marks

A measure of the gigantic size of these amercements can be secured from the fact that the aid exacted at this date from the city of London, with all its teeming population of merchants, is 1,000 marks.[4] One Canterbury moneyer alone, with his wife, is liable for such a sum. Moreover, it is to be observed that John son of Robert owes 400 marks from an amercement which may originally have been even greater. All the sufferers may be found in local documents. Ralph of Rye's daughter Helewysa was still living in Canterbury some years later.[5] John son of Robert (son of Osmund) named in Rental B,[6] seems to be father of alderman Thomas in the next generation, with ground in the upper High Street.[7] This John the moneyer, son of Robert, must surely be John son of Robert the moneyer named in Rental A.[8] Richard Corbeille is father of John Corbeille and grandfather to a second John, as is disclosed by a charter relating to ground in Stour Street.[9] John the elder is named as pledge to his father for the amercement and produces some of the amount due.[10] Richard Deudune was lord of some ground near King's Bridge, sold to Jacob the Jew to make the great stone house,[11] while Solomon the moneyer holds ground a few yards away.[12]

John son of Robert managed to pay off his debt within four years.[13] Ralph of Rye produced one hundred marks straightway, and varying sums in following years, until the figure was reduced to £326 13s. 4d. It stood at this until 1184, when his death is recorded and the sheriff is instructed

---

[1] PR, 19 Henry II, p. 87.   [2] PR, 21 Henry II, p. 220.
[3] PR, 23 Henry II, p. 208. Allen, *Catalogue, ut supra*, p. cxxi.
[4] Stephenson, *Borough and Town*, app. iv.   [5] CAC Reg. E, fol. 375.
[6] B 69, 82.   [7] D 122; LXVIII.   [8] A 32.   [9] LXV.
[10] 25 Henry II, p. 118.   [11] XLIX.   [12] D 291.
[13] PR, 26 Henry II, p. 145.

to find out about his pledges.[1] Solomon and Richard Deudune paid off their debts in three years.[2] As so often may be found in the Pipe Rolls, men who have sinned sufficiently to incur heavy amercements are still entrusted with royal business at a later date. Richard Deudune accounts for the property of a forger in the twenty-ninth year[3] and is found conducting operations on Canterbury castle in the next reign.[4] Another broken moneyer like Ralph of Rye was Richard Corbeille. By 1180 he had reduced his debt to £145 6s. 8d. at which sum it stood until 1184 when miserable renders such as 4s. 11d. and half a mark were proffered. 'Et nichil habet' adequately expresses his utter ruin.[5] The outstanding debts of Ralph of Rye and of Richard Corbeille are repeated year after year in the Pipe Rolls until the beginning of John's reign, when, in the drive to clear the account from long-standing debts, these by now irrecoverable sums were apparently written off.[6]

Solomon the moneyer did not profit from the lesson of a heavy amercement. In 1180 came the 'great persecution of the moneyers throughout England' (in the words of the Canterbury chronicler).[7] In Kent as much as 43s. 4d. was spent 'in carriagio monetariorum' and at the same moment the sheriff accounted for 65s. 7d. of the chattels of Solomon the moneyer.[8] This cannot be connected with his earlier offence as the words *quietus est* are explicitly used, and we are left to infer that Solomon's career met the disastrous and grisly end customary to his dangerous profession. Solomon's wife bought his confiscated house back from the crown for ten marks.[9] A Kentish knight seems to have been involved in the troubles at this time, for Maurice of Wadenhall (a manor near Petham) was amerced three marks 'pro scutellis inventis non sigillatis', probably for illicit possession of unstamped flans.[10]

Some members of the important burgess-family of Chich are named as minters. John Chich signs short-cross issues in the decade 1223–42.[11] In 1230, after the death of Simon Chich, his die was delivered to William 'scissor domini regis'.[12]

[1] See PR, 23 Henry II, p. 208; 24 H. II, p. 123; 25 H. II, p. 118; 26 H. II, p. 145; 30 H. II, p. 146.

[2] PR, 25 Henry II, p. 118.   [3] PR, 29 Henry II, p. 158.

[4] PR, 5 Richard I, p. 165.

[5] PR, 26 Henry II, p. 145; 30 H. II, p. 146; 31 H. II, p. 226; 32 H. II, p. 188.

[6] The debts are still on the roll in 1 John (p. 61), but have disappeared by the next year.

[7] Gervase, RS, i, p. 294.   [8] PR, 27 Henry II, p. 151.   [9] PR, 31 Henry II, p. 233.

[10] PR, 26 Henry II, p. 145. Maurice of Wadenhall is witness to Charter XXXVIII.

[11] Brooke, *English Coins*, p. 111.

[12] CCR, 1227–31, pp. 300, 350. John Chich holds ground in St Alphage parish, c. 1230. (Rental Z, fol. 197v.) W. scissor was Alderman of Westgate in Canterbury. See p. 99.

The moneyers in a given borough were under control from the *cambium regis*. In Canterbury this was sited in the central business quarter, near King's Bridge, close to the houses of the moneyers Solomon, Ordlief, Wiulph, and Lambin Frese.[1] Arnold Ferre, probably another moneyer, has ground close by.[2] This man served about 1189 on the comission which investigated the extinct mint of St Augustine's, and recorded that the abbey had lost the right to maintain a moneyer on its seizure by the king in 1161.[3]

The Canterbury exchange finds frequent mention in the Pipe Rolls. In the fourth year of Richard I, Terric the great Canterbury goldsmith rendered account of a mark of gold to have the exchange at farm.[4] In the sixth year Robert son of Richard (the wealthy citizen who heads the tallage roll of 1198)[5] receives with Terric 500 marks in capital to set up an exchange.[6] The exchange seems at this date to be staffed by its two 'custodes' and a clerk, with 'servientes'.[7] A house for the exchange cost 40s. and a 'fabrica ad monetam faciendam' 20s. Entries in the Pipe Rolls disclose the *cambium* in use as a royal bank, furnishing funds for the expeditions to Brittany and to Wales (1196).[8] Archbishop Hubert figures in the Pipe Roll as owing 100 marks for having the Canterbury exchange at farm from Hilary 6 John.[9] The roll for 10 John embodies an account,[10] standing by itself, headed 'Compotus Terrici de Cantuar'.' From this it appears that Terric was not only concerned with the exchange of Canterbury but was involved in business of the exchanges of York, Carlisle, Chichester and Ipswich. The emergence of Terric's account at this juncture can probably be connected with his death.[11]

The archiepiscopal mint alone at Canterbury would provide material for a prolonged study. Athelstan (as noted above) assigned three moneyers to the archbishop. It is conceivable that the mint lapsed in the convulsions of the Becket crisis. The concession by Richard to archbishop Baldwin of three moneyers with three sets of dies probably marks a re-establishment.

---

[1] The site of no. 20 High Street is probably connected with the exchange.

[2] A. Ferre seems to occupy half a stone house on the n.w. corner of White Horse Lane (the 'Mint'); D 283 n.

[3] *Thorne*, col. 1816, pp. 94–95; Allen, *Catalogue, ut supra*, p. cxx.

[4] PR, 4 Richard I, p. 314; 5 Richard I, p. 171.

[5] PR, 10 Richard I, pp. 207–9.

[6] Chancellor's Roll, 8 Richard I (PRS, NS, no. 7). This roll covers more than one year's business.

[7] Alan, 'clericus cambii' is named in local charters of c. 1220 (e.g. CAC, Ch. Ant. C 749).

[8] Chancellor's Roll, 8 Richard I, intro., pp. xvii, xxiv (PRS, NS, no. 7).

[9] PR, 7 John, pp. 117–18.   [10] PR, 10 John, p. 169.

[11] See p. 175.

THE JEWS

Mr Adler has published a long study of the Canterbury Jewry.[1] Some modest additions may be offered to his remarks, mainly based upon the rentals, which were unknown to him. The Canterbury Jews are exclusively identified with finance, as elsewhere. Mr Adler ranks the community as about third in the kingdom, calculating from figures for contributions to the Northampton *donum*, the corporate subscription to the ransom of Richard I. London produced £486 9s. 7d., Lincoln £287 4s. 11d., and Canterbury £235 19s. 4d. At Canterbury there were some twenty subscribers.[2] A century later, at the time of the expulsion, thirteen houses of Jews came onto the market.[3] The evidence of the rentals (which of course only concerns housing affording rent to Christ Church, or serving as a boundary mark to such housing), does not suggest that the community was very large. The Jews tended to congregate in the central business area. We find them near King's Bridge,[4] opposite the *cambium regis*,[5] close by in Best Lane,[6] and in Stour Street, where the synagogue was situated.[7] White Horse Lane, hard at hand, acquired the name Jewry Lane, and bore it until the seventeenth century. The name indeed still survives attached to its continuation, the alley leading off at right angles into Stour Street.

Where there is any evidence for relations between Jew and Gentile in Canterbury we may discover that they were friendly. There is the well-known affirmation by Gervase of Canterbury that when the monks of Christ Church were being besieged by the archiepiscopal forces in 1189, the Jews prayed in their synagogue and gave more worldly aid in the shape of food and drink.[8] Suggestion of an ordinary day-to-day familiar intercourse between Christian and Jew is offered by the story of Godeliva, a Canterbury woman, who called in a Jewess to administer charms and incantations to her weak foot.[9]

Traces survive of the financial activities of the Canterbury Jews. The Crèvecœur family at Blean a mile away borrowed money,[10] as did the

---

[1] M. Adler, 'The Jews of Canterbury', in *Jewish Hist. Soc. Trans.*, vii, 1915. (The article has been republished in Adler, *The Jews of Medieval England*, 1939.)

[2] Adler, 'Jews of Canterbury', p. 26.   [3] See p. 30.

[4] Somner, *Antiquities of Canterbury*, 1640, p. 120.

[5] Z, under All SS. parish, shows Benedict the Jew, with ground in Stour Street, behind the former dwelling of Jacob the Jew, on the corner of the High Street, succeeded, by 1230, by Cressel the Jew.

[6] Z shows Ysaac the Jew in possession of a stone house, formerly that of Sampson the Jew, 'opposita fronti ecclesie omnium sanctorum', i.e. opposite the east end, in Best Lane.

[7] D 306, n.; F 173.   [8] Gervase, *Opera*, RS, i, p. 405.

[9] *Materials*, ii, p. 7.   [10] LXI.

lord of Lee at Littlebourne.[1] Among citizens we find Amfrid of Burgate selling ground to Terric the goldsmith to find money to liquidate his debts to the Jews,[2] while a woman along Wincheap is also in debt to them. This debt of eighteen marks is distributed as follows: to Sampson of Leicester seven marks; to Isaac ten marks, and to his son 'P.' one mark. Her financial embarrassments include, it should be noted, 60s. owing to the monks of Christ Church for unpaid *gabulum* and reliefs.[3] The monks themselves borrowed money from the Jews. In 1226–7 they repaid as much as seventy-four marks, had on loan for eight years, a figure not including interest.[4] The prior's chapel, still existing in part, was built through loans contracted from creditors, among whom was Benedict the Jew, apparently the man with a dwelling in Stour Street, close to the exchange.[5] The Jews did not monopolize money-lending in Canterbury, for at least one Gentile, Lambin Frese the moneyer, had managed to get control of stock at Goodnestone, some seven miles from the city, from William lord of that manor.[6] The rentals offer an additional name to the list of Canterbury chirographers supplied by Mr Adler, namely Robert the clerk, 'scriptor Judeorum.'[7]

The 'Rothschild of the Canterbury Jewry' was Jacob, dwelling at the corner of Stour Street. He subscribed as much as £115 6s. 8d. to the ransom of Richard I, about half the total for Jews in the city.[8] Flanking Jacob's back wall was the Synagogue which, it is instructive to note, was built on land held by the Jews from a citizen, who in turn held it (at 4d. *per annum*) from the monks of Canterbury cathedral.

BUILDING TRADES

Some masons will naturally be expected in twelfth-century Canterbury. The documents supply the names of seven men styled 'mazon' (and variants) or 'cementarius',[10] but there is nothing, it may be regretted, to connect any of them with the vast building activities of the age. Some of them must have found work in putting up the numbers of stone houses

---

[1] CAC, Ch. Ant. I 166.   [2] LXIV.   [3] CAC, Ch. Ant. C 924.

[4] R. A. L. Smith, *Canterbury Cathedral Priory*, p. 18.

[5] CAC, *TA*, 1222–3; Z under All SS. parish. Several charters among the cathedral archives bear acquittances in Hebrew, usually in form of piece of parchment attached to the seal tag (e.g. A 68, A 90, A 91, I 70, I 78, I 166).

[6] PR, 26 Henry II, pp. 147–8.   [7] F 165.

[8] Adler, 'Jews of Canterbury', note 39; see p. 26.   [9] See D 304–6, n.

[10] Warin (A 5), Alexander (B 61), Serlo (C 28), Eudo (F 363), Lambert (F 408), Richard (F 409), Gerard (LI).

with which Jewish financiers and Christian moneyers were equipping themselves. There are eight carpenters named in the rentals.[1] One glazier is probably engaged on church work.[2] Ingenulph the plumber is on the cathedral staff though it is hard to say whether or not the monks monopolize his services (as in the likewise doubtful case of the caterers).[3] No building assize has been discovered for Canterbury at this age, and at least two thatchers (tector, thecchere) are plying their trade,[4] despite the frequent fires in the city, though where the monks can control building (on their own ground, near the cathedral) we find them insisting on tile.[5] Five painters (pictores) are named.[6] Whether these painters were semi-skilled men daubing doors or windows or whether they might have been responsible for splendid frescoes like the 'Nativity of St John Baptist', and its accompanying magnificent angels, in the cathedral crypt, we have no means of telling.

THE CLOTH INDUSTRY

Several stages of the cloth industry can be detected. There is a wool-monger (wlmangere) named Reginald with ground beside the river in Best Lane.[7] Weavers occur, such as Martin,[8] Adwin,[9] Fulco[10] 'textores', and Hugh[11] and Gilbert[12] 'telarii'. A maker of 'burels' (burarius), called Blackman, has ground in Wincheap[13]. The Canterbury weavers were not as powerful as those of Winchester or York, yet they were sufficiently strong to secure a monopoly of manufacture within a given radius, as is disclosed in a case of 1237, when the crown was induced by Canterbury craftsmen to stop rivals who had set up looms and were dyeing at Sturry (two miles away) and at Littlebourne (four miles away).[14] There does not seem from the evidence of the rentals and charters to be any concentration of the trade at Canterbury in any identifiable locality. The house of Fulco textor stands close to the castle, far away from the main business centre.[15] There is a lane in Canterbury called Webbenelane,[16] suggesting

[1] Bartholomew (F 46), John (A 55), Liefwin (D 98,) Ralph (D 180), Richard (F 633), Warin (F 611), Wibert (B 215).
[2] Nicholas vitrearius (D 75).   [3] See pp. 110–11.
[4] D 203, F 506 (Hamo); XLVII (Wibert).   [5] XXXIX.
[6] Alberic (A 8); Fulco (D 213); William f. Driu (F 467); Osmund, James (II).
[7] F 307.   [8] F 44.   [9] XI.   [10] F 502.
[11] B 57.   [12] XXI.   [13] D 195.
[14] CCR, 1234–37, p. 422. Similar monopolies were secured by weavers at Derby and Lincoln. See R. R. Darlington, *Darley Cartulary*, pp. l–li; Hill, *Medieval Lincoln*, pp. 326–7.
[15] F 502.
[16] Lambeth MS. no. 241 (cartulary of Dover Priory), fol. 171v. The charter mentions J. f. Vivian, the borough reeve of c. 1175.

that some weavers dwelt together there, but this lane cannot be identified. Rental X 2 (c. 1180) names a feltwright (feltewrecte) as a previous occupant of some ground (the site unstated).[1]

Several fullers are named, holding ground, very significantly, close to the river. Gerold and Sired the fullers have tenements close together near St Mildred's mill.[2] The sidestream called 'Thuate' forms the backyard boundary of Eilred the fuller's dwelling.[3]

The term 'mercerius' raises a problem. One side of Mercery Lane is occupied early in the thirteenth century by 'mercerii' who have clearly given it its name. It might be supposed that the occupants of Mercery Lane were mercers in the modern sense of the term, that is, dealers in textiles, especially silks, were it not for the fact that a few of them are also called 'mercator'. There are as many as seventeen 'mercatores' named in the documents (apart from those also called 'mercerii') and we evidently have here representatives of that class of general dealer which is so common in Elizabethan Canterbury and elsewhere. Possibly the application of the expression 'mercator' to certain 'mercerii' is merely a scribal error.[4]

The finishing trades are not well represented. There is a tailor called John named as a witness to a charter.[5] The price of one finished garment has come down, that of the cloak (pallium) worth the substantial figure of one mark rendered in part-payment for ground of Jacob the Jew.[6] It is to be noted that three ells of 'ruchet' for a dresslength were assigned to the widow Godith (c. 1200) for quitclaim of her freebench.[7]

There are many 'parmentarii' scattered around Canterbury. The term can refer to tailors, but since at least five 'parmenters' are also called 'pelliparii', they must probably be classed as skinners.[8]

THE LEATHER TRADE

A few tanners may be found, holding ground near the river, as might be expected, like Peter tannur who has a stone house near Westgate.[9] One of the 'pelliparii', William, may well be the man who did business with the

---

[1] X 2, fol. 13r.   [2] D 210; F 232; Charter LXVII.   [3] D 363.

[4] Solomon, Semer and Suan are called by both terms. Possibly Godwin mercator is Goldwin mercerius. See MERCATOR, MERCERIUS in Index to documents. Wilard mercator may be a moneyer. See p. 114 above.

[5] LX.   [6] LI.

[7] Cartulary of Poor Priests' Hospital, Canterbury, BM, Add. MS. 29,437, fol. 72.

[8] See Index to documents, under PARMENTARIUS, PELLIPARIUS.

[9] BBSA, p. 343. It is not clear where lived and worked the tanners Godwin (F 490), Gerold (xxxv, xxxvi, F 585, 586), Thomas (F 399, XLIX), Martin (PR, 10 Richard I, p. 207, in the tallage list of 1198).

monks at a juncture in the crisis over the secular college. In 1189 their agent overseas wanted to provide a *douceur* for the legate John of Anagni in the shape of a fine grey cloak with a hood of marten skins. The monks heard that William had a hood of Linsey in stock and wanted to buy it for the legate. William affirmed that it was shopsoiled (ex longa detentione perierat) and sold it to someone else. He was then commissioned to go to London to get another, together with the cloak.[1] Unhappily a valuable, if all too brief, record like this of a business man at work in the twelfth century is rarely found. The footwear trade is represented by four corvisers, four cordwainers and one 'sutor'.[2] They are not localized in any one place, but it seems there were several corvisers in Butchery Lane early in the thirteenth century since it is called Corviseria.[3] There are three glovers,[4] with perhaps a fourth, a man bearing the appellation 'Wante', 'le Wante',[5] who may have got it through plying this trade. There are three saddlers,[6] whose products are completed with accessories manufactured by some lorimers.[7] An 'ampoller', Gervase, is probably a maker of leather bottles, though of course he might have worked in earthenware or tin, supplying the little containers in which pilgrims carried away the water of St Thomas.[8]

MILLERS

'Molendinarii' named Robert, Godard, Peter, Reginer, and Sinoth may be found in the rentals.[9] To these may be added Picot le mulner, named (c. 1166) in the list of votaries of St Anselm.[10] A charter of Eastbridge Hospital recording the sale of 16d. rent from ground next to that of Gerard the miller without Westgate, towards 'Scepeschotesmelne', conveyed to Bruning the miller by Benedict the miller, is witnessed by Sinod, Gerard, Hedbricht, Ralph and Ælword, all millers.[11] There must

---

[1] *Epp. Cant.*, p. 306.

[2] See Index to documents, ÆDRIC, WILLELMUS, GILLEBERT, ÆILWIN, corvisers. BRIAN, HUBERT, RICHARD, PETER, cordwainers. ODO, sutor.

[3] See p. 203.　　　　　　　　　　[4] See Index, HELIAS, ROBERTUS, WILLELMUS and GLOVERE.

[5] Rodbert (B 43, 44).

[6] 'Seleir, Sellarius', etc. Reinbert (dead by c. 1166, in B), Robert (F), Jordan (XLVII).

[7] Hereward (B), Richard (F), Henry (Greg., 53).　　　　　　　　　[8] D 144, 155.

[9] Robert appears as a witness and his ground cannot be sited (A 34). Godard (D 208) has ground very close to Hottemelne. Peter has ground in All Saints' Lane, almost opposite King's Mill (F 33). Reginer seems to be connected with Guthwold's mill (F 33). Sinoth has ground near the castle (F 515).

[10] W. Urry, 'St Anselm and his Cult at Canterbury' (in *Spicilegium Beccense*, i, p. 584).

[11] Eastbridge Hospital Charters, no. A 46.

have been many more millers than these in Canterbury, as the tiny head of water in the Stour was heavily overloaded with mill-wheels. On the eastern arm of the river there were St Mildred's mill (subject of Charter XLVI), Hottemelne (which had gone by 1200),[1] King's mill[2] and Abbot's mill.[3] On the western branch stood Westgate mill and Scepeschotesmelne.[4] Below the city were Barton mill and not far away another mill called Guthwold's mill.[5] It is curious that a body of property or ground is attached to more than one mill. Guthwold's mill is associated with meadows, and St Mildred's mill has holdings occupied by tenants. King's mill seems to be connected with eight acres of ground below the city.[6] Mills other than water-mills may be found. There is a 'horsemelne' very close to Westgate, within the walls,[7] and some kind of mill, far away from any water-course,[8] just within Burgate.

Indication of annual profit derived from a mill is offered by the figure for allowances out of the king's mill conceded by Henry II to Becket's sister, at the time of his great penance in 1174 (ten marks, rising later to £11).[9] The mills which archbishop Ralph bought from 'Calvellus', evidently the borough reeve of c. 1100, were acquired for £15. Calvel had evidently paid 20s. *per annum* to the archbishop, probably because the mills were originally members of the archiepiscopal manor of Westgate, Canterbury. The new occupant is to pay but 12d. 'ad recognoscendum curie . . . de Westgat.'[10]

THE EARLY POST-CONQUEST GILDS OF CANTERBURY

Canterbury occupies an important place in the history of the early English gild. A gild of 'cnihtas' existed here in the mid-ninth century, 'the earliest gild on record in England'. Headed by one Æthelhelm, it

---

[1] D 230.

[2] *Thorne*, col. 1807, p. 81, says that King Stephen, being short of money after his capture at Lincoln, bestowed the mill at Estbregge (i.e. King's Bridge), Canterbury, on St Augustine's abbey, in return for the loan of 100 marks. Thorne adds (col. 1827, p. 111) that the mill among other properties was sold by abbot Clarembald (1161–74) and alienated to Henry II. Stephen gave the mill a monopoly when in the hands of the abbey (Elmham, *RS*, p. 383).

[3] Close to the point where the river ran under the city wall in St Radegund's. It finally went out of action after a fire in 1933.

[4] This must be Hooker's Mill. The mill, and Westgate Mill, must be among the twelve manorial mills of Estursete (*DB*, i, fol. 3v.).

[5] F 283–5, 574–8. [6] App. A, § 1.
[7] D 383. [8] D 90.
[9] *Guernes*, pp. 311–12. [10] CCR, v, p. 62.

witnesses a charter,[1] while three 'geferscipas' witness documents a century later.[2]

Domesday Book mentions two gilds in Canterbury, one of clerks and the other of burgesses. The former may easily be disposed of. It is cited in the following terms:

In civitate Cantvaria habet archiepiscopus XII burgenses et XXXII mansuras quas tenent clerici de uilla in gildam suam et reddunt XXXV solidos et unum molendinum de V solidis.[3]

The St Augustine's version of the Survey speaks in substantially the same terms:

Adhuc sunt xxxij mansure et unum molendinum que tenent clerici ciuitatis ad gildam ibique manent xij burgenses qui reddunt eis xxxv solidos et molendinum reddit v solidos.[4]

However, the corresponding section of Domesday Monachorum renders the passage:

Et iterum sunt inibi XXX et II mansurę et unum molendinum quę tenent clerici sancti Gregorii. ad eorum ecclesiam. Ibique manent XII burgenses qui reddunt eis XXXV solidos. Et molendinum reddit V solidos.[5]

The gild of clerks is thus shown to be not a gild in the ordinary sense, a club of lay pattern, but the house of St Gregory, just without the northern walls of Canterbury, while the 'clerks' are the secular canons of that house. The gild of burgesses cannot be so easily explained away, though the suggestion has been made that this is no gild. Domesday Book, after stating that burgesses (burgenses) had forty-five *mansuræ* without the city of which they had gable and custom, while the king had sake and soke, observes:

Ipsi quoque burgenses habebant de rege XXX III acras terræ in gildam suam. Has domus et hanc terram tenet Rannulfus de Columbels.[6]

The St Augustine's version renders this section:

Adhuc idem Ranulfus [de Columbels] tenet xxxiij agros terre quos burgenses semper habuerunt in gilda eorum de donis omnium regum.[7]

[1] Birch, CS, 515; Gross, *Gild Merchant*, i, pp. 183–8. Stenton, *First Century of English Feudalism*, p. 134; *Anglo-Saxon England*, p. 520.

[2] Birch, CS, 1010; Robertson, *Anglo-Saxon Charters*, XXXII, and see notes thereto.

[3] *DB* i. fol. 3r.

[4] PRO 164/27 (White Book of St Augustine's), fol. 23r; Ballard, *Eleventh Century Inquisition*, p. 15. Ballard's text is very inaccurate.

[5] *DMon*, p. 82.   [6] *DB*, i, fol. 2 r.i.

[7] PRO, 164/27 (White Book of St Augustine's), fol. 22v; Ballard, *Eleventh Century Inquisition*, p. 10.

Dr Gross knew only the former version, and does not accept it as a straight-forward reference to a gild. 'I think,' he says, 'the proper translation is "in their geld", i.e. "in their geldable", or lands subject to gelds.'[1] It is difficult to see why he went out of his way to try to dispose of this Canterbury gild, for he knew of other early gilds, in other boroughs, at or not far from the date of Domesday. At Winchester there was a 'chenictehalla ubi chenictes potabant gildam suam',[2] held from King Edward; at Dover there was a 'gihalla burgensium',[3] while in London the pre-conquest gild survived until 1125.[4] Moreover, there is unequivocal evidence, well-known to Dr Gross, for a Canterbury gild existing within the archiepisco-pate of Anselm, which runs from a point of time not much later than Domesday itself.[5]

The expression 'de donis omnium regum' used in Domesday as above, in connection with the holdings of the Canterbury gild, demands com-ment. An institution of the kind was much more likely to be an object of royal imposition than of royal benevolence, and perhaps the phrase merely implies confirmation by the king of benefactions made by individuals. It is worth noting that the gildhall of the burgesses of Dover, not many miles away, is classed as 'elemosina regis'.[6]

A Canterbury document, important in the history of the English borough, supplies proof of the existence of a merchant gild late in the eleventh or early in the twelfth century.[7] An exchange was made between the convent of Christ Church, and the 'cnihtas' of the merchant gild, of housing in the city. The monks owned two 'haws' without Ridingate, and seven within Newingate. These they passed over to the gild in exchange for eight 'haws' within Burgate. The transaction was witnessed by arch-bishop Anselm and the cathedral monks on the one hand and by Calveal, portreeve of Canterbury, and the senior members of the 'heap', the gild, on the other.

This gild, then, owns property, is manned by 'knights' and seems to be headed by the portreeve.

Maitland describes this organization as the earliest merchant gild mentioned in England,[8] but this hardly seems to be true on the evidence available. The 'gilda mercatoria' of Burford (Oxfordshire) may be as early, if not earlier. The Canterbury gild must lie between dates 1093

---

[1] *Gild Merchant*, i, p. 189, n. 6.
[2] *DB*, iv, fol. 531.   [3] *DB*, i, fol. 1r.
[4] Page, *London, its origins and early development*, p. 181.   [5] 1.
[6] PRO, 164/27 (White Book of St Augustine's), fol. 25v; Ballard, *Eleventh Century Inquisition*, p. 25.
[7] 1.   [8] *Domesday Book and Beyond*, p. 191.

and 1109, as is clear from the mention of Anselm, while the Burford gild has been dated to 1087–1107. It would appear that the Burford gild is modelled on a gild of the same kind at Oxford, which must be yet earlier.[1] The 'mercatoria ghilda' of Lewes, Sussex, was in existence at least by 1088, for when Reginald de Warenne restored it (1148–9?), he re-established it in the way held by the burgesses in the time of his father and grandfather. His grandfather, William de Warenne, died in 1088.[2] Another Sussex borough apparently had a merchant gild in the days of William I, the existence of which may be established, by a very short space of time, as earlier even than that of Lewes, for Stephen confirmed to the burgesses of Chichester their 'gilda mercatoria' as in the days of his grandfather.[3] It is curious that Gross, who knew both the Lewes[4] and Chichester[5] gilds, should affirm that the 'earliest distinct references to the Gilds Merchant' related to the Burford and Canterbury examples.[6]

There is, as may be seen, no positive evidence to connect the Canterbury merchant gild with that mentioned in Domesday Book, but it is probable that they are in fact one and the same institution. Each is property-owning, as will have been noticed, though it is difficult to adduce other parallels.[7] The Domesday gild has been plundered of its ground and its acres are in the hands of a protégé of Odo. The bishop of Bayeux has treated the gild with as much gentleness as he has meted out to other Kentish institutions.

The members of the Canterbury merchant gild are 'knights'—cnihtas—like the members of the ninth-century Canterbury gild, the London cnihtengild, and the Winchester gild of the days of king Edward.[8] It has

[1] A charter of William Earl of Gloucester, 1147–73, concedes to the men of Burford 'gildam et consuetudines quas habent burgenses de Oxonfordia in gilda mercatorum.' Another Burford charter (dated to 1087–1107) incorporates the clause relating to the gild, but only the two final words survive in the text available, viz.: . . . 'gildam mercatorum.' (*BBC*, i, pp. xxvii and 203). Ballard adopted his text in the case of these charters from Gross, *Gild Merchant*, ii, pp. 28–29. Gross in turn took them from PRO Misc. Chancery, Gilds, 23, a certificate of 1389. The text of the earlier charter is generally defective owing to damage to the MS. but such text as survives corresponds very closely with that of the charter of 1147–73, and induces the view that the missing text of the gild clause in the earlier charter may have been the same as in the later, thus embodying a reference to the gild at Oxford.

[2] Warner and Ellis, *Facsimiles of Royal and other Charters in the British Museum*, i, p. 31. Gross, *Gild Merchant*, ii, p. 145.

[3] *Gild Merchant*, ii, p. 47. [4] See note 2 above.

[5] See note 2 above.

[6] *Gild Merchant*, i, p. 5.

[7] The Canterbury gild of c. 1100 is discussed by Professor Tait (MEB, pp. 120–3). He seems to incline to the view that this gild may well be identical with the gild of Domesday Book (ibid. p. 121).

[8] For discussion on the 'cniht' see Stenton, *First Century of English Feudalism*, Chapter IV.

been affirmed that the portreeve is head of this Canterbury gild.[1] This is not specifically stated, but the manner in which his name stands in relation to the gildsmen suggests that this is in fact the case. The two groups of witnesses are Anselm and the convent, and Calveal and the senior members of the gild. However, the attendance of the portreeve at a transaction involving the conveyance of real estate is not very surprising, and in fact is to be expected. The idea of unity and community in the gild is admirably expressed by the term 'se heap', which will be found used, in a Latinized form 'acervus', a century later in connection with another local gild.[2]

The 'cepmannegild' of Canterbury, suggests Professor Tait,[3] probably ceased to exist soon after the date of the exchange (c. 1100) but there is a clear reference to a property-owning institution well after the following half-century, bearing exactly the same name. Rental B, in describing a holding on the north-east corner of St Margaret's Street, says that it stretches southwards as far as ground of the 'gilda mercatorum'.[4] This rental cannot fall in date later than 1167.[5] This 'gilda mercatorum' can hardly be anything other than the chapmen-gild of Anselm's day and if it is then this seems to be the latest available mention of it *eo nomine*. When about the year 1220 Susanna de Planaz, the owner of the corner tenement, sold it to the monks of Christ Church[6] the southern boundary is given as the holding of Goldwin 'mercerius' while at a later date the holding is in the hands of his daughter Cecilia.[7] This need not of course imply that the gild did not still exist, for Goldwin and daughter may be tenants of the gildsmen.

An organization called the 'Borough Gild' makes an appearance a generation or more after the last mention of the merchant gild. Perhaps it is the old gild under another name, though there is nothing positive to connect the two. This borough gild is property-owning like the merchant gild. It has ground at the bottom of Hawk's Lane, near the river, classed as 'terra de burchilde',[8] while round the corner in Stour Street, a few yards away, it controls more ground. Lambin son of Sponge occupies a house here, standing partly on territory owing rent to the cathedral, while 'the

---

[1] MEB, p. 121. '. . . the reeve of the city is the head of the gild.' See also p. 120. 'Calveal the protreeve's headship of the Canterbury gild is the first evidence of that close connexion with the government of the borough which made the Norman merchant gild so vital a factor in municipal growth.'

[2] The gild of Westgate. See below.   [3] MEB, p. 121.

[4] B III.   [5] For date, see Chapter II above.

[6] Z, fol. 197r. ([scoppe] quas emimus de Susanna de Planaz).

[7] Ibid.   [8] D 250.

other part of his house,' says Rental D,[1] 'est de burcgilde'. Not far away, just over the Stour, in Crienmeldnelane, there is more ground specified as 'terra de burchilde'.[2] The last-mentioned piece of property is found (if a correct interpretation has been made) in the hands of another gild styled the gild (kilda) of Westgate.[3]

It is most unfortunate that Rental B, the evidence for the existence of the merchant gild as late as c. 1166, should not cover the wards of Westgate and Worthgate where lie the holdings of the 'borough gild' at the end of the century, otherwise we might have had some material for establishing an identity or otherwise between the two gilds. It should be pointed out that as late as c. 1230 there was a gildhall in existence in Canterbury, and that this gildhall had, as a rental[4] puts it, property belonging to it, showing that there was a gild with some surviving spark of vitality. By the end of the thirteenth century, when documents grow more plentiful, no trace of a local gild is to be found. The right to trade in the city, the control of which was with little question the function of the merchant gild, is now confined to freemen, who are admitted under the direct auspices of the burghmoot.[5]

There is mention of a gildhall before the close of the twelfth century in Canterbury, but no evidence is provided as to the type of gild concerned, or where the gildhall stood. Rental C of c. 1180 says that rent due to the monks for certain ground in St Alphage parish is paid to James, porter of the archbishop, and adds that the ground 'pertinet ad gildhalle'.[6] The rent is still collected by James the porter twenty-five years later.[7] Possibly James has some official connection with the gild, and if so, this connection lasts a long time. We might well expect him to hold office in the local gild, for he was alderman of Northgate, and the only known mayor of Canterbury (evidently in 1215) in this early age.[8] Rental D[9] says of the same holding 'hec pertinet ad childhalle'. Other rentals mention the holding and class it as property of the gildhall (as shown) as late as c. 1230.[10] Another piece of ground lying without Newingate is specified at the beginning of the century as 'terra . . . de kildhalle'.[11]

What and where was this gildhall? Early in the thirteenth century local

---

[1] D 226.   [2] D 334.   [3] See below, in account of the gild of Westgate.

[4] Z, fol. 197v. Rent is paid 'de quadam terra que pertinet ad gildhalle'. This is D 65; see below.

[5] A number of rolls of the borough court of c. 1300 (in the city archives) show that the freedom was granted to individuals by a special committee of leading citizens, deputed by the burghmoot (City Archives, R/F).

[6] C 60.   [7] G 60.   [8] See p. 87.   [9] D 65.

[10] See note 4 above.   [11] D 133.

government in Canterbury is apparently associated with the speechhouse, standing in St George's parish.[1] By the early fifteenth century[2] the court and council of the city meet in the gildhall, the building standing on the site of its successor where court and council were still kept until 1949, in the High Street, in Saint Mary Breadman parish. Unfortunately this frontage is unsurveyed in Rental D, though we know there was some building here, as is evidenced by the remains of a handsome stone crypt, constructed about 1180, sited back from the street. Perhaps the crypt was in fact part of the ancient 'gildhalle'. In such case the quality of its workmanship suggests an affluent institution. It is tempting to suppose that the early gildhall was in fact here, and that when perhaps in the thirteenth century the ancient gild owning it became moribund or defunct a move was made from the speechhouse to the gildhall. Parallels may be found in other boroughs.[3] Since, as will be seen below, there was more than one gild in Canterbury, there may well have been more than one gildhall. Even in the little settlement outside the abbey gates at Battle there were two gildhalls.[4] Rental F (§ 280) discloses that there was a gildhall, and by inference a gild, in the little borough of Fordwich, a mile or more below Canterbury. Perhaps this gildhall was on the site of the structure now known as the Town Hall.

A charter of c. 1200 discloses the existence of an institution called the 'kilda de Westgate'.[5] Godere Paumier grants to his son Dunstan four dwellings in Crienemeldnelane, each held from a different lord, one of which is the gild, which receives a rent of 12d. for the holding, at Michaelmas. The charter recording the transaction is, as far as can be discovered, the sole evidence for this gild. The Canterbury merchant gild of c. 1100 is referred to as the 'heap',[6] and it is of interest to note that a term exactly equivalent is used of this gild of Westgate. The rent of 12d. is to be paid 'aceruo . . . kilde' while the sale is published both in the burghmoot of Canterbury and 'coram aceruo . . . kilde.'

There is no hint as to the functions of this gild in the charter. The

---

[1] See p. 91.

[2] Large numbers of burghmoot rolls among the city archives tell of proceedings in 'guyhalla, gihalda' from c. 1400 (J/B/203, etc.).

[3] Compare, for one example, Bridgewater, where the old Tolsey went out of use by the fourteenth century, and municipal government was transferred to the gildhall (*Bridgewater Borough Archives*, ii., 1377–99, ed. T. B. Dilks. *Somerset Record Society*, liv, 1938).

[4] The *Chronicon Monasterii de Bello* (*Anglia Christiana*) p. 20 states: 'Duæ etiam Gilthallæ sunt in eadem villa.' The 'ghildhus' which Walter Map says you might find in every village sounds much more like the village inn than anything else (*Gualterii Mapes De Nugis Curialium*, ed. T. Wright, CS, p. 79).

[5] LX.   [6] See above.

Westgate of Canterbury (which stood not very far away from the property under discussion) gave its name both to a parish and a ward, but the gild is probably unconnected with either of these, as such, and doubtless takes its title from the principal local landmark. It is curious that the ground about 1200 owing rent to the gild of Westgate should seem to be the same ground which at a date close thereafter belongs to a gild with another name, the 'borough gild' mentioned above.[1] Perhaps one gild has become assimilated to the other, or conveyed property to the other.[2] Or perhaps again, the monastic surveyor, with no great interest in, or memory for, the differences between secular institutions out in the town confused the two.

CRAFT GILDS

The St Augustine's version of Domesday makes mention of two classes of tradesmen within Canterbury: Sutores et draparii reddunt xxx solidos.[3]

The passage has inspired references to a craft gild,[4] but this is the only instance noticed where these two trades are found in conjunction, and there is not enough to build on to affirm the existence of any gild. They are allied trades, it must be admitted, representing a clothing interest. Possibly their 30s. render represents a fee for permission to exist in a gild, though it is very odd that no other trade is mentioned if this is the case. Perhaps we merely have payment from certain drapers and certain shoe-makers who happen at the date of Domesday to occupy royal property. Unmistakable references to an early craft gild can be extracted from the rentals. Rental D[5] specifies a holding in Dover Street (Retherchieape) and indicates that it lies next to ground called 'terra smithchilde.' A few yards off, round the corner in Bridge Street, almost opposite Newingate, the same gild (gilda fabrorum) has another piece of ground at a date c. 1216.[6] The same ground is still in the hands of the gild about fifteen years later,[7] but no further reference to it can be traced. Craft gilds in other cities might cost their members dear and large fees were exacted by the crown for licence to exist, as in the case of the weavers' gild at Winchester. No such fees are recorded as paid by the Canterbury gild of

[1] See D 334.

[2] The charter mentioning the gild is a little later, it appears, in date than Rental D, so if any absorption has taken place, the gild of Westgate has absorbed the 'borough gild'. Most probably, as is suggested, the surveyors have confused two different institutions.

[3] PRO, 164/27 (White Book of St Augustine's) fol. 22r; Ballard, *Eleventh Century Inquisition*, p. 9.

[4] Ballard, *Eleventh Century Inquisition*, p. xxii; *Domesday Boroughs*, p. 60.

[5] D 138.   [6] Y, fol. 30r.   [7] Z, fol. 194v.

smiths, but compared with the Winchester weavers they must have been a small and insignificant body, perhaps too small to be worth attention, or again, it is possible that they might have enjoyed a right to exist by long prescription.[1]

The point must not be pressed, but it is worth notice that two of the ancient Canterbury churches bear distinguishing names derived from trades. St Mary Magdalen is called Fishmanchurch, while St Mary in the High Street is named Breadmanchurch. It might be suggested that they bear these names since the relevant trade is carried on around. However, the surrounding tenements near the last-mentioned church are well-surveyed, yet there is never a mention of a baker, while if Hugh piscator takes up property near Fishmanchurch,[2] he is the only man of his trade found near it, and the fishmarket is a long way off, in the High Street, outside Breadmanchurch in fact. It is tempting to wonder if these churches might not have been connected with gilds of fishmongers and bakers.

[1] William Somner mentions the gild of smiths as being the most ancient of the organized trades in Canterbury (*Antiquities of Canterbury*, 1640, p. 108). 'The elder rentalls of Christ-Church bounding out some land of theirs lying without Newingate, make mention both of it [i.e. the gild of smiths] and of certaine ground belonging to it, in these words. *Terra quæ pertinet ad gildam fabrorum.*'

[2] Hugh is probably the man who organized supplies of fish for the monks.

CHAPTER VI

Notes on Tenures

No long account of tenures in Canterbury has been attempted in this study, but attention is drawn to some points arising from the rentals and charters.[1] It is not easy to accept Hemmeon's remark that the boroughs are 'islands, relics of a submerged and ante-feudal continent', projecting above the ocean of feudalism which has flowed over western and northern Europe.[2] The tenure prevailing in medieval Canterbury was a species of gavelkind, the ancient tenure of Kent, and it is not easy to distinguish between the language of a charter whereby a burgess grants away ground within the city walls and that of a charter by which a manorial lord or peasant grants territory out in the countryside. There is certainly little or no difference in the terminology of charters relating to Canterbury, and of those relating to ground all round Kent, in the great cartularies of Christ Church such as Registers A—E. The burgess may use feudal expressions in his grants, but will be subject to gavelet, the ancient forfeiture procedure of gavelkind, if he does not pay his rent to his lord. It may be observed that if the waters of feudalism have seeped into Canterbury, yet much of the remaining countryside remains very dry.

GAVELKIND AND OTHER TENURES IN CANTERBURY

Kent is the province of gavelkind, and features of the custom may be found in the documents below. Charters often specify ground in the city as held at gavelkind, and the main bulk of the holdings in Canterbury of the Christ Church monks is regularly classed in their accounts under the heading *gavelikendes*. Sometimes we hear of ground held *in burgagio*, *de burgagio*, but in the cases noticed the grantors are external lords, and the charters embodying the term are probably drafted by clerks from

[1] Mary Bateson uses the late custumal of Canterbury, which is uninformative on the subject of tenures, for her *British Borough Customs*. The text, drawn up in 1512, represents a re-writing rather than a revision. It mentions as if still functioning, the bailiffs and jurates of the city, who disappeared in 1448 and 1461 respectively. See HMC, ix, app. i, p. 171.

[2] *Burgage Tenure*, p. 5.

outside the city.[1] Terms such as the less-precise 'jure hereditario, in feudo et in hereditate' are frequently employed in charters.

The monks let out a great deal of the holdings in Canterbury on what they called the 'house-and-shop' basis. Gavelkind is concerned with ground, and a complexity arises when irremovable structures occupy the ground like the great stone houses which are being erected in the twelfth century. No longer can the tenant on disposing of his groundplot dismantle the house and move elsewhere. The 'house-and-shop' form of occupation seems to be less a formal custom or tenure than a private arrangement between the monks and their tenants. No doubt there were many such private arrangements made, and when a dispute arose recourse might be had, not to the borough court as in the case of ground held at gavelkind, but to the court christian on grounds of breach of faith. Charter LXVI is evidently the record produced in such a court, of such an agreement, made late in the twelfth century.

SALE AND RENTS

Some instances are found of outright sale in the twelfth century. Wibert, subprior and subsequently prior of Christ Church, buys out completely certain holders of ground along the northern fringe of the cathedral precincts, and in the stretch of ground opposite St Sepulchre's nunnery outside the city walls.[2] However, after this date it does not seem possible to produce examples of outright sale. Hemmeon comments on the general practice in boroughs whereby a vendor will retain an annual rent when disposing of property, suggesting that this practice is due to the feudal conception of tenure.[3] Early in the thirteenth century a Canterbury citizen who held ground by St Margaret's church from no one felt the fact so irregular that he assigned a penny rent to Christ Church 'quia terram illam prius de nemine tenuit'.[4]

The retained rent is regularly seen in Canterbury from the later twelfth century. The real sale-price is usually found in the concluding clause of a charter and is normally called the *gersuma* (*geresuma*, *garsuma* and variants). Hemmeon remarks that there is little constant relation between the initial payment and the retained rent, and perhaps the conditioning factor is the circumstances of the vendor at the time of sale. If he wants ready cash he

---

[1] XL. For Hemmeon's statement on the use of the term 'burgage', see discussion on the burgess-holding below.

[2] VIII, IX, X.   [3] *Burgage Tenure*, p. 80.

[4] CAC, Rental 33, ii. Note at end of roll.

will exact a large *gersuma*, and if he wants an investment he will arrange for a substantial annual payment of rent with a modest *gersuma*. The *gersuma* varies greatly. An outstanding local case of great sale-price is the one hundred and five marks paid to Roger Frese for his house in Stour Street.[1] However, this is a large stone house in a good business area, previously in the hands of the landowner Adam of Charing, and before him in the hands of Lambin Frese the moneyer.[2] It is difficult to find a comparable *gersuma* even in sales made of property in the prosperous central area around Mercery Lane. Quite exceptional is the *gersuma* of forty marks paid by Christ Church to Ralph son of Ralph de Planaz for ground on the corner of St Margaret's Street, opposite Mercery Lane, with promise of 1d. forgable, and undertaking to carry on an annual payment of 4s. 9d. to the lord of Thanington manor, and of 12d. to the nuns of St Sepulchre.[3] The grant includes 'edificia' built or to be built of wood or stone, and may be identified with the 'shops of Susanna de Planaz' (mother of Ralph) appearing henceforward in Christ Church rentals.[4] The *gersuma* with the annual rent is paid not only for ground but in cases where a rentcharge is sold. Bruning the miller sells 16d. *per annum* arising from a messuage in Westgate ward, to Eastbridge Hospital, for 11s. *gersuma* and 2d. annually.[5]

Instances may be found where the saleprice consists of, or incorporates some article in kind. Jacob the Jew in acquiring ground for his stone house, paid eight marks down together with a cloak (pallium) worth one mark, with an annual rent of 14d.[6] Prior Wibert bought ground north of the Precincts for ten shillings and a 'cuppa mazarina'.[7] Godith the widow took three ells of 'ruchet' for a dress-length for quitclaim of her free-bench.[8] Noriot of Newingate and his wife sold their ground (c. 1200) outside the city walls for 40s. *gersuma*, 1d. forgable, 6s. 8d. to Christ Church, their lord, while the wife had 12d. 'ad sotulares et ad caligas'.[9] Some examples of *gersume* and retained rents are supplied below.[10]

[1] XXXVII.
[2] XXXV, XXXVI; D 224.
[3] CAC, Ch. Ant. C 717.
[4] As in CAC, Arrears.
[5] Eastbridge Hospital Muniments, Charter A 46.
[6] LI.
[7] A 3.
[8] Cartulary of Poor Priests' Hospital, Canterbury (BM. Add. MS. 29,437), fol. 72.
[9] CAC, Reg. A, fol. 350r.
[10] Dr Veale tabulates rents with the initial premium from the borough of Bristol. It is worth noting that the retained rent has virtually disappeared by 1300. (*Great Red Book of Bristol*, Introduction, pt. i, pp. 172–9).

Ref.	Subject of grant	Gersuma	Rent p.a.	Other rents or charges
EBH Chr. A 12	messuage 'in venella Judeorum' (Stour Street)	5 M.	4s. 2d.	
EBH Chr. A 40	2s. rent from messuage in St Peter's par.	7s.	16d.	
EBH Chr. A. 62	20d. rent from ground without Westgate	12s.	4d.	
EBH Chr. J1	messuage at King's Bridge	5 M.	3d.	2s. 6d. domino fundi
CAC Reg. A. f. 376	meadow in Westgate ward	40s.	2s.	
CAC Reg. E. f. 123v.	ground at S.W. corner of Butchery Lane	2 M.	3s.	
CAC C 1113	ground 18 ft.× 10 ft., site not stated	2½ M.	12d.	
CAC Ch. Ant. C 1162	messuage outside Burgate	1 M.	½d. forgable	
CAC Ch. Ant. C 1168	ground 3 rods and 3 ft.× 16 ft. in Worthgate ward	12d.	12d.	

Various types of rents are found among the documents. The chief term found for rent arising in Canterbury is *gabulum*, gable. The term is of course not confined to this city, but here it applies properly to rent arising from ground held at the Canterbury species of gavelkind tenure. *Gabulum* is not found paid for ground held at other forms of tenure such as the 'house-and-shop' arrangement of Christ Church, when the expression used is the less-technical *redditus*. This last-mentioned term however is found applied quite frequently to gable. Another expression applied to gable is *census*. This is not common, and is usually of early date.[1] The term *supergabulum* is sometimes met with. It is usually found applied to a second rent from a tenement, from which *gabulum* is already paid, and it appears merely to have the meaning 'additional rent'. Robert 'marescallus' paid 20d. for five *mansure* to the 'ortolanus' of Christ Church while from the same holdings a certain Ivo drew 3s. 3d. *supergabulum*, bestowed by him on Christ Church for an office in the household.[2] Nigel 'piscator' paid 26s. *per annum* for a *mansura* to the sacrist, while an additional 16d. *de super-gabulo* was supplied to the monks for this holding, apparently received as a gift from Lambert Gargate, one of their benefactors.[3]

Another name applied to an additional rent is *forgabulum*. The cases in

[1] II, III (c. 1100).   [2] B 154.   [3] B 212.

which it is found seem to be parallel to those in which *supergabulum* is found. Edwin brother of Martin held an acre of ground without Worthgate (c. 1160) from the chamberlain of Christ Church for 22d. gable. This acre was granted, so it appears, to subtenants at 3s. Prior Wibert bought the ground from Edwin and it now furnished two rents, one of 22d. to the chamberlain, and another of 3s. from the tenants to the prior. The latter rent is specified as forgable.[1] Forgable is paid for ground outside Newingate in addition to ordinary gable.[2] At the end of the century Richard Deudune draws 6d. 'forgavele' from ground sold to Jacob the Jew for which other rents are due.[3]

While *forgabulum* may be merely an additional rent in the twelfth century, it seems to have a more technical significance in the thirteenth. No longer are appreciable sums like 35d. or 3s. paid as forgable, but figures like 1d. are normally exacted.[4] Sometimes it is a rent in kind, of the peppercorn class, and it is clearly now more or less symbolic, a quitrent in fact. In 2 Henry III, William son of Terric the goldsmith sold his stone house for a *gersuma* or initial payment of thirty marks, while an annual rent of 4d. only was retained by the vendor, called *forgabulum*.[5] In 30 Henry III John Ferre sold to Alan the clerk a stone wall lying between their holdings so that the latter could make a leaden gutter thereon, and carry out other construction work. John Ferre retained an annual rent of one penny, styled forgable.[6]

EVEWORK

There is a rent-service arising from a number of holdings at different points in Canterbury called 'evework'. It is exacted over and above the ordinary *gabulum*, and is usually quite small, sometimes only one farthing, though in some cases it is as great as 5½d.[7] or 6d.[8] Whenever the time of payment is named it is always Lammas (ad gulam Augusti, ad vincula sancti Petri), i.e. 1 August. The name of the payment and the date at which it is exacted strongly suggest a commuted labour-service, due at harvest-time. Such labour services are not unknown even in the older and larger boroughs. The burgesses of Leicester were released from a mowing commutation at the end of the twelfth century.[9] In 1193 the men of Lancaster secured emancipation from ploughing and other servile customs.[10]

---

[1] A 35.   [2] A 34. The tenure here is very complex and confusing.   [3] LI.
[4] See A 34, for *forgabulum* of 35d.   [5] CAC, Ch. Ant. C 715.
[6] CAC, Ch. Ant. C 749.   [7] F 386.
[8] F 373.   [9] BBC, i, p. 94.   [10] Ibid., i, p. 93; MEB, p. 84.

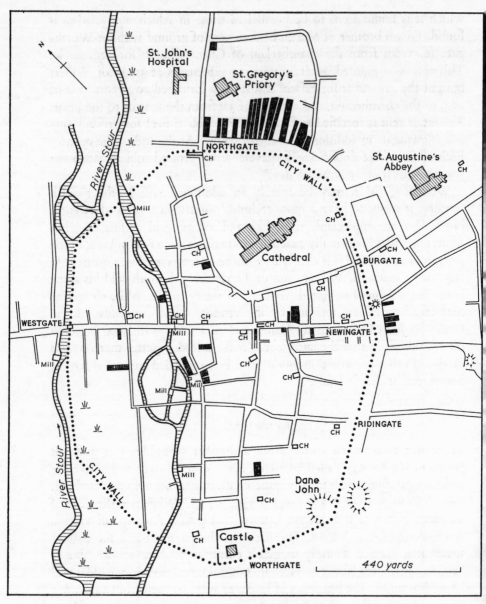

Holdings in Canterbury where Evework is due c. 1150 – c. 1230 are shown as black solids.

The Hereford Domesday remarks that within the city walls each *integra masura* had to cut crops for three days at Marden (a few miles from the walls) and for one day to collect hay wherever the sheriff might ordain.[1] At Bury St Edmunds rep-silver was exacted at Lammas as well as 'sor-' or 'schar-peni' which (in the case of the last-mentioned) amounted to 24s. *per annum*.[2] This commutation had taken place before 1212 and was due from every dwelling in the town and not (apparently) from scattered holdings, as at Canterbury.[3]

No definition of the term evework has been found. The expression seems to be confined to Canterbury, and has not been noticed among the vast mass of manorial material available for the Canterbury estates. In the earlier thirteenth century the meaning of the term has already become dimmed. The small sums due for evework are being assimilated to, or confused with, ordinary *gabulum*. As early as 1218 (or close thereto) the compiler of Rental Y speaks with some vagueness of 'redditus qui dicitur euewerch'.[4]

If evework is a commuted render it may well be asked at what time the commutation took place. There may be some significance in the fact that whereas it is not mentioned in connection with certain holdings in Rental B (c. 1166), it is in fact named as a payment in connection with the same holdings in Rental D (c. 1200). For example the corner-holding where Northgate Street joins Broad Street is held according to Rental B (at the earlier date) by the sons of Sigar Keverel for 6d. at mid-Lent.[5] About thirty-five years later Godefrid son of Keverel pays the same rent with an additional ½d. evework.[6] Further along Broad Street, Anfrid de Chelde pays 14½d. at the earlier date,[7] yet at the later date he owes an additional 2d. for evework.[8] Some of his neighbours render evework c. 1200, which cannot be traced a generation before.[9] The fact that the payment emerges in many cases (in at least thirteen in Broad Street alone)[10] between c. 1166 and the end of the century suggests that at the earlier date it was actually being performed, and that by the later it has been commuted for coin. It may again be asked, if the service was actually performed by citizens,

[1] *Herefordshire Domesday*, ed. V. H. Galbraith and J. Tait, p. 1. (PRS, NS, 25); *DB*, i, fol. 679.

[2] i.e. for the whole borough. Lobel, *Bury St Edmund's*, pp. 29–30, and notes.

[3] See below.

[4] Rental Y (in CAC, Reg. K), fol. 37v. The term disappears by about 1250, though outside the western walls, in the archbishop's manor of Westgate, there is a payment called 'evework' made, not at Lammas, but at mid-Lent, as late as 12 Edward II (Lambeth Roll, no. 1105). The payment is regularly of small sums (½d., 1d., or 1½d.).

[5] B 12. [6] D 7. [7] B 30. [8] D 46.

[9] See next note. [10] D 7, 34, 39, 41, 43, 45, 46, 48, 50, 52, 53, 54, 57.

where did they do it? Since it was due to the monks of Christ Church, the home farm of the priory at Barton, a short distance away along the Sturry Road, would seem to be an obvious place.

It will be instructive to examine the names of those who make this render. Rental F gives the names in convenient form, brought together in one group. There can be no question of servility in connection with many of the names. At the head of the list stands Susanna, wife of a man with a knightly name, Ralph de Planaz, and daughter of John son of Vivian the wealthy borough reeve, lord of hundreds of acres out in the countryside. Susanna is sister to Mary of Tolworth, whose husband is excused scutage for service at the siege of Acre and who serves on the grand assize.[1] Next is Arnold Ferre, evidently the moneyer of the name.[2] Admittedly he is on one occasion called the man (homo) of two monks, but his service to them is no more than that which might be rendered by any free man, and the monks might conceivably be described in modern terms as his clients.[3] Another man with a knightly origin paying evework is William of Shelford, apparently the lord of the hamlet overlooking the river Stour just below Canterbury. John son of Roger the alderman (also in the list) is a landowner, while John Dodekere (likewise producing evework) is a prosperous citizen who controls ground in central Canterbury, owns a great stone house, and serves as 'prepositus' of the city, in company with Geoffrey of Sturry.[4] The name of Hubert Cauvel, a member of the family descended from the first Norman borough reeve, William Cauvel, friend of St Anselm and evidently son-in-law of Vitalis, a knight depicted in the Bayeux Tapestry, will finally dispose of any suggestion that evework has necessarily a servile connotation.[5] The almoner of Christ Church, it should be pointed out, actually pays evework to the monastic treasurers.[6]

Evework at Canterbury arises in many instances from holdings outside the walls, along the fringe of the city moat (as in Broad Street), and might in such cases be interpreted as an agricultural render from ground recently absorbed into the built-up area of the city. However, this explanation can hardly suffice for evework due from holdings in the very centre of the walled area. The first occurrence of the term noted (1153 or before) is in connection with ground at Hottewell a few yards from the actual centre of the circle formed by the walls, where Ralph son of Eilwin Harm pays evework at 2d. to the cellarer of Christ Church.[7]

Rental B shows that in the sixties of the twelfth century evework was

---

[1] For J. son of Vivian and his family see pp. 64–5. [2] See p. 118.
[3] See p. 148. [4] Somner, *Canterbury*, 1703, p. 179. [5] See pp. 51, 63.
[6] F 387. [7] XI.

being collected for holdings along the outer edge of the city moat opposite Newingate,[1] and from holdings within the walls, one in each of the central parishes of All Saints[2] and St Alphage,[3] and two in the parish (likewise central) of St Andrew.[4] Rental D indicates that evework is being paid for ground-plots outside Newingate,[5] from a group of others along the city ditch towards Northgate in Broad Street (those discussed above, of which there is largely no trace in Rental B), from a holding two hundred and fifty yards without Northgate[6] (the dwelling of John the monastic cook), and from a scattered series of tenements within the walls.[7] Rental F devotes a section to evework, and discloses that there are other payments made at Lammas which are not evework,[8] while Rental Z (of c. 1230) names evework in some cases but fails to identify it every time it occurs.[9]

Confusion is clearly arising in the earlier years of the thirteenth century as to what is, or is not, evework, suggesting that there is little practical difference between this and other classes of rents, like *gabulum*. Rental Y specifies a payment of 5½d., evework due at Lammas from the heirs of Odbold to Christ Church. However, another rental of the same date excludes this amount from evework and classes it among payments of *gabulum*.[10] Rental Y gives 3d. evework due at Lammas from the heirs of William of Shelford, but this is classed as *gabulum* in Rental Z (c. 1230).[11] Sometimes evework is combined with *gabulum* without any explanation, as in the case of ground outside Newingate about 1200, from which Lambert and Simon Chig pay 13½d. and 2s. respectively.[12] A generation later Rental Z shows that the former figure is composed of 12d. gable, plus 1½d. evework,[13] while the latter is a consolidated render for 12d. gable at mid-Lent, 6d. at Easter, 4d. at Michaelmas, and 2d. at an unspecified term, probably Lammas, for evework.[14] The process which might be

---

[1] B 91, 92, 93, 94, 96. [2] B 2. [3] B 4.
[4] B 108, 109. [5] D 130, 131, 134. [6] D 25.
[7] D 17 (St Mary de Castro parish), 331 (near Westgate); 289 (in s.e. quadrant of walls). Information about evework in D may be supplemented at almost the same date from F, showing that evework arises in All Saints' Lane, flanking the river, close to King's Bridge (F 410 where 2d. evework arises from ground of Hubert Cauvel, which is next to D 308); 1d. is due to the almoner of Christ Church (F 387, 128, mentioned under D 388; the ground lies in 'Stephen's Lane', within Westgate). Evework arises from D 270 (cf. F 380, 381). F 384 mentions evework (cancelled) evidently from D 269. D 269, 270 may be the ground of Eilwin Harm at Hottemelne (XI) 50 years before.
[8] Apparently F 414 ff. [9] See below.
[10] Y (in CAC, Reg. K.) fol. 38r. calls it evework but a short early thirteenth-century outline rental in Reg. K (fol. 10v.) calls it gable. It probably is in fact gable, since (apart from F 373) it is far larger than in any other instances of evework.
[11] Y (in Reg. K) fol. 37v; Z (in Reg. K.) fol. 193r.
[12] D 129, 128 respectively. [13] Z fol. 194v. [14] Ibid.

expected, whereby evework is assimilated to, and becomes lost in, ordinary *gabulum*, seems here to be working in reverse. Perhaps a clerk with more conscience about detail, and more precise business instincts is drawing up the later rental. The normal course of events, whereby evework is absorbed into *gabulum*, may be found many times and is exemplified in the case of ground of Godere Palmere who about 1200 pays 10d. at mid-Lent, plus 2d. evework, from ground in St Peter's.[1] Some years later his daughter Sarah is paying 12d., an amalgamated render, for the same holding.[2]

The total income derived from evework is very small compared with gross takings in urban rents. In Rental B it amounts to 12½d. from nine holdings (against a rentroll affording over £17 from half of Canterbury).[3] Rental D lists 2s. 10d. from twenty-four tenements at a date when gable brings in £30 or more annually.[4] Rental F records a grand total of over £42 of which only 4s. 5¾d. is evework, derived from forty holdings,[5] while Rental Y registers 3s. 3¾d. from twenty-five against £45 or more from all Canterbury.[6]

In conclusion it must be observed that the only lord to whom evework is found paid in Canterbury is Christ Church.[7] However, there are no rentals surviving for the city other than those produced by the cathedral monks falling before c. 1220 when the term is disappearing. There are, moreover, very few charters before such a date unconnected with the cathedral.

Though Kent is claimed as an area where a money economy is advanced at an early date,[8] and a money economy might be expected to be even more advanced in its leading borough, there are many rents in kind to be found in the rentals and charters. The Welles family pay half a seam of salt for their corpus of holdings at the mid-twelfth century.[9] Chickens are found as a principal rent in kind. Even in central Canterbury as late as c. 1205 two chickens, or 2d. are due from a holding, though it is to be noticed that the render is being commuted.[10] Chickens are often specified as 'presentum' and in such cases are regularly exacted at, or about, Christmas. Four chickens are due 'de presento' for ground at St Sepulchre's outside the walls sold by the Cauvel family in 1149.[11] Two chickens classed

[1] D 336, 332.   [2] Y fol. 29v.   [3] See Index, EVEWORK (B 2, 4, etc.).
[4] Ibid. (D 7, 25, etc.).   [5] F 373 ff.
[6] Y fol. 44r. The total evework from holdings listed in Rental Z apparently amounts to 2s. 3½d. from seventeen holdings, at a time (c. 1230) when gable amounts to about £44 p.a. But, as shown above, evework is in some instances concealed in gable.
[7] As shown above, the archbishop receives it for some holdings outside the city walls.
[8] Cf. *VCH, Kent*, iii, p. 342; R. A. L. Smith, *Canterbury Cathedral Priory*, p. 113.
[9] B 208.   [10] F 54.   [11] VIII.

as 'presentum' are rendered for ground in Wincheap in the thirteenth century,[1] and one and a half chickens are likewise due 'de presento' nearby.[2] Among rents in kind must be included the ploughshare paid for the small island under the north-western city walls. This ploughshare is in process of being commuted c. 1200 and is appreciated at 2d.[3] It is significant that this is due to the manor of Westgate, to which the island is contiguous, and may be classed with the ploughshares used as rent out in the Kentish countryside.

RELIEF

'From this incident,' says Hemmeon, 'the older and larger boroughs were free in the age of charters and custumals, and, using the term in its exact sense of a payment of money from an heir previous to his entering on an inherited estate, it seems that most of them, if not all, had always been free.'[4] Canterbury forms an exception to this generalization, since relief is found there. If however Hemmeon means exclusively relief paid to the lord of the borough the assertion seems valid. The king, as lord, takes no relief (as far as can be traced) for the vast mass of holdings, and no reference to reliefs is embodied in the list of profits from Canterbury contributory to the royal farm, though varying and unpredictable amounts such as tolls and profits of courts are estimated.[5] If however no trace has been found of relief taken by the king (or the 'prepositi' of the city), in respect of holdings directly under his control, yet these holdings are very few in number, and instances where relief is taken would likewise be very few.[6] Others among the greater boroughs knew relief, such as Leicester, where it was abolished by the lord, Earl Robert (1119–68).[7] At Derby, the charter of Henry II forbade the 'prepositus' to take *relevamen* from the sons of burgesses except at a figure which was tolerable, so that they should not be ruined, and so that they might do the king's service.[8]

We are in an exceptional position for the study of relief in Canterbury since the monastic treasurers of Christ Church, who controlled more than a third of the tenements in the city, kept lists of reliefs taken from

---

[1] CAC, Ch. Ant., C 924. [2] Ibid., C 928.
[3] C 23; D 375; F 55; G 24. Note that the word ploughshare has been cancelled in F (c. 1205) and the alternative money render left in the entry.
[4] *Burgage Tenure*, pp. 18–19. [5] Appendix A.
[6] C 2, 39; G 2, 37. See pp. 40–8.
[7] BBC, i, p. 117.
[8] *Cartulary of Darley Abbey*, ed. R. R. Darlington, Introduction, p. l. See remarks on subject of relief, ibid. p. lxvii.

1215 until 1313.[1] Some of these reliefs, though appearing under the heading *relevia*, are more in the nature of an entry-fine than a relief proper, since they are exacted from a purchaser on the sale of a holding, as well as from heirs. It will be found in either case that the amount taken is normally equal to one year's rent.

Rentals Y and Z (c. 1218 and c. 1230 respectively) fall in date within the period during which yearly lists of reliefs were kept. Consequently we might expect to find all the holdings in such rentals mentioned sooner or later in the lists. However, this is by no means the case. No more than about one third of the entries in the rentals finds a corresponding entry in the Reliefs. It does not seem, therefore, as if every tenement in Canterbury were liable for relief. However, it has not proved possible to discover what conditioning factor is involved. Perhaps some tenants managed to establish exemption for their holdings.

There is an occasional mention of relief in the rentals. A marginal note to § 504 in Rental F (relating to ground at Worthgate) indicates that relief is behind (retro). Relief is sometimes, but not often, mentioned in charters. Edmund son of Gilbert 'de aula' grants rent arising from a 'mesuagium' in St Alphage parish, to St John's altar in Christ Church (c. 1220) 'cum omni iure', he says, 'quod ego . . . vel heredes mei ibidem habuimus vel habere potuimus in redditibus releuiis et eschaetis et in omnibus aliis rebus'.[2] About the same time Cecilia, widow of William Silvestre, and daughter of Solomon the mercer, grants to John Turte 6s. 8d. rent from a house in Mercery Lane 'cum pertinenciis scilicet in releuiis'.[3] Christina daughter of Brictieva Blakestre of Wincheap, who was in severe financial straits, granted all her property to her son and daughter-in-law on condition they should pay her considerable debts to the Jews and should also pay the treasurers of Christ Church 60s. 'pro arreragiis gabuli et releuiorum'.[4]

Sometimes charters specify relief due. The charter of c. 1100 whereby ground of Christ Church is granted to William Calvel and heirs without the southern walls gives the rent as 52s. and lays down that when Calvel is dead his heirs shall pay 20s. 'pro redemptione'.[5] The relief here is not, it will be noticed, equal in this case to a year's rent. Charter LXV (1205 or after) discloses arrangements made for relief to be paid at different tenurial levels. John son of John Corbeile holds ground in St Mildred's parish of the

---

[1] Cathedral Library, Lit. MS. D 4; the Reliefs may also be found in the annual treasurers' accounts (CAC, Misc. Accts., I).

[2] CAC, Ch. Ant., C 727.   [3] CAC, Reg. A, fol. 416v.

[4] CAC, Ch. Ant., C 924.   [5] II, III.

fee of Luke of Lower Hardres. John, the tenant, sells the ground to Eudo son of Sigar, who is to pay a *gersuma* of 20s. and a rent of 4d. and 'post decessum' the sum of 4d. *de relevamine*. At the same time the purchaser is to pay 2s. *per annum* to Luke, 1s. *per annum* to Paulinus, probably brother of Luke, with a like sum in relief to each of them or their heirs. The vendor, John, is evidently making the purchaser responsible for services he himself owes to his lords.

Several minor points of interest can be drawn from the list of reliefs. Adam, son of Walter the baker of St Gregory's priory, joined the newly-arrived Franciscans and his brother John paid relief, so it appears, on taking up his holding.[1] One tenant of Christ Church was apparently hanged, and when in accordance with Kentish custom the heirs succeeded after the father 'had gone to the bough', they paid relief as in the case of natural death.[2]

Ref.	Tenant	Annual rent	Relief, as entered in the annual treasurers' lists (Lit. MS. D 4)
Rental D 171	Gunnild Clut	2s.	1215. De Philippo de Tanintune pro terra quadam que fuit Gunilde relicte Clut ii sol.
Rental D 304	Jacob the Jew	6d.	1216. De filiis Jacobi Judei xvi d.
Rental D 305	Jacob the Jew	10d.	
Rental D 1	Sister of Roger f. Hamel	6d.	1216. De herede Rogeri filii Marie vj d.
Rental Z, fol. 200v.	Heirs of Simon Munin	3s. at mid-Lent 3s. at Christmas	1217. De heredibus Simon Munin vi s.
Rental D 227	Henry Deremai	6d.	1216. De terra que fuit Henrici filii Diremai vi d.
Rental D 15	Lieveva wid. of Conrad	8d.	1225. De Waltero filio Liueue relicte Conradi viii d. post mortem eiusdem Liueue.

GAVELET

'The extreme reluctance of ancient law to deprive a tenant of his tenement merely because he has not paid rent is shown by the gavelet procedure of

[1] Reliefs, in Lit. MS. D 4, 1232. 'De Johanne filio Walteri pistoris de sancto Gregorio ix d. post Adam fratrem suum qui est de ordine fratrum minorum.'
[2] This appears to be the interpretation of the entry in the reliefs under 1228: 'De heredibus Mauricii suspensi xij d.'

the Kentish custom.'[1] This process may be found with modifications in Canterbury. The definition embodied in the *Consuetudines Kanciæ*[2] runs as follows:

And they also claim that if any tenant of gavelkind hold back the rent or the service of the tenement which he holds from his lord, the lord, by award of the court from three weeks to three weeks, should seek for the distress upon that tenement until the fourth court, always by witnesses. And if within that time he find no distress upon that tenement by which he can have justice of his tenant, then at the fourth court it should be awarded that he take that tenement into hands in the name of distress just as an ox or a cow, and hold it for a year and a day in his hands without tilling it, within which term if the tenant come and offer his arrears and make reasonable amends for withholding [his dues] then he should have and enjoy his tenements as before. And if he do not come before the year and the day pass, then the lord should go to the next county [court] following by witnesses of his court and cause this process to be pronounced so he may have witnesses, and by award of his court, after that county court has been held, he shall enter and till those lands and tenements as in his own demesne. And if the tenant come afterwards and wish to have his tenements again and to hold them as before, he should make agreement with his lord, as is anciently said:

> Neghe syþe selde
> and neghe syþ gelde:
> and fif pond for þe were,
> er he bicome healder[3]

There is an early mention of gavelet in Canterbury in the charter of Ralph Harm whereby he cedes *mansure* at Hottewelle in central Canterbury to Wibert the sub-prior of Christ Church (in or before 1153). The charter embodies a clause safeguarding the grantee if the rent is not paid and the holding thereby becomes 'gavellate'.[4] Rental D (just over half a

---

[1] Pollock and Maitland, *Hist. Eng. Law*, i, p. 355, n. 1.

[2] The procedure for distress is not actually called 'gavelet' in the *Consuetudines Kanciæ*, but clearly it is in fact. The version given here is the translation in *VCH, Kent*, iii, p. 326. It is to be found in Lambard, *Perambulation of Kent*, ed. of 1596, pp. 553, 581–3. See Sandys, *Gavelkind*, pp. 10–13, 248–51; Somner, *Gavelkind*, ed. of 1726, pp. 31–32. See also Jolliffe, *Prefeudal England*, p. 37; Pollock and Maitland, *Hist. Eng. Law*, i, 355, n.; ii, 271. Dr Neilson has apparently accepted 'gavelet' as a term for a customary rent (*Oxford Studies in Social and Legal History*, ii, p. 47).

[3] This is the version of the formula as given in Sandys, *Gavelkind*, p. 13. There are slightly differing versions of the verse passage. See Sandys, op. cit., pp. 249–50. There is a Latin rendering in the memoranda book of prior Henry of Eastry (BM. MS. Cotton Galba E. IV, fol. 45). The scribe fails to make a reasonably intelligible translation of the lines, lending point to Maitland's observation that the scribes of the fourteenth century could not understand these traditional verses (*Hist. Eng. Law*, ii, p. 271). Maitland suggests that the tenant is perhaps meant to pay eighteen times (ibid., i, p. 355 n.). [4] XI.

century later) shows that there are dwellings which lie gavelet in Canterbury c. 1200, one within Burgate and another without Newingate.[1]

Christ Church, as lord, invoked the process of gavelet on non-payment of rent in Canterbury. The ancient poetic formula names large sums and conditions which seem designed to make re-entry by a defaulting tenant impossible. However, a case of 1230 suggests that the possible return of a tenant was a contingency of which a lord must take due regard, even after a decree of gavelet. One John Saule held ground of Christ Church in St Mary Magdalen parish at 13s. 4d. The rent fell into arrears and the ground was declared gavelet (presumably in the borough court), as from Michaelmas 1230. Saule had died in the meantime, and indeed it is possible that the non-payment is due to his death. However, the monks were dubious about their right to treat the ground as their own. The issue was complicated by the fact that there was a ruinous building on the site. This did not necessarily belong to the monks, and the decree was concerned only with the ground. They were in a quandary for if they repaired the structure at their own expense and the heirs came back, they might lose their outlay. To solve the problem, the treasurers, with the consent of their brethren in Chapter, sold land and building to one John Brand, making express provision safeguarding the rights of John Saule's heirs, should they come again, willing to accept responsibility for the unpaid rents (and presumably the other charges expressed in the verse) and to satisfy John Brand for any repairs he might have carried out.[2]

---

[1] D 91, 137.

[2] Rental Z, fol. 196r. '. . . hec terra fuit gavellate a festo sancti Michaelis anno domini m⁰ cc⁰ xxx⁰. Et quoniam domus desuper penitus deperiit nec volumus [i.e. the monks of Christ Church] eam sumptibus nostris reparare, concessimus hanc terram Iohanni Brand de consensu capituli tenendam de nobis pro iiii s. salvo iure heredum Iohannis Saule si venerint ad respondendum nobis de arreragiis a predicto termino et ad satisfaciendum ei de reparacione edificii.' The cathedral treasurers' accounts for the year 1232–33 record a part-payment of 9s. 4d. 'pro terra Johannis Saule quam vendidimus, salvo cuiuslibet iure, Johanni Brand' (CAC, Misc. Accts., I, sub anno). The term gavelet has not been noticed in Canterbury after the middle of the thirteenth century, though the same or a very similar process may be found at later dates. The prior of Christ Church sued in the borough court of 1294 for possession of 31 tenements in the city, whereof the rent was in arrears. The borough court decreed possession to the prior for a year and a day 'nomine districcionis'. If any defaulting tenant came back prepared to pay the rent in future, and make security for paying the arrears, then he was to have his holding back. At the end of the year and a day the prior was to sue again for the holdings where satisfaction had not been given 'et tunc fiet predicto priori iudicium de seisina secundum consuetudinem civitatis'. Judgment in connection with certain tenements was restricted as the heirs were under age. (From a contemporary transcript of the borough court roll, CAC, Ch. Ant. C 79.) By c. 1400 the civic version of gavelet has disappeared and recourse is had to the ordinary writ 'cessavit per biennium' (rolls of borough court transcribed in CAC, Reg. A, fol. 340v).

THE STATUS OF THE INHABITANTS OF CANTERBURY

The status of the citizens does not appear to have been in any wise lowly in relation to their lords, lay or clerical. Naturally there is a degree of respect to rank and cloth, but apart from this the average citizen has no great regard for his lord and, since he can buy and sell without restraint, he can change his lord, a fact not likely to breed feelings of deference. He may have been responsible at an early stage for the work-service called 'eve-work', but this has been extensively commuted by the earlier thirteenth century. It is unlikely that much humility can have been displayed by some of the wealthy moneyers and goldsmiths, or Jewish financiers, to indigent local knights who came trying to raise a loan. Before the end of the twelfth century the citizens were prepared to take sides against the monks of Christ Church, the greatest lords in the city, a practice they kept up until the end of the Middle Ages. Since the citizens controlled the borough-moot, all lords with ground in Canterbury must come to them as humble suppliants for justice as occasion called.

The writer of one of the *Epistolæ Cantuarienses* speaks in patronizing tones of a leading citizen. At a juncture in the controversy over the secular college at Hackington the monks sent a deputation to archbishop Baldwin. This consisted of two monks with their three 'men' (homines eorum), one of them being Arnold Ferre.[1] Arnold was no menial for he was a citizen of some consequence, probably a moneyer. He subscribed six marks to the Canterbury tallage of 1198,[2] served on the inquisition into the mint of the abbot of St Augustine's in 1189,[3] and in due course appears as one of the joint borough reeves.[4] Perhaps the superiority of the monks was no more than that of clerks over a layman.

There are one or two cases where some degree of subservience in a citizen to churchmen can be disclosed. Professor Tait cites the case in 893 where King Ethelwulf conveys in conjunction with two weirs on the Stour 'unum merkatorem quem . . . lingua nostra *mangere* nominamus', but goes on to say that it would be rash to infer that this 'monger' was personally unfree.[5] There are two remarkable parallels to this grant in the twelfth century. Prior Wibert (1153–67) gave to Emma of Whiteacre and her husband, in exchange for ground north of the Precincts, other ground in Stour Street in central Canterbury, together with the tenant thereof. 'He gave,' says the record, 'to the said Emma and Geoffrey her husband,

---

[1] *Epp. Cant.* no. cccxxvi, p. 311. See D 121, 282, 352.
[2] PR, 10 Richard I, pp. 207–9.   [3] See account of moneyers, p. 118.
[4] Greg., no. 42.   [5] Birch, *CS*, 426; MEB, p. 11.

Ralph surnamed Hearm, with his *mansura* at Hottemelne' and arranged for him to pay a rent equal to rent lost by Emma and Geoffrey.[1] It seems highly improbable that Ralph can have been personally unfree. All that the above may mean may well be that a tenant's holding has been exchanged over his head.

Philip, lord of Hardres some six miles from Canterbury, had a tenant in the city, on ground in St Alphage parish, named Hugh Fagard. Philip took the cross, probably in 1189, and before departing for the Holy Land granted in pure and perpetual alms to God, St Thomas and the monks of Christ Church his ground mentioned above, 'and the aforesaid Hugh [so he says] have I offered up on the tomb of Blessed Thomas the same day that I received the cross at the hands of Geoffrey the subprior, in the presence of many folk standing by and watching'.[2] Again, it is improbable that the tenant can have been unfree. His lord was going off on an expedition from which he might never return and it was important to publicize the conveyance. Hugh was a servant of Christ Church and was all the more likely to acquiesce, if he had any emotions on the subject.

THE BURGESS HOLDING

Domesday Book uses a variety of terms to refer to holdings in Canterbury, such as *domus*,[3] *mansura*,[4] *masura*[5] and *haga*.[6] The expression *burgensis* can clearly connote a dwelling.[7] In the twelfth century *mansura* is found, as in Rental B (c. 1166), where the word is employed with great frequency. At the beginning of the next century the compilers of D and F favour the more imprecise *terra*, even where dwellings are clearly involved. The terms *tenementum*, *mesagium* (with variants thereof) are frequently found in charters, while the dwelling of Lambert Garegate (and this alone in Canterbury) in Burgate Street is called 'managium'.[8] The term 'haw' so much used in Domesday may be found surviving as late as the end of the twelfth century.[9] Of Hemmeon's affirmation: 'Except in the founded boroughs [messuage] ... was the term for an urban tenement in mediaeval England: "burgage" referred to the tenure,' Professor Darlington (in his discussion of the borough of Derby) points out that this can hardly be

---

[1] A 3; XI. Hottemelne is only a few yards from the centre of the circle formed by the walls.

[2] LV.   [3] *DB*, i, fol. 2r.   [4] Ibid.

[5] Ibid., fol. 3v.   [6] Ibid., fol. 10r, v; 14v.

[7] Ibid., fol. 2r. King Edward had 51 *burgenses* of whom eleven were 'vastati' in the fortifications.

[8] XXI–XXIII. Christ Church, Canterbury, has a 'managium' in Norwich (X 2, fol. 22v).

[9] XL.

correct for 'burgage' is in fact found specifying actual holdings in that borough.[1] 'Burgage' seems to be foreign to Canterbury in either sense. It is found there only in a few instances, and then confined to tenure.[2]

The Canterbury burgess-holding exhibits nothing of the symmetry to be encountered in a founded borough. If at a remote date there were holdings of a roughly equal size, yet in the absence of any observable restraint upon mobility, there has been every kind of amalgamation, subdivision and accumulation, so that holdings are, by the age of the rentals, of all different shapes and sizes.

THE HOUSE OF JACOB THE JEW

Owing to the plentiful materials at Canterbury it would be possible to compile a history of a large number of individual tenements in the borough from the twelfth century to the end of the Middle Ages, and thus throw a great light on the question of tenures. The early history of one holding (perhaps abnormally complex) is presented below. The fact is underlined that the burgess-holding in Canterbury, and no doubt in all ancient boroughs, is not a unity, unchanged and unchanging from the earliest times, but has an organic growth, can be broken up, added to, combined with adjacent ground, and cut up again with no reference to its one-time components, until all trace of any original arrangement is completely obliterated.

The holding selected is the house of Jacob the Jew.[3] Towards 1180 there were, running from the eastern corner of Stour Street (Heathen-men-lane), three groundplots, which we will call A (on the corner), B, and C. The last-mentioned had a frontage of 20 feet on the High Street (D 304).

A. This was granted (Charter XLIX) by Richard Deudone (evidently the moneyer of the name, see p. 116), to Jacob for 8½ marks down as *geresumia* and 4s. 6d. *p.a.* The ground was held by R. Deudone from John son of Vivian the borough reeve. There is mention of 6d. 'forgavele', which seems to be the annual profit made by R. Deudone, who apparently paid 4s. *p.a.* to his lord, J. s. of Vivian (4s. being the rent later taken by Susanna de Planaz, J. s. of Vivian's daughter; see below).

B. This (second from the corner) was held for 8d. *p.a.* from the same J. s. of Vivian, by Thomas s. of Osbert. J. s. of Vivian now grants (Charter L), this ground to Jacob, to be held direct from him (J. s. of Vivian) and heirs. It is disclosed that Jacob has already been holding the ground

---

[1] *Burgage Tenure*, p. 61 n.; *Cartulary of Darley Abbey*, ed. R. R. Darlington, pp. lxiii–lxiv.
[2] E.g. XL.   [3] This is today substantially represented by the County Hotel.

from Thomas s. of Osbert at 8d. Thomas has apparently made no profit, except by incidents such as relief. J. s. of Vivian exacts a purchase price of 40s. but is uncertain of his title, for he promises to return this sum if unable to warrant the ground to Jacob.

C. The third groundplot from the corner is held from Christ Church by Benedict son of Thol at 6d. *p.a.* Benedict grants the ground (Charter LI) to Jacob for 14d. *p.a.* and 8d. marks down as *geresumia*, plus a 'pallium', worth one mark.

The Christ Church rental of c. 1180 (X 2, fol. 5v.) incorporates entries showing 6d. taken 'de terra Beneit filii Toli' (clearly D 304, which is C above). X 2 (ibid.) also shows 10d. being paid by Thomas son of 'Osbern' 'de terra ubi Jacobus Judeus manet' (B above). B and C can be seen in D (305, 304).

Having acquired the three holdings Jacob threw them into one and built thereon his stone house, of which substantial traces still remain below ground-level. Rental F shows the sons of Jacob living here about 1205 (F 171, 172). They paid relief to the monks in 1216 on the holding at 16d., i.e. equal to the combined rent due to Christ Church from B and C (10d. and 6d.).[1] Before long Aaron and Samuel, sons of Jacob the Jew, sold the ground to Christ Church, probably for £17 15s. 7d. a figure entered in the Treasurers' Accounts for 1216–17 'pro domo Judeorum'.[2] Susanna de Planaz had by now succeeded to the holdings and rents of her father, John son of Vivian. She now issued two charters:[3]

1. Confirming sale to Christ Church by Aaron and Samuel of ground held by them from Alice, daughter of R. Deudune (grantor of A, above, the corner holding) and of another tenement held by Aaron and Samuel from herself, evidently B above. She reserves right to 4s. rent, apparently the 4s. 6d. once exacted by her father from the mesne tenant R. Deudune minus 6d. 'forgavele'.

2. Susanna's second charter confirms to Christ Church ground of Aaron and Samuel between ground of Alice, d. of R. Deudune (i.e. A, above) and ground of the said A. and S., held of Christ Church (C, above). Susanna exacts a *gersuma* of 20s. and reserves right to 32d. *p.a.* This figure is not explained but looks like the old rent of 8d. multiplied by four, taken by her father J. s. of Vivian for B above, to which this confirmation must refer.

The outpayments made by the monks to Susanna de Planaz after acquiring the house may be read in their schedules *pro defensione terrarum*

[1] Reliefs, *sub anno.*   [2] Treas. Accts., in CAC, Misc. Accts., I, *sub anno.*
[3] CAC, Reg. A, fol. 357.

in Rental Y. The sum of 4s. is paid 'pro . . . parte mesagii quod fuit . . . Jacobi Judei', while 32d. is further paid 'pro quadam parte mesagii quod fuit Jacobi Judei'.[1] The same schedule shows that Christ Church, by acquiring the house of Jacob, has become responsible for the old 6d. 'forgavele' due from the westernmost element in the dwelling (A above), to Alice d. of R. Deudune, original grantor of A.

Having got the great stone house into their hands the monks forthwith let it to a fresh tenant, another Jew, named Cressel, who pays a rent of 11s.[2] This is the house which the lord Edmund gave to his 'valettus' Nicholas Raven after the expulsion of the Jews, for one rose 'forgable' at the feast of the translation of St Thomas, to be rendered up on the same tenement.[3] By the date of the expulsion the holding has apparently been divided up and part joined with vacant ground nearby.[4]

[1] Y, ff. 57r. 59r.   [2] Rental Z, fol. 198r.
[3] CAC, Reg. A, fol. 360v.
[4] K.R. Exchequer Accts., 249/30, printed Adler, *Jews of Medieval England*, p. 116.

CHAPTER VII

The Monks and their Servants: Relations with the Citizens

THE names of several monks may be found in the rentals and charters. In the fifties and sixties of the twelfth century we have (in Rentals A and B), Germanus, Ernulph, Arnold, Henry, James, John, Matthew Prekepelse, Stephen, Julian and Gervase. About 1200 we find (in Rentals D and F), Gervase again, Henry (probably a different Henry from the one above), Nigel, Simon, James of Flanders, Solomon, called 'nephew of George the chamberlain', and a second Solomon, son of William of Hackington. The charters supply the names of Ælric, Alexander, 'ortulanus' (both in 1152), Augustine the cellarer (c. 1176), and Ralph, subsacrist, also c. 1176.[1]

Two of these names are of some degree of interest. Gervase the monk, so it may be learned both from Rentals B and D, brought with him as patrimony when he joined the brethren at Christ Church, two *mansure* in 'Baggeberi', in the northern suburbs of Canterbury.[2] As no differentiation is supplied, we may assume that there was only one monk of the name in the cloister at the period. In such case we evidently have here the historian, Gervase of Canterbury, who gives information about his career which does not conflict in any way with this proposed identification. He was professed, so he tells us, 16 February 1163 at the hands of Becket himself,[3] and was alive as late as c. 1210, as is indicated by internal evidence in the *Gesta Regum*.[4] Another man of letters dwelling in the cloister of Christ Church in the later twelfth century was Nigel called 'Wireker', the

---

[1] See Index to Documents, MONACHI. Since the Henry of about 1166 (in Rental B) was father to the borough reeve of that date, it is unlikely that he can still be a monk about 1200. The lists of monks compiled by W. G. Searle are incomplete (*Cambridge Antiquarian Society*, 8vo series, XXXIV, 1902). He did not exhaust printed materials (for example, the obituaries in appendices viii, xii in Dart, *Canterbury Cathedral*). He seems to have examined none of the MSS. at Canterbury apart from Causton's obituary (Lit. D 12).

[2] B 54, 55; D 26, 28.

[3] Gervase, *Opera*, RS, i, p. 173. Stubbs discusses the various Gervases of the age (Introd.).

[4] R. L. Poole in *DNB*.

satirical poet. Rental D, with Rental F, mentions ground next to St Margaret's church occupied by Agatha de Sarneis, sister of Nigel 'our monk'.[1] Again (as in the case of Gervase) the absence of any qualifying additional name will suggest that this last-mentioned Nigel and the poet are the same man, and we can assume that Agatha's brother is the author of the *Speculum Stultorum* and is precentor of Christ Church. Some additional information may be recovered about the family of Nigel 'our monk'. His sister is called (c. 1180) Agatha, 'filia Gileberti de Sarneis',[2] who is apparently the Gilbert de Sarnais attesting Charter IX (relating to ground at St Sepulchre's, a few hundred yards from the site of Agatha's holding), in company with a Robert 'de Sarnaia', in 1152. Gilbert de Sarnais may with little reserve be accepted as the father of Nigel the monk, who must be brother, not only of Agatha, but of the Ivo son of Gilbert de Sarnais, whose son Nigel bought ground held of St Mildred's church, Canterbury, towards 1200.[3] A short pedigree may be suggested as follows: Gilbert de Sarnais (fl. c. 1150), who had, probably, a kinsman called Robert, was father of three children: Agatha, Ivo and Nigel the monk. Ivo had a son Nigel. Nigel the satirist remarks that he had been in Normandy. Moreover William de Longchamps, with whom Nigel was intimate, and whose kinsman he may have been, was a Norman.[4]

There is a tendency to depict a great monastery as a rival to an adjoining

---

[1] D 266; F 257, 495.   [2] X 2, fol. 13v.   [3] LXVII.

[4] See *Anglo-Latin Satirical Poets*, ed. Wright, RS, i, p. 203; Nigel de Longchamps, *Speculum Stultorum*, ed. J. H. Mozley and R. R. Raymo. It has been suggested by Mr Mozley (in 'Nigel Wirekere or Wetekera', *Modern Language Review*, xxii, 1932, pp. 314–17) that Bale, with whom the name Wireker seems to originate, misread a form 'Wetekre', 'Wetekere', i.e. the hamlet of Whiteacre, lying in Waltham, a few miles s.w. from Canterbury. Convincing support for the theory is offered by an entry in the fine rental of Canterbury holdings at London entered in CAC, Reg. K (fol. 68), where it is stated that ground was bought in Southwark (on behalf of the monastery) by 'Nigellus monachus de Wetehekere'. Whiteacre appears to have given a name to the family of Emma of Wettekera, holding ground north of the Cathedral Precincts (A 6). See p. 59 above. Her husband was Geoffrey de Lisores. William de Longchamps, the supposed kinsman of Nigel the poet, takes a name from Longchamps, just north of Étrepagny, close to Les Andelys. The village of Lisors (canton Lyons-la-Forêt) lies seven miles from Longchamps and Étrepagny. A strong suggestion that Nigel the poet, kinsman so it appears of the Canterbury family of Sarnais, is in fact connected with the family of Emma of Whiteacre (de Lisores), is the existence of Sarness Farm in Waltham, half a mile from Whiteacre. However, Wallenberg, *Place-Names of Kent*, (p. 551), found medieval forms only such as Sarnell. A Norman place of origin for the family called Sarnai(s) near Longchamps or elsewhere has been sought without success. Highly suggestive of a connection between the Sarnai(s) family and Waltham is the presence as witness to a grant there c. 1200, of Ivo, son of Gilbert of Sarnai (Greg., no. 151). See Charter LXVII, and note. If Nigel is related to the Whiteacres, could the Emma to whom he addresses ten lines in a collection of his poems (BM. MS. Cotton, Vespasian D XIX) be Emma of W.? I am grateful to Mr Mozley for engaging in a discussion of this topic.

borough, with little common ground apart from quarrels. Certainly in the case of Canterbury any rivalry must have been tempered by the fact that there were strong family ties and connections of blood between citizens and monks, for many Canterbury families gave a kinsman to the cloister of Christ Church. William of Hackington (lord of the suburban manor) has a son there;[1] the Sarnais family have a brother, evidently the precentor; Hamo the borough-reeve has his father there;[2] one Aaron, holding ground in Old Ruttington Lane, has an uncle Stephen among the brethren,[3] while William the goldsmith is brother to the monk Arnold, evidently the Arnold called 'aurifaber', who summoned up courage to return to the site of Becket's murder after the departure of the knights. Arnold may have been a goldsmith when *in sæculo* and have retained the title when he became a monk.[4] Walter the monk has (c. 1180) a brother (unnamed) out in Canterbury.[5] His contemporary Gilebert the monk has a sister (Reeingard) with ground in the city,[6] while Nicholas the monk, another contemporary, has a brother John among the citizens.[7] The leading citizen, Terric or Theoric, the goldsmith and financier in the days of John, had three sons, William, Philip and John. The last two lead a busy life in the world, while their brother seems to lead a life hardly less busy in religion. He acquired the title 'Master', so had perhaps been to the schools, or possibly, in view of his business ability, was a trained lawyer.[8] We know he had taken the cowl in Christ Church by 1219, for the cathedral treasurers then spent money on him in his illness.[9] He was connected in some capacity with Christ Church by 1216, for he was acting at that date as collector for money derived from the sale of French wine (the wine of St Thomas drawn by the monks from the vineyard at Poissy, the benefaction established by Louis VII).[10] He was concerned in the quarrel with archbishop Edmund in 1239,[11] was one of the eligors of archbishop Boniface,[12] and was chamberlain of the house by 1244.[13] He did a good deal of miscellaneous business for the house, acting as 'nuncius brevium defunctorum' in 1249.[14] Long after his death he was remembered by the brethren through his silver-gilt cup in use among them.[15]

---

[1] F 55.   [2] B 100, 213.   [3] B 175.
[4] X 2, fol. 5v; B 4. *Materials*, iii, p. 148 (FitzStephen).
[5] X 2, fol. 4r.   [6] Ibid., fol. 7v.   [7] Ibid., fol. 10r.
[8] For Theoderic, Terric, the goldsmith see pp. 112, 118. For his family see pp. 174–6.
[9] CAC, Misc. Accts., I, *sub anno*.
[10] Ibid. *sub anno*. For the wine of St Thomas, see *Litteræ Cantuarienses*, RS, i, pp. lxxvi ff.
[11] Gervase, *Opera*, RS, ii, p. 153.   [12] Ibid., p. 186.
[13] CAC, Accounts of Prior/Assisa Scaccarii, 1244.
[14] CAC, Domestic Economy, no. 1.   [15] See p. 113 above.

There are several late professions at Canterbury, as elsewhere. Rental B names as monk one Henry, father of Hamo 'prepositus' of Canterbury.[1] His patrimony consisted of property within the Newingate (held by his son). This is patently a case of late conversion, as must be that of Lambert Gargate, who is found witnessing charters and performing other business at the mid-century. He assumed the habit on his deathbed, and bestowed many scattered pieces of property on the house of his adoption.[2] John Calderun, a leading citizen, retired to the cloister (about 1176), when his wife was still alive, arranging for her to receive a daily corrody of food at the monastic kitchen, together with a periodic issue of raiment.[3] The Shadwell fragment (c. 1180?) remarks of ground near Crinemelne in the south-western quadrant of the city, that it was given by Joseph the priest 'pro Geldewino patre suo'. It sounds as if a son has provided patrimony for his father on the occasion of a late conversion.[4]

The patrimony brought by recruits to the cloister may many times be identified. The case of Geldwin, father of Joseph, has been noticed and, as we have seen, Henry father of Hamo the borough reeve brought property at Newingate, while Gervase the historian brought dwellings in the northern suburbs. Ground close to St Peter's church had been given (so the rentlist of c. 1180 remarks) with Wibert the monk. Could he have been the famous prior?[5] John son of Mary and of Walter 'de sartrino' brought a house near the back gate of the monastery. This John must be John the clerk son of Mary, a member of the *familia* of archbishop Theobald.[6] James of Flanders brought ground in Best Lane in central Canterbury,[7] while Solomon nephew of George the chamberlain brought other ground in Crienemeldnelane, not far off.[8] The island outside the western walls (the modern Miller's Field) was given by William of Hackington with his son.[9] When Geoffrey son of Luke the mercer became a monk, his brother joined with him in giving ground near St Alphage church.[10]

Professor Knowles has shown that the servants of a great monastic house were commonly equal in number to the monks.[11] This seems to be the case at Canterbury. Christ Church was one of the largest houses in the country and the ménage there in the twelfth century was little short of a scandal. There is a schedule at Lambeth[12] confirming in a remarkable way

---

[1] B 215; D 126.   [2] XX, XXIV; B 84.   [3] XLVII, XLVIII.
[4] CAC, Shadwell MSS., no. 13.   [5] X 2, fol. 14r.
[6] B 126; XVII. See Saltman, *Theobald*, Charter no. 35.
[7] D 293.   [8] F 55.   [9] Ibid.
[10] Z (fol. 197v) describes the ground as 'terram quam Godefridus filius Luce mercerii monachus noster et Robertus frater eius dederunt nobis'.
[11] *Monastic Order*, pp. 439–41.   [12] MS. 1212, ff. 356–65.

that in this house the servants were in fact equal in number to their masters. This schedule is the result of an enquiry of 1276, giving the state of affairs in this year, but it is clear that it refers back to a point of time long before, even beyond living memory, since it is observed that the establishment was set down 'as far as it could be found out' and that there was no one 'who knew completely what it ought to be'. The schedule (so it appears) reflects conditions at least early in the thirteenth century, and very likely within the twelfth century, in the age of the rentals. The number of servants does in fact amount to about one hundred, the exact number not being ascertainable since the precise figure for some juniors is not given. Among the various departments the sacristry takes pride of place with fifty-one servants. Some few unimportant people owe no particular allegiance, while the remainder are distributed among the department of the cellarer, the 'chamber', and the prior's household. At the top of the scale stand great men like the 'magister cocus' and the 'camerarius prioris', while at the other end the list tails off into part-time staff such as the cleaner-out of the main drain who came to do his job on Mondays, a pot-maker, getting a specific issue of food for every dozen pots produced, a washerwoman, given a meal every time the laundry came back, and other casual workers and odd-job men.

The names of many servants may be found in the Rentals and charters. About 1166 we find Eadmer Checherelle 'our servant',[1] Bartholomew 'dapifer' or 'senescallus',[2] Thomas 'our servant',[3] Vavasur 'our servant',[4] also called 'the cook',[5] Dunstan, servant,[6] Godefrid the baker,[7] Hugh servant of the infirmary,[8] Ivo the cook,[9] with two gatekeepers, Malger[10] at the front gate and William at the back gate (porter of the *curia mona-chorum*).[11] The monastic brewhouse is staffed by Reginald[12] and Walter,[13] while Roger[14] and Walter[15] the bakers, are colleagues to Godefrid, named above. The prior has a staff of his own, among whom William 'camerarius prioris' makes an appearance.[16]

Rentals D and F provide additional names at the end of the century. There is the monastic plumber, Ingenulph, son of Norman the plumber, perhaps himself predecessor in office to his son.[17] We have the names of Simon of the bakehouse,[18] Robert, porter of the infirmary,[19] and William of the almonry.[20] Members of the archbishop's household may be pointed

[1] B 16. [2] B 7, 17, etc. [3] B 48. [4] B 52.
[5] F 114. [6] B 56. [7] B 118. [8] B 122.
[9] B 211. [10] B 71. [11] B 209. [12] B 185.
[13] B 155. [14] B 176. [15] B 66, 67.
[16] B 205; A 34. He was a layman as is shown by the fact that he was married.
[17] D 95. [18] D 127. [19] F 60. [20] D 2; F 117 n.

out at this juncture, such as Godwin 'stablier', who occupies a dwelling adjacent to the archiepiscopal stables,[1] and James the porter (alderman and mayor of Canterbury), who comes of a family of cathedral porters.[2]

There are several 'piscatores' named in the documents,[3] unexpected in an inland borough. They are however, not fishermen, but suppliers of fish, and are probably on the cathedral staff, for the ordinance of 1276 enjoins that the 'piscator' shall receive an issue of food every time he goes over to the sea coast. The convent was therefore well-supplied with saltwater fish, and perhaps William of Malmesbury's commendation of Canterbury for her fish was prompted by first-hand experience on a visit to Christ Church.[4]

A large establishment of monks naturally required some sort of medical supervision, and accordingly we find an officer charged with this duty named Feramin. William of Canterbury calls him 'physicus quidam Cantuariæ' and says that he 'administered the medical affairs of the brethren'.[5] The medical officer may be found in the treasurers' accounts when they become available. We find a successor of Feramin named William 'physicus' in receipt of a fee of but two marks *per annum*, so he evidently had a private practice in the town.[6] Feramin's pious interests are illustrated by the fact that he founded the hospital of St Jacob for leprous women at the far end of Wincheap.[7] It was Master Feramin who was vouchsafed the splendid vision in the cathedral crypt when he beheld it filled with young Queens weeping for the approaching death of St Thomas,[8] and who saw, in another vision, the Saint riding with King Henry through the Precincts at Canterbury behind the monks' Pentecostal procession, when the Heavens were opened and Thomas' glory made manifest.[9]

There was a practice whereby witnesses were assembled from among the servants, to transactions affecting the monks and their property. A charter of the days of prior Jeremiah (1137–43) relating to cathedral ground at Mersey, Essex, addressed to Ralph the monk (evidently one of the brethren), and the hallimoot of Bocking, is witnessed by Berner 'our steward', William the gatekeeper, Goldward 'de cellario' and Leffwin the cook.[10] A conveyance of ground at Halton, Essex, in 1158 is witnessed

---

[1] For the stables at Stablegate, see p. 201.   [2] For J. 'de porta', see p. 87.
[3] Hugh (xxxix); Aschetin (B 197); Nigel (B 99); Sedewin (B 97).
[4] *De Gestis Pontificum*, RS, p. 3.   [5] *Materials*, i, p. 143.
[6] CAC, Treasurers' Accts., 1216–1217 and other years.
[7] Somner, *Antiquities of Canterbury*, 1640, pp. 78–79; *VCH, Kent*, ii, pp. 209–11.
[8] *Materials*, i, pp. 144–5.   [9] Ibid., i, p. 143; *Guernes*, ll. 6095–120.
[10] CAC, Ch. Ant., M 223.

by Bartholomew the steward, William and Roger 'portarii', William 'camerarius' and Robert 'de molendino' (who probably operated the monastic mill at Barton, below Canterbury), John and Walter the cooks, and William 'de cellario',[1] who may well be the very man who with Richard the cellarer ran down the cloister to open the door when Becket was making his last progress to the cathedral.[2] The cyrograph of 1155 relating to the manors of Patching and Wootton, names as witnesses Bartholomew the steward, with William and Roger 'portarii'. Other domestics are arranged under headings as follows: *coquina*: Walter, John, Sæfugel and William his son. *pistrinum*: Coleman. *bracinum*: Smalman, Wulri, Walter, Reginald, Edmer, 'and besides these, William 'camerarius', Robert 'marescal' and eleven others'. After the porters, and before the kitchen staff, are named the citizens Henry the goldsmith and Humphrey his son-in-law, strongly suggesting that they have some regular connection with the monastery, perhaps a standing arrangement for supplying or repairing plate.[3] In William son of 'Seafowl' we unquestionably have a member of the gild of votaries of St Anselm which was flourishing in the sixties of the twelfth century.[4]

Several individuals mentioned in the documents may be members of the cathedral staff though not specified as such. Sired 'scutellarius' (in Rental D) is probably the monastic scullion, dealing with the 'scutelle ad lavandum' cast out through the dining-room hatch (fenestra) depicted in the Anglo-Norman plan of the cathedral precincts. Sired has the nickname 'drenchedreste' ('drink-the-dregs'), no doubt a tribute to his habits from his colleagues or employers.[5] Hugh 'de domo infirmorum',[6] Richard and Cole 'de balneario',[7] Driw the subporter,[8] must clearly be servants of the cathedral monks. Hugh Fagard, Flagard, who is offered up by his lord about to depart on the crusade,[9] together with his holding, on the tomb of St Thomas, can be shown to be a servant of Christ Church. Sometimes men who seem on the face of it to be departmental heads among the monks themselves prove to be servants, like Henry the sacrist, whose tenancy of property out in the town (in which he was succeeded by his son John) indicates that he is not a monk.[10] There seems to have been a usage within the monastery, whereby the servants within a given

[1] CAC, Ch. Ant., G 2.   [2] *Materials*, ii, p. 11.

[3] CAC, Ch. Ant., W 50, printed Saltman, *Theobald*, app. A.

[4] W. Urry, 'St Anselm and his cult at Canterbury' (*Spicilegium Beccense*, i, p. 582).

[5] D 18; see B 141; F 83. The washing-up at Christ Church must have been very heavy. Cf. Giraldus Cambrensis, *Opera*, RS, i, pp. 51–52.

[6] XLII.   [7] XXI, XLII.   [8] XI.

[9] LV; he is called 'serviens noster' in X 2, fol. 9v.   [10] D 293, 294.

department, say the sacristry, are called 'the sacrists', or, in the case of the cellarers' department, 'the cellarers'.[1]

The servants in a great monastery were not of necessity mere menials to be taken on and dismissed at pleasure. There was property in their office, as exemplified by the case of Ivo the cook. Rental B says this man gave 3s. 4d. *per annum*, being *supergabulum* from housing in the northern suburbs *pro officio suo*,[2] which office is shown by Rental A,[3] to be in the kitchen of Christ Church which affirms that he gave moreover 2s. *per annum* rent for his post. Another sale, or virtual sale, of office in the kitchen is likewise to be found in Rental A. The wife of Wnguin held land at 12d. *per annum* from the knight Alan of Ratling. Prior Wibert wanted the land to advance his frontiers, and bought out the lord. Wnguin's daughter meanwhile married one Robert the clerk, who received the land with her. Wibert, to satisfy the claims of Robert, gave him a post (officium) in the kitchen.[4] No doubt Robert's clerical talents did not go wasting 'inter medios cleros', for there must have been an immense amount of administrative work involved in feeding large numbers of monks, servants, guests (many of high rank, bringing big retinues with them) with corrodians.

It is remarkable how many of the servants were men of landed property. Undoubtedly some of their groundplots out in the town were their own dwelling-places, where they lived with their families. Probably Godefrid the baker dwelt on his holding in Orange Street not far from Christ Church Gate.[5] We know for a fact that John the cook lived upon his groundplot at the corner of 'Baggeberi' outside Northgate, a few minutes' walk from his work in the monastic kitchen.[6] Sometimes we find a servant with much more than his own dwelling-place, as when we discover Thomas, servant of the infirmary, certainly of no great seniority among the staff, in possession of four acres of ground at Fordwich, about two miles from Canterbury,[7] while Godefrid the baker has a couple of acres of ground on the Ashford Road, outside Worthgate.[8] Some of these servants are rich in dwellings in Canterbury and must draw a substantial rent therefrom. Bartholomew the steward had a whole collection of holdings scattered through the northern suburbs.[9] William the gatekeeper controls the site of the slaughter-yard outside the cathedral gate.[10] Anselm 'secretarius' (sacristarius), quite clearly a layman, who is named in a document of

---

[1] There is a list of small payments to servants entered on the end leaf of X 1 where there is mention of 'quatuor sacriste' (X 1, fol. 22v).
[2] B 154. Knowles, *Monastic Order*, p. 441.   [3] A 8.   [4] A 7.
[5] B 118.   [6] B 131.   [7] A 37.   [8] A 19.
[9] B 7, 17, 140, 144, 147, 172, etc.
[10] B 209; D 112.

1143,[1] is well-provided with possessions in Canterbury,[2] and appears to have marshland at some unspecified point.[3] We find the names of monastic servants in the list of members of the gild of St Anselm.[4] This gild must have flourished in the age when Rental B was compiled, and some names are common to both documents. Reinold 'del braccin', a member of the gild, can hardly be other than Reginald 'de bracino ecclesie Christi' in Rental B.[5] Hugh 'de bracino'[6] must have been a colleague. William son of Pagan in the gild is clearly the gatekeeper,[7] of the same name, while William son of Seful among these votaries of St Anselm is named as a Christ Church cook together with his father in a charter of 1155.[8] Solomon the baker in the gild is not classed as a servant in the rentals, but appears among known servants in charters.[9] Elwin of the bakehouse may likewise be a servant. Osbert, Gervase's man, and Liwin, Edward's man, both votaries, may perhaps work for Gervase the cook[10] and Edward the baker.[11] There must have been a great influx of masons, glaziers, labourers, and so forth when large-scale building operations were started at the cathedral. There is not much trace of this transitory population in the rentals. It would be interesting to know what particular duty was performed by Master H. 'cementarius noster' mentioned about 1230, as holding in the Northgate area.[12]

The chief official was the 'senescallus' or 'dapifer'. Berner 'dapifer' appears c. 1140.[13] Bartholomew is named in 1158,[14] while by the end of the century one Martin has taken his place.[15] A connection with the monastic court and its business is underlined by the appearance, almost inevitably, of the name of the steward among witnesses where a transaction is said to have taken place 'in plenaria curia', or where the witnesses are said to be 'de curia nostra'.[16]

The relationship between monks and servants was not always happy. Benedict recounts as a miracle that one domestic, always pestering the brethren for money, saying he would rather take from them than give them anything, having had an attack of fever, and being warned of St Thomas in a dream, astonished the monks by offering a penny at the

---

[1] CAC, Ch. Ant., P 10.   [2] See Index, ANSELMUS, sacrista.
[3] 'De marisco Anselmi sacriste v. sol.' (X I, fol. 14r).
[4] W. Urry, 'St Anselm and his cult at Canterbury' (*Spicilegium Beccense*, i, pp. 571–93).
[5] B 170, 171, etc.   [6] F 115, XVI.   [7] B 75, 77, etc.
[8] CAC, Ch. Ant. W 50. Saltman, *Theobald*, app. A.   [9] VIII. Cf. B 46.
[10] D 65, VIII, etc.   [11] IX, X.   [12] Z, fol. 192v.
[13] See above.
[14] CAC, Ch. Ant. G 2, cited above. He is mentioned in XXI, XXII, XXV, XXXIX, XLIII, XLVIII, etc.
[15] XXXIII, XXXIV, LV, LIX, etc.   [16] E.g. in XXI, XXII, XXXV, etc.

Tomb.[1] The servants displayed their disloyalty during the great controversy over the secular college, in the days of archbishop Baldwin. In the spring of 1188 the monks wrote a letter to their prior (Honorius) prosecuting the cause at Rome, concluding:

> ... the most ruthless and worst of our enemies are our own servants, of whom the ringleader (signifer) is that man of Belial, Godefrid the baker, with John the cook, William the watchman, Gilbert the clerk, Jun of Barton, and Thomas Croc. ... These men above named not only speak evil of us but do it.[2]

William the watchman may perhaps be identified with William 'janitor' of the Court Gate. Jun of Barton (who, we learn from this letter was a servant)[3] witnesses the confirmation to the monks by Juliana, prioress of St Sepulchre's of ground in Wincheap.[4] Gilbert the clerk is evidently the Gilbert the clerk who held ground in Stour Street.[5] John the cook has ground (his dwelling) at the corner of 'Baggeberi'.[6] It is sad to find Godefrid the baker as an enemy of the monks for he is forgetful of benefit received. One of the early Miracles of St Thomas is the recall to life of the dying child of Godefrid the baker, by virtue of the holy blood, while the Saint saved two other children in this somewhat sickly family.[7]

Archbishop Baldwin intruded Felix, a member of his faction, into Christ Church as cellarer. In August, 1189, one of the monks (probably Nigel 'Wireker' himself) wrote to Geoffrey the sub-prior and other monks overseas, complaining of Felix's oppressions, and reporting his statement that the servants (who had been excommunicated) must receive their income (procuracio) so that it should not seem that the convent was persecuting the archbishop in the persons of the servants. This was very unjust as the servants had rebelled, and the monks had suffered want. Now the servants were to be no worse off. It was not reasonable, said the writer of the letter, that the convent should go short so that G(odefrid) the baker and J(ohn) the cook should have their full income.[8] These rebels paid the customary penalty for insubordination, were eventually dismissed, and expelled from the Precincts.[9]

Sometimes figures can be recovered for servants' wages. Probably they all received livery, in accordance with usual medieval practice, and no doubt food. We have the treasurers' accounts from an early date, but these furnish few figures for wages, since most servants were employed by

---

[1] *Materials*, ii, pp. 156–7.   [2] *Epp. Cant.*, *RS*, ccxix.   [3] B 209.
[4] XLII.   [5] D 247.   [6] B 131. See above.
[7] *Materials*, ii, pp. 58–59.   [8] *Epp. Cant.*, *RS*, no. cccxxii.
[9] '... servientes quondam nostros et traditores, a curia nostra expulimus' (ibid., no. cccliv).

the different departments. However, a few figures, like 25s. *per annum* for Ingenulph the staff plumber,[1] or 26s. 8d. for the forester of Blean[2] are recorded by the treasurers, who also pay one Hamo 'clericus' (an office clerk?) £2 a year.[3]

There is no doubt that a large proportion of the inhabitants of Canterbury made a living out of the monks. The hundred servants of Christ Church had many dependants. As we know, Godefrid the baker had a wife and at least three children.[4] St Augustine's abbey supported many servants, and so did St Gregory's priory, on a lesser scale. If the population of Canterbury in the twelfth century amounted to four or five thousand, Mother Church must have nourished well over ten per cent of them. Moreover there were craftsmen and tradesmen selling wares to the monks, the biggest local consumers. One craftsman (Henry the goldsmith) is named among servants in a list of witnesses, as we have seen.[5] Another goldsmith, Terric, at the end of the century had business with the monks. His widow was paid sums totalling no less than £58 12s. after his death,[6] perhaps for commissions executed by him.

Goldsmiths' wares and noble gifts[7] for papal legates stand at one end of the scale while at the other are payments such as 3s. 2d. in 1213 'cuidam figulo pro pottis'.[8] Sometimes not only servants and tradesmen labour for the monks, but also their womenfolk. Ingenulph the cathedral plumber had a wife who supplied ale to the value of £8, a figure four times her husband's annual salary.[9] The wife of Hugh the goldsmith likewise supplied ale, to the value of 28s. 8d.[10] An outstanding milk-bill for 23s. (from before the exile of the monks) was paid in 1215, and it is clear that a perishable commodity like milk cannot have come from a point far from the city and must have been supplied locally.[11]

A further economic tie between monks and citizens was the corrody. The crown had a practice in the fourteenth century of nominating retired civil servants or soldiers to corrodies in the Precincts.[12] In the earlier thirteenth century Gregory IX is found promising that he will in future not intrude nominees into corrodies at Canterbury, from which it is evident

[1] *TA*, under 1198–9 and following years.   [2] Ibid.   [3] Ibid.
[4] See above.   [5] CAC, Ch. Ant., W 50. See above.
[6] *TA*, 1213–16.
[7] Such as the robe and the hood sold to the monks by William the skinner for the papal legate in 1189. See p. 123 above.
[8] *TA*, Michaelmas, 1213.
[9] Ibid. under 1213. The ale had been supplied by 1207, before the expulsion of the monks by John.
[10] Ibid. 1213. This ale had also been supplied before 1207.   [11] Ibid. *sub anno*.
[12] R. A. L. Smith, *Canterbury Cathedral Priory*, pp. 41–2.

that he had already done so or had attempted to do so.[1] The corrodians noticed in the twelfth century are of a different class altogether. They do not dwell within the *curia* and are not nominated from outside. Their corrody is freely negotiated on either side, and is tantamount to purchase of an annuity. The monastery is in fact performing the function of a modern insurance organization.

In the cases discovered within the twelfth century all the corrodians are women, though this has evidently no particular significance. Atheliza who drew rent from housing inconveniently close to the cathedral church, was bought out with a grant *per diem* of two 'plainpains', two jousts of knights' ale, 'ad mensuram Lanfranci', one dish of peas, and one milk dish 'when the monks have it', together with whatever general course (ferculum) the monks had on a particular day. Over and above this she got the spiritual benefit of society within the church, and sepulture on death. The whole of this represented a return for 3s. *per annum* surrendered to the monks, though it should be remembered that the rent was permanently surrendered and the corrody was for life only.[2] The two sisters, Sedegos and Scholastica, entered into a similar arrangement during the priorate of Odo (1167–75). They abandoned claim on some small property of theirs in Canterbury, reserving right to one room 12 feet by 24 feet for the life of the longer-liver, in exchange for the daily issue of one monk's loaf, one 'traversum', one joust of ale, a dish of peas and the general course consumed by the monks on a given day. The food was to be drawn from the kitchen of the monastic infirmary. In addition, one of the sisters (Sedegos) was to have one mark in cash *per annum* during her lifetime.[3] With these issues of food may be compared the sustenance granted to the wife of John Calderun, who professed as a monk late in life, leaving her *in sæculo*. In addition to food she was to have one mantle (pellicia) and footwear (botte) on occasions as issued to the brethren.[4]

In a discussion dealing mainly with economic factors it is easy to lose sight of spiritual relationships between monks and citizens. It is difficult to estimate how far the latter frequented their cathedral in the twelfth century though we can see that at times they took a very lively interest in its affairs. Now and then a hint has survived to show that in the twelfth century the local parish churches did not monopolize the religious life of layfolk in Canterbury. Goscelin tells a story (late in the eleventh century), valuable because of the extreme rarity of glimpses of family life at an early date, of a woman called Mazelina dwelling in the suburbs of Canterbury,

[1] Ibid., p. 42.   [2] xxv.
[3] xliii. The 'traversum' is probably something in the nature of an *entrée*.   [4] xlvii.

who used to go and pray daily at St Augustine's abbey. On one occasion she went off to her devotions taking the doorkeys with her. When her husband came home he could not get into the house, so he sent one of the children round to the abbey to find his wife and get the keys from her. The woman, annoyed at being disturbed, violently smacked the boy, sending him home crying. She was punished by the Blessed Augustine (with a severe swelling in her arm) for breaking the solemn quiet of his church.[1] At the cathedral there was a strong gild (over one hundred and thirty in number) composed of citizens and others from outside Canterbury, banded together to maintain the cult of St Anselm. The list numbers at least one alderman, the wealthy borough reeve, John son of Vivian, some of the monastic servants, with a few country knights.[2]

As in all monastic boroughs, the citizens of Canterbury join battle with the monks over infringements of jurisdiction on either side, or as a result of quarrels over taxation. In the earlier period, however, we find less of conflicts between burgess and religious, and more of cases where the citizens intervene in quarrels among the churchmen themselves. The Latin acts of Lanfranc appended to the Parker MS. of the Old English Chronicle tell how the archbishop subdued a revolt among the monks of St Augustine's against their new abbot Wido. After Lanfranc's death the revolt flared up again, and the rebels inflamed the citizens against Wido to such an extent that they invaded the abbey and tried to kill the abbot in his own house. In the battle several were killed or wounded on either side. Walkelin bishop of Winchester and Gundulph of Rochester came to Canterbury to investigate, and punish offenders. Those guilty among the monks were severely disciplined, and citizens who were unable to exculpate themselves were blinded.[3]

One of the great convulsions which disturbed the peace of the church in the twelfth century, 'a *cause célèbre* familiar to the whole of Christian Europe',[4] was largely played out at Canterbury. Archbishop Baldwin conceived a project for establishing a secular college at Hackington just outside the city, and tried to deprive the monks of Christ Church of many of their resources in order to furnish its endowment.[5] The townsfolk of Canterbury gladly joined in the fray, some on the side of the monks and others on the side of the archbishop. The fiercest enemies of the monks

---

[1] *Acta Sanctorum*, May, vi, p. 407.
[2] W. Urry, 'St Anselm and his cult at Canterbury' (*Spicilegium Beccense*, i).
[3] *Two of the Saxon Chronicles Parallel* . . . ed. C. Plummer, i, app. B (pp. 291-2).
[4] Knowles, *Monastic Order*, p. 319.
[5] The story is told in *Epistolæ Cantuarienses*, RS, ed. W. Stubbs, with introduction.

were found (as shown above) among their own servants, headed by Gode-frid the baker. Another centre of antagonism was formed by the local parish priests, who tried to align their flocks against the monks, attacking them from the pulpits, and defying papal decrees in their malice.[1] Some of the priests, however, supported the monks, in company with citizens described in the relevant correspondence as 'cives nostri'. Among these pro-monastic citizens we may find Arnold Ferre,[2] evidently the same man who served on the commission of enquiry into the mint of St Augustine's abbey,[3] and Ralph, nephew of St Thomas.[4]

In January, 1188, Baldwin arrived at Wingham, six miles from Can-terbury, at a juncture in the conflict. Prior Geoffrey sent out two monks to offer him the customary procession, but the archbishop in a rage ex-communicated them and seized their horses. They made their way back to Canterbury on foot, closely followed by William FitzNeal (the same man who had quitted Becket's service within an hour before his death). The gates of the monastery were closed against him, but he organized an assault, smashed a way through the boundary wall and occupied all the outer offices, up to the cloister and church.[5] A siege of a year and a quarter ensued, when the monks would have starved but for the fact that they were fed by sympathizers out in the town, including the Jews, who actually prayed for the monks in their synagogue.[6]

When news of the attack reached Rome, Clement was overcome with rage, and denounced the offenders in a bull couched in the fiercest language: 'outrage', 'detestable presumption', 'atrocity', he thundered, and declared all involved to be excommunicate, unless they came forward to show sorrow and make restitution. Publication and execution of the bull were entrusted to the prior of Faversham, and to Master Feramin (Farreman) the Canterbury physician whom we have met above. The bull arrived at Canterbury (so it appears) on Good Friday, 15th April.[7] Feramin had some misgivings, and removed himself to London, on the grounds that he wanted to inform the king of what had transpired. He empowered the prior of Faversham to act in his absence and forthwith departed.[8] Warnings were issued, but none of the offenders came forward in penitential wise, so publicly from the pulpit, on Low Sunday, the prior denounced as excommunicate those who had taken possession of the monastic offices, with all their accomplices and sympathizers. The monks published the

---

[1] Gervase, *Opera*, RS, i, p. 425.   [2] D 121, 282. *Epp. Cant.*, cccxxvi.
[3] See p. 118.   [4] D 66.   [5] *Epp. Cant.*, p. lx.
[6] Gervase, *Opera*, RS, i, p. 405. *Epp. Cant.*, p. lxi; nos. clxxvii, clxxxi.
[7] *Epp. Cant.*, p. lxiv; no. cclxix.   [8] Ibid., p. 202.

names of some of the offenders, calling them the principalities and powers of the evil business. These were Godefrid the baker, John the cook, and other servants already mentioned. A violent riot at once broke out in the streets of Canterbury.[1]

Master Feramin had meanwhile fared badly in London. Henry was becoming emancipated from his regard for the monks engendered by the murder of Becket. He flew into a rage when he learned about the bull, and angrily told Feramin that he had better not publish it if he wished to stay in his dominions.

Most of the local clergy treated the bull with contempt, asserting that the papal decree had no force within the archbishop's diocese. They encouraged their parishioners to disregard it and to associate with the excommunicated. One priest, Thomas by name, refused to baptize a dying child until the father had sworn upon the Gospels not to avoid the company of the excommunicated.[2] The pro-monastic party—'cives nostri'—however, piously avoided them. The king seems to have been very well-informed of what was going on in Canterbury and sent down word that those who would not keep company with the excommunicated should be arrested.[3] At once the supporters of the monks, including Ralph, nephew of St Thomas himself, were seized and thrust into the city gaol, no doubt the structure sited (according to Rental D) south of the High Street in Rose Lane.[4] Some members of the archbishop's faction decided to burn it down with the prisoners within it, but were betrayed as they came one night for this purpose, by the barking of local dogs. They made off, but on meeting with some of their rivals, bound and ill-treated them. They also amused themselves going round to the prisoners' houses, tossing up stones on to the roofs to smash the tiles.[5] Probably this scene took place at the dwelling of Ralph, St Thomas' nephew, on the banks of the Stour, in 'The Friars'.[6] Master Feramin earned a share of the popular hatred and an attack was made upon the possessions of his almshouse of St Jacob's at the far end of Wincheap, while stock was carried off from its home farm. Feramin was obliged to get a bull of protection for his old ladies.[7]

The great struggle dragged on for years, into the days of archbishop Hubert Walter. It has left a permanent mark of itself in the siting of an archiepiscopal town-house at Lambeth, while at Canterbury St Thomas' hill perpetuates the memory of the chapel removed to this area from across the fields at Hackington.

[1] Ibid., pp. 201–2.
[2] Gervase, *RS*, i, p. 425; *Epp. Cant.*, no. ccxxvii.
[3] Gervase, *RS*, i, p. 425.
[4] See below, p. 197.
[5] Gervase, *RS*, i, pp. 425–6.
[6] D 66.
[7] Gervase, *RS*, i, p. 427.

The first-recorded struggle of the new series, where the citizens join warfare against the monks, instead of intervening in an ecclesiastical quarrel, is the collision between the city and St Augustine's abbey in 1257, arising from a quarrel over police-jurisdiction in the fields of Barton Manor, the home farm of the abbey. Canterbury was filled with a rioting mob, which attacked the abbey mill in St Radegund's, and advanced upon Barton, all to the sound of the Boroughmoot Horn.[1] It is a measure of the continuity of these struggles that the same scene was enacted two hundred years later. In 1327 took place the great riot against the cathedral monks,[2] while in 1500 there was a pitched battle in the waterside meadows near Westgate between cathedral forces and the citizens.

[1] The dispute is recorded in an exemplification in form of Letters Patent (3 Henry V). Copy in Corporation Archives, Canterbury, Charter 29, and in BM. Add. MS., 32, 311, fol. 8.

[2] A local manifestation of the general disturbances in monastic boroughs in this year. The alleged struggle of 1227 (*Studies . . . presented to F. M. Powicke*, p. 390) is a ghost arising from a misprint in HMC, v, app. p. 433.

CHAPTER VIII

The Inhabitants of Canterbury

IT is not easy to extract much certain information from Domesday Book on the subject of housing and population in Canterbury. Widely divergent figures have been calculated, the least unlikely being those of Ballard,[1] who arrives at two hundred and sixty-six burgesses, plus two hundred and ninety-one burgesses or tenements mentioned under headings for manors out in the countryside, T.R.E., with two hundred and thirty-one burgesses in 1086, and one hundred and sixty-five burgesses or dwellings at the same date. However, these figures (totalling five hundred and fifty-seven, T.R.E., and three hundred and ninety-six in 1086) are obviously far too low. To begin with we have little information about non-manorial holdings of Christ Church, which is by far the largest landholder in the city by the middle of the twelfth century, nor yet of the abbey of St Augustine. Moreover, it seems from the language of Domesday that there is land, and by inference housing, exempt from royal sake and soke, once belonging to a group of immunists like Osbern Biga who, as noted above, is said to have given seventy-two dwellings to Christ Church.[2]

Other immunists whose lands had been exempt from royal sake and soke were, with Christ Church, St Augustine's and Osbern Biga, Queen Edith, Alnod Cild, and Siret of Chilham.[3] It is arguable whether lands in Canterbury which had been theirs, such as four haws connected with the manor of Newington, once held of the queen,[4] or thirteen masuræ related to Chilham, probably held of Sired,[5] can be excluded from totals for the city. At the moment we are probably justified in affirming that

---

[1] Ballard published figures for dwellings, burgesses, etc. in his *Domesday Boroughs* (1904), Statistical Table, pp. 39–40. The figures differ widely from those in J. C. Russell, *British Medieval Population*, chapter xi. Carl Stephenson presents a list of boroughs arranged in apparent order of size, T.R.E., with corresponding figures in 1086. An immediate objection can be raised against Stephenson's figures, for it is clear that he has ignored the haws, burgesses, houses, etc. specified not under a main borough heading in *DB*, but under manors out in the countryside.

[2] The Domesday evidence for the holdings of the cathedral monks is discussed in Chapter II.

[3] *DB*, i, fol. 2r.   [4] Ibid., fol. 14v.   [5] Ibid., fol. 10r.

the figures so far published from Domesday Book for housing or inhabitants in Canterbury are far too small.

The earliest of the Canterbury surveys (Rental B, c. 1166), enumerates rather more than two hundred and twenty *mansure*. The survey covers rather more than half of three of the six city wards, and may point to a total of up to eight hundred in all, though it should be emphasized that one of the three wards (Ridingate) not covered by the survey seems always to have been sparsely populated. However, there was probably housing in the extra-mural suburb lying in the archiepiscopal hundred of Westgate, part of the built-up area of the city, where Christ Church seems to have held no property. There were certainly many dwellings here in the earlier thirteenth century.[1] With the figure offered above may be compared the one thousand two hundred tenements listed in the Winchester survey of 1148.

At the end of the twelfth century the monks of Christ Church record some four hundred tenements in a rental (D) which accounts for a large part of the street frontage of the city, apart from the Westgate suburbs.

We cannot be certain that all these tenements represent houses, and indeed we know in many cases that they do not. However, some of the tenements are large, and may have been covered with more than one dwelling. It is often assumed that a medieval household consisted of an average of five souls. We know one household where there was a father (Godefrid the baker) his wife and three boys, but we do not know if this was the total number under his roof. Terric the goldsmith had a wife, three sons, and possibly a stepson, but it is most unlikely that this wealthy craftsman and financier had no apprentices, or clerk (quite likely in view of the far-distant ramifications of his business), while his wife undoubtedly enjoyed the services of living-in maids. On the other hand there are eighty or more priests and clerks, whose households may have consisted of no more than themselves and a housekeeper. We may be certain that Thomas, priest of St Martin's, in close contact with St Thomas, whose antipathy to clerical marriage was well-known, had no wife and family, yet we know the names of three priests with families, one priest having a son who was himself a priest. The question how far the priests and clerks were heads of families offers a wide margin of doubt in the question of population.

There are many shops in Canterbury in the twelfth and earlier thirteenth centuries. Where information is available these shops generally prove to be very small, often only 7 feet wide or even narrower. They may have

---

[1] See account of suburbs in Chapter IX.

been mere lockups, or possibly even no more than permanent stalls. Did anyone live in any of them?

Another important subject demanding discussion is the racial origin of the inhabitants. Rental B was compiled just one century after the Norman Conquest, and it is striking to observe the substantial number of English names therein. The impression is gained that a generation later, in Rental D, about 1200, the proportion of English names has fallen. It is of course, unwise to place too much reliance upon Christian names as evidence of race. Godparents supply misleading names. However, we may observe that families who we know must be of continental stock, like the Cauvels, usually employ continental Christian names, while it is difficult to believe that men called Eadward se Vinge, Edwin Winter, Edward son of Odbold, Elfsi Attharewelle, can be anything but English, or that Ralph Wastecar, Richard Bonemfant, and John Caudrun are not of immigrant families. However, admixture can be seen, if evidence of names can be relied upon, actually taking place, when we find names such as Ethelburga, widow of William, and Eadilda, widow of Geoffrey.[1]

There are ethnological elements other than Norman or English. There is a man (c. 1200) with a Danish name (Wlfketel), in Stour Street,[2] which bears the name 'Heathenmenslane',[3] possibly a memory of some earlier Scandinavian enclave. Toli, occupying ground round the corner, looks like another Dane.[4] William son of Heremann outside Ridingate seems to be a German, like William 'Teutonicus' in the tallage roll of 1198.[5] Some Flemings have holdings scattered round the city, such as Lambin 'Flandrensis'[6] or Sedegos, widow of Baldwin of Flanders.[7] The name of one Fleming, Ertin, 'natione Flandrensis, civis vero Cantuariensis', is supplied by a miracle story of St Thomas.[8] There is an Irishman named Roger,[9] and a Humphrey 'Scottus' in 1152.[10] Around 1180 a man called Pantaleone, perhaps an Italian, is named in the cathedral rentlist.[11]

There does not seem to be a well-defined urban patriciate in Canterbury in the twelfth century. True, the Normans, or men with continental names seem to dominate the borough, and to monopolize for a long time the office of reeve. Yet there are at least two aldermen with English names,

---

[1] For these names, see Index. Nicknames probably do not offer much help, as they might be applied from any quarter. One man is called 'seven-eight' in French, and 'eighteen' in English (William de setuit uel eachtene, X I, fol. 28r).

[2] D 225. [3] XLIX. [4] D 304.

[5] PR, 1 Richard I, p. 208. [6] B 122; D 71; F 250, 251, etc. [7] B 44.

[8] *Materials*, ii, p. 81. There is a 'Michael Flandr' in the Tallage Roll of 1198 (PR, 1 Richard I, p. 208). Ground in Best Lane was given when James of Flanders became a monk (D 293).

[9] Z, under All Saints' parish. [10] IX, X. [11] X 1, fol. 127v.

Wlnoth and the wealthy Edward son of Odbold.[1] Two or three of the families with continental names do appear to stand out and have affinities with knightly manorial lines out in the countryside. The Cauvels descend from William the borough reeve of Anselm's day, founder of the nunnery outside Ridingate. Their cousins are of the line of Vitalis, evidently the Vitalis depicted in the Bayeux Tapestry, and one of the Cauvels at least is classed as a knight. There is no evidence that they engage in trade.[2] Another family with knightly connections is that of John son of Vivian whose daughters marry manorial lords, one of whom is a crusader.[3]

There is a wealthy group of merchants dwelling in stone houses like Henry the goldsmith;[4] Robert son of Richard,[5] who endows both cathedral and abbey with his housing and shops in the central business area, or Theoderic the goldsmith, craftsman and financier;[6] and affluent aldermen such as William of Ridingate ward,[7] and Edward son of Odbold, apparently of Westgate ward, the founder of Eastbridge Hospital.[8] In the same moneyed group come the minters, Mainer the rich, founder of the hospital of St Mary in Stour Street, his son Wiulph the rich, and Ralph of Rye, who can pay a large proportion of an amercement of 1,000 marks.[9] There are Jews, handling large sums of money, such as Jacob of Canterbury, who subscribed £115 6s. 8d. towards the ransom of king Richard.[10] Among professional men (to use a convenient modern term), we have Master William son of Terric,[11] Master Feramin the physician,[12] Peter the doctor and his son John the doctor.[13]

The greatest single profession was unquestionably that of the priests and clerks. As many as eighty names can be discovered in the rentals and charters; these are merely mentioned incidentally, and there may well have been many more.[14] They themselves embody a long social scale from the archbishop and his entourage, the archdeacon (men of the calibre of Roger of Pont l'Évêque and Thomas Becket), the vicearchdeacon, down through priests enjoying private means such as Thomas of St Martin's[15] to

[1] B 213, 217, etc. It is almost completely certain that E. f. Odbold was alderman of Westgate late in the twelfth century. See account of the aldermanry, Chapter V.

[2] Though it must be noticed that Calveal, portreeve, seems to be head of the merchant gild (Charter I).

[3] For these families see Chapter III.   [4] B 5; D 68.

[5] See Index, ROBERTUS f. Ricardi.

[6] For Theoderic, see discussion on goldsmiths, Chapter VI.

[7] BBSA, p. 163.

[8] See account of aldermanry of Westgate, Chapter V.

[9] For the moneyers, see Chapter VI.   [10] For the Jews, see Chapter V.

[11] CAC, Ch. Ant. C 715.   [12] D 237, 253, etc.

[13] B 93; BBSA, pp. 601, 602.   [14] See p. 109 above.   [15] B 115, 208.

'clerici' and 'capellani', ministering in the occasional little private chapel maintained by a rich citizen like John son of Robert.[1] There will always be a group of failures in a large profession, and the philanthropist Alexander of Gloucester was moved to establish an almshouse for the poor priests (in the former house of Adam of Charing, in Stour Street) about 1220.

William of Sens the French architect (builder in part of the cathedral choir), is temporarily a member of the local community; another architect may probably be seen in Master H. 'cementarius'.[2] The wants of the neighbourhood and city are catered for by a large mass of tradesmen: goldsmiths, mercers, weavers, tanners, smiths, shoemakers, dyers, carpenters, and so forth. The staff of the archbishop's palace and of the monastic houses live to a large extent out in the city, and play a part in its politics. Some of these are great men among their fellow-citizens, such as James the gatekeeper, alderman of Northgate and first mayor of Canterbury.[3] John the cook is not without private resources (in the shape of his house).[4] The daughter of Hamo 'dapifer' of St Augustine's, son of the cook, marries into the powerful Cornhill family.[5] Some hundred servants of Christ Church alone (fifty of whom are mentioned in the documents) play a part in the general life of Canterbury.[6]

Below the ranks of tradesmen and monastic servants the evidence becomes less clear. There must have been hundreds of indigent people who leave little or no trace of themselves, like the 'paupercula quædam Brithiva', 'poor, blind, unlettered', who figures in a miracle of Becket.[7] Some of these poor people acted as lower monastic servants or odd-job men such as the individual who went round weekly to clean out the cathedral drain, or who stood waiting hungrily for someone to hire them, like their fellows at Lincoln.[8] There are many occupations unaccounted for in the rentals, such as washerwomen and fuel-vendors, hawkers or entertainers. At the bottom of the social scale there are beggars, who have left a trace of themselves in the name of the alley outside Newingate which they must have haunted, called the beggars' lane (Lodderelane).[9] Odd corners of boroughs are occupied by 'unthanks' or squatters. We may see in the name 'Unthankeswei' a colony of these squatters in the

---

[1] Z (under St Peter's parish).

[2] Z, fol. 192v. (c. 1230.) There was a good deal of building going on in this period.

[3] See pp. 87–8.

[4] For Johannes 'cocus' and other property-owning monastic servants, see pp. 160 ff.

[5] See p. 57.

[6] The monastic servants are discussed in Chapter VII.

[7] *Materials*, ii, p. 41 (Benedict).   [8] Hill, *Medieval Lincoln*, p. 176.

[9] D 127. Wallenberg, *Place-names of Kent*, p. 606.

mid-twelfth century, in a corner of the old archiepiscopal fields, outside the northern walls.[1]

There must have been a considerable transient population. The country knights rode in and out of the city, which has always formed a natural meeting-place for the eastern half of Kent, far more so than the distant and desolate heath at Pennenden. Devotion to the saints brought them in, as in the case of William son of Archebold, probably of Farleigh on the Medway, who made arrangements for a corrody from the cellarer's department of Christ Church, for himself and two men, when he came to Canterbury once, or twice, in each year 'ad visitanda sanctorum loca'.[2] When the archbishop moved into his palace he brought with him a crowd of clerks, officials, menials and retainers. Becket surrounded himself with 'eruditi' and young men of the status of prince Henry. Sometimes the king himself came, with bishops and barons, each with an entourage of his own.

It would be possible to construct a family tree for a great many citizens in the twelfth and thirteenth centuries. The ancestry of some of them can be carried back a long way. John (son of Robert son of Osmund) holding ground in Palace Street about 1166, must have a grandfather born in the days of Henry I, or perhaps even in the time of William II.[3] The genealogy of one Canterbury family can be recovered from an unusual source. Mainer, scribe of the splendid Bible in the library of Ste-Geneviève in Paris, appends a colophon to his work in which he calls himself 'scriptor Cantuariensis' and goes on to say that his grandfather and grandmother were named Ulger and Elvera, that his father was named Wimund, and his mother Liveva, and that she lived happily for eighty years and more. He had one brother named Ralph, with others called Robert and Girold, a couple of wastrels, classed as 'spoliator et prædo' respectively, and another brother called John, with a sister Dionisia.[4] It is satisfying to observe in Rental B a certain widow, holding ground in Burgate ward in Canterbury, named Liveva, whose husband was called Wimund (a mercer).[5]

An account of the family of Terric the goldsmith offers an interesting picture of a citizen household of the more prosperous class. Terric is first traced in a rental of about 1180,[6] and is certainly one of the great men of

---

[1] B 32, 173; D 31; F 89.   [2] CAC, Ch. Ant. L 251 (temp. prior Odo).
[3] B 69, 82, 123.
[4] Wright, Political Songs (Camden Soc.), p. 354. James, Ancient Libraries of Canterbury and Dover, p. lxxxix. Dodwell, Canterbury School of Illumination, p. 110. A. Grabar and C. Nordenfalk, Romanesque Painting, p. 174.
[5] B 58, 59. Rental X 1 (fol. 14) notes that Wimund (the mercer) had a brother John.
[6] X 2, fol. 3v.

the city in the last years of the century, He employs journeymen, is farmer of the royal exchange, and acts as agent for king John in making purchases, while the ramifications of his business on behalf of the crown reach to the uttermost parts of the realm.[1] As becomes a leading citizen, Terric acts as borough reeve, his colleague in office being Eudo son of Sygar.[2] By 1200 he has a big stone house (where he dwells) in Burgate Street, quite close to the cathedral gate.[3] Before long he takes over the holding of Ralph, nephew of St Thomas, on the river Stour, and there builds another stone house.[4] His death may have taken place by 1208, when a special section appears in the Pipe Roll, headed 'Account of Terric of Canterbury'.[5] The cathedral obituary discloses that he died on 2 June, and it is highly probable that this was in 1208. The entry in the obituary shows that he was a spiritual brother of the monks, and moreover one of their benefactors. For the sake of his soul and that of his wife Matilda, William their son gave to Christ Church 15s. rent arising from two stone shops standing opposite St Mary Magdalen church in Burgate.[6]

Terric had three sons, William, Philip and John. William was clearly the intellect of the family, and enjoyed the title 'Master'. Eventually he took the cowl at the cathedral and rose to office in the house.[7] Philip and John, sons of Terric, remained in the world and are named in a great number of charters as witnesses to sales. Since relief was paid after their deaths (1231 and 1246) their names serve to provide a limiting date for these charters.[8] Philip 'Terri' married Cecilia, daughter of Goldwin the mercer (who had ground not far from Terric's house),[9] and had two sons, John and Terri.[10] John the third son of Terric married and had two sons, John and William.[11] John son of Terric served the abbey of St Augustine as seneschal.[12]

---

[1] For Terric's business activities see p. 118.   [2] See p. 85.

[3] D 99; F 194, 554.

[4] Y, fol. 29v, showing rent paid 'de terra que fuit Radulfi nepotis sancti Thome super quam noua domus Terrici aurifabri sita est'.

[5] PR, 10 John, p. 169.

[6] BM MS. Arundel 68, fol. 30v. 'iiij° non. Jun. Item obiit Terricus aurifaber frater et benefactor noster pro cuius anima et anima vxoris sue Matildis Willelmus Terrici filius eorum dedit ecclesie Christi quindecim solidos redditus de ij^{abus} scoppis lapideis que opposite sunt ecclesie sancte Marie Magdalene in Burgate qui expendentur in refectorio in die patrum et matrum anniuersario.'   [7] See p. 155.

[8] Reliefs, sub annis. The occurrence of their names is of particular value in calculating the termini ad quos for bailiffs, aldermen and other civic officials whose names are found in charters.

[9] CAC, Reg. A. fol. 375r. She evidently married twice as BM. MS. Cotton Claudius D X (cartulary of St Augustine's) indicates she married W. Brussel (fol. 88).

[10] Reliefs, 1231.   [11] Ibid., 1246.   [12] BBSA, p. 390.

The name of Terric the goldsmith's wife was (as shown above) Matilda. She had a son Roger, never named as son to Terric, so perhaps he was a stepson.[1] Terric the goldsmith in common with other citizens invested in real estate out in the country, securing a stretch of marshland under Westbere on the Stour, some three miles below Canterbury.[2] He had four acres of land outside the city, in the field called Gore,[3] with a meadow half a mile from the walls in Wincheap.[4] He had furthermore a dwelling (producing 1s. *per annum* to the cathedral monks) in Dover.[5] Terric's property must have been very extensive, for in the thirteenth year of king John account was rendered of £69 'de exitibus terrarum Terrici de Cantuar' ',[6] while in 1214 his wife Matilda, with her son Roger, made fine at a figure of £100 with the king, to have land, chattels, and debts of Terric.[7]

The Chiches are one of the most important citizen families. In the period 1255–81 four of them (Thomas, Thomas II, Stephen and John) serve as bailiffs of Canterbury.[8] The first Thomas was involved in the lawsuit over this office, prosecuted *coram rege* in 1259.[9] Somner says that the family were hereditary aldermen of Burgate ward.[10] The first mention of the family noticed is in the cathedral rental of c. 1180, when Arnold Chich, goldsmith, holds ground in Best Lane.[11]

The usual drift of population from country and country town to the capital is reversed in the case of the Cokins. The progenitor of the Canterbury line is called Augustine of London.[12] His son William married Margaret, one of the Cauvel womenfolk, and with her acquired the family residence at the west end of St Margaret's church, about 1200.[13] William Cokin founded the short-lived charity in St Peter's Street,[14] and had a son William II who became bailiff of the city in the mid-thirteenth century, and is also named as alderman of Northgate ward.[15]

Many citizen families disappear in daughters. Alderman Alan has a dwelling opposite Newingate in the middle of the twelfth century.[16] He has a sister, Aliz and a son Adam, who since he lives beside Newingate

---

[1] See below.

[2] Cathedral Library, Lit. MS. C 20 (cartulary of St Laurence, Canterbury), p. 67.

[3] Duncombe and Battely, *Three Archiepiscopal Hospitals*, p. 236.

[4] CAC, Reg. A, fol. 375r.   [5] CAC, Reg. H, fol. 15v.

[6] PR, 13 John, p. 243.

[7] *Rotuli de Oblatis et Finibus . . . Tempore Regis Johannis* (Rec. Commrs.), p. 517.

[8] Somner, *Antiquities of Canterbury*, 1703, p. 180.

[9] See p. 90.   [10] See p. 102.   [11] X 2, fol. 13r.

[12] CAC, Reg. E, fol. 115r.   [13] Ibid.

[14] Duncombe and Battely, *Three Archiepiscopal Hospitals*, pp. 304 ff.

[15] Somner, *ut supra*; CAC, Reg. A, fol. 380v.   [16] B 92.

Cross is called Adam 'de cruce'.[1] Adam died by 1233 when his widow paid relief.[2] His son John must have died at the same time since his sisters Christina and Godelef paid relief for his holdings in the same year.[3] Mainer the rich, 'prepositus' of Canterbury, the moneyer who founded the hospital in Stour Street, had a son Wiulf, also called the rich. Wiulf seems to have had no male heir and his daughter Alice married Roger of Sheppey the goldsmith.[4] The family of alderman Humphrey disappeared among girls. Humphrey had a son, but Constance and Agnes, sisters to this son, rendered relief for their brother's ground in 1220.[5] The line of Solomon the mercer with his holding on the corner of Mercery Lane in the days of Becket can be followed through almost a century. Solomon married Godeleva and had a daughter Cecilia, espoused to William Silvestre, who had at least three daughters, Godlief, Beatrice, and Christiana.[6] The children of Godlief, namely Henry, William and Beatrice, paid reliefs in 1235, and in 1255 Walter the priest and William his brother, sons of Beatrice daughter of William Silvestre, paid again.[7] In 1257, Christiana, daughter of William Silvestre, styled as widow of William Samuel, gave in pure and perpetual alms certain rents in Mercery Lane to Eastbridge Hospital, Canterbury.[8]

It has been shown that the landowning families out in the countryside control ground in Canterbury. The converse of this applies for there are several burgesses who have interest in territory far beyond their city walls. Many leading citizens of Lincoln hold ground in the country.[9] Burgesses of Cambridge hold land at Newnham, Chesterton, Histon, Impington, Coton and so forth. 'Six mayors of Cambridge and many more bailiffs can be shown to have held land in the county before 1307.'[10]

We have seen above that Terric of Canterbury the goldsmith acquired land at Westbere, and had ground at Gore. John Hanin, almost certainly Terric's grandson, bought a stretch of ground at Harmondsole on the Stone Street, about three miles from Canterbury.[11] Alfred the parmenter and Cecilia his wife bought ground at Godmersham half-way to Ashford. After his death the widow sold the ground (towards the end of 1223) for

---

[1] X I, fol. 18v.; F 657.   [2] Reliefs, sub anno.   [3] Ibid.

[4] See Index, MEINERUS, dives; BM. MS. Claudius D X, fol. 111v.

[5] Reliefs, sub anno.

[6] B 81, 222; F 622; CAC, Reg. E, fol. 122v (quitclaim of freebench by 'Cecilia f. Salomonis merc.', widow of W. Silvestre).

[7] Reliefs, sub annis.   [8] Duncombe and Battely, Three Archiepiscopal Hospitals, p. 315.

[9] Hill, Medieval Lincoln, pp. 392–5. See account of leading families ibid., appendix v.

[10] Cam, Liberties and Communities in Medieval England, chapter ii ('The Early Burgesses of Cambridge in Relation to the Surrounding Countryside').

[11] CAC Reg. E, fol. 223v.

six marks *gersuma* and 1d. quitrent to Christ Church, Canterbury.[1] The wealthy mercer Goldwin owed ten marks (according to the Pipe Roll of 3 John) to have seizin of the ville of 'Ebbeton' (Heppington?—two miles from Canterbury) whence he had been disseised by William son of William, just as he had it before the king's crossing to Germany.[2] One does not expect to find a town-dwelling smith in the capacity of a rural landowner, yet we may discover William 'faber', son of Alfred 'faber' of Broad Street, in possession of four acres of land at Ickham, three miles from Canterbury.[3] However, a smith need be no mere shoer of horses, and this one with his stone house and forge may well be classed as a substantial industrialist. Rental F remarks that ground was bought at Chartham (four miles from the city) from Robert Pin who, since he is mentioned in a small society without differentiation, is probably the man of the same name in All Saints' lane, with ground outside Northgate at the date (c. 1205).[4] The ground held by one citizen in Thanet is mentioned in interesting circumstances. Becket had bestowed land in the island on one R. son of Henry, 'Cantuariensis civis', and the grant was confirmed by Alexander III (probably at Sens, while Becket was there). A letter was sent by the pope himself to Henry II asking for leave for the man to return from exile to his wife and home.[5] Might the suppliant be Robert son of Henry, whose widow Christiana is holding a plot of ground ceded by Christ Church to St Augustine's abbey in 1177?[6]

Relations between a manorial lord and citizens in Canterbury are disclosed in the Curia Regis rolls at the beginning of John's reign.[7] There was a dispute between two ladies, Matilda, and Christina of Canterbury, wife of William son of Odo, who must be the man shown in Rental D, of the same date, as holding in Wincheap Street.[8] A group of four men, Solomon 'de Fraxino', who seems to have dwelt in the Tonford area, above Canterbury, Ailmer 'bedellus', and two citizens, Arnold Chich, with his neighbour in Mercery Lane, William Wineday,[9] went up to the Curia to bear record of proceedings in the court of Hamo de Crèvecœur, lord of Nackington, in connection with thirty-nine acres of ground of this manor, in dispute between Matilda and Christina. A charter produced

---

[1] Ibid., fol. 264r. The Alfred parmenter in Rental A (§ 28) is far too early for identification with this other A. parmenter.

[2] PR, 3 John, p. 290.

[3] D 58; Y, fol. 25v. The tenant of c. 1220 pays 12d. *p.a.* 'de iiii acris terre que fuerunt Willelmi fabri filii Aluredi fabri de Cant' in uilla de Iecham'.

[4] D 309; F 281. See D 8, n.   [5] *Materials*, v, pp. 170, 171.

[6] XXVI, XXVII.   [7] *Rotuli Curiæ Regis*, ii, p. 72.

[8] D 178.   [9] D 115, 116.

as evidence was stigmatized as spurious, since Arnold Chic and William
Wineday, named as witnesses therein, rejected it, affirming that they were
not present at an alleged conveyance of ground. Christina offered half a
mark to have inquisition into the business by legal testimony of the neighbourhood and of the Portmoot. It is of interest to see a Canterbury woman
laying claim to a long stretch of ground in a manor two miles from the
city walls, with a project for inquisition jointly between the neighbourhood and the borough court.[1] A charter in the cartulary of St Gregory's
priory shows that there were many citizens in control of ground at
Nackington.[2] The priory acquired here thirty-eight acres of ground of
which ten were said to lie adjacent to ground of William Cokin (either
the William Cokin who served as alderman of Worthgate, or his son of
the same name), and also adjacent to the land of the heirs of Ralph 'de
porta' (son of James 'de porta', mayor of Canterbury, alderman of Northgate, and 'portarius' of the archbishop's palace). Other acres are classed as
lying next to ground of John Chich, of Maynard the rich (evidently the
second man of this name, rather than the moneyer of a previous generation), and of the heirs of Osmund Polre. Roger Blund,[3] John the cook,
alderman Thomas, the heirs of Lambin of Flanders, Philippus 'de celario',
all citizens in Canterbury, have interest in ground at Nackington. John,
son of Terric the great Canterbury goldsmith, had thirteen acres at
Nackington, granted by him to the priory of St Gregory. It is remarkable
that at least a dozen citizens can be shown to hold ground in the territory
of a single manor.[4]

Surnames of burgesses are beginning to crystallize at the end of the
twelfth century. In the case of the Cauvel family this process has taken
place much earlier, for it is clear that the family name, which may have
been a personal description in the eleventh century is well-established as a
surname early in the twelfth. The name 'Chamberlain', evidently deriving
from office in the monastery, seems to have become a family name by
c. 1200.[5] The genesis of the name 'Lucas' may be watched. About 1200
Luke the mercer has ground in St Alphage parish, while thirty years later
his son, called Robert 'filius Luce mercerii', and then, quite simply, Robert

---

[1] Charter no. 212 in the cartulary of St Gregory's priory (Greg.) appears to be connected
with this case. A. Chich and W. Wineday are named as witnesses.
[2] Greg., no. 225. [3] *Albus*, cf. F. 265.
[4] Greg., no. 189. This charter shows that the heirs of Ralph 'de porta' have a 'grange' here.
The leading families of Cauvel, and of Vivian of Wiht and his descendants have land in the
country. See pp. 61–5.
[5] B 20 (c. 1166); D 108 (c. 1200); Z 197r, where (c. 1230) the same property (in St
Andrew's, on the Parade) is classed as a stone house in the hands of Robert 'camberlanus'.

Lucas, is in possession.[1] The common Canterbury surname Terry can be taken back to its origins. Theoderic (Theoric, Terric, Tieri, Terri, and variants) the goldsmith is a leading citizen at the end of the twelfth century. His sons and their sons are called 'filii Terri', and then in time, Terri, Terry.[2] Early burgesses do not, like manorial lords, bear surnames derived from places, apart from landmarks within Canterbury itself, or Kentish towns like Dover and Sandwich.

SOME MINOR ACTORS IN THE STORY OF THOMAS BECKET

Sometimes minor characters are introduced into the story of Becket with no explanation. One such character is Adam of Charing. Guernes tells how in the course of one of his abortive efforts to escape from the realm in the year 1164 Becket put out to sea from Romney, and that when the vessel was some way out the crew, realizing what they were doing, talked together in company with Adam of Charing. They foresaw that they and their kin would suffer at the king's hands if they helped his enemy escape, and therefore put the ship back.[3]

Adam of Charing may be found in Rentals D and F, named as tenant of the great stone house in Stour Street which had been built by the moneyer Lambin Frese just before his flight.[4] Adam bought the house for the modest sum of twenty marks, paid off in instalments.[5] He was alive, so it appears, within the financial year 1204-5, but was dead by late in 1207, when his heirs were negotiating with the sheriff of Kent, according to the Pipe Roll, for his property held at the date of his death.[6] The transfer of the property from Adam into the hands of the sheriff can actually be detected in Rental F, for the word 'vicecomes' has been added to his name.[7] Adam is mentioned in the *Epistolæ Cantuarienses* which recount the great struggle over the establishment of a secular college at Hackington, projected by archbishop Baldwin and bitterly resisted by his monks. At a meeting between the contestants in 1189 Baldwin called in Adam of Charing to give an opinion.[8] Adam made an evasive answer, clearly

---

[1] D 71, 72.   [2] See account of the family, above.

[3] *Guernes*, ll. 1361-5.

Li notunier k'i ierent unt ensemble parlé
Et Adam de Cherringes ...

[4] PR, 26 Henry II, p. 148.

[5] PR, 31 Henry II, p. 233; 32 H. II, p. 191; 33 H. II, p. 208, etc.

[6] PR, 9 John, p. 36; *Rot. de oblatis et finibus . . . tempore regis Johannis* (Rec. Commrs.), 1835, p. 373.

[7] F 246, 489.   [8] *Epp. Cant.*, no. cccxxiv.

trying to avoid giving offence to either faction. The cathedral sacrist became enraged and asked him what he was talking about. 'Weren't you there watching at Hollingbourne,' he demanded, 'when two country-fellows were put on trial-by-battle for a theft, and I had the loser hanged, acting as justice for the convent?—and you yourself have often pleaded in our court!' Adam had much land in Kent and at the end of his life was engaged in a dispute with archbishop Hubert over the manor of Charing whence he took his name.[1] Theobald had bestowed on him a sheepfold at Teynham,[2] while in 1196 abbot Roger of St Augustine's granted him thirty acres at Lenham (not many miles from Charing).[3] Adam entered into a final concord in 1190 in connection with other ground at Lenham.[4]

Adam of Charing is often found engaged in public business. He suffered an amercement of one hundred marks in 1164 for some unexplained offence, soon after Becket's final flight.[5] Whatever his offence may have been (and the large amercement makes it appear serious), he is soon in the king's confidence, being employed in exploitation of the resources of the see of Canterbury during the archbishop's exile.[6] Adam secured a special mention in the list of excommunications launched from across the sea by Becket against his enemies, in 1169.[7] After the murder he capitulated, like the rest of the Saint's foes, and founded the leper hospital at Romney in honour of the martyrs SS. Stephen and Thomas, at New Romney, near the stretch of sea where he had thwarted the projected escape in 1164.[8]

Becket made a regular practice of undergoing scourging, and had flagellants at various points. The office was performed when the arch-bishop was at Canterbury by Thomas, priest of St Martin's.[9] This indi-vidual may be found in Rental B, holding the ground immediately to the east of All Saints' church. He has a brother Luke who holds ground close at hand.[10]

[1] PR, 7 John, p. 117.   [2] Saltman, *Theobald*, no. 52.   [3] BBSA, p. 483.
[4] Ibid., pp. 526–7.   [5] PR, 11 Henry II, p. 105; 12 H. II, p. 112; 13 H. II, p. 200.
[6] PR, 13 Henry II, pp. 201–2.
[7] *Materials*, vi (*Epistles*). No. 488 (Becket to the clergy of London); cf. no. 494 (Becket to Rotrou of Rouen); no. 502 (Becket to William, subprior, and the convent of Canterbury). See *Eng. Hist. Docs.* ii, pp. 750–1. Since Adam's fellow-commissioners for expending funds of the see are not mentioned among the excommunicates, it is probable that he offended in some other way.
[8] *Monasticon*, vi, p. 640. Adam of Charing and his son Ivo, who evidently predeceased him, appear among witnesses to the judgment in the county court of Kent in 1176, when the monks of St Augustine's won a victory over their tenants in Thanet. (Warner and Ellis, *Facsimiles of Royal and other Charters in BM*, i, no. 57.)
[9] FitzStephen, *Vita* (*Materials*, iii, p. 22) . . . 'disciplinam secretam, nudato ad flagella dorso, recipiebat; cum erat . . . in vicinia Cantuariæ a Thoma presbytero sancti Martini.'
[10] B 208; (Luke) 115, 116.

When Becket fled overseas in 1164 Henry expelled his kinsfolk,

Thome genus damnat exilio,[1]

and the king coming to Canterbury, 12 July 1174, sought pardon from Roesia the Saint's sister, and made amends by granting her profits of the King's mill.

La surur saint Thomas merci quist et cria,
E en adrescement un molin li dona.
Bien valt dis mars par an la rente qu'ele en a.[2]

The Pipe Rolls show that payment was started in the very quarter of the year within which the grant was made. Her ten marks were advanced to £11 from 1176.[3] Roesia died probably in the year 1184–5, for her son John receives payment thenceforward.[4] Ralph, another nephew of Becket, may be found in Canterbury, holding ground a little downstream from the mill, north of the present Blackfriars' Bridge.[5] His mother is named as tenant here about 1180, and perhaps she dwelt here.[6] Ralph was living at Canterbury at the date of the great struggle between the monks and their archbishop, and became involved therein as a supporter of the former, suffering imprisonment and narrowly escaping death. In 1188 he was flung into the local gaol and nearly burnt therein when his enemies plotted to set it on fire.[7]

Some members of the knightly class who play a part in the story of Becket are lords of land in Canterbury. Alan of Ratling, excommunicated in 1169, whose wife may be the Æliz restored to health by intervention of the Saint, holds ground in the High Street, within the northern walls, and near St George's church. William of Eynesford, probably the third of the name, who stood surety for Becket, and was later excommunicated, holds ground in Newingate ward according to Rental B. It must be William IV who is lord of the ground forming the site of Eastbridge Hospital, and of St Helen's church with other ground near King's Bridge.[8]

There is one name of exceptional interest in the story of the actual murder of Becket, to be found in Rental D,[9] as that of a former holder

[1] *Oxford Book of Medieval Latin Verse*, 1st ed., no. 67.   [2] *Guernes*, ll. 6038–40.
[3] PR, 21 Henry II, p. 208; 22 Henry II, p. 205.
[4] PR, 31 Henry II, p. 224. The name of John is introduced in this year with that of his mother, and his name stands alone henceforward. Roesia evidently died (in 1185?) on 13 August, on which day her anniversary was celebrated by the monks (BM. Arundel 68, fol. 38r).
[5] D 66.   [6] X 1, fol. 5r.   [7] See p. 198.
[8] For Alan of Ratling see p. 56, above; for the Eynesford family, see p. 54.
[9] D 343. J.f. Vivian, the borough reeve, who appears in another miracle story (above, p. 84) also has had interest in the site.

of ground in St Peter's parish, namely Robert del Broc. This is probably a chief actor, after the four knights themselves, in the events of 29 December 1170. It was Robert de Broc, nephew of Becket's bitter foe, Ralph de Broc, who led the charge round by the kitchen of the palace to find another entry into the hall. Robert had plenty of opportunity to acquire ground locally as he was for years in charge of the archbishop's palace during the exile.[1]

William de Capes who holds ground in King Street[2] is with little question Becket's marshal, who after his master's flight from Northampton in 1164 went to Henry imploring him to call off those who were attacking the *familia*, left in the lurch. It was Ralph de Broc who was ordered to stop the attacks.[3] William de Capes followed his master into exile and kept watch while Becket was undergoing his penitential immersions in the drains under the abbey at Pontigny.[4] He obtained the post of janitor of the *curia monachorum*, or keeper of the back gate of the monastery, and was set on a special sentry duty with one of the monks at a juncture in the great struggle over the secular college in the days of archbishop Baldwin.[5] At the request both of Henry II, and of archbishop Richard (as is shown in the charter granting the office of janitor), William de Capes had been assigned the 'corrody of one monk', evidently the daily issue of food as received by one of the brethren. The grant is stated to have been made for the honour and reverence of Thomas the glorious martyr. The monks obtained from archbishop Richard a charter safeguarding themselves, and laying down that the corrody was issued personally to William de Capes, and that the concession was not to be construed as a right to any future keeper of the gate.[6] Richard, nephew of William de Capes, is cited as witness to delivery of Becket's letters of excommunication against Gilbert Foliot, served in St Paul's cathedral.[5] William, according to a charter in the cartulary of St Gregory's, Canterbury,[8] had a 'man' named Reginald, probably an assistant gate-keeper.

The accounts of the Miracles of St Thomas embody the names of local inhabitants. The children of Godefrid the baker (who occurs in Rentals A and B), were cured through relics, by Easter 1171.[9] John son of Vivian the borough reeve is named in one of the innumerable anecdotes, and is

[1] *Materials*, ii, p. 10.   [2] Greg., nos. 74, 75, 76.
[3] *Guernes*, ll. 2046 ff. Ralph was commissioned by the king to proclaim protection of the *familia* throughout Northampton.
[4] Ibid., ll. 2637, 3634.   [5] *Epp. Cant.*, RS, p. 313.
[6] CAC, Ch. Ant. C 179.
[7] *Materials*, vi, p. 604 (*Epistles*, Master William to Becket).
[8] Greg., no. 73.   [9] See pp. 6, 162.

head of a family with ground throughout Canterbury.[1] Master Feramin the physician, to whom were vouchsafed visions relating to St Thomas, is mentioned in Rental D.[2] William, priest of 'Bourne' (most probably Bishopsbourne), well-known to the Canterburians both through the nearness of his village and for his attractive personality, wisely calculated that relics of St Thomas were likely to become of considerable value. He was lucky enough to find the very cloak which Becket had on when he was slain, all bloodstained, which the then possessor was ready to sell. He bought it and also obtained possession of some of the blood.[3] This William can hardly be other than William, 'presbiter de Burnis', holding ground near St Margaret's church in Rentals A and B, very close indeed to the date of the murder.[4]

The chronicles and contemporary correspondence make mention of individuals who cannot always be identified with certainty. The Reginald the citizen who gave warning to Becket just before the murder might be one of several Reginalds of the same date occurring in Rental B.[5] One would give much to identify the house where dwelt Gilbert, whose 'large dwelling' close to the palace gate served as the advance headquarters for the four knights.[6] Unhappily much of the frontage opposite the gate where the house was probably situated stands unsurveyed in the contemporary rentals.[7]

[1] See pp. 64–5.   [2] See pp. 110, 158.   [3] *Materials* (Benedict), ii, pp. 58, 59.
[4] A 24; B 223.   [5] B 32, 49, 156, 170, etc.

[6] No Gilbert dwelling near the palace gate about 1170 has been found, yet there is a Gilbert 'de aula' who may be found in possession of ground east of the Stour, and apparently not far from the palace, about 1215. Gilbert must have taken his name from the great hall of the archbishop's palace, which dominated Palace Street opposite St Alphage church. (Greg., no. 72, in which is mentioned Peter, prior of St Gregory's from c. 1215, and James 'de porta', who died by the end of the same year.) At the end of the twelfth century the ground opposite the gate can be accounted for (D 76, LIII, LIV).

[7] There are other anecdotes which mention inhabitants of Canterbury, such as William, son of a citizen, cured of a tumour (*Materials*, ii, p. 55); Brithiva, a poor woman, saved from blindness (ibid., p. 41); Atheldrida, cured of a fever (ibid., p. 54); Goditha, wife of Matthew of Canterbury, saved from swellings in the legs (ibid., p. 56).

CHAPTER IX

Topography

THE GROUND-PLAN OF MEDIEVAL CANTERBURY

THERE is little relation between the layout of medieval Canterbury and the Roman grid which has emerged as a result of systematic excavation in the last few years. The only points where medieval streets correspond with those of the Roman period are just within and just without the gates which, of Roman origin, force the streets for a short distance into an ancient axis. Even Watling Street, which might be credited with Roman origin, is clearly of much later date, for it has been shown that on its somewhat erratic course down from Ridingate it roughly bisects the vast Hadrianic theatre discovered in 1950.[1]

The most striking fact which may be learned from the Surveys (Rentals B and D) is that within the walls the modern ground-plan can be carried back into the twelfth century.[2] A few modest alleys have disappeared and a new street (Guildhall Street) cut, but otherwise within the walls the layout is much the same as in the reign of king John. Indeed Rental B (as far as it goes) shows that in some of the central areas the layout was just the same thirty or forty years earlier. Outside the walls a ground-plan can be observed in Rentals B and D showing that there was little change between the age of the crusades and of the Napoleonic wars, when a wide barrack area spread across the northern suburbs, replaced in time by several streets of little houses. Rental B takes the ground-plan back into the sixties of the twelfth century, evoking the comment that the extra-mural suburbs are very much more populous in the age of Becket than c. 1800. Indeed there are frontages occupied by dwellings in Rental B which were empty even in the mid-twentieth century. About 1166 there is an extensive stretch of housing flanking New Ruttington Lane (Baggeberi), yet in maps of the area of c. 1654 and 1752 this thoroughfare is depicted as no

[1] *Journal of Roman Studies*, xli, p. 139.
[2] The first good printed map of Canterbury is that of W. and H. Doidge, published 1752. There is an admirable large-scale manuscript map in the city archives, 6 feet by 7 feet, c. 1640.

more than a country lane running between hedges. Perhaps this district was never built up for many centuries following the conflagration raging here in 1224.[1]

The extra-mural suburbs go far to discredit a conception of medieval citizens crowded together for safety within the borough walls. There were dwellings outside the fortifications before the Conquest. Domesday Book states that the burgesses had forty-five *mansuræ* sited 'extra muros'.[2] Charter I mentions a couple of houses without Ridingate, naming their occupants. Two anecdotes among the Miracles of St Augustine show that in the age of Anselm there was a man and his family living in a house in the suburbs, while a German pilgrim put up in the house of a faithful matron, said to be in front of the abbey gate, evidently in the neighbourhood of Lady Wootton's Green, outside the city walls.[3] Perhaps the most surprising feature, disclosed in Rental B, is the existence early in the reign of Henry II of a long ribbon growth reaching out to Barton on the Sturry Road, to a point half a mile beyond Northgate.[4] It seems that the suburbs have straggled out and linked up with the first hamlet along the Sturry Road at the Barton. It is clear that we have dwellings along the road and not agricultural plots, owing to the continual use (in Rental B) of the expression *mansura*. The documents are not informative about the occupations of individuals holding *mansure* here. We know that one of them at least was not a peasant, for he was John the monastic cook of Christ Church dwelling at the corner of Baggeberi (New Ruttington Lane).[5] Another occupant was Osbert the vinedresser (*vinitor*) with a *mansura* close to the vineyard of Christ Church.[6] Further in towards the city we find that Baggeberi is built up, while there are more dwellings in and near Old Ruttington Lane.[7] Moreover the edge of the defensive ditch facing the city wall east from Northgate is occupied by a continuous frontage of *mansure*,[8] while there are even dwellings in the ditch itself (apparently choked up at this point) backing on to the city wall.[9] There are four *mansure* next to the gate under the wall, together with a smithy. These holdings, it may be remarked, are in unpleasant proximity to the open drain which just here received the effluent from prior Wibert's great sewer discharging through the city wall.[10]

[1] Note appended to the Colton Rental in Cathedral Library, Lit. MS. D 4.
[2] *DB*, i, fol. 2r.　　　　　　　　　　　　[3] *Acta Sanctorum*, May, vi, pp. 407–9.
[4] See Map 1b.　　　　　　　　　　　　　　[5] B 131; D 25.
[6] D 35, D 13, 14. O. 'vinitor' need not necessarily have lived at the *mansura*, but it is very close indeed to the vineyard.
[7] B 57–61, 193, 194.　　　　[8] B 12–31.　　　　[9] B 7–10.
[10] See Jacob, 'Chichele and Canterbury' (in *Essays Presented to F. M. Powicke*), p. 395.

Rental D does not show (at the end of the century) such extensive suburbs, and furthermore does not use the term *mansura* in connection with ground either inside, or outside the walls. The ground-plots, as far as it surveys them, are merely called *terre* though there is no reason to suppose that the dwellings surveyed in B, thirty-five years before, have all disappeared. It is quite possible, as has been suggested, that the holdings surveyed in B in Baggeberi and along the Sturry Road, which do not appear in D, have been transferred for administrative purposes to the manor of Colton, evidently lying close to the Barton. The frontage in Broad Street, facing the walls, occupied by *mansure* in B, is surveyed in great detail in D.[1] The holdings are merely called *terre* in accordance with normal practice in D, but we learn from the nearly-contemporary Rental F that there were some stone houses here.[2] Rentals B and D both survey holdings lying east from Ruttington Lane, in Broad Street,[3] and in a lost lane called Dudelane, some yards from Havelock Street,[4] all outside the walls. Both B and D survey a group of holdings outside Burgate,[5] and further up Bridge Street, outside Newingate.[6] According to B there are nine dwellings round the corner on the north side of Dover Street.[7] Since Rental B surveys only the three northern wards of Canterbury, we have to rely principally on D for evidence about the Wincheap area. Unfortunately it merely describes as *terre* the long row of holdings running to a point half a mile beyond Worthgate,[8] and most probably certain of these *terre*, such as the piece of ground 150 feet by 300 feet in the hands of Robert of Cockering,[9] are open ground. Indeed this particular piece of ground has not been built upon till this day. However, the narrow frontage on the street and long stretch of ground running far back, which character-ize so many holdings here, point much more to a dwelling with a back garden than anything else. Rental F mentions a *mesagium* in Wincheap, close to 1205.[10] There seem to be at least eight *mesagia* on the east side of Wincheap, beyond the walls within St Mary de Castro parish by c. 1230,[11] and several more on the other side in St Mildred's, at the same date.[12] Henry Barate as shown in D (200) has a house (domus) some way outside Worthgate, early in the reign of John.[13]

[1] D 7, 34, 39–59, 63, 64.   [2] F 105, 106.   [3] D 35, 36, 77, 78.
[4] D 79, 80.   [5] B 195–8; D 81–87.   [6] B 91–98; D 127–36.
[7] B 99.   [8] D 167 ff.   [9] D 177.
[10] F 268.   [11] Z, ff. 206–7.   [12] Ibid.

[13] Henry Barate (see p. 215 below) was charged with supervising works on the castle, which is very close at hand. This is suggestive that he lived in his *domus* in Wincheap, and that William the clerk who has ground hard by, on the very edge of the castle ditch, may also have lived here since he is evidently W. the priest, also charged with supervision of the castle works (PR, 5 Richard I, p. 165; D 200; F 233).

Unfortunately, since the surveys do not cover ground without the Westgate of Canterbury, we can learn but little of what was probably the principal extra-mural suburb of the city. In the later Middle Ages this district (lying outside the borough and its jurisdiction, and within the archiepiscopal manor and hundred of Westgate) formed a populous built-up area flanking the main road running out of Canterbury towards London. No detailed rental of the area at an early date has been traced, though some evidence may be extracted from the cartulary of St Gregory's priory.[1] In the earlier thirteenth century there was a 'messuage' in the possession of the priory with a frontage of 19 feet on a street outside the city gate. This stood between two other *mesagia*.[2] There seem to be at least four 'messuages' (all apparently outside Westgate) mentioned in another charter,[3] and six messuages in St Dunstan's parish, and therefore some distance from the gate, in yet another.[4] More messuages (one in the hands of the 'claviger' of Westgate) are named in other charters.[5] There are two messuages described as lying south of an alley leading to the river outside Westgate 'on the left as you leave the gate, under the city wall on the opposite bank of the Stour'. This is not readily intelligible, and if the messuages lay in on the right leaving the gate it would be easy to site them in North Lane. If on the left they would find a site in among the mill ponds. Probably the scribe made an error and the dwellings lay along the eastern side of North Lane, in the tanners' quarter of the later Middle Ages. It is significant that John the tanner witnesses the charter in question.[6]

It is possible that some of the ground-plots without the walls about 1200 (certainly in the Wincheap area) had not been in existence for any great time, as they were evidently cut out of big fields flanking the highway, at no remote date. Two charters (XLI, XLII) record the grant of three acres of ground some distance from Worthgate, probably a little after 1170, while at the end of the century these three acres are no longer classified as a single unit but are cut up into nine tenant-holdings, while the rentals are at pains to explain that they all lie together.[7] Highly significant is the fact that the ancient field-names are attached to blocks of holdings in Wincheap, though at the beginning of the thirteenth century memory of these field-names is fading. There were evidently fields called 'Seven Acres', 'Woodland', and 'Holteche'. The compiler of Rental D (c. 1200) is confused as to what is 'Holteche', or even as to a correct form of the name, which he renders 'Holt Oga'.[8] It is not impossible that 'Seven Acres' can be traced back into the past, for the schedule of property of Christ

[1] Greg.   [2] Ibid., no. 57.   [3] Ibid., no. 59.   [4] Ibid., no. 60.
[5] Ibid., nos. 61, 62.   [6] Ibid., no. 54.   [7] F 601–7.   [8] D 183.

Church claimed to have been drawn up in the days of Lanfranc mentions *gabulum* drawn 'de vij acris'.[1] The plan of dwellings in Broad Street, strongly suggests that these have been cut out of two fields, one 300 feet by 520 feet, and another of 140 feet depth with an undetermined length upon the street.[2]

It must be emphasized that the rentals as a rule are merely a record of territory owing rent to the monks, and the absence of any mention of dwellings in a district does not mean that none exist. However, the available evidence, discussed above, points to the fact that there were in the twelfth century at Canterbury extensive suburbs, one lying outside Northgate, another on the London side of the city beyond Westgate, with houses outside both Burgate, and Newingate, while the Wincheap area is becoming built-up in the later twelfth and earlier thirteenth centuries.

Inside the walls Rental B shows that in the period c. 1166 there is a concentration of dwellings belonging to Christ Church around Best Lane[3] and Orange Street, near the river, with some blocks of dwellings in the upper High Street.[4] There is a central row of shops running up the middle of the street from St Andrew's church.[5] Again, we have only the Christ Church evidence, and we may well guess that if (say) Orange Street and Best Lane are populous, then the Mercery Lane area, more in the centre of things, is also inhabited and busy, as we find it a generation or so later in Rental D, assuming that the *terre* named in it along Mercery Lane incorporate dwellings.[6] Indeed the narrow frontages here point to congestion. This rental gives a strong impression that the central business area of Canterbury in the age of John was what it has always been in later centuries, the High Street—lower Burgate district. In the 1230's we have additional evidence from the rolls of arrears of rent, which provide lists of long rows of shops running down Burgate, along the south side of the Parade, and in Mercery Lane.[7] In D the holdings run fairly continuously all down the High Street. Even where there are gaps, as around the site of the Guildhall, we have material evidence for occupation, in the remains of the once handsome vaulted cellar just west of Guildhall Street perhaps constructed about 1180 by the 'gilda mercatorum'.[8] The territory finding a place in the documents thins out in the direction of the Dane John, and this perhaps reflects the actual state of affairs, since the ground

---

[1] The schedule (CAC, Reg. K, ff. 69v–70r) is discussed in Chapter II.
[2] D 42–53, 54–58.
[3] B 1–3, 114–21, etc. See map.
[4] B 104 ff. See map.
[5] B 219–21.
[6] D 115.
[7] CAC, Arrears.
[8] See below.

within the north-eastern quadrant of the walls has always been thinly occupied and indeed is in the same state today. If there are big extra-mural suburbs at Canterbury it can certainly be affirmed that the people dwelling within them have not been forced out of the walled area for sheer want of space. There are other districts inside the walls where it can readily be assumed that there is but little population. In St Mary Queningate and St Michael Burgate parish there actually appears to be a drop in the number of inhabitants between c. 1165 and c. 1200, for ground classed as *mansure* in B,[1] is called 'terre deserte' in D.[2] Moreover, ground in private occupation not far off has been thrown into the cathedral cemetery in the interval. Considerable stretches of ground forming the various monastic precincts are probably less densely populated by their inmates than they would be if they were occupied by housing. Certainly there must have been many people dwelling within the boundary of the palace of the archbishop flanking Palace Street when he was in residence, but it is improbable that these can have outnumbered the inhabitants of twenty-seven dwellings, with probably many more, evicted by Lanfranc to build the palace. Again, at the other end of Canterbury the castle yard made space for a garrison which was probably in peaceful times of less strength than the occupants of over forty houses on this site, demolished by 1086.[3]

Within the walls, as has been remarked above, some modest by-ways have disappeared since the twelfth century. The religious have been chiefly responsible for this change in the layout since they absorbed several such by-ways into their precincts. The rentals show that at Canterbury, as at Oxford and Cambridge, many canonical or academic lawns were originally streets of houses.[4] Prior Wibert secured the housing north of the cathedral *curia* while his successors acquired the access road within the city wall, bringing the boundary of the Precincts up to the wall itself. To the south, by virtue of royal and private charters, the boundary-wall was moved forward and secular dwellings pushed back.[5] On the east it is clear that the post-medieval clerical gardens were occupied by the parish of St Mary Queningate with that church standing in the middle. In the

---

[1] B 69, 205–7.   [2] D 88.

[3] Eleven dwellings whereof the king had sake and soke were destroyed, patently at the site of the castle (see account of holdings of the king, Chapter III). There were eleven more, given by the abbot, at the castle, to the king, for the churches of St Andrew and St Mary de Castro. We know the names of the inhabitants. See Appendix B. If the compensation given by the king to the abbot and archbishop, at fourteen and seven dwellings respectively, is roughly equivalent to houses requisitioned from them at the castle, then a total of about 43 may be reached. See Chapter III.

[4] As shown by Salter for Oxford, and by Willis and Clarke for Cambridge.

[5] For the Precincts, see below.

thirteenth century the friars further reduce the number of inhabited streets. West of the river the Blackfriars absorbed one lane and across the water disturbed the layout, when the dwelling of Ralph, nephew of Becket, clearly defined in Rental D, was thrown into the friary church-yard.[1] The Greyfriars truncated the long track shown as running south from the High Street in Rental D.[2] The Austin Friars secured licence in 1408 to enclose two lanes running across their precinct. One of these seems to be 'Lambertes Lane Wrenne', of which the inhabitants are named in Rental B.[3]

To the catalogue of lost thoroughfares may be added the lane called Stephen's Lane or Neele's Lane named in the rentals near Westgate, which is today exactly blocked by a sixteenth-century house.[4] Clearly some citizen has quietly appropriated a little-used alley. Horse-mill Lane, well-defined in the twelfth century, has disappeared by the eighteenth.[5] It is of much interest to see how some of these lost lanes survive if not in physical fact at least in an invisible manner. The 'parvus vicus' of c. 1200[6] north of the High Street within Westgate, now quite lost, survives today in an intangible form as the parish boundary between St Peters' and Holy Cross, and indeed the lost Stephen's Lane above marks another stretch of the same frontier. In the same class of survival is the ward-boundary Burgate–Northgate, which perpetuates the line of an ancient obliterated back-garden wall parallel with Mercery Lane.[7] These ancient boundaries and lanes are sometimes extraordinarily tenacious of life. At the sale a few years ago of property north of St Peter's church, Canter-bury, it was discovered that the vendors had no documentary title to a strip of ground about six feet wide running up the middle of the garden. It was quite easy to account for this lack of title for the strip of ground was none other than the old 'eastern lane' described on this axis in Rental D at the end of the twelfth century.[8]

A remarkable fact emerging from the study of the rentals is that not only has the general twelfth-century plan of Canterbury survived largely unaltered to this day, but in many instances the ground-plot occupied by a citizen of 750 years ago has also survived, sometimes in depth and some-times in length, and occasionally in both. This is less surprising than may appear at first sight for private owners are tenacious of their rights and

---

[1] A later thirteenth-century note added to Rental Z shows that the 'eastern lane' (D 313–318) has (in its northern section) been absorbed by the friars (fratres predicatores tenent per cartam conuentus cyrographatam). The holding of Ralph is D 66.

[2] D 332–64.   [3] *VCH, Kent*, iii, p. 199.   [4] D 386.

[5] D 378. It re-appeared in due course as St Peter's Place.

[6] D 370.   [7] See p. 104.   [8] D 313–18.

return to claim their ground after devastations by fire or water. Indeed, as has been suggested, Rentals B and D may well be surveys carried out after the fires of 1161 and 1198 to mark out the rights of Christ Church and its tenants. It can be affirmed that the holdings of c. 1200 of which dimensions are yet intact past the middle of the twentieth century have survived more than one local disaster like the conflagration of 1247,[1] when much of the city with St Mildred's church, was destroyed, or the alarming experience of 1272 when a great fount of water suddenly gushed up from the bowels of the earth and did considerable damage to housing in the city.[2]

Some examples of survivals of dimensions as given in Rental D, c. 1200 are offered below.

Solomon the mercer enjoys frontage of 30 feet on the south-eastern corner of Mercery Lane (D 110), while the modern frontage here is today 30 feet.
The frontage on St Margaret's Street, south of Hawk's Lane, is 74 feet in D 257, and survives unchanged, though the holding has been divided.
The frontage running west from St Peter's Lane on the High Street (D 321), 37 feet survives unchanged though the holding is now divided into two.
The north-western corner of Broad Street (D 7) is shown to have a frontage of 54 feet while the frontage is still 54 feet.

One admirable example where both length and breadth survive and the holding remains undivided is provided in the case of Robert of Cockering's ground-plot east of Wincheap Street. Rental D (177) gives the dimensions as 150 feet on the street, and 300 feet depth, precisely the figures for the recreation ground here today.

Examples of this kind can be multiplied, though caution must be exercized, for it is not difficult to find coincidences in the maze of alleys, yards and walled spaces into which the ancient well-defined ground-plots of central Canterbury have been cut up. Cases where survivals can with confidence be picked out have been indicated on the plans accompanying this study.

DOMESTIC AND BUSINESS ARCHITECTURE

Several substantial fragments of twelfth-century dwellings survive today in Canterbury, but largely out of sight. Two severies (out of eight) of a handsome vaulted cellar, originally 28 feet by 48 feet, are to be seen under shops at the corner of White Horse Lane. Not far off, on the other side

---

[1] Gervase, *Opera* (RS), ii, p. 203.
[2] *Annales Monastici* (RS), iv, p. 248; Gervase, ii, p. 272.

of the street, the sidewalls and shafts once supporting a fine vault of six severies (destroyed despite the strongest protests in 1922), survive beneath 21 High Street. Immediately opposite, below the County Hotel, there are footings and a worn back doorstep, which can hardly be anything but remains of the stone house of Jacob the Jew. All over the central area there are cellars of great antiquity, usually supporting on their chalk and flint walls structures of a much later date. The cellars indicate that as a rule the front of a citizen's house was flush with the street, though sometimes, as in the case of a house in Palace Street opposite the palace, there is suggestion that the house was set back, leaving a small yard in front. In the case of this house (no. 17) it appears that the living quarters were mounted over a semi-basement, to which an arched door led down by steps, while there were windows having a wooden lintel. There was a chamber over a high vaulted basement on the site of the old Guildhall, possibly the meeting place of the 'gilda mercatorum' in the twelfth century. The central pillar, still *in situ*, points to a date c. 1180. The structure on the south-east corner of Mercery Lane is mounted upon a remarkable double cellar extending to some 30 feet below the ground-level. At the bottom there is a low vaulted chamber, perhaps of early to mid-thirteenth century date, equipped with a well. Above this chamber is a roomy basement, still completely below ground-level, substantially of the same date, with moulded doorways. Below no. 43 Burgate Street, on the site of the great stone house mentioned in Rental D, is a cellar embodying a doorway with a flat arch once leading up into a central courtyard. The arch may be of earlier thirteenth-century date.

There are at least thirty stone houses in Canterbury in the age of the rentals, some without the city walls. It is curious that these stone houses have almost all disappeared above ground-level. They were probably made of the local materials, chalk with flint facing, a type of construction that has to be thick to last. It was probably change of fashion (back to wooden framing) which removed the stone houses, rather than decay, for the walls of churches built in the same way have survived in sound condition. One complete domestic building has come down to us in the shape of Eastbridge Hospital. However, it was not the private house of its founder Eadward son of Odbold, who we know dwelt north of St Peter's church, and the structure was probably put up for its special institutional purpose and therefore cannot be claimed as an example of a citizen's house at the end of the twelfth century.[1]

Most citizens must have dwelt in a house framed of wood, of which

[1] A plan is given in *Journal of British Archæological Association*, lxxvi, p. 103.

the Kentish countryside offered unlimited quantities. One man has a
house half wooden and half of stone.[1] The widespread fires which could
wipe out a suburb as in 1224,[2] or the whole city in 1161[3] and 1198,[4] or at
least part of the city with the gaol (as in 1186 or 1187)[5] must have made
business-men fearful for their stock, tallies and bullion. We find the
leading merchants and financiers in possession of stone houses, like Henry
the goldsmith,[6] Terric, goldsmith and financier,[7] Jacob the Jew,[8] or
Wiulph the moneyer.[9] Some stone houses reach considerable size. The
example east of the Buttermarket appears (from the evidence of Rental
D) to have been 45 feet by 90 feet.[10]

Roofing material was undoubtedly thatch for the most part. The
cathedral monks when letting out some shops close to their church probably about 1178, indicate that the roofing is of tile and insist that repairs
shall be done in the same material.[11]

The impression gained is that the citizen was not cramped for space in
his tenement. Of course we can never be sure that a man has for his
physical occupation all the ground assigned to him in the rentals, and it
may well be that he has let off portions. Some ground-plots in the central
area are very large by modern standards. John Dodekere has ground at
the corner of Butchery Lane 65 feet by 80 feet[12] while not far away there is
another holding 70 feet by 130 feet.[13] Rental D, which gives measurements,
is unhappily less informative about subdivisions than Rental B. The latter
is sometimes at pains to explain that there are several *mansure* on a plot of
ground,[14] but without any dimensions we cannot assess the amount of
frontage available to each tenant. However, it does seem that scores of
modern shops do business today in half the space occupied by a twelfth-
century citizen.

CROSSES

Rental F makes mention of a cross standing outside Newingate. It is
patently from this cross that Adam 'de cruce' son of alderman Alan takes
his title.[15] There is a man called John 'de cruce' having a messuage which
from its description may lie opposite the west end of St Dunstan's church,
close to the point where stood the cross in the later Middle Ages. The
charter relating to the messuage in question names an Augustine 'de cruce'

[1] D 318.   [2] Above, p. 21.   [3] Above, p. 7.
[4] Above, p. 13.   [5] PR, 33 Henry II, p. 205.   [6] D 68.
[7] D 99; F 194, 554.   [8] D 306.   [9] D 283.
[10] D 107–10.   [11] xxxix.   [12] D 103.
[13] D 105.   [14] E.g. B 32.   [15] F 187.

as witness.[1] It is possible therefore that the St Dunstan's cross was already in existence in the early thirteenth century.[2] There was a cross called Tiernecrouch at the end of St Margaret's Street in the fifteenth century. The corner here is called Tierne, Thierne in Rental A (c. 1165) but the cross has not been recorded at an early date.[3] There are other crosses at various points in Canterbury in the Middle Ages, such as the High Cross in the Buttermarket, Oaten Hill Cross, and Barnacle Cross on Wincheap Green.[4] In all cases the crosses stand at road-junctions.

CITY WALLS AND GATES

The documents show that the city walls are running in the twelfth century on the same lines as in later ages. Indeed recent excavation has disclosed that the walls are originally Roman throughout their length. The main gates in use are Westgate, Northgate, Burgate, Newingate, Ridingate and Worthgate. There is no mention of Wincheap Gate nor of any postern on its site, but since no ground is surveyed close to this point there is no call for a mention of it. Queningate is named in Rental B and in Charter XLV (c. 1175). Since the gate serves as a landmark it has evidently not yet been blocked up and forgotten. Churches apparently surmount at least three of the gates. It may be remarked that there is no mention of any towers attached to the walls, and it is highly probable that the towers were only added in the fourteenth century. Northgate (surmounted by St Mary's church) is depicted, with a long stretch of the city wall running eastward, in the twelfth-century plan of the Precincts. At least three towers (as in the later Middle Ages) might be expected to appear in this stretch had they been in existence in the twelfth century. There is some sort of turret on or just inside the wall in the plan, where today stands the second tower from Northgate, but this turret may have some connection with the waterworks system. The defensive ditch along the wall appears several times in the documents.[5] It is styled 'fossa del bali' at the point near Worthgate where it serves both as moat to the city wall and to the castle as well.[6] The crown naturally interested itself in maintenance of defences of a leading borough like Canterbury. During Becket's exile funds of the

---

[1] Greg., no. 60.
[2] The later medieval cross is depicted in the corner of the plan of Canterbury in Somner, *Antiquities of Canterbury*, 1703.
[3] A 27.
[4] For Tiernecrouch, the High Cross, Oaten Hill Cross, and Barnacle Cross, see Somner, *Antiquities of Canterbury*, 1640, pp. 20, 144, 149.
[5] See Index to Documents, CANTUARIA civitas; murus; fossa.   [6] F 233, 504.

see were devoted to this purpose.[1] An entry in the Pipe Roll uses wording
which suggests that St Augustine's abbey (lying outside the walls) was
responsible for repairs to a stretch of the fortifications.[2] Queen Eleanor
induced the monks of Christ Church to help with repairs to the walls,
when Richard had fallen into captivity. In the next reign Hubert de
Burgh, with the citizens, obtained barricades (cleias) for the defences.
These barricades might have been employed about the walls, or again
they might have been used in the outer defences, based on the bars which
seem to have been in existence.[3]

THE BARS

The rentals and charters prove the existence of a series of bars spanning
main roads approaching Canterbury. There is a bar at St Sepulchre's (as
early as 1149), some three hundred and thirty yards outside Ridingate.[4]
There is another bar in Wincheap, just two hundred yards without
Worthgate,[5] and another in Sturry Road, at Coldharbour Lane, nearly
half a mile from Northgate. There is evidence for a bar or obstruction
of some kind in the late thirteenth century at a point called 'Bordiche' in
Longport, a quarter of a mile from Burgate 'between the belltower and
the Barton'. It was stated (before John de Reygate and his colleagues,
justices itinerant in 7 Edward I), that this bar was in use 'tempore werre', a
valuable indication of the purpose of the bars, otherwise unexplained.[6] It
is to be remarked that each bar is sited on a main road just before the point
where side roads branch off round the city walls or across the fields. The
bars must have been part of a scheme of outer defence and it will be remembered how important was the 'fléel' or bar at Lincoln below Stone-
bow in breaking up the charge of the baronial party in 1217.[7] There is no
evidence that a defence scheme incorporating the Canterbury bars was

[1] PR, 13 Henry II, pp. 201–2.

[2] PR, 20 Henry II, p. 2. 'et pro muro ciuitatis qui pertinet ad eandem abbatiam claudendo
Lxxv.s.7 vi.d. per breue regis'.

[3] CAC, Ch. Ant. C 49; HMC, v, app. p. 433. Somner, *Antiquities of Canterbury*, 1640,
p. 9.

[4] VIII; A 10, D 148.

[5] D 187; where it is called 'barra'. Rental Y (c. 1218) speaks of a stone house in Wincheap
'infra barras'.

[6] Cathedral Library, Lit. MS. E 19 (Register of St Augustine's abbey, embodying, *inter
alia*, transcripts of *quo warranto* proceedings), fol. 61v. 'Jurati dicunt quod abbas sancti
Augustini appropriauit sibi quoddam fossatum quod vocatur Bordiche quod solebat ad ciuitatem Cant' pertinere ad faciendum barreras tempore guerre ad defensionem dicte ciuitatis si
necesse fuerit.'

[7] *Histoire de Guillaume le Maréchal*, ed. Meyer, ii, 16948.

carried in a circle round, and some distance from, the walls. Indeed, the man-power needed to occupy such a perimeter would have been enormous. There is no bar, it should be pointed out (as far as the evidence shows) outside Westgate, but the city jurisdiction ended here on the river. However, jurisdiction counts for little in warfare and one might expect a bar somewhere along St Dunstan's Street, especially on the London side of Canterbury. Some of the citizens take their names from bars, as Luke del bar, on the Sturry Road,[1] and Nigel Bar in Longport.[2]

WELLS

There are several wells about the city bearing special names. The monks recorded in their obituaries a grant claimed to have been made by archbishop Athelhard (793–805) of six *mensurae* in Canterbury next to 'Eadburgewelle'.[3] In the twelfth century there is a well in the alley leading to the cathedral gate from the Buttermarket called Sunwin's well, evidently taking its name from Sunwin the smith dwelling hard by.[4] In Broad Street close to the edge of the defensive ditch is to be found a well called 'fons de Cueningate' deriving a name from the adjacent Roman arch in the city wall.[5] Along the Sturry Road, at Coldharbour Lane, perhaps on the opposite side of the road, there is a well, from which Elfsi attharewelle (one of the members of the gild carrying on the cult of St Anselm) takes his title.[6] In Stour Street, close to the bottom of Hawk's Lane, there is a well called Hottewelle.[7] Perhaps it had a 'hot' taste owing to its chemical property. A well sunk close to this point in the seventeenth century had a marked chemical content.[8]

THE GAOL, PILLORY AND ORDEAL-PIT

The Canterbury gaol makes an appearance in the Pipe Roll of 1166, in common with those of Rochester, Huntingdon, Cambridge, Malmesbury, Aylesbury, Bedford and Sarum, and can, like them, be associated with the provision for erecting gaols in the Assize of Clarendon. The expenditure

---

[1] Z, fol. 191v.   [2] BBSA, p. 343; BM. MS. Cotton, Claudius D X, fol. 141.
[3] Dart, *Canterbury Cathedral*, app. viii. Are these the six 'jugera' of Birch, CS, 317?
[4] B 77, 89.   [5] B 61.
[6] Z, fol. 191v. At this point (c. 1230), 'Lucas del bar' pays rent 'de terra vbi grangia domini prioris fuit contra puteum ad barram citra bertonam'.
[7] D 247.
[8] Somner, *Antiquities of Canterbury*, 1703, pp. 191–2 ('*Reflections* upon Chartham News', by N. Battely).

on the Canterbury gaol is surprisingly small (6s. 8d.)[1] but since the Assize says[2] that such structures are to be made of the king's timber, where available, the cost is probably merely for labour in bringing wood down from the royal forest of Blean, and for setting it up. There is heavy expenditure ten years later (apparently as a result of the Assize of Northampton) when no less than £9 16s. 6d. is laid out on the gaol.[3] Sums of money are spent on it in several years, varying from £4 9s. 9½d. in 31 Henry II,[4] to 10s. in 8 John.[5] The Pipe Roll of 33 Henry II shows that a conflagration had raged through Canterbury in which the gaol had perished (periit) resulting in costs of 51s. 5d. to restore it.[6]

It was in the Canterbury gaol that Ralph, nephew of St Thomas, was imprisoned, together with other citizens supporting the monks, in 1188 (during the crisis over the secular college at Hackington).[7] The site of the gaol is clearly defined in Rental D, as standing in the block south of the High Street, east of Rose Lane, in St George's parish.[8]

Another instrument of justice finds a place in the rentals. Rental F[9] indicates that the 'pillori' is in the High Street, by Wiulph the moneyer's house, just below White Horse Lane, and not as in the days of Elizabeth I, at the end of Pillory Lane (Rose Lane). No mention of the borough gallows has been found. In later centuries the site was at Hollow Lane, in Wincheap. Ground at this point is surveyed in D, but this rental is silent on the subject. We learn, however, that in the thirteenth century the prior of Christ Church kept his gallows out at Horsfold, beyond the vineyards, east of the Sturry Road.[10] We may perhaps point out the site of another item in the judicial equipment of the age. There is a fifteenth-century rental listing sums due to the crown in Canterbury which applies the name 'Hosdelpette' to the field flanking the river outside the city walls in St Mildred's parish.[11] The name as it stands is not readily intelligible, and it is tempting to guess that the scribe has misread as 's' a long 'r' in (perhaps) a thirteenth-century original. Have we in this riverside meadow (just where it might be expected) the ordeal-pit of Canterbury?

[1] PR, 12 Henry II, p. 111.   [2] § 7 in the conventional numeration.
[3] PR, 22 Henry II, p. 206.   [4] PR, 31 Henry II, p. 224.
[5] PR, 8 John, p. 48.
[6] PR, 33 Henry II, p. 205.
[7] Epp. Cant. Nos. ccxviii, ccxxvii, ccxxix; Gervase, Opera, RS i, pp. 425–6.
[8] D 106, 117, 119; F 265; XLVII.
[9] 308.
[10] Hundred Rolls (Rec. Com.) i, p. 203.
[11] CAC. Rental 71. The list embodies the name of Andrew Brytwold, an early-thirteenth-century citizen.

THE ALMSHOUSES

St Thomas' Hospital at Eastbridge, where the main street crosses the river, was founded by Edward son of Odbold, on ground of William of Eynesford (IV), son of the man who stood surety for Becket in 1164.[1] Rentals X 1, X 2, show that the hospital was in existence by 1180. Ralph, nephew of the Saint, was an early Master of the institution. The ground where stands Maynard's (Mainer's) hospital off Stour Street is surveyed in Rental D but is classed merely as the ground of Mainer.[2] Possibly he has not yet founded his hospital. There is no mention of the existence of Cokin's hospital which probably occupied the ground of William Cokin, described in Rental D, on the south side of St Peter's Street.[3] This foundation was united with Eastbridge Hospital by bull of Innocent III in 1203,[4] and had probably gone out of independent existence some time before. It is curious that the documents do not mention St John's hospital, already eighty years old by the date of Rental B. The origins of the Poor Priests' hospital are disclosed in Charter XXXVI. Lambin Frese the moneyer had a workshop near Christ Church Gate. It was probably here that the fire started resulting in the destruction of the cathedral choir in 1174.[5] The monks induced Lambin to move by giving him ten marks, and offering him two adjacent dwellings, those of Godwin Grom and of Gerold the tanner, 'towards Hottemelne, near the ford'.[6] Lambin threw the holdings into one and built himself a stone house thereon. On his flight in 1180,[7] Adam of Charing, Becket's enemy, took over the house. Adam died by 1207[8] and Roger the clerk, Lambin's son, managed to acquire the site.[9] He sold it to Alexander of Gloucester the philanthropist, who set in the building the hospital of St Mary to shelter poor priests, a function it performed into the reign of Elizabeth.[10]

SALT HILL

The rentals make a contribution to the study of archaeology for they show the existence of a now lost tumulus called Salt Hill. William Somner sites it at Oaten Hill[11] but this is too far away from the dwellings opposite

---

[1] *DMon*, pp. 45–47. See account of the Eynesford family in Chapter III.   [2] D 211.
[3] D 366.   [4] Duncombe and Battely, *Three Archiepiscopal Hospitals*, pp. 305, 307.
[5] Gervase, *RS*, i, p. 3.   [6] XXXVI.
[7] For Lambin Frese as a moneyer, see p. 115.   [8] PR, 9 John, p. 36.
[9] Lambin compounded for his offences at 20 marks (PR, 2 Richard I, p. 151; 4 Richard I, p. 311).
[10] XXXVII.   [11] *Antiquities of Canterbury*, 1640, pp. 148–9. See B 91, D 130, F 188.

Newingate which are said to lie at Salt Hill. There are or have been at least eight tumuli in Canterbury in addition to Salt Hill which may be associated with the not far-distant Dane John group. These are evidently Roman burial mounds of the same type as the Bartlow Hills in Essex. That Salt Hill was a Roman burial mound is strongly suggested by the discovery in 1867–8 at the very point calculated from the evidence of the rentals, of a leaden coffin containing the remains of a girl. The coffin was 6 feet from the surface and but 3 feet from some earlier surface. It is likely, if the mound and coffin can be associated, that when the former was cleared the excavators failed to dig low enough to reach the coffin and its contents. Salt Hill must have disappeared between 1420, when it still served as a landmark, and the earlier seventeenth century, when the industrious antiquary William Somner would have known of it.[1]

The name of the greatest of the Canterbury tumuli appears as 'Dan jvn' in Rental D,[2] and this seems to be the earliest instance of the name, half a century before any supplied by Wallenberg.[3] The tumulus (from its name) must patently once have served as the basis for the castle, before removal of the last-mentioned to another site (certainly by 1089).[4]

THE 'HOLY STONE'

Another contribution to archaeology may perhaps be provided by the documents. Rental F[5] says of certain ground of the heirs of Sunwin Hare, in St Peter's parish, that it lies 'near Halistane'. Rental D,[6] without mentioning this last name, indicates that the same ground must lie at the end of Crienemeldnelane (St Peter's Grove), close to a point on the city wall where it meets the river. In the thirteenth century Robert Calvel of Hackington grants away seven poles of ground along the *venella* leading towards 'Halistane'.[7] A charter of the same date remarks of ground in Criene Mill Lane that it lies 'versus le Halistane'.[8] Rental Z says of the ground of Sunwin Hare that it lies (c. 1230), 'apud Halistone'.[9] The Hundred Rolls, late in the century, say of a meadow at Canterbury that it is situated 'apud Holistun extra muros'.[10]

What this 'holy stone' might have been is far from clear. It might have been some sort of monolith, perhaps like that still to be seen in the precincts of St Augustine's abbey. Since the 'holy stone' serves as a landmark

---

[1] W. Urry, 'Salt Hill, a lost Canterbury tumulus' (*Archæologia Cantiana*, lxi, pp. 141–7).
[2] D 159.   [3] *Place-Names of Kent*, p. 605.
[4] See account of St Mildred's Church, below.   [5] 130.   [6] 355.
[7] CAC, Ch. Ant. C 759.   [8] Ibid., C 900.
[9] Z, fol. 199v.   [10] *Hundred Rolls* (Rec. Commrs.), i, p. 203.

for siting ground both inside and outside the city walls it must clearly have a position at, or upon the walls, and must stand near the river bank, opposite St Mildred's church.

ST GREGORY'S PRIORY AND THE HOUSE
OF THE ARCHDEACON

The priory established by Lanfranc was in existence by 1085.[1] Remains found in 1958 may be part of the cloister and suggest that the priory church lay at an acute angle with Northgate Street. Rental D indicates that the south-west corner of the graveyard was at a point 132 feet from the corner of Broad Street.[2] In the twelfth century the eastern part of the priory precinct was still occupied by the house of the archdeacon, placed here by Lanfranc. Rental B shows that the house was reached by an entry running off Old Ruttington Lane, north of Unthanksway.[3] The official occupants of the archdeacon's house numbered some distinguished men. Roger of Pont l'Evêque, Becket's bitter enemy, who in 1170 briefed the four knights at Bur and paid their expenses for the journey to Canterbury,[4] was succeeded in 1154 as archdeacon by Becket himself, who was in turn followed (in 1163), by Geoffrey Ridel. These active men of affairs and politicians can hardly have spent much time at Canterbury in their official residence, and their duties were performed by a vice-archdeacon whom we meet occasionally in the rentals.[5] In 1227 the house of the archdeacon was bestowed on the priory, by charter of Stephen Langton.[6]

STAPLEGATE

William Thorne, the chronicler of St Augustine's abbey, says that king Ethelbert accommodated the Roman missionaries in Canterbury in a place called 'Stablegate', so-called from the fact that the beasts which had been out on the road laden with baggage were stabled here. Thorne also remarks that there had been in this place an oratory for the king's family, where worship and sacrifice to their gods were maintained.[7] This information can probably be dismissed as some more of Thorne's fanciful history. Speculation as to the origin of the name Stablegate, Staplegate seems to be concluded by an entry in Rental F[8] stating that a holding in the 'Borough'

---

[1] Greg., *Introduction*, p. ix. Dickinson, *Origins of the Austin Canons*, p. 104.
[2] D 7.   [3] B 160.   [4] *Guernes*, ll. 5126 ff.   [5] See p. 110.
[6] Langton, *Acta*, ed. K. Major (Canterbury and York Society), no. 103.
[7] *Thorne*, col. 1759, p. 5.   [8] 462.

(which flanks Staplegate) 'lies next to the stable of the lord archbishop'. It is clear therefore that the stables were separate from the main area of the palace, and were on the other side of the road. Probably there was a gateway on the palace side of the stables, from which the area in time took its name.[1]

STREET-NAMES

The local street-names are on the whole very unstable. The surveyors often avoid using any name, and speak of 'the way leading to the castle' or 'to the church of St Margaret', as the case may be. Some names have however, shown great vitality, like 'Drutintune' (Old Ruttington Lane), which emerges at a remote date,[2] and appears in the rentals,[3] or Mercery Lane,[4] Burgate (called indifferently Burgate and Burgate Street as today),[5] and Wincheap.[6]

It is curious that the name Watling Street, which might be supposed by far to antedate the rentals and charters, does not appear until the sixteenth century. The average street name in early Canterbury was quite evanescent. Some names derive from the principal inhabitant of a street or from the man living at the corner. The names of the streets tend therefore to change from generation to generation, like that of the lane within Westgate 'which used to be called "Neele's Lane", and now that Stephen the clerk lives there it is called "Stephen's Lane"'.[7] The wealthy inhabitant of All Saints' Lane endows it with the name 'John son of Robert's Lane'.[8] Opposite St George's church there is an alley (c. 1166) in which dwells Lambert Wrenne, whence the lane is called 'Lambertes Lane Wrenne'.[9] The beggars (lodere) outside Newingate have evidently given the name 'Lodderelane' to Ivy Lane.[10] The name of Dudelane,[11] the lost alley near Lady Wootton's Green is perhaps derived from a proper name, and is probably the 'Doddyslane' which finds mentions in this area in the sixteenth century. Butchery Lane is not supplied with any name in Rental D, though F calls it Sunwineslane at one point (perpetuating the name of Sunewin the smith, whose workshop once stood at the corner), and 'Cor-

---

[1] For Staplegate, see Somner, *Antiquities of Canterbury*, 1640, p. 133; *Thorne*, col. 2203–6.
[2] Wallenberg, *Place-Names of Kent*, p. 607.
[3] See Index to Documents, DRUTINTUNE.   [4] D 110; F 540, etc.
[5] See Index to Documents, BURGATE.
[6] See account of markets, Chapter V.   [7] D 386; Z, fol. 200v.
[8] In the Rental of c. 1300, in CAC, Reg. J, fol. 109r. This rental embodies much earlier material. See F 33.
[9] D 213.   [10] D 127.   [11] B 64, 194; D 79; F 121–6.

veseria' at another,[1] the name applied to the lane in an early thirteenth-century charter.[2] In later years it is called Salcock's Lane and Clement's Lane.[3]

Of particular interest is the name Rithercheape, Retherchieape, applied to Dover Street.[4] The name was still current in the sixteenth century but forgotten by 1640.[5] The occurrence in the twelfth century goes a long way to connect Dover Street with the 'hrytheraceap' named in a Canterbury charter of 1003[6] and with the 'ryther ceap' outside the eastern walls in a charter of 923.[7] The interpretation is clear enough: it is the cattle market. Dover Street was called 'cattle market' in the days of Henry II and John, and the street, or the area around it, was probably so-called in the age of Alfred. Since the cattle market of Canterbury was held at the end of Dover Street under the eastern walls until 1955, a modern institution can be carried back, so it appears, to a remarkably distant date.

Another name which has a sound of high antiquity is 'Hethenman-nelane' applied to Stour Street.[8] Could the 'heathens' who gave the lane its name be a colony of Danes once dwelling here? In the twelfth century there is one man with a Scandinavian name (Wlfketel)[9] along this lane and another with ground next door but one to the lane, called Toli.[10] The turnings running off 'Hethenmannelane' are in some cases supplied with proper names. The alley going down to the river near Maynard's Hospital is called Geroldeslane, apparently after Gerold the fuller whose niece owns ground here c. 1200.[11] This ground is occupied by one Erges-bold but perhaps Gerold once lived on it. Hospital Lane seems to be 'Crocchereslane'[12] which is not to be confused with another Crocker's Lane outside Westgate at the end of the Middle Ages. Hellelane in St Mildred's is evidently Rosemary Lane, which is in fact a slight hill.[13] Rental A takes the name Tierne[14] back into the mid-twelfth century. It seems to be applied to the road-junction at the bottom of Watling Street, rather than any of the streets conjoining here. The meaning is apparently 'turning' which is appropriate for the double turn from St Margaret's to Castle Street. Along the Dover Road, according to Rental D, near St

[1] F 175 295. [2] CAC, Ch. Ant. C 697.
[3] CAC, Reg. J, fol. 243r. [4] B 99; D 138; F 526.
[5] Somner seems to think it is near the Old Dover Road, *Antiquities of Canterbury*, 1640, p. 149.
[6] OS. *Facsimiles of A.S. MSS.*, iii, no. 36. *Eng. Hist. Docs.*, i, p. 540. See *Archæologia Cantiana*, lxix, pp. 41 ff.
[7] Birch, *CS*, 637. [8] XLIX. [9] D 225. [10] D 304.
[11] D 210. [12] D 217. [13] D 213.
[14] A 27. See Somner, *Antiquities of Canterbury*, 1640, pp. 344–5.

Laurence priory, there is a track called Holestrate,[1] now clearly Puckle Lane. Coldharbour lane leads down to a bridge called Longbridge.[2]

THE CATHEDRAL PRECINCTS

Fortunate is the student of twelfth-century documents who has a contemporary map to guide him. Much of Rentals A and B would hardly be intelligible without the Christ Church waterworks plan bound into the Canterbury Psalter, with which it is possible to interpret what otherwise would be some very difficult passages.[3] The plan shows the location of features in the Precincts which are near enough to the boundary wall to serve as landmarks to the surveyors setting out housing just outside. Rental A mentions dwelling-places 'behind the brewhouse' or 'behind the bakehouse'. The plan indicates that the 'bracinum' and 'pistrinum' stood (and indeed in substance still stand) just within the boundary wall, which ran some way within the northern city wall. On the south side of the Precincts, just within the wall, stood (neatly depicted in the plan) the detached 'campanile, clocarium', mentioned in Rental B.[4] The mound on which this stood still survives south of St Anselm's chapel. This belltower finds a mention in contemporary literature, for it was here, at Pentecost, 1169, according to William of Canterbury, that Master Feramin's mystic vision was enacted, when a Voice came from Heaven and the future glory of St Thomas was manifested.[5] The rentals and charters confirm in a remarkable manner the accuracy of minor features in the map and promote confidence in its general fidelity to fact. The boundary wall is drawn with a double right-angled turn behind the belltower. Now this corner is specifically mentioned in Rental B and housing in the town intrudes into the corner, such as the dwelling of Lifwin Cruc.[6] It may be remarked at this juncture that anyone living here must have been deafened by the monstrous bells put into the tower by prior Wibert.[7] This housing was dangerously close to the cathedral from the point of view of fire and the monks cleared the area in the seventies of the century.[8]

The southern gate (cemetery gate), of the Precincts is shown piercing the wall. This must not be confused with the later gate which stood some way to the west. The approach to the mother church of England was most unimpressive, for the constant stream of visiting magnates and pontiffs had to pick its way under an outer arch through a winding and apparently

[1] D 139.
[2] Z, fol. 191v.
[3] See p. 3.
[4] B 70, 84; C 2; D 89, etc.
[5] See pp. 110, 158.
[6] B 84.
[7] Stahlschmidt, *Church Bells of Kent*, p. 192.
[8] xxv–xxxi.

narrow alley past congested dwellings, a well called Sunwin's well,[1] Sunwin the smith's forge,[2] round a bend, along the face of the wall, and so into the graveyard. In this alley started the fire in which three 'domunculæ' were half-burned down, sparks from which set fire to the cathedral choir in 1174.[3]

Professor Willis carried out the most exhaustive examination[4] of the plan as it affected the cathedral and conventual buildings within the boundary wall, but left almost undiscussed the waterworks system outside. The rentals make a contribution to the study of this question. The supply-pipe (if we follow it backwards) passes in the plan through the city wall, thence over a bridge, through a 'pomerium', then through a 'vinea', across a field (campus) and back to the catchpits. The 'pomerium' is clearly the 'gardinum et ortus' bestowed in 1227 on St Gregory's priory by Stephen Langton as part of the dwelling-place of the archdeacon of Canterbury.[5] The brethren of St Gregory's agreed to allow the monks to send in workmen for maintenance purposes in connection with the waterpipe and promised a basket of apples annually as a sign of goodwill.[6] There is a graphic illustration of the accuracy of Rental D, connected with the waterpipe. The system still functions today in a modified form, and the conduit runs down Military Road, crossing Broad Street at an angle, and so under the wall. According to D[7] the ground now occupied by the southern end of Military Road was, c. 1200, in the hands of one William son of Drogo. Rental G (the out-payments) of the same date, records that one penny *per annum* was paid to William son of Drogo 'for the aqueduct passing through his ground'.[8] The plan shows that the pipe now runs back through a vineyard. Rental B agrees in the existence of a vine-growing area, but shows that there were in fact two vineyards, not one, an upper and a lower. The lower vineyard alone was of great size, stretching from the backs of houses in Northgate eastward to beyond Military Road. Moreover, it must come down (from a point opposite Coldharbour Lane) as far as the backs of houses in Baggeberi (New Ruttington Lane), so the lower vineyard must have extended to about eight acres.[9] There was a vinepress (torcular) at the back of Northgate Street opposite Coldharbour Lane,[10] and a 'domus de vinea' (vinedresser's house,

---

[1] B 77, 89.   [2] B 75.

[3] Gervase says that the three 'domunculæ' were sited 'ante portam extra muros atrii' (*Opera, RS*, i, p. 3).

[4] *Architectural History of the Conventual Buildings of the Monastery of Christ Church in Canterbury.*

[5] *Acta Stephani Langton* . . . edited by K. Major (Canterbury and York Society), no. 103.

[6] Greg., app. i, 5.   [7] D 43.   [8] G 30.   [9] B 132, 184.   [10] C 25; F 20.

or toolshed?) not far away.[1] The waterpipe crossed Baggeberi towards its eastern end near the 'sandpet', which must today be represented by the depression in which lies the old military cemetery.[2] The 'campus' indicated in the plan is well beyond any houses, and is therefore not mentioned in the rentals.

The area of the cathedral precincts is by no means static and unchanging for the documents show that it was steadily increasing in size through the twelfth century, and later. There seems to have been a definite effort to establish something like a scientific frontier, which was achieved at the end of the Middle Ages, when the whole quadrant flanked by the archbishop's palace on the west, by Burgate Street on the south, and by the city wall on north and east, was included within the liberty of Christ Church. Charters IV, V, VI show that ground adjacent to the precincts was being brought into that area in the reign of Henry I, and this addition of ground may undoubtedly be associated with the reconstruction of the cathedral choir (finished by 1130) which greatly extended the length of the building, demanding much more space on the east. Further extension was conducted under prior Wibert (1153–67). Back behind the 'bracinum' and the 'pistrinum' ran the monastic boundary wall. In between this and the city wall was a wide passage (VIA INTER MVRVM CIVITATIS & MVRVM CVRIE in the twelfth-century plan) with a track along the inner face of the city wall. Fronting on this track was a series of dwellings, which, crowding up to the monastic offices, introduced a secular and alien atmosphere. Wibert determined to buy out the occupants, and the record of his acquisitions in this quarter may be found in Rental A. Once possession had been obtained of the holdings they were evidently cleared of buildings and thrown into the Precincts, and a new wall was constructed along the frontage, upon the track.[3] In the next century a further advance was made, and a royal charter (dated 1232) was secured permitting the monks to appropriate the lane and to move their frontiers up to the city wall itself.[4] The right of the monks to this lane was challenged by the jurors in the investigations of 1274–5[5] and again in 1305.[6] On the latter occasion the title was defended with the aid of the charter of 1232.

The disaster of 1174 prompted the monks to take drastic action to prevent a recurrence of such a calamity. The fire which destroyed the 'glorious

[1] B 139.   [2] B 179, 181. The military cemetery is flanked today by the waterpipe.
[3] A 1–8. One holding here owed rent to the archbishop, which was not bought out. The rent is classed as paid for ground 'within the new wall'. See Rental C, § 21.
[4] Reg. E, ff. 56–57. Somner prints it in part (Antiquities of Canterbury, 1640, p. 191). He assigns it however to the reign of Henry II, though Hubert de Burgh is named as a witness.
[5] Hundred Rolls, i, p. 203.   [6] Somner, Antiquities of Canterbury, 1640, p. 191.

choir' started in buildings north of Burgate, south of the cathedral.[1]
It was decided to bring all this ground, with its congested dwellings, under
the control of the priory, and a measure of the anxiety of the brethren to
effect their policy can be seen in the fact that no less than three royal
charters[2] (one of these in duplicate) were secured to confirm acquisitions
made in this small stretch of ground. One tenant, Lambin Frese the
moneyer, was not only given two holdings away in another parish in
exchange for his ground before the cathedral gate (at the exact point,
it may be observed, where the fire started) but was given the sum of ten
marks to encourage him to go.[3] Another measure of the monks' anxiety is
the fact that they gave in exchange to St Augustine's abbey, ground with
tenants elsewhere in Canterbury for holdings of the abbey in the Burgate
area which it was designed to clear.[4] They abandoned some of their land
in London to the Cornhill family,[5] in exchange for ground north of
Burgate (dwelling on the subject of 'frequent fires' and the danger thereof
to the cathedral), and furthermore sacrificed their own rents in clearing
the dangerous property.[6] Having done all this they then built a new
boundary wall very much to the south, but north of Burgate Street. This
wall which still exists in part ran on a line 25 feet back from the street.[7]
The strip of ground in front, on the town side, was let out, cut up into
plots bearing shops. This allocation had started very soon after the building
of the new wall, and by the earlier thirteenth century all or most of the
frontage was thus occupied.[8]

THE PARISH CHURCHES

Names are known of a number of pre-conquest churches in Canterbury.
St Martin's was used as an oratory by Queen Bertha before the coming
of the Roman missionaries. The chronicler William Thorne tells an

---

[1] See the account of the old cathedral gate, above.

[2] XXVIII, XXXI, XXXII, XXXVI.

[3] XXXV. See account of L. Frese the moneyer (Chapter V).

[4] XXVI, XXVII, XXVIII.   [5] XXIX, XXX, XXXI, XXXII.

[6] B 72–80, 84–89; XLVII, XLVIII. Rent due to the crown for ground in the cleared area was
not liquidated, and payment was continued. See C 2.

[7] It may be seen in cellars on the north side of Burgate Street. A great deal of it was
exposed during excavations in 1950. It was supported on the cathedral side by buttresses with
quoins of Caen stone, bearing mason's marks corresponding to those on the choir (in
building, c. 1180).

[8] Charter XXXIX (1177–9 or 1186–8, probably the earlier date) illustrates the re-allocation
of the ground. It is significant that strict provision is made that the materials used for repair
of the shops mentioned in the charter shall be of non-inflammable material. The List of
Arrears of 1234 (CAC, Arrears) shows the frontage occupied by shops.

engaging story of the conversion of a heathen temple into the church of St Pancras.[1] Bede, in recounting a miracle of St Mellitus, makes mention of the church of the Four Crowned Martyrs.[2] These last two dedications have all the signs of having been imported at an early date from Rome. The charter of 804, whereby ground in Canterbury is granted to the nuns of Lyminge 'ad necessitatis refugium', uses the church of St Mary as a landmark in siting the ground.[3] At the beginning of the ninth century there was a church of St John the Baptist in Canterbury, within the city walls.[4] It was in the church of St John Baptist that archbishop Cuthbert's body was buried in 758 when the break occurred in the long-standing tradition among his predecessors of sepulture at St Augustine's abbey. The church is stated to have been built by Cuthbert next to the cathedral (juxta principalem ecclesiam).[5]

The only parish church in Canterbury in use in the later medieval period which can be traced back to pre-Conquest days is St Martin's,[6] though three others are mentioned very soon after the invasion. The dedication of St Mildred's would suggest that this church was not established by a Norman. After the death of Abbot Scolland (September, 1087) Lanfranc hallowed Wydo as the new abbot of St Augustine's and brought him to the brethren there, demanding that they should receive him. They would not, and the archbishop then ordered all who would not to leave, at which nearly all departed, and Lanfranc carried on without them. As he was going home word was brought to him that the monks who had gone off were all round by St Mildred's church, sitting under the castle wall. When dinner-time came along, and they became hungry, they decided to submit.[7] This anecdote proves the existence of St Mildred's by 1089 (the date of Wydo's consecration), while SS. Andrew and Mary de Castro can be taken back even a little earlier, for William I in exchange for dwellings belonging to the abbey, cleared to build the castle, gave to the abbey the two churches in question.[8]

A general remark which may be made of Canterbury churches in the twelfth and thirteenth centuries is that they were large in number and small in size. There were no less than twenty-two parishes and churches, and the local ecclesiastical history of the later middle ages is marked by a

[1] *Thorne*, col. 1760, p. 6.
[2] *Eccl. Hist.* bk. ii, cap. viii (Bede, *Opera*, ed. Plummer, i, p. 94).
[3] Birch, *CS*, 317.   [4] Ibid., 345.
[5] William of Malmesbury, *De Gestis Pontificum, RS*, p. 15.
[6] St Pancras was not apparently parochial.
[7] *Two of the Saxon Chronicles Parallel*, ed. Plummer, i, p. 290.
[8] White Book of St Augustine's (PRO), fol. 15v. See Appendix B.

steady diminution of this number, with a corresponding increase (where it can be traced) in the size of surviving churches. St Peter's church has been enlarged, as is quite clear from the survey of c. 1200 (Rental D), for the ground whereon stands the fourteenth- or fifteenth-century chancel of the present church is in private hands at the earlier date.[1] The architecture of the church bears out the evidence of the documents, for the substantial Norman elements in the building are all confined to the west end. St Alphage has apparently been extended in a westward direction, while the present capacious fourteenth-century church of Holy Cross must obviously be very much larger, perhaps four times as large, as the chapel nearby on top of the Westgate which it replaced in about 1380. The church of St Mary Queningate (judged from the foundations discovered in 1919) was hardly more than a mere room, about 38 feet square. While the churches themselves were small it may be pointed out that the parishes which they served were correspondingly small. Not only was St Mary Queningate parish tiny in extent, but it seems to have been almost uninhabited. The adjacent parish of St Michael Burgate was likewise tiny in area, and bereft of population, for the rentals show that a considerable proportion was classed (as shown above) as 'terre deserte'.[2] Holy Cross parish extended (and extends) merely from a few yards without Westgate to a few yards within. Even when parishes were of larger proportions, it seems that the housing within them was sometimes very sparse, as in the case of St Edmund Ridingate.[3] There was much unevenness in the size of parishes, for St Mildred's parish, in contrast with the little parishes above, had a longer axis of some 1200 yards, and comprised well-populated areas both within and without the walls. St Mary Northgate parish must have contained a large population in the later twelfth century and it is difficult to see how it could have been confined to the small church within that gate. It is highly probable that originally there was a modest area within the city walls in this parish with a tract of empty ground outside the northern walls which (c. 1166), had been built up within recent years, with a consequent disproportionate increase in the number of parishioners.[4]

As has been remarked above, the number of churches diminished as

[1] The ground of Odbold, 74 feet by 120 feet in D 312, runs right across the site of the chancel and eastern part of the church of St Peter as extended in the fourteenth century. The eastern part of the churchyard represents Odbold's ground 37 feet × 125 feet (ib.).

[2] F 151-8.

[3] D surveys only two holdings in the intra-mural area of this parish. There may have been more, of course, not held of Christ Church.

[4] There is actually a contemporary drawing of this church, in the plan of the Precincts, incorporated in the Canterbury Psalter. See pp. 3, 204 above.

time went on. St Helen's had a brief and transitory life. It seems to have gone by about 1230 for its parish has by then been incorporated in the adjoining parish of All Saints.[1] St Mary Queningate, which in the later Middle Ages lost most of what was left of its parochial area, due to the continuing advance of the cathedral frontiers, had apparently been dismantled by about 1400, for no documents after this date referring to the area appear to make any mention of it. St Edmund Ridingate does not seem to have survived the fourteenth century, for after this period St Mary Bredin parish has absorbed all dwellings within it. St Mary de Castro died a lingering death from the later fifteenth century. St John's, standing in the desolate area on the fringe of the Dane John, never a prosperous church, was 'profaned into a malthouse' by the seventeenth century.[2]

There is evidence in the documents for certain chapels in Canterbury standing outside the parochial system. The charters of 1177[3] make mention of ground north of Burgate Street 'on which a chapel was constructed'. What the dedication or purpose of this chapel might have been is nowhere shown. It may well have been a private chapel, like that possessed by the leading citizen John son of Robert, attached to his house in All Saints' Lane.[4]

The names of churches in existence c. 1200 are given below:

All Saints	Holy Cross
St Alphage	St John Baptist
St Andrew	St Margaret
St Dunstan	St Martin
St Edmund Ridingate	St Mary Breadman
St George	St Mary Bredin
St Helen	St Mary de Castro

[1] C. E. Woodruff discusses this church in *Archæologia Cantiana*, liv, pp. 5–9. His siting seems to be wrong since it is in the middle of All Saints' parish (on the n.e. corner of Stour Street). The true site would seem to be somewhere between the old Guildhall and the City Library. The church (parish) is mentioned in Rental D (§§ 291–2), the 'Particulars of the Farm' (Appendix A, § 15), c. 1234, in the charter of W. of Eynesford (IV?), in *Cal. Charter Rolls*, v, pp. 200–1. There is still a *capellanus* c. 1234 (App. A), though in the great Christ Church Rental of c. 1230 (Z) there is no mention of the parish at all, and it has evidently been absorbed into All SS. However, the precise relative dates of App. A (the 'Particulars'), and Rental Z are not certain.

[2] Somner (*Antiquities of Canterbury*, 1640, pp. 324–9) provides notes upon the parish churches which are supplemented by Hasted, *Kent* (fol. ed. vol. iv).

[3] XXVI, XXVII.

[4] Z, fol. 199r. Rent is paid by the alderman of Westgate 'de duabus domibus lapideis que sunt inter capellam Johannis filii Roberti et nouum cellarium magistri Willelmi Curteis'.

St Mary Magdalen	St Mildred
St Mary Northgate	St Paul
St Mary Queningate	St Peter
St Michael Burgate	St Sepulchre

To the above may be added St Pancras standing within the confines of St Augustine's abbey, though it was not apparently parochial.

It is possible to get back to the very foundation of several Canterbury parish churches. St Edmund Ridingate was founded by Hamo, son of Vitalis[1] one of the invaders, while St Mary Bredin was founded by the son of this Hamo.[2] St Helen was established on a burgage belonging to William of Eynesford (probably William IV, died 1197).[3] It may be inferred that the church was founded by this William or one of his progenitors. It might well of course, on the other hand, have been founded by a tenant of the Eynesfords, but William gives it to Leeds priory[4] with apparently no reference to such a tenant or his kin. The nunnery of St Sepulchre was founded by William Cauvel,[5] probably William Cauvel borough reeve of Canterbury at the end of the eleventh century, who may have been among the invaders like Vitalis above. The church was not only the priory church, but also a parish church, for as Rental D shows,[6] there was a well-defined parish of that name (later in the Middle Ages assimilated to that of St Mary Bredin). It seems as if St Mary Magdalen church was founded upon royal soil, for according to the *Particulars of the Farm*, 20d. was rendered annually to the crown for the ground whereon this church stood.[7]

A few facts may be recovered about the glebe attached to certain of the churches. St George's church has a plot of ground with a frontage as great as 220 feet, on the north side of Dover Street,[8] a few hundred yards from the church, outside the walls. It enjoys furthermore some pieces of ground nearby in 'New Street'[9] (Chantry Lane) with three acres of ground a long way from the walled area, near St Laurence priory out on the Dover Road.[10] St Michael Burgate church owns three acres close to those of St George's near St Laurence, according to Rental D,[11] while Rental B shows that this church possesses a *mansura* in Old Ruttington Lane (at the mid-twelfth century).[12] St Mildred's has land within its own parish let out to

---

[1] See account of the family of Vitalis in Chapter III.
[2] Ibid.   [3] CCR, v, pp. 200–1.   [4] Ibid.
[5] *Valor Ecclesiasticus*, i, p. 30. See account of the Cauvel family, Chapter IV.
[6] 139–49.   [7] Appendix A, § 4.   [8] D 138.
[9] Ibid. The priest of St George's owns ground close-by though it is not certain whether in his official or private capacity.
[10] D 139.   [11] Ibid.   [12] B 57.

a tenant 'in chief', who sells it to another, still to be held 'in chief'.[1] The grantor retains a rent of 2d. *per annum* and ensures that the rent (census) due to the church shall be continued by the grantee. The rent is not stated, but it may be observed that the capital sum passed is one mark. This is probably the same ground granted to the church of St Mildred by the son of the grantee some years later.[2]

About 1230 the 'parochiani' of St Mary Queningate hold a plot of ground just outside Queningate.[3] Hamo son of Vitalis in founding St Edmund Ridingate church assigns thereto four acres of ground to provide the Holy Bread (ad panem benedictum).[4]

SS. Mary Northgate, Michael Burgate, with Holy Cross embody a curious feature, for they stand on top of city gates. In the case of St Mary Northgate the chancel alone seems to have been incorporated in the gate, as may be judged from the admirable little vignette of this church, in the age of the rentals, incorporated in the twelfth-century plan of the cathedral waterworks in the Canterbury Psalter. Roman city gates sometimes were equipped with an upper chamber of some size, beneath which the roadway passed through a vaulted tunnel (as at Lincoln in the case of the Newport). Now that it is known, following the excavations of the last few years, that the whole circuit of the Canterbury city walls is of Roman origin, it is tempting to wonder if St Michael Burgate and Holy Cross Westgate were not in fact formed from such chambers over Roman gates, for indeed the orientation would have been exactly right. Westgate and the church on top were certainly very old even by 1379, when reference is made to the 'ancient tumbledown gate',[5] and Burgate with its church was sufficiently ruinous to require rebuilding in the later fifteenth century.[6]

---

[1] LXVII.   [2] BBSA, pp. 580–1.

[3] Z, fol. 194r '. . . tenent hanc terram parochiani de Queningate'.

[4] See account of the family of Vitalis in Chapter III.

[5] Letters Patent of 3 Richard II, printed in Somner, *Antiquities of Canterbury*, 1703, appendix lxxii, empowering a committee of citizens to take over ground for reconstruction of church of Holy Cross previously standing on top of 'quædam antiqua debilis porta vocata Westgate'.

[6] Somner, *Antiquities of Canterbury*, 1640, p. 16. It is nowhere positively stated that St Michael's was on top of Burgate, but the fact can be deduced from the rentals, without very much doubt. Rental B describes a line of holdings running south down Burgate Lane, of which the northernmost lies 'next to Burgate church, towards the south' (B 69, 93, 205, 206 207). Rental D, thirty years later, surveys the same ground, now vacant, and says it runs 'from Burgate southwards'. Ground to the north of the gate 'on the other side' is in the hands of Hamo Coppe (D 88, 89). The last-mentioned ground is described in Rental F as 'under the city wall, next to Burgate church' (F 155), while a related charter (XXXIII) says the ground is 'next to Burgate church, within the city wall, towards the north'. The site of the church and gate coincide, and the only intelligible solution is that the church is on top, a parallel to the case of Holy Cross.

A further fact about the architecture of a parish church may be recovered from the documents. Rental F puts an end to the discussions revolving round the name of St Mary Bredin church, for ground which in Rental D is described as next to St Mary Bredin[1] is in Rental F next to St Mary's 'which used to be made of wood'.[2]

Two of the twelfth-century Canterbury churches enjoy a mention in contemporary literature. Guernes de Pont Ste-Maxence says that on the day of his famous penance in 1174 Henry II dismounted at Harbledown outside the city, then walked down to St Dunstan's, 'la premiere iglise qu'en la vile trova', and within that church stripped himself to his shirt for the final stage in his pilgrimage.[3] Giraldus Cambrensis relates in the *Gemma* a disgraceful story (some gossip no doubt picked up on a visit to Canterbury) of gross sacrilege perpetrated in his own church by the clerk serving at St Mary's, avenged in a dramatic fashion by the Virgin herself, who caused her image to descend from the altar where it presided, and, picking up a candle on the way, to beat the offending clerk therewith. He fled in terror to Rochester where he enrolled himself as a monk. Three years later he came back to Canterbury and preached to the congregation to which he was once well-known, inducing in his hearers a reverence for the Virgin by recounting his own experience.[4] Gerald does not, unhappily, tell us which of the four Canterbury churches dedicated to St Mary was concerned in the anecdote.

THE ARCHBISHOP'S PALACE

Two valuable hints on the obscure topography of the archiepiscopal palace at Canterbury are offered by the Rentals. They are of exceptional interest among the fresh material relating to the city, since, belonging to the age of Becket, they throw light on to the immediate background of the great moment of crisis in the reign of Henry II.

The evidence afforded by Rental F that the stables of the palace stood detached from the main precinct of the palace at Stablegate, Staplegate (discussed above), is of interest in view of the frequency with which horses and mules enter the story of Becket's life. Of immense importance for the elucidation of the confused sequence of events during the saint's last

---

[1] D 160. D supplies the earliest English form of the name 'Bredene cherche'. Cf. O.E. 'bred'=board.

[2] F 266. Rental X 2 (c. 1180) mentions the same ground (fol. 6r) and says that it is 'prope ecclesiam ligneam i. sancte [Marie] in Radingate bertha'. The MS. is damaged and the name *Marie* is missing.

[3] *Guernes*, ll. 5937, ff. [4] *Opera, RS*, ii, pp. 106–7.

moments, is the casual observation in Rental B that a tenement, which can
hardly be anywhere else than at the end of Turnagain Lane, lies 'opposite
the archbishop's garden wall, on the other side of the road towards the
west.'[1]

The narratives of the murder agree generally that, having armed themselves, the knights returned to the hall of the palace to find the door
closed against them.[2] Robert de Broc, who during the exile of Thomas
had had charge of the Palace and other archiepiscopal possessions, called
to the party to follow him, for he would find another way in.[3] A charge
was made southwards past the kitchen, at the west end of the hall, into a
garden or orchard, through some bushes, where on the southern, garden,
side an entry was effected into the hall.[4]

The garden mentioned in Rental B, which was compiled some five
years or so before the murder, can hardly be other than the garden (orchard) of the narratives, and the mention thereof is strongly suggestive
that the layout of the palace, as it was reconstructed by archbishop Hubert
Walter and his successors, reproduced in general the features of the ancient
Lanfrancian palace which it succeeded. There must have been a great hall,
running east-west, opposite St Alphage church. On the northern side was
the vast courtyard, where the knights armed, and on the south, opposite
Turnagain Lane, lay the garden.

THE CASTLE

The castle has been mentioned above. The names of many citizens dwelling on its site before it was built may be discovered.[5] The area, just within
Worthgate, was clearly populous in early days. Half the tithes of the site

---

[1] B 123.

[2] 'Osbertus et Algarus et quidam alii servientes archiepiscopo, viso quod irruerent armati,
ostium aulæ clauserunt, et repaguli obice firmaverunt' (FitzStephen, *Materials*, iii, p. 137).
'. . . gladiisque exsertis in ostia domus exterioris, quam pueri metuentes obseraverant, im-
pingunt' (William, *Materials*, i, p. 130).
'. . . ad januas aulæ accesserunt, quas obseratas reperientes, nulla vi, quamquam id totis nixi-
bus tentaverint, effringere potuerunt' (Anonymous, *Materials*, iv, p. 74).

[3] Benedict (*Materials*, ii, p. 10), says that Robert de Broc knew 'all the ins and outs of the
palace'. 'Sequimini me, introducam enim vos alia via' (Anonymous I, *Materials*, iv, p. 74).

> 'Or me siwez,' fait il, 'seignur franc chevalier;
> Jo vus metrai laienz par un altre sentier.'
>
> (*Guernes*, ll. 5398–9).

[4] 'Par devers la quisine sunt entré el vergier' (*Guernes*, l. 5400). 'Eo [i.e. de Broc] . . .
ducente venerunt per pomerium' (Anonymous I, *Materials*, iv, p. 74). '. . . irruentes a
virgulto' (William, *Materials*, i, p. 130).

[5] See account of holdings of *dominus rex* in Chapter III.

were granted by Hamo, sheriff of Kent, to Leeds priory.[1] The castle keep was patently in existence by the later twelfth century, but the date of its construction has not yet been determined. Work was being done upon the castle under the supervision of two citizens dwelling hard at hand, in the reign of Richard I.[2] Canterbury castle enjoyed the same appellation as that of London, being commonly referred to as 'turris'.[3] A 'janitor' of the castle named Peter occurs in Rental F.[4] Perhaps the 'janitor' of the castle is identical with the 'portarius' of Canterbury who receives a salary over a long period of time, according to the Pipe Roll, for doing justice for the county.[5] In such case the grisly practices enforced by the judicial system of the age were probably performed by Peter 'janitor de castello'.

THE MAPS OF CANTERBURY
c. 1166 and c. 1200

Four maps have been provided as follows:

1a. Canterbury c. 1166, small-scale, giving a general view of the holdings surveyed in the northern and eastern sections of the city, based on Rental B with some material added from Rental A of the same age.
1b. The same, large-scale, providing details of each holding.
2a. Canterbury c. 1200 or a little later, small-scale, giving a general view of the holdings surveyed throughout the city, based principally on Rental D (c. 1200), supplemented with some information from Rental F (c. 1205), and from contemporary charters. Some further information has been added from Rental Y (c. 1218) and from Rental Z (c. 1230–3), and from the Lists of Arrears, 1234.
2b. The same, large-scale, providing details of each holding, including measurements, as far as known.

The principal difficulty in plotting the *mansure* of Rental B, c. 1166, is that their size and shape are not known. So many changes have taken place in the interval between the date of B and of D (where measurements are known) that it is not often that the ground-plot in the one can be identified in the other. Even if one knew that a given ground-plot had remained substantially the same, it cannot be known for certain that an adjacent

[1] Leeds (Kent) abbey cartulary in Kent County Record Office, fol. 2r.
[2] Henry Barate and William 'clericus'. See p. 187, n. 13.
[3] D 215; F 230, 245, etc.   [4] F 238, 516, 517.
[5] 'pro justicia facienda' (PR, 7 Henry II, p. 39); 'quia facit iusticiam comitatus' (PR, 17 Henry II, p. 136). The salary is normally 20s.

ground-plot has not been added, or that a slip of ground has not been sold off in the meantime. In Maps 1a and 1b the general configuration of the ground has been followed from 2a and 2b, but positive identifications as to size, shape or occupation must not be read into the earlier plan through coincidences with anything in the latter. Where there is no guidance of any kind in D as to shape or size of holdings, the *mansure* in B have as a general rule been drawn as parallelograms, as in the case of the map of medieval Oxford, prepared by Dr Salter.

In the case of Maps 2a and 2b, Rental D has, as indicated, been adopted as the basis, supplemented by material from F. Considerable blanks are left in the map through want of material in D and F, as in the case of the northern side of Burgate, which can hardly have been unoccupied at that date. Omission is unquestionably due to the fact that the structures here were let out on the 'house-and-shop' basis, and were entered in a different species of rental. As the map would be seriously incomplete, and misleading, if this and similar areas were left unsurveyed, shops and other buildings here and elsewhere have been supplied from the earliest surviving list of such houses and shops, of 1234 (CAC, Arrears, *de domibus et scoppis*).

While D offers figures for length and breadth of holdings, it does not give complete indication as to shape, as of course angles at the corners of a holding are not suggested, nor indeed do we know that a given measurement will apply to opposite sides of each holding. We can only assume we have some four-sided figure. However, the ancient ground-plan of Canterbury survives very largely today outside the bombed areas, and we have a record of the devastated districts set out in the large-scale ordnance surveys of the last century. It would clearly be wrong to ignore the general configuration as disclosed in the maps, and in the ground-plan today. For example, many of the present holdings in Wincheap Street on the eastern side run off at an acute angle, sometimes as low as 65° with the street frontage. It would plainly be wrong to ignore this layout, and accordingly holdings here have been made to conform with it, even when no positive identification can be pointed out between an ancient and a modern holding. Confirmation that there are substantial grounds for following such a scheme at least in this district is that occasionally a ground-plot (like that of Robert of Cockering) has patently survived intact both in length and breadth, and incorporating the early medieval slight bank and ditch 300 feet from the road, as disclosed in D. In other cases, where coincidences in measurement can be found in this way then the precise shape of the modern holding can with confidence be followed.

It is not difficult on the whole to site the holdings. Landmarks surviving today, or of which the site is well known, such as churches, city gates and so forth are used by the surveyors. Sometimes they move across a district such as St Alphage parish, without giving an ascertainable survey-point, but on the whole it can reasonably be claimed that the holdings in the maps are not sited more than a few yards out.

Parish and ward boundaries have been supplied in part only. The frontiers between the pre-1835 wards, and between the old ecclesiastical parishes are on the whole known but it is far from certain that they were the same in the twelfth century. Indeed, in the case of the parishes many changes have come about owing to disappearance of so many churches. It would be merely misleading to try to supply continuous boundary-lines which for much of their length must be merely guesswork. Where holdings lie on either side of a road, or of a branch of the river, and are said in the surveys to be in different parishes or wards, then the boundary can at such a point be defined within a few feet, and can be added to the map.

It will be remarked that in no case in Rental D is a fraction of a foot mentioned. It is unlikely that every holding embodied dimensions of a precise number of feet and we know in one case at least that this was not so. The surveyors have clearly dispensed with inches and have worked to the nearest foot. Where D (107) says ground has a frontage of 61 feet, a contemporary charter (CAC, C 697) supplies the figure at 60 feet 6 inches.

A NOTE ON THE LINEAR FOOT, AS USED BY THE SURVEYORS IN RENTAL D

More than one foot was in use in England in the twelfth century. An Old English foot of $13\frac{1}{5}$ inches survived the Conquest, and was employed alongside the modern foot of 12 inches. By the Statute of 33 Edward I this 12-inch foot was imposed as the standard.

It is obvious that the 12-inch foot is in fact used, from the correspondence between clearly-defined boundaries of today, and those described in the rental. A most striking confirmation lies in the back-boundary of dwellings off Broad Street (the wall of St Gregory's priory). Here the wall largely runs in 1965 at 300 (modern statute) feet from Broad Street as far as a point 520 feet from Ruttington Lane, and then drops to 130 feet. Exactly the same layout is displayed in the figures in Rental D (34, 39–54; Map 2b, Sheet 2). Again, the distance between All SS Lane and the river is today 70 feet, which is the figure given in Rental D (308).[1]

[1] For linear measurements in use in England in the Middle Ages, see F. G. Skinner, 'The English yard and pound weight', in *Bulletin of the British Society for the History of Science*, I, pp. 179–87.

THE RENTALS

NOTE ON TRANSCRIPTION

The transcription has offered little difficulty except in the case of Rentals F and G, where the original draft of the texts has been heavily altered in attempts made to bring them up to date as changes in tenancy have occurred. There are great numbers of cancellations and substitutions of names, and so forth, in other hands. In many cases names and other information have been rubbed out, or scraped off, and fresh material written in. As a further complication the MS. has suffered extensively from fire, and entries at the top or bottom of several folia have been wholly, or partly, destroyed. It is not practicable to indicate every minor erasure though where a word, or passage of greater length, has been deleted, then attention is drawn thereto.

Some scattered crosses, ticks and other marks in the Rentals have not been reproduced. Paragraph signs have been omitted. Proper names have been supplied with a capital letter.

The points which are added in the MSS. to numerals have not been reproduced. Apart from this the punctuation has been followed where possible, though it has proved difficult, especially in the case of Rental B, to decide whether a point is, or is not, part of a contraction of an adjacent word. The points following tenants' names in Rentals D and F have not been reproduced, since they are given very inconsistently in the MSS. The use of *j* in numerals has been followed though often (especially in B) it is of such varying lengths that it cannot be decided in many instances whether or not it should be transcribed as *i*.

A series of symbols, as below, has been adopted. In some instances (as in the much-altered, heavily-corrected totals at ends of terms of payment) it is not possible to give a clear representation of what appears in the MS. by the use of such symbols, and in these cases recourse is made to a footnote.

a The passage has been added in another hand.
c The passage has been cancelled.
d The passage has been erased.
e The passage is written over an erasure.
i The passage is interlined.
m The passage is written in the margin.
p The passage is written in lead point.
r The passage is written in red ink.

Rental A

The Roll of Wibert, Prior of Christ Church, Canterbury, 1153–67, containing the list of property acquired by him for the Cathedral. Rental 87 in the Chapter Archives.

[1] [T]erra illa quę est retro bracinum nostrum & iacet inter murum ciuitatis & murum curię nostrę᾽ hoc modo acquisita est ad opus ecclesię nostrę.

[2] In primis Wibertus prior emit de Johanne Pinel & uxore sua & heredibus eorum terram quam ipsi ibi habebant᾽ pro marca argenti. Quę terra iacet proxima terrę Cophini. ad orientalem plagam. (De hac terra dabuntur Willelmo Capel singulis annis vi d. in medio quadragesime).ᶜ

[3] Post hanc terram emit predictus prior Wibertus a Goditha filia Elfwini Euerga 7 a Vauasur uiro suo & heredibus eorum᾽ totam terram suam pro v marcis argenti. De qua terra dabuntur singulis annis de gablo vi d.᾽ in curia archiepiscopi. (& v d. Willelmo Capel)ᶜ. & hoc in medio quadragesime. Quidam etiam miles. nomine Radulfus de Ældeham habebat singulis annis vi d. de gablo de eadem terra. quos prior Wibertus emit ab eo & ab uxore sua. pro x sol. 7 pro cuppa mazarina. Sic enim tenuit Elfwinus Euerga. pater scilicet predicte Godithe᾽ totam terram illam de tribus dominis. (Emit autem prior postea a Willelmo Capel vi d. qui dabantur ei de terra Johannis Pinel᾽ 7 v d. qui dabantur de terra Euerga.)ⁱ

[4] Juxta istam terram iacet terra quę fuit Ricardi de celario. quam idem prior emit a Roberto filio predicti Ricardi de celario pro marca argenti᾽ concedente matre sua Æthelburga.

[5] Post istam terram iacet terra quę fuit Dunstani & uxoris sue. pro qua dedit sepedictus prior Wibertus Dunstano & uxori sue & heredibus eorum terram unam extra Nordgate in escambium᾽ quam ipse emerat pro xx sol.᾽ ab uxore Warini cementarii. Pro ista terra scilicet extra Nordgate posita᾽ singulis annis dabunt nobis Dunstanus & uxor sua & heredes eorum xxvi d. de gablo in medio quadragesimę. & nos totidem d. ipso die in curia archiepiscopi pro eadem terra dabimus. (Hanc terram (tamen)ⁱ postea calumpniatus est Godefridus filius Warin 7 prior dedit ei xii d. ut calumpniam suam omnino remitteret.)ⁱ

[6] Post terram uero Dunstani ad orientalem plagam᾽ iacet terra quę fuit cuiusdam uiduę nomine Modlief. quam prior emit de ea pro xi sol. Tenebant autem Robertus filius Ricardi de celario & Dunstanus uicinus suus & Modlief uidua. predictas terras suas de Emma de Þettekera & de uiro suo Gaufrido de Lisores. & reddebant eis singulis annis de gablo. Robertus filius Ricardi᾽ x d. Dunstanus᾽ xii d. & Modlief. x d. Prior autem pro supradictis tribus terris. terra scilicet Roberti filii Ricardi. & pro terra Dunstani & uxoris sue & pro terra Modlief uidue᾽ dedit predicte Emme & Gaufrido uiro suo Radulfum cognomento Hearm cum mansura sua que est apud Hottemelnam. quam ipse de nobis tenebat hereditario iure. Dabit ergo

---

¹ The initial 'T' is omitted, perhaps for insertion by rubricator.
² For ground and rents mentioned here see C 21, G 22, xII, xIII.
⁵ See B 56, C 19, D 9, F 59, G 20.

idem Radulfus Hearm & heredes eius Emme & Gaufrido uiro suo & heredibus
eorum semper in posterum xxxii d. de gablo in medio quadragesime. pro escambio
scilicet predictarum terrarum√ de quibus ipsi antea totidem denarios habebant.
Quando autem factum est hoc escambium√ dedit prior predictę Emmę unum
bisantum. & Gaufrido uiro suo dimidiam marcam argenti. & Waltero nepoti
eiusdem Gaufridi ij sol.

[7] Post has terras proxima iacet terra que fuit Alani de Retlinge. quam uxor
Wungwini de ipso tenebat hereditario iure. & reddebat (ei)ⁱ singulis annis xij d.
Tenet autem ipse Alanus terram unam de ęcclesia nostra quę est prope ecclesiam
sancti Georgii. de qua singulis annis (nobis)ⁱ reddere solebat xxvi d. Prior ergo &
conuentus relaxauerunt Alano xiiij d. de predictis xxvi d.√ pro escambio predicte
terre que retro murum nostrum iacet. ita quod deinceps xij d. de gablo tantum dabit
de terra illa quam tenet apud sanctum Georgium. Robertus uero clericus qui
filiam Wnguini postea accepit uxorem simul cum predicta terra. que iacet retro
murum nostrum√ liberam & quietam omnino nobis eam concessit. pro officio
scilicet uno in coquina nostra quod ei dedimus.

[8] † Huic terre proxima (est)ⁱ terra Odonis quam ipse dedit cum filia sua
Drogoni filio Alberici pictoris. Emit ergo prior illam a predicto Drogone pro xx
sol. presente & annuente uxore sua. (Tenebat autem Drogo eandem terram de
Iuone filio Rogeri de osteleria. 7 dabat ei inde singulis annis ii sol. quos idem Iuo
dedit nobis pro officio suo. quod habet in coquina nostra.)ⁱ

[9] Terram Cofini que iacet proxima porte de Nordgate emit Wibertus prior
(pro iiij marcis)ⁱ a Willelmo Capel. de quo ipse Cofinus (eam)ⁱ tenebat√ ita quod
Cofinus deinceps tenebit de nobis [memb. 2] ita libere 7 quiete√ sicut prius tenebat
de Willelmo Capel & per idem gablum quod ei reddere solebat. Hoc est iij sol. 7
vi d. in medio quadragesimę. Nos autem dabimus Willelmo Capel (7 heredibus
suis)ⁱ singulis annis v d. de eadem terra. pro omni consuetudine & seruitio. Hęc
conuentio facta est coram hallimoto nostro. presente & annuente Luca fratre eiusdem
Willelmi Capel.

[10] Item has terras emit Wibertus prior propria pecunia sua a Baldewino
Caluello & heredibus suis√ ad opus ęcclesię suę. Jacent autem omnes simul iuxta
barram sancti Sepulchri extra ciuitatem.

[11] Ædricus corueisier tenet quendam ortum. de quo reddit x d.

[12] Willelmus filius Siredi reddit vij sol. de i acra terre & dimidia. 7 una uirgata.

[13] Rogerus uicinus suus ij sol. de dimidia acra.

[14] Baldewinus xij d. de una uirgata.

[15] Haymo presbiter iij sol. 7 vi d. de una acra.

[16] Ricardus ij sol. de dimidia acra.

---

⁷ D 123, F 195, 527, xix. A. of Ratling is probably the man excommunicated by Becket in
1169. See account of Ratling family, Chapter III.

⁸ Cf. B 154. The significance of the cross before 'huic' is not clear.

⁹ 'Hallimotum': evidently the high court of the priory.

[17] Henricus presbiter vi sol. de una acra & dimidia.

[18] Willelmus filius Heremanni ij sol. de dimidia acra. Omnes isti reddunt mediatatem gabli sui ad festum sancti Johannis꞉ & mediatatem ad festum sancti Michaelis. Summa huius gabli est xxiiij sol. & iiij d.

[19] Item extra Weuergate tenet Godefridus pistor duas acras de quibus reddit iiij sol. ad iiiijᵒʳ terminos. Has duas acras emit Wibertus prior a Gregorio de Kenefelde & Simone fratre suo & heredibus eorum.

[20] Et iuxta has acras tenet Siwardus rufus i acram quam prior emit ab Edeua uidua que fuerat uxor Willelmi filii Osmundi. & a filiabus suis. & a Willelmo corueisier. de qua reddit predictus Siwardus rufus ii sol. in natali domini. (Sex autem denarii tantum sunt de adquisitione prioris. nam xviij dantur ad cameram. sicut antiquitus dari solebant.)ⁱ

[21] Infra ciuitatem tenet Frewinus terram quam prior emit de Eadwardo Lamb. & iacet in angulo iuxta domum Lamberti Wrenne. & reddit de gablo viij d. ad purificationem sancte Marie. 7 viij d. ad uincula sancti Petri.

[22] Willelmus presbiter de Burgate tenet terram que fuit Eilwini secretarii. & reddit inde iiij sol. & iiij d. ad duos terminos. mediatatem scilicet in media quadragesima꞉ & mediatatem ad festum sancti Michaelis. Hanc terram habuit prior a sacrista pro quodam prato quod ei dedit in escambium apud Fordwic. Quod pratum prior emit a Willelmo Boue concedente Haimone filio suo primogenito.

[23] Johannes Beiuin tenet quandam terram que iacet apud Burgate inter carnifices. de qua reddit iiij sol. 7 vi d. ad duos terminos supradictos. Ricardus nepos Rogeri coci habet partem eiusdem terre in orto suo. pro qua reddit iiij d. ad natiuitatem sanctę Marie. Hanc terram emit prior a Rogerio coco pro v marcis.

[24] Willelmus presbiter de Burna (tenet)ⁱ terram quandam de qua reddit xxv d. in medio quadragesime. 7 vi gallinas ad natale domini. Hanc terram emit prior ab Agemundo presbitero. & iacet contra ecclesiam sancte (Marie)ᶜ (Margarete)ⁱ ad orientalem plagam prope ortum Benedicti presbiteri in quodam angulo.

[25] Relicta Bosonis reddebat xx d. de quadam terra que iacet apud Hottemelnia [sic]. Hanc terram emit prior de Radulfo Hearm. & iacet modo uacua.

[26] Eadwardus Odbold tenet terram unam que est uicina predicte terre. de qua reddit xij d. in medio quadragesime.

---

¹⁰⁻¹⁸ The acquisition of ground at St Sepulchre's bar is recorded also in D 140-7, and in VIII-X.

¹⁹ 'Weuergate' is Worthgate, Canterbury. G. 'pistor' occurs in a miracle story of Becket. This ground appears to be part of four acres bought from Kenfield family. See F 620, 621, 666-8.

²¹ B 218 (where Freawin is called 'monetarius'), F 612.

²² B 85.

²³ Clearly B 86, though the vendor is there named as alderman Gregory, and not as R. 'cocus'. Cf. D 92, F 613, 658. Passage 'hanc . . . marcis' is probably added in a different, contemporary, hand.

²⁴ The ground of A. the priest is probably subject of VII. Cf. B 223, C 36, G 35.

²⁶ F 615.

[27] Radulfus Wadecac prebiter [sic]. & Alur(e)idus & Godardus uphealdere. tenent duas mansuras apud Therne. & reddunt Aluredus 7 Godardus x d. & presbiter xvi d. ad festum sancti Michaelis. Has mansuras emit prior a Simone & Nigello de Sepinduna. & a Raginaldo de Tuniforde & filiis suis.

[28] Aluredus parmentarius tenet terram unam ante portam cimiterii nostri. de qua reddit xxvij d. ad duos terminos. medietatem scilicet in die sancti Stephani protomartiris᷑ 7 medietatem ad festum sancti Johannis Baptiste. Hanc terram emit prior a Colemanno & filia sua.

[29] Item prior emit a Gregorio de Kenefelde 7 a Simone fratre suo & heredibus eorum terram unam que iacet iuxta domum Salomonis merc'. prope ecclesiam sancti Andree. Hanc tenet ipse Salomon pro xiij d.

[30] Item emit idem prior a Waltero pistore nostro & a filiis suis pratum quoddam pro vi marcis. Istud pratum iacet apud Settinge. ante portam Willelmi de Suliford'.

[31] Item emit pro quinque sol. terram unam quę est apud Castwisle in Wald' quam terram uendidit ei quedam femina que uocatur Ælueua. concedente filia sua quam habebat unicam. 7 item fratre suo qui inde habuit xii d. a priore. Hanc terram tenent Ottoel de Castwisle 7 Willelmus frater eius. & reddunt inde singulis annis priori vi d.

[dorse of roll] [32] Item emit prior de Johanne Perditch terram unam pro vii solidis 7 viii d. de qua Johannes filius Roberti monetarii reddit iiii d. in medio quadragesime. Et uxor Alduini 7 Ansfridus de Stureie iiii d. ad eundem terminum. Terra est [sic]

[33] Item emit prior de Gregorio de Kenefeld pro xxiiii solidis 7 una pellicia ad opus uxoris eius terram unam quam Willelmus filius Pagani portarii tenebat de eodem Gregorio pro ii solidis. quos modo reddit nobis. uidelicet xii d. in medio quadragesime. 7 xii d. ad festum sancti Michaelis. Terra est. [sic]

[34] Item prior emit terram unam extra Niwengate iuxta mansuram Alani aldermanni᷑ de Hugone clerico de Waltham. & de Eilardo fratre suo & nepote eorum Haymone. Ista terra pertinet ad celarium. & Godesman faber dat de ea xx d. de gablo in medio quadragesime. & i d. pro euewerc᷑ ad uincula sancti Petri. Remanent autem de forgable xxxv d. ad opus prioris. quos Godesman faber & Godelief uidua reddunt ei. Godesman scilicet vij d. ad uincula sancti Petri. & viij ad festum omnium sanctorum᷑ Godelief uero x d. ad festum sancti Michaelis. 7 item x d. in medio quadragesime. Huius emptionis testes sunt Willelmus camerarius prioris. Robertus molendinarius. Fulco de Litelchert. Cole longus. Rogerus uigil.

---

27 D 262, 263, F 618, 619, 662, 663.   28 B 89. See C 39, G 37.
29 B 222, D 110, F 622, 660.   30 Settinge, now lost, about ¾ mile from Northgate.
31 Castwisle is in Tenterden, Kent. F 643.
32 This entry and 33 are written in a small cursive hand.
33 Possibly B 78.   34 See D 130 n.

[35] Item emit idem prior pro xxii(ij)ⁱ solidis unam acram extra Weuergate ab Edwino fratre Martini cognati Germani monachi√ annuente uxore sua & heredibus suis. Hęc terra pertinet ad cameram & reddit ibi xxxij d. de gablo in festo sancti Michaelis. † Remanent autem iii solidi de forgable quos dabunt priori homines qui eandem acram tenent. Warinus scilicet filius Siwardi√ x d. Johannes carpentarius. x d. Ricardus cartere viij d. Wulfeach viij d. Terminus huius gabli√ ad festum sancti Johannis baptiste.

† Warinus filius Siwardi viii d. Johannes carpentarius viii d. Ricardus cartere viii d. Wulfeach viii d.

[36] Item emit predictus prior a Roberto de Wude pro sex marcis & iiii solidis circa xiiii acras terre in Tanet. que iacent prope domum Godwini cornmangere√ annuente fratre suo & uxore sua cum heredibus eorum coram hallimoto de Muneketuna√ apud Brochesende. Hanc terram tenet de priore hereditabiliter. Robertus de Suanetuna frater Ernulfi monachi. & dabit inde singulis annis de gablo viij solidos 7 iiii d. quattuor scilicet solidos 7 ii d. in media quadragesima√ 7 totidem ad festum sancti Michaelis.

[memb. 2] [37] Item emit Wibertus prior de Thoma seruiente infirmorum iiijᵒʳ acras terre pro xxx solidis annuente uxore sua & heredibus suis. concedente etiam Iuone de Wika√ † de quibus predictus Thomas easdem acras tenebat. Iste acre iacent apud Fordwic. & sunt due arabiles. & due pratum. Tenet autem eas Godwinus parkier. & reddit inde singulis annis quinquaginta duos d. Ex quibus octo dabuntur Iuoni & heredibus suis de gablo√ per singulos annos. Quadraginta iiijᵒʳ uero qui remanent√ ad opus prioris sunt.

† & heredibus suis. & Willelmo Capel√ qui iure propinquitatis terram luonis post eum clamat.

[38] De [   ]
[39] [   ]obis
[40] De [   ]
[41] Terra illa est [   ] contra domum [   ] ag[   ]ex alia parte uie.
[42] De quadam terra extra Niuing[a]te [   ]xxx d.
[43] [   ]
[44] [   ]

---

³⁵ D covers the same ground (179–82), amounting there to 4,500 square yards, i.e. nearly one acre. See F 603–6, 636–9.

³⁶ 'Muneketuna'. Monkton, Thanet. See F 617, 661.

³⁷ Wyke (later The Mote), adjacent to Fordwich, near Canterbury.

³⁸⁻⁴⁴ There is a considerable area of erasure here. Text given has been recovered under ultra-violet lamp.

⁴² The reading 'Niuing-' is doubtful.

Rental B

A Survey of Cathedral holdings in the wards of Northgate, Burgate and Newingate, Canterbury, compiled 1163–7. Rental 31 in the Chapter Archives.

[1] (In Norg' bertha ad cellarium)ᵃ
(In Norð gatha [*sic*]. Ad cellarium. Bertha.)ʳ.
Rodbertus presbiter filius Rogeri Caiteuel xxvi d. in media quadragesima de duabus mansuris 7 dimidia. Mansure ille sunt in parochia omnium sanctorum citra Sturam uersus east. Juxta domum Lamberti Segode.

[2] Rodbertus sacerdos filius Caiteuel 7 Osbertus se cocchere ii d. ad uincula sancti Petri ad euewerc. Terra illa est in parochia omnium sanctorum prope terram Willelmi filii Henrici aurifabri unde reddit [   ] 7 [   ] ad sacristariam.

[3] Osbertus se cockere xiiii d. in media quadragesima. Terra illa est in parochia omnium sanctorum iuxta terram Rodberti filii Rogeri Caiteuel uersus north.

[4] Willelmus frater Ernaldi monachi xii d. in media quadragesima. 7 i d. ad euewerc ad uincula beati Petri. de terra quadam que est in parochia sancti Elfegi. 7 iacet iuxta domum Hugonis seruientis nostri uersus occidentem.

[5] Sanctimoniales de sancto Sepulchro x d. in media quadragesima. de terra que fuit Clerebaldi. Terra iacet retro domum Henrici aurifabri uersus sud 7 est in parochia sancti Elfegi.

[6] Agnes filia Simonis clerici xxxii d. in media quadragesima de mansura quadam que est in parochia sancti Elfegi. 7 est citra Sturam iuxta terram Geldewini presbiteri uersus austrum.

[7] Bartholomeus dapifer noster iii ob. de mansura quadam que est extra Norgate proxima porte in fossa.

[8] Salomon filius Turte iii ob. in media quadragesima de mansura que iacet proxima illi mansure.

[9] Rodbertus Pin iii d. in media quadragesima. de i mansura que iacet proxima illis mansuris.

[10] Willelmus dispensator iiij d. in media quadragesima de i mansura que iacet proxima illis mansuris.

---

[1] The first heading has been supplied as guide to rubricator. 1–3 cover ground on west side of Best Lane, but it is difficult to trace connections in survey of same ground in D (293, 302–3). *Bertha* is local term for a ward. See p. 94.

[2] *Evework*. Apparently a commuted labour service. See pp. 137–42. The missing rent is either 12d. (116, below) or 2s. (117, below).

[3] The adjacent tenement is 45 below.

[4] Apparently on south side of Turnagain Lane.

[5] Behind south side of Orange Street? See 119 below.

[6] D 66, n.e. of the later Blackfriars Bridge.

[7] This and 8–10 are east of Northgate, on the city moat.

[8] F 434. Y (c. 1216, fol. 39r) says R. Turte pays 1½d. from the smithy outside Northgate, on the corner going to St Augustine's.   [9] F 111.

[11] Salomon filius Chiet iiii d. in media quadragesima de fabrica extra Norgate super fossam.

[12] Filli [sic] Sigari Keuerel vi d. in media quadragesima de terra que incipit a cimiterio sancti Gregorii uersus septentrionem 7 durat usque ad angulum strete in uno continenti uersus austrum.

[13] Walterus sacerdos filius Alwoldi fabri iiij d. in media quadragesima de i mansura que est proxima terre filiorum Sigari Keuerel uersus orientem.

[14] Osbertus presbiter filius Salomonis sacerdotis vii d. in media quadragesima de i mansura que iacet proxima predicte mansure uersus orientem.

[15] Salomon filius Kiet vii d. in media quadragesima de mansura proxima predicte mansure uersus orientem.

[16] Eadmerus Checherelle seruiens noster ii d. in media quadragesima de j mansura que est proxima predicte mansure.

[17] Bartholomeus dapifer noster ii d. in media quadragesima de i mansura que est proxima predicte mansure. uersus orientem.

[18] Terra que fuit Elfwini Sewite reddit vij d. in media quadragesima que est proxima predicte mansure. uersus orientem. Hanc terram emit Walterus quando fuit prior.

[19] Cristina uxor Reulini vij d. in media quadragesima de mansura que iacet proxima predicte mansure. uersus orientem.

[20] Æthelburga uxor Willelmi camerarii v d. in media quadragesima de mansura que est proxima predicte mansure uersus orientem.

[21] Terra que fuit Eadwini Winter v d. in media quadragesima. que iacet proxima predicte mansure. uersus orientem.

[22] Willelmus de Suliforde xviii d. in media quadragesima de ii mansuris que sunt iuxta terram que fuit Winter uersus orientem.

[23] †Terra que fuit Mathei Prekepelse monachi nostri xxiii d. 7 ob. in media quadragesima que iacet proxima mansuris Willelmi de Sulif' uersus orientem 7 durat usque ad domum Alberici aurifabri in uno continenti. quam terram tenent Rodbertus cocus seruiens noster. 7 Nigellus filius predicti Alueredi [sic] aurifabri. 7 reddunt ultra gabulum cellariiͦ iiij s. ad domum hospitum.

---

11 D 61, F 76.

12 D 7, F 93, 409. Note is added in hand of fifteenth century 'et Drayton tenet'.   13 D 64.

14–31 These holdings, with 12 and 13, run from corner of Broad Street to Old Ruttington Lane. The corresponding sections of D are 7, 34, 39–60, 63, 64, but changes in tenancy, with amalgamation and subdivision of holdings, make individual identifications on either hand very difficult.

16 For E. Checherelle, see 31 below.

18 The prior is either Walter I, durus dens (1143–9), or Walter II (1149–53).

22 This is one holding, not two mansure, in D 53 and F 92, 382.

23 'Domus A. aurifabri' is 25 below, i.e. ground of A. de Chelde where A. aurifaber dwells. The 4s. rent due to the 'domus hospitum' is not recorded in B among rents due 'ad domum hospitum'. B 22, ground of Suliford family, is D 53, and B 23, 24 must be D 47–52, with 119 feet frontage. The narrow frontages in D point to subdivision of a larger holding. B 23 is F 102.

[24] Rodbertus Seret ix d. in media quadragesima de i mansura que iacet infra predictam terram que fuit Mathei.

[25] Anfridus de Chelde xiiii d. 7 ob. in media quadragesima. de mansura Alberici aurifabri ubi ipse Albericus manet.

[memb. 2] [§ 26] Albricus aurifaber vii d. 7 quadrantem in media quadragesima. de mansura proxima domui sue uersus orientem.

[27] Relicta Nigelli coci xxx d. in media quadragesima. 7 ad festum sancti Michaelis xxx d. de mansura proxima predicte mansure uersus orientem.

[28] Salomon filius Kiet xxii d. in media quadragesima. de mansura proxima predicte mansure uersus orientem.

[29] Lieza filia Egelwecheri Ruffi v d. in media quadragesima. 7 Euerardus Tod v d. eodem termino de eadem mansura de terra que fuit Alboldi. que est proxima predicte mansure uersus orientem.

[30] Johannes filius Rogeri coci xv d. in media quadragesima de iii mansuris. que iacent proxime predicte terre uersus orientem.

[31] Ædmerus Checherelle xv d. in media quadragesima. de mansura que est proxima predicte mansure uersus orientem. 7 habet plures mansuras in Drutintune que pertinent ad illam mansuram in uno continenti.

[32] Terra que fuit Matildis viii d. in media quadragesima. terra illa iacet in Drutintune 7 incipit a terra Eadmeri Checherelle 7 exstenditur uersus septentrionem usque ad Unþancheswei in uno continenti. De quibusdam mansuris que sunt super hanc terram reddit Reginaldus aurifaber Wiberto priori xliiij d. 7 Johannes cocus reddit x d. priori de quodam orto qui est super eandem terram. Omnes iste terre 7 mansure sunt extra Norgate 7 incipiunt a cimiterio sancti Gregorii 7 exstenduntur per circuitum prope fossam ciuitatis per Drutintune usque ad Unþancheswei.

[33] Ricardus Bonemfant 7 filia Willelmi fratris sui xv d. in media quadragesima. 7 ad festum sancti Michaelis v d. de terra que iacet proxima iuxta bertunam nostram uersus septentrionem.

[34] Ælfegus sebaggere v d. in media quadragesima. de ii ortis citra bertunam uersus austrum.

[35] Osbertus uinitor x d. in media quadragesima. de mansura que iacet proxima illis ii ortis uersus austrum.

[36] Liuieua uxor Conredi viij d. in media quadragesima de mansura que iacet proxima mansuris Ricardi 7 Willelmi Bonemfant uersus austrum.

[25] D 46, F 95.   [26] D 45?   [27] Probably D 44; F 78, 433.
[30] D 39, F 116, 408.   [31] D 34, F 98, 395.
[32] D 31, 32. This ground lies on west side of Old Ruttington Lane, north of the corner holding (31 above). The rents of 44d. and 10d. are not recorded in this rental, nor in Wibert's Roll (A). The final word is underlined (possibly by W. Somner). See F 89, 90, 96, 440, 432.
[33] Probably D 11, F 84, 436. The ground lies on the Sturry Road, beyond the Barton.
[34] This and 35–37, 41 lie on western side of Northgate Street.
[35] Probably D 13, F 91.   [36] D 15, F 85.

[37] Raenilda relicta Gilleberti vi d. in media quadragesima de mansura que iacet proxima predicte mansure uersus austrum.

[38] Siredus 7 filii fratris sui vi d. in media quadragesima. de ii mansuris que iacent contra mansuram Elfsi Attharewelle. ex alia parte uie prope nouum gardinum.

[39] Lieuiua 7 Gunnilda filie Lifwini longi iiii d. in media quadragesima. de ii mansuris que iacent proxime predictis mansuris uersus austrum prope gardinum nouum.

[40] Ælfegus baggere iiij d. (in media quadragesima)ᶜ ad uincula beati Petri de terra que iacet proxima predictis mansuris uersus austrum. prope nouum gardin-um.

[41] Matildis filia (W)ⁱl(i)ᶜfwini v d. in media quadragesima. de mansura que iacet contra mansuram Æliz filie Henrici aurifabri ex alia parte uie uersus occidentem prope gardinum nostrum.

[42] Jordanus qui habet filiam Reginaldi iiij d. in die festo sancti Elfegi de ii mansuris que iacent contra molendinum monachorum uersus orientem.

[43] (In Norg' bertha ad elemosinariam.)ᵃ
(In Norðgate bertha ad elemosin'.)ʳ
Rodbertus Lewante vj d. in media quadragesima. Terra illa est in parrochia sancti Elfegi iuxta terram Rogeri de Hardes.

[44] Sedegos relicta Baldewini Flandrensis xii d. in media quadragesima. de terra quadam que est in parrochia sancti Elfegi iuxta terram Wante uersus orientem.

[45] Item Sedegos iii s. [blank] de mansura quadam que est in parrochia omnium sanctorum iuxta domum Osberti Seco(c)ⁱchere uersus north.

[46] Amfrida relicta Salomonis pistoris vi d. in media quadragesima. de mansura quadam que est in parrochia sancti Elfegi 7 iacet uersus north contra domum que fuit Baldewini Flandrensis.

[memb. 3] [47] Egenilda uxor Arnoldi xii d. in media quadragesima. 7 in natiuitate beati Iohannis xii d. de mansura que iacet proxima mansure Elfsi Atþar-pelle uersus austrum prope uineam.

[48] Tomas seruiens noster vi d. in natiuitate beati Johannis de mansura que iacet in Baggeberi uersus septemptrionem iuxta mansuram Alueredi clerici.

[49] Reginaldus de curtillagio vj d. in natiuitate beati Johannis. 7 ad natale domini vj d. de terra que iacet proxima predicte terre uersus occidentem.

[50] Bartholomeus. [blank]

---

³⁸ The monastic garden seems to lie west of Northgate Street, north of Coldharbour Lane.
³⁹ Probably D 19, F 81.
⁴³ The first heading is supplied in small characters as guide to rubricator.
⁴⁴ Sedegos and B. of Flanders may have been members of the gild of St Anselm. See p. 165.
⁴⁵ The house of O. Secocchere is 3 above.
⁴⁷ The surveyor has moved out into the northern suburbs again.
⁴⁸ 'Baggeberi' is New Ruttington Lane.

[51] (Ad domum hospitum in Nogate [*sic*] bertha.)ᵃ

(Ad domum hospitum in Norðgate bertha.)ʳ

Sedegos relicta Baldepini Flandrensis ii s. infra xv dies past [*sic*] pascha de terra quadam que est in parrochia sancti Elfegi 7 iacet iuxta terram Elfpini filii Semeri uersus occidentem.

[52] Vauasur seruiens noster xx d. in media quadragesima. 7 ad festum sancti Michaelis xx d. de mansura que fuit Willelmi de Maidestane. mansura illa iacet iuxta monasterium sancte Marie infra Norgate uersus austrum in angulo strate. 7 reddimus de ea xij d. curie de Westg'. in media quadragesima.

[53] Cole xii d. 7 Egelwardus xii d. in media quadragesima. de ii^bus mansuris que pertinent ad mansuram quam Uauasur tenet. 7 iacent proxime mansure Vauasur. uersus occidentem.

[54] †Tomas de curtillagio xvj d. in media quadragesima. de una mansura que data fuit cum Geruasio nostro monacho. 7 iacet iuxta mansuram Johannis coci uersus orientem in Baggeberi.

[55] Nicholaus de elemosinaria xvj d. in media quadragesima. 7 ad festum sancti Michaelis xvj d. de mansura que data est nobis cum Geruasio nostro monacho. que iacet proxima terre Fredemundi in Baggeberi uersus orientem.

[56] De terra que fuit parini quam prior Wibertus emit de Eluiua relicta Wariniⱱ reddit Regenilda relicta Dunstani priori xxvj d. in media quadragesima. 7 prior reddit ad curiam de Westgate xxvi d. eodem termino. Hanc terram dedit prior Wibertus Dunstano seruienti nostre pro concambio terre sue que est retro bracinum nostrum iuxta murum ciuitatis. Hanc terram dederunt monachi sancti Augustini cum quadam parte terre que est iuxta illam archiepiscopo nostro pro iii s. quos solebant dare super altare nostrum pro multonibus 7 panibus 7 medone.

[57] (In Burgate bertha ad sacristariam.)ᵃ

(In Burgate berthe ad sacristariam.)ʳ

Beatrix relicta Hugonis telarii xviij d. in media quadragesima. de mansura que iacet in Drutintuna ex alia parte uie uersus orientem iuxta quandam mansuram que pertinet ad ecclesiam de Burgate uersus austrum.

---

⁵¹ The first heading is supplied in small characters as guide to rubricator. The ground of Sedegos is probably 44 above. See D 67 n.

⁵² D 4, F 114, 460. For the render to Westgate, see C 20, G 21. Added to this entry in hand of fifteenth century is note: 'Estmerus Mersch tenet et ante ipsum T. Olyue.' E. Merssch is witness to grant of ground in Broad Street (very close to site of B 52) in charter dated 27 October 7 Henry VI (Bodley Chrs., 151). This holding is on corner, south of St Mary Northgate church.

⁵³ D 5, F 119, 463. The note 'Estmerus Mersch, etc., added to 52, is repeated here.

⁵⁴ D 26. Gervase is with little question the historian. The *mansura* of J. cocus is 131 below.

⁵⁵ Apparently Rental D, 27, 28. See F 288, 289, 468, 469; XVI n.

⁵⁶ See A 5, D 9, F 59. The ground of Warin lies outside Northgate, opposite St Gregory's graveyard. For the sheep, bread and mead, paid for the Holy Oils, see pp. 76–9. The passage 'bracinum . . . ciuitatis' is underlined. For the payment to Westgate, see C 19, G 20.

⁵⁷ The first heading is supplied in small characters as guide to rubricator. 'Ecclesia de Burgate': St Michael's.

[58] Liuiua uxor Wimundi xii d. in media quadragesima. de i mansura que iacet proxima predicte mansure uersus austrum.

[59] Item eadem Liuiua vii d. in media quadragesima. de alia mansura que iacet proxima predicte mansure uersus austrum.

[60] Egeliua uxor Reginaldi aurifabri vij d. in media quadragesima. de mansura que iacet proxima predicte mansure uersus austrum.

[61] Hugo Coffin xx d. de terra que iacet in angulo de Drutintuna uersus austrum contra fontem de Cueningate. quam tenent Maria relicta Alexandri cementarii. 7 Egeliua filia Militis.

[62] Egeliua filia Militis v d. in media quadragesima. 7 ad festum sancti Michaelis iiii d. de mansura que iacet proxima predicte mansure uersus orientem.

[63] Anneis relicta Adam de Cnolle xix d. in media quadragesima. de mansura que iacet proxima predicte mansure uersus orientem extra Cueningate.

[64] Simon iuuenis x d. in media quadragesima de mansura que iacet in introitu de Dudelane uersus occidentem. 7 exstenditur usque ad domum Sergant.

[memb. 4] [65] Sergant x d. (aut viij d.)ⁱ in media quadragesima. de mansura que iacet proxima predicte mansure uersus orientem.

[66] Walterus pistor noster iii s. in natiuitate beati Johannis. terra iacet contra monasterium sancti Martini ex alia parte uie uersus sud.

[67] Idem Walterus pistor [*blank*] terra incipit a domo Gilleberti le corueisier 7 exstenditur usque ad monasterium de Cueningate. 7 ex alia parte monasterii iacet alia pars terre quam tenet Willelmus (b)ⁱ sacerdos de Burgate. 7 alia pars terre istius tenamenti [*sic*] iacet in orto Willelmi filii Gregorii.

[68] Iohannes filius Rogeri xix d. in media quadragesima. terra iacet infra Burgate. contra terram Rodberti le macecrier (c)ⁱ ex alia parte uie uersus occidentem.

[69] Iohannes filius Rodberti filii Osmundi xx d. in media quadragesima. de terra que iacet in parochia de Burgate contra murum ciuitatis iuxta domum Marcheri fabri uersus north.

---

⁵⁸⁻⁵⁹ See note to D 36.

⁶⁰ Evidently D 37.

⁶¹ On eastern corner of Old Ruttington Lane. See F 77, 121 ff. This is difficult to reconcile with ground at the corner in D (38).

⁶³ See D 78 n.

⁶⁴ Dudelane, now lost, ran in from Broad Street, opposite Queningate. See D 79.

⁶⁵ D 80, where rent, in doubt here, is given as 10d.

⁶⁶ Possibly F 352, C 46, G 46.

⁶⁷ The letter *b* is also added (by Somner?) to name of W. priest of Burgate, 85 below. The ground here is apparently associated with 70 below. See D 90.

⁶⁸ The letter *c* is added (by Somner?) to the name of R. le macecrier where it occurs (202) below.

⁶⁹ Burgate parish is St Michael's. See 57 above, and 206 below. See D 88, n.

[70] Willelmus (e)ⁱ filius Gregorii vi d. ad festum sancti Michaelis de terra que iacet retro clocarium nostrum uersus orientem. iuxta murum cimiterii nostri prope domum Lifwini Cruche.(d)ⁱ

[71] †Matildis relicta Walteri Witepese xii d. ad natale. 7 in media quadragesima xii d. 7 in natiuitate beati Johannis xii d. 7 ad festum sancti Michaelis xii d. de mansura que fuit Lambert Garegate que iacet prope ecclesiam de Fismannech(i)ⁱrche uersus orientem.

[72] Eadilda uxor Galfridi xx d. ad festum sancti Michaelis. de i mansura que iacet iuxta terram que fuit Rodberti filii Godsolti contra murum cimiterii nostri uersus sud.

[73] Johannes Calderun x d. in media quadragesima. de terra que fuit Rodbert Gogge. terra iacet iu(x)ⁱta terram Willelmi (e)ⁱ filii Gregorii uersus sud.

[74] Alfredus xx d. 7 Godardus xx d. in media quadragesima. de terra que fuit Osberti Curteis. 7 iacet proxima predicte terre uersus austrum.

[75] Willelmus filius Pagani x d. in media quadragesima. de terra ubi fuit fabrica Sunepini fabri uersus sud.

[76] Malgerus portitor ii s. 7 vi d.

[77] Willelmus filius Pagani xxviij d. [blank] de terra que fuit Colemanni. 7 iacet prope puteum Sunewini uersus north.

[78] Item idem Willelmus ii s.d. [sic; blank] de mansura ubi Sunewinus manebat que iacet iuxta predictam terram uersus north. prope murum cimiterii nostri.

[79] Lambinus Frese ii s. in media quadragesima. 7 ad festum sancti Michaelis ii s. de mansura 7 de fabrica que iacent proxime predicte mansure Sunewini ante portam cimiterii nostri.

[80] †Liuiua relicta Berneri iiii s. ad pascha. 7 ad (fest)ᶜ natiuitatem beate Marie iiij s. de terra que iacet ante portam cimiterii nostri uersus sud. iuxta domum Lambini Frese.

[81] Salomon le merchier x s. ad pascha. 7 ad festum sancti Michaelis x s. de mansura que iacet prope ecclesiam sancti Andreeᵛ uersus north.

[82] Johannes filius Rodberti Osmundi iiii s. ad pentecosten de terra que est iuxta terram Eluiue uxoris Brumman. uersus sud.

[83] Terra que fuit Brummanni xl d. ad pascha. terra iacet prope scorcheriam uersus sud.

---

⁷⁰ 'Clocarium': the independent cathedral belltower, north of Burgate Street. The house of L. Cruche is 84 below. The letter e is added (by Somner?) to the name of W. f. Gregorii below (73), and d is added to that of L. Cruche (84). See D 90.

⁷¹ See C 26 n. ⁷³ XLVII, XLVIII. ⁷⁵ F 212, 530. ⁷⁸ Possibly A 33.

⁷⁹ By terms of XXXV, XXXVI L. Frese relinquishes this ground in exchange for ground in Stour Street. ⁸⁰ The significance of the cross is not clear.

⁸¹ F 294, 533, D 109 (where rent is only 5s.). See 222 below, and n. This entry has been placed under the wrong ward (Burgate for Newingate).

⁸²⁻⁸³ These probably lie south of the shambles within Burgate. Cf. A 23.

[84] (In Burgate bertha ad domum hospitum.)ᵃ
    (In Burgate bertha ad domum hospitum.)ʳ
Lifwinus (d)ⁱ Cruc iii s. ad pentecosten xviij d. 7 ad festum sancti Andree
xviij d. de terra quam Lambertus Garegate concessit ecclesie nostre pro anima sua.
terra iacet in angulo retro clocarium nostrum uersus [memb. 5] orientem.

[85] (in Burg' bertha priori.)ᵃ
    (In Burgate berthe priori.)ʳ
Willelmus (b)ⁱ sacerdos de Burgate xxvj d. in media quadragesima 7 ad festum
sancti Michaelis xxvj d. de terra que fuit Egelwini (a)ⁱ secretarii nostri. terra
iacet proxima terre Walteri pistoris. prope monasterium de Cuueningate uersus sud.

[86] Johannes Beiuin xxvij d. in media quadragesima. 7 ad festum sancti Michaelis
xxvij d. de terra quam emit de Gregorio aldermanno. terra iacet in macellario de
Burgate iuxta domum Ricardi.

[87] Ricardus filius Suanehilde iiii d. ad festum sancti Michaelis de eadem terra
uersus occidentem.

[88] Hamo de Denstede xl d. [blank] de terra quam emit de Lifwino Chenting
que terra iacet in macellario de Burgate uersus north ex alia parte uie contra terram
quam Johannes Beiuinus tenet.

[89] Alfredus parmentarius xiij d. 7 ob. ad natale domini. 7 xiij d. 7 ob. in
natiuitate beati Johannis. de terra que fuit Coleman. que iacet inter domum Malgeri
ani toris. 7 inter puteum Sunewini fabri.

[90] Fabrica que est proxima terre Iuonis uersus north. reddit viij d.

[91] (in Niwingate bertha ad cellarium.)ᵃ
    (In Niwingate bertha ad cellarium.)ʳ
ohannes filius Rogeri coci ii s. in media quadragesima. terra iacet in Salthelle.
que terra fuit Winedei Oxe. extra Nipingate uersus orientem. iuxta terram sancti
Augustini quam tenet Hamo filius Rogeri. 7 ad uincula beati Petri i d. ad euewerc.

[92] Alanus aldermannus ii s. 7 i d. in media quadragesima. de mansura que
iacet proxima predicte mansure uersus austrum que mansura pertinet ad eandem
mansuram in qua idem Alanus manet. que iacet contra portam de Nipingate uersus
orientem. 7 ad eueperc ad uincula iii d.

⁸⁴ The first heading is supplied in small characters as guide to rubricator. For the letter *d* see
70 above.

⁸⁵ The first heading is supplied in small characters as guide to rubricator. For the letter *b* see
67 above. The letter *a* is added to the name Egelwin where it occurs 201 below. This holding
(85) is A 22.

⁸⁶ One of prior Wibert's acquisitions. See A 23, D 92, F 613, 658.

⁸⁸ For J. Beivin see 86 above.

⁸⁹ Somner has added the note: 'Vide rotulum Wiberti [i.e. Rental A] ubi iacere dicitur ante
portam cimiterii.' See A 28, C 39, G 37.

⁹¹ The first heading is supplied in small characters as guide to rubricator. The two holdings are
south of Ivy Lane on the edge of the moat. For Salt Hill see p. 199. J. and H. sons of Roger are
evidently kin by marriage of Reginald of Cornhill I. See p. 57.

⁹² D 130, n.

[93] Petrus medicus xij d. in media quadragesima. de mansura que iacet proxima predicte mansure. uersus septemptrionem. 7 ad euerperc iii ob. ad uincula.

[94] Hugo filius Simeri sacerdotis [*blank*] de terra que iacet iuxta domum Alani. uersus austrum. 7 ad eueperc [*blank*].

[95] Josep faber xvj d. in media quadragesima. 7 ad festum sancti Michaelis xvj d. de mansura que fuit Godwini se uinge. que terra iacet extra Nipingate contra fossam uersus orientem.

[96] Willelmus filius Baldri x d. in media quadragesima. de mansura que iacet proxima predicte mansure uersus austrum. 7 ad eueperc ad uincula j d.

[97] Sedepinus piscator xv d. 7 ad festum sancti Michaelis xv d. de mansura que iacet proxima predicte mansure uersus austrum.

[98] Mauricius filius Eadwardi se uingge xii d. in media quadragesima. 7 ad festum sancti Michaelis xij d. de mansura proxima predicte mansure uersus austrum.

[99] Eadwardus Odbold viij s. 7 iiij d. ad festum sancti Michaelis. de terra que fuit Eadwardi de Stocche. terra iacet in Rithercheape. in qua sunt ix mansure. iie mansure iacent iuxta domum Nigelli piscatoris uersus orientem. 7 iie inter duas mansuras Alani aldermanni. ve alie mansure iacent post predictam terram Alani. 7 exstenduntur uersus orientem usque ad terram quam Reulinus tenet de sancto Augustino.

[100] Elis filius Þinedei vj d. [*blank*] in media quadragesima. de i mansura que est infra Nipingate contra mansuram Hamonis prepositi. que iacet prope Nipingate (infra murum)i iuxta terram de qua Hamo prepositus reddit sacristarie ii s. uersus austrum.

[101] Willelmus filius Henrici x d. in media quadragesima. de terra quam tenuit Anselmus secretarius. que terra iacet proxima predicte terre uersus austrum.

a   [102] Brictiua filia Reinberti le selier xii d. ad festum sancti [*blank*] 7 ad natale domini xij d. de terra que iace(t)i prope monasterium sancti Georgii. iuxta terram que fuit Elredi de Gildingis uersus occidentem.

a   [103] Herewardus le loremier xii d. in natiuitate beati Johannis. 7 ad natale domini xij d. de terra que iacet proxima predicte terre uersus occidentem.

[104] Eadilda filia Eadmeie vi d. in media quadragesima. de i mansura que iacet in Lambertes lane Þrenne ex alia parte uie uersus occidentem iuxta domum Mauricii filii Eadpardi uersus sud.

---

94 This is D 132, though some re-arrangement or subdivision has taken place in interval (c. 1166–c. 1200) since in D (131) another holding lies next to Alan's. Probably F 521.

96 D 134, F 198, 394.   97 D 135, F 186, 524.

98 Probably D 136.

99 D 138, F 526. 'Rithercheape' is Dover Street.   100 See 213 below.

101 Possibly F 513

102 The letter a is added to this, and following entries, apparently by William Somner.

104 F 183.

a [105] Cristina uxor Reulini vi d. in media quadragesima. de terra que fuit Willelmi Scutel. terra iacet proxima terre Lamberti Þrenne uersus north. 7 v d. eodem termino de terra que fuit Wlfric Belming. que est proxima predicte terre uersus sud. item idem eodem termino xvj d. de mansura in qua manet. que est proxima predictis terris uersus north in parochia sancti Georgii.

a [106] Willelmus de Lidesingis xx d. 7 (a)ⁱ Godpinus Muchet xx d. in media quadragesima. de terra que fuit Godpini Stethese que iacet proxima predicte terre uersus occidentem.

[107] Godeliua relicta Ade filii Gode xx d. in media quadragesima. de mansura que iacet proxima predicte (n)ᶜ terre uersus occidentem.

[108] Egeldreþa relicta Ricardi le cordepantuer i d. ad eueperc ad uincula beati Petri. de terra Alueredi de Þellis.

a [109] Cecilia filia Geroldi xiij d. in media quadragesima. de terra que iacet proxima terre filiorum Alueredi de Þellis. uersus occidentem in parrochia sancti Andree. 7 ii d. ad eueperc. ad uincula beati Petri.

[110] Item eadem Cecilia iiii s. 7 iij d. in media quadragesima. de terra que fuit patris sui. terra iacet contra terram que fuit Rodberti Godsolt. ex alia parte uie uersus sud in parrochia sancti Andree.

[111] Hereueus camerarius xiii d. ad pascha de terra que iacet contra monasterium sancti Andree uersus (sud).ᶜ norh.

a [112] Filia Godefridi de Mallingis xliiij d. in media quadragesma. de terra que iacet contra monasterium Andree uersus sud 7 exstenditur uersus orientem usque ad terram Geroldi. 7 uersus austrum usque ad terram gilde mercatorum. de hac terra redduntur heredibus Godefridi xxi s. 7 v d.

[113] [Column II] (In Norgat bertha ad sacristariam)ᵃ
(In Norðgate bertha ad sacristariam.)ʳ
De terra que fuit Eluordi sapere quam Hubertus Caluellus modo tenet xxxii d. ad duos terminos. ad mediam quadragesimam xvj d. ad festum sancti Michaelis xvj d. terra illa iacet prope monasterium omnium sanctorum uersus northeast.

[114] Paganus seruiens noster ii d. in media quadragesima. terra illa iacet contra domum Simonis Crudde uersus east. in parochia omnium sanctorum.

¹⁰⁵⁻¹⁰⁷ These lie north of the High Street, near St George's church.
¹⁰⁹ See D 104, n.
¹¹⁰ Probably D 106, F 217. The 'terra Geroldi' mentioned in 112 below is evidently this holding.
¹¹¹ This must lie between Mercery and Butchery Lanes. The holding of Matilda widow of Gerard (216 below) lies here too. The neighbour to the west of Herveus is Solomon the mercer (81 above, 222 below). See D 108.
¹¹² If the 'terra Geroldi' is 110 above, this (112) must occupy most of the frontage between St Margaret's Street and Rose Lane. The rents suggest it is a large holding, and it is probably subdivided. For the Malling family see pp. 53–4 and for the gild of merchants, Chapter V.
¹¹³ The first heading is supplied in small characters as guide to rubricator.
¹¹⁴ Lies in Best Lane. Probably D 297, F 161.

[115] Lucas frater Thome de sancto Martino xii d. in media quadragesima de i mansura que iacet iuxta domum Pagani uersus north. in parochia omnium sanctorum.

[116] Willelmus filius Henrici aurifabri xii d. in media quadragesima. terra illa iacet iuxta domum Luce uersus north in parochia omnium sanctorum.

[117] Willelmus filius Henrici aurifabri ii s. in media quadragesima. Terra illa iacet iuxta terram illam de qua reddit xij d. in parochia omnium sanctorum.

[118] Godefridus pistor x d. in media quadragesima. 7 ad festum sancti Michaelis x d. de terra que fuit Osberti Grasporee terra iacet contra terram Elfwini filii Semeri ex alia parte uie uersus north.

[119] Willelmus filius Henrici aurifabri viii d. ad festum sancti Michaelis de mansura in qua ipse manet que est in parochia sancti Elfegi. 7 iacet iuxta terram Elfwini filii Semeri uersus orientem.

[120] Ædieua relicta Eadmundi xxxi d. in media quadragesima. de terra quadam que est in parochia sancti Elfegi. 7 iacet iuxta mansuram Willelmi filii Henrici uersus orientem.

[121] Goditha relicta Elfwini filii Semeri xxii d. in media quadragesima de mansura quadam que est in parochia sancti Elfegi. 7 iacet iuxta mansuram Edieue relicte Eadmundi uersus orientem.

[122] Hugo seruiens de domo infirmorum xxii d. in media quadragesima. 7 xxii d. ad festum sancti Michaelis. de mansura quadam. 7 iacet uersus austrum contra domum Lambini Flandrensis.

[123] Johannes filius Rodberti filii Osmundi iiii d. in media quadragesima. de terra que fuit Godric Muissun. terra iacet contra (murum)ⁱ gardini archiepiscopi ex alia parte uie uersus occidentem. iuxta domum Hugonis seruientis nostri uersus suth.

[124] Æliz filia Henrici aurifabri xii d. in media quadragesima. 7 ad festum sancti Michaelis xii d. de terra quadam que est in parochia sancti Elfegi. 7 iacet contra domum Willelmi filii Henrici aurifabri uersus septentrionem.

[125] Eadwardus filius Odboldi xii d. in media quadragesima. 7 ad festum sancti Michaelis xii d. de mansura que fuit Anselmi secretarii nostri. 7 iacet iuxta domum in qua manet Æliz filia Henrici aurifabri.

[126] Goldwardus scoche ii s. in media quadragesima. 7 ad festum sancti Michaelis ii s. 7 ob. de mansura quam accepimus cum Iohanne monacho filio Marie. Mansura illa iacet retro murum elemosinarie nostre uersus occidentem iuxta

---

115 Thomas of St Martin's is probably Becket's flagellant. See 208 below and p. 181.
118 For Godefrid the baker, who appears among the miracles of St Thomas, see pp. 6, 162, 183.
119 See 5 above, n. See D 68 n. 122 Apparently on s.e. corner of Turnagain Lane.
123 Robert de Broc led the four knights into the garden of the archbishop, at a point opposite this house, on the day of Becket's murder, three or four years after the compilation of the rental.
124 In Orange Street. See D 74.
126 In the 'Borough'. C 17, D 3, F 115, 461, G 19, XVI, XVII.

mansuram que fuit Edieue matris Jacobi monachi nostri. de qua reddimus curie de Westgat' iiii d. in media quadragesima. quos Goldwardus dat nobis ultra iiii s. 7 ob.

[**127**] Amfridus mercator xvj d. infra xii dies natiuitatis domini. 7 in natiuitate beati Johannis xvj d. de terra que fuit Ordmeri se Cat que iacet prope uineam iuxta mansuram Æliz filie Henrici aurifabri uersus austrum.

[**128**] Azo x d. ad purificationem beate Marie. 7 ad uincula beati Petri x d. de mansura que iacet proxima mansuris Salomonis filii Turte uersus austrum prope gardinum nostrum.

[**129**] Filia H. aurifabri viii d. in natiuitate beate Marie de mansura que iacet proxima predicte mansure uersus austrum iuxta gardinum nostrum.

[**130**] Elfsi Atharewelle ii s. [*blank*] de iii mansuris que iacent iuxta granciam prioris uersus septentrionem prope gardinum nostrum.

[memb. 2] [**131**] Johannes cocus xxx d. in media quadragesima. 7 ad festum sancti Michaelis xxx d. de mansura que iacet in angulo uie de Baggeberi.

[**132**] (In Norg' ad ort'.)ᵃ
(In Norðgate berthe ad ort'.)ʳ
Maria 7 Wluiua soror eius xii d. in media quadragesima de mansura que iacet proxima uie que est inter duas uineas uersus austrum.

[**133**] Wluiua relicta Richewardi xij d. in media quadragesima. 7 iiii d. in natiuitate beati Johannis. de mansura que iacet proxima predicte mansure uersus austrum.

[**134**] Elfsi Atþarpelle [*blank*] de mansura que iacet proxima predicte mansure uersus austrum. iuxta uineam.

[**135**] Elemosinarius noster xii d. in media quadragesima. de ii mansuris que iacent proxime predicte mansure uersus austrum prope uineam.

[**136**] Sacrista noster xii d. in media quadragesima. de mansura que iacet proxima predictis mansuris uersus austrum prope uineam.

[**137**] Æliz filia Henrici aurifabri viij d. in media quadragesima de mansura que iacet proxima predicte mansure uersus austrum prope uineam.

[**138**] Salomon filius Turte xii d. de quibusdam mansuris que iacent prope mansuram Matildis filie Wlwini uersus austrum iuxta gardinum.

[**139**] Amfridus mercator xi d. in natiuitate beati Iohannis de mansura que iacet proxima domui nostre de uinea uersus austrum prope uineam.

---

[127] The surveyor has now moved out into the northern suburbs around Northgate Street.
[128] D 22, F 48, 415, 419.
[130] D 24? The prior's grange must lie at the corner of Coldharbour Lane.
[131] 'Baggeberi is New Ruttington Lane. This ground here held from sacrist is by him held from the 'ortolanus' (165, below). D 25, F 68, 412, 441, C 47, G 47.
[132] The first heading is supplied in small characters, as guide to rubricator. For the vineyards see p. 205.
[134] The well, from which Elfsi took a name, was sited in Northgate Street, almost opposite Coldharbour Lane. See p. 197.　　　　　　[136] See C 25, G 25.

[**140**] Bartholomeus dapifer noster vj d. in natiuitate beati Iohannis de mansura que iacet iuxta domum Azonis uersus austrum prope gardinum nostrum.

[**141**] Siredus Drinchedreste vj d. ad festum sancti Martini de mansura que iacet proxima mansure Amfridi mercatoris uersus austrum prope uineam.

[**142**] Emma filia Eadwardi vi d. ad festum sancti Martini de mansura que iacet proxima predicte mansure Siredi uersus austrum prope uineam.

[**143**] Matildis relicta Bosonis iiii d. in natiuitate beati Iohannis de mansura que iacet proxima predicte mansure uersus austrum.

[**144**] Bartholomeus dapifer noster. [*blank*] de mansura que iacet proxima predicte mansure uersus austrum prope uineam.

[**145**] Salomon Ocher de terra que fuit Rodberti de pratis viii d. 7 ob. in dominica palmarum. 7 viii d. 7 ob. ad festum sancti Michaelis. terra iacet prope nouum ortum uersus orientem.

[**146**] Godwinus buþelibag vii d. ad uincula beati Petri de mansura que est prope granciam prioris uersus occidentem ad portam gardini nostri.

[**147**] Bartholomeus dapifer xiiii d. [*blank*] de mansura que iacet contra portam gardini nostri ex alia parte uie uersus austrum.

[**148**] Elfsi Atþa(re)ⁱ pelle iiii d. de quadam parte eiusdem mansure.

[**149**] Salomon Kiet viii d. in assumptione beate Marie de orto quodam qui iacet contra granciam prioris uersus austrum ex alia parte uie.

[**150**] Godeliua uxor Eadwini parmentarii x d. in natiuitate beati Johannis. de mansura que iacet contra ortum Salomonis ex alia parte uie uersus orientem.

[memb. 3] [**151**] Ernaldus parmentarius iiij d. 7 ob. in media quadragesima. 7 ad festum sancti Michaelis iiij d. 7 ob. de mansura que est proxima predicte mansure uersus austrum.

[**152**] Eluiua soror Ernaldi iiij d. 7 ob. in media quadragesima. 7 ad festum sancti Michaelis iiij d. 7 ob. de mansura proxima predicte mansure uersus austrum.

[**153**] Walterus de bracino vi d. in media quadragesima. 7 ad festum sancti Michaelis vi d. de mansura que est proxima predicte mansure uersus austrum.

[**154**] Rodbertus marescallus x d. in media quadragesima. 7 ad festum sancti Michaelis x d. de (v)ⁱ mansuris que iacent proxime predicte mansure uersus austrum. de his v mansuris dedit Iuo ortolano xi d. tres autem solidos 7 iii d. quos habebat Iuo de supergabulo. dedit nobis pro officio suo.

[**155**] Walterus de bracino viii d. in media quadragesima. 7 ad festum sancti Michaelis viij d. de mansura que iacet proxima iuxta ortum Salomonis Kiet uersus austrum.

¹⁴¹ D 18, where Sired is called 'scutellarius'. See F 83.
¹⁴⁷ The 'via' is Coldharbour Lane.
¹⁵⁰ Probably F 20, said to lie 'beyond where the winepress used to be', and 338.
¹⁵⁴ For Ivo and his office see p. 160. Cf. A 8.

[156] Reginaldus cocus vi d. in media quadragesima. 7 in natiuitate beati Iohannis vj d. de mansura que iacet proxima predictis v mansuris que fuerunt Iuonis uersus austrum.

[157] Eadruna relicta Alfrici xviij d. ad festum sancti Martini de ii mansuris que iacent proxime predicte mansure uersus austrum.

[158] Matildis relicta Bosonis iiii d. in natiuitate beati Johannis de i mansura que iacet proxima predictis mansuris uersus austrum.

[159] Eadem Matildis reddit ii d. in natiuitate beati Johannis de quadam parte uie qua itur ad ortum nostrum supra quam partem pars domus sue fundata est.

[160] Willelmus dispensator vi d. ad festum sancti Martini de mansura que iacet in angulo uie qua itur ad domum archidiaconi.

[161] Rogerus clericus v d. in natiuitate beati Iohannis de mansura que iacet proxima predicte mansure uersus septentrionem.

[162] Godpinus filius Alewi v d. in natiuitate beati Iohannis de i mansura que iacet proxima predicte masure uersus septentrionem.

[163] Alboldus ij d. in natiuitate beati Iohannis de mansura que iacet proxima predicte mansure uersus septentrionem.

[164] Matildis relicta Bosonis iiii d. in natiuitate beati Johannis de i mansura que iacet inter mansuram Reginaldi coci. 7 inter v mansuras que fuerunt Iuonis prope uineam.

[165] Sacrista noster xix d. in media quadragesima. de mansura quam tenet Iohannes cocus unde reddit sacristarie v s.

[166] Haenilda vj d. in natiuitate beati Johannis de mansura que iacet proxima post quandam mansuram quam Iohannes cocus tenet de altari in Baggeberi uersus orientem.

[167] Rodbertus Basset. 7 relicta Fredemundi viij d. in natiuitate beati Johannis de i mansura que iacet proxima predicte mansure uersus orientem.

[168] Alfredus filius Radulfi hostiarii nostri de bracino vj d. in natiuitate beati Johannis de mansura que iacet proxima mansure Nicholai de elemosinaria que data fuit cum Geruasio nostro monacho in Baggeberi uersus orientem.

[169] Radulfus de uinea xiiij d. in natiuitate beati Johannis. de terra que iacet in Baggeberi uersus austrum. 7 incipit a domo Nicolai 7 exstenditur usque ad domum Goldfing.

[170] Goldfing v d. in natiuitate beati Johannis de terra que iacet proxima predicte terre uersus orientem. 7 exstenditur usque ad terram Reginaldi de bracino nostro.

160–163 On west side of Old Ruttington Lane. The house of the archdeacon was the official residence in this age of Roger of Pont l'Évêque, Becket and Geoffrey Ridel. See p. 201.

164 For the *mansure* of Ivo see 154 above.

165 See 131 above. This is D 25, F 68, 412 and 441.

168 See 54 above.

[171] Reginaldus de bracino v d. ad vincula beati Petri de mansura que iacet proxima predicte terre uersus orientem.

[172] Bartholomeus dapifer v d. ad uincula beati Petri. de quodam orto qui iacet proximus terre Reginaldi uersus orientem in Baggeberi.

[173] Ediua relicta Brichnodi vi d. in media quadragesima. 7 in natiuitate beati Johannis v d. de mansura que iacet in Drutintune iuxta Unþanchespei uersus septentrionem.

[174] Iohannes cocus xii d. in natiuitate beati Iohannis de mansura que iacet proxima predicte mansure in Drutintune uersus septeptrionem [sic].

[175] Aaron nepos Steffani monachi vi d. ad festum sancti Michaelis de mansura que iacet proxima predicte mansure. uersus nort.

[176] Rogerius pistor noster [blank] de terra que iacet in Baggeberi uersus austrum 7 incipit ab orto Bartholomei dapiferi 7 exstenditur usque ad terram sancti Martini uersus orientem.

[177] Iohannes cocus vi d. in natiuitate beati Johannis de terra que iacet contra predictam terram ex alia parte uie uersus septentrionem. 7 incipit a terra sancti Martini 7 exstenditur usque ad ortum Osmundi uersus occidentem.

[memb. 4] [178] Osmundus de eodem orto iiii d. in natiuitate beati Iohannis.

[179] Azo Scache iiij d. de orto qui iacet proximus orto Osmundi uersus occidentem in Baggeberi prope sandpet.

[180] Liueua relicta Berneri x d. ad festum sancti Michaelis de terra que iacet proxima orto Azonis uersus occidentem in Bagge.

[181] Nicolaus de elemosinaria v d. in media quadragesima. 7 in natiuitate beati Iohannis vj d. de mansura que iacet proxima predicte mansure uersus occidentem prope sandpet.

[182] Alueredus clericus iii d. in natiuitate beati Iohannis de mansura que iacet proxima predicte mansure uersus occidentem. in Bagg'.

[183] Elemosinarius noster ix d. in natiuitate beati Iohannis de terra que fuit Egelpini Cudie in Baggeberi que iacet proxima terre Alueredi clerici uersus occidentem.

[184] Willelmus filius Gode de Certeham iii d. in natiuitate beati Johannis de mansura que iacet in Baggeberi iuxta terram que fuit Egelwini Cudie uersus occidentem prope uineam nostram.

[185] Reginaldus de bracino iii d. in natiuitate beati Johannis. de mansura que iacet proxima predicte mansure uersus occidentem.

[186] Æliz relictaWlsi vj d. in media quadragesima. 7 in natiuitate beati Johannis vj d. de mansura proxima predicte mansure. uersus occidentem.

176 Apparently part of the glebe of St Martin's church.
181 Sandpet: approximately the Military Graveyard.
182 'Bagg': Baggeberi, New Ruttington Lane.

[187] Alfredus parmentarius vi d. in natiuitate beati Johannis. de mansura que iacet proxima predicte mansure. uersus occidentem. in Baggeberi.

[188] Aldiua relicta Gerri viij d. in natiuitate beati Johannis de mansura que iacet proxima predicte mansure uersus occidentem.

[189] Wlfwinus Cari xij d. in natiuitate beati Johannis de mansura que iacet proxima predicte mansure uersus occidentem.

[190] Suanehilda uxor Egenulfi viij d. in natiuitate beati Johannis de mansura que iacet proxima predicte mansure. uersus occidentem.

[191] Brictiþa filia Semeri vi d. in natiuitate beati Iohannis. de mansura proxima predicte mansure uersus occidentem.

[192] Liuid relicta Wlnodi ix d. in natiuitate beati Johannis de mansura que est proxima predicte mansure uersus occidentem. in Baggeberi.

[193] (in Burgate bertha ad cellarium.)ᵃ
(In Burgate bertha ad cellarium.)ʳ
Wluiua relicta Ingenulfi xv d. in media quadragesima. de mansura que iacet in Drutintuna ex alia parte uie uersus orientem iuxta terram sancti Gregorii uersus austrum quam Wlfwinus mercator tenet.

[194] Ricardus Fladewold x d. in media quadragesima. de ii terris prope Dudelane. una terra iacet prope bertunam que fuit Rogeri coci. 7 sunt ibi vi mansure. in alia terra sunt iiij mansure. 7 tota terra ista iacet contra ortum sancti Augustini ex alia parte uie uersus occidentem.

[195] Wibertus Kide xxii d. in media quadragesima. 7 vi d. super altare sancti Dunstani in festo sancti Dunstani. de mansura que iacet extra Burgate contra fossam iuxta domum Alexandri parmentarii uersus sud.

[196] Galfridus filius Reimundi viij d. in media quadragesima. de mansura que iacet proxima predicte mansure uersus sud contra fossam.

[197] Aschetinus piscator ii s. in media quadragesima. de mansura que iacet proxima predicte mansure uersus sud extra Burgate.

[198] Walterus pistor viij d. ad festum sancti Michaelis. terra iacet extra Burgate proxima predicte terre uersus orientem.

[199] Ospardus de Acholte xxxii d. in media quadragesima. terra iacet proxima predicte terre uersus orientem.

[200] Eadilda relicta Osberti xviii d. 7 ob. in media quadragesima. terra iacet proxima predicte terre uersus orientem.

[201] Johannes filius Rogeri [   ] de terra que iacet proxima terre que fuit Egelpini (a)ⁱ uersus austrum.

---

¹⁹³ The first heading is supplied in small characters as guide to rubricator.
¹⁹⁵ D 82.   ¹⁹⁶ Evidently D 83, F 282.
¹⁹⁷ Possibly D 84. See note thereto.   ¹⁹⁸ Probably D 86.
¹⁹⁹ F 100. See D 86 n.
²⁰¹ In the blank space Somner has inserted 'aldermanni 1ˢ'.

[202] Rodbertus le macecrier (c)ⁱ xii d. ad festum sancti Michaelis de terra que iacet proxima predicte terre uersus sud.

[203] Eadpardus Odbold xii d. ad festum sancti Michaelis de terra que iacet proxima predicte terre uersus sud.

[204] Eilliua relicta Jacobi xvi d. in media quadragesima. de terra que iacet proxima predicte terre uersus sud.

[memb. 5] [205] Willelmus camerarius prioris xxij d. in media quadragesima. de terra que iacet iuxta monasterium de Burgate uersus sud.

[206] Willelmus filius Gregorii xii d. in media quadragesima. de terra que iacet proxima predicte terre uersus sud. iuxta murum ciuitatis.

[207] Willelmus filius Winedei x d. in media quadragesima. de terra que iacet proxima predicte terre uersus sud. iuxta murum ciuitatis.

[208] Filii Alueredi de Wellis xxx d. in media quadragesima. 7 ad festum sancti Michaelis dimidiam summam de sale. de terra quadam que iacet contra murum cimiterii nostri ex alia parte uie uersus sud. iuxta terram Eadilde uxoris Elredi Wran. uersus orientem. Quandam partem illius terre tenet Johannes filius Rogeri cum filia Liueue relicte Berneri. apud Andresgate. Aliam partem tenet Sigarus filius Anseri que est iuxta illam quam tenet Johannes uersus austrum. Aliam partem tenet Muriela que fuit uxor Rogeri filii Æliz in parochia sancti Georgii. Aliam partem tenet relicta Ricardi le cordewanier. que est iuxta domum Willelmi filii Osmundi. Aliam partem tenet Thomas (sacerdos)ⁱ de sancto Martino. que est citra monasterium omnium sanctorum uersus orientem. aliam partem tenet sacrista sed nescimus ubi iacet.

[209] Willelmus janitor curie monachorum ii s. de scorcheria in media quadragesima. que iacet ante portam cimiterii nostri uersus sudwest.

[210] Iohannes Perditc ii s. in media quadragesima. de terra que fuit Willelmi janitoris que iacet prope scorcheriam uersus occidentem.

[211] Iuo seruiens noster ii s. in media quadragesima. de terra que iacet proxima predicte terre uersus north.

[212] (In Nipingate bertha ad sacristariam.)ᵃ
　　　　(In Niwingate bertha. ad sacristariam.)ʳ
Nigellus piscator xiii d. in media quadragesima. 7 ad festum sancti Michaelis xiij d. de mansura [blank] hanc mansuram dedit nobis Lambertus Garegate. 7 habemus de supergabulo xvi d.

[213] Hamo prepositus ii s. [blank] de terra que iacet prope Nipingate infra ciuitatem uersus austrum. contra murum ciuitatis. ex alia parte uie uersus occiden-tem. 7 est inter domum Wlnodi aldermanni. 7 inter domum Brictiue relicte

²⁰² See 68 above, and n.　　　　　　　　²⁰⁷ This abuts on to n. side of 69 above.
²⁰⁸ The ground of S. s. of Anser may be that in D 115. See C 12, G 15. For Thomas priest of St Martin's, probably Becket's flagellant, see 115 above, and n.
²¹² The first heading is supplied in small characters as guide to rubricator. D 137. See 99 above.
²¹³ D 126. See F 50, 176, 181, 529.

Godpini fabri. quedam tamen pars camere predicte Brictiue est super eandem terram. Hanc terram dedit nobis Henricus pater Hamonis quando monachatum suscepit.

[214] Rodbertus mercator xx d. in natiuitate beati Iohannis. 7 ad festum sancti Michaelis xx d. de mansura que iacet proxima terre quam Willelmus filius Þinedei tenet de sancto Augustino. uersus occidentem. 7 est in parrochia sancti Georgii ex alia parte uie uersus sud.

[215] Lambertus Wrenne ix d. 7 ob. 7 Wibertus carpentarius iiii d. 7 ob. ad festum apostolorum Petri 7 Pauli. de mansura que iacet retro domum Eadilde filie Eadmaie ex alia parte uie uersus sud.

[216] Matildis uxor Gerardi xii d. in media quadragesima. 7 ad festum sancti Michaelis xii d. terra iacet contra monasterium sancti Andree uersus north. que data fuit nobis cum Iuliano monacho nostro.

[217] Elias filius Þinedei xii d. [blank] de mansura ubi Þulnodus alderman manebat.

[218] (In Nipingate bertha priori.)ᵃ
(In Niwingate bertha priori.)ʳ
Freapinus monetarius viij d. ad purificationem beate Marie. 7 ad uincula beati Petri viii d. de terra quam Þibertus prior emit de Eadpardo le Lamb. terra iacet in Lambertes lane Wrenne inter duas mansuras eiusdem Lamberti. ex alia parte uie uersus sud.

[219] Wimundus de i soppe xviij d. ad pascha. 7 ad festum sancti Michaelis xviij d.

[220] Walterus de alia soppe iii s. ad eosdem terminos.

[221] Johannes de alia soppe xxxi d. ad pentecosten. 7 ad festum sancti Martini xxxi d. iste soppe sunt super terram que fuit Godsolt. que terra iacet prope terre [sic] de Þicham. uersus occidentem in parrochia sancti Andree. Post hanc terram jacet terra quam dedit nobis Egelnodus clericus cum filio suo.

[222] Salomon le mercier vij d. ad pascha. 7 ad festum sancti Michaelis vi d. de terra quam emit de Gregorio 7 de fratre suo Simeone de Keningefelde. terra iacet contra monasterium sancti Andree. uersus north. iuxta terram Hereuei camerarii.

[223] Willelmus sacerdos de Burnis [blank] de terra quam emit de Agemundo sacerdote. terra iacet iuxta terram Willelmi de Einesford uersus north. contra terram Willelmi bouis uersus occidentem.

²¹⁶ D 108? On n. side of High Street close to or next to 111 above. See F 213, 532.
²¹⁷ Cf. D 126, F 50, 176, 181, 529.
²¹⁸ The first heading is supplied in small characters as guide to rubricator. The holding of Freawin was one of prior of Wibert's acquisitions. See A 21, and cf. F 612.
²²² One of prior Wibert's acquisitions. The note 'iuxta . . . camerarii' in fact applies to 81 above. A 29, D 110, F 622, 660.
²²³ Near n. end of St Margaret's Street. See vii, and C 36, G 35. W. of Eynesford is evidently Becket's guarantor. See pp. 55, 182. At the end of the text Somner has added: 'A roll elder than the time of prior Wibert'. This is incorrect since Wibert is mentioned above (32). Cf. A 24.

Rental C

A list of outpayments made by the monks of Christ Church, Canterbury, for ground held by them of various lords, and held in turn by tenants, mainly in the city of Canterbury. Lit. MS. D 4, in the Cathedral Library, ff. 17–20. With this is collated a version in Rental X 2, ff. 23–26.

DATE: about 1180.

[Lit. MS. D 4, fol. 17v.]
Hoc est gablum quod debemus diuersis hominibus de diuersis terris quas tenemus de eis.

[**1**] Ad festum sancti Martini.
Heredibus Ricardi de Grauene ii sol. de terris quas Hagenild. relicta Heremer & Emma relicta Bartholomei dapiferi tenent & dant nobis inde iiii sol. 7 iiii d.

[**2**] Ad festum sancti Andree.
Prepositis huius uille xx d. de terra Kenting'. que est inclusa infra nouum murum retro clocarium nostrum.

[**3**] Heredibus Hugonis filii Euerardi xlii d. de terra quam Johannes Dodekere tenet 7 dat nobis inde x sol.

[**4**] Heredibus Aluredi de Well' xv d. de terris quas Robertus filius Malgeri portarii. [*sic*]

[**5**] Ad natale domini.
Golduino mercier (Thome filio Johannis filii Roberti)ᵃⁱ xxx d. (Heredibus Berneri)ᵃᵉ xxx d. de terris quas Johannes caretier tenet 7 dat nobis annuatim xx sol.

[fol. 18r.] [**6**] Robin filio Simeri (heredibus Berneri)ᵃⁱ xv d. de terra quam Reginaldus aurifaber tenet 7 dat nobis annuatim inde dimidium marcum.

[**7**] Ad purificationem.
Roberto scriptori de (Ha)ᵃᵉkint' xii d. 7 ob. de terra quam (Dauid)ᶜ de Werting'. tenet 7 dat nobis inde annuatim iii sol. (Tantumdem ad)ᵃᵉ natiuitatem beate Marie. (quiet')ᵐᵖ

---

¹⁻⁴ These sections are written twice. Firstly (fol. 17r.) in a very large hand, and secondly (fol. 17v.) in a smaller hand, the principal hand of the text. The version in the larger hand omits *de* following *Ricardi*; *Hagenild* is written *Hak–*; *relicta* is written *rel* without contraction; *dapaferi* for *dapiferi* (all in 1). The text is that of the version in the smaller writing, though *Euerardi* has been adopted from the other version in preference to the reading *-adi* in the second version.

¹ D 261, F 15, 357, G 1.
² G 2. For royal dues collected by the *prepositi*, see p. 86.
³ D 99, F 194, 544, G 3.   ⁴ D 257, G 4, 5, 54, F 250, 299, 485, and 33 below.
⁵, ⁶ See D 115 n. G 7, 8, 9, and 38, 49, 67 below.
⁶ X 2 omits 'Robin filio Semeri' and adds (dapiferi) ᵃᵉ after (heredibus Berneri)ᵃⁱ.
⁷ This is mentioned under D 212. See F 303, 514, G 10.

[8] In media quadragesima.
Apud Andresg'. heredibus Aluredi de Well' xii d. de terra quadam ubi
magna domus lapidea fundata est.   (quiet')ᵐᵖ

[9] (Item de terra Cruke (ii sol.)ᶜ xxx d.)ᵃⁱ

[10] Item eisdem xii d. de terra que est iuxta illam. quam Willelmus
Winedei tenuit 7 dedit nobis xii sol. Tantumdem ad festum sancti Michaelis.
                                                                          (quiet')ᵐᵖ

[11] Item Willelmo filio Winedei iii d. de eadem terra quam emimus de eo 7
heredibus eius pro xiiiiᵒʳ marcis.   (quiet')ᵐᵖ

[12] Iuoni filio Sigari filii Anseri 7 heredibus eius iii d. de quadam terra apud
Andresgate quam emimus de eo 7 heredibus eius pro xxv marcis.   (quiet')ᵐᵖ

[fol. 18v.] [13] Item heredibus Aluredi de Well' de eadem terra xxx d.
                                                                          (quiet')ᵐᵖ

[14] Item heredibus [blank] de Raculf. de eadem terra xli d.   (quiet')ᵐᵖ

[15] Sedegos xl d. de terra Eluiue relicte Bruman quam heredes Willelmi filii
Pagani portarii tenent de nobis 7 dant inde annuatim xx sol. Tantumdem ad
assumptionem sancte Marie.

[16] Elemosinar' nostra [sic] ii sol. de terra quam Wibertus camerarius abbatis
de Bello tenet 7 dat nobis inde annuatim vi sol.   (quiet')ᵐᵖ

[17] Liueue relicte Berneri dapiferi xii d. (7 ob.)ᶜ de terra quam Robertus Godiuere tenet. 7 dat inde iiii sol. 7 ob.   (quiet')ᵐᵖ

[18] (Item reddit viii d. de terra quadam in Bagguri. quam).ᶜ   (quiet')ᵐᵖ

[19] Curie de Westgate de terra quadam extra Norgate xxvi d. quam tenent
heredes Dunstani seruientis nostri. 7 dant nobis inde xxvi d.   (quiet')ᵐᵖ

[20] Item eidem curie xii d. de terra Willelmi de Meidestane quam Robertus
de porta infirmorum tenet 7 dat nobis xl d.   (quiet')ᵐᵖ

[21] Item eidem curie vi d. de terra Eurega que est retro bracinum nostrum infra
nouum murum.   (quiet')ᵐᵖ

---

⁸ This is close to s.w. corner of Mercery Lane. See D 116, F 262 and n. G 11, 12, 72, 73. X 2
adds, following heading: (Heredibus Willelmi Caluel ii sol.)ᵃ and for 'Apud . . . ubi' reads
'Heredibus Æluredi de Welle xii d. de quadam terra apud Andresg' ubi,' etc.
⁹ D 97, G 13, 40, and 41, 73 below.
¹⁰ The term 'juxta illam' refers to ground covered by 8 above. This is D 116, and 58 below.
See F 262 and n.
¹¹ G 14.
¹² G 15. The ground is probably at s.w. corner of Mercery Lane, where Anser has ground
(B 208, D 115).
¹³ G 16.   ¹⁴ G 17.   ¹⁵ See 54 below, and D 112, n.
¹⁶ G 18, LIII, LIV. See D 76, F 210, 569.
¹⁷ B 126, D 3, F 115, 461, G 19, XVI, XVII.
¹⁹ A 5, B 56, D 9, F 59, G 20.   ²⁰ B 52, D 4, F 114, 460, G 21.
²¹ A 3, G 22, XII, XIII. The words 'retro bracinum' are underlined.

[**22**] Item eidem curie iiii d. de terra quam relicta Goduini de stabulo 7 Reginaldus filius Mar [*sic*] tenent 7 dant nobis x d. Rogerus vi 7 relicta Goduini iiii.

(quiet')ᵐᵖ

[**23**] Item eidem curie i uomerem. uel ii d. de quadam insula que est extra Westgate de qua heredes Odboldi dant nobis xx d.   (quiet')ᵐᵖ

[**24**] (Item xii d. de terra Bartholomei dapiferi ubi)ᵃᶜ (mansit.)ᵃ

[fol. 19r.] [**25**] Ortolano nostro xii d. de terra que fuit Wilfwini sacriste 7 est ultra torcular uinee quam tenet.   (quiet')ᵐᵖ

[**26**] Sanctimonialibus de Mallinges iiii sol. de terra quam Paulina tenet. 7 dat nobis inde per annum xiii sol. 7 viii d.   (quiet')ᵐᵖ

[**27**] Haimoni filio Radulfi presbiteri xvi d. de terra que est inclusa terre quam Osbernus presbiter dedit 7 est extra Wurgate.   (quiet')ᵐᵖ

[**28**] (Roberto Pin pro terra quam Serlo cementarius tenet x d.)ᵃ

[**29**] Relicte Clutessiue viii d. 7 ob. de terra quadam que est extra Wuregate. quam Elmerus Waldeis tenet 7 dat nobis annuatim iiii sol.   (quiet')ᵐᵖ

[**30**] (   )ᵈ Roberto Pin (xvi)ᶜ (xij)ⁱ d. de terra quam Matildis filia Elfegi tenet 7 dat nobis iii sol. per annum. (Tantumdem ad festum sancti Michaelis.)ᵃ

(quiet')ᵐᵖ

[**31**] Filiis Wulbaldi de Herebaldune v d. de terra quadam que est iuxta ecclesiam sancti Petri. quam heredes Odboldi tenent 7 dant nobis annuatim ii sol.

(quiet')ᵐᵖ

[**32**] Heredibus Wimundi dapiferi pro iiii pedibus de terra Albin. iiii d.

(quiet')ᵐᵖ

[**33**] Ricardo Caluel xiiii d. de quadam terra que est in parrochia sancte Margarete proxima terre quam Willelmus Picot tenet 7 dat nobis x d.   (quiet')ᵐᵖ

[**34**] (Johanni coco ii d.)ᵃ

[**35**] (Henrico filio Willelmi mercatoris ii d. de quadam parte terre que fuit Pauline.)ᵃ

[fol. 19v.] [**36**] Benedicto nepoti Benedicti presbiteri iiii d. de quadam terra que est uicina predicte terre. uersus norht.   (quiet')ᵐᵖ

---

²²D 1, 2, G 23. See F 117, n, 462.   ²³D 375, part of F 55 (see n.), G 24.

²⁴X 2 omits the corresponding entry and substitutes (Heredibus Willelmi Caluel ii sol. pro parte terre ubi fundata est quadripartita domus lapidea iuxta magnam domum lapideam contra portam cimiterii.)ᵃ See 75 below.

²⁵B 136? G 25. A line is left blank following this entry.

²⁶B 71, D 93, G 26, 31, 33, 44; xx–xxiii. See 32, 35, 52 below.

²⁷G 27. See D 167–76, F 1–9, 326–74. See 55 below, and n.

²⁸D 8, F 70, 429, G 41.   ²⁹G 29. See 48 below.   ³⁰See 63 below.

³¹D 312 (ground of Odbold, next to St Peter's church). See F 472, G 32.

³²Connected with 26, above.   ³³G 34. See 4 above.

³⁵Relates to 26 above.

³⁶Relates to 33 above, not to 34, 35, which are interpolations. G 35.

[37] (Johannes filius Roberti filii Osmundi vii d. de quadam terra que est in parrochia sancti Ælfegi. quam tenet Hugo Fagard 7 dat nobis inde annuatim iii sol. 7 iii d.)ᶜ

[38] Golduino mercier xxx d.

[39] Prepositis huius uille ii sol. 7 vi d. (de terra Aluredi parmentarii. ante portam.)ᵃ

[40] (Presbitero de Brocheᵛ xiii d. de terra (quam)ⁱ Johannes de parco tenet. 7 dat nobis inde. xvi d.)ᵃ   (quiet')ᵐᵖ

[41] (Item heredibus Alure de Welles xxx d. pro terra Cruke.)ᵃ   (quiet')ᵐᵖ

[42] Ad pascha.
Gerusio Chese xxx d.

[43] Roberto filio Simeri xv d.

[44] Mariote uidue iii sol. de terra Briennii cordewaner quam Robertus filius Ricardi tenet 7 dat nobis [i]nde annuatim xvi sol.   (quiet')ᵐᵖ

[45] Ad festum sancti Johannis.
Abbati de Feueresham v d. de terra qu(ad)ᶜam magister hospitalis [fol. 20r.] sancti Thome tenet. 7 dat nobis inde media quadragesima iii sol.

[46] Curie sancti Martini iii sol. de terra quam Johannes filius Walteri pistoris tenet 7 dat nobis ad festum sancti Michaelis iii sol. 7 i d.

[47] Ortolano nostro xix d. de terra Blancard quam Johannes cocus tenet 7 dat nobis inde annuatim v sol. 7 viii d.   (quiet')ᵐᵖ

[48] Relicte God' Clutessune viii d. 7 ob. de terra quam Elmerus Waldeis tenet.
                                                              (quiet')ᵐᵖ

[49] Golduino xxx d.

[50] (Cecilia filia Roberti xlv d.)ᵃ

[51] (Cristine.)ᵃ

---

³⁷ D 72, F 203, 566.
³⁸ 5 above. Above this entry are remains of a note in lead point: '[   ]arii ante portam.'
³⁹ B 89? See G 37.
⁴⁰ G 38. Evidently subject of XLVII, XLVIII. X 2 adds, following this section: Symoni de Blen xiii d. Summa xxxij s. x d. ob.
⁴¹ Connected with 9, above. X 2 reads for this entry: (Laurent' Welles xxx d. pro terra Kruke.)ᵃ and adds: (Roberto Pin x d. pro terra ubi Serlo macun manet.)ᵃ
⁴² This is 65 below. X 2 adds in margin (Christine filie Berneri dapiferi de eadem)ᵃ.
⁴³ This is 66 below.
⁴⁴ Mariota holds at corner of St Peter's Grove in D 364. The adjacent holding in D (365) is said to have belonged to Brien. Mariota evidently has interest in two holdings. The 3s. is for the easternmost. See G 69, 70, and 69, 70, 71 below. X 2 adds at this point: Ad pentecosthen. Heredi Johannis aldermanni xii d. (Pro terra que fuit Lamberti Gargate. tantumdem ad festum sancti Michaelis.)ᵃ. See 26, above.
⁴⁵ D 367, F 137, G 45.
⁴⁶ B 66, F 352, G 46.
⁴⁷ B 131, 165, D 25, F 68, 412, 441, G 47.
⁴⁸ G 48. See 29 above.
⁴⁹ See 5 above.

[52] (Ad pentecosten.
Heredibus Johannis filii Rogerii aldermanni de terra Gargate xii d.)ᵃ

[53] Ad festum sancte Magarete [sic].
Sanctimonialibus de Berekinges v sol. 7 ii d. de quadam terra quam Johannes
Dodekere tenet 7 dat nobis inde annuatim xix sol.   (quiet')ᵐᵖ

[fol. 20v.] [54] (In assumptione sancte Marie.
Sedegos filie Bruman xl d. de terra quam heredes Willelmi filii Pagani
tenent 7 dant nobis inde annuatim xx sol.)ᶜ

[55] In natiuitate sancte Marie.
Monialibus sancti Sepulcri iii sol. de quadam terra que est extra Wuergate. quam
Osbernus presbiter dedit nobis que reddit nobis annuatim xx sol. 7 vi d.   (quiet')ᵐᵖ

[56] Roberto scriptori de Hakintune xii d. 7 ob.   (quiet')ᵐᵖ

[57] In equinoctio autuntali [sic].
Heredibus Willelmi de Malling' iiii d. de terra Æduini Scrideman. quam Elmer
Waldeis tenet 7 dat nobis inde annuatim iiii d.   (quiet')ᵐᵖ

[58] Ad festum sancti Michaelis.
Heredibus Aluerdi de Well' xii d. de terra Willelmi filii Winedei. Tantumdem in
media quadragesima.

[59] Heredibus Willelmi de Maling' ii sol. de vii acris extra Wuure [fol. 21r.]
gate.

[60] Jacobo portario archiepiscopi x d. de quadam terra que est in parrochia
sancti Ælfegi 7 pertinet ad gildehalle.   (quiet')ᵐᵖ

[61] Haimoni clerico de Forduico 7 sociis suis ii sol. de quadam terra apud
Forduic ubi weruum nostrum est.   (quiet')ᵐᵖ

[62] Symoni de Valbadun xii d. de terra quadam que est iuxta terram Mansel
quam Johannes Dodekere tenet.   (quiet')ᵐᵖ

[63] Roberto Pin (xij d.)ᵃᵉ Tantumdem in media quadragesima.

[64] Curie sancti Martini (x)ᵃ viii d. de terra quadam que est ultra ulterius
uiuarium nostrum. quam Eaduardus fullo tenet 7 dat nobis inde annuatim iii sol.
7 ii d.   (quiet')ᵐᵖ

[65] [blank]. xxx d. Tantumdem ad pascha.

[66] Robin filio Simeri mercier xv d. Tantumdem ad pascha.

[67] Golduino mercier xxx. [sic] Tantumdem ad natale 7 pascha 7 sanctum
Johannem.

---

⁵² G 44. See 26 above.   ⁵³ D 103, F 30, 295, 365, 531, G 55, xxiv. See 62 below.
⁵⁴ See 15 above.   ⁵⁵ See 27 above. G 56, xli, xlii.
⁵⁶ See 7 above. G 57.   ⁵⁷ D 190? G 58, 59.   ⁵⁸ See 10 above.
⁶⁰ D 65, F 315, 486, G 60.   ⁶¹ G 77.   ⁶² G 61. Connected with 53 above.
⁶³ See 30 above. X 2 adds: (hanc terram tenet Ernaldus Chic et dat nobis (blank))ᵃ.
⁶⁴ G 63.   ⁶⁵ 42, above.   ⁶⁶ 43 above.
⁶⁷ 5 above.

[68] Item curie sancti Martini xvi d. de terra Warini Kien quam tenent Willelmus clericus 7 relicta Gaufridi marascal 7 relicta Eilmeri 7 Hukelot se frode. 7
dant nobis inde per annum vi sol. 7 iiii d.   (quiet')^{mp}

[69] Mariote uidue ii [sic] de terra Brien (corduaner.)^a

[70] Auitie xii d. de eadem terra.

[71] (Godithe filie Helewis$^\vee$ (de eadem terra)^i xii d.)^a

[72] Simoni clerico viii d. 7 ii gallinas de terra Warini Kien.

[73] (De terra Cruke$^\vee$ xxx d.)^a

[74] (Johanni filio Roberti$^\vee$ (filii Osmundi)^i viii d. de terra quam Ingenulf
tenet.)^a

[75] (De terra ante portam ij sol. heredibus Willelmi Calwel.)^a

^{68} G 64. See D 29, F 65, 66, 445, 446. ^{69} G 69. See 44 above. ^{70} G 70.
^{72} G 75. See 37 above. X 2 adds (Johanni coco pro terra de Baggeberi.)^{ac}
^{73} C 76, 78. X 2 reads: (Laurentio de Welle xxx d. de terra Cruke.)^a and adds (Hugoni
aurifabro xii d. pro quadam terra que est retro domum Wimundi mertier.)^a
^{74} This relates to D 95.
^{75} G 80, xxxviii. See 24 above. X 2 adds: (Heredibus Johannis alderman xii d.)^{ac} (Prepositis
huius ville xx d. pro terra presbiteri de Broke.)^{ac}

Rental D

A survey with measurements, bound into Register H in the Chapter Archives, of Cathedral
holdings in the city of Canterbury, compiled c. 1200.

[Register H, fol. 218r.].

[1] (Parrochia de Northgate intra portam.)^r

Soror Rogeri filii Hamel'	vj d.	Ad festum sancti Michaelis	Terra iacet retro murum elemosinarie nostre. Latitudo eius ad aquilonem xxvi pedum. Longitudo a uico ad occidentem c et x pedum.
[2] Relicta Godwini stablier	iiij d.	Ad mediam quadragesimam	Terra iacet iuxta predictam terram uersus nort. latitudo uersus nort xxvij ped. longitudo uersus west c et xx ped.
[3] Heredes Roberti Goddiuere	ij sol. et ob. et ij sol.	Ad mediam quadragesimam Ad festum sancti Michaelis	Hec terra iacet iuxta predictam terram. Latitudo eius uersus north xxvij ped. Longitudo uersus west c et lvj ped.

^{1} F 462. C 22, G 23. This ground lies on w. side of the 'Borough'.
^{2} C 22, G 23. See F 117, n. ^{3} B 126, C 17, F 115, 461, G 19, xvi, xvii.

[4]

Robertus	xx d.	Ad mediam	De terra Vauersur. hec terra est in
portarius	et	quadragesimam	angulo duarum uiarum iuxta ec-
	xx d.	Ad festum	clesiam de Northgate. latitudo eius
		sancti	xliij ped. uersus north. longitudo
		Michaelis	lx ped.

[5]

Robertus	xij d.	Ad mediam	Hec est iuxta terram Vauersur.
de Tanet	et	quadragesimam	latitudo xxj ped. uersus west.
	xij d.	Ad festum	longitudo uersus suth lx ped.
		sancti	
		Michaelis	

[6]

Relicta	ij sol.	Ad mediam	Hec terra proxima est terre que
Wlnoth	et	quadragesimam	fuit Ionathe clerici. latitudo uersus
	ij sol.	Ad festum	west xxvij. ped. longitudo uersus
		sancti	suth lx ped.
		Michaelis	

(extra portam.)ͬ

[7]

Terra	vj d.	Ad mediam	Hec iacet in angulo a uia que ducit
Godefridi		quadragesimam	ad sanctum Augustinum usque ad
filii		et ob. de	murum cimiterii sancti Gregorii.
Keuerel		heuewer	latitudo uersus east liiij ped. long-
			itudo uersus north c et xxxij ped.

[8]

Serlo	xv d.	Ad mediam	Cum terra Hunfridi. hec iacet ex
machum	et	quadragesimam	alia parte uie uersus west. latitudo
	xv d.	Ad festum	uersus north xxiiij p. longitudo
		sancti	uersus west lxxx p. et xviij p.
		Michaelis	

[9]

Osbertus	xxvj d.	Ad mediam	Hec terra fuit Dunstani seruientis
Spinke		quadragesimam	nostri que est terre [sic] Walteri

⁴ B 52, C 20, F 114, 460, G 21. Rental Y (fol. 191) shows that c. 1218 a stone house, held from Dover priory, stands between 3 and 4 above.

⁵ B 53, F 119, 463.

⁷ B 12, F 93, 409. F says the ground is not next, but next but one to St Gregory's churchyard.

⁸ F 70, 429. The ground was held from Robert Pin by the monks (C 28, G 41). He sold it to them specifying the subject of sale as ground held by Serlo the mason and Humphrey the parmenter (evidently the Hunfridus here). (Reg. H, fol 31v.).

⁹ A 5, B 56, C 19, F 59, G 20. This ground, with (apparently) 10, was passed by St Augustine's abbey to the archbishop to liquidate claim for money for the holy oils. See p. 76.

Bues in eodem uico. latitudo
uersus north xxxvj p. longitudo
uersus west cc et xxij p.

[10]
Nicholaus   x d.   De terra que iacet iuxta terram
filius   Osberti Spinke. latitudo uersus
Baldewini   north xij p. longitudo uersus west
                                                 cc 7 xxij p.

[11]
Michael   xv d.   Ad mediam   Hec terra iacet ultra Bertonam.
filius   et   quadragesimam   latitudo eius uersus north c 7
Brictwoldi   v d.   Ad festum   xxiiij p. longitudo uersus west
Bonenfant   sancti   usque ad terram de Bertona.
                             Michaelis   [blank]

[12]
Terra quam   xlij d.   Hec uacua est. latitudo cuius habet
tenuit   uersus north c p. uersus west lxxij
Johannes   ped.
cocus

[13]
Osbertus   v d.   Ad mediam   Hec iacet iuxta predictam terram.
de uinea   quadragesimam   latitudo eius uersus north lvij ped.
                                                 longitudo eius uersus west sicut alia.

[14]
Michael   xv d.   Ad mediam   Hec est iuxta terram Osberti de
filius   quadragesimam   uinea. longitudo eius sicut alia
Brithwoldi   uersus west.

[15]
Lieueua   viij d.   Ad mediam   Latitudo eius uersus suth lvij p.
relicta   quadragesimam   longitudo sicut alia.
Conradi

[16]
Simon   vj d.   Ad mediam   De terra que est iuxta terram Con-
Hecchefot   quadragesimam   radi uersus suth. latitudo eius uersus
                                                 suth lx ped. longitudo sicut alie.

[17]
Michael   v d.   Ad festum   Latitudo eius uersus suth lxij p.
filius   sancti   longitudo sicut alie.
Brithwoldi   Michaelis
Bonenfant

---

[11] B 33? F 84, 436?   [12] B 34? This and 13–19 lie towards the Barton, on the Sturry Road.
[13] B 35? F 91?   [15] B 36, F 85.

[18]

Heredes	vj d.	Ad mediam	Hec terra est iuxta terram Brith-
Siredi		quadragesimam	woldi. latitudo uersus suth liiij p.
scutellarii			longitudo sicut alie.

[19]

Meinerus	viij d.	Ad mediam	De terra Liefwini Lunʒ que est
filius		quadragesimam	iuxta terram Sired. longitudo
Sedewen			uersus suth lxxx p. 7 iiijᵒʳ latitudo
			uersus west lxij p.

[20]

Godelief	x d.	Ad uincula	Hec est contra domum Emme
relicta		sancti	relicte Bartholomei dapiferi uer-
Eadwini	et	Petri	sus orientem. longitudo eius uersus
parmentarii	x d.	Ad natiuitatem	east c et lij p. latitudo uersus suth
		sancte Marie	lxvj p.

[fol. 218v.] [21]

Donum Emme relicte Bartholomei dapiferi ex alia parte uie uersus west. longitudo eius uersus west lxxij p. longitudo uersus suth lxix p.

[22]

Relicta	x d.	In aduincula	Juxta terram Emme uersus suth.
Ace	et	sancti Petri	longitudo eius de north uersus suth
Scache	x d.	Ad natiuitatem	lxxviij p. latitudo uersus west
		sancte Marie	lxxij p.

[23]

Odo	vj d.	Ad mediam	Hec est iuxta terram Ace Scace
sutor		quadragesimam	uersus suth. latitudo eius uersus
	vj d.	Ad festum	suth xviij p. longitudo uersus west
		sancti Michaelis	lxxij p.
	viij d.	Ad purificacionem	
		Sancte Marie	

[24]

Willelmus	viij d.	Ad mediam	De terra Elfsi ate Welle iuxta
de		quadragesimam	grangiam prioris. longitudo eius
Cherteham	viij d.	Ad festum	uersus suth lxxviij p. latitudo
		sancti Johannis	uersus west lxxij p.
		Baptiste	
	viij d.	Ad uincula	
		sancti Petri	

¹⁸ B 141, F 83.   ¹⁹ B 39? F 81?   ²² B 128, F 48, 415, 419.

²³ F 57.   ²⁴ Possibly B 130; F 49, 60, 339.

[25]			
Adam filius Bartholomei coci	xxxiiij d. xxxiiij d.	Ad mediam quadragesimam Ad festum sancti Michaelis	i d. de heuwerc. De terra Blanchard in angulo de Bageberi uersus suth quam tenuit Iohannes cocus. longitudo uersus suth liiij p. latitudo uersus lest xlij p.
[26]			
Terra quam tenet Thomas de orto	xvj d.	Ad mediam quadragesimam	De una mansura que data fuit cum Geruasio nostro monacho. et iacet iuxta terram Blanchard uersus orientem in Bageberi. longitudo uersus lest xxxix ped. latitudo uersus suth xxx iij p.
[27]			
Heredes Symonis de pistrino	x d. x d.	Ad mediam quadragesimam Ad festum sancti Michaelis	Hec terra est proxima terre Fredemundi uersus orientem. latitudo uersus least x p. 7 dimid. longitudo lxxxiiij p.
[28]			
Wlueua uidua	x d. x d.	Ad mediam quadragesimam Ad festum sancti Michaelis	De eadem terra. Terra ista est eiusdem latitudinis et longitudinis cuius et predicta. Iste eciam date sunt cum Geruasio.
[29]			
Cristina uidua	xix d. xix d.	Ad mediam quadragesimam Ad festum sancti Michaelis	De terra Warini Chien. hec iacet uersus lest. latitudo eius del north al suth xxiiij p. longitudo a uico al east usque ad fossam abbatis. [blank]
[30]			
Relicta Hugonis le frode	xij d. xij d.	Ad mediam quadragesimam Ad festum sancti Michaelis	De eodem tenemento. latitudo uersus suth xlvj p. longitudo uersus least sicut et alia.
[31]			
Salomon le flamang	vj d.	Ad mediam quadragesimam	De terra que fuit Willelmi Malban que iacet iuxta Unthonchesweie

---

[25] B 131, where J. cocus is tenant of the sacrist and he in turn tenant of the 'ortolanus' (ibid. 165). See C 47, G 47. This (D 25) is F 68, 412, 441.

[26] B 54. Gervase appears to be the historian. See p. 153.

[27], [28] Evidently B 55. See F 288, 289, 468, 469.

[29] F 65, 66, 445, 446. The 'fossa abbatis' is the boundary ditch of St Augustine's abbey. See C 68, 72; G 64.   [30] F 67, 447.

[31] Apparently part of ground of Matilda held at 8d. in B 32. This is F 96, 432.

	vj d.	Ad festum sancti Michaelis	uersus suth. latitudo uersus suth xxxij p. longitudo uersus west lxxviij p.

[32]

Robertus le Blund	viij d.	Ad mediam quadragesimam	De terra que iacet iuxta terram que fuit Chekerel. latitudo al suth c et xij p. longitudo uersus west c 7 xxi p.
	item xx d.	Ad mediam quadragesimam	
	xx d.	Ad festum sancti Michaelis	

[33]

Nigellus filius	xv d.	Ad mediam quadragesimam	De terra Landri. latitudo uersus suth l ped. longitudo uersus least c et lxxiiij p.
Aubri	xv d.	Ad mediam quadragesimam	

[34]

Symon presbiter et	iij d. et qua.	De heuewerc	Hec terra est iuxta terram Roberti Blund. latitudo uersus west lx p. longitudo a terra Roberti usque ad magnum uicum uersus suth cc et iij p.
Iohannes filius Eadmeri	ix d.	Ad mediam quadragesimam	

[35]

Symon pelliparius	ix d.	Ad festum sancti Michaelis	Hec terra iacet contra terram Symonis presbiteri uersus least. latitudo eius uersus suth⸝ xxxvi p. longitudo uersus least c et lxxij p. sicut terra Nigelli.

[36]

Wimundus	ij sol.		Latitudo eius uersus least xlviij p. longitudo uersus suth liiij p.

[37]

Reginaldus aurifaber	viij d.	Ad mediam quadragesimam	De terra que est iuxta terram Wimundi ad suth. latitudo eius ad suth xlij p. longitudo uersus least xlviij p.

[32] The 'terra . . . Chekerel' is 34 below. This must be part of B 32. It is F 89, 90, 440.

[33] On eastern side of Old Ruttington Lane, close to, or next to 35 below, and near site of B 57. F notices only one of the payments (103).

[34] Eadmer is called Checherelle, Gekerel, in B 31, F 98, 395. See 32 above.

[35] F 443, where S. pelliparius is called parmentarius. The ground is approximately site of B 59, and lies on the eastern side of Old Ruttington Lane, opposite 34 above.

[36] B 58 and, or 59. See F, 61, 62, and 466. Wimund is called 'mercier' in X 2 (fol. 4r.).

[37] Evidently B 60.

[38]

Deinde   x d.   Longitudo cuius liiij p. latitudo
terra usque   similiter.
ad magnum
uicum

[39]

Johannes   iij sol.   De terra que est iuxta Druthinton'
filius   et   post terram Symonis presbiteri
Rogeri   iij d.   De heuewer   uersus west. cuius latitudo lxxxij
p. uersus west. longitudo c et
lxxx p.

[fol. 219r.] [40]

Heredes   ix d.   Ad mediam   De terra iuxta predictam terram
Hugonis   quadragesimam uersus west. latitudo eius uersus
de aula   ix d.   Ad festum   west xvij p. longitudo uersus
                    sancti Michaelis north c et lxxx p.

[41]

Gerardus   viij d. Ad mediam   De terra proxima predicte terre.
presbiter   quadragesimam latitudo eius uersus west xvj p.
         viij d. Ad festum   longitudo uersus north sicut alia.
                    sancti Michaelis
         et j d. De heuewerc

[42]

De terra que fuit Willelmi Corbin
que est proxima terre Gerardi.
latitudo eius uersus west xxxij p.
longitudo uersus north ccc et xxx
p.

[43]

Willelmus   x d.   De terra proxima uersus west.
filius   et j d. De heuewerc   latitudo eius uersus west xxxij p.
Droconis   longitudo uersus north sicut alia.

---

[38] This occupies the site of B 61. The figure in col. 4 is written liijj. 'Vicus' is Broad St.

[39] B 30, where John s. of Roger cocus is tenant of three *mansure*. The ground still seems to be three *mansure* c. 1200. Cf. F 408 where J. s. of alderman Roger pays evework for three *mansure* outside Northgate. This appears to be F 116.

[40] F 58, 444, where the ground lies between that of alderman John and of William Sprot.

[41] F 86, where W. Sprot is tenant of ground 'que fuit Gerardi presbiteri', and 438. The evework is listed at 403.

[42] F 73 where Adam careteir pays rent for ground between that of W. Sprot (41 above) and that of W. s. of Driu (i.e. W. f. Droconis, 43 below). A. careteir is apparently A. Corbin of F 467. A portion of a letter, written in error, appears above this entry.

[43] The cathedral waterpipe passes through here. See G 30.

[44]			
Willelmus marescallus	xxx d.	Ad mediam quadragesimam	De terra Wiberti Kide et Aliz filie sue. de terra proxima uersus
	xxx d.	Ad festum sancti Michaelis	west. latitudo eius uersus west lxij p. longitudo uersus north sicut alia.
[45]			
Alicia soror Nigelli	viij d. et j qua.	Ad mediam quadragesimam De heuewerc	De terra proxima predicte. latitudo eius uersus west xxviij p. longitudo uersus north sicut alia.
[46]			
Amfridus de Chelde	xiiij d. et ob. et ij d.	Ad mediam quadragesimam De heuewerc	De terra proxima uersus west. latitudo eius uersus west xlij p. longitudo uersus north sicut alia.
[47]			
Nigellus filius Aubri			˙De terra proxima uersus west. latitudo eius uersus west xix p. longitudo uersus north sicut alia.
[48]			
Heredes Roberge relicte Willelmi coci	ij sol. et j d.	Ad mediam quadragesimam De heuewerc	De terra proxima uersus west. latitudo eius uersus west xix p. longitudo uersus north sicut alia.
[49]			
Item Nigellus			De terra proxima uersus west. latitudo eius uersus west xx p. longitudo uersus north sicut alia.
[50]			
Sunewine	xij d. et j d.	Ad mediam quadragesimam De heuewerc	De terra proxima uersus west latitudo eius uersus west xx p. longitudo uersus north sicut alia.
[51]			
Item Nigellus	iiij sol.		De terra proxima uersus west. Latitudo eius uersus west xj p. longitudo uersus north sicut alia.
[52]			
Suanus mercator	xxi d.	Ad mediam quadragesimam	De terra proxima uersus west. Latitudo eius uersus west xxx p.

44 F 78, 433. Probably B 27.

45 Appears to be B 26, next to B 25, which is D 46.   46 B 25, F 95.

47–52 For the identification of these holdings (lying along the defensive ditch east of Northgate) see B 23, notes.

48 F 113, 404, 454.   50 F 101, 393.   52 The evework is apparently F 407.

| | xxi d. | Ad festum sancti Michaelis | longitudo uersus north sicut alia. |
| | et j ob. | De heuewerc | |

[53]

| Henricus de Suliford | xviij d. | Ad mediam quadragesimam | De terra quam heredes Wlsi tenent de eo que est proxima predicte |
| | et ij d. | De heuewerc | terre uersus west. latitudo eius uersus west xxx p. longitudo uersus north sicut alia. |

[54]

| Relicta Ailwardi | xij d. | Ad mediam quadragesimam | De terra proxima uersus west. latitudo eius uersus west xxv p. |
| | et j ob. | De heuewerc | longitudo uersus north c et xl p. |

[55]

| Bartholomeus faber | ix d. | Ad festum sancti Michaelis | De terra Iohannis clerici filii Cristine. hec proxima est predicte |
| | xij d. | Ad mediam quadragesimam | terre. latitudo eius uersus west xv p. longitudo uersus nort sicut alia. |

[56]

| Item Bartholomeus faber | xij d. | Ad festum sancti Michaelis | De terra proxima predicte terre uersus west. latitudo eius uersus |
| | xij d. | Ad mediam quadragesimam | west xxx p. longitudo uersus north sicut alia. |

[57]

| Willelmus Driv | iij sol. | Ad mediam quadragesimam | De terra proxima uersus west. latitudo cuius uersus west xxviij p. |
| | et j d. | De heuewerc | longitudo uersus north sicut alia. |

[58]

| Willelmus faber filius Alfredi | xij d. | Ad mediam quadragesimam | De terra quam Radulfus faber filius Alfredi de eo tenet. latitudo |
| | xij d. | Ad festum sancti Michaelis | eius uersus west xxx p. longitudo uersus north sicut predicta. |

[fol. 219v.] [59]

| Godardus presbiter | ix d. | Ad natiuitatem domini | De terra proxima terre Willelmi fabri uersus west. latitudo eius |

---

[53] B 22, F 92, F 382 (evework).

[55–57] From F 104–6 it seems that D 55–57 were given by John the clerk son of Christina, and that the whole was called 'terra Herloc'. X 2, fol. 6r. shows that Lefwin Herloc was tenant at some date before 1180. The tenure is obscure in the case of these holdings. D 57 is clearly F 104. D 56 seems to be F 105. See F 104–6, 451, 452, 455.

[58] F 94, 431.   [59] Probably F 21, 342.

| | ix d. | Ad festum sancti Johannis Baptiste | uersus west xvi p. longitudo [blank]. |

[60]

| Salomon Keth | viij d. | Ad mediam quadragesimam | De mansura quadam proxima illi que fuit Osberti presbiteri filii Salomonis sacerdotis. |

[61]

| | iiij d. | Ad mediam quadragesimam | De fabrica extra Northgate super fossam. |

[62]

| | xxij d. | Ad mediam quadragesimam | De mansura proxima quondam terre relicte Nigelli coci. |

[63]

| Sanctimoniales sancti Sepulcri | iiij d. | Ad mediam quadragesimam | De terra Cole uersus west. latitudo uersus west xxiiij p. longitudo uersus north sicut alia. |

[64]

| Gilebertus filius Moysi | | | De terra que est iuxta terram Keuerel uersus least. latitudo eius uersus west xl p. longitudo uersus north sicut alia. |

[65] (Parrochia sancti Ælfegi.)ʳ

De terra uacua que iacet ad suth contra domum Geruasii coci damus x d. Jacobo de porta. hec pertinet ad childhalle. latitudo eius a uico ad orientem xlv p. longitudo ab alio uico ad suth lx p.

[66]

| Radulfus nepos sancti Thome | ij. sol. | Ad mediam quadragesimam | De terra Elesmoth. hec est proxima terre que fuit Geldewini presbiteri. latitudo eius uersus suth iuxta Sturam lxxxx p. longitudo a Stura uersus lest c et x p. |

---

⁶⁰ Appears to be B 15, which is F 77. The holding of O. the priest s. of Solomon mentioned in the descriptive note is B 14.

⁶¹ B 11, F 76.   ⁶² The site of this is uncertain.   ⁶³ Possibly F 74, or 108.

⁶⁴ B 13. This lies in Broad Street, next but one to Northgate Street. 'Terra Keuerel' is 7 above (the corner holding).

⁶⁵ For the payment of 10d. to J. de porta see C 60, G 60. This holding is F 315, 486. It lies at s.w. corner of St Alphage lane.

⁶⁶ B 6, F 206. For Becket's kin and entourage, see pp. 180–4.

[67]
Nicholaus   ij   Ad pascha   De mansura sua. terram illam
filius   sol.   dedit nobis Lieuenoth de Northe-
Baldewini   wede cum Laurencio filio suo.
                                            hec est iuxta terram que fuit
                                            Elfwini filii Semeri uersus occi-
                                            dentem.

[68]
Robertus   vj d.   Ad pascha   De terra que est iuxta domum
de porta   lapideam Henrici aurifabri uersus
                                            suth. latitudo uersus suth lxvij p.
                                            longitudo uersus least lxx p. De
                                            hac terra habet predictus Henricus
                                            ad domum suam lapideam xij p. in
                                            latitudine 7 xxx p. in longitudine.

[69]
Symon   xij d. Ad festum   De duabus terris que sunt iuxta
capellanus   omnium   predictam terram Roberti portarii.
filius   sanctorum   latitudo unius uersus least xl p.
Walteri   xxxij d. Ad mediam   latitudo alterius xxx p. longitudo
Bues   quadragesimam   utriusque lix p.

[70]
Willelmus   xxij d.   De terra que proxima est terre
filius   Willelmi de Sandwiz. latitudo eius
Lamb'   xxvij p. longitudo uersus suthwest
                                            c et xxvj p.

[71]
Moniales   De terra que est inter domum
de sancto   Luce mercatoris et domum Lam-
sepulcro   bini flandrensis. latitudo eius uersus
                                            suth xiiij p.

[72]
Feraminus   xix d. Ad mediam   De terra proxima Luce mercatori
et uxor   quadragesimam   ubi manet que ad nos pertinet.
eius filia   xix d. Ad festum
Hugonis   sancti Michaelis
Flagard

---

⁶⁷ F 292.

⁶⁷⁻⁷⁶ Owing to absence of surviving landmarks it is difficult to site these holdings. The holding of N. s. of Baldwin may be B 51, lying west of the ground of E. s. of Semer at 2s. rent. This last-mentioned ground appears to lie on s. side of Orange Street.

⁶⁸ The stone house of H. the goldsmith may be B 119, east of the ground of E. s. of Semer (see last section). In this case the holding of R. *de porta* (D 68) would lie in the Dancing School Yard.   ⁷⁰ This possibly lies in Sun Street.   ⁷² C 37, F 203, 566.

[73]

| | xiij d. | Ad natale
domini | De terra Philippi de Ha(r)ᶦdres.
latitudo domus ab occidente ad |
| | xiij d. | Ad natiuitatem
sancti
Johannis
Baptiste | uicum xxxvi p. latitudo orti a suth
uersus north lxxx p. longitudo ab
oriente ad occidentem c p. |

[fol. 220r.] [74]

Heredes	xii d.	Ad mediam	De terra que est contra domum
Alicie		quadragesimam	lapideam Henrici aurifabri ex alia
filie	xii d.	Ad festum	parte uie ad north. latitudo eius
Henrici		sancti Michaelis	uersus west xlviij p. longitudo
aurifabri			uersus north lxxxxij p.

[75]

De terra quam tenet Nicholaus
uitrearius que est inter terram
predicte Alicie et Anselmi secretarii.

[76]

Moniales	iii	Ad mediam	De terra Wiberti clerici que
de Scapeia	sol.	quadragesimam	quondam fuit Anselmi secretarii.
	iij	Ad festum	hec iacet inter terram Nicholai
	sol.	sancti Michaelis	uitrearii et terram Iacobi de porta.
			latitudo uersus north xlviij p.
			longitudo a uico uersus west c et
			lxiij p.

[77] (Parrochia sancti Pauli.)ʳ

| Reginaldus | ix d. | De duabus terris. scilicet illa de |
| aurifaber | x d. | Hopilonde. et altera. quarum ut-
raque est in exitu de Trutintune.
latitudo terre Reginaldi uersus lest
xx p. latitudo terre de Hopilond'
uersus lest xxvi p. longitudo
utriusque uersus north lxxxiiij p. |

---

⁷³ F 40, 367; LV.

⁷⁴ Apparently B 124.

⁷⁵ The 'ground of Alice' here seems to be different from the ground of her heirs in the last section. It (75) evidently lies in Palace Street.

⁷⁶ C 16, G 18, F 210, 569; LIII, LIV.

⁷⁷ X 1 (c. 1180) shows that Reginald the goldsmith succeeded Alexander the mason as tenant. This connects 77, here, with B 61, and F 121. The name Hopilond is probably the quasi-surname of an earlier tenant. There was a knightly family of the name in Westbere and Chislet (BBSA, pp. 419, 420). See F 121–6, n.

[78]

| Alfredus filius Oswardi de Haccolte | xix d. | | De terra que est iuxta domum Reginaldi aurifabri uersus lest latitudo eius uersus lest xl p. longitudo uersus north sicut predicta. |

[79]

| Symon juuenis | x d. | Ad mediam quadragesimam | De terra proxima uersus lest que est in introitu de Dudelane. latitudo eius uersus lest xxiij p. longitudo uersus north lxxvij p. usque ad terram que fuit Sergant. |

[80]

| Sergant | x d. | Ad mediam quadragesimam | De terra proxima uersus lest. latitudo eius uersus west xl p. longitudo uersus northeast xlij p. |

[81]

| Symon de Lindeseia | xv d. xv d. | Ad natale Ad festum sancti Johannis Baptiste | De terra que est iuxta fossam ciuitatis contra sanctum Augustinum. latitudo eius de north in suth xxvi p. longitudo de west in east lxvij p. |

[82]

| Willelmus Rabel | xxij d. et vj d. | Ad mediam quadragesimam super altare sancti Dunstani in festo eius | De terra Alicie filie Wiberti Kide. hec iacet iuxta terram predicti Symonis uersus suth. latitudo eius uersus suth xxvij p. longitudo uersus east l p. |

[83]

| Gaufridus filius Reimundi | iiij d. iiij d. | | De quadam parte terre de terra Hasketini. hec est proxima predicte terre uersus suth. latitudo cuius uersus [blank]. |

[84]

| Terra Hasketin | ij sol. | | Hec iacet uacua 7 est proxima predicte. latitudo eius uersus suth xxi p. longitudo uersus east xxiiij p. |

---

78 B 63, F 123?   79 B 64.   80 B 65.

81 F 32, 290, 341, 572. This seems to be the ground of Alexander parmenter in B (195), north of the ground of Wibert Kide on the moat, without Burgate (D 82).

82 B 195.   83 B 196, F 282.

84 Possibly B 197 where the ground is on the corner, opposite Burgate. Here, however (D 84) it is next but one to the corner. Possibly D 85, on the corner, was originally combined with 84.

[85]
Willelmus   ij sol.   De terra proxima uersus suth.
marescallus   latitudo eius uersus suth xiiij p.
                                                         longitudo ad east xxiiij p.

[86]
Filia   viij d.   Ad festum   De terra quam tenet de ea Robertus
Markere   sancti   filius Ricardi. que fuit quondam
                               Michaelis   Helye de Bremlinge. hec est
                                                         proxima predicte terre uersus east.
                                                         latitudo eius uersus east xxx p.
                                                         longitudo uersus north lxxx p.

[87]
Reginaldus   xx d.   Ad mediam   De terra proxima uersus least.
Blundus   quadragesimam   latitudo cuius xxv p. uersus least.
                                                         longitudo uersus north lxxv p.

[fol. 220v.] [88]
(Parrochia sancti Michaelis de Burgate.)ʳ

                                                         Terra iacet uacua a porta de Bur-
                                                         gate uersus suth usque ad fabri-
                                                         cam Markere. longitudo eius cc
                                                         et lxx p. latitudo a muro usque
                                                         ad uicum xx p. Hec de diuersis
                                                         mansuris solebat reddere vj sol. et
                                                         x d.

[89]
                                                         Ex alia parte eiusdem porte uersus
                                                         north terra Hamonis Coppe quam
                                                         dedimus ei in concambium terre
                                                         retro clocarium. longitudo eius
                                                         uersus north lx p. latitudo a muro
                                                         usque ad uicum xx p. Deinde de
                                                         terra ista usque ad ecclesiam de
                                                         Queniggate [sic] cccc p. et x in
                                                         longitudine. latitudo xx p. hec
                                                         tota iacet uacua. In medio fere
                                                         huius terre habent monachi sancti
                                                         Augustini lxxx p. in longitudine.

---

[86] Rental Z (c. 1230, under par. of St Paul), shows that the n.w. corner of Church Street is occupied by John f. Robert (f. Richard) holding from Alfred de Ocholte who holds from Christ Church at 32d. This probably falls between 85, 86. Z indicates that John Chiche held ground opposite on s. side of Church Street. See B 199.

[88] B 69, 205–7, occupied c. 1166, and now vacant.

[89] F 155; XXXIII, XXXIV. For 410, read 310, for which only there is room.

[90]

	xij d.	De terra Willelmi filii Gregorii. hec terra est ex alia parte uie uersus west. longitudo eius uersus north l p. de uico uersus west l p. De hac terra et de molendino inquirendum est per Basiliam uiduam.

[91]

Johannes filius Rogeri aldermanni	xij d.	De terra cuius media pars iacet in orto Gregorii Frese et media pars in orto Henrici Chuchere. longitudo unius xxx p. latitudo xx p. Similiter et alia. inde est gauelate.

[92]

Henricus Chuchere	iiij sol. et vj d.	De quadam terra quam emit Wibertus prior. hec est in uico de Burgate uersus suth. latitudo eius xxxv p. longitudo uersus suth lxxx p.

[93] (Parrochia sancte Marie Magdalene de fismanne cherche.)ʳ

Paulina relicta	xli d.	Ad natale domini	De terra Lamberti Gargate. hec terra iacet iuxta Fismane chereche uersus lest. latitudo eius iuxta uicum ad west liij p. longitudo uersus suth c et x p. latitudo orti uersus west lxxx p. et x.
Johannis aldermanni	xlj d.	Ad pascha	
	xlj d.	Ad festum sancti Johannis	
	xlj d.	Ad festum sancti Michaelis	

[94]

Terra que fuit Hamonis Vnderdune inter terram Lamberti Gargate et Fismanne chereche. latitudo eius uersus west xx p. longitudo uersus suth c et v p.

---

⁹⁰ This seems to be ground of W. s. of Gregory in B 70.

⁹¹ For gavelet, the Kentish process of distress, see p. 145. The word 'inde' is plainly written but the context would appear to require 'hec' or 'ista', for which 'inde' may be a mistranscription.

⁹² Appears to be A 23, B 86, F 613, 658.

⁹³ B 71. See C 26, 32, 35, 52, G 26, 31, 33, 44; XX–XXIII.

[95]

Ingenulfus filius	xviij d.	Ad mediam quadragesimam	De terra proxima terre Iohannis filii Roberti et Thome filii sui.
Normanni plumbarii	xviij d.	Ad festum sancti Michaelis	latitudo eius uersus west lxvj p. longitudo uersus suth lxxxiij p.

[96]

Filius Alfredi de Welles	De terra que est iuxta domum Liefwini Cruke uersus lest. latitudo eius uersus west xix p. longitudo uersus suth c et v p.

[97]

Tera [*sic*] Liefwini Cruke que est de gauelikende. latitudo eius iuxta uicum uersus west xxvij p. longitudo uersus suth a uico cc et xx p. latitudo orti del est al west lix p.

[98]

Liefwinus carpentarius	xl d.	Ad mediam quadragesimam	De terra proxima predicte terre uersus west latitudo eius uersus
	xl d.	Ad festum sancti Michaelis	west iuxta uicum xxj p. longitudo uersus suth lxxx et xiiij p.

[99]

Theoricus aurifaber	x sol.	De terra ubi manet. latitudo eius uersus west lx p. longitudo uersus suth c et liij p.

[100] [fol. 221r.]

(Parrochia sancti Andree.)ᴿ

Theoricus aurifaber	De terra que est iuxta terram Basilie uidue uersus suth latitudo eius uersus suth iuxta uicum xl p. longitudo uersus east lx p.

---

⁹⁵ For Ingenulph, staff-plumber to the monks, see pp. 157, 163. He holds ground to the north of his holding 18 feet long on Iron Bar Lane, and 36 feet long on the side nearer to the Precincts. Ground to the north of this is held by David of Burgate, holding in turn from Terric the gold-smith (Y, fol. 28r.). D 95 is F 199, 564. See XVI n. It was held by the monks from John s. of Robert s. of Osmund (C 74, G 79).

⁹⁷ C 9, 41, 73; G 13, 40. Probably a subject of LVI.

⁹⁸ F 305, 563. Y (c. 1216), fol. 34r., says of this holding: Hanc emit Robertus quondam abbas Cestrie de eodem Lefwino 7 dedit huic ecclesie [Christ Church, Canterbury] et est inter terram canonicorum sancte Radegundis [near Dover] et terram que fuit Lefwini Cruke.

⁹⁹ F 194, 554. F indicates that the house of Terric was of stone. The heirs of Terric paid (c. 1230), 19d. to Christ Church 'de terra Hugonis filii Everardi supra quam quedam pars predicte magne domus lapidee [i.e. of Terric] sita est' (Z, fol. 196v.). See C 3, G 3.

¹⁰⁰ This lies on the eastern side of Butchery Lane.

[101]
Reginoldus
Blundus

De terra proxima ad suth. latitudo eius uersus suth xxviij p. longitudo uersus east lxvi p.

[102]

De terra Godardi que est proxima terre Reginaldi Blundi. latitudo eius uersus suth xxix p. longitudo uersus east lxvj p.

[103]

Johannes	iiij. sol.	Ad natiuitatem
Dodekere	et ix d.	domini
	iiij sol.	Ad pascha
	et ix d.	
	iiii sol.	Ad festum
	et ix d.	sancti
		Johannis
		Baptiste
	iiij sol.	Ad festum
	et ix d.	sancti Michaelis

De terra que est iuxta magnam stratam uersus east. latitudo eius uersus east lxv p. longitudo a magno uico uersus north lxxx p. iuxta hanc terram uersus east terra Willelmi Malemie.

[104]

Mater	xv d.
Willelmi	
Siluestre	

De terra proxima uersus east. latitudo eius uersus east xx p. longitudo uersus north lxxx p. et iiij.

[105]
Heredes
Alfredi
de Welles

De terra proxima iuxta illam. latitudo eius uersus east lxx p. longitudo a magno uico uersus north c et xxx p.

[106]

Item	v sol.	In die
mater		Mercurii
Willelmi		post mediam
Siluestre		quadragesimam
	et ij d.	De heuewerc

De terra Geroldi. hec terra iacet ex alia parte magne strate uersus suth in angulo uie que ducit ad gaiole. latitudo eius ab east ad west iuxta magnam stratam xxxiiij p. longitudo a magna strata ad suth xl p.

---

¹⁰¹ F 175, where R. Blund holds at a rent of 2od. next to ground of Godard Uphaldere, in Sunwin's Lane, i.e. Butchery Lane.   ¹⁰² F 537.

¹⁰³ F 30, 295, 365, 531; XXIV. For outpayments due, see C 53, 62; G 55, 61.

¹⁰⁴ This appears to be B 109, in which case the rent of 15d. in D was originally 13d. *gabulum*, plus 2d. evework. See F 217.

¹⁰⁶ Probably B 110. D 106, here, and 104 above are F 217, while evework of 2d. is covered by F 376.

[107]

Ab angulo magne domus lapidee i.
a uico qui uenit de Burgate usque
ad magnam stratam uersus suth
sunt cc et l p. Item a uico uersus
west usque ad domum Mahaut
relicte Gileberti camerarii lxi p.

[108]

Mahaut relicta Gileberti camerarii	ij sol.	

De terra proxima. latitudo eius
uersus west lx p. longitudo a
magna strata uersus north c p.

[109]

Salomon mercator	v sol.	Ad festum sancti Michaelis

De terra proxima uersus west.
latitudo eius uersus west lix p.
longitudo uersus north c p.

[110]

Item Salomon	xiij d.	Ad mediam quadragesimam

De alia terra iuxta predictam
latitudo eius usque ad angulum
de Merceria xxx p. longitudo
uersus north xlviij p. post illam
usque ad forum ante portam ecclesie terra monachorum sancti
Augustini. a magna domo lapidea
uersus west́ usque ad terram
monachorum sancti Augustini xlv
p. longitudo a foro ad suth usque
ad terram Mahaut́ lxxiij p. Ex
alia parte fori uersus west terra
Wimundi. latitudo eius a suth

---

107 This covers the western side of Butchery (Sunwin's) Lane. However, the modern frontage
on the lane is but 234 feet 8 inches, well short of the figure (250 feet) given here. The surveyors
may have measured up to the stalls in the street, the *scope* of B 219–221.

108 Evidently F 213, 532. See B 111, 216.　　　　　　　　　　109 B 81, F 294, 533.

110 A 29, B 222, F 622, 660. The tenants of the monks of St Augustine's can be supplied from
other sources. North of the ground of Solomon the mercer is to be found Dionisius mercerius
and wife (Cartulary of St Laurence, Canterbury, Cathedral Library, Lit. MS. C 20, pp. 75, 76).
The ground is classed as 'de tenemento Johannis filii Roberti filii Ricardi', subsequently St
Augustine's. Next come eight shops belonging to Goldwin the mercer, granted by his daughter
to the abbey (BBSA, pp. 585, 586). Next there is a shop held by Luke the mercer from Robert
s. of Richard, granted by him to the abbey and confirmed by his son John (BBSA, pp. 590, 591).
Next is the holding of Charles the mercer (ibid.). Early in the thirteenth century the ground
next to the north was quitclaimed to the abbey by Christina, daughter of Andrew of Flanders
(BBSA, 584, 585). The Corporation of Canterbury still collects here ancient rents of the abbey,
bought from the Crown at the Dissolution. See p. 67. These lie on east side of Mercery Lane.

uersus north iuxta nouam portam
xxxv p. latitudo eius in orto a
north uersus suth x p. longitudo
domus cum orto lx p.

[III]
Gilebertus   iiij sol.
de Bereham

De terra proxima predicte uersus
suth. latitudo eius a north ad suth
xxxiiij p. longitudo de east ad
west lvij p.

[II2]
Jacobus de   v sol.   Ad natiuitatem
porta   domini
heres   v sol.   Ad pascha
Willelmi   v sol.   Ad festum
filii   sancti
Pagani   Johannis
              v sol.   Ad festum
                        sancti Michaelis

De terra de scorcherie que est
proxima terre Symonis le feiner.
latitudo eius de east ad west xxi p.
longitudo de north uersus suth
(x(x)ⁱiiij p.)ᶜ xxiij p.

[fol. 221v.] [II3]
Item   xxvj d.
Jacobus
de porta

De terra proxima uersus suth.
latitudo uersus suth xxxv p. longitudo uersus west [blank].

[II4]
Robertus
filius
Ricardi

De terra proxima uersus suth.
latitudo uersus suth xij d. longitudo uersus west [blank].

[II5]

Juxta predictam terram Arnoldus
Buche et Johannes et alter Johannes
tenent mansuram. sed non de
gauelikende. latitudo uersus suth
xxvij p. longitudo uersus west c et
v p. similiter et alie. Juxta illos
ad suth Arnoldus Chic. latitudo
eius xv p. Juxta eum Reginaldus

---

111 F 215, 536. Y (fol. 40v.) c. 1216, says of this holding that the tenant of G. of Barham is
Simon fenarius. See next section.
112 The ground of S. le fenier is 111 above. See note. This (112) and holdings listed in 113–15
lie along the western side of Mercery Lane. Section 112 is C 15, 54; F 29, 296, 359, 539.
113 Probably F 216, 540.
115 The ground not held at gavelkind is probably held on the 'house and shop' basis. See p.
36. For the ground of Arnold Chic see LII. The ground of Anser (see B 208) is at the s.w.
corner of Mercery Lane. See C 5–11.

aurifaber. latitudo eius uersus suth
xv p. Juxta illum ad suth filia
Alfredi de Welles. latitudo eius
ad suth x p. Juxta illos usque ad
magnam stratam terra Anseri.
longitudo eius usque ad magnam
stratam liij p. latitudo uersus west
xxvij p.

[116]
Willelmus
filius
Winedei

De terra proxima. latitudo eius
uersus west xviij p. longitudo
uersus north [*blank*]. Juxta eum
domus lapidea.

[117] (Parrochia sancti Georgii.)ʳ

Lambertus	xiiij d.
Werne	item
	iiij d.

De terra que est iuxta carcerem
ciuitatis uersus suth. latitudo eius
[*blank*].

[118]
| Elfegus | xij d. |
| Lamb | |

De terra proxima ad orientem.
latitudo eius iuxta uicum xxiiij p.
longitudo eius lxx p.

[119]
Item	vj d.
Lambertus	
Werne	

De quadam terra que iacet inter
iiijᵒʳ uicos iuxta carcerem uersus
north. latitudo eius uersus north
lx p. Juxta illam est alia terra
uersus north de qua contencio est
inter Robertum filium Hamonis
et predictum Lambertum. latitudo
eius uersus north lx p. longitudo
utriusque ab east ad west lxxxx
p.

[120]
Johannes	xvj d.	Ad mediam
filius		quadragesimam
Rogeri		
Blundi		

Latitudo terre eius xxx p. longitudo
de north uersus suth lxxxxij p.

---

¹¹⁶ This and the stone house next door lie west from Mercery Lane. The stone house appears
to be that flanked by S. Munin's ground (F 262). This last-mentioned ground was flanked c.
1230 by ground of the heirs of J. Chich, and described as opposite St Mary Breadman church
(Z fol. 199v.). See C 8.
¹¹⁷ For the prison, evidently established following the Assize of Clarendon, see pp. 197–8.
¹²⁰ F 265.

[121]

| Arnoldus Ferre | xx d. | Ad mediam quadragesimam | De terra proxima terre Rogeri Blundi uersus east. latitudo eius de |
| | et j d. | De heuewerc. | east ad west xxvij p. longitudo a magno uico uersus suth lxxx p. et vij. |

[122]

| Robertus filius Emme | xx p. | Ad festum sancti Iohannis Baptiste | De terra que est iuxta domum Thome filii Iohannis filii Roberti uersus suth. latitudo eius de east ad west xxvij p. longitudo a magno |
| | xx p. | Ad festum sancti Michaelis | uico uersus suth lxxxxiij p. |

[123]

| Thomas de Rethlinge | vj d. | Ad mediam quadragesimam | De terra que est contra ecclesiam sancti Georgii. latitudo eius de |
| | vj d. | Ad festum sancti Michaelis | east ad west xxx p. longitudo a uico uersus north lxxij p. |

[124] Terra Odboldi iacet uacua ante ecclesiam sancti Georgii. latitudo eius xxij p. longitudo a uico uersus suth lxxx p. et x.

[125] Item ibidem terra Odboldi uacua iacet. latitudo eius ab east ad west lxxiiij p. longitudo a uico uersus suth lxxx p. et x.

[126]

| Robertus Polre | xij d. | Ad mediam quadragesimam | De terra que iacet prope Newingate infra ciuitatem uersus suth |
| | xij d. | Ad festum sancti Michaelis | contra murum ciuitatis. ex alia parte uie uersus west. et est inter domum Wolnod aldermanni et domum Brithtiue relicte Godwini fabri. quedam pars camere predicte Brithtiue est super eandem terram. Hanc terram dedit nobis Henricus pater Hamonis quando monachatum suscepit. latitudo eius uersus suth xl p. longitudo uersus west a uico lxxx p. |

[fol. 222r.] [127]

| Eluiua relicta Pardic | xxv d. | Ad mediam quadragesimam | De terra que est iuxta Lodderelane uersus suth. latitudo eius uersus |
| | et vij d. | Ad uincula sancti Petri | suth xxvij p. longitudo a magno uico uersus east lxxx p. et xij. |

---

[121] F 214, 375.　　　　[122] See F 351, 525.　　　　[123] A 7, F 195, 527; XIX.

[126] B 213, F 176, 181, 529. See F 50, n.

[127] This and 128–137 lie outside Newingate. The same ground is covered by B 91–98, but it is difficult to effect identifications. Close to the site of 127 stands Salt Hill, a lost tumulus. See p. 199. This (D 127) is F 188, 416. Lodderelane is Ivy Lane.

[128]
Symon   ij sol.   De terra proxima uersus suth.
Chig   latitudo eius uersus suth xxij p.
                                                 longitudo a uico uersus east lxxx
                                                 et x p.

[129]
Lambertus   xiij d.   De terra proxima uersus suth.
                 et ob.   latitudo eius uersus suth xiiij p.
                                                 longitudo uersus east sicut alia.

[130]
Heredes   xxv d.   Ad mediam   De terra proxima contra portam
Alani   quadragesimam   de Newingate. latitudo eius uersus
aldermanni   et iij d.   De heuewerc   suth xliiij p. longitudo a uico uersus
                             ad gulam   east c et xiij p. latitudo orti de
                             Augusti   north ad suth c et lij p.

[131]
Heredes   xx d.   Ad mediam   Hec terra est proxima predicte
Ailrici   quadragesimam   terre heredum Alani uersus suth.
seocher   et j d.   De heuewerc   latitudo eius uersus suth xxiij p.
                             ad gulam   longitudo uersus east lxxx et vj p.
                             Augusti

[132]
Hugo   De terra proxima uersus suth.
filius   latitudo eius uersus suth vij p.
Semeri   longitudo uersus east sicut terra
presbiteri   Ocher.

[133]
Hamo   xxj d.   Ad mediam   De terra proxima de kildhalle.
frater   quadragesimam   latitudo eius uersus suth xxiiij p.
Rogeri   xxj d.   Ad festum   longitudo uersus east c et lxiij p.
decani   sancti Michaelis

[134]
Johannes   x d.   De terra proxima uersus suth.
Dodechere   et j d.   De heuewerc   latitudo eius uersus (suth)ⁱ xx p.
                             Ad gulam   longitudo uersus east lxxx et ix p.
                             Augusti

128–129 F 189, 310, 398. A holding in the hands of the gild of smiths next to that of S. Chig
has been omitted in D. Rental Y (fol. 30r.), c. 1216, says that the 13½d. paid in D 129 arises 'de
terra proxima [to that of S. Chig] uersus austrum preter quandam terram que pertinet ad gildam
fabrorum'. For the early Canterbury gilds see p. 124.

130 B 92, F 187. Evework is F 402. See A 34. F indicates that a cross stood here in the roadway, giving a name to Adam de cruce, alderman Alan's son. See F 608, 642, 657.

131 F 178, 397.   132 Probably F 521. See B 94 and n

133 For the gilds see D 128–9 n., above.   134 B 96, F 198, 394.

[135]

Filius Sedewen	xv d.	Ad mediam quadragesimam	De terra proxima uersus suth latitudo eius uersus suth xxxij p.
	xv d.	Ad festum sancti Michaelis	longitudo uersus east c et xxx p. latitudo orti de north ad suth lxx p.

[136]

Johannes clericus	ij sol.		De terra proxima uersus suth. latitudo eius uersus suth xxvij p. longitudo uersus east lxxx p.

[137]

Nichellus Broch	xlij d.		De terra proxima uersus suth. latitudo eius uersus suth xxxij d. longitudo uersus east lxxx et ix p. Hec est gauelate.

[138] In his terris continentur ix mansure secundum antiquas rotulas.

De terra Eadwardi filii Odboldi	viij sol. et iiij d.	Ad festum sancti Michaelis	De terra Eadwardi de Stoche in Retherchieape. latitudo eius uersus east c et x p. longitudo a uico uersus north c et xxxiiij p. Juxta eam terra smithchilde. Juxta illam item terra Eadwardi. latitudo uersus east cc et ij p. longitudo uersus north c et xxxiiij p. post eam terra Hamonis de Suford. deinde terra que pertinet ad ecclesiam sancti Georgii. longitudo eius uersus east cc et xx p. latitudo uersus north [blank]. Item ibidem terra pertinens ad sanctum Georgium in uico qui uocatur Niewestrete. longitudo eius a uico uersus north cccc et xxxv p. latitudo a uico uersus west cc et lxxv p. hanc tenent heredes Roberti mederere. Juxta uicum qui est ab occidente et ducit ad sanctum Sepulcrum. terra iacet quam tenet sacerdos sancti

[135] B 97, F 186, 524. [136] B 98?

[137] B 212, where the total rents amount to 42d, as here. F 185, 523. Rental Y (fol. 42r.), c. 1216, states that the ground lies 'extra Newingate in angulo sicud itur ad sanctum Sepulcrum', i.e. corner of Dover St. For gavelet, the Kentish process of distress, see pp. 145–7.

[138] B 99, F 526. B is probably one of the 'ancient rolls'. For the gild of smiths, see p. 131. 'Retherchieape' is Dover Street. See p. 203. New Street is Chantry Lane.

Georgii que fuit terra Buterclunch
nescimus quomodo uel per quem.
hec nostra fuit. longitudo eius ab
east uersus west c et x p. latitudo
uersus suth lx p.

[139] (Parrochia sancti Sepulchri.)ʳ

Tres acre iacent citra hospitale
sancti Laurencii uersus suth que
pertinent ad sanctum Georgium.
Item tres acre citra predictas tres
que pertinent ad ecclesiam de
Burgate. iuxta Holestrate uersus
west.

[140]

| Johannes Rose | ij sol. | Medietatem ad festum sancti Michaelis. Et alteram medietatem ad festum sancti Johannis Baptiste. Et eodem modo singuli subsequentes. | De dimidia acra. |

[fol. 222v.] **[141]**

| Heredes Johannis clerici | vj sol. | | De acra et dimidia. Juxta predictam. |

[142]

| Nicholaus filius Aldithe | ij sol. | | De dimidia acra iuxta predictam. |

[143]

| Arnoldus | vj sol. et viij d. | | De una acra terre iuxta predictam. |

---

¹³⁹ St Laurence priory stood on the Dover Road, about ¾ mile from Ridingate. 'Holestrete' is
apparently Puckle Lane, leading south from the Old Dover Road. The passage 'pertinent...
Georgium' is underlined.

¹⁴⁰ Part of this ground (lying opposite St Sepulchre's, on the Dover Road) is subject of
VIII-X. See A 10-18. It is difficult to identify the holdings as described in the different rentals,
and charters. D 144 may be F 625, 651. D 147 may be F 628, 646.

[144]
Geruasius   xij d.   De una uirgata terre iuxta pre-
ampollarius   dictam.

[145]
Rogerius   ij sol.   De dimidia acra iuxta predictam
de Helle   uersus west.

[146]
Robertus   ij sol.   De dimidia acra iuxta predictam
presbiter   uersus west.

[147]
Relicta   iij sol.   De tribus uirgatis terre iuxta
Alfredi   predictam uersus west.
Pete

[148]
Ædwardus   viij d.   De terra que iacet citra barram
parere   sancti Sepulchri uersus suth. lati-
                                   tudo eius a uia proxima ad west
                                   xliij p. longitudo a magna strata
                                   uersus suth c et xv p.

[149]
Arnoldus   viij d.   De terra proxima uersus west.
de monte   latitudo eius uersus west xxvj p.
                                   longitudo uersus suth c et x p.

[150] (Parrochia sancti Ædmundi.)ʳ
Magister   ij sol.   De terra que est ex alia parte
Radulfus   strate uersus north prope terram
                                   Iohannis aldermanni. latitudo eius
                                   uersus west iuxta stratam lv p.
                                   longitudo a strata uersus north cc
                                   et lxvj p.

[151]
Heredes   iij sol.   De terra iuxta predictam uersus
Roberti   et ij d.   west quam terram Ricardus Deu-
le mederere   dune tenuit de heredibus Roberti
                                   le mederere pro iij sol. et iij d. hec
                                   uacua est. Reginaldus Blundus
                                   tenet partem de eadem terra super
                                   quam grangia sua stat. has duas

---

148 For the bars spanning approach roads to Canterbury see p. 196.
150 This ground lies on the north side of the Old Dover Road, west of Oaten Hill. Master
Ralph is the vice-archdeacon. See p. 109. See F 320.
151 Possibly F 278, 571.

terras Reginaldus Blundus defor-
ciat et ecclesie et heredibus Roberti
le mederere. latitudo unius terre de
east ad west xliij p. longitudo
utriusque terre a strata uersus
north cc et lxvj p. latitudo terre
Reginaldi Blundi infra portam
suam de est ad west c et ix p.

[152]
Johannes
filius
Rogerii
aldermanni

De terra proxima iuxta strata
[*sic*] uersus west. latitudo eius
uersus west lx p. longitudo a
strata uersus north clx p. hanc
tenent moniales sancti Sepulcri.

[153]
Item
idem
Iohannes

De terra proxima terre Hamonis
de Soford. latitudo eius uersus
west xxxiiij p. longitudo uersus
north c et lxx p.

[154]
Item
idem
Johannes

De eodem tenemento uersus suth
ex alia parte strate. latitudo eius de
east ad west l p. longitudo uersus
suth cc lviij p.

[155]
Geruasius   ij sol.
ampollarius

De terra Cathebite. latitudo eius
uersus west xlviij p. longitudo a
strata uersus suth cc et lviij p.
Deinde terra Elfegi Lamb iuxta
illam uersus west.

[fol. 223r.] [156]
Item   xl d.
Johannes
filius
Rogeri
aldermanni

De terra proxima uersus west cum
predictis terris suis. latitudo eius
uersus west xlvj p. longitudo
uersus suth cc et lviij p.

[157]
Robertus   xij d.
Diue

De terra proxima uersus west.
latitudo eius uersus west xxxij p.
longitudo uersus suth cc et lviij p.

[152] See F 190, n.   [153] For the Shoford family see p. 51.
[155] F 277.
[157] There is a short stroke over the name Dive, not apparently a contraction.

[158]
Heredes
Lambini
Frese

De terra Walteri pistoris. hec terra iacet infra portam de Radingate contra ecclesiam sancti Eadmundi uersus north. querend' est de relicta Lambini.

[159]
Willelmus   vj d.
Petitfant

De quadam terra Rogeri aldermanni et Johannis filii sui. que iacet iuxta uicum qui ducit uersus Danjvn.

[160] (Parrochia sancte Marie de Bredene cherche.)ʳ

Johannes   iiij d.
Tretel

De orto quodam qui (est)ᵃⁱ iuxta ortum Alfrei Gosse in angulo duarum uiarum uersus suth prope ecclesiam sancte Marie. latitudo utriusque terre a uico ad east c et x longitudo ab angulo uersus suth cc et xxiiij p.

[161]
Heredes   xxij d.   Ad sanctum
Willelmi   Anselmum
Kaudrun

De domo sua que est prope ecclesiam sancte Marie uersus north.

[162]
Item   xvj d.
idem

De terra uacua que est inter domum et predictam ecclesiam. latitudo utriusque terre ab ecclesia uersus north lxxx p. longitudo a uia ad west c et xxx p.

[163] Juxta terram Johannis del Parc. terra Willelmi Geruot pertinet ad ecclesiam sancti Georgii. latitudo eius xxxv p. longitudo de north ad suth lxxx p.

[164]

De terra Walteri pistoris. latitudo terre de east ad west. xxxij p. longitudo a uico uersus suth c et x p.

[165] (Parrochia sancti Iohannis Baptiste.)ʳ

Hugo   xvj d.
aurifaber

De terra Wlboldi. hec iacet in eodem uico et eadem parrochia. latitudo eius uersus west l p. longitudo a uico uersus suth c et x p.

---

¹⁵⁸ For St Edmund's church, founded by Hamo f. Vitalis, alias de Shoford, see p. 52.

¹⁵⁹ This seems to be the first recorded instance of the name Dane John.

¹⁶⁰ For St Mary Bredin's church, founded by William f. Hamonis, alias de Shoford, see p. 52. The ground of A. Gosse seems to be F 266.

[166]

Ex opposito eius uersus north terra Wimundi. latitudo eius uersus west xxx p. longitudo a uico uersus north c et vij d.

[167] (Parrochia sancte Mildrithe.)ʳ

| Robertus aurifaber seruiens Terrici | iij sol. | Hee terre dant medietatem ad festum omnium sanctorum et alteram ad assumpcionem sancte Marie | De terra proxima terre Osberti filii Willelmi citra sanctum Jacobum. latitudo eius de suth ad north lxxxxij p. longitudo a uico uersus east ccc p. |

[168]

Alfwinus　　xxvj d.

De terra proxima uersus north. latitudo eius uersus north lij p. longitudo uersus east sicut alie.

[169] [fol. 223v.]

Goda
uidua　　xviij d.

De terra proxima uersus north. latitudo eius uersus north liij p. longitudo uersus east sicut alie.

[170]

Henricus
Cod　　ij sol.

De terra proxima uersus north. latitudo eius uersus north lxxvi p. longitudo uersus east sicut alie.

[171]

Gunnild　　ij sol.

De terra proxima uersus north latitudo eius uersus north lxxvj p. longitudo uersus east sicut alie.

[172]

Item
Gunnild　　xxj d.

De terra proxima uersus north. latitudo eius uersus north lxx p. longitudo uersus east sicut alie.

[167] F 1 and 326.

[167–187] These holdings lie on the e. side of Wincheap, north of Hollow Lane. Sanctus Jacobus: the hospital of St Jacob south of Hollow Lane, founded by Master Feramin. Osbert priest of Thanington (apparently O. f. Willelmi) gave ground near St Jacob's to Christ Church (XLI, XLII). See C, 27, 55, G 27, 56. The ground given by Osbert is not clearly defined in D, but from comparison with F, appears to be (D) 167–76.

[168] F 2 and 327.

[169] Evidently F 3 and 328.

[170] F 4 and 329.

[171] F 5 and 330.

[172] F 602 (part of ground called 'Seven Acres').

[173]
Cristina   xl d.   De terra proxima uersus north.
                                                     latitudo eius uersus north xlvj p.
                                                     longitudo uersus east sicut alie.
                                                     hucusque donum Osberti presbi-
                                                     teri.

[174]
Henricus   ij sol.   De terra proxima uersus north.
parmentarius   latitudo eius uersus north xx p.
                                                     longitudo uersus east sicut alie.

[175]
Iuette   ij sol.   De terra proxima uersus north.
relicta   latitudo uersus north xxv p.
Elfwini   longitudo uersus east sicut alie.
                                                     et hec est de dono Osberti presbi
                                                     teri.

[176]
Petrus   xxx d.   De terra proxima uersus north.
filius   latitudo eius uersus north xx p.
Warini

[177]
Robertus   De eodem tenemento. latitudo
de   partis eius uersus north cl p.
Cokeringe   longitudo utriusque uersus east
                                                     sicut alie.

[178]
Willelmus   De terra proxima uersus north.
filius   latitudo eius uersus north clxxviij
Odonis   p. longitudo uersus east sicut alie.

[179]
Relicta   viij d.   Ad festum   De terra proxima uersus north.
Warini   sancti Michaelis   latitudo eius uersus north xxviij p.
                    x d.   Ad festum   longitudo uersus east sicut alie.
                                sancti Iohannis

---

[173] F 6 and 331.

[174] F 7 and 332. This appears to be part of the gift of Osbert, though the remarks under 173 and 175 seem to exclude it.

[175] F 8 and 333.   [176] F 9 and 334.

[177] The phrase 'de eodem tenemento' probably means that 176 and 177 were originally part of a single piece of ground. The groundplot no. 177 survives intact today in the form of the Wincheap Recreation Ground. This is F 607.

[178] See F 241, 423; cf. 497, 601.

[179] This and 180–2 cover approximately one acre and represent the acre acquired by prior Wibert (d. 1167). This is A 35. See F 603–6, 636–9.

[180]

Radulfus			De terra proxima uersus north.
carpentarius			latitudo eius uersus north xl p.
			longitudo uersus east sicut alie.

[181]

Symon			De terra proxima uersus north.
			latitudo eius uersus north xxxviij
			p. longitudo uersus east sicut alie.

[182]

Relicta	viij d.	Ad festum	De terra proxima uersus north.
Wlfeach		sancti Michaelis	latitudo eius uersus north xxxiij p.
scilicet	viij d.	Ad festum	longitudo uersus east sicut alie.
Kila		sancti Iohannis	

[183]

Willelmus	viij d.	Ad festum	De terra proxima uersus north que
filius		sancti Michaelis	dicitur Holt Oga. latitudo eius
Winedei	x d.	Ad festum	uersus north cc et vj p. longitudo
uel Liueua		sancti	uersus east sicut alie.
relicta		Johannis	
W [blank]			

[184]

Willelmus	v sol.	Ad festum	De terra proxima uersus north.
gener		omnium	latitudo uersus north c et lxxx p.
Brithiue	et	sanctorum	et x. longitudo uersus east sicut
	v sol.	Ad festum	alie.
		sancti Iohannis	

[185]

Alfredus	xxviij d.		De terra proxima uersus north.
			latitudo eius uersus north lxvij p.
			longitudo uersus east sicut alie.

[186]

Osbertus	xv d.		De terra proxima uersus north.
Pret			latitudo eius uersus north xx p.
			longitudo uersus east sicut alie.

[187]

Elfegus	viij d.		De terra proxima uersus north. lati-
King			tudo eius uersus north usque ad bar-
			ram lx p. longitudo uersus east ccc p.

183 There was ground in Wincheap called Holtege, evidently meant here. Cf. F 14, 36–8, 360–2, 581–4. See F 498.

184 F 14, part of Holtege. 186 Possibly F 27, 507. See D 205 below.

187 Probably F 272. For the bars on approach roads, see p. 196. St Mary de Castro parish starts at this point. The tenants beyond this point are supplied partly by F 242, 268.

[188] Ex alia parte strate uersus west iuxta semitam que ducit ad prata terra Lamberti Gargate que pertinet ad sanctum Laurentium. quam tenet Godefridus.

[189]
Robertus aurifaber   iiij sol. et iiij d.   De terra proxima predicte terre que fuit Anselmi. latitudo eius uersus north xlvj p. longitudo uersus west ccc p.

[224r.] [190]
Terra de Tanintune   Latitudo eius uersus north c et xx p. longitudo uersus west sicut alia.

[191]
Osbertus Grom   xxj d.   Ad festum sancti Michaelis   De terra proxima predicte. latitudo eius uersus north c et xiiij p. longitudo uersus west sicut alie.

[192]
Alexander filius Wlnodh   iiij sol.   Ad iiij terminos   De terra proxima uersus north. latitudo eius uersus north lxiij p. longitudo uersus west sicut alie.

[193]
Godrun   ij sol. et vj d.   De terra proxima uersus north. latitudo eius uersus north lv p. longitudo uersus west sicut alie.

[194]
Willelmus capellanus. Paganus de Westgate   iiij sol.   De terra proxima uersus north. latitudo eius uersus north lvj p. longitudo uersus west sicut alie.

[195]
Robertus de Cokering' Blakemannus burarius   De terra proxima uersus north. latitudo eius uersus north xxx p. longitudo uersus west sicut alie.

[188] The surveyor has crossed to the western side of Wincheap, and has moved back to the still-existing alley (semita) leading down to the meadows by the river. The cartulary of St Laurence priory (Cathedral Library Lit. MS. C 20, fol. 76) records confirmation by Basilia domina de Tanintune of a *mansio* at Thanington, bought by Lambert Garegate, and given to the priory. This ground (D 188) lies at the border of Thanington manor. See 190 below.

[189] F 26, 51, 346, 427.

[190] Evidently part of the adjacent manor of Thanington. See C 57, G 58, 59.

[192] F 244.

[196]
Willelmus   xvj d.   De terra proxima uersus north
capelain   latitudo eius uersus north lx p.
                                                       longitudo uersus west sicut alie.

[197]
Liueua   De terra Boidini. hec proxima
neptis   est predicte. latitudo eius uersus
Geroldi   north cc et xvj p. longitudo uersus
          Petrus   xiij d.   Ad mediam   west sicut alie.
[198]   de   quadragesimam
Alfredus castello   De terra proxima uersus north.
de Rod-   defendit   latitudo eius uersus north l p.
intone   ista   longitudo uersus west sicut alie.
          et
[199]   dat   xiij d.   Ad festum
Terra   sancti   De terra proxima uersus north
Sired   Michaelis   latitudo eius uersus north lxvj p.
                                                        longitudo uersus west sicut alie.

[200]
Henricus   xij d.   Ad festum   De quadam parte domus sue que
Barate   sancti Michaelis   est de terra Walteri pistoris. lati-
                                                       tudo partis huius uersus north xl p.
                                                       longitudo uersus west sicut alie.

[201] (Johannes de sancta Margareta)ᵃ
Godardus   xij d.   De terra Wiching. hec proxima
frater   est predicte uersus north. latitudo
Willelmi   eius uersus north xxx. [sic] longi-
Picot   tudo uersus west sicut alie.

[202]
Gleduse   iiij d.   Ad festum   De terra proxima uersus north.
Fairhegne   sancti Michaelis   latitudo eius uersus north xix p.
                                                       longitudo uersus west sicut alie.

[203]
Hamo   vj d.   Ad pascha   De terra proxima uersus north
tector.   et   latitudo eius uersus north xix (p.)
Wimarca   j ob.   longitudo uersus west sicut alie.

¹⁹⁷ Possibly F 586. Lines connect 197–99 and the note 'Petrus de castello', etc.
¹⁹⁹ Possibly F 232, 592.
²⁰⁰ Evidently F 589, part of ground called Woodland, outside Worthgate. A line connects
'Ad festum', etc. with xij d. in 201.
²⁰¹ Appears to be F 596, part of Woodland.
²⁰² F 593. Likewise part of Woodland. A line connects the rent with 'ad . . . Michaelis', in
200, probably meaning that the last-mentioned note has been added to the wrong entry.
²⁰³ Probably F 506.

[204]

| Matheus de Chileham | xij d. | Ad festum sancti Michaelis | De terra proxima uersus north. latitudo eius uersus north xlij p. longitudo uersus west sicut alie. |

[205]

| Osbertus Pret | xv d. | | De terra proxima uersus north. latitudo eius uersus north [blank] longitudo uersus west sicut alie. |

[206]

| Godith uidua | xx d. | Ad festum sancti Michaelis | De terra proxima uersus north. latitudo eius uersus north lxxxviij |
| | xx d. | Ad mediam quadragesimam | p. longitudo uersus west sicut alie. |

[207]

| Robertus presbiter | xx d. | | De terra proxima uersus north. latitudo eius uersus north xx p. longitudo uersus west sicut alie. |

[208]

| Godardus molendinarius | xxij d. | | Pro una acra terre. |

[209]

| Item idem | xiiij d. | | De orto quodam. |

[fol. 224v.] (Hee terre sunt extra Wrgate.)ʳ

[210]

| Liuiua neptis Geroldi fullonis et Ergesboldus sedet super. | xij d. | | De terra que est in Geroldeslane uersus suth et pertinet ad molendinum sancte Mildrʾ. latitudo eius a uico uersus suth l p. longitudo ab east ad west lxviij p. |

[211]

| Meinerus diues | | | De terra uacua et de domo ex alie parte uie uersus east contra domum suam. latitudo terre ab angulo uiarum uersus suth xxx p. longitudo uersus east xlix p. |

²⁰⁵ Possibly F 27, 507.

²⁰⁷ Possibly F 233, 504. The surveyor has worked inwards from the country and has reached the city moat at Worthgate, just without the castle.

²⁰⁸, ²⁰⁹ The sites are uncertain, though 208 may be part of Woodland.

²¹⁰ xlvi records grant to Christ Church of St Mildred's mill, with ground of Gerold the fuller, by Hugh of Dover. The Survey is now in Stour St.

²¹¹ For Mainer the rich, provost of Canterbury and moneyer, see pp. 85, 114. The 'domus ex alia parte uie' is the site of his still-existing almshouse (Maynard's Hospital). See F 302.

[212]

Juxta ortum predicti Meineri diuitis. terra uacua quam tenemus de
Roberto persona de Hakint'. et
iuxta illam uersus north terra
Ilgerii. latitudo utriusque iuxta uicum uersus north lxxx p. longitudo
a uico ad Sturam c et lxx p.

[213]
Willelmus   ii d.
Timpan

De terra que est in uico qui
dicitur Hellelane. latitudo eius
iuxta uicum de east ad west xlij
p. longitudo a uico uersus suth
usque ad ortum Fulconis pictoris
lvij p.

[214] Terra uacua que est iuxta domum que pertinet ad sanctum Gregorium
habet in latitudine ab east ad west xl p. in longitudine uersus suth c p. Juxta illam
ad east terra Osberti Pret. latitudo eius uersus suth lx p. longitudo iuxta uicum
uersus east lxvj p.

[215]
Wiulphus   ix d.   Ad pascha
filius   ix d.   Ad festum
Meineri   sancti Michaelis

De terra quam tenet. latitudo eius
a north ad suth iuxta uicum qui
uadit ad turrim xxvi p. longitudo a
uico uersus west lxxx p. et iij.

[216]

Pro parte orti qui est ad west.
latitudo eius xx p. longitudo xxx
p.

[217]
Brithtiua   x d.   Ad mediam
relicta   quadragesimam
Pic

De terra que est in angulo de
Crocchereslane. latitudo eius xl p.
uersus suth longitudo eius a magno
uico uersus west lxx p.

[218] (Parrochia sancte Marie de castello.)ʳ
Robertus filius Ricardi tenet terram quandam de hospitali de Ierusalem et est
iuxta terram Pic. que ut dicitur fuit nostra. longitudo eius a terra Pic uersus suth
lxx p. latitudo a uico uersus est lxviij p.

---

²¹² See C 7, G 7, 10, F 303, 514.
²¹³ Hellelane is probably Rosemary Lane.
²¹⁴⁻²¹⁶ The sites of these holdings are uncertain. 214 probably lies in Rosemary Lane or in
Hospital Lane. The 'uicus qui uadit ad turrim' in 215 is Castle Street. 215 is possibly F 309,
502.
²¹⁷ Crocchereslane is probably Hospital Lane.

[219] Alanus Wischard	x d.		De terra proxima uersus suth. latitudo eius uersus suth xxxiij p. longitudo a uico uersus east xliiij p.
[220] Willelmus de Bagtheberi			De terra proxima uersus suth. longitudo eius iuxta uicum uersus suth lxxxiiij p. latitudo a uico uersus east xlvj p.
[221] Helyas se glouere	vij d. et j d.	Ad mediam quadragesimam de heuewerc ad gulam Augusti	De terra Golde. hec terra iacet iuxta quandam terram de sancto Augustino. latitudo eius iuxta uicum uersus east xlv p. longitudo ab eodem uico uersus north c et xiiij p.
[222] Willelmus presbiter of Wede- chereche			De terra proxima uersus east. et pertinet ad elemosinariam nostram.
[223] Hamo clericus de Wald'	viij d. viij d.	Ad mediam quadragesimam Ad festum sancti Michaelis	De terra proxima uersus east. latitudo eius uersus east xxxv p. longitudo uersus north lxxx p. et xvij.

[219] F 311; 542? A section has probably been omitted between 218 and 219. Each is on a different side of Castle Street, and 219 cannot lie next to 218 (to the south).

[221–223] These lie on the north side of St Mary's Street. 221 is F 270.

[fol. 225r.] [224] (Parrochia sancte Margarete.)ʳ

Adam de Cherringe	xlij d.	Ad mediam quadragesimam	De terra Lambini Frese ubi fecit sibi domum lapideam super Stur-
	xlij d.	Ad festum sancti Michaelis	am. la[titudo] a uico ad Sturam lxxx p. longitudo ab angulo uie uersus north c et xxx p.
[225]			Terra que fuit Wlfketel uacua. que est contra domum Lambini Frese ex alia parte uie uersus east. longitudo eius uersus east lxxiij p. latitudo ab angulo uersus north xxviij p.
[226] Lambinus filius Sponge	x d. et viij d.	Ad pascha Ad festum sancti Michaelis	De terra proxima uersus north super quam pars quedam domus eius stat. latitudo eius uersus north xxx p. longitudo uersus east lxxiij p. alia pars domus eius est de burcgilde.
[227] Henricus Deremai	vj d.	Ad festum sancti Michaelis	De terra proxima uersus north latitudo eius uersus north xxiii p. longitudo uersus east iuxta uicum lvj p.
[228] Robertus de Hottewelle	ix d.	Ad mediam quadragesimam	De terra Willelmi de Pluchele. hec proxima est terre Lambini Frese uersus north latitudo eius uersus north lij p. longitudo a uico ad Sturam lxxx et vj p.

[224] F 246, 489; xxxv–xxxvii. Site of Poor Priests' Hospital. For Lambin Frese the moneyer
see p. 114 and for A. of Charing, Becket's enemy, see p. 180. The letters within square brackets
have been destroyed by fire.

[225] F 255, 491.

[226] F 110, 298, 488. For the borough gild see p. 128.

[227] See F 228, 483.

[228] F 249, 484.

Rental E

A survey of Cathedral holdings in the parish of St Margaret, Canterbury, compiled c. 1200, based on the same material as the corresponding passage in Rental D.

[E1] De parochia sancte Margarete.
Terra Lamberti Frese de qua reddit. ad mediam quadragesimam xlij d. et ad festum sancti Michaelis xlij d. super Sturam latitudo a vico ad Sturam iiij^{xx} ped. longitudo ab angulo uersus north c xxx ped.

[E2]
Terra Wlfchetel contra domum Lamberti Frese ex alia parte uie uersus east. longitudo eius uersus east lxxiii ped. latitudo ab angulo uersus north xxviii ped.

[E3]
Terra Lambini filii Sponge de qua reddit ad pascha x d. et ad festum sancti Michaelis viii d. proxima uersus north super quam quedam pars domus eius stat latitudo uersus north xxx ped. longitudo uersus east lxxiij ped. alia pars domus eius est de burghilde.

[E 4]
Henricus Diremay reddit vi d. ad festum sancti Michaelis de terra proxima uersus north. latitudo eius xxiii ped. longitudo uersus east lvi ped.

[E 5]
Robertus de Hottewelle reddit ad mediam quadragesimam ix d. de terra Willelmi de Plukele proxima terre Lamberti Frese uersus north latitudo xlij ped. longitudo ad Sturam iiij^{xx} vi ped.

[229]

Item idem	ix d.	Ad mediam	De terra Henrici Deremai. longi-
Robertus	et	quadragesimam	tudo eius a uico uersus west li p.
	ix d.	Ad festum	latitudo uersus suth xiiij p.
		sancti Michaelis	

[230]

Item idem	xij d.	Ad mediam	De terra sua. latitudo eius usque
Robertus	et	quadragesimam	ad Sturam xxx p. longitudo
	xij d.	Ad festum	uersus suth iuxta Sturam liij p.
		sancti Michaelis	

[231]

Latitudo terre ubi Hottemeldne aliquando stabat xxx p. longitudo similiter.

[232]

Arnoldus de	xxviij d.		De terra Rogeri se Desie que est
Geddinge			ultra Sturam contra domum Lamb'
			Frese. latitudo eius a Stura uersus
			west xxxiij p. longitudo a Stura
			uersus suth lxx p.

[233]

Item idem	xij d.		De terra Corbeil que est iuxta
Arnoldus			predictam terram. latitudo eius a
			Stura uersus west xxx et iij p.
			longitudo ab alia terra uersus suth
			cc et xxx p.

[234]

Beringerus	xij d.	Ad festum	De terra proxima terre Martini.
filius	et	sancti Michaelis	latitudo eius uersus west xliiij p.
Godwini	xij d.	Ad mediam	longitudo sicut alia.
filii		quadragesimam	
Eue			

[235]

Item	xij d.	Ad mediam	De ortulis suis de Hotte med.
Beringerus		quadragesimam	longitudo eorum de suth ad north c
			et lxx p. latitudo ab east ad west xl p.

[236]

Willelmus	vj d.	Ad mediam	De terra Brunman se dore de
Picot		quadragesimam	Hottemed. longitudo eius de north
			ad suth c et lvj p. latitudo xxxiij p.

231 F 496.

232–246 These holdings lie in the area later occupied by the Greyfriars. It is difficult to site all the various holdings of Beringer (234, 235, 238, 241, 245, 246). 232 is probably F 253. Cf. F 355.

[E 6]

Item idem Robertus reddit ad mediam quadragesimam xviii d. et ad festum sancti Michaelis xviii d. de terra Diremay. longitudo a uico uersus west li ped. latitudo uersus suth xiiii ped.

[E 7]

Item idem Robertus de terra sua reddit ij sol. latitudo usque ad Sturam xxx ped. longitudo iuxta Sturam uersus suth liij ped.

[E 8]

Latitudo terre ubi Hottemelne fuit xxx ped. et longitudo similiter.

[E 9]

Terra Arnoldi de Geddinge de terra Rogeri Desie. reddit xviii d. et est ultra Sturam contra domum Lamberti Frese latitudo a Stura uersus west xxxiij ped. longitudo a Stura uersus suth lxx ped.

[E 10]

Item terra eiusdem Arnoldi de terra Corbeil iuxta uersus [sic] suth. reddit xij d. latitudo a Stura uersus west xxxiij ped. longitudo uersus suth cc xxx ped.

[E 11]

Terra Beringerii filii Godwini filii Eue. reddit xii d. et est proxima terre Martini. latitudo uersus west xliiij ped. longitudo sicut alia.

[E 12]

Idem Beringerius tenet v ortulos in Hottemed et reddit xij d. quorum vnus habet in longitudine de suth ad north c lxx ped. latitudo de east ad west xl ped.

[E 17]

Terra Willelmi Picot de terra Bruman Sedore de Hottemed habet in longitudine de suth ad north c lvj ped. in latitudine xxxiii ped.

[237]
Magister
Feraminus

De terra iuxta predictam ad suth. latitudo lxxx p. longitudo c p.

[238]
Item predictus
Beringerus

De terra iuxta predictas terras quam tenet pro predictis xij d. latitudo eius a terra Picot uersus suth xxxij p. longitudo de suth ad north c et xxxvj p.

[239]
Item Willelmus
Picot

De terra [blank] latitudo eius lvj p. longitudo a Stura uersus suth lx p.

[240]
Item   ix d.   Ad mediam
Willelmus   et j ob.   quadragesimam
Picot et
Godardus
frater
eius

De terra. [sic] latitudo a Stura uersus west l p. longitudo ab alia terra ad suth c et lv p.

[241]
Item
predictus
Beringerus

De terra quadam quam tenet pro predictis xij d. iuxta Sturam prope molendinum sancte Mildrethe. latitudo a Stura uersus west xlviij p. longitudo a Stura uersus north c et xxx p.

[242]
Henricus Harm   ij d.

De terra proxima uersus west.

[243]
Robertus de
Hottewelle

De terra proxima uersus west. latitudo xlviij p. longitudo sicut alia.

[244]
Item idem
Robertus

De terra quam tenet de Godere le Palmere. latitudo eius a terra Beringeri uersus north l p. longitudo a Stura uersus west lxviij p.

[245] [fol. 225v.]
[Ber]ingerus tenet terram iuxta predictam. pro predictis xij d. latitudo eius uersus north lx p. longitudo uersus west sicut alia.

<hr />

[237] F 220.   [239] This may be F 251.

[E 18]

Terra magistri Firmini proxima uersus suth habet in latitudine uersus suth iiii^xx ped. in longitudine a Stura uersus west c ped.

[E 13]

Secundus ortus habet in latitudine a terra Picot uersus suth^v xxxij ped. In longitudine de suth ad north^v c xxxvij ped.

[E 19]

Item alia terra Willelmi Picot latitudo lvi ped. longitudo a Stura uersus suth^v lx ped.

[E 20]

Item terra Willelmi Picot et Godardi fratris eius reddit ix d. ob. latitudo a Stura uersus west l ped. longitudo a terra [blank] uersus suth^v c lv ped.

[E 14]

Tercius ortus est iuxta Sturam prope molendinum de sancta Mildr'. longitudo a Stura uersus north^v c xxx ped. latitudo a Stura uersus west. xlviii ped.

[E 21]

Henricus Harm reddit ii d. de terra iuxta tercium ortum Beringerii uersus (suth)^c west.

[E 22]

Terra Roberti de Hottewell' proxima terre Henrici uersus west. latitudo xlviij ped. longitudo [blank].

[E 23]

Item terra eiusdem Roberti quam tenet de Godere Palmere. latitudo eius a quarto orto Beringerii uersus north. l ped. longitudo (usque ad quintum ortum B.)^i a Stura uersus west^v lxviii ped.

[E 15]

Quartus ortus est iuxta terram Roberti de Hottewelle quam tenuit de Godere Palmere. latitudo eius uersus (north)^c (suth)^i. lx ped. longitudo uersus west a Stura^v lxviij ped.

[246] Item idem tenet terram prope aliam pro predictis xij d. longitudo eius (a)ᶜ de suth ad north lxxx p. et x. latitudo uersus west lxx p.

[247]

| | iiij sol. | Ad festum sancti Michaelis et totidem ad mediam quadragesimam | De terra que fuit Gileberti clerici iuxta Hottewelle. latitudo eius a fonte uersus east xxx p. longitudo a uico uersus north c et xx p. |

[248]

| Godieua relicta Laurencii | iij sol. | | De terra proxima uersus east. latitudo eius de domo Gileberti usque ad uicum uersus east xx p. longitudo uersus north c et xlij p. |

[249]

| Item eadem G. | xij d. | | De orto proximo uersus east. latitudo eius uersus east xx p. longitudo eius uersus north lxx p. |

[250]

| Cecilia filia Bartholomei senescalli | j d. | Ad mediam quadragesimam | De terra uacua que est iuxta terram Godardi fratris Willelmi Picot. latitudo eius iuxta uicum uersus west l p. longitudo a uico uersus north lxiiij p. Juxta illam terra de burchilde. |

[251]

| Odo spicier | xij d. | | De terra Iohannis Belesmains que est proxima terre de burchilde uersus east. latitudo eius iuxta uicum uersus east l p. longitudo a uico uersus north lxx p. |

[252]

| Relicta Eilredi se Prude | v d. v d. | Ad mediam quadragesimam Ad festum sancti Michaelis | De terra proxima uersus east. latitudo eius iuxta uicum uersus east l p. longitudo a uico uersus north lxx p. |

247-249 These three holdings are surveyed (as part of St Mary Breadman parish) under 271-3 below.

251 For the gild see Chapter V. The survey is now in Hawk's Lane.

252 F 256, 494.

[E 16]

Quintus ortus est iuxta quartum ortum uersus north. longitudo eius uersus north iiiij^{xx} et x ped. latitudo uersus west$^\vee$ lxx ped.

[E 24]

Terra Gileberti clerici iuxta Hottewell' reddit iiii sol. latitudo a fonte uersus east xxx ped. longitudo a uico uersus north$^\vee$ vj^{xx} ped.

[E 25]

Terra Godiue relicte Laurentii proxima uersus east$^\vee$ reddit (i)^{e}iij sol. latitudo de domo Gileberti usque ad vicum uersus east$^\vee$ xxv ped. longtitudo uersus north c xlij ped.

[E 26]

Eadem Godiua reddit xij d. de orto proximo uersus east. latitudo uersus east xx ped. longitudo uersus north lxx ped.

[E 27]

Terra Cecilie filie Bartholomei senescalli. reddit [*blank*] iuxta terram Godardi fratris Willelmi Picot. latitudo iuxta vicum uersus east l ped. longitudo a vico uersus north lxiiii ped. Juxta illam est terra de burghilde.

[E 28]

Odo Specier reddit xii d. de terra Johannis Belesmayns proxima terre de burghilde uersus east. latitudo iuxta vicum l p. longitudo uersus north lxx ped.

[E 29]

Relicta Elredi Prude reddit x d. de terra proxima uersus east latitudo l ped. longitudo uersus north lxx ped.

[253]
Magister
Feraminus

De terra proxima uersus east. latitudo eius iuxta uicum uersus east xl p. longitudo a uico uersus north [*blank*]

[254]

Juxta illam uersus east terra Wilardi mercatoris que dicitur nostra aliquando fuisse.

[255]
Jacob   ij sol.

De terra Willelmi Mauueisin. que est contra domum Samsonis presbiteri ex alia parte uie uersus suth latitudo eius a terra proxima uersus west quam idem Jacob tenet de Mainero diuite liij p. longitudo a uico uersus suth lxxiij p.

[256]
Ricardus
Cauuel

De terra Robin Boisun que est proxima terre Veisin. latitudo eius iuxta uicum uersus east xxxiiij p. longitudo a uico uersus suth lxxiij p.

[257]

Terra Iohannis Caldrun que fuit Malgeri portitoris iuxta predictam terram iacet uacua uersus east usque ad magnam stratam. latitudo eius a predicta terra Ricardi Caluel uersus east ad stratam xlij p. longitudo ab angulo uersus suth lxxiiij p.

[258]
Willelmus   x d.   Ad mediam
Picot   quadragesimam

De terra proxima uersus suth. latitudo eius uersus suth iuxta uicum lv p. longitudo a uico uersus west lxxx p.

---

253 For the career of Master Feramin, see pp. 110, 158.

257 'Magna strata': St Margaret's Street. Subject of XLVII, XLVIII, LXII. See C 4, 33, F 250, 299, 485, G 4, 5, 34.

258 This was taken over by L. Fleming, tenant of 257, as part of his stone house. See F 250. There is some confusion here, as the total given for the frontage Hawk's Lane—Therne is 219 feet, greater than the actual distance (209 feet). Some frontage has been counted twice, perhaps due to intrusion of L. Fleming's house into his neighbour's ground.

[E 30]

Terra magistri Firmini proxima uersus east usque ad terram Wilardi. latitudo iuxta vicum xl ped. longitudo [*blank*].

[E31]

Jacob reddit ii sol. de terra Willelmi Mauueisin. contra domum Sampsonis presbiteri uersus suth ex alia parte vie. latitudo eius a proxima terra uersus west quam idem Jacob tenet de Maynero le Riche liii ped. longitudo a vico uersus suth√ lxxiii ped.

[E 32]

Terra Ricardi Cauuel de terra Robin filii Boisun proxima terre Veysin. latitudo eius iuxta uicum uersus east xxxiij ped. longitudo a vico uersus suth lxxiii ped.

[E33]

Terra Johannis Caudrun que fuit Malgerii portarii proxima uersus east usque ad magnam stratam. latitudo xlii ped. longitudo ab angulo uersus suth lxxiiii ped.

[E 34]

Item Willelmus Picot reddit x d. de terra proxima uersus suth latitudo super vicum lv ped. longitudo a vico uersus west iiijˣˣ ped.

[259] Dauid de Wertinge	x d.	Ad mediam quadragesimam	De terra que est iuxta Therne in uico qui ducit ad domum Lamb' Frese. latitudo eius de east ad west xlviij p. longitudo a uico uersus north lxxx p. et x.
[260] Willelmus de Eilwordtune	xviij d.	Ad mediam quadragesimam	De terra proxima uersus (w)ieast. longitudo eius uersus (w)ieast c et l p. latitudo a uico uersus north c et xxx p.
[261] Elfegus Lamb			De terra quam emit Wibertus prior que est contra terram predicti Willelmi de Eilwordt' uersus suth ex alia parte uie. latitudo eius [blank].
[262] Liedbricht	viij d.		De terra Wiberti prioris que est in angulo uersus suth iuxta Therhne. latitudo eius [blank].
[263] Godardus huphaldere	v d. et v d.	Ad mediam quadragesimam Ad festum sancti Michaelis	De terra proxima uersus suth. latitudo eius iuxta uicum uersus suth (xlvii)c (xlviij)i p. longitudo a uico uersus west lxxv p.
[264] Willelmus Winedei			De terra proxima uersus suth. latitudo eius iuxta uicum uersus suth xxx p. longitudo a uico uersus west lxxv p.
[265] [fol. 226r.] Osbertus se Lithle	ij sol.		De terra Lamberti se Gode que est iuxta terram monialium sancti Sepulchri uersus suth. latitudo eius iuxta uicum uersus suth xxxvij p. longitudo a uico uersus west lxxv p.

[259] Probably F 196, 510.
[260] F 254.
[261] This is not mentioned in A (list of Wibert's acquisitions).
[262] A 27 (ground of A. Wadecac).
[263] A 27 (ground of A. and G. uphealdere).

[E 35]

Dauid de Wertinge reddit x d. de terra in vico de Thierne qui ducit ad domum Lamberti Frese. latitudo de east ad west xlviij ped. longitudo a vico uersus north iiij^{xx} et x d.

[E 36] (nota)^m

Willelmus de Eilwart' reddit xviij d. de terra proxima uersus west (latitudo)^c uersus west longitudo cl ped. latitudo a vico uersus north c xxx ped.

[E 37]

Terra Elphegi Lamb contra terram predicti Willelmi uersus suth ex alia parte vie latitudo eius [*blank*]. longitudo [*blank*].

[E 38]

Terra Liedbricht in angulo uersus suth iuxta Thierne reddit viii d. latitudo [*blank*]. longitudo [*blank*].

[E 39]

Godardus Vphaldere reddit x d. de terra proxima uersus suth. latitudo iuxta uicum uersus suth xlviii p. longitudo a vico uersus west lxxv ped.

[E 40]

Terra Willelmi Winedei proxima uersus suth latitudo iuxta vicum xxx ped. longitudo versus west lxxv ped.

[E 41]

Osbernus se Litle reddit ij sol. de terra Lamberti se Gode iuxta terram monialium sancti Sepulcri uersus suth. latitudo iuxta vicum uersus suth xxxvij ped. longitudo a vico uersus west lxxv ped.

[266]
Agatha   ij sol.
soror
Nigelli
monachi
nostri

De terra que est inter terram Willelmi Caluel et Johannis Suetman. latitudo eius iuxta uicum uersus suth lxxij p. longitudo a uico uersus west lxxx p. et x.

[267]
Willelmus
Caluel

De terra proxima que est inter ecclesiam sancte Margarete et predictam terram Agathe.

[268]
Jordanus   xii d.   Ad mediam
frater   et ob.   quadragesimam
Symonis   xij d.   Ad festum
monachi   et ob.   sancti Michaelis
nostri

De terra Eadmundi clerici quam emit Wibertus prior. hec iacet inter terram que fuit Willei Caldrun et terram Amfridi mercatoris. latitudo eius de east ad west lx p. longitudo de suth ad north c et lxxiij p.

[269] (Parrochia sancte Marie Bredmanne.)ʳ
Dirifa   v d.   Ad mediam
et   quadragesimam
Godieua

De terra que est in angulo duarum uiarum contra Hottewelle. latitudo eius ab angulo uersus suth xxxviij p. longitudo ab angulo uersus east lxvj p.

[270]
Godardus   viij d.
frater
Willelmi
Picot

De terra proxima uersus suth. latitudo eius a uico uersus east lxv p. longitudo a predicta terra Dirife uersus suth lxxx et xvij.

[271]
Johannes   iiij sol.
Uolt

De terra que fuit Gileberti clerici que est iuxta Hottewell' latitudo eius a fonte uersus east xxx p. longitudo a uico uersus north c et xx p.

²⁶⁶ F 257, 495. For Nigel the monk, probably the precentor, and satirical poet, N. 'Wireker', see p. 153. This ground lies south of St Margaret's church.

²⁶⁸ This is not mentioned among Wibert's acquisitions in Rental A. The site is uncertain.

²⁶⁹ F 184, 384. The site is at s.w. corner of Jewry Lane.

²⁷⁰ This and 269 must lie in Stour Street, between Jewry Lane and Hawk's Lane. The figure 97 feet is erroneous as this is almost exactly the whole frontage between the two lanes. The surveyor has clearly given the combined frontage for the two holdings.

²⁷¹ This, 272 and 273 are also surveyed as part of St Margaret's parish (247-9 above). 271 is F 258, 479; cf. F 54. The arrangement here is difficult to follow. Perhaps 273 and 275, which have the same dimensions, are the same ground surveyed twice.

[E 42]

(Agnes)^c (Agatha)ⁱ soror Nigelli monachi nostri reddit ij sol. de terra inter terram Willelmi Caluel. et terram Johannis Swetman latitudo iuxta vicum lxxij ped. longitudo a vico uersus west iiij^{xx} et x ped.

[E 43]

Terra Willelmi Cauuel est inter terram predicte Agathe et ecclesiam sancte Margarete de qua Willelmus Cokin. pater istius Willelmi dedit i d. de redditu nobis quia terram illam prius de nemine tenuit.

[E 44]

Jordanus frater Symonis monachi nostri. reddit xxv d. de terra Admundi clerici inter terram Willei Caudrun et terram Amfridi mercatoris latitudo de east ad west lx ped. longitudo de suth ad north c et lxxiij ped.

[272]
Godieua   iij sol.   De terra proxima uersus east.
relicta   latitudo eius de domo Gileberti.
Laurentii   usque ad uicum uersus east xxv
                                             p. longitudo uersus north c et xlij
                                             p.

[273]
Item   xij d.   De orto proximo uersus east.
eadem   latitudo eius uersus east xx p.
Godieua   longitudo uersus north lxx p.

[274]
Willelmus   De terra Harm. latitudo eius a
de Bernefeld   terra predicte Godieue uersus east
                                             iuxta uicum xl p. longitudo a uico
                                             uersus north c et xlij p.

[275]
Heredes   De terra proxima uersus east.
Odboldi   latitudo eius uersus east xx p.
                                             longitudo a uico uersus north lxx
                                             p.

[276]
Robertus   De terra proxima uersus east.
filius   latitudo eius uersus east lxxx p.
Ricardi   et x. longitudo uersus north
                                             [blank].

[277]
Symon   ij sol.   Ad mediam   De terra proxima uersus east in
filius   quadragesimam   angulo. longitudo eius ab angulo
Withgar   uersus north lxxiiij p. latitudo uer-
                                             sus west. [sic]

[278]
Item   xi d.   Ad mediam   De terra que est opposita pre-
idem   quadragesimam   dicte terre in angulo uersus suth-
Symon   east. latitudo eius iuxta uicum xij
                                             p. longitudo a uico uersus east
                                             lxxvij p. latitudo orti cum domo
                                             lapidea de north uersus suth lxx
                                             p.

273–277 These holdings lie on the n. side of Jewry Lane.

277 F 260, 478 where Simon is called S. de Boctune. Rental Y (fol. 29r.) c. 1216 calls him S. de la Tune.

278 F 261. This lies in the corner at the east end of Jewry Lane.

[279]

Johannes			De terra proxima uersus west.
Fretecoc			latitudo eius uersus west xxxvij p.
			longitudo a uico uersus suth lxvj p.

[280]

Heredes	xlij d.	Ad natale	De terra proxima uersus west.
Johannis		et totidem	latitudo lxiij p. longitudo uersus
filii		ad festum	suth lxvi p.
Viuiani		sancti Michaelis	

[281]

Frumbold	xij d.	Ad festum	Latitudo eius de suth ad north
filius		sancti Martini	xx p. longitudo a uico uersus west
Hachenild	xij d.	Ad festum	lxxx p. et xiij p.
relicte		sancti Johannis	
Hemeri		Baptiste	

[282] [fol. 226v.]

Vicecomes	xvj d.	Ad festum	De terra proxima uersus north
de Kent		sancti Martini	que est iuxta terram Arnoldi
			Ferre. latitudo eius a terra Frum-
			bold usque ad terram Arnoldi Ferre.
			iuxta uicum xxiij p. longitudo
			a uico uersus west lxxx p. et xiij.

[283]

Wiulfus	xvj d.	Ad mediam	De domo lapidea.
filius		quadragesimam	
Meineri			
diuitis			

[284]

Heredes	xlij d.	Ad natiuitatem
Iohannis		domini
filii	xlij d.	Ad festum
Viuiani		sancti Michaelis

[285]

Item	v sol.	Ad mediam
idem	et iij d.	quadragesimam
[sic]		

---

²⁷⁹⁻²⁸⁰ These holdings lie on the south side of Jewry Lane. For John s. of Vivian, adminis-
trator of the see during Becket's exile, provost of the city, and an actor in one of the Becket
miracles, see pp. 64, 84.   ²⁸¹ C I, G I, F 15, 357. See 283 n., and 306 below, n.

²⁸³ F 308. It seems that the stone house stands on the corner of White Horse Lane and that
A. Ferre (see 282) and Wiulph each hold half. Rental Y (fol. 33v.) c. 1216 describes the holding
as 'medietas domus lapidee que est contra pillorium que fuit Wiulphi diuitis.'

²⁸⁴ Probably F 28, 480.   ²⁸⁵ F 142.

[286]

| Item | iij sol. | | Terra ubi camera eius est inter domum suam 7 domum Tyerbe ad Andresgate. |

[287]

| Item | xv d. | | De terra retro domum suam. ubi |
| idem | | | pomerium eius est. |

[288]

| Item | x d. | | De terra Acelote. |

[289]

Item	v sol.	Ad festum	
idem	et vj d.	sancti Iohannis	
	et ij d.	de heuew'	
		ad gulam	
		Augusti	

[290]

Thomas	vj sol.		De terra Huphaldere. [*blank*] mag-
mercator	et		istro Feramino [*sic*]
	viij d.		

[291] (Parrochia sancte Helene.)ʳ

De terra Willelmi de Withelmes-
tune que est contra terram Salomonis monetarii ex alia parte uie
uersus north. latitudo eius ab east
uersus west iuxta uicum xliiij p.
longitudo a uico uersus suth
lxxx p. et v.

[292]

Proxima terra iuxta iuxta [*sic*]
illam uersus west xvj p. longitudo
uersus suth. lxvj p. Alia pars eiusdem domus pertinet ad sanctum
Augustinum.

[293] (Parrochia omnium sanctorum.)ʳ

Henricus	xiiij d.	Ad festum	De terra que est in parrochia
sacristarius		omnium	omnium sanctorum. hec data fuit
	et	sanctorum	cum Iacobo Flandrensi. hec habet
	iiij d.	Ad mediam	in longitudine uersus suth iuxta
		quadragesimam	uicum c et xxx p. iuxta Sturam

²⁸⁶ F 263, 349.   ²⁸⁷ F 264.   ²⁸⁸ Probably F 143.
²⁸⁹ It is difficult to identify the site of this, and of 290.
²⁹¹ For Solomon and other Canterbury moneyers, see pp. 113–18.
²⁹³ See p. 156 for James, monk.

	et xiiij d.	Ad pascha	xxx p. latitudo eius a uico ad
	et xl d.	Ad festum sancti Michaelis	Sturam uersus west c et xvij p.

[294]

Johannes filius Thome Slupe — xij d. — De terra que est fere contra terram Henrici ex alia parte uie uersus lest. latitudo eius iuxta uicum uersus suth xxxiij p. longitudo a uico uersus lest lvj p.

[fol. 227r.] [295]

Arnoldus Chig — ij sol. et iij d. ij sol. et iij d. — Ad festum sancti Michaelis / Ad mediam quadragesimam — De terra proxima uersus suth. latitudo eius uersus suth lij p. longitudo a uico uersus east lxxx et xvj p.

[296]

Robertus filius Ricardi — xvj d. — De terra proxima uersus suth quam tenet Arnoldus Bucke. latitudo eius uersus suth xxij p. longitudo a uico uersus east lxxx et x p.

[297]

Bonefacius filius Henrici de monasterio — ij d. — Ad mediam quadragesimam — Latitudo terre iuxta uicum uersus suth xxij p. longitudo a uico uersus east c et xiiij p.

[298]

Augustinus sacerdos — xij d. — De terra proxima uersus suth quam tenet Arnoldus Bucke. latitudo eius iuxta uicum uersus suth xxij p. longitudo a uico uersus east lxxx p. et x.

[299]

Anfridus de Chelde — De terra proxima uersus suth. latitudo eius iuxta uicum uersus suth lxvi p. longitudo a uico uersus east lxxx p. et x.

[294] F 159, 160. This and 295–301 are on the eastern side of Best Lane. See B, 1n.

[295] F 165, 550.   [296] F 167, 552.

[297] F 161, where A. Bucke holds the ground and dwells here. Probably B 114. Rental Y c. 1216 (fol. 29v.) says that Boniface s. of Henry sacrista pays 2d. at Midlent 'de terra proxima domui lapidee que fuit Ernaldi Bucke' [i.e. D 298.]

[298] A stone house stands here in the earlier thirteenth century. See last note.

[300]
Bartholomeus
Berebraid

De terra proxima uersus suth. latitudo eius iuxta uicum uersus suth xxi p. longitudo a uico uersus suth lxxx p.

[301]

De domo lapidea que proxima est predicte terre.

[302]
(Odo   xvj d.   Ad mediam
spicerius)ᶜ   quadragesimam
(Robertus
filius
Salekin
de Douora)ᵃ

De terra proxima terre monachorum sancti Augustini. latitudo eius a terra sancti Augustini uersus north xxij p. longitudo a uico uersus west usque ad Sturam c et ij p.

[303]
(Rogerus   v sol.
marescallus   et vj d.
               (est in manu
               nostra.)ᵃ

De terra proxima uersus north. latitudo eius iuxta uicum uersus north lxviij p. longitudo a uico uersus west c et ij p.)ᶜ

[304]
Jacobus.   vj d.   Ad mediam
Iudeus   quadragesimam

De terra que fuit Toli. latitudo eius de east uersus west iuxta uicum xx p. longitudo eius a uico uersus suth [blank]

[305]
Item   x d.   Ad mediam
idem   quadragesimam
Jacobus

De terra Thome filii Osberti. que est proxima predicte terre. latitudo eius iuxta uicum [blank]

³⁰⁰ See F 274.

³⁰² F 169. This and 303 lie on the western side of Best Lane. It is south of and probably next to 293 above. South of 302 is the stone house of Goldwin the mercer (Ch. Ant. C 761). South of this is the ground of Simon Cruddde, later Vivian the mercer, son of Ordnoth the dyer (ibid.); to the south of this is the dwelling of Alphage Lamb (ibid.). This ground belonged to Eastbridge Hospital (Hospital muniments, charter J 33, J. Tretel s. of R. Tretel to A. Lamb, c. 1200). The boundary of this ground to the south was the alley running e.–w. to the King's mill (ibid.). This ground with perhaps some adjoining was formed into All Saints' churchyard (BBSA, p. 617). The lane to the mill ran along the north side of the church (HMC, ix, app. ii, p. 169, col. 2).

³⁰³ See F, 31, n.

³⁰⁴⁻³⁰⁵ These (F 172, 171) are two of the three holdings formed into the house of Jacob the Jew (XLIX–LI).

[306] Domus lapidea Jacobi Iudei stat super utramque terram.

[307]

ij sol.	Ad mediam quadragesimam	De terra Willelmi de Einesfordia que iacet iuxta hospitale de East-
(xij. sol.)ᶜ	Ad [blank]	brege contra domum Jacobi Iudei.

[308]

xij sol.   De terra que fuit Normanni fullonis in uico proximo ultra East-
brege latitudo eius a terra Caluel
uersus suth iuxta uicum xlij p.
longitudo a uico uersus east lxx p.

[309] (Parrochia sancti Petri.)ʳ

Robertus   De terra que iacet in predicto
Pin   uico contra terram Normanni
uersus west latitudo eius iuxta
uicum uersus suth l p. longitudo a
uico uersus west lx p.

[310]

Johannes   De terra proxima uersus suth.
filius   longitudo eius uersus suth usque
Thome   ad magnam stratam lxvj p. lati-
Slupe   tudo eius ab angulo uersus west
iuxta stratam xxxvij p.

[311]

Eadwardus   De terra proxima uersus west.
Odbold   latitudo eius iuxta stratam uersus
west xliij p. longitudo a strata
uersus north lxx p.

---

³⁰⁶ Rental Z, c. 1230, (fol. 198r.) indicates that the house of Jacob stands between the synagogue and the High Street (inter scolam Judeorum et magnam stratam). Y, c. 1216 (fol. 29v.)
says that Thomas mercator pays 4d. 'de terra super quam pars scole Iudeorum sita est uersus
[blank'.] Y also shows that south of the synagogue is a holding of Benedict the Jew paying 12d.
to Christ Church. The holding backs on to that of Frumelin (Frumbold) in White Horse Lane
(D 281). South of Benedict's ground is that of Samuel the dyer. Rent is paid (Y, fol. 31v.) 'de
quadam terra inter scolam Judeorum et terram Samuelis tinctoris juxta stratam que est uersus
west et terram Frumelini que est uersus east.' See F 173.

³⁰⁷ F 138. For the Eynsford family see pp. 54–5, 182.

³⁰⁸ The 'vicus' is All Saints' Lane. This is probably the dwelling of Peter the miller (F 33,
318, 350, 476).

³⁰⁹ See F 33, n. William Somner has added to this entry the note: 'V[ide] vt infra fo. 178 in
pede'. See next note.

³¹⁰ F 133, 474. This lies on the s.w. corner of All SS. Lane. Somner has added to the entry:
'V[ide] le knobb. book. fol. 179.' This 'knobb. book' is clearly Reg. K, where (in Rental Z)
on fol. 178 (old foliation) at the bottom is the entry corresponding to 309 here, while on fol.
179 (old foliation) occurs the entry corresponding to 310 here.

[312] Juxta predictam terram terra quam tenet Robertus filius Ricardi de Hospitalariis. Item idem Robertus de terra Odboldi. latitudo eius a terra Hospitalariorum uersus west iuxta stratam xxxvij p. longitudo a strata uersus north c et xxv p. Item Odboldus uersus west proxima predicte terre. latitudo eius uersus west iuxta stratam lxxiiij p. longitudo a strata uersus north c et xx p. Juxta ecclesiam sancti Petri uersus north terra Odbold. latitudo eius a uico uersus east [blank] longitudo a predicta ecclesia uersus north c et lxvj p. usque ad terram Gileberti.

[fol. 227v.] [313]

Terra
Serun

Juxta predictam terram uersus north. latitudo eius uersus north lxxx p. et xiij. longitudo eius a uico uersus east usque ad Sturam [blank]

[314]

Ex alia parte uie uersus west terra Odboldi iuxta terram Willelmi de Mares. longitudo eius uersus suth c et lxxxiiij p. latitudo eius a uico orientali ad uicum occidentalem lx p.

[315]

Salomon   xij d.
clericus
Godesmanni

De terra que est in angulo uersus west prope ecclesiam sancti Petri. latitudo eius ab angulo uersus north xxxvi p. longitudo a uico uersus west lxxvij p.

[316]

Juxta illam uersus north terra Odboldi. longitudo eius iuxta uicum uersus north cc p. iij^bus p. minus. latitudo a uico uersus west c et lxiij p.

[317]

Ex alia parte uie uersus east terra Godardi de Boctune quam tenet Odbold. hec iacet contra terram Iohannis de Doura. latitudo eius a uico uersus east lx p. longitudo uersus north lx p.

³¹² For R. s. of Richard and his holdings from the Hospitallers, see p. 68. The ground of Odbold next door is F 472. See C 31, G 32.

³¹³ F 148. Z (Reg. K, fol. 199v. under St Peter's parish) says that Edward son of Odbold (founder of Eastbridge Hospital, and probably alderman of Westgate) dwelt here.

³¹⁴ The 'vicus orientalis' is the now lost lane, running parallel to St Peter's Lane (vicus occidentalis).   ³¹⁵ F 146.   ³¹⁷ See F 151–8, n.

[318]

Johannis	xxxij d.
filius	
Thome	
Slupe	
Idem	xvj d.

De terra quam tenet de Hamone filio Liefwini super quam stat pars lapidee domus sue scilicet usque ad fenestram et iuxta illam tota domus lignea. latitudo eius uersus north usque ad predictam fenestram xxxvij p. longitudo eius a uico uersus east usque ad Sturam. [sic] alia pars domus sue stat super terram sancti Gregorii.

[319]

Contra illam iacet terra quam emit Iohannes clericus de Hamone filio Liefwini. latitudo orti qui est inter terram Godefridi et Brunman lxij p. longitudo orti c et xx p.

[320]

Terra Odboldi que est iuxta ecclesiam sancti Petri uersus west. latitudo eius ab angulo uersus suth usque ad terram Goldere clerici xx p. longitudo eius uersus west xxij p.

[321]

Goldere
clericus

De terra proxima uersus suth. longitudo eius uersus suth usque ad stratam lxxx p. latitudo eius ab angulo uersus west iuxta stratam xxxvij p.

[322]

Odbold. de terra proxima. latitudo eius iuxta stratam uersus west xxx p. longitudo a strata uersus north lxxx p.

---

[318] F 420. Y, c. 1216 (fol. 38v.) says that the rent of 32d. arises 'de terra proxima domui sue [i.e. of John Slupe] uersus austrum et quedam pars camere sue stat super eandem terram.' Z, c. 1230, (Reg. K, fol. 199r.) calls the holding 'quedam pars domus sue [J. Slupe] a fenestra uersus austrum.' and adds 'reliqua pars eiusdem domus stat super tenementum sancti Gregorii.' This is the stone house of John Slupe west of the island in the Stour granted by Henry III to the Blackfriars, 10 March 1237 (Cal. Charter Rolls, i, p. 226; Arch. Journal, lxxxvi, 154).

[321] F 134, where Goldere is called son of Elias Cath. This holding lies at the w. corner of St Peter's Lane.

[323]

Thomas de Dene	ij sol.	Ad mediam quadragesimam	De terra que fuit Thome filii Eaddrun. latitudo eius iuxta strat-
	et	Ad festum	am uersus west xxviij p. longitudo
	ij sol.	sancti Michaelis	a strata uersus north lxxx p.

[324]

Heimeri

Ad ecclesiam sancti Petri de terra ubi manet.

[325]

xij d.

Terra Odbold que fuit Berebraid que est inter terram regis et Gode-fridi de balio. longitudo eius a terra regis uersus north lxxx et xiiij p. latitudo eius a uico uersus east lxx p.

[326]

Ex alia parte strate terra Odboldi iuxta terram cononicorum [*sic*] de Ledes. latitudo eius uersus east lxv p. longitudo a strata uersus suth iuxta uiam lxviij p.

[327]

Heredes
Iohannis
filii
Viuiani

De terra proxima uersus suth. latitudo eius uersus suth xxv p.

[328] [fol. 228r.]

Cuppere

De terra que iacet proxima iuxta terram Widonis et terram Eadgari rustici.

[329]

Willelmus
del Blen

De terra que est in exitu uie illius iuxta stratam uersus east. Deinde Ricardus Caluel.

[330]

Juxta illam uersus east terra Od-boldi. latitudo eius iuxta stratam xxx p. longitudo uersus suth usque ad terram Pin.

---

[324] A line connects 'Heimeri' with 'Terra' in 325.

[325] This appears to lie in the lost alley running north within Westgate. The ground of G. de Balio is 370 below.

[326] The surveyor has crossed to the s. side of the High Street.

[331]

Heredes	xviij d.	Ad mediam	De terra proxima. latitudo eius
Willelmi	et ob.	quadragesimam	uersus east iuxta stratam xxiiij p.
pelliparii	xviij d.	Ad festum	longitudo a strata uersus suth
	et ob.	sancti Michaelis	[blank]
	et j ob.	de heuewerc	
		ad gulam	
		Augusti	

[332]

Liefwinus	v d.	Ad mediam	De terra Iohannis Swin. latitudo
pelliparius		quadragesimam	eius uersus east xxxiiij p. longitudo
	et v d.	Ad festum	a strata uersus suth iuxta uiam
		sancti Michaelis	que dicitur Grienemeldnelane lxxx
			p.

[333]

Juxta illam ad austrum terra sancti Gregorii.

[334]

Terra Odbold est proxima predicte terre sancti Gregorii. latitudo eius ad austrum iuxta uicum lx et xvj p. Juxta illam ad austrum terra de burchilde.

[335]

Alepot

De terra proxima. latitudo eius iuxta uicum uersus suth xxiij p. longitudo eius a uico uersus west lxx p.

[336]

Godere	x d.	Ad mediam	De terra proxima uersus suth.
se	et	quadragesimam	latitudo eius uersus suth iuxta
palmere	ij d.	de heuewerc ad	uicum xl p. longitudo a uico
		gulam Augusti	uersus west c et lxxxiiij p.

[337]

De terra Pacoc proxima predicte terre. latitudo eius iuxta uicum uersus suth xxxi p. longitudo a uico uersus west [blank].

---

331 F 145, 391, 471.
332 Probably F 140, 141. Crienemeldnelane is St Peter's Grove.
334 For the gilds, see p. 124.
336 LX. Apparently F 129, 388.

335 Probably F 449.
337 Probably F 136.

[338]
Godwinus   viij d.   Ad mediam   De terra proxima. et de eadem
Brodhadfed   quadragesimam   terra latitudo uersus suth iuxta
                                            uicum xxx p. longitudo a uico
                                            uersus west c p.

[339]
Cristina   ij d.   De orto quodam qui est de terra
                                            Pacoc. latitudo eius et longitudo
                                            lxx p.

[340]
                                            Juxta terram Pacoc uersus suth
                                            terra Odboldi. latitudo eius uersus
                                            suth xv p. longitudo uersus west
                                            [*blank*].

[341]
                                            Juxta illam uersus suth terra sancti
                                            Gregorii.

[342]
                                            Juxta terram sancti Gregorii. item
                                            terra Odbold. longitudo eius uersus
                                            suth liiij p. latitudo a uico uersus
                                            west xl p. Juxta illam uersus suth
                                            terra sancti Gregorii.

[343]
                                            In angulo de Grienemeldnelane
                                            terra Odboldi de terra Iohannis
                                            filii Viuiani quam habuit Robertus
                                            del Broc. latitudo eius c et xv p.
                                            longitudo cc et lxxx p.

[344]
Heredes   De terra Wlfwardi Swirhod.
Iohannis
filii
Viuiani

[345]
Radulfus   De terra Eadgari rustici latitudo
de Baluerle   eius iuxta uicum uersus suth lxx p.
                                            longitudo a uico uersus west c et x
                                            p.

[338] F 139?

[343] The tenurial relationships here are obscure. Robert del Broc is probably the man who accompanied the four knights who murdered Becket.

[346]
Hubertus
Caluel

De terra proxima uersus suth.
latitudo eius uersus suth xxvij p.
longitudo uersus west c et x p.

[347]

E contra uersus east terra filiorum
Liefwini de Westgate. latitudo eius
iuxta uicum uersus suth lxvi p.
longitudo a uico uersus c et xx p.
[*sic*] Juxta illam est terra sancti
Gregorii.

[fol. 228v.] [348]

E contra terra Salomonis mercatoris.

[349]

Juxta illam uersus suth terra Gold-
wini mercerii quam tenet de
sancto Gregorio.

[350]

Juxta illam uersus suth terra Huberti Caluel quam tenet Leticia
relicta Iohannis filii Viuiani. latitudo eius uersus suth (l)ⁱ xxx p.
longitudo uersus west c et xxx
p.

[351]

Juxta predictam terram uersus suth
terra Odboldi. latitudo eius uersus
suth xliij p. longitudo uersus west
c et xxx p.

[352]

Juxta illam est terra quam tenet
Cecilia de Arnoldo Ferre.

[353]

Juxta quam est terra Iohanins
clerici ad austrum. terra Iohannis
Belesmains. latitudo eius uersus
suth c et xxiij p. longitudo a uia
uersus west cc et lxxx p. et x. Juxta
illam uersus suth terra sancti
Gregorii.

³⁴⁷ F 135, where the ground is described as two gardens.

[354]

Contra portam Philippi de Hardres terra Odboldi. latitudo eius iuxta uiam del suth uersus north lxviij p. longitudo a uia uersus west c et xlviij p.

[355]

Heredes   viij d.   Ad mediam
Roberti   quadragesimam
Godiuere

De terra proxima. que fuit Sunwini Hare. latitudo eius iuxta uiam del suth uersus north lxx p. longitudo a uia uersus east c et xlviij p.

[356]

Odbold de terra proxima uersus north que fuit Henrici Caluel. latitudo eius iuxta uiam uersus north lxx p. longitudo a uia uersus west c et xlviij p.

[357]
Wimundus

De terra que fuit Wlfwardi Swirhod. quam tenet de heredibus Johannis filii Viuiani.

[358]
Godesman

De terra proxima eiusdem Swirhod. latitudo eius xliiij p. longitudo liiij p.

[359]

Juxta terram Odbold que est in angulo terra Augustini sacerdotis de sancto Martino quam tenet de sancto Gregorio.

[360]

Ter(r)ia Odboldi iuxta predictam terram uersus north. latitudo eius uersus north iuxta uicum xlvj p. longitudo a uico uersus east usque

---

354, 356 The word 'west' should evidently be 'east' in either case. The two holdings have the same depth as 355, east of the lane, and all three seem to be subdivisions of a larger tenement. Z, c. 1230 (fol. 199v.), says of the ground of Sunwin Hare at Halistone (i.e. D 355): quam tenuit Robertus Godiuere contra portam Philippi de Hardres (cf. D 354) . . . inter duas terras Odboldi. Unam [sic] que jacet uersus north [i.e. D 356] fuit Henrici Cauuel.

355 F 130 (called ortus).

360 Thuate seems to be the now lost branch of the Stour running s.–n. west of the eastern main stream.

ad aquam que dicitur Thuate.
Juxta illam est domus et terra
magistri Radulfi de sancto Martino.

[361]

Juxta illam uersus north terra
Odboldi. latitudo eius iuxta uicum
uersus north xxxv p. longitudo a
uico uersus orientem usque ad
Thuate [*blank*].

[362]

Juxta predictam terram uersus
north est terra sancti Gregorii
usque ad uiam de Crienemeldne.

[363]

Ex alia parte uie illius terra Odboldi que fuit Eilredi fullonis.
latitudo eius a predicta uia uersus
north xxxviij p. longitudo uersus
suth usque ad Sturam.

[364]
Meinerus
fullo

De terra Sedewini. latitudo eius
iuxta uicum uersus north lxxx p.
et iij. longitudo a uico uersus
orientem xxvj p. Juxta predictam
terram terra Odboldi que pertinet
ad elemosinariam nostram. Juxta
illam terram uersus north usque ad
stratam est terra Mariotte que
pertinet ad sanctum Gregorium.

[365]
Robertus
filius
Ricardi

De terra proxima uersus east que
fuit Brien. latitudo eius iuxta
stratam uersus orientem xxxvj p.
longitudo a strata uersus suth usque
ad Sturam [*blank*].

³⁶³ The word 'suth' must be an error for 'east'. F 55 says that the ground of Eilred the fuller
is three houses from the mill (Crienemeldne in D 362). The houses must lie along the side-
branch of Crienemeldnelane running east towards the mill. The descriptive note is probably not
completed here since the 'longitudo' of the holdings does not extend to the river, owing to the
houses.
³⁶⁴ The ground of Sedewin is F 132, which shows that Meiner is son of Sedewin.
³⁶⁵ See C 44, where Brien is called 'cordewaner', and C 69, 70, 71, with G 69, 70.

[366]

Juxta illam uersus east terra Willelmi Cokin quam tenet de sancto
Gregorio. Juxta quam terra Cecilie
uxoris Rogeri marescalli quam
tenet de monachis de Fauresham.

[fol. 229r.] [367]
Hospitale
de Eastbrege

De terra quam habet de nobis
iuxta illam. latitudo eius iuxta
uicum uersus orientem xlvij p.
longitudo a strata uersus suth usque
ad Sturam [blank].

[368]

Juxta illam uersus east terra Willelmi Hering.

[369]

Deinde usque ad Eastbrege terra
Eustachii de Merewerthe.

[370] (Parrochia sancte crucis de Westgate.)ʳ
Radulfus
de Baluerle

De terra que est in paruo uico
uersus north prope domum Godefridi de balio et iacet contra terram
Odboldi uersus west. latitudo eius
a uico uersus west lxxx p. et vi.
longitudo iuxta uicum uersus suth
c et xxxiiij p. Juxta illam uersus
suth est terra sancti Augustini
usque ad stratam.

[371]
Eillewis

De terra que est iuxta predictam
terram uersus west latitudo eius
uersus west iuxta stratam l p.
longitudo a strata uersus north c et
xxviij p.

366 This is evidently the site of Cokin's Hospital, declared united with Eastbridge Hospital by
bull of Innocent III (1203) Bunce, MS. account of Canterbury Charities, in City Archives, i, p. 527.
367 F 137. This ground, like that of Cecilia in 366, was held of Faversham abbey (C 45; G 45).
369 This ground was shared by Hamo s. of Arnold the dyer on west, and his brother Ralph
on the east, who occupied 42 feet frontage from Eastbridge, with 77 feet depth. Gunnora, d. of
Eustace of Mereworth, granted rent of 3s. from this ground to Eastbridge Hospital before 1232
(Eastbridge Hospital Muniments, Charters C 1, C 2).
370 The remainder of the rental is manifestly incomplete. Z, c. 1230, shows that Christ Church
drew rents extensively in Holy Cross parish, and entries in Z in this respect can be identified
in Y, c. 1216. It is improbable that the monks drew only two rents c. 1200 (as here in D), and it
must be assumed that the names of tenants and rents in cols. 1 and 2 are largely incomplete.

[372]

Terra Odboldi est iuxta predictam terram uersus west. latitudo eius iuxta stratam uersus xxxv p. [*sic*] longitudo a strata uersus north c et xxviij p.

[373]
Radulfus
de Baluerle

De terra proxima uersus west. latitudo eius iuxta stratam uersus west usque ad angulum iuxta Westgate xxxviij p. longitudo ab angulo uersus north c p. duobus minus.

[374]

Odbold de terra Nigelli filii. [*sic*] longitudo eius iuxta uicum uersus north c et lxiii p. latitudo a uico uersus east lviii p.

[375]
Odbold   xx d.

De terra Viuiani Binnewicth extra portam de Westgate et nos de eadem terra debemus curie de Westgat (   )ᵈij d.

[376]

Infra portam de Westgate terra proxima uersus suth est Sturstani.

[377]

Juxta illam uersus east terra sancti Augustini.

[378]

Juxta illam ad austrum terra Eillewis quam tenet Petrus filius Godwini de Radulfo de Baluerle. longitudo eius a terra sancti Augustini uersus suth xxxvij p. et est in uico qui uocatur Horsmelnelane.

[379]

Ibidem est domus lapidea. longitudo eius xl p. latitudo xl p.

---

[375] This ground is the small island outside Westgate for which a ploughshare or 2d. was due to the manor of Westgate. See F 55; C 23; G 24. An erasure occurs between 'Westgat' and 'ij d.'

[380]

Terra Odbold proxima predicte terre uersus suth. longitudo eius iuxta uicum uersus suth lxxviij p. latitudo a uico uersus west lxxiij p.

[381]

Contra terram sancti Augustini est ortus quidam qui fuit Odbold. latitudo eius lxv p. longitudo lxxiij p.

[382]
Radulfus
filius
Liefwini
de Westgat'

De terra Elfegi Bigke. latitudo eius lxx p. longitudo c p.

[383]
Radulfus
de Baluerle

De terra ubi fuit Horsmelne. hec est iuxta terram sancti Iacobi. latitudo eius iuxta uicum lvij p. longitudo a uico uersus east similiter lvij p.

[384]
Radulfus
de Baluerle

De terra proxima uersus north. latitudo eius uersus north de terra que dicitur Saltcoc. xl p. longitudo a uico uersus east lvij p.

[fol. 229v.] [385]
Johannes
filius
Walteri
pistoris

De terra proxima uersus north. longitudo eius usque ad stratam lx p. latitudo iuxta stratam uersus east l p.

[386]

Juxta illam est terra Odbold que fuit Trukelin. latitudo eius iuxta stratam uersus east xxx p. usque ad proximam semitam que dicitur Neeleslane. longitudo a strata uersus suth c et iij p.

---

381 This holding occupies approximately the site of the nave of the fourteenth-century church of Holy Cross.

382 The site is uncertain though the ground probably lies in St Peter's Place.

383 Sanctus Iacobus is St Jacob's Hospital, Wincheap.

386 Neeleslane is now lost. It ran south from the High Street, west of Black Griffin Lane.

[387]

Geruasius de   ij d.

Hosprenge

De terra proxima uersus suth. longitudo eius uersus suth iuxta uicum lxxv p. latitudo uersus west xxxi p.

[388]

Contra illam uersus east est Stephani clerici quam dedit ad elemosinariam nostram [sic]. longitudo eius ab angulo uie usque ad stratam. [sic] Juxta illam uersus est est terra canonicorum de Ledes.

[387] F 275.

[388] F (§ 128) shows that the almonry of Christ Church paid rents to the treasury for this ground. See 326 above, and n.

Rental F

A schedule of Cathedral tenants in Canterbury, together with their rents, and descriptive notes of their holdings, arranged under terms within the year at which their payments fall due.

DATE: about 1206.

[Register H, fol. 1r.]

[   ] (hac ciuitate 7 [   ] is locis.)ʳ

[1]

[   ] Wadeis   xviii d.

[2]

Ælfwinus coruesier   xiii d.

[3]

Radulfus de Warewic   ix d.

[4]

Henricus Cod   xii d.

[5]

Gunnild relicta   xii d.

Has terras dedit
Osb' presbiter de
Tanin[   ] 7
sunt extra Wrgate.
citra hospitale
sa[ncti] Jacobi.
in uno continenti
iuxta regiam uiam
versus orientem.

[1–9] The ground covered lies on the e. side of Wincheap, nearly half a mile from the walls. See D 167–76. The corresponding payments at Ascensiontide are 326–34 below.

The whole of this folio has been badly damaged by fire (in 1670). The heading should probably read when complete: 'Gabulum' or 'Redditus de hac ciuitate 7 aliis locis.' A term of payment should be indicated, probably 'Ad festum omnium sanctorum.'

[5] For payment of 3s. to St Sepulchre's nunnery see C 55, G 56. Tanin[tun'] has been damaged by fire. See XLI, XLII.

Cluth (Johannes
filius)ᵃᶜⁱ   Et de hiis reddimus
(Philippus de Tanintun')ᵃⁱ   monialibus de
                                                     sancto Sepulcro
                                                     iii sol. ad
                                                     natiuitatem sancte
                                                     Marie.

[6]
(Cristina mater Thome)ᶜ   xx d.
(Tomas)ᵃᵉⁱ (capellanus)ᵃⁱ

[7]
Henricus filius Eilbrict   xii d.

[8]
Henricus 7 Simon filii   xii d.
Ælfwini

[9]
(Johannes filius Roberti   xv d.)ᵃ   (De terra que fuit Petri filii
filii Ricardi   Warini.)ᵃ
Isti tantumdem reddunt ad (ascensionem)ᵃᵉ domini.

[10]
(Item ad eundem terminum.)ᵐʳ
(   )ᵈ

[11]
(Parochia sancte Margarete.)ᵐʳ   Terra est supra Sturam ultra
(   )ᵈ   Ottemell' Binnewict.)ᶜ

[12]
Willelmus Hactetene   xii d.
(mercator)ᵃ

[13]
(Parochia sancti Ælfegi)ʳ
(Willelmus bracur   viii d.)ᵃᵉ   Et ad mediam
(Cecilia filia Malgeri   vi d.)ᵃᵉ   quadragesimam iiii d.
                                                     Ad pascha xiiii d.
                                                     Ad festum sancti Michaelis xl d.

[14]
(Willelmus gener Brictieue   v sol.)ᶜ   De terra que dicitur Holteche. 7
                                                     fuit de dominio nostro de Bertona.
(Summa xii sol. 7 v d.)ᵃ

¹⁰, ¹¹ The names of tenants have been entirely deleted. See 464 below, n.
¹² 204 below?   ¹³ 174, 306, 307, 549, below.
¹⁴ D 184. Holteche is one of the great fields flanking Wincheap, now (c. 1200) cut up into
plots. See D 183 n.

[15]
[   ]
Frumbaldus filius Hachenild   xii d.

[16]
([P]arochia sancte Marie)ᵐʳ
[   ] (manne)ᵐʳ   De eadem terra.
Heredes Emme relicte   xvi d.
Batholomei [sic] senescalli
(Reginaldus de Cornhelle.)ⁱ
   [fol. 1v.] [17]
[   ] Heredes Gualteri [   ]
(Summa iiii sol.)ᵃ

[18]
De iiii acris que sunt ultra Ber-   Heredes Willelmi de   ii sol.
tonam nostram. 7 dicuntur   Suliford
Nunneland.

[19]
Terra est apud Horsfald   Thomas filius Ærnoldi de   ix d.
                           Horsfald'.

Summa (ii sol. ix d.)ᵃ
   [20] (Ad natale domini)ᵐʳ
Terra est ultra ubi fuit torcular   Godelef relicta Ædwini   xvi d.
uinee nostre.   parmentarii

[21]
De terra proxima lapidee domui   (Salomon de Sesautre.)ᵃᵉ   ix d.
Willelmi fabri.

[22]

                           (Radulfus Braibecun)ᵃ   xii d.
   [23] (Sancte Mildrithe.)ᵐʳ
Terra est extra Wrgate. 7 dat   Cristina filia Brictieue   ii sol.
(dat)ᶜ ad natiuitatem sancte   (Relicta Terrici aurifabri.)ᵃⁱ
Marie. (de terra Godefridi Me.
dermangere [sic])ᵃⁱ

---

¹⁵ D 281, C 1, G 1, and 357 below. The heading has been almost entirely obliterated by fire. D 281, 282; Y, fol. 23r. where the corresponding entries occur, show that the missing passage may be restored as 'Terminus sancti Martini.'

¹⁶ C 1; G 1; D 282. Evework is probably 396 below. The portion in square brackets here, and in 17, has been destroyed by fire. The heading to 16 may probably be completed [Bred]-manne. Lines connect 16 in col. 3 with col. 2 in 15 and 16.

¹⁸, ¹⁹ The money denomination is almost obliterated by fire and should probably be 'sol'. This and 19 lie in the northern suburbs. The placenames are both lost. Nunneland must be on the Sturry Road, beyond Barton Mill, and Horsefold must be in the region of the Old Married Quarters of the Barracks. See 337 below.   ²⁰ Possibly B 150, 338 below.

²¹ Probably D 59, 342 below.   ²² 453 below.   ²³ 425 below.

[24]
Et tantum ad tres reliquos ter-   (Reginaldus de Cornhulle   xxvii d.)ᵃ
minos anni. pro terra que iacet
sursum domum suam uersus
Sturam. in qua sunt vi acre de   [25]
prato. 7 quinque terre arabilis.   (Ricardus de castello   xxvii d.)ᵃ

[26]
In Wenchiape de terra que fuit   Robertus aurifaber   xii d.
Anselmi sacriste nostri.

[27] (De terra que fuit Eilmeri Wadeis.)ᵃᵐ
Extra Wrgate de terra que fuit   De terra Osberti Pret
Ricardi Corbeill'.   (Johannes Turte)ᵃⁱ   vii d. ob.

[28] (Sancte Marie Bredmann')ᵐʳ
De domibus suis ubi ipsa manet   Relicta Johannis filii   xlii d.
in Litlepettelane.   Viuiani   (7 tantumdem
                                                                              ad festum sancti
                                                                              Michaelis)ᵐ

[29] (Sancte [sic] Andree.)ᵐʳ
De escorgeria. Tantumdem ad   Heredes Willelmi filii   v sol.
tres reliquos terminos de terra   Pagani (Jacob portarius)ᵃⁱ
quadam. cuius partem tenet de
illis Hugo aurifaber.

[30]
De terra que est iuxta magnam   (Johannes Dodekere)ᶜ   iiii s. ix d.
stratam uersus east contra ter-   (Heredes Terrici aurifabri.)ᵃⁱ
ram nostram. (Et tantumdem
in festo sancti Johannis.)ᵃ

[31] (Parochia omnium sanctorum)ᵐʳ
De terra que fuit Pauie.   Rogerus marascallus noster   xii d.

[32] (Sancti Pauli)ᵐʳ
De terra quadam que est iuxta   Simon de Lindeseia   v d.
fossam ciuitatis contra sanctum
Augustinum.

²⁴, ²⁵ 239, 240, 344, 345, 499, 500, below. The site of this ground is evidently without
Worthgate. Lines correct 24, 25 in col. 2 with the note in col. 1.
²⁶ 51, 346, 427 below; D 189.   ²⁷ 507 below; possibly either 186 or 205 in D.
²⁸ 480 below; probably D 284.
²⁹ See D 112, n. Payments at other terms in F are 296, 359, 539. The word 'escorgeria' is
underlined.
³⁰ The rent is paid not only at St John's but at Easter and Michaelmas. See 295, 365, 531
below. C 53, 62; D 103; G 55, 61. xxiv.
³¹ D 303. Possibly 170, 548 below.   ³² 290, 341, 572 below; D 81.

[33] (Sancti Petri.)ᵐʳ
De terra ultra Sturam contra   Petrus molendinarius   xii d.
domum Roberti filii Ricardi.
ex altera parte magne strate.

[34] (Sancte Margaret[e])ᵐʳ
De terra quadam que est in   Hugo aurifaber   vi d.
Therne.

[35] (Sancte Marie M[   ])ᵐʳ
Terra est in Ottemede.   Relicta Rogeri Desie   vi d.

[36]

         (Haimo filius Roberti   vi d.)ᵃ
         de Rodint'

[37]
De Holtege   (Henricus clericus   viii d.)ᵃ

[38]

         (Henricus Barath   iiii (d.)ⁱ iii qua.)ᵃ

[39]
[   ] (ubi grangia   Robertus Batur)ᵃ   [   ]
prioris fuit [   ]
[fol. 2r.] [40]
[   ]   xiii d.   De terra Philippi de Har[   ]
                                 (Robertus Fareman vi d.)ᵃ

[41]
([   ] mercerius   v. sol.)ᵃ

[42]
(Johannes Saule   xl d.)ᵃ

---

³³ 318, 350, 476 below. The words 'magne strate' must be an error, as the thoroughfare seems to be All Saints' Lane, not the High Street. Y, 1216 (fol. 24r.) says that this holding lies 'in uenella Iohannis filii Roberti contra terram eiusdem Iohannis mediante uenella.' Z, c. 1230, agrees and shows that the ground of P. the miller lies in All SS. Lane, backing on to the river Stour. The holdings are evidently D 308 while the house of R. s. of Richard becomes D 309. However, the rent in D is 12s., not 4s. over the four terms, as here.

³⁴ 356.   ³⁵ Probably D 232.

³⁶⁻³⁸ 312-14, 360-62, 581-83 below. Lines connect 'De Holtege' to col. 3 of 36-8.

³⁹ The missing portion of the descriptive note (destroyed by fire) should probably read 'De' or 'Pro terra'. There are slight traces of more writing following 'fuit'.

⁴⁰ D 73; 367 below, whence the missing note (col. 1) can be supplied (as H. Fagard), and the name P. de Hardres (col. 3) completed. The donation of P. de Hardres is subject of ʟᴠ. The MS. is badly damaged at the top of fol. 2. Many of the entries here are affected by fire, and are added in an untidy fashion. It is not certain whether some notes form independent entries or are additions to other entries.

⁴¹ The missing name is Johannes. See 369 below.

⁴¹⁻⁴⁵, ⁴⁷ Cf. 316, 317, 321, 322, 323, 324, 368, 369, 370, 371, 372, 556, 557, 558, 559, 560, below.

[43]
(David de Burgate   ii sol.)ᵃ

[44]
(Martinus textor 7   iiii d.)ᵃ
Ricardus frater eius

[45]
(Fulco de Wenchepe   xv d.)ᵃ

[46]
(Bartholomeus carpentarius   xii d.)ᵃ

[47]
(Heres Reginaldi Ioie   xii d.)ᵃ
                              (Summa xlv s. viii d. i qua.)ᵃ

[48] (Ad purificationem sancte Marie)ᵐʳ
Heredes Hazonis Scache   viii d.

[49]
(Nortgate.)ᵐʳ   De terra Holeman'.
Guillelmus de elemosinaria   viiii d.

[50]
(Sancti Georgii.)ᵐʳ
Simon de Bremling'   x d.   De terra ubi Polre manet.

[51]
(Sancte Mildrithe)ᵐʳ
(Robertus aurifaber)ᵉ   xii d.   De terra Anselmi sacriste. que pos-
                                              tea fuit Elmeri le Wadeis.

[52]
Robertus filius   iiii d.   Terra est in Hallelane.
Fulconis pictoris

[53]
(Sancti Petri)ʳ   vi d.
Heredes Ricardi (mercer)ᶜ
(Godesman)ᵃᶜⁱ (Martinus)ᵃ

[54]
(Sancte Margarete)ᵐʳ
De terra que fuit Roberti   ii galline Hanc terram tenent (heredes)ⁱ
sellarii. (Goldvinus mercier)ⁱ   uel ii d.   Johanni(s)ᵃⁱ le Volt (scilicet ipse
                                                 Goldwinus)ⁱ de elemosinaria nostra.
                                                 7 elemosinarius de nobis (per iiiis.)ᵃ

⁴⁶ 366, 428, below.   ⁴⁷ The figure xlvs. in the total has been altered from xliiis.
⁴⁸ See 415, 419 below. See B 128; D 22.
⁴⁹ 60, 339 below. See D 24, and 414 below. Lines correct 48 and 49 with 'De terra' in col. 3.
⁵⁰ This is associated with B 213; D 126. Cf. 176, 181, 529, below.
⁵¹ See 26.   ⁵⁴ 501 below.

[55]

(Sancti Petri)ᵐʳ · · · · · · · · · · iiii s. iiii d.

[56]

(Simon fenier de terra · · · · viii sol.
Lefwini decani · · · · · · · · · vi d.)ᵃ
(Item tantumdem
ad iiiᵉˢ terminos)ᵃ

Summa (xvii sol.)ᵃ

Et tantumdem ad Pentecosten de diuersis mansuris. Due illarum mansurarum sunt extra Æstbrege ab aquilonari parte uie. iuxta 7 ultra terram que fuit Wlfwini sadelere. 7 reddunt (nobis)ᵃⁱ iiii sol. Tercia que fuit Æilredi fullonis reddit ii sol. 7 est in Crinemelnelane. tribus domibus citra molendinum. Hec data fuit ecclesie cum Salomone nepote Georgii camerarii. Quarta reddit xii d. 7 est citra Westgate in proximo uiculo qui ducit ad austrum. Quinta est parua insula extra Westgate ad aquilonem. 7 reddit nobis xx d. 7 nos inde reddimus j uomerem ad curiam de Westgate. uel ii d. Hanc terram dedit Willelmus de Hakintun'. cum Salomone filio suo.

[57]

(Ad mediam quadragesimam)ʳ
(Parochia de Norgate.)ᵐʳ

Walterus Bes · · · · · · · · · · · vi d.
· (vacat)ᵃ

De terra Odonis sutoris que est iuxta terram Willelmi de Cherteham.

[58]

Heres Hugonis de aula · · · · ix d.

Terra est inter terram Johannis aldermanni 7 terram Willelmi Sprot.

[59]

Relicta Dunstani · · · · · · · · xxvi d.

De terra quadam extra Nortgate. quam emimus de uxore Guarini mazonis.

[60]

Willelmus de · · · · · · · · · · · viii d.
elemosinaria

De terra Holeman.

⁵⁵ 335 below. The third *mansura* is D 363. The fourth is probably D 380. The fifth is D 375; C 23; G 24. This is apparently entered again at 421 below.

⁵⁶ 325, 358, 562 below.   ⁵⁷ D 23. Cf. 99 below.   ⁵⁸ D 40; 444 below.

⁵⁹ A 5, B 56, C 19, D 9, G 20. This is the ground passed by St Augustine's abbey in connection with the Holy Oils. See B 56, n.

⁶⁰ See 49 above, n.

[fol. 2v.] [61]
Willelmus frater   xii [ ]   [   ]
Johannis

[62]
Item idem   vi d.

[63]
(Parochia de [   ]te)ᵐʳ
Heredes Walteri   iiii sol.   De Settinge.
pistoris

[64]
Item idem   xv d. ob.

[65]
(Nortgate)ᵐʳ
(Henricus)ᵃᵉ filius   ix d. (ob.)ᵃ
Æilmeri.

[66]
(Walterus filius   (ix d. ob.)ᵃᵉ
Eilmeri.)ᵃ   De terra que fuit Guarini Chien.
(retro vi d. ob.)ᵃ   in fine de Drutintune.

[67]
Relicta Hugonis   xii (d.)ᵃᵉ
Frode (Item eadem)ᵃ

[68]
Adam filius   xxxii d.   Terra est in angulo iuxta Bage-
Bartholomei coci   berie.

[69]
(Item idem)ᵃ   (xii d.)ᵃ

[70]
Serlo mascun   viii d.   De quadam terra extra Nortgate
                                                   ubi ipse manet. iuxta terram que
                                                   fuit Sigari salsarii nostri. Item idem
                                                   ii s. ad festum sancti Michaelis.

[71]
Gilebertus de terra   iiii d.
Walteri presbiteri

---

⁶¹, ⁶² Probably D 36, and 466 below.   ⁶⁴ 459 below.
⁶⁵⁻⁶⁷ See 445–7 below; D 29, 30. A series of lines connects the note in col. 3 with the rents in 65–67.
⁶⁶ Lines connect 'De terra...' (col. 3) with 65–67.
⁶⁸ B 131, 165; C 47; D 25; G 47; and 441 below. Evework is 412 below.
⁷⁰ D 8; G 41; and 429 below.

[72]
Geruasius Hog de   xv d.   Terra est iuxta acram Simonis coci.
Horsfalde

[73]
Adam careteir   (ii sol.)ae   Terra est inter terram Willelmi
                                    Sprot. 7 terram Willelmi filii Driu.

[74]
Moniales sancti   vii d.
Sepulcri

[75]
Salomon Chet   x d.   De terra ubi ipse manet.

[76]
Item idem   iiii d.   De terra quadam super fossam extra
                            Nortgate ubi fabrica quondam fuit.

[77]
Item idem   viii d.

[78]
Alitia filia Wiberti Kide   xxx d.   De terra que est inter terram
(Heredes eius)ai   Willelmi pictoris 7 Radulfi Braba-
                                        cun. que fuit (Kide).d

[79]
Item eadem   xxii d.   De eadem terra.

[80]
Item eadem (retro iiii d.   xii d.   De terra que fuit Aschetini. prope
de Lorekin)aem   Bertonam nostram.

[81]
Alitia heres Leifwini Lun3   iiii d.

[82]
Matheus se lodere de   viii d.
terra Heggesfot.

[83]
Heres Sired Drinkedreste   vi d.   Terra est ad Bertonam prope
                                    mansuram que fuit Rikewardi.

---

73 D 42, and 467 below. Evework is 379 below.
74 Possibly D 63. Evework is 400 below.
75–77 Evework at 378 below must be for one of these holdings, probably for 75.
76 B 11; D 61.   77 Possibly B 15; D 60.
78 Probably B 27; D 44; 433 below. An attempt has been made to delete the name Kide
(col. 3).
80 The Barton lay half a mile from Northgate.
81 Evework is 413 below. See B 39, D 19 n.   83 B 141; D 18.

[84]
Michael Bon Enfant   xv d.   Terra est iuxta curiam de Bertona.

[85]
Liueua relicta Conradi   viii d.   Terra est iuxta terram Osberti de
                                                   vinea.

[fol. 3r.] [86]
Willelmus Spr[   ]   viii d.   De terra que fuit Gerardi presbiteri.

[87]
(Bartholomeus de terra   ii d. ob.)ᶜ
Willelmi stamere

[88]
Robertus de scalieres   v d.   Terra est extra Nortgate. 7 est
                                                   iuxta terram Suani mercerii.

[89]
Robertus Blundus   viii d.   Terra est in Drutintun'. iuxta
                                                   Huntonches wei.

[90]
Item idem   xx d.

[91]
Willelmus Pertrich   v d.   De terra que fuit Osb' de vinea est
                                                   iuxta Bertonam. [sic]

[92]
Heres Guillelmi de Suliford   xviii d.   Terra est extra Nortgate iuxta
                                                   terram que fuit Guillelmi de
                                                   Hungreford parmentarii.

[93]
Godefridus filius   vi d.   Terra est proxima cimiterio sancti
Guarini Keuerel   Gregorii. uersus aquilonem preter
                                                   unam mansuram.

[94]
Willelmus filius   xii d.   Terra est extra Nortgate iuxta
Aluredi fabri   domum lapideam Radulfi fratris
                                                   sui.

---

⁸⁴ Probably B 33; D 11. Cf. 436 below.   ⁸⁵ B 36; D 15.
⁸⁶ D 41, 438 below. The MS. is damaged by fire. The name Sprot can be completed from 403,
438 below. Evework is 403 below.
⁸⁷ The entry is damaged by fire, and the name Bartholomeus and following words partly
obliterated.
⁸⁸ In D 52 Suan mercerius has ground without Northgate, not, however, flanked by that of R.
de scalieres.
⁸⁹ This, with 90 is 440 below, and D 32. See B 32.
⁹¹ Probably D 13 and B 35.   ⁹² B 22; D 53. Evework is 382 below.
⁹³ B 12; D 7. Evework is 409 below.   ⁹⁴ D 58; 431 below.

[95]
Heredes Philippi de   xvi d. ob.   Terra est extra Nortgate contra
Chelde   aque nostre ductum.

[96]
Salomon Flandrensis   vi d.   Terra est in Drutintun'. ubi manet.
(Item idem)ᶜ

[97]
Laurentius filius   v d.   Terra est iuxta domum lapideam
Ætelburge   Bartholomei fabri.

[98]
Heredes Ædmeri Gekerel   x d.   Terra est in fine vici de Drutintune.
(Item idem   x d.)ᶜ

[99]
(Heredes Walteri Bes.)ᵃ   (ii d.)ᵃ

[100]
Heredes Oswardi de   xxxii d.   Terra est extra (Bur)ᵃᵉcgate.
Ocolte (per Burgat')ᵃᵐ

[101]
Heres Sunewini carnificis   xii d.   Terra est extra Nortgate iuxta
(Augustinus presbiter)ᵃⁱ   terram heredum Galfridi mares-
                                                calli uersus east.

[102]
Heres Nigelli filii Albri   xxiii d. ob.   Terra est extra Nortgate prope
                                                fossam muri iuxta terram Goldstani
                                                parmentarii.

[103]
Item idem de terra Landri   xv d.

[104]
Willelmus filius Driu   iii sol.   De terra Herloc. quam nobis dedit
                               (ii d.)ᵃ   Johannes clericus.

[105]
Bartholomeus faber   xii d.   De eadem predicta terra super
                                                quam stant domus lapidee Radulfi
                                                7 Bartholomei.

[106]
Heres Nigelli filii Albri   iiii d. ob.

⁹⁵ B 25; D 46. For the 'aqueduct' supplying the cathedral, see p. 205. Cf. 340 below.
⁹⁶ B 32; D 31, 432 below.
⁹⁷ This ground probably lies without Northgate, in Broad Street. There is some confusion
here and identification with entries in D is difficult. See D 55–57, n.
⁹⁸ B 31, D 34. Evework is 395 below. See 363 below.   ⁹⁹ See 57 above.
¹⁰⁰ B 199. See D 86.   ¹⁰¹ D 50. Evework is 393 below.   ¹⁰² See B 23 n.   ¹⁰³ D 33.
¹⁰⁴⁻¹⁰⁶ For identifications, and of 451, 452, 455 below, see D 55–57 n. See 389 below. Lines
connect 105 and 106 with 'De eadem' in col. 3.

[107]

Maria filia Ælueue (vxor   xii d.   De terra Spinke que iacet ante
Svani mercerii.)ai   hostium ecclesie sancte Marie de
                                              Norgate.

[108]

Moniales sancti Sepulcri   xxxvii d.   De terra que fuit Sedegos relicte
                                              Baldwini Flandrensis 7 est extra
                                              Norgate iuxta terram Salomonis
                                              Keth.

[109]
(Sancte Margarete)mr
Adam mercier   xv d.   De terra que fuit Reingard'.

[110]
(Item idem)a   viii d.   De terra que fuit Lambini Spange.

[111]
(   )d   (iii d.   De terra que fuit Roberti Pin
                                              super fossam de Norgate.)c

[112]
(Relicta Roberti sacur   vi d.)a   De terra que fuit Willelmi vigilis.
                                              prope ecclesiam de Norgate.

[fol. 3v.] **[113]**
[Norg?](ate)mr
Joseph filius Roberge   xii d.   [   ]

[114]
Robertus portarius de   xx d.   Terra est in angulo duarum uiarum
infirmaria   [   ] de Nortgate. 7 fuit
                                              Vauersuri coci.

[115]
Relicta Roberti Godiuere   ii sol.   Terra ista interiacet terre Arnoldi
                                    ob.   coci 7 terre [   ]di. que fuit
                                              Hugonis del braccin.

[116]
(Johannes filius   xviij d.)a
Rogeri alderman

107 Adjacent to 119 below.
108 The holding of S. Keth is 75, or 76 above. The holding of the nuns is 435 below, and
possibly D 63.
109 493 below.   110 D 226; and 298, 488 below.
111 B 9, the third holding eastward from Northgate backing on to the city wall. See B 7-10,
n.   112 465 below.
113 The text is defective here through damage by fire. This is 454 below, and 404 below (evework). D 48.
114 B 52, C 20; D 4; G 21, and 460 below.
115 B 126; D 3, and 461 below.
116 B 30; D 39. Evework is 408 below.

[117]
Relicta Arnoldi coci   iiii d.   De terra que fuit Golwardi Scache.
                                                      7 interiacet terre Simonis de bal-
                                                      neario. 7 terre relicte Roberti
                                                      Godiuere.

[118]
(Erna(l)ᶦdus   iiii d.)ᵃᵉ
cocus

[119]
(In parochia sancti Pauli.)ᵐʳ   Terra est ante ostium ecclesie de
Robertus cognatus   xii d.   Nortgate iuxta terram Rodberti
Gileberti de Tenet   portarii nostri.

[120]
(Ricardus filius Ricardi)ᶜ   xvi d.   Terra est extra Burgate iuxta
(Relicta Terrici aurifabri.)ᵃⁱ   terram Roberti filii Ricardi.

[121]
Heredes Alexandri cementarii   x d.

[122]
Simon parmentarius   ix d.
(Walterus filius Eilmeri)ᵃⁱ

[123]
Heredes Oswardi   xix d.   Omnes iste mansure sunt extra
de Ocolte   murum contra fontem de Quene-
(Queningate)ᵃᵐ   gate. in uno continenti inter Dude-
                                                      lane 7 Drutintune.

[124]
Heredes Radulfi   x (d.)ᵃ
7 Hugonis Coffin

[125]
Godeleif vxor   x(ii d.)ᵉ
Stephani de porta

[126]
Thomas filius   vii d.
Reginaldi aurifabri

---

¹¹⁷ Appears to be D 2. See B 126.
¹¹⁹ The heading is obviously wrong as the ground is in St Mary Northgate parish. The ground
is B 53; D 5, and 463 below.
¹²¹⁻¹²⁶ The ground between Old Ruttington Lane and Dudelane is surveyed in B (61–64) and
D (77–79) but is difficult to identify in the various rentals. In F the holdings are not apparently
in geographical order. F 124 may be B 61. F 123 is probably D 78, and B 63. The word Queningate in the margin (123) is underlined. Lines connect each section from 121 to 126 with the
word Queningate. A line connects 121 and 126 to the para. 'Omnes . . . Drutintune'.

[127]
Item idem   v d.   De terra Æileue matris sue. Et iiii
                                                    d. ad festum sancti Michaelis.

[128]
(Sancti Petri)ᵐʳ
Elemosinarius   xviii d.   De terris que fuerunt Stephani clerici
noster   7 x d.   et Henrici presbiteri fratris eius.

[129]
Godere Palmere   x(ij)ᵃd.   Ex una parte iacet terra Humfridi
(Dunstanus filius)ᵃⁱ   aldermanni. ex alia parte terra
                                                    Nigelli presbiteri.

[130]
(Heredes Sunewini Hare)ᶜ   (viii d.)ᶜ De quodam orto prope Halistane
                                                    iuxta terram Henrici Caluel.

[131]
Robertus filius Ricardi   viii d.   De eadem terra.

[132]
Manerius filius Sedewin   (ix)ᵃᵉd.   Terra est in Crienemellane.

[133]
Johannes filius   iii sol.   Terra est iuxta domum lapideam
Thome Slupe   Roberti filii Ricardi in qua ipse
                                                    manet.

[134]
Goldere filius   xii d.   Terra est in angulo super magnam
Helie Cath   stratam sicut itur ad ecclesiam
                                                    sancti Petri.

[135]
Heredes Liefwini   ix d.
de Westgat'   De duobus ortis citra Halistane.
Item idem   ix d.
(xxiiii s. xi. d. ob.)ᵃᵐ (Summa iiii lib. v sol. viij d. ob.)ᵃ

[136]
(Secundum capitulum.)ʳ
(Sancti Petri)ᵐʳ
Vitalis Pacoc   iiii d.   De duabus terris que sunt prope
                                                    Crienemelnel[   ]

---

¹²⁷ 450 below.   ¹²⁸ This is the holding mentioned under D 388. Evework is 387 below.
¹²⁹ Possibly D 336, LX. Evework is 388 below.
¹³⁰ D 355. Halistane is underlined. For the 'Holy Stone' see p. 200.   ¹³² D 364.
¹³³ D 310, and 474 below. See 33 above, n.   ¹³⁴ D 321.
¹³⁵ D 347. 'Halistane' is underlined. The second total has been much altered, erased etc.
'viij d. ob'. has been altered from 'vij d. ob'.
¹³⁶ Apparently D 337. The descriptive note has been damaged by fire, but should clearly end
'-l[ane]'.

[137]
Magister hospitalis   iii sol.   De terra que fuit Eluredri presbi-
sancti Thome   teri. que est prope monasterium
                                 sancti Petri iuxta regiam uiam
                                 uersus suth contra magnam domum
                                 que fuit Olboldi.

[fol. 4r.] [138]
Item idem   ii sol.   De domo lapidea retro hospitale.
                                 hanc terram dedit nobis Willelmus
                                 de Einesford.

[139]
Cecilia filia   viii d.   De eadem terra.
Goduini Bradhefed

[140]
(Haimo filius   iii d.)ac
Lewini pelliparii

[141]
Edith filia   v(iij)ᵃd.
Johannis Swin

[142]
Susanna filia   v sol. iii d.
Johannis filii Viuiani

[143]
Item eadem   (x)ᵃᵉ d.

[144]
Johannes filius   xxx d.
Henrici Caluel

[145]
Heres Willelmi parmentarii   xviii d. ob.   Terra est contra ecclesiam sancti
                                 Petri uersus suth.

[146]
Heredes Salomonis clerici   xii d.   Terra est retro ecclesiam sancti
(Cecilia vxor Rogeri   Petri.
marescalli.)ai

[147]
Humfridus vicealdermannus   x(viij)ᵃᵉ d.

¹³⁷ C 45; D 367; G 45.   ¹³⁸ D 307.
¹³⁹ This is apparently D 338 and part of 136 above, not 138 as suggested by the note.
¹⁴⁰ This with 141 is evidently D 332.   ¹⁴² D 285.   ¹⁴³ Probably D 288.
¹⁴⁵ D 331, and 471 below. Evework is 391 below.
¹⁴⁶ D 315.
¹⁴⁷ 475 below.

[148]
Heredes Serun de Boctune   vi d.   De terra ubi Æduordus filius
                                               Odboldi manebat.

[149]
Heredes Odboldi   iii sol.

[150]
Item idem   vii d.

[151]
(vacat)ᵐ
Johannes filius Wlbald   xvi d.   Terre deserte.

[152]
Willelmus Gernun   iiii d.

[153]
Godardus de Boctune   xvii d.

[154]
Dauid 7 fratres eius   vi d.

[155]
Haimo Coppe   vi d.   Terra ista in manu nostra est. 7
(terre deserte)ᵃᵐ   iacet sub muro iuxta ecclesiam de
                                               Burgate.

[156]
Godvine   ix d.

[157]
Cristina filia Roberti   xii d.

[158]
Liuieua filia Walteri   vii d.
presbiteri

[159]
(Omnium sanctorum)ᵐʳ
Johannes Slupe   vi d.

[160]   Terra est iuxta domum lapideam
(Item   (ii d.)ᵃ   Arnoldi Child uersus north.
Radulfus de
Hakentune)ᵃ

---

¹⁴⁸ D 313.
¹⁵¹⁻¹⁵⁸ It is difficult to identify most of these 'waste plots'. 155 is D 89 (in St Michael's parish);
153 may be D 317 (in St Peter's), in which case it appears that groundplots scattered across the
city have been grouped together in the rental. William Somner has added the note at 158
'Vide inter redditus assise versus finem libri.' This reference is to D (at the end of Reg. H, while
F is at the beginning). The passages 'terre deserte' and 'sub . . . Burgate' are underlined. 'Vacat'
in margin is rendered va–cat, the line spanning 151–158. This line is joined by another to
'terra deserte' (see 155).   ¹⁵⁹ This with 160 is D 294.

[161]
Bonefatius filius Henrici   ii d.   Hanc terram tenet de eo Ærnold
                                              Bucke. ubi ipse manet.

[162]
Haimo de Ewerlande   x d.   De terra quadam que est contra
                                      terram Frederich.

[163]
Item idem   vi d.   De alia terra que est iuxta predic-
                             tam uersus suth.

[164]
(Sancti Ælfegi.)mr
Item idem   xii d.   De terra que fuit Humfridi auri-
                              fabri iuxta terram que fuit Anselmi
                              sacristarii uersus suth.

[165]
(Robertus clericus   (xxvii)aed.   De terra que fuit Arnoldi de
scriptor Iudeorum)ae   Chigh.

[166]
(Item idem   xviii d.)ae

[167]
Johannes filius Roberti   viii d.   De terra proxima predicte terre.
filii Ricardi

[fol. 4v.] [168]
([O]mnium sanctorum.)mr
(Item idem   xviii d.)c   De terra que fuit Beatr[icis].

[169]
Odo specier   xvi d.   De terra Liede ex opposito [   ]
                                 Ærnoldi Chig.

[170]
Rogerus marescallus   xxvi d.   De eadem terra.

[171]
Filii Jacobi Judei   x d.   De terra que fuit Thome filii
                                      Osberni.

---

161 D 297. Perhaps B 114. Lines connect 159 and 160 with 'Terra' in col. 3.
162 This and 163 evidently lie in Best Lane. They are 544 and 543 below.
164 D 76 is ground of A. the sacrist, secretary, in St Alphage, but the adjacent holdings there do not correspond with that in the descriptive note here. See 210, below.
165 D 295, and 550 below.   167 D 296, and 552 below.
168, 169 The passages within square brackets have been destroyed by fire.
169 D 302. Ground of A. Chig is 165 above.
170 548 below, and possibly D 303. See 31 above.
171 D 305.

[172]
Item ipsi

vi d.

De terra que fuit Benedicti filii Toli super quam domus lapidea est ubi ipsi manent.

[173]
(Thomas)ᵃᵉ mercator

iiii d.

(De terra in qua scola Judeorum sita est.)ᵃ

[174]
Willelmus le bracur

iiii d.

(De terra Henrici sacriste.)ᵃ

[175]
(In parochia sancti Georgii.)ᵐʳ
Reginaldus Blundus

xx d.

Terra est iuxta terram que fuit Godardi uphaldere in Sunwines-lane.

[176]
(Heres Roberti Polre)ᶜ

(xii d.)ᶜ

De terra que est iuxta propriam domum ubi ipse manet.

[177]
(Osmundus Polre)ᵃᵉ

vi sol.
viii d.

Pro iiiiᵒʳ acris extra ciuitatem que dicuntur Faxmalde.

[178]
(Relicta Elrici Oker)ᶜ
(Simon Chich.)ᵃⁱ

xx d.

De terra que iacet extra Niwegate inter terram Ade filii Norioth. 7 terram Willelmi filii Suani merca-toris.

[179]
Milesent (relicta
Ricardi loremier.)ᵃ

xii d.

[180]
Haimo

xxi d.

[181]
Simon filius Helie de
Bremling'. 7 fratres eius

vi d.

De tercia mansura infra Niwegate uersus suth.

[182]
Eugenia filia
Petri

xii d.

---

¹⁷² D 304. See XLIX–LX.　　　　　¹⁷³ See D 281, 306 n.
¹⁷⁴ See 13 above.　　¹⁷⁵ D 101.　　¹⁷⁶ Apparently part of D 126. See 50, above.
¹⁷⁷ The name Faxmalde, Foxmolde, is now lost. It lay somewhere near Ridingate.
¹⁷⁸ D 131. Evework is 397 below. See 608 and 642 below, and A 34.
¹⁸¹ See 50 above. The whole of the passage in col. 3 is underlined.
¹⁸² For evework see 401 below.

[183]
(Edilda filia Eadmei)ᶜ   vi d.   De terra que fuit uxoris Lamberti
(Hugo longus.)ᵃⁱ   Wrenne. 7 est in Lamberteslane
Wrenne ex alia parte uie uersus
occidentem iuxta domum Mauritii
filii Æduordi uersus suth.

[184]
Diriua 7 Goditha   vi d.

[185]
(Aluredus de   (xviii d.)ᵃ
Steuerl(i)ⁱnge)ᵃ

[186]
Filie Sedewini   xv d.   Terra est extra Niwengate.

[187]
(Heres Alani alderman')ᶜ   xxv d.   Terra est extra Niwe(n)ᵃgate
(Adam de cruce.)ᵃ   opposita parte [*sic*] ante crucem.

[188]
(Heredes Pardic)ᵃ   xxv d.   De terra que est iuxta Loddereslane
(Ricardus clericus   uersus suth apud Salthelle.
de Milestede.)ᵃ

[189]
(Hugo faber)ᶜ   xii d.   Terra (ista)ⁱ est proxima predicte
(Simon Chich)ᵃⁱ   terre.

[190]
(In parochia sancti Ædmundi.)ᵐʳ
(Willelmus filius   xl d.)ᶜ
(Johannis)ᵃᵉ aldermanni

[191]
(Stephanus filius Osberti   xii d. ob.)ᵃᵉ   (De terra Rogerii alderman de
de sancto Laurencio   Radingate)ᵃ

[fol. 5r.] [192]
(Willelmus 7 Amfridus   xxx d.   De terra que est in fine scopparum
filii Hugonis)ᶜ   nostrarum uersus west de Burgate.
(Heredes Terrici aurifabri)ᵃⁱ

---

[183] B 104.   [184] D 269. Evework is 384 below.

[185] 523 below. Y, c. 1216 (fol. 42r.) says that A. de Staverling pays this rent 'de terra que fuit Nigelli Broch'. This is ground of N. Broch outside Newingate. It is B 212; D 137.

[186] B 97; D 135, and 524 below.

[187] B 92; D 130, and 402 (evework) below. See 657 below. Cf. A 34.

[188] D 127 and 416 below.   [189] See D 128, and 310, 398 below (for evework).

[190] This with 191 is covered (among others) by D 152–54; F 190, 191 are 511, 512 below.

[192] 561 below. The passage 'in fine scopparum' is underlined.

[193]
Terricus aurifaber   iii sol.   De terra Eastmundi.

[194]
Item idem   v sol.   De terra quam tenuit Johannes Dodekere.

[195]
(Sancti Georgii)mr
Alanus de Rettlinge   vi d.   Terra ista iacet iuxta ecclesiam sancti Georgii uersus west.

[196]
Heres Dauid de Wertinge   xi d.

[197]
Willelmus de Hottemelne   v d.   De terra que fuit Osberti Pret.

[198]
(Johannes Dodekere)c   x d.   De terra Baldri.
(Radulfus le Prude)ai

[199]
(Sancte Marie Magdalene)mr
Ingenulfus plumbarius   xviii d.   De terra ubi ipse manet.

[200]
Item idem   xviii d.   Pro particula terre que fuit Hamonis Hunderdune. ubi quedam pars camere sue lapidee stat.

[201]
Johannes de Welles et   xxx d.
Laurencius frater eius

[202]
(Wlfwinus frater Semeri   vi d.   Terra est retro terram Hamonis de
mercatoris)c (Heredes   de orto.   Vnderdune.
Terrici aurifabri.)i

[203]
(Sancti Ælfegi)mr
Heres Hugonis Fagard   (xix d.ob.)a   De terra Rogeri Holeman. que est iuxta (terram)a Elfwini filii Semeri uersus suth.

---

193 Possibly 553 below.

194 C 3; D 99; G 3; and 554 below.

195 A 7; D 123, and 527 below. xix.

196 Probably D 259, and is 510 below.

197 508 below.

198 B 96; D 134. Evework is 394 below.

199 D 95 and 564 below.

200 565 below.

201 Apparently part of corpus of holdings in B 208.

202 Lambert s. of Semer the merchant had ground c. 1200 in Semereslane (Canterbury Lane) in St M. Magdalen's. (Greg., no. 46).

203 C 37; D 72, and 566 below.

[204]
Willelmus Eactetene · ii sol.

[205]
Item idem · vii d.

[206]
De terra Radulfi · ii sol. · Terra est super Sturam contra
nepotis sancti Thome · terram Helie pelliparii. que fuit
(Stephanus de Buriston'.)ⁱ · Guarini Kien.

[207]
Heres Cecilie vxoris · x d. · Terra est contra domum Nicholai
Roberti Diue · filii Bald'.

[208]
Elemosinarius noster · vii d. · De terra que fuit Henrici de
monasterio. 7 pro ea recipit iii
sol.

[209]
Heres Semeri (Johannes · xxii d. · Quorum x d. de terra Semeri.
filius Roberti filii Ricardi)ᵃⁱ · 7 xii d. de Willelmo filio Lamb'.
terre sunt iuxta domum lapideam
Nicholai filii Bald'.

[210]
Moniales de Scapeia · iii sol. · Terra ista iacet iuxta terram Jacobi
de porta. et fuit Wiberti camerarii
de Bello.

[211]
Hospitalarii per manum · xi d. · De terra ubi Lucas mercerius
Roberti filii Ricardi · manet.

[212]
[ ] (Andree.)ᵐʳ
(Johannes Dodekere)ᶜ · xii d. · De terra ubi fuit fabrica Sunwini.
(Heredes Terrici aurifabri.)ᵃⁱ

[213]
Robertus filius Matildis · xviii d. · Terra est iuxta ecclesiam sancti
Andree uersus north.

---

²⁰⁴ See 12 above. · ²⁰⁶ B 6; D 66.
²⁰⁷ 567 below. The house of N. s. of Baldwin is D 67.
²¹⁰ C 16; D 76; G 18 and 569 below; LIII, LIV.
²¹¹ The holding of Luke mercerius may be that in D 72.
²¹² See B 75. This is 530 below. The passage in square brackets (sancti?) has been destroyed by fire.
²¹³ 532 below, and evidently D 108. See B III, 216.

[214]
Arnoldus Ferre

xxi d.

Terre est ex opposito contra domum lapideam (Johannis filii Roberti.)a

[215]
Heres Galfridi
de Bereham

ii sol.

De terra ante portam ubi Simon fenarius manet.

[fol. 5v.] [216]
Jacobus de porta 7
fratres eius

iii sol.

De lescorcherie.

[217]
(Cecilia filia Geroldi)c
(Willelmus Siluestre)i

v sol.
iii d.

De duabus terris quarum una est prope a[   ] iuxta terram filiorum Aluredi de Welles uersus occidentem 7 altera iuxta terram Godsoldi ex altera parte uie uersus suth.

[218]
(Heres Salomonis mercier)c
(Item idem)ai

xiii d.

De cellario suo lapideo.

[219]
Godiech

xx d.

De terra que fuit Ricardi Corbeill' extra Wrgate.

(xlix s. ix d. ob.)am (Summa c 7 ix s. et ii d. ob.)ae

[220]
(Capitulum iii)am
Magister Faraminus

viii d.

Terra est in Ottemed.

[221]
Item idem

ii sol.

Terra est prope ecclesiam sancti Jacobi 7 fuit Estrilde.

[222]
Beringerius filius Goduini

xii d.

---

214 D 121. Evework, probably for this holding, is 375 below.

215 D 111, and 536 below.

216 The slaughteryard is D 112, and 29 above, and 296, 359, 539 below. The note 'De lescorcherie' has been added here in error. The ground here is probably D 113, and 540 below (on w. side of Mercery Lane). 'De lescorcherie' is underlined.

217 In B 109, 110; D 104, 106. Evework is 376 below. The passage in square brackets, a[ndresgate?], is destroyed by fire.

219 The second total has been altered.

220 D 237. For Master Feramin, see p. 158.

221 St Jacob's hospital (founded by Feramin) stood at the far end of Wincheap.

222-225 See D 232, n. Lines connect 222 and 225 with 'In Hottemede' in col. 3.

[223]
Willelmus Picot   iii d.ob.   In Hottemede sunt terre iste.
(retro iii ob.)ᵃᵐ

[224]
Godardus frater eius   v d.
(retro i ob.)ᵃᵐ

[225]
Brunman filius Dore   vi d. ob.

[226]
(Item Samuel tinctor)ᵃ   (iiii d.)ᵃ   (De terra quam filia Dore uendidit huic ecclesie.)ᵃ

[227]
Robertus filius Willelmi   xii d.   De terra ubi ipse manet. 7 de terra
de Hottemelne   quam habet in Ottemede.

[228]
Item idem   vi d.

[229]
Item idem   ii d.   De terra Dierremei.

[230]
Guillelmus se stamere   xvii d.   De terra Bald' Caluel iuxta turrim.

[231]
(Relicta Æilmeri le   xii d.   (De terra que fuit Eilmeri Waldeis)ᵃ
Wald)ᶜ (eis)ᵈ
(Robertus aurifaber)ᵃⁱ

[232]
De terra Milesent   xii d.   De terra (Siredi fullonis.)ᵃⁱ (Turgis
(Robin capelein)ᵃⁱ   que est iuxta terram Henrici Barat in Wenchiape.)ᶜ

[233]
(Willelmus)ᵉ presbiter   xii d.   De terra extra Wergate iuxta fossam del bali.

[234]
Heres Odboldi   xi d.

²²⁷⁻²²⁹ It is difficult to identify these in D owing to repetition of the same names. The scribe of F has become confused as the lines (see below) show, entering the wrong descriptive paragraphs opposite names and rents. F 227 may be 482 below. F 228 may be D 227 and 483 below. Lines connect 227 and 229 with 'De terra ubi' in col. 3, and 228 with 'De terra Dierremei' in col. 3.

²³⁰ 'Turris' is Canterbury Castle.   ²³¹ 509 below; cf. 599 below.
²³² D 199? cf. 592 below.   ²³³ D 207; 504 below.

[235] Item idem	xii d.	
[236] Relicta Æilwordi Pich	v d.	
[237] Heres Willelmi Glouere	v d.	
[238] Petrus janitor de castello	vii d. ob.	De Medlande.
[239] (Reginaldus de Cornhelle	xxvii d.)ae	(Et tantumdem ad reliquos ter-
[240] (Ricardus de castello	xxvii d.)ae	minos de xi acris super)a [ ]
[241] Heres Guillelmi filii Odonis	xviii d.	Terra est in Wenchiape.
[242] Dionisia filia Ruchaued	xiiii d.	De Wodland in Holtege.
[243] Item eadem	vii d. ob.	De terra Roberti spellere.
[fol. 6r.] [244] Alexander filius Wlnoth	ii sol.	De terra Anselmi sacriste que est iuxta terram Æilmeri Waldeis extra Wrgate.
[245] Moniales sancti Sepulcri	iiii d.	De terra Kene que est citra turrim in Hallelanehund'.
[246] (Adam de Cerring'.)c (Vicecomes.)ai	xlii d.	De domo lapidea que fuit Lambini Frese.
[247] (Æiluord Smal(s)ipon	vii d.)c	De uno orto qui est prope Hotte- melne.

---

237 301 below.   238 517 below.

239, 240 See 24 and 25 above. The explanatory note has been damaged by fire. It should prob-ably conclude: 'super[ius notatis].' Lines connect 239 and 240 with '(Et tantumdem' in col. 3.

241 Probably D 178. See 423, 497, 601 below.   242 348 below.

244 D 192.   245 Near the s. end of Castle Street.

246 D 224, and 489 below. xxxv–xxxvii. Adam of Charing enters the story of Becket. See p. 180.

247 487 below. The ground evidently lies within the later Greyfriars' precinct.

[248]
(Cristina vxor Rogeri   j d.)ᶜ   De terra que fuit Goduini Wende-
de Hoiland'.   malt iuxta terram Godardi molen-
                                               dinarii.

[249]
Robertus de Hottewell'   ix d.   De terra que fuit Willelmi de
                                               Plukele 7 est iuxta terram Lambini
                                               Frese uersus north.

[250]
(Lambinus Flemeng   x d.   De terra que fuit Willelmi Picot.
                                               super quam pars domus sue lapidee
                                               stat.)ᵃᵉ

[251]
(Item idem)ᵃᵉ   v d.   De terra eiusdem que est in Hot-
                                               temed.

[252]
Godardus (molendinarius)ᵉ   ix d.

[253]
(Relicta Rogeri Desie)ᶜ   xiiii d. De terra sua Binnewith.
(Petrus cordewanier)ᵃⁱ

[254]
Heredes Willelmi (7   xviii d. Terra est in Therne.
Godefridi)ᵃⁱ de Ailwortun'

[255]
Osbernus (Willelmus Drauet)ᵃⁱ   xii d.   De terra que fuit Wlf ketel iuxta
                                               domum Spange.

[256]
Filie Æilredi Prude   v d.

[257]
(Agatha filia Gileberti   xii d.   Terra est iuxta ostium ecclesie
de Sarneis)ᶜ   sancte Margarete.
(Milo de balneario)ᵃⁱ

[258]
(Johannes le Volt)ᶜ   ii sol.   De terra Liueue de fonte iuxta
(Goldwinus mercier)ⁱ   Hottemelne.

[259]
Elemosinarius noster   ii sol.

---

[249] D 228; and 484 below. Ground of L. Frese is 246 above.   [250] See D 258, n.
[251] Probably D 239.   [253] Probably D 232. Cf. 355.
[254] D 260.   [255] D 225, and 491 below.
[256] D 252, and 494 below.   [257] D 266, and 495 below.
[258] D 247, 271; and 479 below. See 54 above.

[260]
Simon filius Wictgari 7   ii sol.   Terra est prope Hottemelne. 7
frater eius   fuit Æilredi Snake presbiteri.

[261]
Item idem   xi d.

[262]
Simon Munin   iii sol.   Terra est in Andresgate iuxta
(   )ᵈ   domum nostram lapideam.

[263]
Relicta Johannis filii   iii sol.   De terra ubi camera eius est. inter
Viuiani   domum suam et domum Tieberge
                                                        ad Andresgate.

[264]
Item eadem   xv d.   De terra que est retro domum
                                                        propriam ubi pomerium eius est in
                                                        Andresgate.

[265]
Johannes Albus   xvi d.   Terra est contra carcerem uersus
                                                        aquilonem.

[266]
(Relicta Aluredi Gosse)ᶜ   vi d.   Terra est prope ecclesiam sancte
(Heredes Reginaldi Blundi)ᵃⁱ   Marie que quondam lignea fuit.

[267]
Walterus presbiter   vi d.   De terra Æstrilde infra Wergate.

[268]
(Willelmus le Noble)ᵃ   xii d.   De quodam mesagio in Wen-
                                                        chiape. quod est inter mesagium
                                                        Luce clerici. 7 mesagium Dionisie
                                                        filie Ruchheued.

[fol. 6v.] [269]
Simon filius Wrmenild   vi d.

[270]
Helias se glouere   viii d.   Terre est prope ecclesiam sancte
                                                        Marie de turri.

[271]
(Ricardus juuenis de Wald'   viii)ᵃᵉ d.   De terra que fuit Gunnilde de
                                                        Hethe.

---

²⁶⁰ D 277, and 478 below. See 635 below.   ²⁶¹ D 278.
²⁶² 477 below. See D 116 n.   ²⁶³ D 286, and 349 below.
²⁶⁴ D 287.   ²⁶⁵ D 120.
²⁶⁶ D 160. 'Eccl. sancte M. . . . lignea', i.e. St Mary Bredin.
                                                  ²⁶⁸ 520 below.
²⁷⁰ D 221. 'Eccl. sancte M. de turri', i.e. St Mary de Castro.
                                                  ²⁷¹ 541 below.

[272] Ælfegus King	xii d.	De Wodland. De terra que fuit Roberti spellere.
[273] Basilia relicta Hugonis filii Euerard (Heredes Terrici aurifabri.)ai	xix d.	Terra iacet infra Burgate retro clocarium nostrum.
[274] Heredes Heilewis de Westgat'.	iii sol. ob.	(De terra proxima terre que fuit Bartholomei Berebred uersus west.)a
[275] Heredes Geruasii de Ospreng'.	ii d.	
[276] Heredes Hagemundi	vi d.	Terra est extra Radegate.
[277] Geruasius sefugel (Releuium retro.)acm	ii sol.	De terra Æduardi Cattebite que est extra Radingate citra barram sancti Sepulcri.
[278] Reginaldus Blundus	(v)e ii. d.	De terra que fuit Roberti le mederere.
[279] Hugo de Forduic	xv d.	
[280] (Godelief filia)ae (Salomonis)ai de Forduic	xv d.	Terra est in Forduic iuxta Gidhalle. [sic]
[281] Heres Wace de Cherteham	xii d.	Hanc terram emit Wace de Roberto Pin in Cherteham.
[282] (Heres Alexandri filii Reimunt)c (Robertus Tolekere.)ai	iiii d.	(De terra proxima que fuit Osberti Chide extra Burgate.)a

272 Probably D 187. The passage 'retro . . . nostrum' is underlined.
273 See C 3 n., LVI.   274 D 300.   275 D 387.
277 D 155.   278 D 151, and 571 below.
280 Fordwich was the port of Canterbury. This seems to be the earliest reference to its Gild-hall. Lines connect 279 and 280 with the word 'Terra' in col. 3.
282 B 196; D 83.

[283]
(Walterus pistor)ᵃᵉ   (ix d.)ᵃ

[284]
(Willelmus et Walterus   vii d.)ᵃ   (De molendino Guthwaldi.)ᵃ

[285]
(Reginerus molendinarius   xv d.)ᵃ
(xvii s. iii ob.)ᵃᵐ (Summa tercii capituli lxx sol. ix d. ob.)ᵃ
(Summa tocius in media quadragesima
    xiii lib. v sol. v d. ob. exceptis terris desertis)ᵃ

[fol. 7r.] [286]
Geruasius Hog   xii d.   Terra est apud Horsfalde.

[287]
Jordanus de Langebreg'   iiii d.   De duabus mansuris que iacent
                                                       contra molendinum domini archie-
                                                       piscopi 7 nostrum uersus orientem.

[288]
Relicta Simonis de   x d.   De terra que fuit Thome de orto in
pistrino   Bageberi.

[289]
Wluitha uidua   x d.

[290]
Simon de Lindeseia   v d.

[291]
(Gilebertus de Bereham   vi d.)ᵃ

[292]
Nicholaus filius Bald'   ii sol.   De mansura sua ubi manet.

[293]
(Heres Willelmi filii   vi d.
Henrici aurifabri.)ᶜ
(Hamo de Ewerlande)ᵃⁱ

[294]
(Heres Salomonis merceir)ᶜ   x sol.   Terra est iuxta ecclesiam sancti
(Willelmus Siluestre)ⁱ   7 tantumdem   Andree uersus north.
                                     ad festum
                                     sancti Michaelis

---

²⁸³⁻²⁸⁵ For Guthwold's mill see 574–78 below. In 285 the totals have been extensively
erased and rewritten. The figure 5d. in the total for all Lent has been altered from 4d. Lines
connect 282–4 with 'De molendino' in 284, col. 3.

²⁸⁶ The heading destroyed here by fire must be 'Pascha'.

²⁸⁷ B 42. These mills were at Barton, half a mile from Northgate.

²⁸⁸⁻²⁸⁹ B 54, 55; D 26–28; 468, 469 below. Lines connect 288, 289 with 'De terra' in col. 3.

²⁹⁰ n. 32 above.   ²⁹¹ 555 below.   ²⁹² D 67.   ²⁹⁴ B 81; D 109; 533 below.

[295]
(Johannes Dodekere)ᶜ   iiii sol.   De terra que est iuxta magnam
(Heredes Terrici   ix d.   stratam uersus east contra terram
aurifabri)ªⁱ   nostram que est in corueseria citra
                                                       illam uersus west mediante uenella.

[296]
Jacobus portarius 7   v sol.   Et tantumdem ad tres reliquos
fratres eius   terminos anni.

[297]
Osbertus filius Goduini   xii d.   Terra est in Therne.

[298]
(Lambinus Sponge   viii d.)ᶜ   De terra que est ex opposito contra
                                                       domum lapideam que fuit Lambini
                                                       Frese.

[299]
Lambinus Flameng   xl d.   De domo lapidea que est ex oppos-
                                                       ito mediante strata contra domum
                                                       lapideam Roberti de Paris.

[300]
(Beatrix relicta Salomonis.   v d.)ª
                                                       Terra est iuxta turrim.
[301]
(Robertus filius   v d.)ª
Willelmi glouere

[302]
Heredes Meineri diuitis.   iii d.   Terra est retro pistrinum suum.

[303]
(Johannes mercier)ᶜ   xv d.   Terra est super Sturam iuxta
(Stephanus de   terram que fuit Ricardi Corbeille.
Buristune.)ªⁱ   7 totidem ad festum sancti Michae-
                                                       lis. 7 damus inde xxv d. Roberto
                                                       scriptori de Hakint'.)ª

[304]
(Johannes filius)ªⁱ   vi d.ob.   Extra Wrgate.
Hamo(nis)ª tector(is)ª
(de Wenchiape)ª

---

²⁹⁵ See 30 above, n. 'Corueseria' is underlined.
²⁹⁶ See 29 above.
²⁹⁸ See 110 above.
²⁹⁹ Connected with 250 above. It is 485 below.
³⁰¹ See 237 above, n. Lines connect 300 and 301 with 'Terra' in col. 3.
³⁰² Connected with D 211.
³⁰³ D 212; C 7; G 7, 10; 514 below.

[305]
(Terra Lefwini carpentarii.   xl d.   Hanc terram custodit monacus ille qui habet anniuersaria in custodia.)a

[306]
(Willelmus bracur   viii d.)a   Terra est in parochia omnium sanctorum inter terram Helie parmentarii 7 terram que fuit Reginaldi wlmangere.

[307]
(Relicta)a Henrici   (vi d.)a
sacriste

[308]
Wiulphus filius Meineri   xvi d.   De medietate domus lapidee que est contra pillori.

[309]
(Item idem)a   (xii d.   De terra Karoli de Iecham. Terra est uersus turrim iuxta regiam uiam.)a

[310]
Heres Hugonis fabri   vi d.
(Simon Chich)ai

[311]
Wischard nepos   v d.
Ædmeri (Willelmus Pikace)a

[312]
(Haimo filius   vi d.)a
Roberti de Rodint'

[313]
(Henricus clericus   xii d.)a   (De Holtege.)a

[314]
(Henricus Barath   iiii (d.)i
     7 iii qua.

[315]
(Willelmus filius   (xviii d.   De quadam terra in parochia sancti Ælphegi. que pertinet ad Gildhalle.)a
Baldwini de la Forestalle.)a
(de Cherteham)ai

---

305 D 98; 563 below.
306, 307 See 13 above. Lines connect 306, 307 with 'Terra' in col. 3.
308 D 283.   309 502 below, and possibly D 215.
310 See 189 above, and note.   311 D 219. Possibly 542 below.
312-314 See 36-38 above. Lines connect 312-14 with (De Holtege.)a in col. 3.
315 C 60; D 65; G 60; and 486 below.

[316]
(Fulco de Wenchepe   xv d.)ᵃ

[317]
(Bartholomeus carpentarius   xii d.)ᵃ

[fol. 7v.] [318]
Petrus molendinarius   xii d.

[319]
(Lvcas monetarius   xviii d.)ᵃ

[320]
Magister Radulfus   xii d.   Terra est extra Radingate iuxta
quondam vicearchidiaconus   terram Reginaldi Blundi.

[321]
(Johannes mercerius   v so.   Robertus Fareman.
                                                vi d.)ᵃ

[322]
(Johannes Saule   xl d.)ᵃ

[323]
(Dauid de Burgate   ii sol.   Martinus textor 7 Ricardus frater
                                                eius iiii d.)ᵃ

[324]
(Reginaldus Joie   xii d.)ᵃ

[325]
(Simon fenier   viii s. vi d.   De terra Lefwini decani.)ᵃ
(Svmma lxviij so. 7 ix d. i qua.)ᵃ

[326]
(In ascensione domini)ʳ
Robertus aurifaber   xviii d.   (De terra que fuit Eilmeri le
                                                Wadeis.)ᵃ (Idem xii d. in festo
                                                sancti Johannis.)ᵃ

[327]
Æilwinus coruesier   xiii d.

[328]
Radulfus de Warewich   ix d.

[329]
Henricus Codh   xii d.

[330]
Gunnild Clut   xii d.
(Johannes filius)ᵃⁱ

---

³¹⁶⁻³¹⁷ See 41–47, above.   ³¹⁸ See 33 above, n.   ³²⁰ D 150.
³²¹⁻³²⁴ See 41–47 above.   ³²⁵ 56 above. ix d. in the total has been altered from v d.
³²⁶⁻³³⁴ See 1–9 above.

[331]
Turbertus presbiter   xx d.
(Thomas filius eius)ai

[332]
Henricus filius   xii d.
Eilbricti

[333]
Ælfwin(i)ae le ca(r)itere   xii d.
(Henricus filius)ai

[334]
(Petrus filius Warini)c   xv d.
(Johannes filius Roberti
filii Ricardi.)ai
(Summa x sol. 7 iii d.)a

[335]
(Ad Pentecosten)r
Heres Odboldi   iiii sol.   De quinque mansuris supra-
                                            iiii d.   nominatis in purificatione sancte
                                                         Marie.

[fol. 8r.] [336]
(Ad festum sancti Johannis Baptiste.)r
Lefstanus de Horsfalde   iii sol.
                                                         Terre sunt apud Horsfalde.
[337]
Thomas filius Ernoldi   ix d.

[338]
Godelief relicta   xvi d.
Ædwini parmentarii   et tantumdem ad natale domini.

[339]
Willelmus de elemosinaria   viii d.   De terra que fuit Holeman.

[340]
Relicta Nigelli filii   xii d.   Terra ista est contra aque nostre
Alberici aurifabri   ductum.

[341]
(Simon de Lindesie   v d.)ae

[342]
(Salomon de Sesautre)ae   ix d.   De terra que adiacet domui lapidee
                                                         Willelmi fabri.

---

335 55 above.   337 19 above. Lines connect 336 and 337 with 'Terre' in col. 3.
338 20 above.   339 49 above.   340 Close to site of 95 above.
341 See 32 above, n.   342 See 21 above.

[343]
Relicta Galfridi marescalli   v d.   De terra extra Norgate que est iuxta terram que fuit Sunewini carnificis uersus west.

[344]
(Reginaldus de Cornhelle   xxvii d.)ᵃ

    (De terra que fuit Cristine filie Brithweue de Wenchiape.)ᵃ

[345]
(Ricardus de castello   xxvii d.)ᵃ

[346]
(Robertus aurifaber   xii d.   De terra que fuit Eilmeri le Wadeis.)ᵃ

[347]
(Heres Milesenth)ᶜ   viii d.   De terra Turgis.
(Robin capelein)ᵃⁱ

[348]
Dionisia filia Rucheued   xiiii d.   Extra Wrgate de Wodland.

[349]
Relicta Johannis   v sol.   De terra Tieberge iuxta cameram
filii Viuiani   suam lapideam.

[350]
Petrus molendinarius   xii d.

[351]
Robertus filius Emme   xx d.   De terra que est iuxta terram que
    7 tantumdem   est Thome filii Johannis filii Rob-
    ad festum   erti super uenellam qua itur uersus
    sancti Michaelis   suth.

[352]
(Gaufridus de Settinge.)ᵃᵉ   iii sol.   De terra quadam que pertinet ad
    j d.   socam sancti Martini. 7 est contra
    ecclesiam sancti Martini super uiam
    a meridie.

[353]
Cecilia filia Edieue   vi d.   De terra que fuit Aschetilli belli.
(Stephanus presbiter)ᵃⁱ
(Heredes Terrici
aurifabri)ᵃⁱ

---

³⁴³ See 101 above for holding of Sunwin the butcher.
³⁴⁴ For this and 345 see 24, 25 above, n. Lines connect 344 and 345 with 'De terra, etc.' in col. 3.
³⁴⁶ See 26 above, n.   ³⁴⁸ 242 above.   ³⁴⁹ See 263 above, n.
³⁵⁰ See 33 above, n.   ³⁵¹ D 122, and 525 below.
³⁵² Evidently B 66. See C 46; G 46. The words 'ad . . . Martini' are underlined.

[354]
Willelmus Picot   v d.   De Hottemed.
(Lambinus Flemeng)ai

[355]
Relicta Rogeri Desie   vi d.   De terra Binnewith.

[356]
Hugo aurifaber   vi d.   In Therne.

[357]
Frambaldus filius   xii d.   De terra que interiacet domui
Haghenilde   lapidee Wiulphi filii Meineri 7
                                               terre que fuit Emme relicte Bar-
                                               tholomei senescalli.

[358]
(Simon fenier de   viii.
terra Lefwini   sol.
decani   vi d.)a

[359]
Jacobus de porta   v sol.   De escorgeria.
7 fratres eius

[360]
(Haimo filius   vi d.)a
Roberti de Rodint'.

[361]   (De Holtege.)a
(Henricus clericus   xii d.)a

[362]
(Henricus Barath   iiii(d.)i
                                  7 iii
                                  qua.)a

[363]
[E](udo cementarius   ix d.   In Drudint'. de heredibus Edmeri
                                               Chekerel.)a

[364]
[Rob](ertus le batur   viii d.)a
[fol. 8v.] [365]
(Johannes Dodekere)c   iiii sol.
(Heredes Terrici aurifabri)a   ix d.

354 See D 232, n.   355 See 253 above.   356 34 above.   357 See 15 above, n.
358 See 56 above, n.   359 29 above. The word 'escorgeria' is underlined.
360–362 See 36–38 above, n. Lines connect 360–2 with (De Holtege.)a
363 Connected with 98 above.
364 There are further traces of writing (damaged by fire) relating to this entry.
365 See 30 above n.

[366]
(Bartholomeus   xii d.
carpentarius)ᵃ

[367]
Heres Hugonis Fagard   xiii d.   (De terra que fuit Philippi de Hardres.)ᵃ

[368]
(Fulco de Wenchepe.   xv d.)ᵃ

[369]
(Johannes mercerius   v sol.   Robertus Fareman vi d.)ᵃ

[370]
(Dauid de Burgate   ii sol.   Martinus textor 7 Ricardus frater eius. iiii d.)ᵃ

[371]
(Johannes Saule   xl d.)ᵃ

[372]
(Heres Reginaldi Ioie   xii d.)ᵃ
(Svmma lxvi sol. vi d. iii qua.)ᵃ

[373]
(Ad vincula sancti Petri. Evewerc.)ʳ
Heres Johannis filii   vi d.
Viuiani (Susanna)ᵃⁱ

[374]
(Item idem   ii d.)ᵃ

[375]
(Ærnold Ferre   j d.)ᶜ

[376]
Willelmus Siluestr'   ii d.

[377]
Johannes Tretel   j d.

[378]
Salomon Keth   iii ob.

[379]
(Adam caretier)ᶜ   ( )ᵈ   De terra Willelmi Corbin.

---

[366] 46.   [367] See 40 above, n.   [368–372] See 41–47 above.

[372] The total has been extensively altered, the figure given as it now stands. The amount lxvi sol. has been altered from lxiiij sol.

[373] For evework, apparently a commuted agricultural service, see p. 137. In the notes below the numbers refer to sections of F to which evework in question relates, as far as can be traced. 'Evewerc' in the heading is underlined.

[375] 214?   [376] 217.   [378] 75–77?

[379] 73. The amount has been completely erased.

[380]
Godard Picot   j d.

[381]
Item idem   i(ob.)ᵉ

382]
Heres Willelmi   ii d.
de Suliford

[383]
Item idem   j d.

[384]
(Heredes Godieue   j d.)ᶜ
7 Dierewif

[385]
Osbertus filius   ii d.
Heilewis

[386]
Heredes Odboldi   v d. ob.

[387]
Elemosinarius noster   j d.
(de terra que fuit
Stephani clerici)ᵃⁱ

[388]
(Dunstanus filius   (   )ᵈ
Palmere)ᶜ (de terra que
fuit Alepot)ᵃⁱ

[389]
Heres Nigelli   ii d.
filii Albri

[390]
(Radulfus Brabecun)ᶜ   (ob.)ᶜ
(De eadem terra.)ᶜⁱ

[fol. 9r.] [391]
Heres Willelmi parmentarii   ᐧ ob.

[392]
(Johannes frater   (iii ob.)ᵃ
Nicholai monachi)ᶜ
(de terra Matildis)ⁱ

---

³⁸⁰, ³⁸¹ These may relate to D 270.   ³⁸² 92.   ³⁸⁴ 184.   ³⁸⁷ 128.
³⁸⁸ 129. The amount has been completely erased.
³⁸⁹ 451, 452? Identification is difficult as N. f. Albri has interest in many different holdings.
See 104–6 above.   ³⁹¹ See 145, above n.

[393]
Heres Sunewini carnificis j d.
(Augustinus presbiter)ai
(de terra Johannis Rati)ai

[394]
Johannes Dodekere j d.
(de terra Balderi)i

[395]
Simon 7 Johannes filii iii d. (qua.)a
Ædmeri Chekerel
(de terra que est inter
terram Mathei fabri 7
Drutintun'. quam tenet [sic]
de herede Nigelli)i

[396]
Heredes Emme relicte j(d.)a
Bartholomei dapiferi

[397]
Heres Elurici Oker j d.

[398]
Hugo faber ii d.
(Simon Chich)i

[399]
(Johannes filius Thome vi d.)c
tanur

(400]
Heres Cole j ob.

[401]
Eugenia filia iii ob.
Petri clerici

[402]
Heres Alani aldermanni iii d.
(Adam de cruce)i

[403]
(Willelmus Sprot j d.)c
(de terra Gerardi
presbiteri)i

---

³⁹³ 101. 'Johannis' seems to have been altered from Osb. ³⁹⁴ 198.
³⁹⁵ 98. ³⁹⁶ 16? ³⁹⁷ 178. ³⁹⁸ 189, 310?
⁴⁰⁰ 74. The corresponding entry in Y, c. 1216, (fol. 37v.) says that this ground renders eve-work at ½d. as above, and that the nuns of St Sepulchre pay 7d. at Midlent, clearly 74 above.
⁴⁰¹ 182. ⁴⁰² 187. ⁴⁰³ 86, 438.

[404]
Joseph filius Roberge   j d.

[405]
(Heredes Philippi de   ii d.)ᶜ
Chelde

[406]
(Willelmus filius Driu   j d.)ᶜ

[407]
Suanus mercator   ob.

[408]
(De tribus mansuris extra Norgate. quarum unam tenet Radulfus Brabacun. 7
alteram relicta Ædmeri de balneario. 7 terciam filia Lamberti mascun.)ᶜ
Johannes filius   iii d.
Rogeri aldermanni

[409]
Ricardus mascun   j ob.
(Adam capellanus)ᵃⁱ
(de terra Keuerel)ⁱ

[410]
Heredes Huberti Caluel   ii d.
(de terra que est iuxta
terram Petri molendinarii)ⁱ

[411]
Heredes Simonis   ii d.
de Bremlinge
(de terra que fuit
Winedei Litel)ⁱ

[412]
Adam filius Bartholomei   j d.
(de terra que fuit Blanchardi)ⁱ

[413]
(Filia Liefwini Lun3   iiii d.)ᶜ
(Summa de euewerc   iiii sol. iiii d. i qua.)ᵃ

[414]
(Item redditus eadem die)ʳ
Willelmus de elemosinaria   viii d.   De terra Holeman.

---

⁴⁰⁴ 113, 454.   ⁴⁰⁷ Apparently D 52.   ⁴⁰⁸ 116.   ⁴⁰⁹ 93.
⁴¹⁰ Apparently next to 33 above, but not apparently entered in F, apart from here (410).
⁴¹² 68, 441.
⁴¹³ 81. 'euewerc' is underlined. The total has been extensively altered. The amount 4d. has
been altered from 9d. See 418 below.
⁴¹⁴ See 49 above, n. Lines connect 414 and 415 with 'De Terra Holeman'.

[415]
(Heredes Azonis Scage)ᶜ　　　　x d.
(Johannes filius Norman)ᵃⁱ

[416]
Eluiua relicta　　　　vii d.
Randulfi Pardich

[417]
(Johannes Slupe　　　　vi d.)ᵃ

[418]
(Filia Lefwini Lun3　　　　iiii d.)ᵃ
(Summa redditus preter euewer　　ii s. xi d.)ᵃ
(Summa tocius vii sol. iij d. qua.)ᵃ

[fol. 9.v.] [419] [(　　　)ʳ]
Heredes Azonis Scage　　　　x d.　　Terra est iuxta terram Willelmi
　　　　　　　　　　　　　　　　　　de Cherteha[m]　[　　]　man-
　　　　　　　　　　　　　　　　　　suram.

[420]
Johannes filius　　　　xxxii d.　　Terra est iuxta domum suam
Thome Slupe　　　　　　　　　　lapideam uersus suth.

[421]
Heredes Odboldi　　　　xx d.

[422]
Heredes Willelmi　　　　v sol.　　De molendino de Suliford.
de Suliford

[423]
Avitia filia　　　　xvi d.　　Terra est extra Wrgate.
Willelmi filii Odonis

[424]
Heres Hamonis filii　　　　viii d.　　De vii acris extra Wrgate.
Randulfi presbiteri

[425]
(Cristina filia Brictieue)ᶜ　　ii sol.　　De terra Henrici Cod.
(Relicta Terrici aurifabri)ᵃⁱ

---

⁴¹⁵ See 48 above, n.　　　　　　　　　　　⁴¹⁶ See 188 above, n.
⁴¹⁸ The same entry, cancelled, is 413 above. 'euewer' is underlined.
⁴¹⁹ See 48 above n. The passage in brackets is destroyed by fire. The heading 'Terminus natiuitatis beate Marie' occurs at the head of the corresponding group of rents in Y (fol. 38v.).
⁴²⁰ D 318.
⁴²¹ Apparently the small island outside Westgate covered by 55 and 335, above.
⁴²² Suliford is Shelford, west of the river below Canterbury.
⁴²³ See 241 above, and 497 and 601 below. Probably D 178.
⁴²⁴ The ground called 'Seven Acres' beyond Worthgate is covered by 601–6 below, but this does not appear therein.　　　⁴²⁵ 23 above. Lines connect 'ii sol,' with col. 3 in 425, 426.

[426]
Osbertus filius   ii sol.   In Wenchiape.
Goduini tanur

[427]
(Robertus aurifaber)ᵃᵉ   ii sol.   De terra que fuit Eilmeri Waldeis.

[428]
(Bartholomeus carpentarius   xii d.)ᵃ
Summa xix sol. ii d.

[429]
(Ad festum sancti Michaelis)ʳ
(i capitulum)ᵐʳ
Serlo machun   ii sol.

[430]
(Emma de Horsfolde)ᵃᵉ   iiii d.   Terra est apud Horsfalde.

[431]
Willelmus filius   xii d.   De domo lapidea ubi ipse manet.
Aluredi fabri

[432]
Salomon Flemeng   vi d.   De terra quadam in Trutindune.

[433]
Alitia filia Wiberti Kide   xxx d.   Terra est iuxta terram Willelmi
                                               pistoris que est uersus suth. 7
                                               terram Willelmi Brabacun que
                                               est uersus west.

[434]
Heredes Salomonis Turte   iii ob.   De fabrica extra Norgate quam
                                               Radulfus faber tenuit.

[435]
Moniales de sancto   xxxvii d.
Sepulcro

[436]
Michael Bon Enfant   v d.

[437]
Jordanus de coquina   xii d.   De parua terra iuxta Bertonam.

---

⁴²⁷ 26 above.   ⁴²⁸ 46 above.
⁴²⁹ 70 above. The heading is written in the second principal hand of this rental. See 536
below, n.
⁴³⁰ For Horsefalde see 19 above, n.   ⁴³¹ 94 above.   ⁴³² 96 above.
⁴³³ See 78 above, n.   ⁴³⁴ B 8.   ⁴³⁵ 108 above.
⁴³⁶ See 84 above, n.

[438]
Willelmus Sprot (viiii)ᶜ De terra quadam extra Norgate
(ix)ᵃᵢd. que fuit Gerardi presbiteri. (cum
euewerc.)ᵃ

[439]
(Heredes Walteri Bes)ᵃ vi d.

[fol. 10r.] [440]
Robertus le Blund xx d. De terra que iacet iuxta terram
[   ].

[441]
Adam filius xxxii()ᵈd. In Bageberi. In angulo iuxta uiam.
Bartholomei coci

[442]
Item idem (xii d.)ᵃ

[443]
Heredes Simonis ix d. Terra est in Drutintun' contra
parmentarii terram que fuit Ædmeri Chekerel.

[444]
Heredes Hugonis de aula ix d. Terra est extra Norgate iuxta
mansuram Ædmeri Chekerel.

[445]
(Henricus filius Ailmeri)ᵃᵉ ix d.(ob.)ᵃ

[446]
(Walterus filius Eilmeri ix d. ob.)ᵃ

[447]
Hugeloth se Frode xii d. In Drutintune.

[448]
Relicta Gaufridi v d.
marescalli

[449]
Rodbertus Pin ii d. (De terra Alepot.)ᵃ

[450]
Thomas filius iiii d. De terra matris sue.
Reginaldi aurifabri

[451]
Relicta Nigelli filii Albri xii d.

---

⁴³⁸ See 86 above, n.
⁴⁴⁰ See 89 above, n. The passage within square brackets has been destroyed by fire.
⁴⁴¹ See 68 above, n.   ⁴⁴³ D 35.   ⁴⁴⁴ 58 above.
⁴⁴⁵⁻⁴⁴⁷ See 65–67 above, n.   ⁴⁴⁹ Probably D 335.   ⁴⁵⁰ 127 above.
⁴⁵¹, ⁴⁵² See 104–6 above, n.

[452]
Item eadem   iiii d.   De terra Herloc.
                                             ob.

[453]
Radulfus Brabecun   (x)ᵃᵉ ii d. (7 ob.)ᵃ

[454]
Joseph filius Roberge   xii d.
                                     7 tantumdem
                                     ad mediam
                                     quadragesimam

[455]
Bartholomeus faber   xii d.   De terra Herloc.

[456]
Reinerus (7 frater   (x)ᵃᵉ viii d.
eius)ᶜ (de Northwode)ᵃ

[457]
Item idem   (iiii)ᵃᵉ d.

[458]
(Johannes de Norewde)ᵃᵉ   x d.

[459]
Heres Johannis filii Walteri   xv d. ob.
pistoris
Item idem   iiii sol.   (Ex his soluti sunt ii s. viii d.)ᵃ

[460]
Robertus de porta   xx d.   De terra Vauesur.
infirmorum   7 tantumdem
                                     ad mediam
                                     quadragesimam

[461]
Relicta Roberti Godiuere   ii sol.

[462]
Rogerus filius Marie   vi d.   Terra iacet retro murum ele-
Wido clericus   mosinarie nostre. iuxta stabulum
                                                         domini archiepiscopi.

[463]
Robertus cognatus Gileberti   xii d.   Terra est ante ostium ecclesie de
de Taneth   Norgate iuxta terram Roberti de
                                                         porta.

---

⁴⁵³ 22 above.   ⁴⁵⁴ 113 above.   ⁴⁵⁵ See 104–6 above, n.
⁴⁵⁹ The payment of 15½d. is noted at 64 above.   ⁴⁶⁰ 114 above.   ⁴⁶¹ 115 above.
⁴⁶² D 1. See G 23, G 22. The words 'Retro . . . archiepiscopi' are underlined.
⁴⁶³ 119 above.

[464]
(Petrus)ᵃᵉ (cordewanier)ᵃ — (xiiij d.)ᵃ — Terra est supra Sturam ultra Ottemell'. Binnewith.

[fol. 10v.] **[465]**
De terra Willelmi vigilis (relicta Roberti le sacur)ᵃ — vi d.

[466]
Willelmus frater Johannis de Bremble — vi d. — De terra que fuit Wimundi le mercier in Drutintune.

[467]
Adam Corbin — ii sol. — Terra est iuxta terram Willelmi pictoris filii D[r]iu.

[468]
Wluiua relicta Goduinet — x d.

In Bageberi de terra que fuit Thome de orto.

[469]
Simon de pistrino — x d.

[470]
(Ricardus filius Ricardi de Burgate)ᶜ (Heredes Terrici aurifabri)ᵃⁱ — xvj d. 7 tandumdem ad mediam quadragesimam

[471]
Heres Willelmi parmentarii — xviii d. ob. — Terra est contra ecclesiam sancti Petri.

[472]
Heredes Odboldi — xii d. — De terra Goduifie que data fuit cum Wiberto monacho. et est iuxta domum Roberti filii Ricardi. Et damus inde v d. heredibus Wlbaldi de Herebaldune.

[473]
(Editha filia Suin)ᵃᵉ — v(iij)ᵃᵉ (d.)ᵃ

[474]
Johannes filius Thome Slupe — iii sol.

---

⁴⁶⁴ Possibly 11 above.   ⁴⁶⁵ 112 above.   ⁴⁶⁶ See 61, 62 above, n.
⁴⁶⁷ 73 above.   ⁴⁶⁸, ⁴⁶⁹ See D 26–28, note.   ⁴⁷¹ 145 above.
⁴⁷² Ground of Odbold next to St Peter's is mentioned at D 312. See C 31; G 32.
⁴⁷⁴ 133 above.

[475]
Humfridus   xviij d.
vicealdermannus   7 tantum
(releuium retro)[am]   ad mediam
quadragesimam

[476]
Petrus   xii d.
molendinarius   7 tantum
ad tres relinquos
terminos

[477]
Simon Munin   iii sol.   De terra Radulfi de Wingeham. 7 est a(d)[ai] Andresgate contra ecclesiam sancte Marie.

[478]
Simon de Boctune   ii sol.   Terra est in uico sicut itur a(d)[i] Hottemell'.

[479]
(Johannes le Volt)[c]   ii sol.   De terra que fuit Liuiue ad fontem.
(Goldwinus mercier)[i]
(xxi s. 7 (viij d.)[i] ob.)[am] (Summa Lxi sol. viii d. 7 ob.)[a]

[480]
(Capitulum ii)[mr]
Relicta Johannis filii
Viuiani   xlii d.

[481]
Henricus filius   vi d.   Terra est contra terram Godardi
Dieremei   molendinarii.

[482]
Heres Roberti   xii d.   In Hottemelle.
filii Willelmi

[483]
Item idem   vi d.   De terra que fuit Dieremei.

[484]
Item idem   ix d.   De terra Willelmi de Plukele.

[485]
Lambinus Flameng   xl d.

[475] 147 above.   [476] See 33 above, n.   [477] 262 above.
[478] 260 above.   [479] 258 above. The second total has been extensively altered.
[480] 28 above.   [481] See 227-9 above.   [482] 227 above?
[483] See 228 above, n.   [484] See 249 above, n.   [485] 299 above.

[486]
(Willelmus filius Bald' de   xviii d.   (De quadam terra in parochia
la Forestalle.)ª (de   sancti Ælphegi [   ] pertinet
Cherteham)ai   ad [   ]halle.)ª

[fol. 11r.] [487]
(Relicta Æilwardi   vii d.)c   De quodam orto prope Hottemell'.
Smalpon

[488]
(Adam mercier)ae   viii d.   De mansura que iacet contra dom-
                                                um lapideam que fuit Lambin Frese.

[489]
Adam de Cerringe   xlii d.   De domo lapidea que fuit Lambin
(vicecomes)ai   Frese.

[490]
Osbernus filius   xii d.   Terra est in uico qui dicitur
Goduini tanur   Therne.

[491]
(Willelmus Drauet)ae   xii d.   De terra Wlfketel iuxta domum
                                                Spange.

[492]
Beringerus filius   xii d.   De terra que est proxima iuxta
Goduini filii   terram Martini.
Eue

[493]
Adam le mercier   xv d.   De terra que fuit Reingard 7
                                                iacet iuxta domum lapideam Lam-
                                                bini Flameng.

[494]
Filii Æilredi se Prude   v d.   Terra non longe est ab ecclesia
                                                sancte Margarete uersus suth.

[495]
Agatha de Sarnais   xii d.   Agatha de domo lapidea iuxta
                                                ecclesiam sancte Margarete.

[496]
Relicta Rogeri se Desie   v d.   De loco ubi Hottemelne fuit. (de
                                                terra que fuit Willelmi de Plukele
                                                in Ottemell'.)c

---

486 315 above. The passages within square brackets have been destroyed by fire. They may
be restored by reference to 315 above.
487 247 above.   488 110 above.   489 246 above.   491 255 above.
492 See 222 above, n.   493 109 above.   494 256 above.
495 257 above. The name Agatha (second instance) is underlined.
496 D 231. Hottemelne is underlined.

[497]
Auitia filia Willelmi   xviii d.   Terra est in Wenchiape.
filii Odonis

[498]
(Heres Willelmi Winedei)c   xxx d.   Extra Wrgate ultra Holtege.
(Johannes de Dudindale)ai

[499]
(Reginaldus de Cornhelle   xxvii d.)ae
                                               (De Medlande.)a
[500]
(Ricardus de castello   xxvii d.)ae

[501]
Elemosinarius noster   ii sol.   De terra que fuit Roberti le seleir
                                               prope Ottemelne. (quam Gold-
                                               vinus mercier tenet.)a

[502]
Heres Karoli de Iecham   (xii)aed.   Terra est uersus turrim in regia
(Wiulphus filius Meineri)ai   uia iuxta domum Fulconis textoris.

[503]
(Item idem   iiii d.   De ortulo quodam iuxta Halis-
                                               tane.)c

[504]
(Robertus)c (Willelmus)ai   xii d.   Terra est extra (Wrgate)e iuxta
presbiter (releuium retro)am   fossam del bali.

[505]
(Item idem)a   (respondet de quodam mesagio
                                               iuxta sanctum (Sepulcrum.)e
                                               Quere cum redditu (Wiberti
                                               prioris)e)a

[506]
Haimo tector   vii d.   Extra Wrgate.

[507]
Relicta Osberti   vii d. ob.   Terra est extra Wrgate.
Preth (Johannes Turte)ai

[508]
Willelmus de Ottemelle   v d.   De terra que fuit Osberti Preth.

---

497 See 241 above.
498 May be connected with D 183. An attempt has been made to erase the tenant's name.
499, 500 See 24, 25 above, n. Lines connect 499 and 500 with (De Medlande).a
501 54 above.   502 309 above.   504 233 above.
505 This should appear among Wibert's rents (608–69 below) but it is not possible to identify
it there.
506 Possibly D 203.   507 27 above.   508 197 above.

[509]
R(obertus aurifaber)ᵃᵉ   xii d.   De terra (que fuit Eilmeri le Wadeis.)ᵃᵉ

[510]
Dauid de Wertinge   x d.   Terra est in Ottemellane iuxta domum Malet.

[511]
(Stephanus filius Osb' de sancto Laurencio   xii d. ob.)ᵃ   (De terra que fuit Rogerii aldermanni de Radingate)ᵃ

[512]
(Willelmus filius Johannis aldermanni de Rading'   xviii d.)ᵃ

[fol. 11v.] [513]
Relicta Wlnothi   ii sol.   De terra Anselmi sacriste.

[514]
(Johannes mercier)ᶜ   xv d.   Terra est super Sturam iuxta
(Stephanus de Buristune)ⁱ   7 tantumdem ad Pascha   terram que fuit Ricardi Corbeill'. 7 damus pro ea Roberto scriptori xxv d. ad duos terminos.

[515]
Sinothus molendinarius   iiii d. ob.   De terra Wimundi monachi uersus turrim in Wrgate berthe.

[516]
Petrus janitor de castello   iiii d. ob.

[517]
Idem   vii d. ob.   De Medland que fuit Johannis filii Geroldi.

[518]
Dionisia filia Ruchefed   vii d. ob.   In Holtege iuxta terram Roberti spellere.

[519]
Willelmus se stamere   xvii d.   Terra est iuxta castellum.

---

[509] 231 above.   [510] 196 above.   [511], [512] 190, 191 above.

[513] Probably B 101, ground of A. the sacrist within Newingate, close to that of Hamo the provost. (See B 100, 101), which according to B 213 is next to that of alderman Wlnoth.

[514] 303 above.

[515] Lines connect 515, 516 with 'De terra' in 515, col. 3.

[517] 238 above.

[518] This must lie in Wincheap. Cf. 242, 348 above.

[520]
Willelmus le noble   xii d.   (De quodam mesagio in Wen-
                                               chiape quod est inter mesagium
                                               Luce clerici 7 mesagium Dionisie
                                               filie Ruchheued.)ᵃ

[521]
Heres Suani mercatoris   xxi d.   Terra est extra Niewegate iuxta
                                               terram que fuit Æilrici soker.

[522]
Hugo faber   iiii d.
(Simon Chich)ⁱ

[523]
(Aluredus de Steuerl(i)nge   xviii d.)ᵃ

[524]
Filie Sedewini   xv d.   De tercia mansura a predicta
                                               uersus suth. (extra)ᵃᵉ Niwegate.

[525]
(Robertus)ᶜ filius   xx d.
Emme (Baldewinus
de Hee)ᵃⁱ

[526]
Heredes Odboldi   viii sol.   In Ritherchiape de terra que fuit
                                   iiii d.   Eadwordi Stocche. in qua sunt
                                               ix mansure. 7 due illarum iacent
                                               iuxta domum Nigelli piscatoris
                                               uersus orientem. 7 due inter duas
                                               mansuras que fuerunt Alani al-
                                               dermanni. 7 quinque iacent post
                                               predictam terram que fuit Alani.
                                               7 extenduntur uersus orientem
                                               usque ad terram quam Reulinus
                                               tenuit de sancto Augustino.

[527]
(Alanus)ᶜ (Thomas)ᵃⁱ   vi d.   Terra est iuxta ecclesiam sancti
de Rethlinge   Georgii uersus west.

[528]
(Dauid de Burgate   ii sol.)ᵃ

[520] 268 above.   [521] Possibly D 132. Cf. 178 above. See B 94 n.
[522] Probably connected with 189 above.   [523] 185 above.
[524] 186 above.   [525] 351 above.   [526] B 99; D 138.
[527] 195 above.   [528] See D 95 n.

[529]
Robertus Polre   (ii sol.)ae   Terra est iuxta domum ubi manet. 7 est inter terram que fuit Goduini fabri. 7 terram Wlnothi alder- manni.

[530]
(Johannes Dodekere)c   xii d.   De terra ubi fuit fabrica Sunwini.
(Heredes Terrici aurifabri)ai

[531]
(Item idem)c   iiii sol.
(Heredes Terrici   ix d.
aurifabri)ai
(xxxii s. ix d.)am (summa lxxii sol. vii d.)a

[532]
(Capitulum iii)amr
Robertus   xviii d.   De domo lapidea. que est contra
camberlangus   ecclesiam sancti Andree.

[533]
Willelmus Siluestre   x sol.   Terra est contra ecclesiam sancti
(retro ii sol.)am   Andree ubi manet. que fuit Sal- omonis le mercier.

[534]
(Robertus Faraman   vi d.)a

[535]
(Martinus textor 7   iiij d.)a
Ricardus frater eius

[536] [fol. 12r.]
Galfridus de Bereham   ii sol.   De terra que est iuxta domum
                                   nostram.

[537]
Relicta Godardi uphalder'   xx d.   Terra est iuxta domum lapideam
                                   Johannis Dodekere.

[538]
(   )d

[539]
Jacobus de porta   v sol.   Et tantum ad tres reliquos ter-
7 fratres eius   minos.

---

529 See 50, above, n.   530 See 212 above, n.
531 30 above. The second total has been extensively altered.   532 213 above.
533 294 above.   534 See 40 above, n.
536 215 above. The second principal hand of this rental starts here.
537 D 102.   538 The whole entry has been erased.   539 29 above.

[540]
Item idem iii sol. Terra est in Merceria cuius partem ipsi tenent 7 Hugo aurifaber partem.

[541]
Ricardus (juuenis de viii d. De terra que fuit Gunnild' de Wald')ae Hethe.

[542]
(Radulfus Colekin)c v d.
(Willelmus Pikace)a

[543]
Hamo de Ewerlande vi d. De terra quadam uersus suth que est iuxta subscriptam.

[544]
Item idem x d. Terra ( )d est contra terram que fuit Frecheric.

[545]
Item idem xii d.

[546]
(Heredes Walteri xii d. De terra que fuit magistri Augus-Bes)ae tini.

[547]
(Item idem iii d. De terra que fuit Bartholomei fabri.)a

[548]
Rogerus marescallus xxviii d. De terra que fuit Liece.

[549]
Willelmus Braszur (ii s. Terra est iuxta terram Helye
iiii d.)ae pelliparii que fuit Garini Kie(n).ae
(Cecilia filia Malgeri xii d.)a

[550]
Robertus scriptor xxvii d. De terra que fuit (Arnoldi Chigh.)ae
Iudeorum

[551]
(Item idem)ac (ix d.)c

[552]
(Johannes filius Roberti (viii)aed. (De terra proxima predicte terre.)a
filii Ricardi)ae

---

540 See 216 above, n.   541 271 above.   542 See 311 above.
543 163 above.   544 162 above.   548 31 above.
549 13 above. Lines connect 549 and 550 with 'Terra' in col. 3.
550 165 above.   552 167 above.

[553]

(Terricus aurifaber)ᵃ	iii (sol.)ᵃ	(De terra que est inter terram que
Item idem	xii d.	fuit Roberti filii Ricardi 7 terram
		heredum Reginaldi Blundi.)ᵃ

[554]

Item idem	v sol.	(De terra super quam magna
		domus lapidea fundata est contra
		scopas Roberti abbatis.)ᵃᵉ

[555]

(Gilebertus de Bereham	vi d.)ᵃᶜ

[556]

Johannes mercerius	v sol.

[557]

(Robertus glouere	v d.)ᵃ

[558]

(Johannes Saule)ᵃᵉ	xl d.

[559]

(Hugo longus	xiiij d.)ᵃ

[560]

Heres Ioie	xii d.

[561]

Anfridus 7 frater eius	xxx d.	Terra est a(d)ᵃⁱ Burgate iuxta
		scoppas nostras.

[562]

(Simon fenier	viii sol.	De terra Lefwini decani.)ᵃ
	vi d.	

[563]

(Terra Lefwini carpentarii	xl d.)ᵃ

[fol. 12v.] [564]

Ingenulfus plumbarius	xviii d.	De terra Normanni patris sui.
(Auicia filia		
Ingenulfi plumbarii)ᵃⁱ		

[565]

Item idem	xviii d.	De quadam particula terre que fuit
(Isabele filia eiusdem		Hamonis de Hunderdune.
Ingenulfi)ᵃⁱ		

[566]

Heres Hugonis Flagard	xix d 7	Terra est iuxta terram Luce mer-
	ob.	cer.

---

⁵⁵³ See 193 above, n.　　⁵⁵⁴ 194 above.　　⁵⁵⁵ 291 above.

⁵⁵⁶⁻⁵⁶⁰ See 41–45, 47 above, n.　　⁵⁶¹ 192 above.　　⁵⁶² See 55 above, n.

⁵⁶³ 305 above.　　⁵⁶⁴ 199 above.　　⁵⁶⁵ 200 above.　　⁵⁶⁶ 203 above.

[567]
Heres (Cecilie)[i] uxoris Roberti   x d.   Terra est contra domum Nicholai
Diue   filii Bald'.

[568]
Relicta Willelmi Palmere   (v)[ae]d.

[569]
Moniales de Scapeie   iii sol.   Et tantumdem ad mediam quadragesimam de quadam domo lapi-
dea in qua Jacobus de porta manet
7 de altera domo ante illam.

[570]
Magister Radulfus   xii d.   Terra est ubi orrea (sunt)[ai] Regin-
vicearchidiaconus   aldi Blundi.

[571]
Reginaldus Blundus   xxi d.   Terra est ubi orrea eius sunt extra
Redingateṿ 7 remanserunt retro
per multos annos xii d.

[572]
(   )[d]
Symon de Lindeseie   v d.

[573]
Cristina filia Radulfi   vii d.   Terra est in Norwuthe ubi mansura sua est.

[574]
(Molendinum Gudwaldi   vi sol.
    7 viii d.)[c]

[575]
(Walterus pistor)[a]   (ix)[e] d.

[576]
Walterus (et)[ai]   vii d.
Willelmus   (De molendino Guthwaldi.)[a]

[577]
(Reginerus molendinarius)[a]   (x)[e]v d.

[578]
Willelmus filius   xxv d.
(Godith)[ai]
(Godelief)[ce]

---

[567] 207 above.   [569] This must be connected with 210 above.
[570] 320 above.   [571] 278 above.
[572] See 32 above, n. There is an extensive erasure above the name of S. de Lindeseie.
[573] 'Northwuthe': Whitstable?
[574-578] See 283-5 above. Lines connect 575-8 with 'De molendino' in col. 3.

[579]
(Lucas monetarius)ae

(xii)c
(xviii)id.

De terra que est iuxta domum
(nostram)i lapideam de Estbrege.

[580]
(Milesent relicta
Ricardi lorimer

xii d.)a

[581]
(Haimo filius
Roberti de Rodint'

vi d.)a

[582]
(Henricus clericus

xii d.)a

(De Holtege.)a

[583]
(Henricus Barath

iiii d.
iii qua.)a

[584]
(Fulco de Wenchape

xv d.)a

(xxi s. x d. iii qua.)am
(Summa tercii capituli iiii lib. ix. sol. viii d. iii qua.)a
(Summa tocius de festo sancti Michaelis xi lib. iiii sol. ii d. iii qua. item xx d.)a
(Summa sine redditu Wiberti prioris xxxvi l. xi s. viii d. ob. de toto anno)a

[fol. 13r.] [585]
(Item ad terminum sancti Michaelis de Wodland extra Wrgate.)r
Petrus de turri

xxi d.

[586]
Item idem

xiii d.

De terra que fuit Johannis filii
Geroldi le tannur.

[587
Heres Johannis filii
Walteri pistoris

vii d. 7
ob.

[588]
Dominus de Tanintune

xii d.

[589]
Eilardus (filius Gileberti
de Ostrinhangre)a

xiii d.

(Hec terra est in Wenchiape. 7
Henricus Barate tenet illam.)a

---

579 See 319 above. The stone house is evidently close to the site of the present G.P.O., near King's, or Eastbridge.

581–583 See 36–38 above, n. Lines connect 581–4 with (De Holtege).a

584 The totals (in many different hands) are extensively erased.

585 For Woodland, the field without Worthgate, see p. 27.

586 See D 197–9 n. Lines connect 585 and 586 with 'De terra' in col. 3.

588 The boundaries of Thanington manor lie adjacent to 'Woodland'.

589 Westhanger, Kent. This is evidently D 200.

[590]
Siricus de Feleberge   xii d.

[591]
Ælfegus King   xvi d.

[592]
Milesent de terra Thurg'   x d.
(Robin capelein)ai

[593]
Gladuse Fair Hege   iiii d.

[594]
(Cristina filia Britief)c   xxi d.   (De terra Henrici Cod.)a
(Relicta Terrici aurifabri)ai

[595]
Osbertus filius   xxi d.
Godwini

[596]
(Goddardus molendinarius   xii d.   De terra Wikinge)a
7 frater eius

[597]
Willelmus filius Godiue   x d.

                                                De eadem terra.

[598]
Godiua de terra Ricardi   x d.
Corbaille

[599]
Relicta Æilmeri Waldeis   iiii d.
(Robertus aurifaber)ai

[600]
De terra Roberti spellere
(Henricus Barat)ai   xii d.
Svmma xvi so. et vi d. 7 ob.

[601] [fol. 13v.]
Item ad terminum sancti Michaelis. Gabulum de vii acris extra Wrgate.
Auicia filia Willelmi   xxxii d.
filii Odonis

---

590 Felborough in Chilham, Kent.   591 May be connected with D 187.
592 Cf. 232 above.   593 D 202.   596 D 201.
597 Lines connect 597 and 598 with 'De eadem' in col. 3.
599 Cf. 231, 509 above.
600 Possibly D 200. The figure vi d. in the total has been altered from xi d.
601 The heading has been partly picked out in red ink. For the field 'Seven Acres', see pp. 26,
188. See 241 above.

[602]
Gunnild relicta Chuut   xxi d.
(heredes Willelmi filii
Gunnilde Clut)ᵃᵉⁱ

[603]
(Wlfeach)ᶜ   viiii d.   (De)ᵃ [*sic*]
(Elueua filia Wlfech)ᵃ

[604]
(Johannes carpentier)ᶜ   viii d.   (De mesagio de quo ipse dat x d.
(Willelmus filius   ad festum sancti Johannis.)ᵃ
Warini)ᵃⁱ

[605]
(Willelmus le Noble)ᵃᵉ   viii d.   (   )ᵈ (quam emit Nigellus monachus ad luminare sancti Stephani.)ᶜ

[606]
(Piroth filius Warini)ᶜ   viii d.
(Johannes filius Roberti
filii Ricardi)ᵃⁱ

[607]
Robertus filius Hamonis   xxxii d.
(de Cokeringe)ᵃ
Svmma ix so. 7 ix d.

[608] [fol. 14r.]
Redditus Wiberti prioris   Ad festum omnium sanctorum.
(Heres Eilrici Hoker)ᶜ   viii d.   De terra Hugonis clerici de Wal-
(Simon Chigh)ᵃⁱ   tham que est extra Niwengate.

[609]
Ad natiuitatem domini
Eadwardus fullo   xviii d.   De terra que est proxima ulteriori
(uinee)ⁱ nostre. Hanc terram emit
prior de Symone de Horsfalde.

[610]
(Columbel clericus   x d. ob.)ᵃ

Et tantumdem ad tres reliquos
[611]   terminos.
(Henricus filius   iiii d.
Warini carpentarii   ob.)ᵃ
Summa ii sol. ix d.

---

⁶⁰² D 172.

⁶⁰³⁻⁶⁰⁶ The descriptive note to 603 is incomplete. For these holdings see A 35, n. See 636–9 below.

⁶⁰⁷ D 177.   ⁶⁰⁸ A 34. See 642, 657 below. See D 130 n.   ⁶⁰⁹ 634, 665 below.

⁶¹⁰, ⁶¹¹ 623, 624; 640, 641; 652, 653, below. Lines connect 610 and 611 with 'Et tantumdem' in col. 3.

[612]
Ad purificationem sancte Marie.

Ælphegus Lamb   vi d.   De terra quam prior emit de
                                            Eadwardo Lamb 7 est in angulo
                                            iuxta domum Lamberti Wrenne.

[613]
Ad mediam quadragesimam.

Johannes filius Beiuin   xxvii d.   De terra (quadam)ⁱ quam prior
                                            emit de Rogero coco apud Burgate.

[614]
(Willelmus le Noble)ᵃᵉ   viii d.

[615]
Heres Odbold   xii d.   De quadam terra apud Hotte-
                                             melne.

[616]
Jordanus frater   xij d. 7
Jonathe clerici   ob.

[617]
Heres Roberti de   iiii sol.   De vii acris apud Muneketune.
Suanetune   7 ii d.

[618]
Ælfred 7 Godardus   v d.   De quadam terra apud Therne.
Huppeheldere (Thomas
mercator)ᵃⁱ

[619]
(Hubertus cordewanier)ᵃ   viii d.   De quadam mansura proxima
                                             predicte quam Radulfus Watkeke
                                             prius tenuit.

[620]
(Robertus aurifaber.   xviii d.)ᵃ
de terra Eilmeri   De (tribus)ᶜ (iiii)ⁱ acris terre quas
Waldeis   prior emit de Gregorio de Kene-
                                             feld.
[621]
Henricus filius   xviii d.)ᵃ
Johannis carpentarii
7 Willelmus filius Warini
(Willelmus filius Warini retro de ix d.)ᵃᵐ
        (Summa xiii sol. ii d. ob.)ᵃ

---

⁶¹² Cf. A 21; B 218.   ⁶¹³ A 23, and appears to be B 86, D 92; it is 658 below.
⁶¹⁵ A 26   ⁶¹⁶ 669 below.   ⁶¹⁷ 661 below; A 36.
⁶¹⁸, ⁶¹⁹ A 27; see D 262, 263; and 662, 663 below.
⁶²⁰, ⁶²¹ These with 666, 667, 668 below, are A 19. Lines connect 620 and 621 with De (tribus)ᶜ
in col. 3.

[622]
(Ad Pascha.)am
Godelief relicta   vi d. 7 ob.   De quadam mansura que est
Salomon mercatoris   scilicet   iuxta domum suam quam prior
                                   Willelmus   emit de Gregorio de Kenefeld.
                                   Siluestre

[623]
(Columbel clericus   x d. ob.)a

[624]
(Henricus filius   iiii d. ob.)a
Warini carpentarii

[625]
Ad festum sancti Johannis Baptiste.
Geruasius filius   vi d.   De terra Bald' Caluel iuxta barram
Seuugel   sancti Sepulchri.

[fol. 14v.] [626]
Heres Osmundi   xii d.
filii Merkere

[627]
(Swanild relicta Eilmeri   vi d.)c
(Eilredi)ci stamere

[628]
(Ricardus Pete   xviij d.)ae   De terra que fuit Willelmi filii
                                                   Sired.

[629]
Robertus P(ollard)ae   xii d.   De eadem terra.

[630]
Johannes filius   iii sol.
Henrici presbiteri

[631]
Emma filia Rogeri   (vi)aed.
attenhelle

[632]
(Heres vxoris Morin)a   (vi d.)a

[633]
Ricardus carpentarius   xii d.(ob.)a

---

622 A 29; B 222; D 110. See 660 below.   623, 624 See 610, 611 above, n.
625 D 144 and 651 below.   626 656 below.   627 645 below.
628 D 147 and 646 below.   629 647 below.   630 655 below.
631 648 below.   632 649 below.   633 654 below.

[634]
Eadwardus fullo   x d.   De terra quadam iuxta uiuarium
                                                nostrum.

[635]
Heredes Wichgari de   vi d.
Boctune
(Simon de la Tune)ai

[636]
(Petrus filius Warini)c   x d.
(Johannes filius
Roberti filii Ricardi)ai

[637]
(Warinus filius   x d.
Johannis carpentarii)c
(Willelmus filius Warini)ai

[638]
(Ricardus caretier   viii d.)c   In Timbercheppe.

[639]
Wlfeach   vii(i)ed.   De quodam orto.

[640]
(Columbel clericus   x d. 7 ob.)a

[641]
Henricus filius   iiii d. 7 ob.)ae
Warini carpentarii

                                                Summa xiij sol. xi d. 7 ob.

[642]
A. Ad uincula sancti Petri.
Heres Elurici Oker   viii d.
(Simon Chich)i

[643]
Otuel de Castwise   vi d.   De quadam terra in Waldo quam
                                                prior emit de quadam femina
                                                nomine Eluiua.

                                                Summa xiiii d.

634 See 609 above, n.
635 May be connected with 260, 261 above.
636–639 See A 35. See 603–6, above.
640, 641 See 610, 611 above, n. The total has been much altered.
642 See 608 above, n. For the significance of the letter A in the margin see 644 below.
643 A 31.

[644]
B. Ad festum sancti Michaelis.
Arnoldus filius Lithulf
(de quodam orto)   vii(i d.)ᵃ

[645]
(Suanild relicta   (vi d.)ᵃᶜ
Eilmeri (Eilredi)ᶜⁱ
stamere)ᶜ

[646]
(Ricardus Pete   xviij)ᵃᵉd.

[647]
Robertus (Pollard)ᵃᵉ   xii d.

[648]
Emma filia Rogeri   (vi)ᵃᵉd.
attehelle

[649]
(Heres uxoris Morin   vi d.)ᵃᵉ
attehelle

[fol. 15r.] [650]
(Maria filia Godelief   viii d.   (De quodam messagio iuxta bar-
attehelle)ᵃ   ram sancti Sepulcri.)ᵃ

[651]
Geruasius filius Seuugel   vi d.

[652]
(Columbel clericus   x d. 7 ob.)ᵃ

[653]
(Henricus filius   iiii d. 7
Warini carpentarii   ob.)ᵃ

[654]
Ricardus carpentarius   xii d. 7 ob.

[655]
Johannes filius   iii sol.
presbiteri

[656]
Heres Osmundi   xii d.
filii Markere

⁶⁴⁴ The scribe has entered payments for St Peter ad Vincula (642, 643) in col. 2 of fol. 15r.
and payments for Michaelmas (644-9) in col. 1. As these are in the wrong order he has added
A (642) and B (644) to indicate correct order, which has been adopted in this edition.
⁶⁴⁵ 627 above.   ⁶⁴⁶ 628 above.   ⁶⁴⁷ 629 above.   ⁶⁴⁸ 631 above.
⁶⁴⁹ 632 above.   ⁶⁵¹ 625 above.   ⁶⁵², ⁶⁵³ See 610, 611 above, n.
⁶⁵⁴ 633 above.   ⁶⁵⁵ See 630, n.   ⁶⁵⁶ 626 above.

[657]
A(dam de cruce filius)ae
Alani aldermanni   (iiii)ae d.

[658]
Johannes Beiuin   xxvii d.

[659]
(Adam filius Eilgari   xxxii d.   De iiiior acris terre in Fordwiz.)c
de Stureie

[660]
Godelief relicta Salomonis   vi d.(ob.)a
mercatoris (Willelmus Siluestre)ai

[661]
Robertus de Suanetune   iiii sol.
                                   et ii d.

[662]
Relicta Alredi uppeheldere   v d.
(Thomas mercator)ai

[663]
(Hubertus cordewanier   viiii d.)a

[664]
(Jacobus de porta   xii d.)ac

[665]
Eadwardus fu(llo)ae   xviii d.

[666]
Robertus aurifaber   xviii d.)a

[667]
(Henricus filius   ix d.)a   (De (tribus)c (iiii)i acris que
Johannis carpentarii   notantur in media quadragesima.)a

[668]
(Willelmus filius   ix d.)a
Warini

[669]
Jordanus frater   xii d. et ob.
Jonathe clerici
(Summa xxv sol. vi d. ob. de termino sancti Michaelis)a
(Summa tocius lix sol. vi d. ob.)a

---

657 See A 34, n.   658 See 613 above, n.   659 A 37.
660 622 above.   661 617 above.   662, 663 See 618, 619 above, n.
665 See 609 above, n.   666–668 See 620, 621 above, n.
669 This is 616 above. The totals have been extensively altered, added to, erased, etc.

Rental G

A list of outpayments made by the monks for ground held by them from various lords, and held in turn by tenants, mainly in the city of Canterbury. Register H in the Chapter Archives, ff. 22–24. The entries in Rental G correspond very closely with those in Rental C. To save repetition reference is made in the notes below to the relevant section in C, where references to corresponding sections in other rentals will be found.
DATE: about 1206.

[fol. 22r.] [1]
(Pro defensione terrarum)ʳ
(Ad festum sancti Martini.)ʳ
Heredibus Ricardi de Grauene ii sol. de terris quas Frambaldus filius Hagenil. 7 Emma relicta Bartolomei dapiferi (Reginaldus de Cornhell')ⁱ tenent et dant nobis inde iii sol. et iiii d.

[2]
(Ad festum sancti Andree)ʳ
Prepositis huius ciuitatis xx d. Pro terra Kenting que est inclusa infra murum nostrum retro clocarium.

[3]
Heredibus Terrici aurifabri iii sol. vi d. De terra [blank] .

[4]
Laurencio de Welles   vii d. ob   De terra quam Lambinus Flan-
[5]   drensis tenet de nobis. 7 dat nobis
Thome filio Luce de   vii d. ob.   annuatim vi sol. viii d.
Hardres.   Summa vi sol. v d.

[6]
(Ad natale.)ᵐʳ
Johanni pellipario de Norg' xxvii d. ob. pro quadam terra in Merceria que fuit Augustini pelliparii super quam pars (noue)ⁱ domus nostre lapidee stat.

1–30 These sections cover the first folio of this rental (Reg. H, fol. 22r.–v.). The original text has almost completely disappeared owing to erasures, and substitution of fresh entries. These fresh entries are made in a variety of different hands.
    ¹ C 1.   ² C 2.
    ³ C 3. Somner has added to this entry the note: 'Vi[de] li[brum] tub[erosum] & lib[rum] vet[erem] cum putr[ido] tegm[ine].' It is not easy to identify the 'old book with the rotten cover', but the 'liber tuberosus' is clearly Reg. K, referred to by Somner as the 'knobbed book'. See D 310 and n. There are several rentals in the volume (such as Y and Z), and it is not certain what may be the subject of Somner's note above.
    ⁴, ⁵ C 4. See 34 below. Lines connect 4 and 5 with para. in col. 3.
    ⁶ See 51 below.

[7]
Johanni filio Thome alderm'   xxx d.

[8]
Heredibus Bernerii dapiferi   xxx d.

Pro terris in Merceria que sunt inter (nouam)ⁱ domum nostram lapideam 7 terram Svani mercerii.

[9]
Item heredibus eiusdem xv d. Pro terra quam emimus de Reginaldo aurifabro. super quam pars domus nostre lapidee noue in Merceria stat.

Summa viii s. vi d. ob.

[10]
(Ad purificationem sancte Marie)ʳ
Roberto scriptori de Hakint' xij d. 7 ob. de terra quam Stephanus de Aldintone tenet. 7 dat nobis (inde)ⁱ xxx d. Hec terra est super Sturam iuxta terram que fuit Ricardi Corbaile in parochia sancte Mildrih'.

[11]
(Ad mediam quadragesimam)ʳ
Thome filio Luce de Hardres   xii d.

[12]
Laurencio de Welles   xii d.

De duabus terris. Scilicet de terra ubi uetus domus nostra lapidea de Andresgate stat✓ xii d. Et de altera que est iuxta illam que fuit Willelmi Winedei super quam pars noue domus nostre lapidee stat✓ xii d.

[13]
Item eidem Laurencio xxx d. Pro terra Cruke. que est in parochia sancte Marie Magdalene. que est iuxta terram que fuit Lefwini carpentarii versus est. (Isti dantur Matildi uxori Samuelis de Feldwarelande)ᵐ

[fol. 22v.] [14]
Heredibus (Willelmi filio Winedai)ᶜ (Terrici aurifabri)ⁱ iii d. de (eadem)ᶜ terra quam emimus de (eo)ᶜ (Willelmo filio Winedei)ⁱ 7 heredibus eius. pro xiiiiᵒʳ marcis. apud Andresgate. super quam pars noue domus nostre lapidee stat.

[15]
Eudoni filio Eudonis filii Sigari. 7 heredibus eius iii d. de quadam terra (que fuit Anseri)ⁱ apud Andresgate quam emimus de eo 7 heredibus eius (pro)ⁱ xxv marcis 7 est iuxta predictam terram Winedai. (de Eudone filio Sigari filii Anseri.)ᵐ

[16]
Item eidem xxx d. Hos solebat accipere heredes Aluredi de Welles.

⁷⁻⁹ See C 6, and 36, 43, 52, 53, 54, below. Lines connect 7 and 8 with 'pro terris' in col. 3.
¹⁰ C 7.
¹¹, ¹² See C 8, 10, 11, and below, 72, 73. Lines connect 11 and 12 with 'De duabus' in col. 3.
¹³ C 9, and 40 below.   ¹⁴ C 11. xiiiiᵒʳ has been altered from iiiiᵒʳ.
¹⁵ C 12.   ¹⁶ C 13.

[17]

Item eidem xli d. Hos solebat recipere quidam homo de Raculve.

[18]

Elemosinario nostro ii sol. de terra quam tenent mon(i)ᵢales de Scapeie et dant nobis inde annuatim vi sol.

[19]

Heredibus Berneri dapiferi xij d. de terra quam (heredes)ᵢ Roberti Goddiuere tene(n)ᵃᵗ 7 da(n)ᵃᵗ inde iiii sol. et ob.

[20]

Curie de Westgate de terra quadam extra Norgate xxvi d. quam tenent heredes Dunstani seruientis nostri et dant nobis inde xxvi d.

[21]

Item eidem curie xij d. de terra Willelmi de Meidestane quam Evdo de Chich tenet 7 dat nobis xl d. 7 (est in parochia de Norg'. iuxta ecclesiam de Norg'.)ᵃ

[22]

Item eidem curie vi d. de terra Euerga que est retro bracinum nostrum infra nouum murum.

[23]

Item eidem curie iiii d. de terra quam relicta Godwini de stabulo et Rogerus filius Marie tenent. 7 dant nobis x d. (distringat quia nescimus tenementum)ᵃᵐ

[24]

Item eidem curie (i uomerem uel)ᶜ ii d. de quadam insula que est extra Westgate de qua heredes O(d)ᵢboldi dant nobis xx d.
(distringat quia nescimus tenementum)ᵃᵐ

[25]

Ortolano nostro xij d. de terra que fuit Wlfwini sacriste 7 est ultra torcular uinee nostre.

[26]

Monialibus de Mallinges iiii sol. de terra que fuit Lamberti Gargate (quam tenent heredes Johannis mercier. 7 Johannes Saule)ᵃ 7 heredes Reginaldi Ioye 7 dant nobis inde xxxvij sol. 7 iiii d.

[27]

Hamoni filio Radulfi presbiteri xvi d. de terra que est inclusa ter(ra)ᵃᵉ quam Osbernus presbiter dedit (nobis)ᵃⁱ 7 est extra Wregate.

[28]

Hamoni de (E)ᵢwerlande. xij d. de terra quam (Robertus scriptor Iudeorum tenet)ᵃ et dat nobis iii(i)ᵃ sol. (vi d.)ᵢ per annum.

¹⁷ C 14.   ¹⁸ C 16.   ¹⁹ C 17.   ²⁰ C 19.
²¹ C 20.   ²² C 21.   ²³ C 22.   ²⁴ C 23.
²⁵ C 25.   ²⁶ C 26. With this are associated 31 and 33, below.
²⁷ C 27. See 56 below.   ²⁸ 62 below.

[29]

(Johanni filio Wluordi Clut viii d. ob. de terr)ᵃᵉa quadam que est extra Wuregate quam Eilmer (Waldeis tenuit 7 dedit nobis annuatim iiii s. quam nunc tenet Robertus aurifaber.)ᵃ

[30]

(Willelmo filio Droconis i d. pro ductu aque nostre que transit per terram eius.)ᵃ

[fol. 23r.] [31]

(Heredibus Pauline ii d.)ᵃ

[32]

Heredibus Wlbaldi de Herebaldune v d. de terra quadam que est iuxta ecclesiam sancti Petri. quam heredes Odboldi tenent 7 dant nobis inde annuatim ij sol.

[33]

Heredibus Wimundi dapiferi pro iiii pedibus de terra Albin iiii d.

[34]

Ricardo Caluel xiiii d. de quadam terra que est in parochia sancte Margarete uersus north proxima terre Willelmi Picot. Hanc terram tenet Lambinus Flammeg [sic]. 7 dat nobis annuatim dimidiam marcam.

[35]

(Benedicto nepoti Benedicti presbiteri iiii d. de quadam terra que est uicina predicte terre versus north.)ᵃ

[36]

(Johanni filio Thome alderman')ᵃ xxx d. (Pro terra pro qua damus ei ad natale xxx d.)ᵃ

[37]

Prepositis istius ciuitatis ii sol. vi d. (De terra que fuit Aluredi parmentarii ante portam cimiterii ueterem.)ᵃ

[38]

(Presbitero de Broke xiii d.)ᵃᶜ

[39]

(Simoni del Blen xviii d. pro terra quam Simon fenarius tenet de nobis in parochia sancti Andree.)ᵃ

[40]

(Laurentio de Welles xxx d. pro terra Cruke.)ᶜ

[41]

(Heredibus Roberti Pin x d. pro terra quam Serlo macun tenet 7 dat nobis inde ii s. viii d.)ᶜ

---

²⁹ C 29. See 48 below.   ³⁰ D 43.   ³¹ C 26.   ³² C 31.

³³ C 26. See 31 above, 44 below.   ³⁴ C 33.   ³⁵ C 36.

³⁶ See 7 above.   ³⁷ C 39.   ³⁸ C 40.

³⁹ See 81 below. S. fenarius holds in St Andrew's parish at the corner of Butchery Lane (Ch. Ant., C 697).

⁴⁰ See 13 above.   ⁴¹ C 28.

[42]

Heredibus Willelmi Caluel ii sol. pro parte terre ubi fundata est noua domus iuxta magnam domum lapideam contra minorem portam cimiterii.

(Summa xxxvi s. ix d. ob.)ae

[43]

(B. Ad pascha.)r

Heredi Berneri dappiferi xxx d. Item eidem xv d. (Pro terris pro quibus damus ei ad natale xlv d.)a

(Summa iii s. ix d.)a

[44]

(Ad pentecosten.)r

(Willelmo filio Johannis alderm' xii d. Pro eadem terra de qua damus monialibus de Malling' iiii sol. in media quadragesima.)ae

[45]

(Ad festum sancti Johannis Baptiste)r

Abbati de Fauersham v d. de terra quam magister hospitalis sancti Thome tenet et dat nobis (annuatim)c iii sol. (in media quadragesima.)a

[46]

Curie sancti Martini iii sol. de terra quam Johannes filius Walteri pistoris tenet 7 dat nobis (annuatim)c (ad festum sancti Johannis)ai iii sol. 7 i d.

[47]

Ortolano nostro xix d. de terra Blanchard quam Johannes cocus tenuit 7 dedit nobis inde annuatim v sol. 7 viii d.

[48]

(Johanni filio Wluordi Clut viii d. 7 ob.)a de terra quam Eilmerus Waldeis ten(et)c (uit)a.

[49]

(A. In annunciatione beate Marie.)r

(Hamoni de Blen militi xii d. De bosco apud Blen quem Nicholaus monacus emit ab eo. Et debet recipere hos xii d. ad mesagium suum de Blen secundum cartam suam.)a

[50]

(Simoni de Blen xiii d. pro duobus campis quos emimus ab eo apud Blen.)a

[fol. 23v.] [51]

(Johanni pellipario de Norg' xxvii d. ob. pro terra de qua damus eidem ad natale xxvii d. 7 ob.)a

---

42 80 below; xxxviii. See C 24 n., and 75.   43 8 above.   44 C 52. See C 26.
45 C 45.   46 C 46.   47 C 47.   48 C 48. See 29 above.
49 71 below.   50 See 81 below.   51 See 6 above.

[52]
(Johanni filio Thome alderm'	xxx d.)ᵃ

Pro terris pro quibus damus
eisdem ad natale v s.)ᵃ
[53]
Heredi Berneri dapiferi	(xxx d.)ᵃ

[54]
Item eidem xv d. (pro terra de qua damus ei ad natale xv d.)ᵃ

(Summa xiiii sol. iii d.)ᵃ
[55]
(Ad festum sancte Margarete)ʳ
Sanctimonialibus de Berkinge v sol. 7 ii d. de quadam terra quam Johannes Dodekere tenuit 7 dedit nobis inde xix sol. (quam nunc tenent heredes Terrici aurifabri.)ᵃ

[56] (In natiuitate sancte Marie)ʳ
Monialibus sancti Sepulcri iii sol. de quadam terra que est extra Wregate quam
Osbernus presbiter dedit nobis que reddit nobis annuatim xx sol. 7 vi d. (ad duos
terminos scilicet ad festum omnium sanctorum. 7 ad ascensionem domini.)ᵃ

[57]
Roberto scriptori de Hakint' xij d. 7 ob. (de terra de qua damus ei ad purificationem
xii d. ob.)ᵃ

(Summa iiii sol. ob.)ᵃ
[58]
(In equinoctio autumnali)ᶜʳ
(Heredibus Willelmi de Mallinges iiii d. de terra Eadwini Scrideman quam Eilmerus Waldeis tenet 7 d(e)ᶜ(a)ⁱt nobis annuatim iiii d.)ᶜ

[59] (Ad festum sancti Michaelis)ʳ
(Heredibus Willelmi de Mallinges (scilicet domino de Tanintune)ⁱ iiii d. de terra
Eadwini Scrideman quam Robertus aurifaber tenet 7 dat nobis iiii d)ᵃ (Item eisdem
ii sol. de vii acris extra Wrgate.)ᵃ

[60]
Jacobo portario archiepiscopi x d. de quadam terra que est in parochia sancti Elfegi.
et pertinet ad gildhalle. (quam tenet Willelmus nepos domini O. de Vnderd'.)ᵃ

[61]
(Heredibus Stephani de Denint')ᵃᵉ xij d. de terra quadam que est iuxta terram
Mansel quam Johannes Dodekere tenuit.

[62]
Hamoni de (E)ᵃⁱwerlande xii d. (de terra que fuit Roberti)ᶜ (De terra quam)ᵃᵉ
tenet Robertus scriptor (Iudeorum)ⁱ. et dat nobis inde annuatim iiii s. vi d.

52–7 8 and 9 above. Lines connect 52 and 53 with (Pro terris . . .) in col. 3.
55 C 53.	56 C 55. See 27 above.	57 C 56.
58, 59 C 57. The word 'det' has been corrected by insertion of a above the line, while e in
det has been cancelled by a dot.
60 C 60.	61 C 62.	62 28 above.

[63]

Curie sancti Martini xviii (d.)ⁱ de terra que est ultra ulterius uiuarium nostrum quam Eadwardus fullo tenet 7 dat nobis inde anuatim iii sol. x d.

[64]

Item e(i)ⁱdem curie xvi d. de terra Warini Kien quam tenent (Henricus 7 Walterus filii Elmeri 7 relicta Gaufridi marescal)ᵃᵉ et (Elphegus)ᵃᵉ se Fwrode et dant nobis inde annuatim vi s.

[65]

(Heredibus Walteri Bes x d. De eadem terra.)ᵃ

[66]

Heredi Berneri dapiferi   xxx d.

[67]   (Pro terris de quibus damus eisdem
(Johanni filio Thome alderman   xxx d.)ᵃ   ad natale v sol.)ᵃ

[68]

(Item eidem xv d. pro terra de qua damus ei ad natale xv d.)ᵃ

[69]

(Mariote uidue ii sol. de terra Brien corduanarii)ᶜ

[70]

Auicie xij d. (heredibus Heilewis de Westgate)ᵃⁱ de (eadem)ᶜ terra (Briani corde-wanier.)ᵃ

[71]

(Hamoni de Blen militi xii d. De bosco quem Nicholaus monacus emit ab eo. Et ipse debet recipere hos xii d. ad capitale mesagium suum de Blen secundum cartam suam.)ᵃ

[72]

(Laurencio de Well'.   vi d.)ᵃ

                                                          (De terra Willelmi Winedei apud
                                                          Andresgate de qua damus eisdem
[73]   xii d. in media quadragesima.)ᵃ
(Thome filio Luce de
Hardres   vi d.)ᵃ

[fol. 24r.] [74]

(Heredibus Odboldi)ᵃ xii d. de(eadem)ᶜ terra (Godwif filie Heilewis.)ᵃ

[75]

Simoni filio Eadmeri de balne(n)ᶜo x d. de terra Warini Kien)ᶜ

[76]

Laurentio de Wælle xxx d. de terra Cruke.

---

⁶³ C 64.   ⁶⁴ C 68.   ⁶⁶ Lines connect 66 and 67 with (Pro terris . . .) in col. 3.
⁶⁸ 'Eidem': probably heir of Berner in 66.   ⁶⁹ C 69.   ⁷⁰ C 70.   ⁷¹ 49 above.
⁷², ⁷³ See 11, 12 above. Lines connect 72 and 73 with (De terra . . .) in col. 3.
⁷⁵ C 72.   ⁷⁶ C 73.

[77]

Hamoni clerico de Fordwico 7 sociis suis ii sol. ubi waruum nostrum est.

[78]

Hugoni aurifabro xii d. pro quadam terra que est retro domum Wimundi mercier.

[79]

(Johanni filio Roberti filio Hosmundi viii d. de terra quam Ingenulf tenet et dat nobis inde iii sol.)c

[80]

Heredibus Willelmi Caluel ii sol. (De terra pro qua damus eisdem ii sol. in media quadragesima.)a

[81]

Simoni de Blen xiii d. (de duobus campis apud Blen. Item eidem xviii d. de terra quam Simon fenarius tenet de nobis.)a

[82]

(Willelmo   xii d. pro terra de qua damus   )d

[83]

(Nicholao filio Baldwini. x sol.)ac

[84]

(Johanni et Jacobo filiis Molonis de (Filethes)i xx sol. pro terra quam Adam de Saxinherste dedit huic ecclesie apud Ketinghelde iuxta Apuldre. quorum cartas habemus.)a

(Summa xlix sol. ii d.)a   (Summa tocius anni vi l. xiiii s. iii d.)a

---

77 C 61.   78 See C 73 n.   79 D 95.
80 C 75, 42 above.   81 39, 50 above.
82 This passage has been subject to erasure, and only the words above remain legible.

84 Fileth is in Adisham, E. Kent. Ch. Ant., C 159 records the grant by John de Filethes to Adam de Saxingherste of land at Ketinghelde 'que iacet infra nouum clausum de Apeldre et extra illud inclausum. et in susanna terra,' reserving a rent of 10s. p.a. Presumably the charter of James de Filethes reserves the remaining 10s. The figure xiiii in the second total has been altered from v s.

THE CHARTERS

THE SEALS OF CHRIST CHURCH, CANTERBURY

To save repetition among the descriptions of charters below, notes are given of the first two seals of Christ Church, Canterbury, which are attached to several of these charters. The third medieval seal (in use c. 1220–1540) and the seal *ad causas* (in use from the mid-thirteenth century) are not attached to charters in this collection and have not been described.

1. *The first seal*. Circular, 1⅞ inches in diameter, bearing representation of the Cathedral, with porch, turrets, ribbed roof, and central spire. Inscription on raised rim: †SIGILLVM ECCLESIAE CRISTI. Reproduced in *Catalogue of Seals ... Department of MSS., BM*, i, pl. ix; Woodruff and Danks, *Canterbury Cathedral*, 1912, opposite p. 45; Warner and Ellis, *Facsimiles of Royal and other Charters in BM*, i, no. 29 (in facsimile of Charter no. IX below). The matrix of this seal is probably eleventh century. The seal is found attached to documents temp. Anselm (e.g. no. III below) and was in use as late as 1152 (no. IX below).

2. *The second seal*. Circular, 3⅜ inches in diameter, bearing on obverse a detailed representation of the Cathedral, ribbed roof, with central tower and spire, surmounted by an angel; two turrets at each end of the structure. Figure of the Saviour in niche in centre. Reproduced in *Catalogue of Seals in . . . Department of MSS., BM*, i, pl. ix; *VCH, Kent*, ii opposite p. 114; Woodruff and Danks, *op. cit.*, opposite p. 45. Inscription round the rim runs: SIGILLVM ECCL'E XPI CANTVARIE PRIME SEDIS BRITANNIE. It is asserted in *Catalogue of Seals in . . . Department of MSS., BM*, i, p. 190 (where the last word of inscription is rendered BRITTANIE) that this seal was used from 1175 until the beginning of the fifteenth century. Both limiting dates are incorrect. This seal is found attached to a charter temp. Theobald bearing the seal of that archbishop (Ch. Ant. C 163) dated by Dr Saltman 1155–1161 (*Theobald*, no. 31). As mentioned above, the first seal was still in use in 1152 so the second seal must have been introduced between then and 1161, the date of the death of Theobald.

Examples of the second seal often bear the impression of a counterseal, vesica-shaped (2½ inches × 1⅔ inches), displaying a figure of the Saviour, seated on a rainbow. The inscription round the rim runs: EGO SVM VIA VERITAS ET VITA (see nos. XXIII, XXV, etc., below).

The second seal seems to have gone out of use c. 1220 as the third seal makes its appearance at this time. It displays the murder of Becket in great prominence and its manufacture may without doubt be associated with the enthusiasm for the Saint engendered by the festivities attending the Translation (1220).

I

Record of exchange between the merchant gild of Canterbury and the convent of Christ Church, of haws at Canterbury.

DATE: 1093–1109.

Ðis beoð þa gehþorfe betpux ðan hirede æt Xpescircean. 7 þan cnihtan on Cantpareberig of cepmannegilde. Se heap on ceapmannegilde let þam hirede to hande VIII hagan piðinnan[1] Burhgate mid sace 7 socne spa hi hit selue hæfden and se hirede let heom to hande þær to gænes nigan hagen tpegen pið utan Readingaten. on þam anen sit Ælfric. 7 on þam[2] oðram Bruman. Ða seofan sindan pið innan Nipingate. ðæreon sittað[3] Sipord Cutfert 7 Brihtric 7 Goldpine 7 Herepord. 7 Þillelm 7 Þulfgeue 7 Ælfpine mid sace 7 socne. spa se hirede hit[4] hæfde. Ðærto is gepitnesse Anselme ærceb. 7 se hired æt Xpescircean. 7 Calueal portgerefa 7 ða yldista men of pam heape. Ðis to gesputelian se hired hæfð an geprit 7 se heape an oðer.*

TEXT: The MS. has not been traced, and may have been destroyed in the fire in the Cathedral Audit House in 1670.

PRINTED: Somner (*Antiquities of Canterbury*, 1640, p. 365) in OE type. His MS. corrections are in his annotated copy in the Cathedral Library, as follows: [1]piðinnam for piðimam, [3]sittað for þittað. He has not corrected the use of 'wyn' for 'thorn' as the initial for [2]þam. Battely reprinted the text in his (1703) edition of Somner's *Antiquities* (p. 179), without incorporating the corrections, although he had access to the annotated copy. He added an error of his own: [4]hic. Gross (*Gild Merchant*, ii, p. 37) prints the text, from *Antiquities*, 1703. He corrects the reading [1]piðimam and [2]pam, but reproduces the ghost-words [3]þittað and [4]hic; 'æ' is rendered 'ae' and 'Xpes-' as 'Xres-', *passim*.

The text above is that of the 1640 edition of *Antiquities* with Somner's two corrections and the reading [2]þam.

NOTE: The transaction must be referred to a time when archbishop Anselm was in England. The earliest possible date appears to be late in 1093 (Eadmer, *Historia Novorum*, RS, p. 41). Anselm was in exile from November 1097 (ibid. p. 88) returning to England September 1100 (p. 119). He was abroad again from April 1103 (p. 149) until August 1106 (p. 183). For the early Canterbury gilds see above, Chapter V, and for Calveal the portreeve and his family, see Chapter III.

* I am very grateful to Professor Bruce Dickins for checking the text above, and for discussing the problems connected with it.

II

Grant by archbishop Anselm to William Cauvel and his heirs of nine pieces of ground outside the city of Canterbury, near the castle, for 52s. *per annum* to be paid to the cellarer of Christ Church, and 20s. relief on death, for all services, except three forfeitures, *murdrum*, *furtum*, and *verecundia*.

DATE: 1095–1107.

ANSELMUS archiepiscopus. omnibus fidelibus & amicis suis salutem. Sciatis me concessisse Willelmo Caluello & hẹred(e)ᵃᵉ su(i)ᵃᵉ [*sic*] extra ciuitatem Cantuariam circa castellum nouem partes terrẹ inter terram arabilem & prata. ea conuentione ut ipse Caluellus & hẹrede( )ᵈ [*sic*] sui singulis annis dent celarario fratrum Lii solidos pro omni re prẹter tres forisfacturas. id est murdrum. & furtum si ipse Caluellus uel herede( )ᵈ [*sic*] sui fecerint. & prẹter si uerecundiam ipse siue hẹrede( )ᵈ [*sic*] sui fecerint monachis ẹcclesiẹ uel seruientibus eorum. Horum uero denariorum una medietas dabitur in media quadragesima. & altera in festiuitate sancti Michaelis. Caluello autem mortuoΎ pro redemptione quam hẹrede( )ᵈ [*sic*] facere solent hẹrede( )ᵈ [*sic*] sui xx solidos dabunt. & censum quem pater prius dederat. ipsi deinceps similiter dabunt. Testes horum sunt. Godefridus de Tanit'. Ælfredus filius Godwini. Gotsoldus. Radulfus frater ipsius Caluelli. Radulfus Wastecarn. Edwinus filius Pitegos. Valete.

ENDORSEMENTS: Twelfth century: De terra W. Caluel. Thirteenth–fourteenth century: Cant.

SEAL: On strip, riband below torn off. Seal of archbishop Anselm in uncoloured wax. Figure of archbishop in chasuble and pallium, with maniple; holds staff and book. Legend almost entirely lost. Maximum size of seal 2⅞ ins. (vertical) by 2½ ins.

SIZE: 4⅛ ins× 7 ins.

TEXT: Original charter, CAC, Ch. Ant. C 1193.

NOTE: Date is limited as 1 above. It may further be limited to June 1095 when Anselm received the pallium, depicted in the seal. (*Historia Novorum, RS*, p. 73). The charter may have been issued at Canterbury since it is in the 'Canterbury hand' and local men appear such as G. of Thanington, and R., brother of W. Cauvel. Charter III is limited to the priorate of Ernulph (1096–1107). The text in both Charters II and III is corrupt. Where the terms 'hẹrede' or 'hẹrede sui' occur they have been altered from some earlier form. The hand of II is larger than that of III but they may both be the work of the same scribe. Witnesses in either charter, G. of Thanington, F. of Chilham, W. Folet and R. son of Herengod, may be identified in Domesday Book. See pp. 48, 53. Verecundia, the third forfeiture, is defined as 'injuria', 'contumelia', by Ducange, citing III, below, from Somner. Cf. Cowel, *Law Dictionary, Vercundium* ('Injury, trespas, damage'), also citing III, below, from Somner.

III

Grant by prior Ernulph and the convent of Christ Church of the same ground as in Charter
II above, with consent of archbishop Anselm.
DATE: 1096–1107.

ARNULFVS prior. & tota congregatio ęcclesie Christi. omnibus fidelibus & amicis
suis salutem. Sciatis nos c[onsenti]en[te] archiepiscopo ANSELMO concessisse
Caluello & hęrede sui [*sic*] extra ciuitatem circa castellum nouem p[art]es terrę
inter terram ar[a]b[i]lem & prata. ea conuentione ut ips[e] Caluellus & hęrede
[*sic*] sui singulis annis dent celarario¹ Lii solidos pro omni re. pręter tres forisfacturas.
id est murdrum. & furtum si ipse Caluellus uel he[r]ede [*sic*] sui fecerint. & pręter
si uerecundiam ipse siue hęrede [*sic*] sui fecerint monachis ęcclesię uel seruientibus
[e]orum. Horum uero denariorum una medietas dabitur in media quadragesima.
& altera² in festiuitate³ sancti Michaelis. Caluel[l]o autem mortuo⸍ pro redemptione
quam hęrede [*sic*] facere solent hęrede [*sic*] sui xx solidos dabunt. & censum quem
[pater] prius dederat. ⁴ipsi deinceps similiter dabunt.⁴ Testes horum sunt. Folbertus
de Cill'. Willelmus Folet. Rogerus filius He[ren]godi. Robertus de Mala Uilla.

ENDORSEMENTS: Twelfth century: De terra Calvelli, and in different hand, extra Wrgate'.
   Fifteenth century?: Sancte Mildrede.
SEAL: First seal of Christ Church, Canterbury, in cream-coloured wax, rim damaged, on
   strip, projecting from top left-hand corner of MS., the strip forming part of the document.
   Riband at bottom torn off. 'Note that this Charter hath a seal appendant on a labell pro-
   ceeding from the side-margent, round, and about the bignesse of a five shillings peece of
   silver, the wax yellow, stamped; but on the one side with the form of a Church . . . The
   inscription in the ring of it is this: †SIGILLVM ECCLESIAE CRISTI.' (Somner, *Gavelkind*,
   1726, app. I).
SIZE: 3 ¹⁄₁₀ ins. × 8⅛ ins. excluding seal-strip.
TEXT: Original charter, CAC, C 885, extensively injured by damp; text is defective. Passages in square brackets are missing and have been supplied from Somner's text, and from
   parallel charter of Anselm, II, above.
PRINTED: Somner, *Gavelkind*, editions of 1660 and 1726, app. I. Somner has reduced spelling
   to classical form and has introduced minor variations of no consequence. More substantial
   variations: ¹celerario; ²altero (in 1660 ed. only); ³festo; ⁴ipse deinceps similiter dabit
   (1726 ed.), ipse . . . dabunt (1660 ed.).

IV

Writ of Henry I notifying grant to abbot Hugh and the monks of St Augustine's, of ground given them by the monks of Holy Trinity (Canterbury Cathedral) in exchange for other ground used to enlarge the cathedral cemetery, whether land of the king or that granted to Holy Trinity by Hugh Maminot, his wife and heirs, or that of any other.

DATE: 1109–1114.

HENRICUS Dei gratia rex Anglorum Cantuariensi archiepiscopo et Radulfo Roffensi episcopo et Hugoni abbati de sancto Augustino et Hamoni dapifero et omnibus baronibus et fidelibus suis Francis et Anglis de Kentẏ salutem. Notum sit vobis me concessisse Hugoni abbati de sancto Augustino et monachis eiusdem ecclesie omnes illas terras quas monachi sancte Trinitatis Cantuarie eis dederunt pro escambio terre quam ab eis receperunt ad amplificandum cimiterium suum siue de mea sit siue sit de terra quam Hugo Maminot et vxor et heredes eius ecclesie Christi Cantuarie contulerunt. siue sit de terra alicuius alterius quam ipsi monachi habuissent in manu eorum. Volo enim et precipio ut predictus abbas cum monachis suisẏ ita bene et honorifice teneant eas terras sicut ipsi melius tenebant suam quam in escambio dederunt. T' Rogero episcopo Salesb'. et Rogero [sic] episcopo Linc'. et Rannulfo cancellario et Hamone dapifero et Willelmo de Albinni et Rannulfo Meschinoẏ apud Brantonam.

TEXT: Transcript of later thirteenth century in BM Cotton Claudius D X, fol. 72. Other versions in MS. History of St Augustine's abbey (fifteenth century), attributed to Thomas of Elmham (Trinity Hall MS., Cambridge); BM Add. MS., 29,437, fol. 105 (seventeenth century).

PRINTED: *Historia Monasterii sancti Augustini Cantuariensis*, RS, p. 359, from MS. at Trinity Hall. Spelling has been reduced to classical form. No name was supplied for the bishop of Lincoln (among witnesses) in this MS. and the incorrect form Rogero was adopted from Claudius D X. It should read Roberto (Robert Bloett, bishop 1094–1123). Précis in Farrer, *Itinerary*, no. 269 (p. 58); and in *Regesta*, ii, no. 1077.

DATE: As calculated by Farrer (*Itinerary*, no. 269, same date as no. 258), is June 1109–August 1111, or July 1113–1 April, 1114.

NOTE: For Hugh Maminot and his Canterbury holdings, see p. 27 above.

V

Writ of Henry I announcing that he has granted licence to archbishop William to occupy certain ground of St Augustine's abbey for enlargement of the cathedral precincts, and to pass over in exchange ground of the same value belonging to the cathedral monks.

DATE: 1123–31.

H. REX Anglorum. archiepiscopo Cantuar'. 7 toti conuentui monachorum de sancta Trinitate de Cantuaria. 7 conuentui monachorum abbatię sancti Augustini.

7 vicecomiti. 7 omnibus baronibus 7 fidelibus suis Francis 7 Anglis de Chentẏ salutem. Sciatis me concessisse Willelmo archiepiscopo Cantuar' ut capiat terram quam sanctus Augustinus habet in Cantuaria iuxta curiam monachorum sancte Trinitatis ad incrementum curię monachorum illorum. Et det sancto Augustino 7 monachis suis escambium terrę illius de proprio monachorum sancte Trinitatis in eadem uilla. adualens terrę illius. Et volo 7 precipio ut bene 7 in pace 7 honorifice teneant hanc terram monachi de sancta Trinitate in perpetuo iure. sicut melius tenent alias terras suas 7 (sicut)ⁱ terram illam quam monachi de sancto Augustino habent in escambio melius tenuerunt. t' Gaufrido cancellario. 7 G. de Glint'. apud Roth'.

ENDORSEMENTS: Contemp.: Cartha Henrici regis de escambio terre curie nostre contra monachos sancti Avgustini. Thirteenth century: .I. (XIII.)ᶜ

SEAL: Henry I, on strip. Riband torn off.

SIZE: 4⅞ ins × 7⅝ ins.

TEXT: Original charter CAC. Ch. Ant., A 64. Late thirteenth-century versions in CAC, Reg. A, fol. 146, Reg. E, fol. 50v.–51r., Reg. I, 63v. No material variants.

PRINTED: *Regesta*, ii, no. CCLIII, where passage melius . . . (sicut)ⁱ is omitted by homoioteleuton, and ę is rendered *e*. Précis, ibid. no. 1703.

NOTE: Both Charters V and VI were evidently issued at the same time. The mention of archbishop William and of Geoffrey (Rufus) the chancellor gives an earlier limit of Feb. 1123 (Farrer, *Itinerary*, p. 104). G. de Clinton was evidently dead by 1132 (ibid. p. 143). There were two successive Hughs, abbots of St Augustine's: Hugh Fleury, died 24 April 1126; Hugh of Trottescliff, instituted abbot 12 June 1127 (ibid. p. 118; d. 1151). Henry visited Normandy many times within these limits, and there may have been unrecorded visits. The known visits to Normandy confine the charters to limits June 1123–August 1131.

VI

Writ of Henry I notifying confirmation of grant of ground made to the monks of St Augustine's abbey, by archbishop William with the monks of Christ Church, Canterbury, in exchange for ground of the former taken over to enlarge the cathedral precincts.

DATE: same as no. V.

H. REX Anglorum. archiepiscopo Cantuar'. 7 toti conuentui monachorum de sancta Trinitate de Cantuaria. 7 vicecomiti. 7 omnibus baronibus 7 fidelibus suis Francis 7 Anglis de Chentẏ salutem. Sciatis me concessisse monachis de sancto Augustino in perpetuo jure terram illam quam Willelmus archiepiscopus 7 monachi de sancta Trinitate eis dederunt 7 concesserunt in escambio pro terra sua quam habuerunt iuxta curiam monachorum sanctę Trinitatis in Can[tu]aria.[1] quam eis concesserunt[2] ad incrementum curie sue. Et volo 7 precipio ut bene 7 in pace 7 honorifice 7 quiete teneant. sicut melius tenent alias terras suas. 7 sicut melius tenuerunt[3] terram illam quam monachi de sancto Augustino habent concessione illorum. t' [   ] canc' 7 G. de Glint'. apud Rothom'.

ENDORSEMENTS: Contemp.: Carta Henrici regis confirmans essambium terrarum inter nos 7 sanctum Avgustinum. quod debuit fieri ad incrementum curię nostrę. .I. .XIII.

SEAL: Henry I on strip. Riband torn off.

SIZE: 4¾ ins.×7 3/16 ins.

TEXT: Original charter CAC, Ch. Ant., A 63. ¹MS. is damaged here and letters *tu* missing; ²followed by an erasure; ³first letter *t* written in a confused manner. Versions without material variant in CAC, Reg. A, fol. 146r, Reg. E, fol. 51, Reg. I, fol. 63v.

PRINTED: *Regesta*, ii, no. CCLIV (where ę is rendered e). Précis ibid., no. 1704.

VII

Notification by archbishop Theobald and the convent of Christ Church, Canterbury, that Achemund the clerk may hold, at a rent of 6d. *per annum* to Christ Church, the land devised, given and granted to him by his uncle in his lifetime as his inheritance.

DATE: 1139–50.

T. DEI gratia archiepiscopus ęcclesię Christi Cantuarie 7 primas totius Anglie 7 totus eiusdem ęcclesię conuentus. omnibus ciuibus Cant'. Francis 7 Anglis salutem 7 gaudium. Sciatis quod concedimus 7 uolumus. quod Achemundus clericus teneat tam libere 7 quiete 7 in pace 7 sine omni calumpnia terram suam quam Wibertus sacerdos sancte Margarite auunculus suus diuisit ei 7 dedit 7 concessit habendam sicut hereditatem propriam dum sanus 7 incolumis adhuc fuerit√ testimonio. Radulfi decani. 7 Geldewini sacerdotis. 7 Rodberti Caluelli. 7 ita quod singulis annis reddet vj denarios super magnum altare ęcclesię nostrę die dedicationis eiusdem. Valete in Christo.

ENDORSEMENT: Twelfth century: De terra Agemundi clerici.

SEAL: First seal of Christ Church, on strip projecting from left-hand end of MS. Riband torn off.

SIZE: 2⅛ ins× 8 1/10 ins. exclusive of strip.

TEXT: Original charter, CAC, C 579.

PRINTED: Saltman, *Theobald*, no. 33.

NOTE: Date is that assigned by Saltman. See Rental A 24; C 36; G 35.

VIII

Notification by Baldwin Cauvel to the inhabitants of Canterbury, of sale to Wibert, subprior, for use of Christ Church, of one acre one rood of ground at St Sepulchre's bar, Canterbury.

DATE: 1149.

C Y R O G R A P H V [M]

NOTUM sit omnibus habitatoribus ciuitatis Cantuarię quod Wibertus supprior emit a me Baldewino Caluello annuentibus omnibus filiis meis terram ad opus ęcclesię Christi quam tenuit Siredus de patre meo Willelmo Caluello & postea de me. Terra autem illa iacet prope portam ęcclesię sancti Sepulchri uersus australem partem iuxta barram. & continet unam acram & uirgatam. pro qua idem Siredus solebat dare singulis annis quinque solidos de gablo. & presentum iiii°ʳ gallinas. Hanc itaque terram ego Baldewinus Caluellus concedentibus filiis meis trado ęcclesię Christi liberam ab omni gablo & omni seruitio quietam in perpetuum possidendam. in presentia eiusdem ęcclesię conuentus & in presentia etiam hallimoti quod pertinet ad cellarium ipsius ęcclesię. quatinus tantorum testimonio ista uenditio & emptio rata semper in posterum & inconcussa permaneat. Isti sunt testes ¹huius conuentionis & presentes fuerunt coram conuentu Baldewinus Caluellus & filii eius Willelmus & Stephanus. Bartholomeus dapifer. Ricardus de cellario. Henricus aurifex. Anselmus secretarius. Nigellus cocus. Geruasius cocus. Walterius cocus. Ælwinus camerarius. Johannes hostiarius bracini. Salomon pistor. Willelmus de Horsfald. Semannus. Johannes filius Rogeri coci. Withelardus pistor. Winedeius filius Æstrildis. Sigarus de Mearstham. Coleman uentilator. Goldwardus. Æilwinus scretarius [sic]. Arnoldus aurifaber. Iuo mercator. Boso. Malgerus portarius. Hęc acta sunt anno dominice incarnationis millesimo centesimo xlix. in capitulo ęcclesię Christi Cantuar'.

ENDORSEMENT: Twelfth century: De terra Baldwini Caluelli. quam Wiberto suppriori uendidit ad opus ecclesie Christi iuxta barram sancti Sepulcri.

SEAL: Seal strip and seal which was affixed to strip at bottom of document, missing. Riband missing.

SIZE: 7⅚ ins. × 6⅜ ins.

TEXT: Original charter CAC, Ch. Ant., C 1087. Transcripts in CAC, Reg. A, fol. 347 (early fifteenth century); Reg. H, fol. 29r. (early thirteenth century). No material variants; except that ¹Reg. H omits all following.

NOTE: Rental A, 10–18; D 140–7, cover ground forming subject of VIII–X.

IX

Record of purchase by Wibert, sub-prior of Christ Church, Canterbury, from Baldwin Cauvel, with consent of his sons, for 42s. and an *aureus*, of nearly one acre of ground, with a small garden, near St Sepulchre's bar, Canterbury, free of all rent and service, saving rent due annually to the cellarer of Christ Church. Counterpart of x. The vendor has signed the document with a cross on the feast of St Katherine (25 November).

DATE: 1152.

CYROGRAPVM :

ANNO ab incarnatione domini millesimo c lii°√ Wibertus supprior ecclesie Christi Cant'. emit a Balduino Caluello presentibus 7 concedentibus filiis suis Willelmo scilicet 7 Stephano unam fere acram de terra 7 quendam ortulum quadraginta & duobus solidis. & uno aureo libere & quiete & sine gablo atque omni seruitio in perpetuum possidendos saluo toto gablo quod idem Balduinus Caluellus singulis annis reddere solet cellario eiusdem ęcclesię. quia terra illa de tenura eiusdem ecclesie est. Illa uero acra iacet iuxta duas acras & dimidiam. ad orientalem partem tendens usque ad domum Liuiuę que fuit uxor Godrici de la helle. quas duas acras & dimidiam. predictus Wibertus supprior alia uice ab eodem Balduino annuentibus filiis suis comparauerat quattuor libris 7 duobus solidis & uno aureo. eadem libertate possidendas qua ista. Ortus uero iacet iuxta domum Siredi de la helle. ad occidentalem plagam ubi manere solebat Willelmus filius eiusdem Siredi prope barram de sancto Sepulchro. ubi etiam tota terra illa iacet in uno continenti supra uiam publicam uersus austrum. (Teste Athelardo. Haymone. Ælfrico sacerdotibus Roberto clerico. Willelmo pincerna de sancto Augustino. Odone parente Dauid monachi.[1] Willelmo de Horsfalda. Roberto de prato. Godardo clerico. Salomone de hosteleria. Edwardo. pistore. Osberto ruffo Hoc signum manu Baldewi † ni (Caluelli)[i] factum est in festo sanctę Katerinę virginis 7 martiris. [2][et rogatu eius in ecclesia Christi reseruatur hoc cyrografum.][2]

[*on dorse*]

Willelmo de Berkesora. Humfrido Scotto. Joseph. filio Eilwini camerarii. & aliis multis testibus. Drio. aurifabro. Gileberto de Sarnaia Godefrido fratre eius. Wlmero seruiente nostro. Roberto de Sarnaia Alboldo seruiente nostro. Sedewino piscatore. Garbados. Rogero monacho filio Henrici. Ricardo monacho. Ælrico. Willelmo Baldewino sacrista. Alexandro. monachis eiusdem ecclesie. Goldwardo Scoca. Iohanne de bracino 7 aliis multis.)[a]

ENDORSEMENTS: Twelfth century: Cyrographum contra (W)[c] Baldewinum Caluellum de duabus terris quas uendidit Wiberto priori iuxta sanctum Sepulcrum. Fifteenth century: ij.

SEAL: First seal of Christ Church, in red wax, on tag passing through two slits at bottom of document, which is not folded.

SIZE: $7\frac{1}{8}$ ins. $\times$ $5\frac{5}{8}$ ins.

TEXTS: Original charter, BM Campbell Chr. xxii.2. Transcript in CAC, Reg. A, fol. 347, early fifteenth century. Variations: [1]omitted in Reg. A; [2-2]entirely obliterated in original charter, and is supplied from Reg. A, where it is written in red.

PRINTED: (with facsimile) in *Facsimiles of Royal and other Charters in BM*, ed. Warner and Ellis, i, no. 29.

X

Counterpart of IX.

ANNO ab incarnatione domini millesimo c lii°√ Wibertus supprior ęcclesię Christi Cant'. emit a Balduino Caluello presentibus & concedentibus filiis suis. Willelmo scilicet & Stephano unam fere acram terre & quendam ortulum quadraginta & duobus solidis & uno aureo libere & quiete & sine gablo atque omni seruitio in perpetuum possidendos saluo toto gablo quod idem Balduinus Caluellus singulis annis reddere solet cellario eiusdem ęcclesię. quia terra illa de tenura eiusdem ęcclesię est. Illa autem acra iacet iuxta duas acras & dimidiam ad orientalem partem

tendens usque ad domum Liuiuę quę fuit uxor Godrici de la helle. quas duas acras
& dimidiam predictus Wibertus supprior alia uice ab eodem Balduino annuentibus
filiis suis comparauerat quattuor libris & duobus solidis. & uno aureo. eadem libertate possidendas qua ista. Ortus uero iacet iuxta domum Siredi de la helle. ad
occidentalem plagam ubi manere solebat Willelmus filius eiusdem Siredi prope
barram de sancto Sepulchro. ubi etiam tota terra illa iacet in uno continenti supra
uiam publicam uersus austrum. Teste[1] (Athelardo. Haymone. Ælfrico sacerdotibus.
Roberto clerico. Willelmo. dapifero. Odone. parente Dauid monachi. Willelmo de
Horsfalde. Roberto de prato. Godardo clerico. Salomone de hostelerie. Eduardo.
pistore. Osberto. ruffo. Willelmo. de Berkesore.)[a]

C Y R O G R A P V M :

[on dorse]
(& Humfrido scotto. 7 Joseph filio Eilwini camerarii. 7 aliis multis testibus. Drio
aurifabro. Gileberto de Sarnai. Godefrido fratre eius. Willelmo. seruiente nostro.
Roberto de Sarnai. (Abod)[c] Alboldo. seruiente nostro. Sedewin. piscatore. Garbados.
Rogero filio Henrici monacho. Ricardo monacho. Æilrico. Willelmo. Baldewino
sacrista. Alexandro ortulano. Goldwardo Scoce. Johanne de bracino. 7 aliis multis.)[a]

ENDORSEMENTS: Late twelfth century: Cyrographum contra Baldewinum Caluellum de
ortulo 7 acra terre quam uendidit Wiberto priori iuxta sanctum Sepulcrum.
SEAL: First seal of Christ Church, in red wax, on tag passing through single slit at top of
document.
SIZE: $4\frac{5}{8}$ ins. $\times$ $5\frac{1}{2}$ ins.
TEXTS: Original charter, CAC, Ch. Ant., C 1086. Transcript in hand of thirteenth century in
CAC, Reg. H, fol. 29v., which has [1]testibus his; all following omitted.

XI

Grant by Ralph son of Eilwin Hearm with consent of his heirs to Wibert, sub-prior of
Christ Church, Canterbury, of two *mansure* near Hottemelne in Canterbury. The grantor
undertakes responsibility for $18\frac{1}{2}$d. *gablum* and 2d. evework due from the two *mansure* with
his own dwelling, due to the cellarer of Christ Church. If through non-payment the holdings
become 'gavelet' then Wibert may seize the grantor's dwelling.
DATE: 1153 or before.

Cirographum contra Radulf filium Eilwini Hearm de duabus mesagiis iuxta
Hotemelne.

SCIANT omnes ad ecclesiam Christi Cant' pertinentes quod ego Radulphus filius
Eilwini Hearm concedentibus heredibus meis uendidi Wiberto suppriori duas
paruas mansuras ab omni gablo et seruicio liberas quas ego et omnes heredes mei
semper in posterum secundum pactum defendemus cum mansura mea ubi habito
per decem et octo denarios et obolum quos dabimus de gablo ad cellarium ecclesie

Christi et per duos denarios quos dabimus de euewerc. Quod si forte contigerit quod ego vel heredes mei prescriptos denarios non dederimus ad terminos constitutos et per hoc ille mansure cum mea mansura fuerint gauellate tunc Wybertus supprior et heredes eius (i. ecclesia Christi)ᶦ iuxta conuencionem nostram saisiet et possidebit mansuram meam sine omni contradiccione sicut suam propriam et aquietabit eam uersus cellarium de gablo singulis semper annis. Ille autem prenominate mansure iacent iuxta mansuram meam ad orientalem partem non longe ab Hottemelne. Et ut vendicio et paccio mea certius stare uideatur inter me et predictum Wibertum suppriorem presentis cirographi attestacione conuencionem nostram firmari statui. Teste Willelmo clerico Lund', Bartholomeo dapifero, Geruasio coco, Adwino textore, Driwo supportario, Martino nepote Germani monachi, Osberto clerico, Admero Trote, Withelardo pistore, Alboldo, Osberto de coquina, Roberto Basset, Petro filio Alurici, Dunstano clerico, Raulfo bagger, Nigello coco, Ailwine Hearm, Lamberto Gargato, Adwardo filio Odboldi, Wlnodo Bri, Willelmo port', Rogero port', Leuwino cognato Adwardi filii Odboldi.

TEXT: Transcript in CAC, Reg. A, fol. 402r. (early fifteenth century). See Rental A, 6.

XII

Grant in perpetual alms by Ralph de Ælkeham to Christ Church, Canterbury, of ground against the northern wall of the monastic precinct, which Elfwin Everga and his heirs held of him.

DATE: mid-twelfth century.

RADULFUS de Ældeham. omnibus fidelibus 7 amicis sancte ecclesie 7 suis√ salutem. Sciatis me concessisse Deo 7 ecclesie Cant'. in perpetuam elemosinam√ terram quandam que iacet iuxta murum curie monachorum a parte aquilonari. quam Elfwinus Euerga 7 heredes sui de me tenebant√ & sex denarios. de gablo mihi annuatim inde reddebant. Hanc itaque terram pro salute anime meę 7 parentum meorum defunctorum. 7 pro salute heredum meorum tam presentum quam futurorum√ dedi 7 concessi ecclesie Christi Cant' 7 monachis. in ea Deo seruientibus. ita quiete 7 libere in perpetuum possidendam√ sicut eam melius 7 liberius unquam habui. Et rogo omnes heredes meos 7 successores√ ut hanc donationem meam quam feci pro salute animę meę 7 animarum suarum√ ratam habeant. 7 semper in posterum stabilem 7 firmam esse faciant. Valete:

SEAL: On strip, riband below, circular, c. 1¾ ins. diameter. See under *Size*. Equestrian figure riding to right, pointed helmet, surcoat, with sword and shield, with boss. Seal of brown wax. Inscription: †SIGILLVM [RA]DVL[FI D]E [ÆLDEH?]ANI. Termination of the last word appears thus in facsimile in MS. *Book of Seals*, and in printed version but should evidently read: -AM.

TEXTS: Facsimile drawing in Sir Christopher Hatton's Book of Seals, among MSS. of Earl of Winchilsea and Nottingham, deposited in Northants. County Archives. Charter is described as 'Ex cartis Willelmi le Neue', etc. Original not traced.

PRINTED: *Sir Christopher Hatton's Book of Seals*, presented to F. W. Stenton, 1950, no. 287.

SIZE: Size of facsimile, probably reproducing size of original, is 4⅞ ins. (inc. strip and riband) ×6⅛ ins.

NOTE: The grants recorded in XII and XIII are mentioned in Wibert's roll (Rental A, 3). See C 21; G 21. Ralph de Ældeham is witness to charter of Becket to Leeds priory, Kent (Leeds priory cartulary, MS. in KCC Record Office, p. 4).

XIII

Confirmation by William Capel with consent of his brothers, to the prior and monks of Christ Church, Canterbury, of ground in Canterbury sold to them by Goditha daughter of Elfwin Everga and heirs, saving 5d. *per annum* due to William Capel.

DATE: C. 1153.

WILLELMUS Capel omnibus fidelibus Christi salutem. Sciant tam presentes quam futuri quod Goditha filia Elfwini Euerga et heredes sui terram quam de patre meo et de me iure hereditario tenuerunt Wiberto priori et conventui ecclesie Christi Cant' uendiderunt, et postea quietam mihi reddiderunt. Ego autem, presentibus et consentientibus fratribus meis, concessi priori et monachis ecclesie Christi Cant', ut ipsi eandem terram de me et heredibus meis imperpetuum per idem servitium teneant per quod Elfwinus Everga et heredes sui de patre meo et de me tenere solebant, reddendo scilicet inde v. denarios in medio quadragesime.

CYROGRAPHVM

ENDORSEMENT: Inter nos et Willelmum Capel cyrographum contra Willelmum Capel de terra Elfwini Averga.

SEAL: It is stated (*Proc. Soc. Ant.* Ser. ii, vol. 2, p. 282) that the seal was attached at the upper end.

TEXTS: Original MS. not traced. It was in the Surrenden collection, Pluckley, Kent, and was exhibited at the meeting of the Kent Arch. Soc. 30 July 1858 (*Arch. Cant.* v, p. 325). It was sold Feb. 1863 and exhibited by Rev. T. Hugo, the antiquary (see *DNB*) to the Soc. of Antiquaries (*Proc. Soc. Ant.*, as above). See *Gentleman's Mag.*, 1863, pt. ii, p. 161. We have three texts: 1. In transcripts of Surrenden MSS. by L. Larking, Maidstone Museum ii, p. 186. 2. Printed, *Arch. Cant.* as above. 3. Printed: *Proc. Soc. Ant.*, as above. No material variants between texts, apart from the fact that the initial of Everga in 1. and 3. is rendered Œ- in 2. The form 'Crhisti' (first instance) in 2 is patently a misprint. The word CYROGRAPHVM is given only in 3. The text above is that of 3, with the endorsement from no. 1.

NOTE: See XII, above. For William Capel see above, p. 60.

XIV

Grant by William of Ypres to God and the church of Holy Trinity (i.e. Christ Church),
Canterbury, in perpetual alms, of 20d. rent in Canterbury from the ground of Leuwin
Chentingessune.
DATE: 1155 or before.

W. DE IPRA. archiepiscopo Cant'. 7 vic' de Chent. 7 abbati sancti Austini 7 omnibus burgensibus de Cant'. 7 omnibus fidelibus suis. 7 amicisʸ salutem. Sciant
uniuersi. presentes 7 post futuri. me concessisse 7 dedisse Deo. 7 ecclesie sancte
Trinitatis Cant'. in perpetuam elemosinam xx denarios. de redditu meo de Cant'.
uidelicet de terra Leuwini Chentingessune. Qare [sic]. uolo. 7 firmiter precipio quod
predicta ecclesia. 7 prior. 7 monaci ibidem seruientes. habeant prefatum redditum.
bene. 7 in pace. libere. 7 quiete. ita quod nullus eis inde iniuriam faciat. T'.
Ernulfo comite de Ginis. 7 Radulfo filio comitis. Hamone preposito Cant'. 7
Lamberto Garg'. 7 Johanne Caldrun'.

ENDORSEMENTS: Contemp.: Willemi de Ypra. de redditu xx denariorum. de terra Chettinge.
Thirteenth century: Cantuar'.
SEAL: On strip, in white wax, varnished; circular, size uncertain owing to damage to rim,
but originally about 2¼ ins. Equestrian figure, with shield and uplifted sword, riding to
right.
SIZE: 2½ ins.×7 ins.
TEXTS: Original charter, CAC, Ch. Ant., C 1127. Transcripts in CAC, Reg. A, fol. 462v.,
Reg. E., f. 137v.–138r, both in hand of c. 1300. No material variants.
NOTE: Stephen endowed William of Ypres, leader of his mercenaries, with revenues in Kent.
Gervase indicates that William left England by 1155 (*Opera, RS,* i p. 161; Kate Norgate in
DNB). The name Ernulph, count of Guines, offers difficulty. Ernulph was the second
count, while the count contemporary with William of Ypres was Arnold of Ghent, who
succeeded in 1147, who had a son Ralph (see witness-list in charter). The form 'Ernulfo'
is evidently an error for 'Ernaldo'. The house of Guines held land in Kent as at Newington
(near Folkestone) where Arnold died in 1169 (see Chron. of Lambert of Ardres in Bouquet,
Historiens des Gaules, xiii, p. 438; Stapleton, 'Observations on the succession to the barony
of William of Arques . . . in Kent', *Archæologia,* xxxi, pp. 216–37, 1845). When John of
Salisbury landed on the shores of Guines in 1164 he was welcomed by servants of the
count of Guines. 'procurante Ernulpho nepote eius' (*Pat. Lat.,* 179, p. 111). This charter
must have been executed at or near Canterbury, since Hamo the provost, Lambert
Garegate and John Caldrun attest. The ground of L. Kentingson is very close to that of
the same man, charged with 20d. to the crown. See xxv, below. Garegate and Caldrun
were near neighbours. See B 71, 73.

XV

Writ of Henry II addressed to Hamo and John, borough reeves of Canterbury, ordering them to restore to the prior and monks of Holy Trinity (Christ Church), the way round their cemetery as it was at the death of Henry I, and to do justice concerning those persons who have occupied it during the war.
DATE: c. 1 January 1156?

HENRICUS rex Anglorum et dux Normannorum et Aquitanorum et comes Andegauorum Hamoni et Johanni prepositis Cant' salutem. Precipio quod iuste deliberetis priori et monachis sancte Trinitatis Cant'. viam suam circa murum cymiterii sui sicut fuit tempore regis H. aui mei et die qua fuit uiuus et mortuus et de illis qui eam tempore werre occupauerunt plenarie rectum et justiciam eis faciatis, ne inde clamorem audiam pro penuria recti. Et nisi feceritis justic' vel vicecomes meus de Kent faciet. Teste comite Reginaldo apud Cant'.

TEXT: Copy in hand of early fifteenth century in CAC, Reg. A, fol. 147v.
NOTE: The writ was probably issued at Henry's first visit to Canterbury, at the date indicated. His next visit was not until 1163. Reginald earl of Cornwall was at Canterbury at the earlier date. The *via* was evidently the track along the Precincts boundary wall, north of Burgate Street. The writ is apparently that mentioned in Somner, *Antiquities of Canterbury*, 1640, p. 189.

XVI

Undertaking by prior Wibert and the convent of Christ Church, Canterbury, to pay to the nuns of Minster in Sheppey, a total rent of 44½d. arising from three dwellings in Canterbury. Liviva, widow of Berner the steward, had assigned the rent, received from the monks of Christ Church, to the nuns of Minster on reception of her daughter there.
DATE: 1153–67.

.I. C Y R O G R A P H V M

WIBERTUS prior & conuentus ecclesie Christi Cantuar'. Omnibus fidelibus Christi salutem. Nouerint presentes & futuri. quod nos singulis annis reddere debemus in medio quadragesime sanctimonialibus de Scapeia xliiiior denarios 7 obolum de tribus mansuris in Cantuar' sicut eos Bernerus dapifer & Liuiua uxor eius de eisdem mansuris habere solebant. Uidelicet xix denarios de terra Euerardi Flandrensis. que fuit Colhoppe. quam tenet modo Normannus plumbarius. 7 reddit nobis inde iii solidos. Et xiii denarios de una mansura in Baggeberi. quam tenet modo Nicholaus de elemosinaria. & reddit nobis inde xxiii denarios. Et xii denarios 7 obolum quos ipsi Liuiue reddere solebamus de terra Johannis filii Marie. quam Golduardus Scoche tenet. & reddit nobis inde iiii solidos 7 obolum. Quam quidem terram sanctimoniales de Scapeia adquietare debent in omnibus uersus curiam archiepiscopi de Westgate cum uicina terra quam Hugo de bracino de ipsis tenet. Hos xliiiior denarios 7 obolum predicta Liuiua assensu Hugonis fratris sui 7 heredum Berneri concessit sanctimonialibus de Scapeia imperpetuum. quando filia eius sanctimoni-alis ibi facta est. Ipsas uero tres mansuras quarum duas de nobis tenebat. & tertiam quam nos de ipsa tenebamus⸗ concedentibus heredibus quietas nobis clamauit. 7 quicquid in eis iuris habebat. Saluo predicto redditu qui prefatis sanctimonialibus inde debetur in medio quadragesime. Et tunc sanctimoniales pro eo mittere Can-tuar' debent. Uolumus ergo ut ista conuentio inter nos 7 ipsas sanctimoniales imperpetuum firmiter teneatur. Et ne forte tradatur obliuioni. uel aliquo casu possit infringi⸗ presenti cirographo illam confirmauimus. Valete.

ENDORSEMENT: Fifteenth century?: De iij s. et viij d. de redditu in Cant. de priore Cant'.

SEAL: Fine impression of second seal of Christ Church, with counterseal, on tag passing through fold. Riband is cut from upper edge of fold.

SIZE: $6\frac{3}{10}$ ins.×$9\frac{2}{3}$ ins.

TEXT: Original charter, CAC, Ch. Ant., C 1110.

NOTE: The date is confined to the priorate of Wibert. The ground held by Norman the plumber may be D 95, F 199, 564. The ground in Baggeberi held by N. of the almonry does not tally with description here (B 55, 181), though there Liviva, named in the charter, has ground next to a holding of Nicholas (B 180). Ground held by G. Scoche is subject of XVII, B 126; D 3; F 115; 461. See C 17; G 19.

XVII

Notification by archbishop Theobald, addressed to his men of Canterbury and the hundred of Westgate, that he has granted to the cathedral priory the house and ground, lying next to the new almonry wall, in Canterbury, of John (son of Walter de sartrimo), who has become a monk.

DATE: 1157–61.

T. DEI gratia Cant' archiepiscopus. Angl' primas. 7 apostolice sedis legatus. Omnibus hominibus suis de Cantuaria. 7 de hundreto Westgate⸗ salutem. Sciatis nos concessisse conuentui nostro Cantuariensis ecclesię. domum 7 terram Johannis filii Walterii de sartrimo. que est iuxta nouum murum elemosinarie monachorum. de feodo nostro de Westgata. sicut idem Johannes eam dedit 7 concessit ecclesie Cantuar' 7 conuentui⸗ cum corpore suo ad faciendum se monachum. Et nos ei monachatum concedimus. 7 conuentui Cant' terram eius predictam confirmamus. salua consuetudine 7 censu annuo⸗ quem nobis eadem terra debet. t. Philippo cancellario. archidiacono Norwic'. 7 Johanne de Saresberia. 7 Petro scriptore. 7 Rogero Spec'. 7 Osberno clericis archiepiscopi. 7 multis aliis apud Cantuar'.

ENDORSEMENTS: Twelfth century: Carta Teobaldi archiepiscopi de terra Walterii de sartrino iuxta murum elemosinarie nostre. c. 1200: Carta Theobaldi archiepiscopi de terra Johannis filii Walterii. (.XI.). Late thirteenth century: De Coltona.

SEAL: Of archbishop Theobald in brown wax, on strip, riband below, torn off. Seal when complete was vesica-shaped, $3\frac{1}{4}$ ins.×$2\frac{1}{4}$ ins. Bears figure of archbishop with pall and mitre points worn over ears; figure holds staff while hand is raised in blessing. Inscription of which there is little trace should run: SIGILLV̄: TEOBALDI: DEI: GRATIA: ARCHIEPISCOPI: CANTVARIENSIS. The counterseal (oval) measuring 1⅜ ins.× 1 in. embodies a classical gem, displaying a bearded bust, facing right, filletted hair. Inscription, read from inside, reads: SIGNVM SECRETVM. In this example the inscription is barely legible. See Saltman, *Theobald*, p. 225.

SIZE: 4⅞ ins.× 6 7/16 ins.

TEXTS: Original charter CAC, Ch. Ant., C 1109. Transcripts in the same later thirteenth-century hand in CAC, Reg. C, fol. 13v., and in Reg. E, fol. 91v. No material variants.

PRINTED: Saltman, *Theobald*, no. 35. Date is that given by Saltman. The ground named in charter is subject of XVI.

XVIII

Memorandum of grant by Robert, son of Baldwin and Ada, with warranty, to Lambert Gargate his kinsman, of all rights in the inheritance belonging to him, of the inheritance of Godsold, and to the heirs on whom Lambert had bestowed it.

DATE: Before 23 March 1167.

[A]D sciendum est quod Robertus filius Eadwini 7 Ade con[cessit?] Lamberto Gargate cognato suo omnia iura de he[redita]te que sibi pertinebat de hereditate Godsoldi [   ]eris[1] sui in hereditatem perpetuo. 7 heredibus quibus ipse Lambertus dederat. 7 Robertus in conuentione ha[bet] fide pleuiata Lamberto quod illum inde guarentabit erga omnes feminas 7 homines secundum suum posse. 7 istam conuentionem testificatur Henricus presbiter sancti Georgii. 7 Hamo clericus filius Geroldi 7 Eadwinus filius Roberti sacerdotis. Jordanus filius Wlfwi. 7 Alberb Furdenel 7 Serle filius suus. Robertus li Saracin. Rogerus Richite. Wlmer de Tanintune 7 Hugo iiii ministri regis. Godwine Berembread Heinulf filius Arnold le gode. Nichole filius Henrici aurifabri. 7 Hamo filius Heruei. 7 ista conuen[tio fac?]ta fuit in ecclesia sancti Andree in angulo ori[entali].

ENDORSEMENTS: Twelfth century: Carta Roberti filii Eadwini de terra Godsoldi. De terra Gargate. Late thirteenth century: Facta Lamberto Gargate.

SEAL: No evidence that the document was ever sealed.

SIZE: 4⅗ ins.× 4 ins.

TEXT: Original charter, CAC, Ch. Ant., M 272.

NOTE: The date is provided by the death-date of Lambert Gargate. His obit was celebrated 23 March (Obituary in Cotton Nero, C IX, printed in Dart, *Canterbury Cathedral*, app. xii). He died within the priorate of Wibert (d. September 1167). See XX below. The latest date for the charter appears to be March 1167. The king's 'ministri' are apparently not named individually, since W. of Thanington and N. son of Henry the goldsmith, at least, are local men.

---

[1] It is difficult to determine the complete form of this. Perhaps the scribe has put 'gener' in the third declension.

XIX

Notification by prior Wibert and the convent of Christ Church, Canterbury, of a reduction in rent due to them from Alan of Ratling, for ground near St George's church, Canterbury, in exchange for ground behind the monastic bakehouse.
DATE: 1153–67.

NOTUM sit omnibus presentibus 7 postfuturis. quod ego Wibertus prior 7 conventus ecclesię Christi Cant'. perdonavimus Alano de Retlingæ 7 heredibus suis xiiii denarios de xxvi denariis quos ipse Alanus singulis annis reddere solebat ad altare Christi de terra quadam quam de ipso tenuit Winedei cognomento Butercluncc. 7 iacet prope ecclesiam sancti Georgii. pro escambio cuiusdam terrę iacentis retro pistrinum nostrum inter murum scilicet civitatis 7 murum curię nostrę. quam ipse Alanus 7 heredes sui liberam 7 ab omnibus rebus quietam pro predictis xiiii denariis nobis in perpetuum concesserunt. Reddent autem nobis in posterum de predicta terra quam tenebat Winedei. supradictus Alanus 7 heredes sui annuatim xii denarios. reliqui uero quatuordecim pro escambio predicte terrę quę muro nostro adiacet. eis relaxabuntur. Hoc concambium 7 hanc conventionem tam nos quam sepedictus Alanus cum heredibus suis semper in posterum ratam 7 stabilem esse volumus. 7 presentis cyrographi conscriptione firmamus. Testibus his. Ex parte nostra. Willelmo camerario. Geddewino 7 Iohanne cocis. Et ex parte Alani. Rodberto de Chethamtune. 7 Rodberto clerico de Glinde. 7 Radulfo de Bosgerardo.

C Y R O G R A P H V M

ENDORSEMENTS: Twelfth century: Cyrographum. Contra Alanum de Retlinge. De terra Winedei. Fifteenth century: Northgate.
SEAL: Slit and folded for sealing at top, but no trace of tag or seal remains.
SIZE: 5½ ins. × 7⅜ ins.
TEXT: Original charter, CAC, Ch. Ant., C IIII.
PRINTED: *Literæ Cantuarienses*, RS, iii, app. 37 (with some mistranscriptions; text reduced to classical spelling).
NOTE: Date is limited by priorate of Wibert. The transaction is recorded in Wibert's roll (Rental A, 7). See D 123; F 195, 527. For Alan of Ratling, evidently the man excommunicated by Becket, see p. 56.

XX

Undertaking by prior Wibert and the convent of Christ Church, Canterbury, to the abbess Ermelina and the convent of Malling, Kent, to pay a rent of 4s. *per annum* from houses and ground formerly held of the nuns by Lambert Gargate, and by him bestowed on Christ Church, when taking the cowl there at his death.
DATE: 1153–67.

WIBERTUS prior & conuentus ecclesię Christi Cant' Ermeline abbatisse & conuentui sanctimonialium de Melling'y͛ salutem. Nouerit dilectio uestra & vniuersi tam presentes quam futuri. Lambertum Gargate. quando ad obitum suum habitum monachi suscepit√ dedisse pro anima sua in perpetuam elemosinam ecclesię nostrę terram illam cum domibus & omnibus ad eam pertinentibus. quam ipse de uobis per cartam uestram hereditario iure tenebat. saluo iure ecclesię uestrę & seruitio quod uobis inde facere solebat. Sicut igitur ipse Lambertus singulis annis iiii⁰ʳ solidos pro omni seruitio de predicta terra uobis reddebat in medio quadragesime. & eos per proprium nuntium uestrum vobis transmittebat ueluti carta eius fieri debere testatur√ similiter & nos qui heredes eius sumus in perpetuum faciemus. & tenorem carte quam de uobis habuit in omnibus ecclesię uestrę seruabimus. Valete.

C I R O G R A P H V M

ENDORSEMENT: Twelfth century: Cirographum contra sanctimoniales de Meallinge de terra que (fuit)¹ (Lamberti Garegate).ᵃ

SEAL: No evidence that the charter was ever sealed.

SIZE: 5⅖ ins.× 10⅘ ins.

TEXTS: Original charter, CAC, Ch. Ant., M 245. Copy in fragment of thirteenth-century cartulary bound into CAC, Reg. H (fol. 28r.). No material variants.

NOTE: The priorate of Wibert provides the limiting dates. The *managium* of Lambert Gargate was an important landmark in the Burgate area. It is subject of XXI–XXIII. See B 71; C 26, n.; D 93; G 26.

XXI

Notification addressed to the inhabitants of Canterbury by prior Odo and the convent of Christ Church, of grant to alderman John of the dwelling of Lambert Gargate, near St Mary Magdalen church, Canterbury, for one mark of silver *per annum*. The grantee is responsible for rents to other lords, and will free the grantors at his own expense and trouble if any claim is made in connection with the property. Counterpart of XXII.

DATE: 1167–75.

O D O prior. 7 conuentus ecclesie Christi Cantuar'. Omnibus qui habitant in ciuitate Cantuar√ Salutem. Nouerint presentes 7 futuri quod nos concessimus Johanni ældermanno tenere de nobis hereditario iure managium Lamberti Gargate iuxta fismanne cheriche. ubi ipse Lambertus manere solebat. Sed partem illam que proxima est ecclesie de qua Albinus reddit nobis iiii⁰ʳ solidos√ retinemus in manu nostra. Totum autem reliquum sicut Lambertus illud habuit√ concessimus predicto Johanni. 7 heredibus suis. pro una marca argenti semper in posterum annuatim nobis reddenda ad iiii⁰ʳ terminos. id est ad natale. ad pascha. ad festiuitatem sancti Johannis. ad festiuitatem sancti Michaelis. ad unumquemque uidelicet istorum terminorum√ xl denarios. Et preter hoc√ adquietabit nos de iiii⁰ʳ denariis de gablo uersus heredes Wimundi dapiferi. de quorum terra particula quedam addita est ad predictum managium Lamberti. Similiter uersus Gilebertum telarium 7 heredes eius√ adquietabit nos de duobus denariis de gablo. Et si quis forte calumpniam mouerit uersum nos de predicto managio. uel de aliqua parte eius√ ipse Iohannes.

uel heredes sui proprio sumptu 7 labore nos inde liberabunt. Volumus ergo ut ipse Iohannes 7 heredes sui bene 7 in pace teneant prenominatum managium sicut distinximus. quamdiu conuentionem istam nobis tenuerint. 7 censum nostrum ad terminos constitutos bene reddiderint. Huius rei testes sunt√ Haimo prepositus. Willelmus filius Gregorii. Reginaldus mercator. Semerus mercator. Ruelinus Flandrensis. Ælphegus mercator. Johannes filius Roberti monetarii. Lambinus Frese. Johannes filius Haimonis prepositi. 7 de curia nostra√ Bartholomeus dapifer. Malgerius janitor. Hector. Cole de balneario. et Willelmus bedellus.

C Y R O G R A P H V M

ENDORSEMENT: Twelfth century: De terra Lamberti Gargate.
SEAL: Document is folded and slit at top, but no other trace of seal.
SIZE: 5 ins.× 7⅓ ins.
TEXT: BM. Campbell charters, no. L.F.C.IV.8.
NOTE: See notes to XX, above.

XXII

Counterpart of no. XXI.

C Y R O G R A P H V M

ENDORSEMENT: Thirteenth century?: De terra que fuit Lamberti Gargate. Contra Johannem elderman.
SEAL: Document is folded and slit for seal, but no other trace of seal remains.
SIZE: 5 ins.× 7 5/16 ins.
TEXT: Original charter, CAC, Ch. Ant., C 1123. No material variants between the two versions.

XXIII

Grant by prior Benedict and the convent of Christ Church, Canterbury, for life, to Paulina, widow of alderman John, of ground near St Mary Magdalen church, Canterbury, on same terms as in XXI, XXII.
DATE: 1175–77.

C Y R O G R A P H V M [inverted]

BENEDICTUS prior 7 conuentus ecclesie Christi Cantuar'. Omnibus qui habitant in ciuitate Cantuaria. Salutem. Nouerint presentes 7 futuri quod nos concessimus Pauline relicte Johannis aldermanni tenere de nobis sine omni feodo 7 hereditate managium quod fuit Lamberti Gargate iuxta fismannekirche ubi ipse Lambertus manere solebat. Sed partem illam que proxima est ecclesie de qua Albinus reddit nobis quattuor solidos√ retinemus in manu nostra. Totum autem reliquum sicut Lambertus illud habuit√ concessimus predicte Pauline quamdiu uixerit pro una marca

argenti annuatim nobis reddenda ad quattuor terminos scilicet ad Natale. ad Pascha.
ad festum sancti Johannis. 7 ad festiuitatem sancti Michaelis. ad unumquemque
istorum terminorum xl denarios. Et preter hoc adquietabit nos de quattuor denariis
(in media quadragesima)¹ de gablo uersus heredes Wimundi dapiferi de quorum
terra particula quedam addita est ad predictum managium. Similiter uersus Gille-
bertum telarium 7 heredes eius̸ adquietabit nos de duobus denariis (in media
quadragesima)¹ de gablo. Et si quis forte calumpniam mouerit uersum nos de
predicto managio uel de aliqua parte eius̸ ipsa Paulina proprio sumptu et labore
nos inde liberabit. Volumus ergo¹ ut ipsa Paulina bene 7 in pace teneat prenominatum managium quamdiu uixerit. 7 conuentionem istam nobis tenuerit. 7 censum
nostrum ad terminos statutos² bene reddiderit. Huius conuentionis testes sunt.
prior. supprior. Augustinus celararius.³ Radulfus subsacrista. Bartholomeus
dapifer. Willelmus de Capes.⁴ Walterius le uannur. Matheus Durneis. 7 multi
alii sicut in plenaria curia.

ENDORSEMENT: Twelfth century: De terra Lambert Gargate quam tenuit Paulina uidua
    Johannis aldermanni.
SEAL: Second seal of Christ Church (damaged), in brown wax, on tag; with counterseal.
SIZE: 5⅝ ins× 6½ ins.
TEXT: Original charter, CAC, Ch. Ant., C 772.
PRINTED: Madox prints a version of this charter (*Formulare Anglicanum*, CXCV); spelling is
    reduced to classical form, and accents are added. Apart from immaterial variants, the
    following occur: ¹igitur; ²constitutos; ³celarius; ⁴Capell. Madox says he takes his text
    Ex archivis Eccles. Christi Cantuar'. 'It has the word CYROGRAPHVM Cutt through in a
    Right line'. Madox probably took his text from a counterpart of XXIII, but such counter-
    part is not now to be found in the Chapter archives. The priorate of Benedict provides
    the limiting dates.
NOTE: See notes to XX above.

XXIV

Grant by prior Odo and the convent of Christ Church, Canterbury, of two pieces of ground
in Canterbury, each held from a different lord, to John Dodekere at 19s. *per annum*.
DATE: 1167–75.

ODO prior et conuentus ecclesie Christi Cant' omnibus ciuibus eiusdem ciuitatis
presentibus et postfuturis̸ salutem. Sciatis nos concessisse Johanni cognomento
Dodekere tenere de nobis hereditario iure. terram quam tenemus de sanctimonialibus de Berkinges quam Lambertus Gargate dedit ecclesie nostre. et cum ea̸
terram que illi proxima est quam tenemus de Symone de Valbadun. ea conditione
quod ipse Iohannes et heredes sui reddent nobis inde singulis annis decem et nouem
solidos. ad quatuor terminos. id est ad Natale. ad Pascha. ad festum sancti Johannis.
ad festum sancti Michaelis singulis scilicet istorum terminorum iiii°ʳ solidos et ix

denarios. Volumus ergo ut ipse et heredes sui terras illas bene et in pace teneant√ quamdiu predictos xix solidos bene nobis reddiderint ad terminos constitutos. Rei huius testes sunt.

TEXT: Transcript in CAC, Reg. H fol. 28v. in hand of earlier thirteenth century.
NOTE: The priorate of Odo provides the limiting dates. See C 53, 62; D 103; F 30, 295, 365, 531; G 55, 61. For the Vaubadon family see p. 74.

XXV

Notification by the convent of Christ Church, Canterbury, of grant of corrody in food and drink, with spiritual benefits and sepulture on death, to Atheliza, who has bestowed on the monks 3s. 'forgable' arising from dwellings near the cathedral belltower. The dwellings had been granted to Atheliza and the monks by the royal justices, in compensation for her ground held of the convent, requisitioned to strengthen the castle defences.
DATE: C. 1177?

CONUENTUS ecclesie Christi Cant'. Omnibus fidelibus sancte matris ecclesie. salutem. Notum esse uolumus presentibus 7 futuris quod concessimus huic Athelize corredium unum in curia nostra quamdiu uixerit. videlicet singulis diebus duos planos panes et duas iustas ad mensuram Lanfranci de ceruisia militum. 7 unam scutellam pisarum. 7 alteram de cibo lacteo quando conuentus illum habebit. Et de uno generali ferculo quod ipso die conuentus habuerit√ dabitur ei quantum unus monachus habere debet. Concessimus etiam ei beneficium 7 societatem ecclesie nostre. 7 sepulturam ad obitum suum sicut sorori nostre. Ipsa uero dedit nobis in perpetuum redditum tres solidos quos habebat de forgable de v mansuris quas tenebat de nobis pro iiii͏ͦ͏ʳ solidis annuatim. Ille autem v mansure sunt in angulo retro clocarium nostrum. que date fuerunt nobis 7 huic mulieri in comcambium pro quadam terra extra Wiwergate iuxta fossatum turris. quam predicta mulier 7 antecessores eius de nobis tenere solebant hereditario iure. reddentes nobis inde singulis annis iiii͏ͦ͏ʳ solidos. 7 habebant insuper ad opus suum ualentiam trium solidorum. Et quia eadem terra assumpta fuit ad efforciandam turrim extrinsecus√ preceperunt iusticie regis. scilicet Ricardus de Luci. 7 Ricardus archidiaconus Pictauiensis. 7 Henricus filius Geroldi dari predicte mulieri comcambium in ciuitate de redditu regis ad ualentiam sepedicte terre 7 eiusdem libertatis ad tenendum de nobis hereditario iure pro iiii͏ͦ͏ʳ solidis annuatim sicut aliam terram tenebat. Et sic per considerationem 7 iuramentum proborum hominum ciuitatis√ assignate nobis 7 huic mulieri fuerunt in comcambium v ille mansure. que reddebant ad firmam regis vii solidos. 7 i denarium. videlicet terra filiorum Wlnodi de Chert reddebat xvi denarios. Terra Euerwaker et Samei xx denarios. Terra Pissebolle xvii denarios. Terra Willelmi filii Gregorii xii denarios. Terra Lifwini Kenthing xx denarios. Itaque quantum remanebat huic mulieri de vii istis solidis. id est tres solidos quos habebat de forgable√ dedit ipsa ecclesie nostre sicut diximus in perpetuam possessionem liberam semper et quietam ab omnibus heredibus suis. Et hereditatem quam in terris illis habebatꝩ totam nobis quietam clamauit. Volumus ergo ut ipsa predictum corredium bene 7 plenarie habeat quamdiu uixerit. set sine omni hereditate. ne aliquis propinquorum eius post obitum ipsius illud clamare possit. Quamdiu autem predictum redditum nobis warantizare poteritꝩ hanc ei donationem 7 conuentionem seruabimus. Rei huius testes sunt. Haimo prepositus. Johannes ælderman. Willelmus filius Gregorii. Willelmus nepos Pagani. Semærus mercier. Walterius de Deueneschire. Normannus de Stureie. Elfwinus de Stureie. Bartholomeus seneschal. Godefridus pistor. Walterius pistor. Willelmus Jonathas. Willelmus Noreis. Willelmus filius Seful. Iuo cocus. Osbernus de porta. 7 multi alii.

C Y R O G R A P H V M

ENDORSEMENT: Twelfth century: Cyrographum contra Athelizam de vᵠᵘᵉ mansuris que sunt retro clocarium nostrum.

SEAL: Second seal of Christ Church, with counterseal, on tag affixed to top of document.

SIZE: 8⅛ ins.×7 7/16 ins.

TEXT: Original charter CAC, Ch. Ant., C 1140.

NOTE: The transaction must be connected with the scheme for clearing the ground south of the cathedral, following the fire of 1174. The names of the justices offer difficulty. The Pipe Roll for 12 Henry II (and following years) records exactions (p. 115) 'De plac' Com' Gaufr'. 7 Ric' de Luci,' while that of 14 Henry II (and following years) records (p. 214) those 'De plac' Archid' Pict'. 7 Widon' Dec'. 7 Regin' de Mar' 7 Henr' fil' Ger' Cam'.' If the charter were drawn up c. 1177, as suggested, when the ground was being cleared, it would refer to events of many years before, and it is possible that two separate visits of justices have been confused. See account of king's holdings in Chapter III.

XXVI

Notification by Roger, abbot elect, and the convent of St Augustine's, reciting terms of agreement between them, and prior Benedict with the convent of Christ Church. The former have (at the request of king Henry II) surrendered to the latter, ground producing rents worth 20s. 11d. *per annum*, lying on the south side of the cathedral belltower, dangerous because of fires, while the latter have given in compensation other ground in Canterbury, producing 22s. 2d. The monks of Christ Church are to pay 20d. *per annum* due to the royal farm, charged on a tenement surrendered to them.

DATE: 1177.

R. DEI gratia sancti Augustini Cant' electus eiusdemque loci conuentus. Vniuersis Christi fidelibus ad quos presentes littere peruenerintꝩ Salutem. Uniuersitati uestre notum esse uolumus. qualiter cum Benedicto priore 7 conuentu ecclesie Christi Cant' quasdam terras nostras pro quibusdam terris suis commutauimus. Nos habuimus quasdam terras ex parte meridiana cimiterii ecclesie Christi iuxta campanile eiusdem loci. scilicet quatuor terras Matildis filie Haymonis dapiferi unde solebamus habere annuatim v solidos 7 x denarios. terram Willelmi furbatoris. unde habebamus ii solidos. terram Willelmi filii Richild. unde habebamus viij solidos. set de his viij solidatis solebamus reddere ad firmam regis xx denarios. terram presbiteri Baldewini de Chert 7 Dauid fratris eius unde habebamus ii solidos. Terram Philippi parmentarii. unde habebamus xx denarios. Terram que fuit Euerwecher. unde habebamus x 7 vij denarios. Terram que fuit Mudechin 7 Sedegos. unde habebamus xx denarios. Summa quorum reddituum est xx solidi 7 xi denarii. 7 terram in qua capella una constru(c)ita fuerat. Quoniam uero he predicte terre ecclesie Christi periculose fuerunt propter crebra incendiaⱽ iccirco ad preces domini nostri Henrici regis Anglie 7 fratrum ecclesie Christi concessimus. dedimus 7 assignauimus in concambium fratribus ecclesie Christi has terras liberas 7 quietas ab omni questione 7 querela. saluo tamen eorum iure qui prenominatas terras de monasterio nostro tenebant. Ipsi uero supradicti fratres ecclesie Christi pro iamdictis terris concesserunt. dederunt 7 assignauerunt in concambium nobis ad electionem nostram quasdam de terris suis liberas 7 quietas ab omni questione 7 querela. Saluo quidem iure eorum qui terras illas de ipsis tenere solebant. scilicet terram Roberti filii Ricardi Flawold que reddebat eis annuatim x denarios. Terram in qua Johannes filius Roberti manet que reddebat eis xx denarios. Terram Willelmi filii Winedei que reddebat eis xii denarios. Terram Burwen. que reddebat x denarios. Terram Basilie de Thanintune que reddebat eis xliiij denarios. Terram in qua Ruelinus Flandrensis manet. que reddebat eis xxvii denarios. Terram Christiane que fuit uxor Roberti filii Henrici que reddebat eis xij denarios. Terram Benedicti presbiteri que reddebat eis xii denarios. Terram Cecilie filie Geroldi que reddebat eis xii denarios. Terram Willelmi de Lisinges que reddebat eis xxi denarios et obolum. Terram Godwini Muschet. que reddebat eis xxi denarios et obolum. Terram Brihtiue filie Remberti que reddebat eis ii solidos. Terram Herewordi lorimier que reddebat eis ii solidos. Terram Bartholomei seneschalli. que reddebat eis viii denarios. Terram Galfridi filii Reimundi que reddebat eis viij denarios. Summa quorum reddituum est xxii solidi 7 ii denarii. Preterea xx denarios quos ad firmam regis de terra supradicti Willelmi filii Richild solebamus reddereⱽ ipsi amodo pro nobis reddent. Sane quia uolumus hanc commutationem 7 concambium hinc inde sicut de utriusque partis consensu factum estⱽ firmiter in perpetuum obseruari. propterea ipsam commutationem ecclesie nostre sigillo curauimus roborare. Hec commutatio facta est anno ab incarnatione domini millesimo centesimo lxxvii.

ENDORSEMENTS: Twelfth century: Carta conuentus sancti Augustini de concambio terrarum retro clocarium. Late thirteenth century?: Cantuar'. Duplicata. (.I.)ᶜ. Fifteenth century: In parochia sancte Marie Magdalen'.

SEAL: First seal of St Augustine's abbey, on tag. Circular, 2¼ ins. diameter, in greenish-brown wax; figure of archbishop giving benediction, holding a cross. Inscription runs: SIGILLV̄ SCI ĀVG[VSTINI ĀGLOR' A]PL'I. See Birch, *Cat. of Seals in Dept. of MSS., BM*, i, p. 485. Counterseal: Signet of Roger, abbot (elect, at this date). Vesica-shaped, 1³⁄₁₆ ins. ×⅞ ins; bust of a monk, with inscription: †SIGILL' ROGERI CAPELLANI SCI THOME.

SIZE: 8¾ ins.×9⅛ ins.

TEXT: Original charter, CAC, Ch. Ant., C 1112.

XXVII

Confirmation by archbishop Richard of exchange of lands in Canterbury between Christ Church and St Augustine's abbey as recorded in XXVI.

DATE: 1177.

RICARDUS Dei gracia Cantuariensis archiepiscopus tocius Anglie primas et apostolice sedis legatus᷎ vniuersis sancte matris ecclesie filiis ad quos presentes littere peruenerint᷎ eternam in domino salutem. Ad omnium volumus noticiam peruenire᷎ qualiter dilecti filii nostri Benedictus prior et conuentus ecclesie Christi Cantuar' cum Rogero electo monasterii sancti Augustini et conuentus eiusdem loci quasdam terras suas pro quibusdam terris ad idem monasterium pertinentibus commutauerunt. Prefatus siquidem electus et conuentus sancti Augustini quasdam terras habuerunt ex parte meridiana cimiterii nostri iuxta campanile nostrum in Cantuar' scilicet quatuor terras Geruasii de Cornhelle vnde solebant habere annuatim quinque solidos et decem denarios. Terram Willelmi furbatoris vnde habebant duos solidos. Terram Willelmi filii Ricardi vnde habebant octo solidos᷎ de quibus reddebant ad firmam domini regis annuatim viginti denarios. vnde monachi nostri eos acquietabunt erga regem. Terram eciam Baldewini presbiteri et Dauid de Chert fratris eius vnde habebant duos solidos. Terram Philippi parmentarii vnde habebant viginti denarios. Terram que fuit Everwaker᷎ vnde habebant septemdecim denarios. Terram que fuit Mudekin et Sedegos que reddebat eis viginti denarios. Summa quorum reddituum est viginti solidi et vndecim denarii. Et terram in qua quedam capella constructa fuerat. Quoniam vero hee predicte terre nobis et ecclesie nostre periculose fuerunt propter crebra incendia᷎ idcirco predictus Rogerus electus et conuentus prenominati monasterii ad preces domini nostri Henrici regis Anglie et nostras concesserunt et dederunt et assignauerunt in escambium nobis et ecclesie nostre᷎ has terras liberas et quietas ab omni questione et querela᷎ saluo quidem iure illorum (qui prenominatas terras de monasterio sancti Augustini tenebant. Nos autem pro iamdictis terris concessimus dedimus et assignauimus in concambium eidem electo et conuentui ad electionem ipsorum quasdam de terris nostris liberas et quietas ab omni questione et querela saluo quidem iure illorum)ᵐ qui terras illas de eis tenere solebant᷎ scilicet terram Roberti filii Ricardi Flacwold¹ ²que reddebat illis annuatim decem denarios. Terram in qua Johannes filius Roberti manet que reddebat eis viginti denarios. Terram Willelmi filii Winedai que reddebat eis duodecim denarios. Terram Burewen que reddebat eis decem denarios. Terram Basilie de Tanintone que reddebat eis quadraginta quatuor denarios. Terram in qua Ruelinus Flandrensis manet que reddebat eis viginti et septem denarios. Terram Cristiane que fuit vxor Roberti filii Henrici que reddebat eis duodecim denarios. Terram Benedicti presbiteri que reddebat eis duodecim denarios. Terram Cecelie filie Geroldi que reddebat eis duodecim denarios. Terram Willelmi de Lisinges que reddebat eis viginti et vnum denarios et obolum. Terram Godwini Muschet que reddebat eis viginti et vnum denarios et obolum. Terram Bricthiue filie Reimberti que reddebat eis duos solidos. Terram Herewardi lorimer que reddebat eis duos solidos. Terram Bartholomei senescalli que reddebat eis octo denarios. Et terram Gaufridi filii Reymundi que reddebat eis octo denarios. Summa quorum reddituum est viginti duo solidi et duo denarii.[2] [3]Sane quia[3] volumus hanc commutacionem et escambium hincinde sicut de utriusque partis consensu factum est firmiter et inuiolabiliter in perpetuum obseruari ipsam commutationem presentis scripti nostri patrocinio confirmamus et sigilli nostri munimine roboramus. Facta est autem hec commutacio´ anno incarnacionis dominice millesimo centesimo septuagesimo septimo regnante illustrissimo Anglorum rege Henrico secundo.

TEXT: Transcript of later thirteenth century in BM Cotton Claudius D. X, ff. 72r.–73r.

PRINTED: Somner (*Antiquities of Canterbury*, 1640, app. x), with variations: [1]Richardi Flatbold; [2–2] *omitted*; [3–3] *cumque*; and other minor variations. Thorne recites the counterpart issued by Benedict (*Thorne*, col. 1820) omitting passages corresponding with omissions in Somner's text. Somner (who must have had access to a MS. of Thorne) has apparently conflated the version issued by Benedict and the confirmation of archbishop Richard (i.e. xxvii, here). Thorne was published in *Scriptores* x, 1652.

XXVIII

Charter of Henry II confirming arrangements made by terms of xxvi and xxvii above.
DATE: c. 8 May 1177?

H. DEI gratia rex Anglorum 7 dux Normannorum 7 Aquitanorum 7 comes Andegauorum. archiepiscopis. episcopis. abbatibus. comitibus. baronibus. justiciis. vicecomitibus. 7 omnibus ministris 7 fidelibus suis Francis 7 Anglis totius Anglie. Salutem. Sciatis me concessisse 7 presenti carta confirmasse conuentionem 7 commutationem quam Rogerus electus monasterii sancti Augustini Cant' 7 conuentus eiusdem loci fecerunt Benedicto priori 7 conuentui ecclesie Christi Cant' de quibusdam terris suis quas idem electus 7 conuentus predicti monasterii habuerunt ex parte meridiana cimiterii ecclesie Christi iuxta campanile eiusdem loci. pro quibusdam aliis terris quas. prenominatus B. prior 7 conuentus ecclesie Christi dederunt iamdicto R. electo 7 conuentui pretaxati monasterii in excambium illarum terrarum que sunt iuxta campanile ecclesie Christi sicut supradictum est. Quare volo 7 firmiter precipio quod conuentio illa 7 commutatio inter eos stabilis 7 firma maneat 7 inconcusse teneatur. sicut inter eos facta est 7 utrobique concessa 7 eorum cartis confirmata 7 distincta. T' G. Elyensi. J. Norwic'. R. Bathon'. episcopis. Ricardo de Luci. Willelmo filio Audel' dapifero. Vnfrido de Bohun constabulario. Reginaldo de Curtenai. Thoma Basset. Willelmo de Stut'. Radulfo filio Stephani. Thoma filio Bern'. Eustatio filio Stephani. apud Windesor'.

ENDORSEMENT: Contemp.: Carta H ii confirmans escambium de terris retro clocarium nostrum.

SEAL: Document is folded twice at bottom and is slit, but no trace of seal nor of tag remains.

SIZE: 5⅘ ins.× 8⅓ ins.

TEXTS: Original charter CAC, Ch. Ant., C 73. Copy in BM. Cotton, Claudius D X, fol.
73. Copy in MS. History of St Augustine's abbey (fifteenth century), attributed to Thomas
of Elmham (Trinity Hall MS., Cambridge), fol. 95v.

PRINTED: (from last-mentioned MS.) *Historia Monasterii Sancti Augustini Cantuariensis*, RS,
pp. 461, 462. No material variants.

XXIX

Record of agreement (with permission of the king), between prior H. (Herlewin?) and the
convent of Christ Church, Canterbury; and Gervase of Cornhill with his son Reginald and
Matilda, wife to Reginald. Ground near the cathedral belltower, partly bought by Gervase,
and partly of the inheritance of Matilda, is exchanged for ground in Friday Street, London,
property of the prior and convent. Buildings on the ground near the belltower in Canterbury,
were dangerous to the cathedral on account of frequent fires.

DATE: 1177?

C Y R O G R A P H V M

H. PRIOR & conuentus ecclesie Christi Cantuar'. Uniuersis Christi fidelibus.
Salutem. Sciant presentes & futuri quod hec commutatio facta est inter conuentum
ecclesie Christi Cantuar'. & Geruasium de Cornhell' & Raginaldum filium eius &
Matildem uxorem ipsius Raginaldi filiam Haymonis. Geruasius habebat quandam
terram retro clocarium nostrum. cuius quandam partem ipse Geruasius sumptu
suo emerat. quedam autem pars erat de hereditate Matildis uxoris Raginaldi filii
Geruasii. Et quia edificia terre illius erant periculo ecclesie nostre propter crebra
incendia' Geruasius de Cornhell'. & Raginaldus filius eius & Matildis uxor eiusdem
Raginaldi pro salute animarum suarum ex concessione domini regis dederunt
conuentui in concambium eandem terram pro quadam terra quam ipsi monachi
habebant Lundon' in Frideistrete. quam tenuerunt Teodericus. Johannes presbiter
7 Giffard. quam idem monachi prius concesserant Geruasio in feodum 7 hereditatem pro xx solidis annuatim inde reddendis. Nunc autem eandem terram concesserunt ipsi Gervasio 7 Raginaldo filio eius & Matildi ipsius uxori liberam & quietam
ab omni seruicio in perpetuum tenendam. Vt autem hec conuentio firma sit' presentis cyrographi attestatione utrimque confirmata est. 7 domini regis sigillo robor-
ata. 7 domini Cantuar' archiepiscopi Ricardi testimonio confirmata. His testibus.
[*blank*].

ENDORSEMENTS: Contemp.: Concambium inter nos 7 Geruasium de Cornell'; thirteenth
century: (XXXIIII)ᶜ Cantuar'; sixteenth century: Sancte Magdalene.

SEALS: Originally there were three seals, each tag passing through two slits in the fold at bottom. Fold is exceptionally wide (2⅛ ins. to 2⅜ ins.). 1. Archbishop Richard, in red wax,
vesica-shaped, 3¾ ins ×2¼ ins. originally; damaged at top. Figure of archbishop, bearing
staff, mitre with points at sides; diapered background. Legend: [SI]GILLVM [RICAR]DI DEI
GRATIA CANTVARIENSIS ARCHIEPISCO[PI]. Counterseal, vesica-shaped, 1⁵⁄₈ ins.× 1½ ins.
Half-length figure of archbishop, bearing staff, mitre with points at sides. Legend, very

faint, both on this example and on that attached to charter XXX; it seems to run: RICARDVS DEI GRATIA ANGLIE PRIMAS. 2. Missing, evidently that of Henry II. See last lines above. 3. Seal of Gervase of Cornhill, in red wax, circular, $1\frac{3}{4}$ ins. diameter; design of lion passant, facing left. Legend: SIGILLVM GERVASII JUSTICIE L[V]DONIARVM.

SIZE: $9\frac{1}{4}$ ins.×$9\frac{5}{8}$ ins.

TEXT: Original charter, CAC, Ch. Ant., C 859.

NOTE: (to XXIX–XXXII): Probably one copy of each of the two charters (XXIX with XXX, XXXI with XXXII) was meant for either of the parties concerned, though endorsements show that all copies have been in the cathedral archives ever since, or from a time close to, the date of issue. The charter XXIX, XXX must be confined to the priorate of Herlewin (1177–79) and not that of Honorius (1186–88) since archbishop Richard (1174–84) is mentioned, while G. of Cornhill died 1183–4. Herlewin's succession to the priorate cannot have taken place before June 1177, since his predecessor Benedict was only appointed to Peterborough 29 May (Eyton, p. 215). Henry was at Westminster 13 March 1177 and thereabout (Eyton, pp. 211, 212), then 27 August 1179 and again late 1181 (ibid. p. 244) by which time Herlewin had resigned (Searle, p. 159). The date of XXXI, XXXII seems to be 27 August 1179, which is very likely as the king had been at Canterbury only five days before, when the royal seal may have been attached to XXIX, XXX. The court witnesses in XXXI, XXXII are, apart from the bishops of London and Durham, all named in a charter assigned to 27 August 1179 (Eyton, p. 228).

XXX

Counterpart of no. XXIX.

C Y R O G R A P H V M [*inverted*]

ENDORSEMENTS: Contemp.: Concambium inter nos 7 Geruasium de Cor(n)[1] helle. Thirteenth century: XXXIIII. Cantuar'. Fifteenth century: In parochia Marie Magdalene.

SEALS: Originally three seals, on tags, each passing through fold, which is exceptionally wide ($2\frac{9}{10}$ ins.). 1. Seal of archbishop Richard, in red wax, with counterseal, as attached to XXIX. 2. Missing, evidently that of Henry II (see conclusion of charter, above). 3. Second seal of Christ Church, in red wax, with counterseal.

SIZE: $9\frac{7}{8}$ ins.×$9\frac{5}{8}$ ins.

TEXT: Original charter, CAC, Ch. Ant., C 846. No material variants from text of XXIX.

NOTE: See XXIX.

XXXI

Confirmation by king Henry II of arrangements made by terms of XXIX, XXX. Duplicate of XXXII.

DATE: 27 August 1179?

H. DEI gratia rex Anglorum 7 dvx Normannorum 7 Aquitanorum 7 comes Andegauorum᷎ archiepiscopis. episcopis. abbatibus. comitibus. baronibus. justiciis. vicecomitibus. ministris. 7 omnibus fidelibus suis totius Anglie᷎ salutem. Sciatis me concessisse 7 presenti carta mea confirmasse conuentionem que facta fuit coram me inter H. priorem 7 conuentum ecclesie Christi Cantuar'. 7 Geruasium de Cornhulla. 7 Raginaldum filium eius. 7 Mathildem vxorem ipsius Raginaldi filiam Haymonis. 7 escambium inter eosdem monachos 7 ipsos factum de subscriptis terris sicut cyrographum inde inter eos factum testatur. Videlicet quod Geruasius de Cornhell' 7 Raginaldus filius eius 7 Mathildis vxor eiusdem Raginaldi pro salute animarum suarum ex concessione mea dederunt in escambium conuentui predicto ecclesie Christi quandam terram in Cantuar' quam prefatus Geruasius habebat retro clocarium eiusdem ecclesie. cuius quandam partem ipse Geruasius sumptu suo emerat. quedam autem pars erat de hereditate Mathildis vxoris Raginaldi filii Geruasii. quia edificia terre illius erant periculo ipsi ecclesie Christi propter crebra incendia√ pro quadam terra quam monachi eiusdem ecclesie habebant Lvndon'. In Frideistrete. quam tenuerunt Teodericus. Johannes presbiter 7 Giffard. quam idem monachi prius concesserant Geruasio in feodum 7 hereditatem pro xx solidis annuatim inde reddendis. Nunc autem eandem terram concesserunt monachi illi ipsi Geruasio 7 Raginaldo filio eius. 7 Mathildi vxori ipsius Raginaldi liberam 7 quietam ab omni seruitio in perpetuum tenendam. Quare uolo 7 firmiter precipio quod hec conuentio inter eos facta. secundum quod in cyrographo eorum continetur√ rata sit 7 stabilis. 7 inconcusse teneatur. T. G. Lvndon'. G. Elien'. H. Dunelm'. J. Northwic'√ episcopis. Willelmo de Albinn' comite Suthsex'. Rannulfo de Glanvill'. Reginaldo de Cvrtenai. Willelmo de Lanval'. Thoma Basset. Sehero de Qvinci. Roberto filio Bernardi. Willelmo de Bendeng'√ apud Westmon'.

ENDORSEMENTS: Contemp.: Carta Henrici regis [in another hand] De escambio inter nos 7 Geruasium de Cornhell'.

SEAL: Second seal of Henry II, in red wax, damaged at rim, attached to bottom of document (which is folded twice) by a green lace.

SIZE: 8½ ins.× 6¾ ins.

TEXT: Original charter, CAC, Ch. Ant., C 1208.

NOTE: See XXIX.

XXXII

Duplicate of XXXI.

ENDORSEMENTS: Contemp.: De escambio inter nos 7 Geruasium de Cornhelle. Thirteenth century: Confirmacio Henrici regis de quadam terra retro clocarium nostrum: this passage seems to be written in two different hands.

SEAL: Second seal of Henry II, in red wax, badly damaged, attached by a green lace.

SIZE: 7½ ins× 7¼ ins.

TEXT: Original charter, CAC, Ch. Ant., C 1209. No material variants between texts of XXXI and XXXII.

NOTE: See XXIX.

XXXIII

Sale and grant by Hamo Coppe to the convent of Christ Church, Canterbury, of (1) ground once held by him within Burgate from St Augustine's abbey, the subject of an exchange between the two houses; and (2) ground at St Michael Burgate church, within the gate, given to the grantor in exchange for no. 1. Christ Church has given Hamo Coppe 20s.
DATE: C. 1200.

SCIANT presentes et futuri quod ego Hamo Coppe filius Henrici Coppe vendidi et concessi in perpetuum domino priori 7 conuentui ecclesie sancte Trinitatis Cant'. terram meam infra Burgate quam tenui de ecclesia sancti Augustini de qua dominus abbas et conuentus sancti Augustini. et dominus prior et conuentus ecclesie Christi Cant' inter se per concambium amicabiliter composuerunt. et terram illam que est infra murum ciuitatis Cant'. iuxta ecclesiam de Burgate uersus aquilonem. quam dederunt mihi in concambium alterius predicte terre. Et pro hac uenditione et concessione mea facta et recognita et sacramento et interposita fidei religione firmata in capitali curia ecclesie sancte Trinitatis Cant'. et in burgimoto ciuitatis Cant'. et in bertha de Burgateᵛ predictus prior et conuentus ecclesie Christi Cant'. dederunt mihi uiginti solidos sterlingorum. Igitur ut hec uenditio et concessio mea firma et stabilis sit in eternum presentem cartam meam sigilli mei munimine confirmaui. Hiis testibus. Henrico de Sorene. Martino senescallo. Thoma de Denne. Willelmo de cardino. Johanne mercerio. Willelmo filio Hugonis. Anfrido fratre suo. Malgero filio Roberti. Osmundo de fraxino. Stephano de porta. Roberto de porta. Ada camerario. Willelmo Malueisin. 7 multis aliis.

ENDORSEMENTS: Contemp.: Carta Hamunis Coppe de terra infra Burgate. Thirteenth century: Magdalen' Registratur.
SEAL: Circular, 1⅝ ins. diameter; in brown wax. Design of quatrefoil. Inscription (damaged) runs: SIGIL[L' HA?]MONIS COPPE.
SIZE: 3⅞ ins × 7¾ ins.
TEXT: Original charter CAC, Ch. Ant., C 849.
NOTE: Ground of H. Coppe within Burgate, next to St Michael's church, is mentioned in Rental D, 89.

XXXIV

Confirmation of Alditha, sister of Hamo Coppe, of arrangements recorded in XXXIII, with quitclaim.
DATE: C. 1200.

SCIANT presentes et futuri quod ego Alditha filia Henrici Coppe ratam et firmam habeo illam uenditionem et concessionem quam Hamo frater meus fecit domino priori et conuentui ecclesie sancte Trinitatis Cant'. sicut carta eius testatur de duabus terris illis intra Burgate quarum una fuit de tenura ecclesie sancti Augustini. et altera iacet iuxta ecclesiam de Burgate intra murum uersus aquilonem. Et pro hac uenditione et concessione predicti fratris mei facta et recordata et interposita fidei et sacramenti religione firmata in capitali curia ecclesie sancte Trinitatis Cant'. et in burgimoto ciuitatis Cant'. et in bertha de Burgate que ut firma et stabilis sit in eternum sigillo meo est munita. predictus prior et conuentus dederunt mihi duos solidos sterlingorum. Hiis testibus. Henrico de Sorene. Martino senescallo. Thoma de Denne. Willelmo de cardino. Johanne mercerio. Willelmo filio Hugonis. et Anfrido fratre suo. Malgero filio Roberti. Osmundo de fraxino. Stephano janitore. Roberto de porta. Ada camerario. Willelmo Malueisin. et multis aliis.

ENDORSEMENTS: Contemp.: Carta Aldithe que fuit soror Hamonis Coppe de terra infra Burgate. Magdalen' Registratur.
SEAL: Lost, tag only remains.
SIZE: $3\frac{1}{4}$ ins.$\times 7\frac{11}{16}$ ins.
TEXT: Original charter, CAC, Ch. Ant., C 860.

XXXV

Notification by prior Benedict and the convent of Christ Church, Canterbury, of exchange with Lambin Frese, who surrenders ground before the cathedral gate for two pieces of ground at the ford near Hottemelne, in Canterbury. The monks have given him ten marks to go.
DATE: 1175–May 1177.

CYROGRAPHUM

BENEDICTUS prior 7 conuentus ecclesie Christi Cantuar'. Omnibus qui habitant in ciuitate Cantuaria. salutem. Notum sit tam presentibus quam futuris quod Lambinus Frese reddidit nobis terram suam quam tenebat de nobis illam que iacet ante portam cimiterii nostri. liberam 7 quietam ab omni calumpnia tam sui quam heredum suorum in perpetuum habendam. Nos autem dedimus ei 7 heredibus suis in concambium quandam terram uersus Hottemelne iuxta forde. que fuit Godwini Grom. 7 aliam terram iuxta illam que fuit Geroldi le tanur. tenendas de nobis a Lambino 7 heredibus suis. ita quod ipse 7 heredes sui reddent nobis 7 ecclesie nostre de illis duabus terris singulis annis quinque solidos. scilicet tres solidos de terra que fuit Godwini 7 duos solidos de terra que fuit Geroldi. ad duos terminos. medietatem in medio quadragesime. 7 ad festum sancti Michaelis alteram medietatem. Terram quoque quam reddidit nobis warantizabunt nobis ipse 7 heredes sui contra omnes homines. similiter 7 nos warantizabimus ei 7 heredibus suis contra omnes homines terras quas dedimus eis in concambium. Huius concambii gratia dedimus predicto Lambino. decem marcas in plena curia. 7 saisinam de terra sua recepimus. 7 eum de concambi [sic] saisiuimus. Testibus his. Helya de Silinghelde. Toma de Essedeford. Willelmo de Ludesdune. Willelmo de Langedune. Johanne Herengod. Alano alderman. Ricardo Deudune. Bartholomeo dapifero. Willelmo de Capes. 7 multis aliis sicut in plenaria curia.

ENDORSEMENTS: Contemp.: Carta Lambini Frese de terra ante portam cimiterii. Thirteenth century: Concambium. Fifteenth century: Sancti Andree.

SEAL: Mass of brown wax in which is impressed seal $\frac{5}{8}$ ins.$\times \frac{3}{4}$ ins. on tag, passing twice through fold. Classical gem, design of hound or wolf running, surrounded by inscription (twelfth century) very faint, evidently: SIGILLUM LAMBERTI.

SIZE: $7\frac{1}{2}$ ins.$\times 5\frac{3}{16}$ ins.

TEXT: Original charter CAC, Ch. Ant., F 42.

NOTE: Charters XXXV, XXXVI, XXXVII disclose the origins of the stone house of Lambin Frese, later that of Adam of Charing, Becket's enemy, and later still the Poor Priests' Hospital. See B 79; D 224; F 246, 489. Charter XXXV is limited to Benedict's priorate. The royal charter, XXXVI, cannot be later than April 1179 when Richard de Luci retired from worldly business. Of the many times that the court was at Windsor, 8 May 1177 seems the most likely date for the issue of XXXVI since the king had just been at Canterbury. The later limiting date for XXXVII is 9 May 1227, when H. de Sandford, archdeacon of Canterbury, was consecrated bishop of Rochester.

XXXVI

Charter of Henry II confirming an exchange made between the prior and convent of Christ Church, Canterbury, and Lambin Frese, whereby the former bestow on the latter two pieces of ground at the ford, near Hottemelne, in Canterbury, while Lambin gives up in return his ground in front of the cemetery gate of the Cathedral. Lambin is to pay a total of 5s. rent *per annum* to the prior and convent for the two pieces of ground.

DATE: c. 8 May 1177?

H. DEI gratia rex Anglorum 7 dux Normannorum 7 Aquitanorum 7 comes Andegauorum. archiepiscopis. episcopis. abbatibus. comitibus. baronibus. justiciis. vicecomitibus. 7 omnibus ministris 7 fidelibus suis totius Anglie. Salutem. Sciatis me concessisse 7 presenti carta confirmasse conuentionem rationabiliter factam inter priorem 7 monachos ecclesie Christi Cant' 7 Lambinum Frise. hanc videlicet quod Lambinus reddidit eis terram quam tenebat de illis que iacet ante portam cimiterii liberam 7 quietam ab omni calumpnia tam sui quam heredum suorum in perpetuum habendam. Et eidem monachi dederunt ei 7 heredibus suis in concambium quandam terram uersus Hottemelne iuxta forde que fuit Godwini Grom. 7 aliam terram iuxta illam que fuit Geroldi le tanur. sibi 7 heredibus suis de eis tenendas ita quod ipse 7 heredes sui reddent monachis 7 predicte ecclesie Cant' de illis duabus terris v solidos singulis annis. Scilicet iij solidos de terra que fuit Godwini. 7 ij solidos de terra que fuit Geroldi ad duos terminos. medietatem in medio quadragesime. 7 ad festum sancti Michaelis alteram medietatem. Ipse uero Lambinus 7 heredes sui guarantizare debent monachis contra omnes homines terram quam ipse Lambinus eis reddidit. 7 monachi similiter guarantizabunt Lambino 7 heredibus suis contra omnes homines terram quam ei dederunt in concambium. Quare volo 7 firmiter precipio quod conuentio ista inter eos stabilis maneat 7 inconcusse teneatur sicut inter eos facta fuit 7 utrobique concessa 7 sicut cyrographum inter eos factum testatur. T. Ricardo Wint'. G. Elyensi. episcopis. Ricardo de Luci. Alwredo de sancto

Martino. dapifero. Reginaldo de Curtenai. Roberto Marmion. Willelmo de Lanual'. Thoma Basset. Hugone de Creissi. Willelmo Basset. Willelmo filio Radulfi. 7 Gerardo de Canuilla. apud Windesor'.

ENDORSEMENTS: Twelfth century: Carta H. ii inter nos 7 Lambinum Frese. de terra ante portam cimiterii nostri. Thirteenth century: (XVI)ᶜ
SEAL: Bottom of document is folded three times and slit, but tag and seal have disappeared.
SIZE: 10 ins.× 7⅜ ins.
TEXT: Original charter, CAC, Ch. Ant., C 1207. Transcripts in CAC, Reg. A, fol. 146r., and in Reg. E, fol. 51r. No material variants.

XXXVII

Grant by Roger the clerk, son of Lambin Frese, of messuage in St Margaret's parish, Canterbury, to Alexander of Gloucester and his heirs, for 105 marks, saving 5s. *per annum* rent due to the prior and convent of Christ Church.
DATE: 1227 or before, in a copy of 1422–1423.

SCIANT presentes et futuri quod ego Rogerus clericus filius Lambini Frese ciuis Cantuar' dedi et concessi et hac presenti carta mea confirmaui Alexandro de Glowcestria et cuicumque dare vendere vel assignare voluerit totum illud mesagium meum in parochia sancte Margarete Cant' inter mesagium Roberti de Hottewelle versus aquilonem et introitum Sture versus austrum et inter Sturam versus occidentem et regiam stratam versus orientem. tenend' et habend' imperpetuum ipse et cuicumque dare vendere vel assignare voluerit iure hereditario libere quiete et pacifice. Reddendo inde annuatim priori et conuentui ecclesie Christi Cantuar' in thesauraria sua quinque solidos scilicet in festo sancti Michaelis duos solidos et sex denarios et ad mediam quadragesimam duos solidos et sex denarios pro omnibus seruiciis consuetudinibus et demandis temporalibus omni occasione remota. Pro hac autem donacione concessione et confirmacione facta et recordata in capitali curia predicti prioris et in burgimoto ciuitatis Cant' et in hundredo berthe de Wrgate dedit mihi predictus Alexander centum et quinque marcas in gersumam. Et ne contra istam donacionem concessionem et confirmacionem ego vel heredes mei venire possimus presentem cartam sigilli mei apposicione communiui. Hiis testibus, magistro Henrico de Sanford archidiacono Cant', Johanne Turte, Radulpho fratre suo aldermanno berthe, Henrico de Osprenge tunc senescallo curie prioris, Lambino Flemengo, Thoma spiciario, Gwydone cissore, Adam mersario, Henrico le Jay, Osmundo Polre, Rogero de Gypewiz, Philippo Terrici, Johanne fratre suo, Willelmo decano, et multis aliis. Hec est vera copia cuiusdam carte Rogeri clerici filii Lambini Frese facte Alexandro de Glowcestria vt patet superius sigillo communi hospitalis pauperum sacerdotum Cant' consignate.

ENDORSEMENT: Fifteenth century: Vera copia carte Rogeri clerici filii Lambini Frese sigillo communi hospitalis pauperum sacerdotum Cantuar' sigillata quia carta ipsa originalis dicto hospitali de consilio iurisperitorum liberatur anno regni regis Henrici sexti primo.

SEAL: Fragment of red wax on tag.
SIZE: 4 $\frac{7}{10}$ ins. × 12 ins.
TEXT: CAC, Ch. Ant., C 884; sealed true copy.

XXXVIII

Notification by prior Alan and the convent of Christ Church, Canterbury, that they will pay
to Baldwin Calvel and his heirs 4s. *per annum* for all services, for certain ground in front of
the cemetery gate of the priory, formerly held of Baldwin and his heirs by tenants (named).
DATE: 1179–86.

C Y R O G R A P H V M [*inverted*]

ALANUS prior 7 conuentus ecclesie Christi Cantuar'. omnibus Christi fidelibus
salutem. Nouerit uniuersitas uestra quod nos dabimus Baldewino Caluel 7 heredibus suis singulis annis quatuor solidos pro omni seruitio pro terris que sunt ante
portam cimiterii nostri. pro terra scilicet quam tenuit Æluredus. 7 pro terra quam
tenuit Ælfelmus. 7 pro terra quam tenuit Andreas de predictis scilicet Baldewino 7
heredibus suis. ad duos terminos reddendos scilicet in media quadragesima. duos
solidos, 7 ad festum sancti Michaelis. duos solidos. His testibus. Moritio de Waden-
hal'. Roberto filio Hamonis. Willelmo Misch'. Rogerio aldermanno. 7 multis
aliis.

ENDORSEMENT: c. 1200: De terris ante portam cimiterii.
SEAL: No evidence for sealing.
SIZE: 4 ins. × 5$\frac{3}{8}$ins.
TEXT: Original charter CAC, Ch. Ant., C 1143. The priorate of Alan offers limiting dates.
    For the payment undertaken, see C 75; G 42, 80. See C 24 n.

XXXIX

Notification by H. prior and the convent of Christ Church, Canterbury, of grant to Hugh
piscator and his son, of two shops behind the cathedral belltower, at 5s. *per annum*. The grantors will build the shops and the grantees are to keep them in repair with tile and stone to
minimize danger of fire.
DATE: 1177–9 or 1186–8.

C Y R O G R A P H V M

H. PRIOR 7 conuentus ecclesie Christi Cantuar'. uniuersis Christi fidelibus. Salutem.
Notum sit presentibus 7 futuris quod nos concessimus Hugoni piscatori 7 filiis eius
duas scoppas retro clocarium nostrum tenendas de nobis iure hereditario. Habebunt autem scoppe ille viginti 7 ix pedes in longitudine sicut terra eorum prius
durabat in latum. 7 de illis persoluent nobis annuatim quinque solidos. Scoppas
istas sumptibus nostris faciemus 7 illis committemus. sed postquam ipsi eas rece-

perint✓ propriis sumptibus eas seruabunt 7 cum opus fuerit emendabunt bene de lapide uel tegula ne per incendium periculo esse possint. nec poterunt illas uendere aut cambire uel inuadiare sine assensu nostro. Testibus his. Gileberto presbitero. Hugone Coffin. Bartholomeo dapifero. Rogerio Albo. Malgerio portario. Semero 7 Gaulterio mercatoribus. Johanne Suetman. Helya pellipario. Willelmo Picot 7 multis aliis.

ENDORSEMENT: Later thirteenth century: Carta H. prioris 7 conuentus de duabus scoppis.

SEAL: Second seal of Christ Church, on tag, in brown wax, with counterseal. Seal (in good condition) is thin and translucent.

SIZE: $5\frac{3}{8}$ ins.$\times 7\frac{1}{2}$ ins.

TEXT: Original charter CAC, C 873.

NOTE: The dates given are those of priors Herlewin and Honorius.

XL

Notification by abbot Roger and the convent of St Augustine's, Canterbury, of settlement of dispute between them and Reginald of Cornhill over rents once paid by Haymo son of Roger the cook.

DATE: After January, 1179–1210.

ROGERUS Dei gracia abbas sancti Augustini Cantuar' et conuentus eiusdem loci vniuersis sancte matris ecclesie fidelibus ad quos presens scriptum peruenerit✓ perpetuam in domino salutem. Nouerit vniuersitas vestra quod controuersia que erat inter nos et Reginaldum de Cornhelle de redditu quem Haymo filius Rogeri coci solebat reddere abbati et conuentui sancti Augustini de burgagio in Cantuaria✓ ita terminata est et finita. Omnes haghas et omnes terras de burgagio quas supradictus Haymo die qua fuit uiuus et mortuus hereditario iure tenuit de sancto Augustino intra muros ciuitatis et extra✓ concessimus et presenti carta nostra confirmauimus ipsi Reginaldo et heredibus suis jure hereditario. Tenendas de sancto Augustino et de nobis. Reddendo inde annuatim nobis triginta quinque solidos in duobus terminis anni. In media quadragesima viginti solidos et in natiuitate sancti Johannis Baptiste quindecim solidos. preter tresdecim solidos et quatuor denarios quos reddit ad cellarium sancti Augustini annuatim de Northeham in quatuor terminis anni✓ Et preter septem solidos et nouem denarios quos super altare sancti Augustini reddit annuatim in duobus terminis anni✓ et preter concambium quod fecimus de terra nostra cum monachis sancte Trinitatis. Et in hac pace et propter hanc pacem clamauit ipse Reginaldus nobis quietam terram quandam juxta gardinum nostrum in qua grangie Rogeri coci et granaria aliquando fuerunt✓ quietam dico et liberam de se et heredibus suis in perpetuum✓ quia de dominio nostro est ab antiquo. Hiis testibus magistro Radulfo de Fordam. Elya clerico de Rya. Rogero de Northb' tunc senescallo sancti Augustini. Johanne filio Viuiani. Roberto filio Ricardi. Michaele clerico. Johanne filio Viuiani [sic]. Gilberto fratre abbatis. Willelmo filio Reginaldi. et Radulfo fratre eius. Haymone de Northewode.

Waltero marescallo. Alexandro hostiario. Wylekin coco. Radulfo Barat. Martino de Eastureie.

TEXT: Transcript of later thirteenth century in BM. MS. Cotton Claudius D X, fol. 73v.

NOTE: Roger was not confirmed as abbot until January 1179 (Eyton, p. 225). Reginald of Cornhill is (in absence of information to the contrary) probably Reginald I, who died by 1210 (the suggested limiting date). Haymo son of Roger is Reginald's father-in-law. See Chapter III for the Cornhill family.

XLI

Grant by Juliana, prioress, and the convent of St Sepulchre, Canterbury, to Osbert of Thanington, of three acres of ground outside Worthgate, Canterbury, to hold by hereditary tenure, for 3s. per annum.
DATE: Late twelfth century.

SCIANT presentes 7 futuri quod ego Juliana priorissa ecclesie sancti sepulchri eiusdemque loci conuentus concessimus Hosberto de Tanintun'. tres acras de terra extra Wrgatiam. que acre iacent inter terram predicti Osberti quam tenet de conuentu ecclesie Christi Cant'√ 7 terram que fuit Helie filii Radulfi. iure hereditario de nobis tenendas. ille 7 heredes sui annuatim soluendo iij. solidos ad natiuitatem sancte Marie pro omni seruicio. 7 nos ei 7 heredibus suis acras predictas contra omnes homines 7 feminas warantizabimus[.] Vt hec nostra concessio firma 7 inconcussa permaneat√ presentem cartam 7 sigilli nostri munimine consignamus. 7 testium subscriptorum testimonio confirmamus. Hamone presbitero. 7 Radulf' Caluel. Ham' fil' Widonis. Morin. Will' Pinere. Will' Coc. Warin Chien. 7 multi alii.

ENDORSEMENT: Contemp.: de terra Worgate. Late thirteenth century?: Carta priorisse de sancto sepulchro. facta Osberto de Tanintune. Fifteenth century?: vij.

SEAL: St Sepulchre's priory, circular, 2⅝ ins. diameter, showing an angel seated upon the Sepulchre, beneath a canopy; inscription: + SIGI[ILLVM ECL'E S'] SEPV[LCHRI] CANT-VARIE. N.B. This is first version of the seal. A very close copy was made and was in use by 1278, as on CAC, Ch. Ant., B 319. The second version is illustrated in VCH, Kent, ii, opp. p. 142 (from B 319).

SIZE: 2½ ins.× 5 ins.

TEXT: Original charter, CAC, Ch. Ant., C 1184. Transcript of early fifteenth century in CAC, Reg. A, fol. 348v. No material variants.

XLII

Confirmation by Juliana, prioress, and the convent of St Sepulchre, Canterbury, of grant made by Osbern the priest of Thanington, to St Thomas the martyr, of ground bought by him from the nuns, saving rent of 3s. *per annum* due to them.

DATE: Late twelfth century.

VNIUERSIS sancte ecclesie filiis√ Jvliana prior 7 conuentus sanctimonialium in ecclesia sancti Sepulcri Cantuarie Deo famulantium√ salutem. Nouerint presentes 7 futuri. quod nos concessimus sancto martyri Thome terram nostram iuxta hospitale sancti Jacobi. quam Osbernus presbiter de Tanint' a nobis emit. 7 de nobis tenuit. 7 sancto Thome in elemosinam dedit. Uolumus ergo ut eidem sancto libera 7 quieta remaneat ab omni seruitio. saluo redditu nostro quem a prefato Osberno habuimus. 7 habere debemus. hoc est iij sol. annuatim pro omni seruitio. Qui denarii reddi debent in natiuitate beate Marie in septembri. Testes huius rei sunt. Robertus clericus de sancto Sepulcro. Yun de bertona. Ricardus de balneario. Hugo de domo infirmorum. Joseph frater Roberti cognomento Angeli. 7 alii plures.

ENDORSEMENT: Contemp.: Carta sancti Sepulchri de terra Osberni presbiteri quam dedit sancto Thome. c. 1300: Wenchep'.

SEAL: MS. is folded and slit, but tag and seal have gone.

SIZE: 3⅜ ins. × 7⅝ ins.

TEXT: Original charter CAC, Ch. Ant., C 1161. Transcripts of late thirteenth century in CAC, Reg. A (fol. 374v.), and Reg. E (fol. 106v.) No material variants. Version in Reg. H of early thirteenth century (fol. 28) where all witnesses are omitted.

XLIII

Notification by prior Odo and the convent of Christ Church, Canterbury, that Sedegos and Scolastica, daughters of Elviva, wife successively of Eadulf and of Bruman secretarius, have made grant and quitclaim of their property in Canterbury, in exchange for a corrody of food, drink and use of a room, with pension to Sedegos.

DATE: 1167–75.

ODO prior. 7 conuentus ecclesie Christi Cant'. omnibus ciuibus eiusdem ciuitatis√ salutem. Scire nos uolumus quod Sedegos 7 Scolastica filie Eluiue que fuit uxor Eadulfi. 7 postea Brummani se secretarii [sic]√ concesserunt 7 dederunt ecclesie nostre hereditatem suam. 7 totam terram quam habebant ante portam ecclesie nostre iuxta domum Radulfi Wastekar. 7 de qua reddebant nobis annuatim xl denarios. 7 cartam conuentus quam inde habebant√ nobis redderunt [sic]. 7 per eandem cartam nos inde seisierunt. in capitulo nostro coram multis testibus [   ] alteram terram inter ecclesiam beate Marie 7 domum Viuiani quam clamabant habere [de] nobis hereditario iure√ totam liberam 7 quietam nobis concesserunt in perpetuum. Nos autem predictis duabus sororibus concessimus singulis diebus quamdiu uixerint√ unum panem monachi. 7 unum trauersum. 7 unum iustum de ceruisia nostra. scutellam unam de pisis. 7 ferculum unum de uno generali quod ipso die conuentus habuerit. Quod corredium ipse accipient ad domum infirmorum. Et permittemus ipsas quam diu uixerint√ habitare in una camere [*sic*] domus. habenti xxiiij pedes in longitudine. 7 xij in latitudine. [ita?] quod in camera illa nullam possint clamare hereditatem. nec aliquis de propinquis suis post ipsas. Preterea persone ipsius Sedegos√ sine hereditate dabimus singulis annis quamdiu uixerit dimidiam marcam argenti. medietatem in medio quadragesime√ 7 medietatem ad assumptionem sancte Marie. Scolastice autem sorori sue post obitum ipsius Sedegos√ non dabimus nisi predictum corredium. 7 inhabitationem predicte camere quam diu uixerit. Hanc ergo conuentionem presenti cyrographo[1] illis confirmamus. 7 eam ipsis seruabimus quam diu predictas hereditates nobis warantizare poterunt. Rei huius testes sunt√ Karolus sacerdos. Eadmundus clericus. Hamo prepositus. Willelmus filius Gregorii. Baldewinus Caluel. Sagærus mercator. Wibertus. Reginaldus aurifaber. Hamo aurifaber. Malgerius portarius. Hugo aurifaber. Willelmus portarius. Bartholomeus senescal. Willelmus Noreis. Sanson cocus. Iuo cocus. Godefridus pistor.

CYROGRAPHUM

ENDORSEMENTS: Twelfth century: De terra Sedegos. Fifteenth–sixteenth century: Cantuar'.
SEAL: No evidence of sealing.
SIZE: 5⅛ ins.×6 ins.
TEXT: BM Add. Charter, no. 917.
NOTE: Charter XLIII is confined by the dates of Odo's priorate. XLIV appears to be contemporary with, or a little later in date than XLIII, but cannot be later than 1180 when Lambin Frese the moneyer (for whom see p. 114) fled from Canterbury.

XLIV

Notification by the convent of Christ Church, Canterbury, of grant to William son of Pagan of the dwelling of Elviva widow of Bruman secretarius (at 20s. *per annum*), safeguarding arrangements made with daughters of Elviva, whereby they may have use of a room in the dwelling.
DATE: 1167?–80.

CYROGRAPHVM

CONUENTUS ecclesie Christi Cantuar'. omnibus ciuibus Cant' presentibus 7 futuris. salutem. Sciatis quod nos mansuram illam que fuit Eluiue uxoris Brumanni secretarii 7 que est ante portam ecclesie nostre iuxta domum Radulfi Wastekar√ concessimus Willelmo filio Pagani tenere de nobis hereditario iure. reddendo inde nobis singulis annis xx solidos ad quatuor terminos. id est ad natale. ad pascha. ad festiuitatem sancti Johannis. ad festiuitatem sancti Michaelis. ad. unumquemque

---

[1] This word is damaged and the reading is uncertain.

scilicet terminorum istorum v solidos. Volumus ergo ut ipse Willelmus 7 heredes sui predictam mansuram bene 7 in pace habeant⫟ quamdiu illos xx solidos bene nobis reddiderint ad terminos constitutos. salua conuentione que est inter nos 7 filias predicte Eluiue. quibus concessimus habere in illa mansura cameram unam xxiiiior pedum in longitudine. 7 xiicim in latitudine quamdiu uixerint sine feudo 7 hereditate. Hanc autem conuentionem Willelmo 7 heredibus suis presenti cyrographo confirmauimus. Huius rei testes sunt. Herueus camerarius. Willelmus filius Gregorii. Ricardus de Suthchirche. Leofwinus de Westgate. Lambin Frese. Bricius de Norðewede. Hector. Willelmus Norreis. Osbernus de porta. Willelmus de elemosinaria. Yun. Driu.

ENDORSEMENT: Contemp.: Cyrographum contra Willelmum port' filium Pagani de terra que fuit Eluiue uxoris Brumanni.
SEAL: Second seal of Christ Church, on tag, without counterseal; damaged.
SIZE: 5½ ins.×7⅜ ins.
TEXT: Original charter CAC, Ch. Ant., C 1137.

XLV

Grant by Haimo son of William le Bof in perpetual alms to Christ Church, Canterbury, for love of St Thomas, of ground outside the city wall, between Queningate and Burgate.
DATE: After 1170.

NOTUM sit omnibus fidelibus quod ego Haimo filius Willelmi le Bof concessi in perpetuam elemosinam ecclesie Christi Cant' pro amore sancti Thome terram meam que iacet extra murum ciuitatis inter Queningate 7 Burgate. quam tenuit Æilweker le Uanur. Volo autem ut monachi teneant terram illam omnino liberam sicut ego 7 antecessores mei. 7 nemini inde respondeant. quod facio pro salute anime meę 7 parentum meorum 7 heredum meorum. Et ne aliquis super hac donatione mea illos uexare aut inquietare presumat⫟ predictam terram presenti carta confirmo. Testibus his. Henrico presbitero de Uismanne cherche. Aluredo presbitero de Redingate. Johanne ælderman de Burgate. Wiberno de Redingate. Ailredo clerico de Redingate. Stephano Caluello.

ENDORSEMENTS: Twelfth century: Carta Haimonis le Bof de terra extra Queningate quam dedit sancto Thome. Thirteenth century?: (I).c c. 1300: Registratur. Fifteenth century. Queningate.
SEAL: Document is folded and slit. Tag remains but all trace of seal gone.
SIZE: 4⅞ ins.×7½ ins.
TEXTS: Original charter CAC, Ch. Ant., C 1066. Transcripts of c. 1300 in CAC, Reg. A, fol. 442v., Reg. E, fol. 130v. (same hand as in Reg. A). No material variants.

XLVI

Confirmation by John de Douvres to the monks of Christ Church, Canterbury, his spiritual brethren, of St Mildred's mill in Canterbury, which Hugh de Douvres, uncle of the grantor gave to the monks at his deathbed, for the sake of his soul. The monks are to hold the mill in pure alms with its appurtenances, viz. a piece of meadow beside the mill and ground in the hands of three tenants (named).

DATE: C. 1170.

JOHANNES de Douora. Omnibus fidelibus sancte matris ecclesie presentibus 7 futuris√ Salutem. Sciant presentes 7 futuri me concessisse monachis ecclesie Christi Cantuarię fratribus meis in liberam 7 perpetuam elemosinam pro anima mea 7 parentum meorum 7 heredum meorum molendinum iuxta ecclesiam sanctę Mildrithę Cantuarię situm. cum omnibus pertinentiis suis. quod Hugo de Douora auunculus meus dedit me consentiente predictis monachis ad obitum suum pro anima sua. Cuius ego donationem presenti carta confirmo. 7 stabilem in perpetuum fore constituo. Volo ergo ut idem monachi predictum molendinum in perpetuam elemosinam bene 7 in pace habeant. liberum 7 quietum ab omni seruitio 7 consue-tudine. 7 omni exactione. a me 7 omnibus heredibus meis 7 omnibus hominibus√ sicut liberam elemosinam Hugonis auunculi mei 7 meam. cum omnibus pertin-entiis suis. id est cum prato quod est iuxta molendinum. 7 terra de qua Radulfus de Fordwiz reddit molendino√ xii denarios. 7 terra unde Geroldus fullo reddit xii d. 7 terra unde Ricardus carpentarius reddit vi denarios. Huius rei testes sunt√ Robertus de Luci. Elias de Silinghelde. Alanus de Sutwelle. Marsilius de Herste. Walterius de Hadfelde. Radulfus de Eslinges. Rogerius marescal. Simon filius Reginaldi. Bar-tholomeus dapifer. Johannes cocus. Samson cocus. Rogerius portarius. Malgerius portarius. Hugo hostiarius. Sigarus hostiarius. Radulfus de Nieweham. Robertus de celario. Augustinus rufus. Johannes Dodin. Turstanus. Matheus. Thomas de coquina. Henricus de Gisorz. Osbernus de vinea. Willelmus de Cochefelde. Will-elmus marescal. Wibertus Kide.

ENDORSEMENTS: Contemp.: Carta Johannis de Doura de molendino de sancta Mildritha. Johannis de Doura de molendino sancte Mildrithe. Thirteenth century: (.I.).ᶜ Late thir-teenth century: Sancte Mildrithe. Duplex est.

SEAL: Circular, on tag, damaged, in brown wax, apparently originally 2⅛ ins. diameter. Equestrian figure with sword and shield, riding to right. Fragment of inscription, very faint: [   ] DOVR[   ].

SIZE: 4¼ ins.× 7½ ins.

TEXT: Original charter CAC, Ch. Ant., C 895.

NOTE: For the family de Dovera *alias* of Chilham, see p. 48. Hugh de Dovera the uncle probably died 2 March 1168. The form ę suggests that the charter cannot fall long after that date.

XLVII

Notification by prior Benedict and the convent of Christ Church, Canterbury, of agreement between them and John Calderun. He grants the monks four pieces of ground when taking the cowl among them, while they undertake to supply a corrody of food, clothing and foot-wear to his wife.
DATE: 1175–7.

C Y R O G R A P H U M [inverted]

BENEDICTUS prior 7 conuentus ecclesie Christi Cant'. Omnibus eiusdem ecclesie fratribus[1] 7 amicis. Salutem. Sciant presentes 7 futuri quod Johannes Calderun dedit nobis 7 ecclesie nostre in liberam 7 perpetuam elemosinam quasdam terras quas de proprio catallo suo emerat in ciuitate Cantuaria. Scilicet terram que fuit Gogge. Hec terra iacet iuxta terram Willelmi filii Gregorii ex parte australi 7 perdurat usque ad terram [2]Godardi mercatoris contra terram[2] que fuit Lambin[3] Frese. ex altera parte viculi. 7 est de tenemento nostro. Aliam quoque terram in parrochia sancti Georgii que iacet retro terram Rogerii le Blund ex parte australi iuxta nouum carcerem. De hac terra debemus reddere heredi Agemundi de Wi. singulis annis xiii denarios in medio quadragesime. Duas etiam terras contiguas in parrochia sancte Margarite que iacent inter terram Johannis Suetman ex parte altera viculi 7 terram Godwini Wendemealt iuxta magnum vicum qui tendit uersus turrim. De istis duabus terris debemus singulis annis reddere heredibus [4]Alani de Well'[4] xv denarios ad festum sancti Johannis. 7 alios xv ad festum sancti Andree de illa parte terre que est iuxta magnum vicum. de illa uero parte que est uersus occidentem debemus reddere singulis annis heredibus Radulfi Caluelli xiiij denarios in media quadragesima. Heredes autem Johannis Calderun 7 Mahalt vxor sua affidauerunt nobis quod nunquam aliquid clamabunt in aliqua predictarum terrarum. Preterea uxor eiusdem Johannis 7 filius eius Willelmus affidauerunt nobis quod omnia debita Johannis adquietabunt. nec aliquam uexationem inde sentiemus. Nos autem concessimus iamdicte Mahalt uxori Johannis quamdiu ipsa uixerit singulis diebus unum panem qualem monachi habent 7 unum pleinpein 7 unum trauersum 7 tres galones de ceruisia monachorum 7 unum ferculum gen-erale aut duo sicut unus de monachis in die habuerit. Concessimus etiam eidem Mahalt unam pelliciam 7 unas bottas singulis annis quibus monachi eas habebunt[5] quamdiu ipsa uixerit. Post obitum uero iam dicte Mahalt. nullus heredum. parentum uel amicorum suorum aliquid poterit clamare in predicto corredio sed ab omnium[6] querela 7 exactione liberi 7 quieti erimus nos 7 ecclesie nostra. Vt autem conuentio ista firma sit 7 rata eam predicte Mahalt sigillo nostro 7 huius cyrographi attes-tatione confirmauimus. similiter 7 Johannes Calderun nobis eam sigillo suo con-firmauit tenendam. Testibus istis Benedicto presbitero de sancta Margarita. Bartholomeo dapifero. Willelmo de Capes. Jordano sellario. Wiberto Kyde. Wiberto thecchere 7 multis aliis.

ENDORSEMENT: Contemp.: De terra Iohannis Calderun. Fifteenth century: Sancte Margarete /et sancti Georgii.

SEAL: On tag. Fragment of second seal of Christ Church, with counterseal.

SIZE: 6 ins. × 7⅞ ins.

TEXT: Original charter, CAC, Ch. Ant., C 825.

NOTE: The first piece of ground ('terra . . . Gogge') is B 73. The second is in St George's, near D 120. The outpayment of 13d. is evidently C 40, G 38, where, however, the payment is made not to A. of Wye, but to the priest of the neighbouring village of Brook. The last two pieces are evidently D 257. For William de Capes, the witness who is apparently Becket's marshal, see p. 183.

XLVIII

Counterpart of XLVII; Variants from text are listed below.

C Y R O G R A P H V M

ENDORSEMENTS: Contemp.: Cyrographum contra Johannem Calderun de terris quas dedit ecclesie Christi quando monachatum suscepit. (VI.).c Fourteenth century: Sancti Georgii et sancti [sic] Margarete.

SEAL: In yellow wax, circular, 1⅞ ins. diameter bearing representation of a cauldron, suspended on a hook. Rim of seal damaged; portion of inscription remains: [   ] CALDR[   ].

SIZE: 8⅞ ins. × 6$\frac{1}{10}$ ins.

TEXTS: Original charter CAC, Ch. Ant., C 177. Transcripts of early thirteenth century in CAC, Reg. H, fol. 30v., and of late thirteenth century in Reg. A, fol. 461r. Variants from XLVII: [1]fidelibus; [2-2]Reg. A omits through homoioteleuton; [3]Lambini; [4-4]Aluredi de Welles; [5]habuerint; [6]omni. Reg. H omits witnesses.

XLIX

Grant by Richard Deudune to Jacob the Jew of Canterbury, for geresumia of 8½ marks of silver and 4s. 6d. per annum, of ground held of John son of Vivian, at the corner of the High Street and Hethenmannelane (Stour Street).

DATE: c. 1180.

NOTUM sit tam presentibus quam futuris quod ego Ricardus Deudune concessi 7 dimisi Jacobo Judeo Cant' terram meam quam teneo de Johanne filio Uiuiani que terra jacet juxta terram predicti Jacobi 7 de sinistra parte sicuti homines intrant in uicum qui anglice appellatur Hethenmannelane 7 juxta magnum uicum habendam 7 tenendam de me 7 de heredibus meis illi 7 heredibus suis in feudo 7 in hereditate finabiliter. reddendo unoquoque anno iiij[or] solidos 7 vi denarios duobus terminis. scilicet ad festum sancti Michaelis. duos solidos 7 iij[es] denarios 7 ad mediam quadragesimam duos solidos 7 iij[es] denarios. Et ego Ricardus non possum de hac predicta terra uendere nec dispendere nec inuadiare nisi solummodo vi denarios qui sunt de foregauele. Et ego Ricardus Deudune 7 heredes mei warantizabimus predictam terram Jacobo 7 heredibus suis contra omnes homines 7 contra omnes feminas. Et propter hanc conuentionem 7 concessionem dedit mihi Jacobus viiito marcas argenti 7 dimidiam in geresumiam. Hanc conuentionem tenendam affidaui ego Ricardus pro me 7 pro heredibus meis Jacobo uel heredibus suis. His testibus. Roberto de Westgate. Thoma tanero. Hamone filio Liefwini. Radulfo filio Lief-wini. Liefwino parmentario. Willelmo filio Lambricti. Hunfrido. homine Tieri. 7 totum hundredum. [sic] Ysaac. Judeo nepote Brun Londoniis. Samsone Judeo filio Aaron de Leicestria. Joseph Judeo filio Ysaac Cant'. Simone Judeo nepote Jacobi. Mosse Judeo nepote Brun.

[Note at bottom of document, on fold, at right hand side].

ריקט דודנא מכר קרקעו

(Riqat Dudna' makhar qarqa'o)[1]

ENDORSEMENT: Late thirteenth century: Carta facta Jacobo judeo de quadam terra in par-ochia omnium sanctorum per Ricardum Deudune.

SEAL: Document is folded and slit for sealing but seal and tag are lost.

SIZE: $6\frac{3}{8}$ ins. $\times$ $8\frac{1}{4}$ ins.

TEXT: Original charter CAC, Ch. Ant., C 770.

PRINTED: Adler, 'Jews of Canterbury,' app. iii (with substantial inaccuracies).

NOTE: Richard Deudune is evidently the R. Deodatus amerced heavily in connection with the coinage 24 Henry II. See p. 116. J. f. Vivian was borough reeve in the years following the murder of Becket. See p. 84. L. Wrenne (witness in LI) occurs in B (215). A. of Rat-ling (in LI) is evidently the man excommunicated by Becket. See p. 56. The house of Jacob the Jew was built on three pieces of ground running from the corner of Stour Street See p. 150.

L

Grant by John son of Vivian to Jacob the Jew of Canterbury of ground formerly held by the latter from Thomas son of Osbert, and by him from John son of Vivian at 8d. *per annum*. Henceforth Jacob is to hold direct from John son of Vivian at 8d. *per annum*, paying 40s. down. The 40s. will be returned by the grantor to Jacob if the former is unable to warrant the ground to the latter.

DATE: About 1180.

NOTUM sit omnibus tam presentibus quam futuris quod ego Johannes filius Viviani concessi 7 dimisi Jacobo Judeo Cant' terram quam Thomas filius Osberti tenuit de me. de qua reddebat mihi octo denarios annuatim ad mediam quadra-gesimam. tenendam silicet de me 7 de heredibus meis reddendo annuatim octo denarios sicut predictus Jacobus solebat reddere predicto Thome. 7 propter hanc concessionem 7 dimissionem predictus Jacobus dedit mihi quadraginta solidos

[1] 'Richard Doodna sold his land'. Thanks are due to Dr Avrom Saltman for transliteration and translation.

sterlingorum. 7 terram hanc predictam gwarantizabo predicto Jacobo 7 heredibus suis contra omnes homines 7 contra omnes feminas. 7 si ita evenerit quod terram predictam Jacobo predicto uel heredibus suis per predictum redditum guarantizare non potero dabo ei quadraginta solidos sterlingorum. Teste. [*blank*]

ENDORSEMENT: Late thirteenth century: Carta facta Jacobo Judeo per Johannem filium Viuiani de quadam terra in parochia omnium sanctorum.

SEAL: On tag, passing through fold. Oval, in white wax; embodies Roman gem, with figure in classical draperies, seated on a cross-legged stool; figure has wreathed head and holds a thyrsus. A smaller figure offers an object (patera?) to seated figure. Another stool in background. Gem is surrounded by medieval inscription, not legible. Seal is damaged at rim but longer axis seems to have been $1\frac{1}{4}$ ins. and the shorter 1 in.

SIZE: 4 ins.× $5\frac{3}{4}$ ins.

TEXT: Original charter CAC, Ch. Ant., C 762.

LI

Grant by Benedict son of Tholi to Jacob the Jew of ground held from the monks of Christ Church, Canterbury, at 6d. *per annum*, to be held from Benedict at 14d. *per annum*, with payment of 8 marks as initial *geresumia*, and a cloak worth one mark.

DATE: About 1180.

NOTUM sit tam presentibus quam futuris quod ego Benedictus filius Tholi concessi 7 dimisi Jacobo Judeo Cant' terram meam quam teneo de monachis ecclesie Christi Cant' 7 de terra illa reddo eis annuatim sex denarios. 7 terra illa jacet inter terram predicti Jacobi quam tenet de Thoma filio Osberti 7 inter terram Ysaac filio [*sic*] Benedicti quam tenet de Alano de Retlinge. habendam 7 tenendam de me 7 de heredibus meis illi 7 heredibus suis in feudo 7 in hereditate finabiliter reddendo unoquoque anno xiiiior denarios ad mediam quadragesimam. 7 pro terra predicta dedit mihi Jacobus octo marcas argenti in geresumiam. 7 unum pallium de una marca. Et ego Benedictus 7 heredes mei warantizabimus Jacobo 7 heredibus suis predictam terram contra omnes homines omni occasione remota. 7 hanc conuentionem tenendam affidaui Jacobo 7 heredibus suis. T'. Ricardo sacerdote. Ædwardo clerico. Wluardo clerico. Jordano aurifabro. Petro filio Simonis. Osmundo pictore. Jacobo pictore. Lamberto Wrenne. Lamberto. Bodo. Salomone mercier. Hugone qui est in loco aldermanni. Jacobo bedel Ainulfo Cauast. Gerardo le machun. Staphano le Breac. Simone Langwambe. Joseph Judeo filio Deudune. Bonechose. Joseph de Everwic. Josep. Simone filio Deulesaut. 7 plures alii Christianorum [et Judeorum?]

ENDORSEMENT: c. 1300: Carta facta Jacobo Judeo per Benedictum filium Toly de quadam terra in parochia omnium sanctorum.

SEAL: Bottom of document is torn off and no evidence survives for sealing.

SIZE: $5\frac{3}{4}$ ins.× $5\frac{2}{5}$ ins.

TEXT: Original charter CAC, Ch. Ant., C 763.

LII

Record of exchange between prior Honorius and the convent of Christ Church, Canterbury, on the one hand, and Agnes prioress and the convent of Minster in Sheppey on the other, whereby the former grant to the latter a marsh called 'Leffleddehope', while the latter grant to the former rents worth 10s. arising from Mercery Lane and from St Mary Magdalen parish, Canterbury.

DATE: 1187.

C Y R O G R A P H V M [*inverted*]

S CIANT presentes 7 futuri hanc esse conuentionem inter H. priorem 7 conuentum ecclesie Christi Cant'. 7 inter A. priorissam 7 conuentum ecclesie sancte Sexburgis de Scappeia. Predictus siquidem H. prior 7 conuentus ecclesie Christi Cant'. concesserunt prefate A. priorisse 7 conuentui ecclesie sancte Sexburgis de Scappeia mariscum unum qui uocatur Leffleddehope in excambio pro quodam redditu decem solidorum in Cant'. de duobus mesagiis. quorum unum tenet Ærnaldus de Chiche in uico Mercerie de octo solidis. Alterum tenet Ingeholfus[1] filius Normanni plummarii in parrochia sancte Marie que uocatur ecclesia piscariorum. de duobus solidis. Et si forte iamdicti monachi memoratum mariscum prelibatis monialibus warantizare non poterunt́ prescripte moniales recurrent ad antefatum redditum sine omni placito 7 contradictione. Similiter predicti monachi recurrent ad mariscum prenominatum si sepedicte moniales redditum prefatum warantizare non poterunt. Vt igitur hec conuentio inter eos facta in futuris temporibus rata sit 7 firmá sigillis ecclesiarum suarum eam roborauerunt. Facta est autem conuentio ista anno incarnationis dominice m⁰ c⁰ lxxx⁰ vii⁰. His testibus. Johanne presbitero de Scapeia. Johanne de Well'. Johanne de parco. Willelmo de Capes.

ENDORSEMENTS: Late thirteenth century: Concambium inter nos et moniales de Scapeye Dederunt enim decem solidos redditus in Cant' pro quodam marisco in Scapeya. (.II.)ᶜ. c. 1300?: Cantuar'. Fourteenth century: De diuersis in Cant'. Fifteenth century: Sancti Andree.

SEAL: Vesica-shaped, in brown wax, on tag, 1¾ ins.× 2¾ ins. Female figure, crowned, holding book in left hand and sceptre in right; inscription, damaged: [SIGILLVM ECCL'E SANCTE] SEXBVRGE DE SCAP[EIA]. Missing portions supplied from impression of seal attached to Charter LIV.

SIZE: 3¾ ins.× 5⅝ ins.

TEXTS: Original charter CAC, Ch. Ant., C 773. Transcript of early thirteenth century, in CAC, Reg. H, ff. 30–31. No material variants, apart from omission of witnesses.

NOTE: The marsh 'Leffleddehope' probably lies near Sheppey. The holding of A. de Chiche may be D 115; that of Ingenulph the plumber may be D 95; see F 199, 201, 564, 565.

[1] Clearly a misrendering of 'Ingenolfus'.

LIII

Notification by prior Geoffrey and the convent of Christ Church, Canterbury, that Wibert the clerk, chamberlain to Odo, abbot of Battle, has granted in perpetual alms to the nuns of Minster in Sheppey, certain ground in the parish of St Alphage, Canterbury, for $\frac{1}{2}$ lb. of cumin *per annum*, saving rent of 6s. due to the prior and convent.
DATE: 1191–1207.

C I R O G R A P H U M [*inverted*]

OMNIBUS ad quos presens carta peruenerit. Gaufridus prior et conuentus ecclesie Christi Cant'. Salutem. Nouerit uniuersitas uestra Wibertum clericum domini O. abbatis de Bello camberlanum͛ dedisse in perpetuam elemosinam concessione nostra 7 assensu sanctimonialibus sancte Sexburge de Scapeia totam terram quam habuit in parrochia sancti Ælfegi Cantuar'. que iacet inter masagium Nicholai vitrearii 7 masagium Jacobi portarii domini archiepiscopi. cum omnibus edificiis tam lapideis quam ligneis in eadem terra constructis. ut ea plene 7 integre habeant 7 in perpetuum teneant de predicto Wiberto 7 heredibus suis. reddendo eis annuatim infra octabas sancti Michaelis dimidiam libram cimini. saluo nobis annuo redditu nostro. scilicet sex solidis. quos nobis prefate moniales omni anno in thesauraria nostra pro Wiberto 7 heredibus suis persoluent. ad duos terminos. scilicet in media quadragesima tres solidos. 7 ad festum sancti Michaelis similiter tres solidos. Vt ergo hec concessio nostra nulli in posterum possit uenire in dubium͛ eam sigilli nostri appositione roborauimus. Valete.

ENDORSEMENTS: c. 1200: De domo Wiberti clerici quam dedit sanctimonialibus de Scapaia. Fifteenth century: (xj.)ᶜ.
SEAL: No evidence that this document was ever sealed.
SIZE: $4\frac{1}{8}$ ins. × $6\frac{1}{2}$ ins.
TEXT: Original charter CAC, Ch. Ant., C 738.
NOTE: Charter LIII is limited by the effective priorate of Honorius (1191 until 1207, when he went into exile). For ground forming subject of LIII and LIV see D 76; F 210, 569. For rent due to almonry see C 16; G 18.

LIV

Notification (tripartite) by Agnes prioress, and the convent of Minster in Sheppey, that they have granted to James, son of William, son of Pagan, porter of the archbishop of Canterbury, certain ground in St Alphage parish in Canterbury, which, with stone houses built thereon, was granted to the nuns by Wibert the chamberlain, nephew of Odo, abbot of Battle. The said ground, together with the stone houses, is granted to James and his heirs at 16s. *per annum* rent, with a *gersuma* of 23 marks down.
DATE: Late twelfth century.

CYROGRAPHVM

GRAPHVM [*in left margin*]

NOTUM sit tam presentibus quam futuris. quod ego Agnes priorissa ecclesie sancte Marie 7 sancte Sexburge de Scap' eiusdemque loci conuentus concessimus 7 dedimus 7 presenti carta confirmauimus Jacobo filio Willelmi filii Pagani portario domini Cant' archiepiscopi. terram nostram quam Wibertus camerarius. nepos Odonis abbatis de Bello nobis in perpetuam elemosinam dedit. cum domibus lapideis superedificatis. 7 omnibus pertinentiis suis. in parochia sancti Ælfegi Cant'. que terra adjacet proxima terre iamdicti Jacobi a boriali parte. excepta terra quam nobis retinemus de prefata terra in perpetuum uersus kemin regis cum edificiis suis. que terra habet in latitudine uersus kemin xxxij pedes. 7 in alio capite xxviij pedes. 7 in longitudine lxx pedes. Predictam uero terram cum prescriptis domibus lapideis predicto Jacobo concessimus 7 heredibus suis tenendam 7 habendam de nobis jure hereditario libere 7 quiete in perpetuum. reddendo inde nobis annuatim xvi solidos sterlingorum ad duos terminos. ad festum sancti Michaelis viij solidos. 7 ad mediam quadragesimam viij solidos pro omnibus seruitiis. 7 omnibus consuetudinibus. saluis nobis rationabilibus releuiis. Quod si sepedictus J. dictum redditum ad terminum uel terminos statutos non reddiderit. ipse uel heredes eius√ ad terram nostram libere recuperabimus. donec inde nobis rationabiliter satisfecerit. Et ego A. priorissa 7 dictus conuentus defendemus sepedictam terram cum predictis domibus lapideis erga dominum fundi de omni redditu 7 seruitio 7 consuetudine. 7 warantizabimus eam ipsi J. 7 heredibus eius contra omnes homines 7 contra omnes feminas. 7 pro hac concessione nostra 7 warantizatione memoratus J. dedit nobis xxiij marcas sterlingorum de gersumma. Facta autem fuit hec donatio nostra 7 concessus in capitali curia domini prioris ecclesie Christi Cant'. apud Cant'. 7 ibidem recordata 7 similiter in Burhmoto predicte ciuitatis. 7 ut hec donatio nostra firma permaneat√ eam sigillorum nostrorum munimine roboramus. Hiis testibus Godefrido de la Den'. tunc temporis senescallus curie. Roberto filio Ricardi. Theoderico aurifabro. Laurentio filio Willelmi. Reginaldo Blund'. Roberto filio Hamonis. Golwino mercero. Eudone mercatore. Wiulfo filio Meineri. Willelmo Norr'. Gileberto de aula. Ricardo Deudun'. Ærnulfo Ferre. Rogero de Irlande. Samuele tinctore. Ingenulfo plumbario. 7 multis aliis.

ENDORSEMENTS: C. 1200: Cirographum de uenditione de terra Wiberti clerici quam emit Jacobus de porta. (Thirteenth century: Cant'.) Late thirteenth century: Note, mostly obliterated, of which only the words Scapeya factum are legible. Fourteenth century?: Sancti Elfegi.

SEALS: I. Circular in red wax, 1½ ins. diameter, attached by green lace passing through fold. Bears floral design, with inscription (faint and damaged): SIGILL' IACOBI IAN[ITORIS? ARCH]IEPISCOPI. 2. Vesica-shaped, in red wax, 1¾ ins. × 2¾ ins. attached by green lace passing through fold; female figure, crowned, holding book in left hand and sceptre in right, with inscription: SIGILLVM ECCL'E SANCTE SEXBVR[G]E DE [SCAP]EIA. See LII above. Woodcut of this actual specimen Arch. Cant., VII, 306.

SIZE: 5½ ins. × 7½ ins.

TEXT: Original charter, CAC, Ch. Ant., X 13.

LV

Grant by Philip of Hardres to God, St Thomas and the monks of Christ Church, Canterbury, in free, pure and perpetual alms of ground in Canterbury held by Hugh Fugard. The grantor takes the cross at the hand of Geoffrey, sub-prior of Christ Church, and offers up the tenant with his heirs on the tomb of St Thomas.

DATE: 1189?

OMNIBUS sancte matris ecclesie filiis[1] ad quos presens carta peruenerit Philippus de Hardre filius Henrici de Hardre salutem. Sciatis me concessisse et dedisse et hac mea carta confirmasse Deo et beato Thome martyri et monachis ecclesie Christi Cant' fratribus meis in liberam et puram et perpetuam elemosinam pro salute anime[2] et omnium antecessorum et successorum meorum terram meam que iacet inter terram Luce mercatoris et terram Elye parmentarii in parochia sancti Elfegi quam Hugo Fugard[3] tenuit de me. Volo igitur ut idem monachi predictam terram in perpetuam elemosinam ita bene et in pace habeant liberam et quietam ob omni seruicio et consuetudine et omni exactione a me et ab omnibus heredibus meis et omnibus hominibus sicut pater meus Henricus et ego eam unquam melius et liberius tenuimus cum omnibus redditibus et consuetudinibus ad eam pertinentibus. Hanc donacionem et confirmacionem [4]feci ego[4] Philippus in capitulo coram conuentu ecclesie Christi Cant'. et postea predictam terram et predictum Hugonem qui eandem terram de me tenuit cum heredibus suis obtuli super tumbam beati Thome gloriosi martyris die qua ego accepi crucem per manus Gaufridi supprioris multis astantibus[5] et uidentibus. Huius donacionis et confirmacionis h[ii] sunt testes. [6]Eustacius presbiter de Blen. Johanne [sic] Heringod. Henricus Gredle. Robertus de Westgate. Martinus senescallus. Rogerus marescallus. Elyas parmentarius. Robertus de porta. Gilebertus de tumba. Symon de Sibertewalde. Hugo Fugard.

TEXTS: Transcript of early thirteenth century in CAC, Reg. H, fol. 31r. and of late thirteenth century in Reg. A, fol. 352r. Text above taken from Reg. A. No material variants in H apart from: [1]fidelibus; [2]*followed by* mee; [3]Flagard; [4-4] ego feci; [5] attestantibus; [6] *all witnesses omitted.*

NOTE: Geoffrey became prior in 1191. The ground in question appears to be D 73; F 40, 367.

LVI

Record (indented) of grant by Laurence de Welles, for 5s. *per annum,* to the convent of Christchurch, Canterbury, of messuage once of Lefwin Cruke and his wife Muriel. Counterpart of LVII.

DATE: c. 1200.

C I R O G R A P H V M [*inverted*]

SCIANT omnes ad quos presens scriptum peruenerit. quod ego Laurentius de Welles dedi. et concessi conuentui ecclesie Christi Cant'. mesagium unum in ciuitate Cantuar'. videlicet quod fuit Lefwini Cruke et Muriele uxoris sue. tenen-

dum de me et heredibus meis iure hereditario pro quinque solidis. annuatim solu-
endis mihi et heredibus meis in thesauraria eorum. ad duos terminos. scilicet in
media quadragesima triginta denarios. et ad festum sancti Michaelis triginta denarioš
pro omni seruitio. Quod ut ratum inter me et predictum conuentum. et firmum in
posterum habeatuř presenti scripto et appositione sigilli tam conuentus Cant'.
quam meǐ hinc inde roboratur.

ENDORSEMENT: c. 1300: Carta Laurencii de Well' de v solidis redditus.

SEAL: Tag remains, but seal is entirely gone.

SIZE: $2\frac{3}{8}$ ins. at left hand edge; $2\frac{7}{8}$ ins. at highest point of indented edge, $\times 5\frac{1}{2}$ ins.

TEXT: Original charter, CAC, Ch. Ant., C 1129. The ground may be that mentioned in C 9,
41, 73; D 97; G 13, 40.

LVII

Counterpart of LVI: no material variants.

CIROGRAPHVM

ENDORSEMENTS: Contemp.: Carta Laurentii de Welles. Early thirteenth century: De terra
Cruke. c. 1300: In Burgate. Sanct Marie Magdalene. Registrat'.

SEAL: On tag, circular, in green wax, $1\frac{3}{8}$ ins. in diameter; floral design, inscription (defective)
runs: SIGILL' LOVRANT[II D]E WELLES.

SIZE: $2\frac{7}{8}$ ins. $\times 5\frac{1}{2}$ ins.

TEXT: Original charter, CAC, Ch. Ant., C 857.

LVIII

Grant by Gilbert of Barham to God and St Thomas of 4d. *per annum* due at Michaelmas,
paid by William son of Elvric to the grantor (together with an additional 5d.) for ground in
Canterbury.

DATE: About 1200.

SCIANT omnes quod ego Gilebertus de Berham dedi et concessi Deo et beato
martiri Thome quatuor denarios annuatim in perpetuum ad festum sancti Michaelis.
quos Willelmus filius Elurici debet mihi ad eundem terminum̌ cum aliis quinque.
de terra quadam quam de me tenet. Volo itaque ut predictus Willelmus uel qui-
cumque terram illam habueriť ipsos quatuor denarios ad pretexatum terminum
ecclesie Christi Cant' annuatim persoluat pro anima mea et uxoris mee. et prede-
cessorum et successorum meorum in perpetuum.

ENDORSEMENTS: c. 1200: De iiii denariis Gileberti de Bereham. Thirteenth century: (XXXI)ᶜ.
Cantuar'.

SEAL: On tag, circular, in brown wax; $1\frac{3}{8}$ ins. in diameter; floral design. Inscription (damaged)
runs: [SIGI]LL' GILEBER[TI DE BER?]EHA[M].

SIZE: $2\frac{1}{4}$ ins. $\times 5\frac{5}{8}$ ins.

TEXT: Original charter CAC, Ch. Ant., C 1128.

NOTE: See D 111; F 215, 536.

LIX

Grant in pure and perpetual alms by Robert son of Richard to Holy Trinity Canterbury (Canterbury Cathedral), and the monks serving God there, with consent of his wife and son, of four shops, the rent of which is to be expended every year at his anniversary in refreshment to the convent.

DATE: C. 1200.

NOTUM sit omnibus ad quos presens scriptum peruenerit᷑ quod ego Robertus filius Ricardi. compos mei de consensv 7 consilio Auitie vxoris mee et J. filii et heredis mei dedi et concessi in puram et perpetuam elemosinam de libero empto meo Deo et ecclesie sancte Trinitatis Cant'. et monachis ibidem Deo seruientibus quatuor scopas iuxta domum Terrici aurifabri super celarium mevm in parte occidentali domus Terrici. quarum due habent quindecim pedes in longitudine. ille due scilicet que sunt inter domum Terrici et ostium celarii mei. alie due que sunt ex alia parte ostii celarii mei habent quindecim pedes et dimidium in longitudine. Singule autem habent decem 7 septem in latitudine. Uolo autem quod harum scoparum redditus post obitum meum singulis annis in die anniuersarii mei expendatur in refectione conuentus. Et ut hec mea concessio rata sit et stabilis᷑ illam sigilli mei appositione roboraui. Hiis testibus. magistro Firmino. Godwino mercatore. Terrico aurifabro. Eun preposito. Laurentio fratre meo. Jacobo portario. Martino senescallo. Adam camerario. Roberto portario. Rogero marescallo. et multis aliis.

ENDORSEMENT: Early thirteenth century?: Carta Roberti filii Ricardi de quatuor scopis. [In a different hand] Sancte Marie Magdalene. Reg'.

SEAL: On tag, oval in shape, 1¼ ins.×1 in. incorporating a classical gem bearing design of running hound or wolf. Inscription round edge: †SIGILL' ROB' FILII RIC'. Initial S in inscription reversed.

SIZE: 5¼ ins.×6½ins.

TEXT: Original charter CAC, Ch. Ant., C 856.

NOTE: Robert s. of Richard heads the Canterbury tallage roll of 1198. See pp. 13, 70. The house of Terric (the goldsmith) is D 99. For Master Feramin, visionary and physician, see pp. 110, 158.

LX

Grant by Goder Paumier to Dunstan his son, for a *gersuma* of three marks and 6d. *per annum* rent, of four *mesagia* in Canterbury, one held of the gild of Westgate; a second held of Holy Trinity (the cathedral); a third of Terric the goldsmith; and a fourth of Susanna de Planaz. Rents are to be paid to the lords, including 2d. evework to the cathedral treasury.

DATE: C. 1200.

SCIANT presentes et futuri quod ego Goderus Paumier dedi et concessi et presenti carta mea confirmaui Dunstano filio meo et heredibus suis quatuor mesagia mea cum pertinentiis suis que sunt de proprio purcatio meo. Quorum unum iacet contra Crienemelnelane inter terram que est de tenura ecclesie sancte Trinitatis Cant'. que est uersus suth. et terram Cristine Blakiestre que est uersus north͡ que est de tenura kilde de Westgate. Et alterum mesagium iacet proxime uersus suth juxta predictam terram que est de tenura predicte kilde de Westgate que est de tenura ecclesie sancte Trinitatis Cant'. Et tercium mesagium iacet proxime uersus suth in uno continenti iuxta predictam terram que est de tenura ecclesie sancte Trinitatis Cant'. que est de tenura Terrici aurifabri. Et quartum mesagium jacet uersus west proxime iuxta terram predicti Terrici que est de tenura Susanne relicte Radulfi de Planaz͡ Tenenda et habenda jure hereditario in perpetuum de me et de heredibus meis respondendo dominis predictorum tenementorum de omnibus seruitiis sibi inde annuatim debitis. dando scilicet annuatim aceruo predicte kilde de Westgate scilicet ad festum sancte [sic] Michaelis duodecim denarios sterlingorum. Et thesaurarie ecclesie sancte Trinitatis scilicet ad mediam quadragesimam decem denarios et ad vincula sancti Petri duos denarios de euewerc. Et Terrico aurifabro scilicet ad festum sancti Michaelis triginta denarios. Et Susanne relicte Radulfi de Planaz scilicet ad mediam quadragesimam sexdecim denarios. Et preterea mihi et heredibus meis annuatim reddendo scilicet ad mediam quadragesimam sex denarios sterlingorum pro omnibus seruitiis et consuetudinibus et demandis temporalibus. Et ego Goderus Paumier et heredes mei gu guarantizabimus [sic] predicta quatuor mesagia cum pertinentiis suis predicto Dunstano et heredibus suis contra omnes homines et omnes feminas per predictum seruitium. Pro hac autem confirmatione mea ad stabilitatem eius perpetuam sigillo meo firmiter munita et facta et recordata in burgimoto ciuitatis Cant'. et coram aceruo predicte kilde de Westgate dedit mihi predictus Dunstanus tres marcas sterlingorum in gersamiam. Hiis testibus. Arnoldo Ferre. Johanne Turte. Thoma de Dene. Jacobo de porta. Goldwino mercerio. Eudone filio Sygari. Eudone clerico. Johanne mercerio. Symone Chig. Samuele tincturio. Johanne filio Thome. Roberto Talebot. Galfrido Anglico. Salomone et Rogero filiis Radulfi. Johanne taillur'. Waltero de Tretford. Johanne Pikenet. Arnoldo bedello. et multis aliis.

ENDORSEMENT: Sixteenth century?: Redditus xij d. de quibusdam tenementis in Westgate.

SEAL: Circular, in green wax, $1\frac{3}{10}$ ins. in diameter; fragment only. Floral design. Inscription runs: †s[IGILL' GOD?]ERE.

SIZE: $10\frac{1}{8}$ ins.× 9 ins.

TEXT: Original charter CAC, Ch. Ant., C 1185.

NOTE: The four holdings lie in 'Crienemelnelane' (St Peter's Grove). Cf. D 336, 337; F 129, 136, 388. For the Canterbury gilds see Chapter V.

LXI

Notification by Hugh the goldsmith of terms of a marriage settlement made by him upon his wife Regina, daughter of Elias of Blean. He has endowed her and her heirs with all his houses, messuages, lands and rents which he possesses within and without the city of Canterbury, in return for 1d. 'forgable'.

DATE: Late twelfth century.

SCIANT presentes 7 futuri quod ego Hugo aurifaber dedi 7 concessi 7 hac presenti carta mea confirmaui Regine filie Elie del Blen vxori mee et heredibus suis in liberum maritagium ad hostium ecclesie quando eam desponsaui omnes domos meos 7 omnia masagia 7 omnes terras 7 redditus quas 7 que habeo infra ciuitatem Cantuar' uel extra. tenendum 7 habendum de me 7 de heredibus meis predicte Regine 7 heredibus suis libere quiete jure hereditario in perpetuum. defendendo hec omnia predicta uersus omnes gentes ex omnibus seruiciis inde annuatim debitis. Et reddendo mihi inde annuatim. vnum denarium de forgabulo scilicet ad festum sancti Michaelis. 7 heredibus meis. pro omni seculari exactione 7 querela. Et ego Hugo 7 heredes mei warantizabimus omnia prenominata predicte Regine 7 heredibus suis contra omnes homines. 7 feminas per predictum seruitium. Et ut hec mea donatio firma 7 stabilis in perpetuum permaneat huic presenti carte mee sigillum meum apposui. Hiis testibus. Etardo del Blen. Elia del Blen. Symone del Blen. Johanne filio Wiuiani. Roberto filio Ricardi. Johanne mercerio. Ernaldo Bucce. Elya permentario 7 multis aliis.

ENDORSEMENT: Seventeenth century (probably in hand of W. Somner, d. 1669): Liberum maritagium.
SIZE: 3½ ins.×7¼ ins.
SEAL: Circular, in green wax, damaged, 1 7/16 ins. diameter. Four-stemmed floral design. Inscription (defective) runs: †SIGIL[L' HU?]GO[N]I[S] AURIFAB[RI].
TEXT: Original charter, CAC, Ch. Ant., C 1192.
NOTE: John s. of Vivian, 'prepositus' of Canterbury, named as a witness, was dead c. 1189. Other witnesses such as A. Bucce, R. s. of Richard are found in D.

LXII

Grant by prior Geoffrey and the convent of Christ Church, Canterbury, to Lambin the merchant and his heirs, of ground at the corner of Hawk's Lane, Canterbury, for half a mark *per annum.*

DATE: 1191–1207, probably late.

C I R O G R A P H V M [*inverted*]

OMNIBUS Christi fidelibus ad quos presens carta peruenerit̸ G. prior et conuentus ecclesie Christi Cant'. salutem in domino. Sciatis nos concessisse et presenti carta confirmasse Lambino mercatori et heredibus eius terram nostram que est in par-

rochia sancte Margarete inter uiam que ducit ad domum Wilardi Flandrensis
uersus occidentem⸍ 7 inter d[omum] Willelmi Picot uersus [au]strum. Reddet
autem nobis predictus Lambinus 7 heredes eius singulis annis in thesauraria nostra
de predicta terra dimidiam marcam argenti pro omni seruitio ad duos terminos.
ad pascha scilicet xl denarios 7 ad festum sancti Michaelis xl denarios. Vt autem
hec nostra concessio futuris temporibus firma perseueret⸍ eam sigilli nostri appositione roborauimus. Hiis testibus. Terrico aurifabro. Roberto filio Haymonis. Johanne
Suuetman. Wilardo Flandrensi. Hugone aurifabro. Roberto camberlano. Martino
senescallo. Willelmo de Capes. Willelmo Noreis. Stephano ianitore. Johanne coco.
Waltero pistore. Jordano. 7 multis aliis.

ENDORSEMENT: Thirteenth century: Cirographum de terra Lambini flandrensis que est in
parochia sancte Margarete.
SEAL: Document is folded at bottom, but there is no slit nor any other evidence of sealing.
SIZE: $3\frac{1}{4}$ ins.× $7\frac{3}{10}$ ins.
TEXT: Original charter CAC, Ch. Ant., C 883.

LXIII

Notification (tripartite) by Terric the goldsmith of Canterbury, that he has granted, for
regard of God, and at the petition of the whole Burghmoot of Canterbury, to Amfrid of
Burgate, all his ground at Burgate, with a shop thereon, to hold by hereditary tenure, for
10s. *per annum*.
DATE: C. 1200.

C I R O G R A P H V M [*inverted*]
G R A P H V M [*in left margin*]

SCIANT presentes et futuri quod ego Terricus aurifaber de Cantuar' dedi et
concessi et hac presenti carta mea confirmaui intuitu Dei et ad petitionem totius
burgimoti de Cantuaria Amfrido de Burgate et heredibus suis totam terram meam
apud Burgate que jacet inter ueterem murum monachorum sancte Trinitatis Cantuar' et soppam lapideam que fuit Johannis et Henrici nepotum eiusdem Amfridi
simul cum soppa lapidea que est super eandem terram. tenendam et habendam
libere et quiete de me et de heredibus meis jure hereditario in perpetuum reddendo
inde annuatim ipse et heredes sui mihi et heredibus meis decem solidos sterlingorum.
Videlicet ad natale duos solidos et sex denarios. et ad pascha ij solidos 7 vj denarios.
et ad natiuitatem sancti Johannis Baptiste ij solidos 7 vj denarios et ad festum sancti
Michaelis ij solidos 7 vj denarios pro omnibus seruitiis consuetudinibus et exaction-
ibus. Et ego Terricus et heredes mei warantizabimus predicto Amfrido et heredibus
suis predictam terram simul cum predicta soppa contra omnes homines et omnes
feminas. Et ut hec mea donatio firmam obtineat in perpetuum stabilitatem facta
est hec carta in modum cirographi tripartita. cuius unam partem cum sigillo ipsius
Amfridi signatam penes me retinui. Reliquam retinuit sibi et heredibus suis predictus Amfridus cum sigilli mei appositione confirmatam. Tercia uero pars cum

sigillo meo et sigillo ipsius Amfridi roboratam⩗ in thesauraria sancti Gregorii
Cantuar' sub equa manu reseruatur. Hiis testibus. Jacobo de porta. Goldwino.
Swano et Johanne merceriis. Johanne Blundo. Johanne Turte. Radulfo fratre eius.
Henrico Baratte. Ernoldo Bucce. Ernoldo Ferre. Ernoldo Binnewit. Eudone clerico.
Reginaldo clerico. Et multis aliis.

ENDORSEMENT: Thirteenth century: Carta Terrici aurifabri facta Amfrido de Burgate de
terra sua in Burgate.
SEAL: In brown wax, circular, $1\frac{1}{2}$ ins. in diameter. Design of deer trippant, with tree; inscrip-
tion: SIGILLVM TIRRI.
SIZE: $2\frac{3}{5}$ ins.×$7\frac{1}{10}$ ins.
TEXT: Original charter CAC, Ch. Ant., C 864.
NOTE: The dates given for LXIII, LXIV are suggested by handwriting and name of parties
involved.

LXIV

Notification by Anfrid of Burgate, son of Hugh, of sale and quitclaim to Terric the goldsmith and heirs, of stone shop and ground in St Mary Magdalen parish, Canterbury. The
grantee is bound to pay rent due to the treasurers of Canterbury Cathedral, and has given
three marks to acquit the grantor from the Jews.
DATE: c. 1200.

SCIANT presentes et futuri quod ego Anfridus de Burgate filius Hugonis vendidi
et dimisi et presenti carta mea confirmaui Terrico aurifabro Cant'. et heredibus suis
in perpetuum scoppam meam lapideam simul cum terra que est in parrochia sancte
Marie Magdalene apud Burgate inter veterem murum ecclesie sancte Trinitatis
Cant'. que est uersus west. et scoppam lapideam Johannis et Henrici filiorum Willelmi filii Hugonis. fratris mei que est uersus east. et habet in longitudine quam in
latitudine sua undique sexdecim pedes. et omne jus quod in eadem scoppa et terra
habui liberum quietum de me et de heredibus meis in perpetuum eidem Terrico
et heredibus suis clammaui in capitali curia domini prioris ecclesie Christi Cant'.
et ipsum alligaui ad reddendum redditum predicte scoppe et terre thesaurariis
predicte ecclesie sicut et ego reddere solebam dando illis annuatim triginta denarios
sterlingorum ad duos terminos. scilicet ad festum sancti Michaelis xv denarios et
ad mediam quadragesimam xv denarios pro omnibus seruitiis. Pro hac autem ven-
ditione et dimissione et libera et quieta clammancia mea totius juris mei et heredum
meorum in predicta scoppa et terra facta et recordata in predicta curia et apposito
sigilli mei munimine ad stabilitatem eius perpetuam firmiter corroborata⩗ et ibidem
cautione fidei mee prestita pariter et juratoria pro me et heredibus meis quod nullo
unquam tempore contra confirmationem et tenorem presentis carte ueniemus
uel stabimus⩗ dedit mihi predictus Terricus tres marcas argenti ad acquietandum me
de Judeis Cant'. Hiis testibus. Thoma de Dene. Godefrido de la Dene. Jacobo de
porta. Goldwino mercerio. Eudone filio Sigari. Rogero de la Le. Johanne mercerio.

Ada camerario. Martino senescallo. Gileberto de aula. Eudone filio Sygari. Malgero clerico. Henrico Galle. Henrico Juchgere. Johanne de porta. Willelmo de gardino. Willelmo Veisin. et multis aliis.

ENDORSEMENT: Thirteenth century: Carta Amfridi de Burgate de scoppa lapidea. Facta Terrico aurifabro. Magdalene.

SEAL: Circular, on tag, in green wax, $1\frac{3}{10}$ ins. diameter. Floral design. Portion only of seal remains. Inscription can be partly supplied from impression of same seal attached to CAC, Ch. Ant., C 865: SIGILL' A[B]VRGAT.

SIZE: $6\frac{7}{10}$ ins.$\times$9 ins.

TEXT: Original charter CAC, Ch. Ant., C 866.

LXV

Grant by John son of John Chorbeile of Canterbury to Eudo son of Sigar of the same city, of ground in the parish of St Mildred, Canterbury, on the river Stour, of the fee of Luke of Lower Hardres, with regrant to Eudo of ground sold by him to Richard Chorbeile, grandfather of the grantor. Eudo is to pay 4d. *per annum* rent, with 4d. relief to John, and to the lords of the fee as follows: to Luke 2s. *per annum* and to Paulinus 12d. with relief at the same figures.

DATE: 1205 or after?

SCIANT omnes tam presentes quam futuri quod ego Johannes filius Johannis Chorbeile de Cantuaria. concessi. et dedi. 7 hac presenti carta mea confirmaui. Eudoni filio Sigari eiusdem civitatis. quandam terram meam in parochia sancte Mildrithe. que continet in latitudine versus keminum domini regis⩛ triginta pedes. in longitudine uero⩛ quantum extendit a iam dicto kemino⩛ vsque ad aquam⩛ que vocatur Stura. de feodo Luce de Nider Hardre. que terra adiacet proximo mesagio Salomonis Turte. Preterea. concessi ei. totam illam emcionem terre. quam ipse. fecit versus Ricardum Chorbeile. avum meum. que continet in latitudine versus keminum⩛ viginti. 7 octo pedes. in longitudine autem⩛ quantum extendit a kemino⩛ vsque ad prefatam aquam. que adiacet iamdicte terre versus boream. vt ipse Eudo 7 heredes ejus. habeant 7 teneant has terras prescriptas cum omnibus pertinenciis suis. de me⩛ et heredibus meis. jure hereditario. libere et quiete in perpetuum. reddendo inde annuatim. mihi. et heredibus meis. ipse et heredes eius. quatuor denarios sterlingorum. in media quadragesima. pro omnibus servitiis. 7 omnibus consuetudinibus. omni occasione remota. et post decessum⩛ decessum⩛ [*sic*] Quatuor denarios de relevanime [*sic*]. et faciendo inde per annum omnia servitia dominis fundorum que debentur. videlicet Luce⩛ duos solidos et Paulino⩛ duodecim denarios pro omnibus servitiis. uel heredibus eorum. et post decessum⩛ tantum de relevamine. illis. uel heredibus eorum. Et ego Johannes filius Johannis et heredes mei. warantizabimus has terras superius divisas cum omnibus pertinenciis suis. predicto Eudoni et heredibus suis. contra omnes homines. 7 omnes feminas. de omnibus placitis et omnibus querelis. per servicium prescriptum. Et pro hac donacione mea. 7 warantizatione. 7 concessuꞌ memoratus Eudo dedit mihi. viginti solidos sterlingorum. de gersumma. facta autem fuit hec donatio mea. 7 hic concessus in hundredo de Wuwergatæ. 7 ibi recordata. 7 postea in burgimoto predicte civitatis. Et vt hec donatio mea. firma. 7 incorrupta permaneat. et hic concessus stabilisꞌ sigilli mei munimineꞌ confirmaui. His testibus. Eudone clerico vicecomitis. tunc preposito. predicte civitatis. 7 Ranulfo de sancto Clemente. constabulario. Johanne Turte. tunc aldermanno. de predicto hundredo. Radulfo fratre suo. Meinero divite. Wiulfo filio suo. Henrico Barate. Goldwino mercerio. Reginoldo Albo. Wielardo mercatore. 7 Ricwardo. Anfrido mercatore. Willelmo Drauet.

ENDORSEMENTS: Thirteenth century: Carta Johannis filii Johannis Corbeile. Late thirteenth century: Facta Eudoni filio Sigari de quadam terra in parochia [in another hand] sancte Mildr'.

SEAL: On tag, circular, in brownish-green wax, $1\frac{9}{16}$ ins. in diameter. Inscription: SIGILL' IOHANNIS FILII IOH'IS CORBAILE. The letters N in IOHANNIS are conjoined in one, with the diagonal strokes reversed.

SIZE: 7 ins.×$6\frac{3}{4}$ ins.

TEXT: Original charter CAC, Ch. Ant., C 922.

NOTE: The handwriting and names of witnesses point to date in earlier thirteenth century. R. of St Clement's the constable may have been appointed by terms of the London provision of 1205. See p. 86.

LXVI

Evidence from a lawsuit, probably in an ecclesiastical court, relating to the letting of a house at 16s. *per annum*, to Hugh son of Ebrard, by Brien and his wife Sigrit.

DATE: c. 1200.

TESTES Brienni.

Philippus clericus juratus dicit quod quadam die Jouis post prandium circa horam uespertinam ante ascensionem domini fuit in domo Brienni. 7 ibi audiuit recordationem conuentionis facte inter Hugonem filium Ebrardi 7 Sigrit mulierem de quadam domo conducenda. Modus autem conuentionis hic erat. quod Sigrit confessa fuit coram duobus sacerdotibus 7 aliis qui interfuerunt se concessisse domum de qua fit contentio. predicto Hugoni. pro xvi solidis per unum annum. 7 etiam anno secundo si pensionem bene solueret. eadem conditione si Brien assensum preberet. Brien uero respondit quod ipsa tanquam de re propria disponeret. Cum autem Hugo securitatem de pactione peteret. respondit Sigrit Brien conpetentius illam posse facere 7 pensionem suscipere eo quod uir esset. 7 his dictisꞌ de manu ad manum affirmauerunt. Asserit etiam Brien dixisse predictam pactionem seruare dummodo penes se domus remansisset.

Galfridus Nolo(h)ⁱat juratus concedit de conuentione. 7 de securitate facta. 7 de loco 7 tempore 7 hora. 7 quod Brien pro posse suo pactionem seruaret dummodo penes se domus remansisset.

ENDORSEMENT: None.
SEAL: None.
SIZE: $2\frac{1}{16}$ ins. $\times$ $10\frac{3}{16}$ ins.
TEXT: Original sheet of evidence, CAC, Eccl. Suits, no. 374.
NOTE: The handwriting indicates date. Cf. D 99, n.

LXVII

Grant of ground by William, son of Sired the fuller, to Ivo, son of Gilbert de Sarnai, of ground held at hereditary tenure from the church of St Mildred, Canterbury, to be held from the grantor at gavelkind, for a rent of 2d. *per annum*, and one mark down. The grantee is to pay rent due to the church.

DATE: 1179?–1212.

OMNIBUS Christi fidelibus ad quos presens carta peruenerit Willelmus filius Siredi salutem. Sciatis quod W. filius Siredi fullonis concessi 7 tradidi 7 presenti carta mea confirmaui Iuoni filio Gileberti de Sarnai 7 heredibus suis terram quam tenui hereditarie de eclesia sancte Mildrethe Cant' tenendam de me 7 heredibus meis ad gauelikend' redendo inde mihi 7 heredibus meis singulis annis duos denarios ad festum sancti Michaelis pro omni seruitio ita quod ipse 7 heredes sui censum quod ipsa terra debet annuatim eclesie sancte Milderethe persoluent. 7 tenebunt de ea sicut ego tenui in capite nichil mihi uel heredibus mei [*sic*] in posterum de predicta terra reddentes preter duos denarios predictos. Et propter hanc concessionem sibi 7 heredibus suis factam dedit mihi prefatus Iuo unam marcam argenti in curia domini Rogeri abbatis sancti Augustini Cant'. Vt igitur predictus Iuo 7 heredes sui predictam terram habeant 7 teneant bene 7 in pace per predictum seruitium de me 7 heredibus meis in perpetuum hanc terram eis concessi 7 presenti carta mea confirmaui quam etiam sigillo meo aposito roboraui. Hiis testibus. Roberto filio Ricardi. Ricardo filio Willelmi. Roberto de Cumbe. Milone filio Hugonis. Petro de Westgate. Thoma de Lund'. Willelmo filio Roberti. Edwardo de Dore. Haimone de Cumba Johanne. Galfrido. Rogero. Roberto. Alano. Ricardo. 7 aliis multis.

ENDORSEMENTS: Thirteenth century: Sancte Mildr'. In hand of W. Somner (d. 1669): Gavelkind.
SEAL: Circular, on tag, $1\frac{3}{8}$ ins. in diameter, in greenish-brown wax. Device of crescent moon and stars. Inscription: †SIGILL' WILLELMI FILII SIREDDI.
SIZE: $3\frac{1}{8}$ ins. $\times$ $10\frac{13}{16}$ ins.
TEXT: CAC, Ch. Ant., C 921.
NOTE: Since Roger abbot of St Augustine's, elected 1176, is not styled 'elect' the document probably postdates his confirmation in 1179. See XXV, XVIII, above. For the Sarnai family see pp. 59, 154. The family is probably connected with Sarness in Waltham, Kent, in which case 'Dore' (see witnesses) may be Ansdore at Waltham, and 'Lund', Little London, close to Whiteacre in Waltham.

LXVIII

Grant for two marks down by Matilda, daughter of alderman Thomas, to Reginald of Cornhill II, of all her rights in the stone house, with other structures and appurtenances, in St George's Street, Canterbury, granted by her father to Reginald of Cornhill, father of the present grantee. She reserves rent to herself and her sisters. Matilda confirms grant made by Reginald of Cornhill of the ground to the convent of Christ Church, for support of the altars of SS. Dunstan and Alphage.

DATE: 1209 or later.

SCIANT presentes et futuri quod ego Matildis filia Tome aldermani concessi et hac presenti carta mea confirmaui. Regenaldo filio Regenaldi de Cornhelle Totum jus quod ad me pertinebat in terra cum domo lapidea et edificiis aliis et pertinenciis omnibus quam predictus Tomas pater meus Reginaldo patri predicti Reginaldi concessit et confirmauit. scilicet que iacet in Cant'. inter terram Hvgonis de Neuile que est versus orientem in qua monetarii manere solebant. et inter terram Johannis filli [sic] Lefwini que est versus occidentem. et inter stratam regiam qua itur a sancto Andrea ad sanctum Georgium que est versus austrum. et terram Ingenulfi plumbarii que est versus aquilonem. Tenend' et habend' in perpetuum libere et quiete. et pacifice. sibi et heredibus suis. Reddendo inde annuatim mihi Matildi et Beatrici et Constancie sororibus meis et heredibus nostris xxvii denarios. videlicet in media quadragesima xv denarios 7 ad festum sancti [Mi]caelis xij denarios pro omnibus seruiciis. consuetudinibus et demandis temporalibus donacionem eciam. concessionem et confirmacionem quam predictus Reginaldus de predicta terra cum pertinenciis suis fecit priori 7 conuentui eccllesie [sic] Christi Cant'. ad luminare. et ad alios vsus necessarios altarium sancti Dunstani et sancti Aelfegi hac carta mea confirmaui. sacramento prestito me numquam fvturis temporibus contra supradictam venturam. Et ego Matildis quantum ad me pertinet predictam terram cum pertinenciis suis warantizabo predicto Reginaldo 7 heredibus suis contra omnes homines et omnes feminas per predictum seruicium. Vt autem hec mea concesssio et confirmacio rata maneat et stabilis. eam sigilli mei apposicione communiui. pro qua facta et recordata. in burgimoto ciuitatis Cant' dedit mihi predictus Reginaldus duas marcas argenti. Hiis testibus. Johanne Turte. Willelmo Wyllard. tunc prepositis. Henrico de Osprenges. Roberto de Bermudesie. Arnoldo Ferre. Eudone Chich. Radulfo de porta. Goldwino mercerio. Henrico Jai. Ansalmo mercerio. et mvltis aliis.

ENDORSEMENT: Contemp. [C]arta Matildis filie Thome le alderman. De domo lapidea. Fifteenth century: Sancti Georgii.

SEAL: Tag remains, but seal has gone.

SIZE: 6⅘ ins.× 8½ ins.

TEXT: Original charter CAC, Ch. Ant., C 1196.

NOTE: The elder Reginald is clearly R. of Cornhill I (d. 1209–10); Reginald II died 1249. For the Cornhill family see p. 56. J. Turte and W. Wyllard served as provosts of Canterbury in 1218 (Somner, *Canterbury*, 1703, p. 179). They may have served in other years.

LXIX

Final concord effected before the justices itinerant at Canterbury between James of Wrotham and wife, plaintiffs, and Reginald of Cornhill, whom the prior of Holy Trinity (Canterbury Cathedral) has called to warranty in connection with a messuage in Canterbury. James and wife make quitclaim for 20 marks.

DATE: Easter 20 Henry II, 'in quinque septimanas' (1236).

HEC est finalis concordia facta in curia domini regis apud Cant' a die pasche in quinque septimanas anno regni regis Henrici filii regis Johannis xx° coram Willelmo de Ebor' Willelmo de Insula Radulfo de Norwic' et Hugone de Pleiz iustic' itinerantibus et aliis domini regis fidelibus tunc ibidem presentibus inter Jacobum de Wrotham et Mariam uxorem eius petentes et Reginaldum de Cornhell' quem Johannes prior sancte Trinitatis Cant' vocauit ad warantum per Nicholaum de Ores positum loco ipsius prioris ad lucrandum uel perdendum et qui ei warantizauit de uno mesuagio cum pertinenciis in Cant' et unde placitum fuit inter eos in eadem curia. Scilicet quod predictus Jacobus et Maria remiserunt et quietumclamauerunt de se et heredibus ipsius Marie eidem Reginaldo et heredibus suis totum ius et clameum quod habuerunt in toto predicto mesuagio cum pertinenciis in perpetuum. Et pro hac remissione quietumclamacione siue concordia idem Reginaldus dedit predictis Jacobo et Marie viginti marcas argenti.

TEXT: Transcript of c. 1300 in CAC Reg. E, fol. 150v.

LXX

Quitclaim by Dionisia, widow of Henry le Wode, to Alexander of Gloucester, his heirs or assigns, of all her freebench falling to her on the death of her husband the said Henry le Wode, in land and house, with appurtenances, at Hottewell, Canterbury, north of the bridge.

DATE: About 1220.

NOTUM sit omnibus ad quos presens scriptum peruenerit quod ego Dionisia relicta Henrici le Wode dimisi et quietum clamaui totum francum bancum meum quod mihi accidit uel accidere potuit post mortem uiri mei Henrici le Wode de terra et domo et pertinenciis suis de Othewelle que est ex parte aquilonari pontis Alexandri de Gloucestria et heredibus suis uel cui eam assingnare [sic] uoluerit pro duobus solidis quos mihi dedit premanibus dictus Alexander. Hanc quietam clamacionem sibi fideliter obseruandam in perpetuam coram curia domini prioris affidaui. Vbi scriptum istut lectum [era?]t. et ad maiorem huius conuencionis securitatem hoc scriptum sigillo meo roboraui. Hiis testibus̄ Johanne [T]erri tunc senescallo domini prioris. Willelmo Pedeleuere tunc seruiente. Johanne Turte. Radulpho Turte. Lambino Flemeng. Willelmo Cokin. Adam mercerio. Paulino de Othewele. Seberno pistore. Rogerio de Rouecestre. Arnaldo budello. Willelmo clerico. et multis aliis.

ENDORSEMENT: Contemp.: Scriptum Dionisie de franco banco suo. Later thirteenth century: factum Alexandro de Gloucestre. Cant.

SEAL: On tag, circular, in red wax, $1\frac{2}{5}$ ins. in diameter. Star-like design. Inscription (damaged) runs †SIGILL' DIANIS[RE]LICTE HENRICI.

SIZE: $2\frac{3}{10}$ ins. × $6\frac{3}{5}$ ins.

TEXT: Original charter CAC, Ch. Ant., C 1163.

NOTE: Alexander of Gloucester founded the hospital of Poor Priests at Hottewell in Canterbury. See XXV–XXXVII above. For bedels and other civic officials, see Chapter IV.

Particulars of the Farm of the City of Canterbury (1234?)

[City of Canterbury: Corporation Archives. Register A 2, fol. 64r.]

Hec est inquisicio facta (anno regni regis E. tercii xlv°)ⁱ de exitibus, redditibus, placitis, consuetudinibus, stallagio ciuitatis Cantuar' per sacramentum istorum per preceptum domini regis scilicet Ricardi filii Rogeri, Reginaldi de Cornhelle, Hamonis de Valoynes, Willelmi de Hardres, Ade Rabel, Willelmi de Beche, Alani de Tyncham, Henrici de Osprynge, Johannis Turte, Johannis filii Terry, Johannis filii Roberti, Henrici le Jay, Roberti le mercer, Thome le spycer, Arnoldi Bynnewyth et Nigelli Talebot.

Sequuntur particule de quibus firma ciuitatis Cantuar' debet oriri per annum.

[1] De molendino et decem acris terre que appreciantur xviij li.

[2] De stallagio xx marce que annuatim paiantur hospitali de Herebaldoune de elemosina regis.

[3] De Barbecane v s. qui debentur in compoto super scaccarium.

[4] De ecclesia beate Marie de Burgate xx d.

[5] De domo Dauid de Burgate de conuentu sancte Trinitatis de domo lapidea contra veterem portam xx d.

[6] De eodem conuentu de quodam prato xviij d.

[7] De Johanne filio Roberti de quadam terra apud sanctum Dunstanum.

[8] De herede Thome de Wikebeche de domo Roberti Pollard xij d.

[9] De Roberto Parys de domo sua vbi manet xij d.

[10] De Roberto fabro de quadam terra super fossam de Northgate vj d.

[11] De herede Bartholomei fabri super eandem fossam viij d.

[12] De Petro filio Petri capellani de domo Alexandri le mercer x d.

[13] De Alexandro le mercer de eodem tenemento (super fossam)ⁱ viij d.

[14] De abbate (de Langedone)ᶜ (sancte Radegundis)ⁱ de tenemento proximo xij d.

[15] De Johanne capellano de sancta Elena iuxta portam suam viij d.

[16] De Gilberto aurifabro de domo proxima viij d.

[17] De herede Walteri Bovys de tenemento extra Northgate xiij d.

[18] De Hugone le longe de domo sua ob.

[19] De Baldewino nuncio de curtilagio suo vj d.

[20] De herede Couell' de domo Warifi aurifabri xij d.

[21] De Andrea de Brythewolde de terra infra portam suam ij d.

[22] De Thoma fabro de quadam terra extra Newengate xij d.

[23] De aldermanno de Westgate (de quodam tenemento infra Westgate)ᶦ iiij s. vj d.

[24] De Alfredo Hocholte de quadam terra sub muro de Westgate extra xx d. ob.

[25] De Thoma filio Ade de tenemento proximo ecclesie sancte Marie de Bredene vj s. viij d.

[26] De Roberto de Cornhelle de domo vbi manet xxj d.

[27] De monialibus sancti Sepulcri de quodam tenemento infra Redyngate xviij d.

[28] De Ricardo sacerdote de quadam terra ex opposito domus sue vj d.

[29] De Willelmo de Bosinton' de terra sua infra Burgate iij d.

[30] De Alfredo Markare de domo sua sub muro de Newyngate iiij d.

[31] De Simone de balneario de domo sua j d.

[32] De Rogero Kynce de terra sua sub muro de Westgate vj d.

[33] De Willelmo Malemeyn de terra quam Willelmus Burre tenet xviij d.

[34] De xx li. et xiij s. ij d. super placitis et huiusmodi casibus, etc.

The handwriting suggests a date in the fifteenth century. The interlineation giving 45 Edward III is obviously wrong as the names of the inquest belong to the earlier thirteenth century. If Robert the mercer is Robert son of Luke the mercer in Rental Z, c. 1230, then the last eight names are to be found in this rental. Reginald of Cornhill is probably Reginald II (d. c. 1249). Hamo de Valoynes is possibly Hamo the younger named 1216–17 (*Rot. de Oblatis et Finibus . . . Tempore Regis Johannis*, p. 556), and may be the Hamo whose son Hamo holds half a fee in Tremworth, Wye, near Canterbury (*Holder of Fees in Kent, anno 38 Henry III*, ed. J. Greenstreet; *Arch. Cant.* xii, p. 217). William is lord of Hardres, near Canterbury. Adam Rabel is evidently the man received back into fidelity and service to the king in 1217 (*Rot. Litt. Claus.*, i, p. 320). Henry of Ospringe is seneschal of Christ Church 'in the year after the Interdict' (CAC, Ch. Ant., L 357). Canterbury was granted in fee-farm to its citizens in 1234, and this is probably the inquest held preparatory to the grant. Perhaps the date 45 Edward III is that of some earlier transcript.

The Earliest List of Citizens of Canterbury
(*Temp*. William I)

[White Book of St Augustine's, PRO, E 164/27, fol. 15v., in a hand of the thirteenth century.]

[BM Roy. MS. I.B. xi, fol. 146v., in a hand of the twelfth century.]

Memorandum de escambio castelli. Gable de excambiacione terre quam rex Willelmus accepit ad castellum.

De excambio castelli. Glable [*sic*] de excambitione terre quam rex Willelmus accepit ad castellum.

Elred	xij d.		Ælred	xij d.
Godwin	x den.		Gowine	x d.
Hefsi [*sic*]	xij d.		Leifsi	xij d.
Osward	x d.		Osward	x d.
Wulfsi	x d.		Þulsi	x d.
Wlfred	xiiij d.		Þulfred	xiiij d.
Sired	vj d.		Sidred	vj d.
Ketel	x d.		Ketel	x d.
Wlword	x d.		Þulford	x d.
Wlfric	viij den.		Þulfric	viij d.
Buct	xij d.		But	xij d.

De terra ista quam rex Willelmus accepit ad castellum suum Cant' abbas Scotlandus recepit ab eo in scambium ecclesiam sancti Andree apostoli 7 ecclesiam sancte Marie ante castellum.

Item de eodem. De terra sancti Augustini quam rex Willelmus accepit ad castellum Cant' abbas Scotlandus recepit ab eo in scambium ecclesiam sancte Marie ante castellum 7 ecclesiam sancti Andree.

Index to Documents

Note: Individuals with territorial names or with well-defined stable surnames have been listed thereunder and not normally under their Christian names. It has not proved practicable, where a Christian name (such as Brictiva or Liviva) is spelt in a whole variety of different ways, to give every minor variation in spelling in every entry including the name. The terms 'widow', 'wife', 'heir' are not given, unless her, or his name is supplied. Territorial names have been identified where possible.

The letters A to F refer to Rentals, the numbers attached to the various sections therein following the letters. Roman numerals in small capitals (I-LXX) refer to Charters. App. A, B, refer to Appendices.

f.	filius, -ia	nep.	nepos	ux.	uxor
hrs.	heres	p.	pater	vid.	vidua
m.	mater	rel.	relicta	v.r.	variant reading

A. *see* AGNES

AARON
de Leicestria, Judeus *see* JUDEUS
nep. Steffani monachi, B 175

ABBAS, Robertus (Cestrensis), F 554
see AUGUSTINI, sancti, abbatia

ABBATIA sancti Augustini *see* AUGUSTINI, sancti, abbatia

ACE Scace, Scache *see* SCACHE

ACELOTA, D 288

ACHEMUNDUS *see* AGEMUNDUS

ACHOLTE (OCHOLTE, OCC-, HACC-, HOCC-, etc.) [Ockholt], Oswardus de, B 199, F 100, 123; Alfredus f. eius (A. de Acholte, Hoch-, etc.), D 78, App. A, 24

ADA m. Roberti, XVIII

ADAM
f. Bartholomei (coci) *see* BARTHOLOMEUS cocus
camerarius, XXXIII, XXXIV, LIX, LXIV
capellanus, F 409
careteir, caretier, F 73, 379
de cruce, f. Alani aldermanni, F 187, 402, 657
f. Eilgari de Stureie, F 659
f. Gode; Godeliva vid. eius, B 107
mercier, mercerius, F 109, 110, 488, 493, XXXVII, LXX
f. Norioth, F 178
p. Thome, App. A, 25

ADMUNDUS *see* EADMUNDUS
ADWINUS textor, XI
ÆDIEVA *see* EDIVA
ÆDMERUS *see* EADMERUS
ÆDMUNDUS *see* EADMUNDUS
ÆDRICUS *see* EDRICUS
ÆDUINUS (-WINUS) *see* EADWINUS
ÆDUORDUS (-UARDUS, -WARDUS) *see* EADWARDUS
ÆILEVA *see* EILEVA
ÆILMERUS *see* EILMERUS
ÆILWARDUS (-UARDUS) *see* EILWARDUS
ÆILWECHER (-WEKER) *see* EILWEKER
ÆILWINUS (-UINUS) *see* EILWINUS
ÆLDEHAM [Aldenham?], Radulfus de, A 3, XII
ÆLDERMAN, -MANNUS *see* ALDERMANNUS
ÆLFEGUS *see* ELFEGUS
ÆLFELMUS *see* ELFELMUS
ÆLFREDUS *see* ALFREDUS
ÆLFRICUS *see* ELFRICUS
ÆLFWINUS *see* ELFWINUS
ÆLIZ *see* ALICIA
ÆLRICUS monachus ecclesie Christi Cantuar., IX, X
ÆLUREDUS *see* ALFREDUS
ÆLVEVA *see* ELVIVA
ÆRNALDUS (-NOLDUS) *see* ARNOLDUS
ÆSTBREGE (-BREGGE, etc.) *see* EASTBREGGE
ÆSTRILDIS *see* ESTRILDIS

447

ÆTHEL- *see* ETHEL-

AGATHA soror Nigelli monachi, A. de Sarnais (-ai) *see* SARNAI

AGEMUNDUS (ACH-)
  clericus, VII
  presbiter, sacerdos, A 24, B 223

AGNES, A.
  priorissa de Scappeia [Minster abbey, Sheppey] LII, LIV
  f. Simonis clerici, B 6

AILREDUS *see* EILREDUS

AILRICUS Seocher *see* OKER

AILWARDUS, D 54

AILWINUS *see* EIL-

AILWORDTUN' (-WORTUN') *see* EIL-

AINULFUS *see* EINULFUS

ALANUS, LXVII
  p. Ade de cruce *see* ADAM de cruce
  aldermannus, A 34, B 92, 94, 99, D 129, 131, F 187, 402, 526, 657, XXXV
  prior ecclesie Christi Cantuar' *see* ECCLESIA CHRISTI

ALBERICUS (AUBRI, ALBRI, etc.)
  aurifaber, B 23, 25, 26; Nigellus f. eius *see* NIGELLUS
  pictor, p. Droconis, A 8

ALBINNI (ALBINN')
  Willelmus de, IV
  Willelmus de comes Suss', XXXI

ALBINUS, C 32, G 33, XXI, XXIII

ALBOLDUS, B 29, 163, XI
  serviens ecclesie Christi, IX, X

ALBRI *see* ALBERICUS

ALBUS *see* BLUNDUS

ALDERMANNERIA *see* BERTHA

ALDERMANNUS (ÆLD-)
  see ALANUS
      GREGORIUS
      HUMFRIDUS
      JOHANNES
      JOHANNES, de Burgate
      JOHANNES, de Radingate
      ROGERUS
      ROGERUS, de Radingate
      THOMAS
      TURTE, Johannes, de Wrgate
      TURTE, Radulfus, de Wrgate
      WLNOD
      WESTGATE
  VICEALDERMANNUS *see* HUMFRIDUS, HUGO
    qui est in loco aldermanni

ALDINTUNE [Aldington, Kent], Stephanus de, G 10

ALDITHA
  soror Hamonis Coppe *see* COPPE
  m. Nicholai, D 142

ALDIVA rel. Gerri, B 188

ALDUINUS, A 32

ALEPOT, D 335, F 388, 449

ALEWI, Godwinus f., B 162

ALEXANDER
  cementarius, B 61, F 121
  hostiarius, XL
  le mercer, App. A. 12, 13
  monachus, ortulanus, IX, X
  parmentarius, B 195
  f. Reimunt, F 282
  f. Wlnoth, -dh, D 192, F 244

ALFEGUS *see* ELFEGUS

ALFREDUS (ALUREDUS, ALUEREDUS, ALFREUS, ELVREDUS, ÆLFREDUS, etc.), D 185
  aurifaber [*sic*, Albericus?] *see* ALBERICUS
  clericus, B 48, 182, 183
  faber, p. Willelmi, F 94, 431
  f. Godwini, II
  f. Markere, App. A, 30
  parmentarius, A 28, B 89, 187, C 39, G 37
  presbiter (Elvredus), F 137
  presbiter (Aluredus), de Redingate [St Edmund], XLV
  p. Radulfi fabri, D 58
  f. Radulfi hostiarii de bracino ecclesie Christi, B 168
  et Godardus Uppehealdere (Uph-, -haldere, etc.) *see* GODARDUS
  p. Willelmi fratris Radulfi, F 94
  p. Willelmi fabri, D 58

ALFRICUS, *see* ELF-

ALFWINUS *see* ELF-

ALICIA (-ITIA, ÆLIZ, etc.)
  f. Henrici aurifabri *see* HENRICUS
  heres Liefwini Lunʒ, Longi, *see* LONGUS
  soror Nigelli, D 45
  m. Rogeri; Muriela ux. eius, B 208
  f. Wiberti Kide *see* KIDE
  rel. Wlsi, B 186

ALUREDUS, *see* ALFREDUS

ALURICUS *see* ELFRICUS

ALWOLDUS faber, p. Walteri sacerdotis, B 13

AMFRIDA rel. Salomonis pistoris, B 46

AMFRIDUS (AN-, ANS-), F 561
  de Burgate, LXIII, LXIV; Willelmus frater eius, p. Johannis et Henrici, *ibid.*
  f. Hugonis, F 192
  mercator, B 127, 139, 141, D 44, 268, LXV

AMPOLLARIUS, Gervasius, D 144, 155

ANDREAS, XXXVIII
  'de Brythewolde', App. A, 21

ANDREE, sancti, ecclesia et parochia, A 29, B 81, 109, 111, 112, 212, 216, 221, D 100 ff., F 29, 212, 213, 294, 532, 533, G 39, XVIII, LXVIII, App. B

ANDRESGATE [road-junction, Mercery Lane-High Street, Canterbury], B 208, C 8, 12,

BAGGBERI (contd.)
168, 169, 172, 176, 179, 180, 182, 183,
184, 187, 192, C 18, 72 v.r., D 25, 26,
F 68, 288, 289, 441, 468, 469, XVI, *and see*
BAGGURI
Willelmus de, D 220
BAGGERE, -ER
Ælfegus se, B 34, 40
Raulfus, XI
BAGGURI (BAGGEBERI?), C 18
BAGTHEBERI, etc. *see* BAGGEBERI
BALDERI (BALDRI), terra, F 198, 394
BALDRI, Willelmus f., B 96
BALDWINUS (BALDE-), A 14
Flandrensis *see* FLANDRENSIS
p. Nicholai *see* NICHOLAUS
nuncius, App. A, 19
presbiter, de Cert (Chert) *see* CHERT
sacrista monachus ecclesie Christi, IX, X
BALI *see* CASTELLUM
BALIO, Godefridus de, D 325, 370
BALNEO (BALNEARIO, 'BALNENO') (ecclesie
Christi)
Cole de, XXI
Eadmerus de p. Simonis *see* EADMERU
Milo de, F 257
Ricardus de, XLIII
Simon de, F 117, App. A, 31
BALVERLE [The Beverley, Canterbury?],
Radulfus de, D 345, 373, 378, 383, 384
BARATE (BARATH, BARATTE, etc.)
Henricus, D 200, F 38, 232, 314, 362, 583,
589, LXIII, LXV
Radulfus, XL
BARBECANE *see* CASTELLUM
BARRA
sancti Sepulcri *see* SEPULCRI, sancti, barra
[in Wincheap] *see* WENCHIAPE
BARTHOLOMEUS, B 50, F 87, 105–6
carpentarius, F 46, 317, 366, 428
cocus, p. Ade, D 25, F 68, 69, 441, 442
(cocus), p. Ade, F 412
dapifer, senescallus (ecclesie Christi), B 7,
17, 140, 144, 147, 172, 176, C 24, VIII,
XI, XXI, XXIII, XXV, XXVI, XXVII, XXXV,
XXXIX, XLIII, XLVI, XLVII; p. Cecilie *see*
CECILIA
Emma rel. eius, C 1, D 21, 22, F 16, 356,
369, G 1
faber, D 55, 56, F 105, 455, 547, 697, App.
A, 11
BARTONA (BERT-, -UNA) ecclesie Christi *see*
ECCLESIA CHRISTI
Rogeri coci, B 194
Yun de *see* YUN
BASILIA vid., D 90, 100
rel. Hugonis f. Everard, F 273

BASSET
Robertus, B 167, XI
Thomas, XXVIII, XXXI, XXXVI
Willelmus, XXXVI
BATHON', Ricardus episcopus *see* EPISCOPI
BATUR, Robertus, F 39, 364
BEATRIX
rel. Hugonis telarii, B 57
rel. Salomonis, F 300
f. Thome aldermanni, F 168, LXVIII
BECHE, Willelmus de, App. A
BEDELLUS (BUDELLUS)
Arnoldus, LX
Jacobus, LI
Willelmus, XXI
BEIVIN, Johannes, A 23, B 86, 88, F 613,
658
BELESMAINS (-MAYNS), Johannes, D 251, 353,
E 28
BELLO, Odo abbas de, avunculus Wiberti,
camerarii eius, *see* WIBERTUS
BELLUS, Aschetillus, F 353
BELMING, Wlfric, B 105
BENDENG', Willelmus de, XXXI
BENEDICTUS
Judeus p. Isaac *see* JUDEUS
presbiter, A 24, XXVI, XXVII; avunculus
Benedicti, C 36, G 35
presbiter de sancta Margareta, XLVII
prior ecclesie Christi *see* ECCLESIA CHRISTI
f. Tholi, LI, F 172
BEREBRED (BEREM-, -BRAID), D 325
Bartholomeus, D 300, F 274
Godwinus, XVIII
BEREHAM [Barham, Kent]
Galfridus de, F 215, 536
Gilbertus de, D 111, F 291, 555, LVIII
BERINGERIUS (-RUS), f. Godwini f. Eve, D
234, 235, 238, 241, 244, 245, 246, E 11,
12, 13, 21, 23, F 222, 492
BERKESORA [Berksore, Upchurch, Kent]
Willelmus de, IX, X
BERKINGES (BERE-) [Barking (abbey)], moni-
ales de, sanctimoniales de, G 53, G 55,
XXIV
BERMUDESEIE [Bermondsey, Surrey?], Rob-
ertus de, LXVIII
BERN', Thomas f., XXXI
BERNARDI, Robertus p., XXXI
BERNSFELD, Willelmus de, D 274
BERNERUS, C 5, 6
dapifer ecclesie Christi, G 8, 9, 19, 43, 53,
54, 66, XVI; p. Christine, C 42 v.r.;
Liviva (-veva etc.), rel. eius, B 80, 180,
208, C 17, XVI
BERTHA, ALDERMANNERIA (ALDIR-, -MAN-
RIA), WARDA, HUNDREDUM, etc.

GALLE, Henricus, LXIV

GARBADOS, IX, X

GARDINO (CAR-), Willelmus de, XXXIII, XXXIV, LXIV

GARDINUM
see ARCHIEPISCOPUS
AUGUSTINI, sancti, abbatia
ECCLESIA CHRISTI

GARGATE (GARE-), LII
Lambertus (Lambinus), B 71, 84, 212, C 26, v.r., 44 v.r., 52, D 93, 94, 188, G 26, XI, XIV, XVIII, XX, XXI, XXIII, XXIV

GAUFRIDUS (GALFRIDUS)
Anglicus, LX
cancellarius, V
Eadilda ux. Galfridi, B 72
marescal, C 68, F 101, 343, 448, G 64
Nolohat, LXVI
prior ecclesie Christi *see* ECCLESIA CHRISTI
f. Reimundi (Rey-), B 196, D 83, XXVI, XXVII

GAULTERUS *see* WALTERUS

GAVELET (GAVELLATE, etc.), D 91, 137, XI

GAVELIKENDE, tenura de, D 97, 115

GEDDEWINUS, cocus, ecclesie Christi, XIX

GEDDINGE [Geddinge, Barham, Kent], Arnoldus de, D 232, 233, E 9, 10

GEKEREL *see* CHEK-

GELDEWINUS, presbiter, sacerdos, B 6, D 66, VII

GEORGII, sancti, ecclesia, monasterium; et parochia, A 7, B 102, 105, 208, 214, D 117, 123, 124, 138, 139, 163, F 50, 175, 195, 527, XIX, XLVII, LXVIII
presbiter, sacerdos, D 138; Henricus, XVIII

GEORGIUS, camerarius (ecclesie Christi) monachus, avunculus Salomonis monachi ecclesie Christi, F 55

GERARDUS
le machum, LI
Matildis ux. Gerardi, B 216
presbiter, D 41, 42, F 86, 403, 438

GERMANUS, monachus (ecclesie Christi), A 35, XI

GERNUN, Willelmus, F 152

GEROLDESLANE, D 210

GEROLDUS, B 112, D 106
p. Cecilie (Cecelie), B 109, 110, F 217, XXVI, XXVII
fullo, XLVI; avunculus Liveve, D 210
p. Hamonis clerici, XVIII
Henricus f. G. justicia regis, XXV
p. Johannis, F 517
avunculus Livive, D 197
le tanur, XXXV, XXXVI; p. Johannis, F 585, 586

GERRI, Aldiva rel., B 188

GERVASIUS
ampollarius, D 144, 155
cocus, D 65, VIII, XI, LXV
Hog (de Horsfalde), F 72, 286
monachus ecclesie Christi, B 54, 55, 168, D 26, 28
Sefugel, (Fugel etc.) *see* SEFUGEL

GERVOT, Willelmus, D 163

GIFFARD [of London], XXIX, XXXI

GILBERTUS (GILLE- GILE-), D 312, F 71
de aula, LIV, LXIV
aurifaber, App. A, 16
camerarius, Mahaut rel. eius, D 107, 108
clericus, D 247, 248, 271, 272, E 24, 25
f. Moysi, D 64
presbiter, XXXIX
Raenilda rel. G., B 37
fr. Rogeri abbatis sancti Augustini, XL
telarius, XXI, XXIII
de tumba, LV

GILDA
burchilde (burcgilde), D 226, 250, 251, 334, E 3, 27
cepmannegilde, I
gilda fabrorum, smithchilde, D 138
kilda de Westgate, LX
mercatorum, B 112

GILDHALL (CHILDEHALLE, -HALLA, etc.), C 60, D 65, 133, F 315, 486, G 60
in Fordwic, F 279, 280

GILDINGES [Ileden, Barham, Kent], Elred de, B 102

GILEBERTUS (GILLEB-) *see* GILBERTUS

GINIS, Ernulfus [*sic*, for Ernaldus?] comes de, p. Radulfi, XIV

GISORZ, Henricus de, XLVI

GLADUSE *see* FAIRHEGNE

GLANVIL, Rannulfus de, XXXI

GLINDE, Robertus clericus de [Glinde, Sussex], XIX

GLINT' (CLINT'), G. de, V, VI

GLOVERE
see HELIAS
ROBERTUS
WILLELMUS
WILLELMUS (p. Roberti)
see also LE WANTE

GLOWCESTRIA (GLOUC-, etc.)
Alexander de, XXXVI, LXX

GOD', Clutessune, C 48

GODA, vid., D 169

GODARDUS, B 74, D 102
clericus, IX, X
mercator, XLVII
molendinarius, D 208, 209, F 248, 252, 481, 596
presbiter, D 59

MEINERUS (MAIN-, MAYN-, -IUS)
Dives, le Riche [monetarius], D 211, 212, 255, E 31, F 302; p. Wiulphi [monetarii], D 215, 283, F 308, 357, 502, LIV, LXV
fullo, D 364
f. Sedewin, D 19, F 132
MERCATOR
  see AMFRIDUS
    EACTETENE
    ELFEGUS
    EUDO
    GODWINUS
    IVO
    LAMBERTUS
    LUCAS
    REGINALDUS
    ROBERTUS
    SAGÆRUS
    SALOMON
    SEMERUS
    SUANUS
    THOMAS
    WALTERUS
    WILARDUS
    WILLELMUS
    WLFWIN
  see also MERCERIUS
MERCATORUM GILDA *see* GILDA
MERCERIA [Mercery Lane, Canterbury], D 110, F 540, G 6, 7, 8, LI
MERCERIUS (MERCHIER, MERCEIR)
  see ADAM
    ALEXANDER
    ANSELMUS
    GOLDWINUS
    JOHANNES
    LUCAS
    RICARDUS
    ROBERTUS
    SALOMON
    SEMERUS
    SUANUS
    WIMUNDUS
  see also MERCATOR
MEREWORTH, Eustachius de, D 369
MERKERE *see* MARKERE
MESCHINUS, Rannulfus, IV
MICHAEL (f. Brictwoldi, etc. Bonenfant), D 11, 14, 17, 18, F 84, 436
clericus, XL
MICHAELIS, sancti, ecclesia et parochia; ecclesia de Burgate [St Michael, Burgate], B 57, 67, 69, 205, D 88, 139, F 155, XXXIII, XXXIV
Willelmus sacerdos, presbiter, ecclesie sancti Michaelis de Burgate, A 22, B 85

MILDRIDIS (-IDE, -ITHE, etc.), sancte, ecclesia et parochia, D 167, F 23, 51, G 10, LXV, LXVII
molendinum, juxta, apud sanctum Mildr-, D 210, 241, E 14, XLVI
MILESENT (-ENTH), F 232, 347, 592
rel. Ricardi lorimier, F 179, 580
MILESTEDE, Ricardus clericus de, F 188
MILITIS, Egeliva f., B 62
MILO
de balneario, F 257
f. Hugonis, LXVII
MISCH', Willelmus, XXXVIII
MODLIEF, vid., A 6
MOLENDINATOR (-ARIUS)
  see GODARDUS
    PETRUS
    REGINERUS
    ROBERTUS
    SINOTHUS
MOLENDINUM, D 90, F 55
Crienemeldne (-melle) *see* CRIENEMELDNE
domini archiepiscopi Cantuar', F 287
domini regis, App. A, 1
Guthwoldi (Gud-) F 283-5, 574-8
Horsmelne *see* HORSMELNE
Hottemelne *see* HOTTEMELNE
monachorum (ecclesie Christi), B 42, F 287
sancte Mildridis *see* MILDRIDIS, sancte
de Suliford, F 422
MONACHI
[It is difficult to decide, unless his house is named, where a monk belongs, though probably nearly all the monks given below are from Christ Church. Men (such as L. Gargate), who assumed the habit on a death-bed are included]
Ælricus, ecclesie Christi, IX, X
Alexander, ecclesie Christi (ortulanus), IX, X
Augustinus, ecclesie Christi, cellararius, XXIII
David, ecclesie Christi? Odo parens eius, IX, X
Ernaldus, ecclesie Christi, fr. Willelmi, B 4
Ernulfus, ecclesie Christi, frater Roberti de Suanetune, A 36
Georgius, camerarius ecclesie Christi, avunculus Salomonis monachi, F 55
Germanus, ecclesie Christi, avunculus Martini, XI, cognatus Edwini fratris Martini, A 35
Gervasius ecclesie Christi, B 54, 55, 168, D 26, 28
Henricus, ecclesie Christi, p. Hamonis prepositi civitatis Cantuar', B 213, D 126
Jacobus, ecclesie Christi, f. Edieve, B 126

General Index

Note: The following abbreviations are used

CC the Cathedral Church of Christ, Canterbury

bro.	brother	f.	father	neph.	nephew	w.	wife
d.	daughter	m.	mother	sist.	sister	wid.	widow